ITALY

FODOR'S MODERN GUIDES

are compiled, researched, and edited by an international team of travel writers, field correspondents, and editors. The series, which now almost covers the globe, was founded by Eugene Fodor.

OFFICES
New York & London

Editorial Staff for FODOR'S ITALY 1982

Editor	RICHARD MOORE
Area Editor	BARBARA WALSH ANGELILLO
Assistant Editor	THOMAS CUSSANS
Editorial Contributors	LESLIE GARDINER, FRANCES HOWELL RICHARD PARIS, PETER SHELDON DAVID TENNANT
Photographs	PETER BAKER, BARBARA WACE
Drawings	BERYL SANDERS
Cartography	C. W. BACON

FODOR'S®

ITALY

1982

FODOR'S MODERN GUIDES, INC.

Distributed by
DAVID McKAY COMPANY, INC.
New York

ISBN 0-679-00803-9 (David McKay Co., Inc., cloth edition)
ISBN 0-679-00804-7 (David McKay Co., Inc., Traveltex edition)
ISBN 0-340-27504-9 (Hodder and Stoughton edition)

All the following Guides are current (most of them also in the Hodder and Stoughton British edition).

CURRENT FODOR'S COUNTRY AND AREA TITLES:

AUSTRALIA, NEW ZEALAND AND SOUTH PACIFIC
AUSTRIA
BAJA CALIFORNIA
BELGIUM AND LUXEMBOURG
BERMUDA
BRAZIL
CANADA
CARIBBEAN AND BAHAMAS
CENTRAL AMERICA
EASTERN EUROPE
EGYPT
EUROPE
FRANCE
GERMANY
GREAT BRITAIN
GREECE
HOLLAND
INDIA & NEPAL
IRELAND
ISRAEL
ITALY
JAPAN AND KOREA
JORDAN AND HOLY LAND
MEXICO
NORTH AFRICA
PEOPLE'S REPUBLIC OF CHINA
PORTUGAL
SCANDINAVIA
SOUTH AMERICA
SOUTHEAST ASIA
SOVIET UNION
SPAIN
SWITZERLAND
TURKEY
YUGOSLAVIA

CITY GUIDES:

LONDON
NEW YORK CITY
PARIS
ROME
WASHINGTON, D.C.

FODOR'S BUDGET SERIES:

BUDGET BRITAIN
BUDGET CARIBBEAN
BUDGET EUROPE
BUDGET FRANCE
BUDGET GERMANY
BUDGET ITALY
BUDGET JAPAN
BUDGET MEXICO
BUDGET SPAIN
BUDGET TRAVEL IN AMERICA

USA GUIDES:

USA (in one volume)
ALASKA
CALIFORNIA
COLORADO
FAR WEST
FLORIDA
HAWAII
NEW ENGLAND
PENNSYLVANIA
SOUTH
SOUTHWEST
SUNBELT LEISURE GUIDE

SPECIAL INTEREST SERIES:

CIVIL WAR SITES

MANUFACTURED IN THE UNITED STATES OF AMERICA
10 9 8 7 6 5 4 3 2 1

FOREWORD

Italy is a country of striking contrasts, from the snow-covered borders with Switzerland to the sun-drenched rocks of Sicily. It is a country rooted deeply in the history of Western civilization. A country where atavistic memories are stirred by the sight of a statue in a town's ornate square, by a religious procession winding through a vine-clad countryside, by a Roman temple etched against the evening sky. It is a country incredibly rich in remembrances of the past, in supreme works of the imagination, and in still-lovely landscapes from which those works sprang.

But, sadly for the Italians, Italy is one of the poorest members of Europe, markedly so when compared with her affluent neighbors. While her reeling economy makes life difficult for those who live there, it makes for a favorable situation for the visitor. Where shopping, eating, hotel and general travel costs are concerned, Italy currently rates as one of the bargains of Europe. Naturally, with the wild fluctuations in exchange rates and other basic financial factors, we hope that you will regard the prices we quote (as at time of writing, mid-1981) as merely guidelines, intended to help give you some idea of relative costs as you plan your trip.

Unfortunately, there is a catch in Italy being such a desirable budget destination—it is no secret! Michelangelo's *David,* in Florence's Accademia, rises above a sea of jostling admirers that would put a football crowd to shame. At the height of the season, Venice seems to be in extra danger of sinking under the weight of visitors. The press of people on Capri sometimes threatens to force those nearest the edge to have to swim for the mainland. But there is something for everyone in Italy, and the fortitude needed for a swift visit to the most famous highlights, can be more than compensated for by finding the fascinations of the country's byways—the beauty of hidden Tuscan towns; that Signorelli fresco which is all the more effective because you don't have to jostle to see it; the lunch in the little trattoria on a village square, where you can get happily drowsy on local wine. We hope that you will find help in this edition of *Fodor's Italy* for whatever kind of visit you plan.

*

We would like to express our thanks to all those who have assisted us in the preparation of this edition: to the staff of the Italian State Tourist Office in London; the Italian Tourist Office in New York; Dottore Franco Demarinis, Director of Information for Foreign Countries of the ENIT in Rome; the directors and staff of EPT and AAST Tourist Offices throughout Italy; Mr. Leslie Gardiner for putting his knowledge and expertise at our disposal.

Finally we would like to thank Mrs. Barbara Walsh Angelillo for all the hard work and skill which she has once more brought to her task as Area Editor. Her knowledge of, and love for, Italy remains one of the main supports of our enterprise.

*

All prices quoted in this Guide are based on those available to us at time of writing, mid-1981. Given the volatility of current costs, it is inevitable that changes will have taken place by the time this book becomes available. We trust, therefore, that you will take prices quoted as indicators only, and will double-check to be sure of the latest figures.

*

Errors are bound to creep into any guide. When a hotel closes or a restaurant's chef produces an inferior meal, you may question our recommendation. Let us know, and we will investigate the establishment and the complaint. Your letters will help us to pinpoint trouble spots.

Our addresses are:

in the USA, Fodor's Modern Guides, 2 Park Ave, New York, NY 10016;

in Europe, Fodor's Modern Guides, 1-11 John Adam Street, London WC2N 6AD.

We accept advertising in some books, but this does not affect the editor's recommendations. We include advertising because the revenue helps defray the high cost of our annual republishing, and the advertisements themselves provide information for our readers.

EARTHQUAKE REPORT

The effects of the appalling earthquake of late 1980 that shattered much of the Naples area are still evident at the time of writing (mid-1981). Though valiant efforts have been made by the Italians to rebuild their devastated towns and resorts, much yet remains to be done. Large parts of the center of Naples for example are still little more than rubble and parts of the important archeological sites of Pompeii and Herculaneum are liable to remain closed for much of 1982.

The situation regarding hotels is also confused. Though many of the main tourist centers—the islands, Sorrento and Amalfi coasts in particular—escaped the earthquake largely unscathed, many of the inland areas suffered badly. Rebuilding work has begun, but is not well advanced. Consequently, if you plan to visit this part of Italy in 1982, we urge that you check with the Italian State Tourist Office before leaving on your trip, as well as in Italy itself, for the latest information.

CONTENTS

FACTS AT YOUR FINGERTIPS

FACTS AT YOUR FINGERTIPS

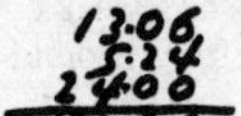

WHAT WILL IT COST. Prices in Italy have been climbing steadily for several years. The simplest way to budget your money is to choose one of the many pre-packaged trips. They will be more expensive than formerly, but still offer good value and a wide variety of costs, depending upon the degree of luxury provided.

For the pay-as-you-go, go-where-you-please traveler, budgeting is more difficult. We suggest below how much it will cost to visit and travel in Italy on four levels: deluxe, comfortably, economically and if you're roughing it. These are minimums, but not bare minimums: that is, they represent about what might normally be spent in each set of circumstances without requiring any undue strain to keep within the limits given.

Keep in mind that costs in Italy are increasing at a rate of about 20% each year. As a result, the prices listed throughout this book will undoubtedly be higher by the time you get there. You can fight this upward trend in prices by keeping your stay in the major tourist centers down to a minimum and giving some time instead to the lesser-known, more inexpensive spots such as the South

Tyrol. Valle d'Aosta, Umbria, Abruzzi and the Marches, Calabria, Apulia and Sardinia (*not* the Costa Smeralda, please). They're all well-equipped with good hotels, and prices are much lower for comparable comfort. Remember, too, that while Milan and Venice are expensive for dining out, you can still eat well in good, reasonable restaurants everywhere else in Italy, including Rome.

Deluxe, as used here, means staying in the best rooms of the best hotels; traveling by plane, chauffeur-driven car and 1st class on trains, in Pullmans or Wagons-Lits; eating at the best restaurants and paying reasonable attention to the smarter nightclubs.

Comfortable travel involves staying at good hotels, with private bath, but not the palaces; eating in good restaurants, but not at the most expensive ones; indulging in moderate doses of nightlife; traveling by 2nd class train, bus or small drive-yourself car.

Economical travel still lets you into comfortable hotels, but without style or much service, and you don't have a private bath; you can eat good food, but in crowded restaurants, since places both cheap and good are bound to be crowded; you'll patronize only an occasional opera or concert, and not in the best seats; you'll ride in buses much of the time.

Roughing it means staying at Youth Hostels or camping; eating where you stay, carrying sandwiches, or patronizing cheap *trattorie*; walking, cycling or taking 2nd class on the trains; and depending for amusement on the movies, the museums, the cafés and your eyes.

You can follow this program at the deluxe level for about 110,000 lire per person per day; on a comfortable level for 65,000 a day; on the economical level for 35,000 a day; roughing it for, say, 18,000 a day. If you spend much time in smaller, inexpensive places, the greatest savings will be for the first two levels, as deluxe and 1st-class hotels will not exist there; travelers on the economical level will go to moderate hotels in smaller places.

At all levels, it is more economical to stay for several days or a week or more at one center, taking advantage of pension terms, and touring around from there.

HOTEL PRICES*

Category City	*Major Resort*	*Major Capital*	*Provincial Capital*	*Budget Resort***	*Southern City*
Deluxe: (L)					
Single	35–60,000	50–70,000	45,000	35,000	45,000
Double	60–95,000	80–120,000	70,000	60,000	55–70,000
Expensive (1)					
Single	45,000	35–60,000	28,000	25,000	30,000
Double	55–70,000	55–75,000	50,000	45,000	50,000
Moderate (2)					
Single	28,000	28,000	23,000	18,000	22,000
Double	25–38,000	30–42,000	25–34,000	26,000	25,000

Category *City*	*Major* *Resort*	*Major* *Capital*	*Provincial* *Capital*	*Budget* *Resort***	*Southern* *City*
Inexpensive (3)					
Single	14,000	14,000	12,000	12,000	14,000
Double	25,000	15–25,000	17,000	18,000	24,000
Pension: (P)					
Single	12,000	15,000	10,000		
Double	12–18,000	24,000	14,000		

* All rooms with bath. For rooms without bath, you will pay 1/3 to ½ less.
**In budget resorts, prices in classes 1 and 2 pensions range from about 13,000 to 16,000 lire per person, with all meals.

The cost of meals varies considerably. Breakfast will usually fall into the 2,500–5,000 lire range, but for lunch and dinner you can spend anything from 15,000 lire per person in a modest restaurant, up to 50,000 in a 1st-class one, including wine and service. Deluxe hotels and chic dinner clubs cost much more. Ordinary wine costs about 5,000 lire a bottle; better vintages start at about 8,000 and range up to 10,000 or more. You can save on restaurant bills by ordering house wine by the carafe. A cocktail costs at least 2,000 lire; try dry vermouth or Campari as aperitifs.

A TYPICAL DAY

Moderate hotel, breakfast and one meal service and taxes included	32,000–37,000 lire
Lunch or dinner at a restaurant	15,000
Transportation, say four tram rides, and one taxi	2,500
Tours, entrance fees, tips	6,000
Cigarettes	1,200
Cafés, say one coffee	400
and one beer	800
Miscellaneous	2,500

Say, 65,000 lire

A man's haircut runs to about 7,000 lire with tip. A woman's shampoo and set is from 8,000 up to 35–40,000 in a top salon. A few other items: 900 lire for a pack of Italian cigarettes, 1,500 for American; 500 for a Havana cigar, opera seats from 2,000 to 8,000 (but first-night seats at La Scala run to 28,000!); about 2,500 for a movie; 10,000 and up for a nightclub.

Hotelcheck Plan. For travelers from America, TWA and the Hilton hotels have a voucher plan covering guaranteed accommodations in Hilton hotels in 20 major centers of Europe plus Turkey and Israel. Rates are $60 for single occupancy, $75 for double occupancy, including taxes, service charges, meals in some cases, but not surcharges. Italy, Rome and Milan are covered by this scheme. Various other conditions may increase the total charge considerably.

RESTAURANTS. We class restaurants in our Practical Information sections as:

Expensive (E). 30,000 lire and up per person; for a full meal and house wine (though in the really expensive spots you'll only find bottled wine).

Moderate (M). 15–30,000 lire per person.

Inexpensive (I). 9–15,000 lire per person.

WHEN TO GO. The main tourist season in Italy runs from mid-April to the end of September, when the weather is best. Spring and early autumn (through October) are fine, especially for city sightseeing. Avoid resorts in August, when they're crowded with vacationing Italians.

You will find a section entitled *Weather Matters* in most of the regional chapters, giving more specific information on that particular area.

Average maximum daily temperatures in degrees Fahrenheit and centigrade:

Milan	Jan.	Feb.	Mar.	Apr.	May	June	July	Aug.	Sept.	Oct.	Nov.	Dec.
F°	41	46	55	64	73	81	84	82	75	63	50	43
C°	5	8	13	18	23	27	29	28	24	17	10	6
Naples												
F°	54	55	59	64	72	79	84	84	79	72	63	57
C°	12	13	15	18	22	26	29	29	26	22	17	14

Off-Season Travel. This has become more popular in recent years as business houses have finally recognized the many advantages of staggering vacations throughout the year and as tourists have come to appreciate the advantages of avoiding the crowded periods. Plane fares are cheaper and so are hotel rates. Italy is ideally suited for off-season vacationing, since its mild climate makes it an outdoor country all year round. The winter is of course the season to hear the famous La Scala Opera at Milan, as well as the operas of Venice, Naples, Rome and other cities. The Italian Riviera and Sicily are attractive in winter. Sardinia and Calabria are good in early spring or late autumn.

BUDGET TIPS. Tuscan towns such as Pisa, Arezzo, Lucca and Siena, the island of Elba (off-season) and beach resorts at Marina di Pietrasanta and Lido di Camaiore are good tourist value. Hotels are reasonable and comfortable, and there's a wide range of moderately priced restaurants. Most expensive spots in Tuscany are the Argentario, Punta Ala, Forte dei Marmi, Viareggio, Montecatini.

In Liguria, there are off-season rates in May and from September thru October, the weather is usually fine, and you avoid the crowds. Smaller resorts such as Laigueglia, 10 minutes from Alassio; Chiavari and Lavagna-Cavi near Rapalto; Arma di Taggia near San Remo; and Diano Marina near Imperia, offer lower rates all year round.

Valle d'Aosta hotels offer excellent facilities at rates lower than those in other Piedmont resorts, and special bargains off-season (from mid-January to mid-April and from September to late December). Inquire about all-inclusive ski-week rates at all Piedmont winter resorts.

Venice is expensive, perhaps even more so than Capri, because hotel and restaurant owners have a unique problem—all supplies have to be ferried in on small boats—which increases their costs. But you can visit off-season; the city has a particular magic from late autumn to early spring (in fact, many in-the-know people prefer it then) and all hotels offer lower rates. Some, such as the 1st class *Metropole* and 2nd class *Concordia,* promote low-cost individual tour packages through CIT. Then, take half-pension terms (you'll be expected to during the summer anyway) and learn to love the *tavola calda,* where you can save enough on two or three meals to splurge with at a top restaurant. Third, use the *vaporetti,* Venice's waterborne buses, to get around in. Gondolas and water taxis are getting more and more expensive.

Prices throughout the Marches are comparatively low. The delightful resorts south of Ancona, especially Numana, Grottamare and San Benedetto del Tronto, are much greener and quieter than big Adriatic resorts like Rimini, and their June or September off-season rates are real budget-savers.

In the Deep South, check on the tourist villages at Ostuni, Tropea, the Gargano, Copanello and Isola Capo Rizzuto. They're ideal for a relaxed singles or family vacation, and their all-in rates are reasonable.

SPECIAL EVENTS. You will find all the most interesting festivals listed under their location in the *Town by Town* section. Here are a few gathered together by month:

January, the Roman Catholic Epiphany celebrations and decorations in Rome's Piazza Navona; the Greek Catholic Epiphany rites at Piana degli Albanesi, near Palermo; at Cortina d'Ampezzo international hockey.

February (sometimes March), pre-Lenten carnivals in many places, particularly the Viareggio Carnival before Shrove Tuesday; Almond Blossom Festival at Agrigento; the Saint Agatha Festival at Catania; the Flower Show at San Remo.

March, nationwide mid-Lent festivals, feasts for the poor, usually on St. Joseph's Day, the 19th; Florence's traditional Scoppio del Carro (this sometimes falls in April).

April, the International Trade Fair at Milan; International Handicrafts Fair, Florence.

May, Musical Festival at Florence; Feast of Sant' Efisio in Cagliari; Annual Fish Festival at Camogli (near Genoa); the Festa dei Ceri, Gubbio; the Sardinian Costume Cavalcade at Sassari.

June, Tournament of the Bridge, Pisa; the now famous Festival of the Two Worlds, at Spoleto (month long); nationwide celebration of Feast of St. John, with the most important observances in Rome and Florence.

July, the Palio at Siena (repeated in August); the Feast of the Redeemer, Venice; International Ballet Festival, Nervi; the Madonna del Carmine festival, Naples. Noantri festival, Rome.

August, Feast of the Assumption of Mary, throughout Italy; Tournament of the Quintana, Ascoli Piceno; Palio of the Gulf, La Spezia; the final of the Palio at Siena. Feast of the Redeemer, Nuoro (Sardinia).

September, The Joust of the Saracen, Arezzo; Joust of the Quintana, Foligno; Historic Regatta, Venice; Feast of the Piedigrotta, Naples.

October, Celebrations in honor of Columbus, Genoa; Annual Truffle Fair, Alba.

November, Feast of the Madonna della Salute, Venice.

December, traditional Christmas celebrations throughout the country.

Note: Check the dates on the spot, as some events are liable to change from year to year.

PILGRIMAGES. The first goal of Catholic pilgrims to Italy is, of course, Rome and its four major churches, and the favored times to go there are Easter and Christmas. Important Easter ceremonies are held also in Florence, Sulmona, Lanciano and Grassina, where there is a Passion Play.

Special pilgrimage days for Loreto are 25 March, 15 August, 8 September and 8 and 10 December. 13 June is the day to visit the tomb of St. Anthony in Padua. The Black Madonna of Tindari, in Sicily, is visited especially on 8 September, and the Madonna of Trapani, on the same island, on 25 March. It would be impossible to list here all the religious ceremonies and processions in devout Italy, but among them special attention might be called to these: 17 January, the blessing of work animals and pets at St. Eusebius in Rome and the Presentation of the Lambs, at St. Agnes, in the same city, 21 January; just before Easter, the Palm Sunday blessing of the palms by the Pope at Rome and just after it, in Genzano, in the Alban hills, on the Sunday nearest Corpus Domini, the beautiful Infiorata procession.

Rome's Trastevere quarter celebrates the feast of the Madonna del Carmine in July; also in July, the unique celebration of the feast of Santu Antine at Sedilo, near Cagliari; September is the month of the miracle of San Gennaro at Naples and of the festival of Santa Rosa at Viterbo, in Lazio: the festival of St. Francis of Assisi occurs in that city in October; and at Christmas a visit to the Christmas crib in the volcanic Grotto of the Doves in Acireale (Catania) is a stirring experience.

Relics. Relics of particular interest to Roman Catholics are to be found in many parts of Italy. The most important are these: at Amalfi, the body of St. Andrew; at Assisi, the remains both of St. Francis and St. Clare; at Loreto, the

Holy House, birthplace of the Virgin; at Pavia, relics of St. [illegible] Perugia, the Virgin's wedding ring; at Portofino, the bones of S[illegible] Rome, St. Peter's chains and fragments of the Cross; at Salerno, th[illegible] Matthew; and at Turin, the Holy Shroud.

Information may be obtained from ENIT—see *Travel Agents* sec[illegible]ow for addresses.

HIGHLIGHTS. In Italy, it is easier to advise you where not to go. For a first trip, with limited time, it might be best to concentrate on the triangle of Italy's most visited cities—Rome, Florence, Venice.

Some highlights of Italy you may wish to take in are: for those interested in antiquity, go to Pompeii and Herculaneum for Roman remains; to Tarquinia (Lazio) for the Etruscan Necropolis; to Paestum (Campania) or Agrigento (Sicily) for Greek temples.

Art lovers can see Leonardo da Vinci's *Last Supper* at Milan, Michelangelo's *Last Judgement* and his amazing frescos in the Sistine Chapel in Rome. Titian's *Sacred and Profane Love* in the same city, the best of Raphael in the Vatican, Tintoretto in Venice, and everything in Florence; Ravenna is worth visiting for its mosaics.

Districts noted for their beauty include the Naples region—Amalfi, Sorrento, islands of Capri and Ischia; the Riviera Levante—Rapallo, Santa Margherita Ligure (and here those in the know go to Portofino); the lake region—Stresa, Como; Fiesole, just outside of Florence; Sicily and Sardinia, to get really out of the workaday world. Wild mountain scenery is found in the Dolomites. For volcanos, there are Etna and Vesuvius.

If you want to ski here, Cortina d'Ampezzo is perhaps the most popular resort; for winter sports in the Piedmontese Alps, try Sestrière.

Swimmers can go to Sardinia, to Rimini on the Adriatic Riviera, to San Remo, Viareggio, or Elba on the western coast, all with sandy beaches; or to Capri, Amalfi, the Tremiti and Aeolian islands for rock bathing.

And for other cities worth visiting: Pisa, of Leaning Tower fame, Assisi, Bologna, Ferrara, Padua, Cremona, the violin capital, Verona, the city of Romeo and Juliet, Siena, Urbino, the port of Genoa, Turin, Palermo, Syracuse, Taormina and dozens more.

TRAVEL AGENTS. When you have decided where you want to go, your next step is to consult a good travel agent. If you haven't one, the *American Society of Travel Agents,* 711 Fifth Avenue, New York, NY 10022; and *ASTA West Coast,* 4420 Hotel Circle Court, Suite 230, San Diego, CA 92108; or the *Association of British Travel Agents,* 50–57 Newman St., London WIP 4AH, will advise you. Whether you select *Maupintour, CIT, American Express, Thomas Cook* or a smaller organization is a matter of preference. Most of them have branch offices or correspondents in the larger European cities.

nformation. CIT (*Compagnia Italiano Turismo*), highly reputed, leading travel agency, 10 Charles II St., London SW1; 600 Fifth Ave., New York, NY 10019; 765 Route 83, Bensenville, Ill. 60106 *Italian State Railway,* 5670 Wilshire Blvd., Los Angeles 90036; 2055 Peel St., Montreal 110; 111 Richmond St. West, Toronto, Ont., M5H 264; as well as 30 offices throughout Italy.

ENIT (Italian Government Tourist Office), Suite 1565, 630 Fifth Ave., New York, NY 10020; 500 North Michigan Ave., Chicago 60611; 360 Post St., San Francisco; 3 Place Ville Marie, Montreal; 201 Regent St., London W1.

In the Practical Information sections at the end of each chapter, you'll also find the following abbreviations; *AAST* (Azienda Autonoma Soggiorno Turismo, Local Tourist Board); *EPT* (Ente Provinciale Turismo, Provincial Tourist Board); *SIT* (Societa Internazionale Turismo, normally the location of the local American Express office).

There are good reasons why you should engage a reliable travel agent. Travel abroad today, although it is steadily becoming easier and more comfortable, is also growing more complex in its details. As the choice of things to do, places to visit, ways of getting there, increases, so does the problem of *knowing* about all these questions. A reputable, experienced travel agent is a specialist in details, and you should inquire in your community to find out which organization has the finest reputation.

If you wish him merely to book you on a package tour, reserve your transportation and even your first overnight hotel accommodation, his services should cost you nothing. Most carriers and tour operators grant him a fixed commission for saving them the expense of offices in every town and city.

If, on the other hand, you wish him to plan for you an individual itinerary and make all arrangements down to hotel reservations and transfers to and from rail and air terminals, you are drawing upon his skill and knowledge and thus he will make a service charge on the total cost of your planned itinerary. This charge may amount to 10 or 15%, but it will more than likely *save* you money on balance. A good travel agent can help you avoid costly mistakes due to inexperience. He can help you take advantage of special reductions in rail fares and the like that you would not otherwise know about. Most important, he can save you *time* by making it unnecessary for you to waste precious days abroad trying to get tickets and reservations.

PACKAGE TOURS are a marvelous way of seeing a country for the first time, as you get good value for money and frequently cover the highlights all in one go. Having sampled Italy by this means, you can then return on your own, or take a more specialized tour, one covering different aspects of the country or just different regions. There are many kinds of package tours, ranging from the fully-escorted (someone with you all the time) to the individualistic fly/drive package, where you hop off your scheduled airplane, pick up a rented car and zoom away to your own particular target.

From the US. Leading all tour operators in Italy is the highly reputed CIT which knows more about things Italian than anyone else in the travel field. See *Travel Agents* section (above) for addresses.

Di Carlo Tours, 151 West 40th St., New York NY 10018, has a *Best of Italy* tour for 9 days at a total land cost of $210 (approx. $23 per day). Tour includes: portage, daily breakfast, restaurant and gift discount cards, 1st class lodgings, an airconditioned coach for sightseeing and for transfers, and a 15% discount on all car rentals. Other meals, sidetrips and airfare are extra. There are also 5 optional extension trips to the southernmost sections of Italy, including a 1-week fly-drive package tour for $139, and a camper package deal.

American Express offers a 15-day *Italian Holiday* tour of most sections of Italy. This fully-escorted tour includes 1st class lodgings, most meals, transportation etc., as well as sightseeing in Rome, Pompeii, Capri, Sienna, Venice, Florence, Milan and many other spots. The land price, during high season, for a shared booking is $1,120, but the single one costs an additional $150.

Extra Value Vacations, 5 World Trade Center, New York, NY 10048, offers a 15-day escorted motorcoach tour of Italy with Alitalia Airlines for $1,439 (book at least 45 days prior to departure). You may also add to a 9-day tour a week in a resort hotel in any of 6 places in southern Italy: Capri, Amalfi, Sorrento, Ischia, Positano or Naples for an additional charge.

These are only a few samples of the many possibilities in a country as popular as Italy. *Maupintour, Thomas Cook, American Express* are other major tour operators with extensive programs to choose from.

From Britain the choices are just as varied. Motor-racing fans will find a friend at *Page and Moy,* 136–138 London Road, Leicester, England. This agency specializes in arranging tours to visit Grand Prix events.

Art lovers should book in with *W.F. & R.K. Swan (Hellenic) Ltd.,* 237 Tottenham Court Road, London, W1, who have several Art Treasures Tours to Italy. One covers the glories of Northern Italy in 15 days for £799; a guest lecturer reveals the wonders of Venice, Ravenna, Siena, etc. The Southern Italy Tour is for 15 days also and costs £618. Sicily has an Art Tour for 15 days and £669. Art Appreciation in the Hill Towns (Perugia, Urbino and so on) is for 15 days and costs £616. All these tours have guest lecturers, skilled in their subject.

Serenissima, 140 Sloane Street, London SW1, also have several expertly guided Art Tours. Their tour of Ravenna and Byzantine Venice is for 8 days at £550.

CIT have a rich multiplicity of programs to offer, fly/drive, weekends, one- and two-week visits, all well worth exploring. A week in Florence, for example, over Easter in a first-class hotel, including flight and accommodations, costs about £310; a week in Venice at the same time of year and in a similar hotel costs about £260. They also offer a wide range of winter holidays. 14 nights in Macugnaga, for example, just on the Swiss border costs from about £230, flight included.

HANDICAPPED TRAVEL. An important source of information in this ever expanding field is *Access to the World* by Louise Weiss (Chatham Square Press); the *Travel Information Center,* Moss Rehabilitation Hospital, 12th St and Tabor Rd, Philadelphia, Penn 19141; *Easter Seal Society for Crippled Children and Adults,* Director of Education and Information Service, 2023 West Ogden Av, Chicago, Ill 60612; *the Society for the Promotion of Travel for the Handicapped,* 26 Court St, Brooklyn, NY 11242.

Tour Operators in the US. *Evergreen Travel Service,* 19505, 44th Avenue West, Lynwood, WA 98036, has operated tours for the handicapped for 16 years, wheelchair travelers and the blind. Tours to Europe, the South Pacific and even one six-week round-the-world tour every other year.

Flying Wheel Tours, 148 West Bridge St., Owatonna, MN 55060. A big agency handling both tours and individual travel.

Rambling Tours, PO Box 1304, Hallandale, Fla. 33009. Specialists in European handicapped travel.

Britain is also very active in this field. One of the major centers for help and advice is the *Royal Association for Disability and Rehabilitation,* 25 Mortimer St., London W1, which has a whole library of pamphlets; *Holidays for the Physically Handicapped* and the *Access* guides among them.

Information on Europe is also available from *Mobility International,* 43 Dorset St., London W1, England, and the *National Society for Mentally Handicapped Children,* 117 Golden Lane, London EC1. The *Across Trust,* Crown House, Morden, Surrey, England have an amazing series of 'Jumbulances', huge articulated ambulances that can whisk even the most seriously handicapped across Europe in comfort and safety and staffed by volunteer doctors and nurses.

ROUGHING IT. If you are one of those who prefer a tent to a hotel room, you should find Italy a veritable paradise. Whether you favor wooded areas, the lakes, mountain areas, or the seashore, you can find a beautifully located camp. There are more than 1,000 campsites in Italy, many with bungalows, and many open all year. The average daily rates run at about 2,500 per person, 2,000 for a car, 1,000 for a motorcycle, 2,500 for a caravan and 1,500 for a tent.

In Italy you can apply to the *Federazione Italiana del Campeggio,* Exit 19, Autostrada del Sole, Prato-Calenzano or Casella Postale 649, 50100 Florence, for a camping license or for an international camping carnet, both of which are valid in the other European and Mediterranean countries. With your application send a passport-size photo. The *Federazione* publishes a fine guide, Guida Camping Italia (Italian Camping Guide), text in Italian, French, English, and German.

YOUTH HOSTELS. The Youth Hostel movement in Italy has developed since the last war. At present there are about 50 hostels, and the number grows every year. Headquarters in Italy is the *Associazione Italiana Alberghi per la Gioventù,* Palazzo Civiltà del Lavoro, Quadrato della Concordia, 00144, Rome, a member of the *International Youth Hostels Federation.*

Ample information about this type of traveling can be obtained from *American Youth Hostels, Inc.,* National Campus, Delaplane, Va. 22025; the *Canadian Youth Hostels Association* national office, 333 River Road, Vanier City, Ottawa, Ontario; the *National Campers and Hikers Association, Inc.,* 7172 Transit Rd, Buffalo, NY 14221; and the *American Camping Association,* 343 South Dearborn Street, Chicago, Ill.

In England the addresses are: *Camping Club of Great Britain and Ireland,* 11 Lower Grosvenor Place, London SW1; the *Youth Hostels Association,* Trevelyan House, St. Albans, Herts; *The Cyclists Touring Club,* 69 Meadrow, Godalming, Surrey.

WHAT TO TAKE. The first principle is to travel light. If you plan to fly across the Atlantic, airline baggage allowances are now based on size rather than weight. Economy class passengers may take free two pieces of baggage, provided that the sum of their dimensions is not over 106 inches and neither one singly is over 62 inches-height, width and length. For first class the allowance is two pieces up to 62 inches each, total 124 inches. The penalties for oversize are severe; to Western Europe $40 to $50 per piece.

Flights within Europe still have the old weight restrictions, 44 lbs. per economy passenger, 66 lbs. first class.

Do not take more than you can carry yourself; it's a lifesaver if you go to places where porters are hard to find. It's a good idea to pack the bulk of your things in one large bag and put everything you need for overnight, or for two or three nights, in another. This obviates packing and repacking at every stop.

The weather is of course considerably milder in Italy than in either the United States or Great Britain all the year round. In the summer season, make your clothing as light as possible—but women should have a scarf, light stole or jacket handy to cover bare shoulders and arms when visiting churches, where pants suits are acceptable but shorts are taboo (they can be strict about this in Italy). It's no longer necessary for women to cover their heads in churches, however. A sweater or woolen stole is a must for the cool of the evening, even during the hot months. In the summer, brief afternoon thunderstorms are common in Rome and inland cities; carry a plastic folding raincoat. And if you go into the mountains, you will find the evenings there quite chilly. During the winter, a medium-weight coat will stand you in good stead, while a raincoat is essential. You'll probably need an umbrella, too, but you can pick it up on the spot (or invest in a good folding one).

The deluxe spots are still dressy, but not formal. Men aren't required to wear ties or jackets anywhere, especially in the summer, except in some of the grander hotel dining rooms and top-level restaurants. Formal wear is very definitely the exception rather than the rule at the opera nowadays. For the huge general papal audiences, no rules of dress apply except those of common sense. For other types of audience, the Vatican Information Office will illustrate requirements.

If you wear glasses, take along a spare pair or the prescription and if you have to take some particular medicine regularly, especially if it is made up only on prescription, better bring a supply. Its exact equivalent may be difficult for the average pharmacist to identify, though it undoubtedly exists.

PHOTOGRAPHY. Those once-in-a-lifetime holiday films are vulnerable to the X-ray security machines on airports. At some, such as London's Heathrow, extra-powerful equipment is used; on most the machines are of the "low-dose" type. Both can cause films to be "fogged", and the more often the film passes through such machines, the more the fog can build up.

Warning notices are displayed sometimes, and passengers are advised to remove film—or cameras with film in them—for a hand check. But many airport authorities will not allow hand inspection and insist that all luggage pass through the detection devices.

There are two steps you should follow. First, ask for a hand-inspection whenever you can. Second, buy one or more *Filmashield* lead-laminated bags, which are manufactured by the American SIMA Products Group. These will protect films from low-dosage X-rays, but should not be relied on against the more powerful machines. The bags are also available in Britain.

TRAVEL DOCUMENTS. It is wise to give obtaining a passport top priority in your planning. Apply several months in advance of your expected departure date.

USA. You must apply in person to the US Passport Agency in New York, Boston, Philadelphia, Washington DC, Miami, Chicago, New Orleans, Detroit, Houston, Stamford (Conn.), Seattle, San Francisco, Los Angeles or Honolulu, or to their local County Courthouse. In some areas selected post offices are also equipped to handle passport applications. If you still have your latest passport issued within the past eight years you may use this to apply by mail. Otherwise, take with you: 1) a birth certificate or certified copy thereof, or other proof of citizenship; 2) two identical photographs 2 inches square, full face, black and white or color, on nonglossy paper, and taken within the past six months; 3) $14 or $10 if you apply by mail with an old passport; 4) proof of identity such as a driver's license, previous passport, any governmental ID Card. Social Security and credit cards are NOT acceptable. US passports are valid for 5 years. If you expect to travel extensively, you may request a 48- or 96-page passport rather than the usual 24-page one. There is no extra charge. If your passport gets lost or stolen, immediately notify either the nearest American Consulate or the Passport Office, Department of State, Washington, D.C. 20524. Record your passport's number and its date and place of issue.

If a resident-alien, file a Treasury Sailing Permit, Form 1040C, certifying that Federal taxes have been paid; apply to your District Director of Internal Revenue for this. You will have to present various documents: 1) blue or green alien registration card; 2) passport; 3) travel tickets; 4) most recently filed Form 1040; 5) W2 forms for the most recent full year; 6) most recent current payroll stubs or letter; 7) check to be sure this is all! To return to the USA you must file an I–131 form 45 days prior to departure. Apply in person at the nearest office of the Immigration and Naturalization Service, or by mail to the Immigration and Naturalization Service, Washington, DC.

Britain. You must apply for passports on special forms obtainable from your travel agency or main Post Office. The application should be sent to the Passport Office for your area (as indicated on the guidance form) or through a travel agent. Apply at least 3 weeks before the passport is required. The regional Passport Offices are located in London, Liverpool, Peterborough, Glasgow, Newport (Mon.), and Belfast. The application must be countersigned by your bank manager, or a solicitor, barrister, doctor, clergyman or justice of the peace who knows you personally. You will need two photos. The fee is £11; validity 10 years.

British Visitor's Passport. This simplified form of passport has advantages for the once-in-a-while tourist to Italy and most other European countries. Valid for one year and not renewable, it costs £5.50. Application must be made in person at a main Post Office and two passport photographs are required—no other formalities.

Visas. Not required by passport holders of the UK, Eire, the USA, and Canada for stays of up to 3 months, but visas are required for citizens of some Commonwealth countries.

Currency Declaration Form. Required to be filled in upon arrival and returned to authorities at departure point.

Health Certificates. Not required for entry to Italy, and neither the USA, Canada or Britain require a certificate of vaccination against smallpox on arrival home as the disease has now been almost totally obliterated throughout the world. Nevertheless, we suggest you be vaccinated wherever you may be going. The simplest way is to be vaccinated before you leave. Have the doctor fill in a standard form, which you can obtain from your steamship company or airline, if they don't hand it to you automatically. Take the form with you to present on re-entering. If you put off vaccination until your return, remember to allow time for the reaction test which checks the efficacy of the vaccination.

GETTING TO ITALY

FROM THE UNITED STATES

BY AIR. The main Italian international airports are Rome and Milan, either one an overnight flight from New York. Leaving New York at 7.30 in the evening, for example, you will arive in Rome or Milan the next morning at about 9, local time.

Alitalia, Italy's national airline, flies from Boston, New York, Philadelphia, Chicago, Montreal and Toronto to Rome and Milan. *Pan Am* and *TWA* fly from

New York direct to Rome and from San Francisco and Los Angeles to Rome via the Polar route.

Remember that there is a luggage allowance, now by size on transatlantic flights, by weight within Europe itself. This is actually a plus, as it forces you to keep baggage to a minimum, vital in these days of airport strikes and no porters.

FARES. It is no secret that airline fare structures are among the most complex and obscure inventions of the 20th century. Nonetheless, certain basic fares can be identified. The standard fares are first-class and economy. At $2,800 return (first-class) New York–Rome and $1,500 return (economy) New York–Rome, these are frankly expensive. Excursion fares (return only; minimum stay 14 days, maximum 90 days) are $1,100 and Apex (return only, minimum stay 7 days, maximum 60 days; must be purchased 21 days in advance) is $920. These last two represent much better value though the conditions under which they must be booked limit them somewhat. All these fares are those of mid-1981 and will certainly change before 1982.

After these basic fares are a whole host of special discounts for groups and charter flights. Though their conditions are also limiting and sometimes a little inconvenient, they certainly represent the best value for money. But consult a travel agent and hope that he can explain their inner mysteries to you. Remember that there is nothing more galling than discovering that the person sitting next to you has paid less than you for an identical seat.

Children between the ages of 2 and 12 travel at half the adult tariff, but are entitled to a full luggage allowance. Infants under 2 not occupying a seat and accompanied by an adult are charged only 10% of the full fare. Although they are not entitled to a free luggage allowance, their food, clothing, and other supplies needed in flight are not weighed. Most airlines provide special bassinets if notified in advance.

BY SEA. Passenger liner service everywhere is increasingly limited and its place taken by passenger-carrying freighters. These take up to 12 passengers in very comfortable single-class accommodations. "Increasingly limited" is, in fact, a polite way of saying "almost non-existent". There is only one major liner still plying for hire across the Atlantic, and that is the *Queen Elizabeth 2, Cunard's* answer to the market for both luxury cruising and those who want to get to Europe in style and comfort. A two-class ship, basically, its 65,000 tons surround 5 decks of staterooms and 3 decks of public rooms. The latter include several restaurants (high up on the ship for good visibility), 2 outdoor pools, 2 indoor pools, bars, and everything else you can think of to make the trip enjoyable. Quite naturally, everything is air-conditioned, and there are stabilizers and all the latest safety equipment.

Unfortunately, the *QE 2* calls only at French and English ports. There is no longer *any* regular liner service between North America and the Mediterranean.

For cargo-liner passage, consult any of the following: *Traveltips Freighter Association,* 163–09 Depot Rd, Flushing, NY 11358; *Ford's Freighter Travel Guide,* 22151 Clarendon Street, Woodland Hills, Calif. 91365; *Pearl's Freighter Tips,* 175 Great Neck Rd, Great Neck, NY 11202; *Air Marine Travel Service,* 501 Madison Ave, New York, NY 10011.

The Mediterranean, Tyrhennian and Adriatic Seas are all popular with cruise ships, some of which are based at Genoa, Naples or Venice. In addition, other cruises from the U.K. such as those operated by the big *P & O* shipping group call at various Italian ports including Genoa, Naples, Syracuse and Venice. Another U.K.-based company, *Swans Hellenic Cruises,* operates a series of high grade voyages always with a "cultural" theme calling at a number of Italian ports. And the Greek-owned *Chandris Line* also operate cruises to various Italian ports with Genoa again as their base.

As we went to press some of these cruise details were still undecided. Again we would suggest that you contact your travel agent.

FROM GREAT BRITAIN

BY AIR. *Alitalia* and *British Airways* fly frequently between Italy and Britain. From Heathrow (London), the two carriers have several daily flights to Roma and Milan and daily flights to Naples, Venice, Pisa, Bologna and Turin. Flying time to Rome is about two hours. *British Caledonian* flies from Gatwick (London) to Genoa. Several other major airlines also fly between London and Rome as the last or first leg on intercontinental flights. There are also direct flights to Milan, Rome and Turin from Birmingham and Manchester on British Airways and Alitalia, and from Dublin to Rome on *Aer Lingus.* Return fares between London and Rome, at the time of writing, are £340 economy, £285 one month excursion (minimum stay 6 days, maximum 30 days), Apex £140 (minimum stay 14 days, maximum 90 days; fare varies according to season and must be bought 30 days before departure).

However, the least expensive (and least comfortable) way of flying to Italy is on a charter flight. These operate from Gatwick and Luton and most northern airports to Rome, Milan, Venice, Pisa, Naples, Genoa, Brindisi and Palermo. You do not need to be on a package tour to make use of them. The best way to find further details is in the national and Sunday press or the magazine Time Out. If you can put up with the inconvenience of flying in the middle of the night and from relatively inaccessible airports, you'll find that there are considerable savings to be had.

BY TRAIN. With the abundance of routes, scenic or fast or often both combined, into and also within Italy, it is only possible to make a small selection.

From London, one of the most convenient ways to travel to Italy by train is to leave Victoria in the early afternoon and travel via Folkestone and Calais. From here there is a through service (mid-May to the end of September) to Milan, Verona and Venice, reaching the latter at about 4.30 the following afternoon. This service also runs over the Christmas, New Year and Easter holidays. At other times, there is a connection at Paris. From Calais, there are both 1st- and 2nd-class sleepers, 1st- and 2nd-class day carriages and 2nd-class couchettes to Venice. These may also be booked to Milan and Verona. There are excellent connections at Milan for Bologna, Florence and Rome. This last is reached in mid-evening. There are also good connections to Genoa and Pisa. Buffet service part of the way.

Another comfortable way to get to Italy is to take the 9 A.M. train from London (Charing Cross) to Dover for the Hovercraft connection to Boulogne and then go by rail-car direct to Paris (Gare du Nord). Take the metro or a taxi across Paris to the Gare du Lyon, and catch the *Palatino* express. This leaves at about 6.50 P.M. and travels via Chambery and the Mont Cenis Tunnel to Turin. Here it divides, part going to Genoa (arriving 5 A.M.), Pisa (arriving 7 A.M.), and Rome (arriving 10 A.M.). The other section goes to Bologna (arriving 7 A.M.) and Florence (arriving 8.30 A.M.). There are 1st- and 2nd-class sleepers and 2nd-class couchettes to all these destinations though day carriages only in Italy itself. There is a buffet car most of the way. Rail and sleeper joint tickets can be issued for the Paris to Italy sections.

BY CAR. Starting from England, the first hurdle is the Channel crossing. Car ferry services to the Continent increase yearly to keep pace with the growing number of carborne tourists, but only a few of them concern people making their way to Italy. There are the routes from Dover or Folkestone to Calais or Boulogne, by ship or Hovercraft; from Newhaven to Dieppe; and Southampton or Portsmouth to Cherbourg or Le Havre. It is conceivable that someone wishing to make a night crossing would go Dover-Dunkirk or Ostend, which costs the same as the shorter routes but takes longer and slightly increases the mileage on the other side. All ferries now have drive on/off loading.

According to the *RAC* the shortest drive to Milan, for example, is from Dieppe, 635 miles, easily covered in 2 days. The *Sealink* crossing takes 3¾ hours and there is a maximum of 6 crossings a day. The single fare in summer for a family plus car is £282 return. The shortest sea routes, which also have very frequent sailings, are from Dover or Folkestone to Boulogne or Calais; 1 hour 15 minutes on *Townsend Thoresen,* 1 hour 40 minutes on *P & O Ferries* and 1 hour 45 minutes on *Sealink.* For a family plus car, the return fare at peak period average out at around £160 to £200. The *Sealink* crossing to Ostend, 4½ hours, and Dunkirk, 2½, is rated the same as to Calais. People traveling from north of London might well use the *Townsend Thoresen* service from Felixstowe to Zeebrugge, 5 hours, with fares at around £240 return for a family and car. There is a useful night service available on this route. The mileage from Zeebrugge to Milan is 643, which makes it the second shortest after Dieppe, to which there is also a night service.

The crossings from Southampton or Portsmouth to Cherbourg or Le Havre take between 5 and 7 hours and add, in the case of Cherbourg, another 60 to the subsequent mileage. *P & O Ferries* sail to Le Havre. Fares on this route vary from £360 to £430 return in peak period for a family plus car. *Townsend Thoresen* cover the other ports. Fare for family and their car are again in excess of £350 return at peak period. The Hovercraft services from Dover to Calais or Boulogne by *Seaspeed,* and Ramsgate to Calais by *Hoverlloyd* make the fastest crossings, in 30, 35 and 40 minutes respectively. *Seaspeed* fares are £60 for a 14 ft. car and two passengers to Boulogne or Calais. The *Hoverlloyd* charge is £50 for the car and up to 5 passengers. All companies reduce their charges hugely in winter. There are, incidentally, no longer any air car-ferries operating out of Britain.

Car-Sleeper Expresses. Motorists who feel the need to save themselves driving several hundred miles can do so by using the *European Autorail* service, which saves time and fatigue but not money. The most direct service from the UK would be from Boulogne to Milan, 15–16 hours, which for a 14 ft. car one way and two 2nd-class passenger fares, including couchettes, would cost around £200 to £260 to do it in comfort with 1st-class sleepers. It is also possible to continue, with a change of trains, to Rome. Alternatively one can simply, and less expensively, reduce the long haul by entraining from Boulogne to Fréjus-St. Raphael on the Mediterranean, whence a brief motorway leads into Italy; or from Calais to Lyss in Switzerland, after which a pleasant but slow drive over the Alps brings one to Italy.

Fly-Drive. Only Alitalia offers a fly-drive service from Britain, and great value it is. When you pay for scheduled airfares for 2 or more people you can get an Avis group 'A' car (that's the small one); if it's 2 adults the unlimited mileage is for 7 days, if it's 3 adults 9 days, if it's 4 adults 11 days. The offer holds good for 18 airports in Italy and there is no need to return the car to the starting point. You can get larger cars and extra days for a supplementary payment. The minimum stay has to be 7 days, maximum one month.

FROM THE CONTINENT

BY AIR. All important Continental cities are linked by air with Milan and Rome, both by the Italian line *Alitalia* and those of the various countries flying to or through Italy. Connections to Venice, Florence and other important Italian cities can be made from these two. Special excursion rates are cheaper than the ordinary return fares, which are double the one-way tariff.

BY TRAIN. There is such a profusion of services to various parts of Italy from the whole of Western Europe (no direct service from Spain) that we have selected only a few of the top trains.

From France. Best train from Paris is the *Palatino* which leaves the Gare de Lyon in the early evening and goes via the Mont Cenis Tunnel and Pisa to Rome, arriving there around 10 the next morning. Also through coaches to Bologna and Florence. Buffet car most of the way. Carries sleeping and couchette cars to both Rome and Florence.

From Germany. From the Rhine Valley area take the *Loreley Express* which goes from Amsterdam via the main Rhine cities, Basle, Milan, Bologna, Florence and Rome. Takes 24 hours from Amsterdam with through carriages and 2nd class couchettes from Basle. Restaurant car part of way. *Holland-Italy* express follows similar route. From Munich the *Mediolanum* (TEE) leaves there in the mid-afternoon and goes via Innsbruck, Brenner Pass, Verona and Milan arriving there around 11.40 P.M.

From Austria. From Vienna the best train is the *Romulus* which leaves the Austrian capital around 8 A.M. and goes via Villach to Udine, Venice, Bologna, Florence and Rome arriving there after midnight. Buffet car all the way. Several trains each day from Innsbruck go through to Italy. For overnight travel between Vienna and Rome use the *Remus* which leaves the Austrian capital about 9.00 P.M., reaching Rome just after 1 P.M. next day, stopping en route at Venice (Mestre), Bologna and Florence. First- and second-class sleepers, second-class couchettes all or part of the way, as well as day cars. Buffet car Venice (Mestre) to Rome and vice versa.

From Switzerland. As many of the expresses from France, Germany and beyond pass through here en route there is no shortage of trains. In addition there are regular services starting from Zurich, Basle, Luzern, etc., to destinations in northern and central Italy.

BY BUS AND COACH. Italy is covered by several services in the Europabus network, the consortium of express bus routes operated by the railways of western Europe. Here are the main routes:

1. Vienna-Caorle-Lido de Jesolo-Venice. About 11 hours for full run every day in summer, costing around £24.
2. Venice-Florence, £20.
3. Florence-Rome, £20.
4. Rome-Naples, £12.

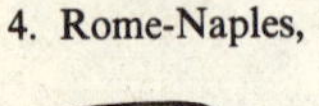

BY CAR. France is where travelers who have brought their cars from the States by sea join forces with those who have brought theirs across the Channel from Britain. Now they have only the dry run across France to Italy. From Cherbourg it is best to make for Vire, Alençon and Orléans on an assortment of roads, most of them major and all acceptable. At Orléans there is the reasonable choice of continuing eastwards along N60 to join the autoroute to carry on down to Chalon or continuing south-eastwards cross country to the same point. The autoroute is farther, much quicker, but imposes a high toll. The cross country route is very much more rewarding in every way except speed.

From Chalon-sur-Saône, there is a treble choice: enter Switzerland on the northwest side of Lake Leman, pass through Geneva and take the 50 mile motorway up to the Mt. Blanc tunnel, which emerges in Italy to join the Mt. Blanc autoroute, or continue on the original autoroute to Grenoble, then take N91 to Briançon and N94 over the frontier into Italy. All the routes are ultimately slow, but the first choice is least so.

Travelers from Le Havre can join the A13 autoroute after crossing the Tancarville bridge (toll), while those from Dieppe should use the D915 to Gisors then head due south to join the autoroute at Mantes. In both cases you can then avoid the terrible traffic in Rouen. From Mantes the autoroute goes to and around Paris; or you can take N191 which makes a wider sweep around Paris through delightful country and then heads back to the Autoroute du Soleil. From Calais or Boulogne motorists can join the autoroute at Arras and stay on it, or take a more *touristique* route via Amiens, Compiégne, Troyes, Dijon and on N5 to Geneva. From Dunkirk the A25 autoroute now runs direct to Lille where it connects with the A1 to Paris and the A6 for the south, right down to the Mediterranean to enter Italy along the Corniche autoroute. It is possible to drive the whole of the autoroute, Lille-Marseilles in one day, but not advisable and would cost a frightening amount in tolls.

Note that road numbers in France are in the process of being changed, but most remain recognizable, as for example N25 out of Dieppe is now D925.

From Hamburg, **Germany**, the conventional route to Italy is on the autobahn E4 past Hanover to Bad Hersfeld, E70 to Wurzburg, E5 to Nürnberg, E6 to Munich and on the Garmisch Partenkirchen where there is a gap of 42 miles in the motorway system to Innsbruck; after which E6 continues right over the Brenner pass to Verona and the east-west autostrada. Dedicated autobahnists can avoid the gap in E6 by taking E11 and E17 east of Munich, but it is about 60 miles longer. However, with the opening of the new St Gotthard tunnel through the Alps, you can now leave the autobahn at Stuttgart and drive down E70 to Schaffhausen, Winterthur and Schwyz and up the emerging motorway to the 9-mile tunnel (no toll). At the bottom of the valley, join the autostrada that runs through to Milan, the pivot of the Italian motorway system. A word of warning, however; let no stranger to Milan tackle the city without first studying a large-scale map of the city minutely. Even then you need nerves of iron.

Drivers from anywhere who have arrived in **Switzerland** have the splendid choice of taking the Mont Blanc or Grand St Bernard tunnels—both tolls—or going over the top of Grand St Bernard, the Simplon, the St Gotthard, the San Bernadino, Splugen, Bernina or Ofen. All these routes are beautiful and exciting. It just depends where you want to be in Italy.

From **Austria,** you can join the route from Germany on the Brenner, which has a toll and is often crowded. Alternatively, you can take the more interesting routes between Landeck, in the Tirol, and Merano, Lienz and Cortina d'Ampizzo and Villach and Tarvisio. This last way is also an excellent route into Yugoslavia. There are a few other minor passes, but they are for intrepid map-readers only.

From **Holland,** motorists can follow E36 to Cologne and then make for Nürnberg and Munich rather than staying on the much more heavily trafficked E4 and E11 via Karlsruhe and Stuttgart. Alternatively they can follow the Breda-Antwerp-Brussels-Namur-Luxembourg-Metz-Nancy-Epinal-Belfort line to Basle, and on.

Another good way from **Holland** or **Belgium** is to continue south from Brussels on 5 to Charleville-Mezières and then join N64 which goes all the way to Belfort. A little ingenuity on this route could bring one to the Rhône Valley routes N6 and 7, which since the advent of the autoroute have recaptured their pre-war charm. After Avignon and Aix-en-Provence you pick up the Riviera road to the frontier at Ventimiglia.

European Thruways. It will have been noticed that the letter "E" frequently appears in the road numbers. These are part of the international superhighway system of Europe, in the process of creation. It includes nearly all the continental motorways but also many lengths of ordinary trunk roads gradually being brought up to standard. They are signed with the letter E and their number in black on green. You can, for example, follow E2 from London to Brindisi; E6 from Oslo to Rome; E7 from Warsaw to Rome, and E14 from Stettin and Prague to Trieste.

Motels. Among the motels that have sprung up along Italy's superhighways and outside its major cities, the *AGIP* chain, owned by the petrol company, is the best value. It offers consistently clean, comfortable rooms at reasonable rates, often below average for the locality. Almost all *AGIP* motels are officially categorized as 2nd-class. The *Italian Automobile Club (ACI)* runs small 2nd- and 3rd-class *autostelli,* rather uneven in quality, strategically sited from central Italy down both coasts to Sicily. Most of the *AGIP* and *ACI* motels are described in the text of the town concerned.

ARRIVING IN ITALY

CUSTOMS. Two still cameras and one movie can be brought in duty-free by each person entering Italy. 10 rolls of still-camera film and 10 rolls of movie film may be brought in duty-free, along with binoculars, a portable phonograph and 10 records, a tape recorder, tapes, and a portable radio. Visitors from non-European countries may bring in up to 400 cigarettes, two bottles of wine and one of spirits per person. European-based visitors are limited to 300 cigarettes, one bottle of wine, and a pint of alcoholic spirits. Other items intended for your personal use are admitted without question as long as quantities are reasonable. There is a restriction on the amount of Italian lire which may be brought in or out of the country.

Although there are technical limitations to what you may export from Italy on your departure they do not apply to ordinary tourist purchases. Any major purchase will likely be shipped to your home directly by the store you bought it from, which will obtain any necessary licenses.

MONEY. Travelers may bring in, or out of, Italy a maximum of 200,000 lire in lire banknotes. However, unlimited amounts of travelers' checks or foreign currencies may be brought in. Tourists are required to provide an official record of all their currency and travelers' checks. When leaving the country, they may not take out more money than they brought in. Purchases of Italian currency have to be recorded.

Money can be changed in Italy not only at banks, travel agencies, and hotels, but, in effect, by anyone. That is to say, you may pay any bill or make any purchase in your own currency as well as in lire. To avoid misunderstandings, be sure to check the exchange rate you are getting; it will be more favorable at exchange and American Express offices, less so in banks, hotels, restaurants and stores.

The exchange rate varies these days. As we go to press, the rate is around 1,200 lire to one U.S. dollar, so that 100 lire equal around 12 cents; 2,270 lire to the £ sterling. We cannot stress strongly enough, however, the importance of keeping a weather eye open for fluctuations, both while planning your trip and while on it. Failure to do so could lose you money.

Two helpful tips about cash. Always carry a few single dollar bills, they will save you changing small travelers' checks, as well as coming in handy for last minute airport shopping.

A very good idea indeed is to stock up with small denomination money for the countries you are going to visit. This can be very useful for immediate needs on arrival, tipping porters, taxis, etc. You can get this in packs of $10, $15 or more from some banks, or from *Deak-Perera,* whose head office is at 29 Broadway, New York 10006.

Travelers' checks are the best way to safeguard your travel funds. In the US, *Bank of America, First National City, Republic Bank of Dallas,* and *Perera Co.* issue checks only in US dollars; *Thomas Cook* issues checks in US dollars, British pounds and Australian dollars; *Bank of Tokyo* in US dollars and Japanese yen; *Barclay's Bank* in dollars and pounds; and *American Express* in US and Canadian dollars, French and Swiss francs, British pounds, German marks and Japanese yen. Most banks charge a 1% service fee. Barclay's checks are free.

Note you can also cash personal checks up to £50 a time with a British banker's card at banks participating in the *Eurocheque* scheme. And don't forget that well-known credit cards, such as *American Express,* are perfectly acceptable for hotel, restaurant and other bills.

Security. It goes without saying that in the country that perfected purse snatching you must at all times keep any money you have on you in a secure place, but there are a couple of other points to bear in mind. The lire is a currency that runs into thousands at the drop of a hat, so it is extremely easy to misplace the odd nought at the end of a number. There are many sorry stories of people changing $200 at banks and coming away with $20 in lire without noticing. Similarly, always check your change. This applies not just in banks but restaurants, rail stations, hotels and shops to name only the most obvious places.

STAYING IN ITALY

HOTELS. Italian hotels are officially classified as deluxe, 1st class, 2nd class, 3rd class and 4th class, and the rates they may charge are fixed by law. These conform, more or less, to our gradings of deluxe, 1st class (1), moderate (2), inexpensive (3) and rock-bottom (4). Generally speaking most conventional tourists will probably prefer not to go below the 2nd class in Italy. This in fact gives them a very wide choice of hotels because while ceilings are established by law for the prices which hotels in any particular category may charge, no establishment is obliged to be placed in any particular category. Many new concerns, in particular, prefer to be placed in the moderate category, in order to obtain special loans, investment allowances, and tax reliefs, even though, in some cases, they *could* qualify as deluxe.

In all hotels you'll find a rate card on the back of the door to your room, or inside the closet door—it tells you exactly what you will pay for that particular room. Any discrepancy between this rate and that on your bill should be cause for complaint and should be reported to the local tourist office.

A hotel's age can be an important index of its comfort. With the exception of the really "grand" old Grand hotels, the older the building, the more likely it won't have efficient heating, air conditioning or plumbing.

See *Hotel Prices* in *Planning Your Trip.*

In Italy, never forget to enquire about supplementary charges. There is a fixed service charge of 15% in most parts of Italy, but in the last few years almost all hotels in all categories have adopted a policy of including service, general, and sojourn taxes in the room rate. Notable exceptions are some hotels in Rome (add 20%), Milan (add 20%), Venice, Florence, and some Aosta Valley resorts (17–20%). When this policy isn't applied, there is also, besides service, a general tax which adds 14% to your bill in deluxe hotels, 9% in the lower hotel classifications. A daily sojourn tax per person is also charged in tourist centers: 200 lire for deluxe hotels, less in lower categories.

In addition, there is a tax on food and beverages in bars of deluxe hotels of 9% and in 1st-class hotels of 3%; and you pay the same tax on restaurant meals taken in hotels other than the one at which you are stopping. You may find a charge for airconditioning, varying from 500 to 1,500 lire per day, in hotels in which this feature is optional. As a rule-of-thumb, when taxes aren't included in room rate, *increase the basic room rate by one-third* and you will approximate your actual bill.

Because hotels in Italy vary widely in quality, it is often safest to patronize hotel chains or group hotels. The *Compagnia Italiana Grandi Alberghi* (CIGA) owns and operates some of Italy's most renowned hotels; the chain has an information office at Rome's Fiumicino airport. CIGA hotels, in short, are the places to stay if you want to be certain of a royal welcome.

Italhotels is not a chain, but an association of individually owned and operated establishments, all offering the maximum in comfort, convenience, and service.

Three local chains are also worth particular attention. In Rome, you have the *Bettoja* chain, all top-drawer places. Equally dependable are the *Fioroni* hotels of Genoa. Sicily has its own association, the *Società Grandi Alberghi Siciliani.*

The Jolly, AGIP and *ACI* chains offer dependable though standardized accommodations—the latter two are especially convenient for motorists.

All this does not mean that 3rd class and 4th class hotels should be completely overlooked. Occasionally they provide the only available accommodation. In the country, an inn graded 3rd or 4th class may in fact turn out to be perfectly clean and friendly and adequate—or even more than adequate. And in addition, there are a very large number of extremely friendly, worthwhile *pensioni.*

Tourist Villages. In the wake of the *Club Méditerranée,* tourist villages are springing up throughout Italy. They offer bungalow accommodations, centralized dining and entertainment services, shops, hairdressers, babysitting and medical services, pools, private beaches and sports facilities. As a rule these villages are isolated and off the beaten track. All-inclusive costs make them a good vacation buy. The best are the *Valtur* villages at Ostuni, Pollino, Brucoli and Capo Rizzuto, and the *Forte* village at Santa Margherita di Pula in Sardinia.

Farm Holidays. *Agriturist,* 6 Piazza Sant' Andrea della Valle, can provide information on staying with a farm family in the Italian countryside. Or you can rent a farmhouse in Tuscany; information from local tourist office, *Azienda Soggiorno,* Via Banchi di Sotto, Siena.

Villa Rental. Also ideal for families is a villa vacation. Through CIT or your travel agent you can rent a fully equipped villa for 2–8 persons, some with maid service included, on the Adriatic or Tuscan coasts, in Sardinia, at Baia Domizia or at Rosa Marina village (see Ostuni). The London based *Villas Italia Ltd.,* 31 Haymarket, offers villas in Tuscany, Rome and Positano. Insist on seeing photos of the villa and get a clear idea of what services are included in the price. Further information on renting villas, farmhouses from ENIT (see *Travel Agents* section above for addresses.) For sea holidays, charter a yacht from Elba's Porto Azzurro—information from *Seasport Holidays,* 3 Common Wood, Farnham Common, Bucks SL2 3TY, England.

MEDICAL SERVICES. Tourists visiting Italy can purchase at certain border offices, the health cards created by the *Roue Blanche Internationelle Sanitaire Touristique.* The tourist is given the card and a booklet in 6 languages—French, English, Italian, Spanish, German and Russian—which contains basic sentences that can be used to talk to a doctor by phone and obtain the necessary assistance. The booklet also contains the names and addresses of all the doctors affiliated with the organization. Most cities have English-speaking doctors. The US or British consulate will furnish their names and phone numbers. The bilingual personnel of the so-called "international pharmacies" in Italy's tourist capitals are always helpful and will suggest suitable remedies.

The *IAMAT* (International Assoc. for Medical Assistance to Travelers Inc.) offers you a list of approved English-speaking doctors who have had postgraduate training in the US, Canada or Gt. Britain. Membership is free; the standard fee schedule is—office calls $15, house and hotel calls $20, and night, Sunday and holiday calls $25. In Italy, IAMAT has member institutions in 32 cities. In the US apply to Suite 5620, 350 Fifth Avenue, New York, NY 10001; in Canada, at 123 Edward St., Toronto, Ontario M5G 1E2; in Europe at 17 Gotthardstrasse, 6300 Zug, Switzerland.

Intermedic is a similar network with an initial membership of $6 for one person, $10 for a family, though the fees are about twice those of IAMAT. In Italy it has 21 correspondent physicians in 9 cities. Write to *Intermedic,* 777 Third Avenue, New York, NY 10017.

Free Medical Care (or reduced cost treatment) for British visitors is available in many European countries, but you have to be prepared with documentation in most cases. One month before leaving Britain, write to your local office of the Department of Health and Social Security for a Form CMI. Fill this in and return it; you will then get a Form E111 to take with you. If you become sick in Italy, take Form E111 to the local office of *Istituto Nazionale per l'Assicurazione Contro le Malattie* (INAM); they will give you a list of doctors and a certificate entitling you to free treatment. In an emergency give Form E111 to the hospital for free treatment (make sure they notify INAM within three days).

Europ Assistance Ltd. offers unlimited help to its members. There are two plans: one for travelers using tours or making their own trip arrangements, the second for motorists taking their cars abroad. Multilingual personnel staff, a 24-hour, 7-days-a-week telephone service which brings the aid of a network of medical and other advisors to assist in any emergency. Special medical insurance is part of the plan. Basic price is £5.75 per person, £16.60 for a car, £5.60 for a caravan or trailer. Write to *Europ Assistance Ltd.,* 252 High St., Croydon, Surrey CRO INF, England, for details. The scheme is only available to residents of Britain.

INFORMATION OFFICES. Official tourist i offices are designated *Ente Provinciale Turisn* they're run by national government, *Azienda* *Turismo* (AAT) if they're sponsored by to... city authorities. Both offer free advice and literature. Make it a rule to stop by these offices on your arrival in each town and pick up their brochures, full of interesting and useful information.

The *Touring Club Italiano,* headquarters in Milan, Corso Italia 10, with offices throughout Italy, offers general tourist information and excellent maps (including a fine series of the *Autostrada del Sole* with service facilities, access roads and connecting highways clearly marked). There are also regional guide books and special-interest (ski, beach) guides. Most TCI material is printed in Italian; some is available in English, but all is so chock-full of useful regional and city maps and basic information that the language barrier is secondary.

SHOPPING. "Made in Italy" has become synonymous with style and quality craftsmanship whether it refers to high fashion or Maserati automobiles. Good buys are usually listed as leather goods, silk ties and dressing gowns, knitwear, gold jewelry, ceramics, straw goods and other handicrafts.

The most important thing to keep in mind when traveling and shopping in Italy is that every region has its local specialties—Venice for glassware, lace and velvet; Naples for coral, cameos and tortoiseshell articles; Vietri for ceramics; Florence for leather goods, straw and raffia products and embroideries; and Milan and Como for silks, to mention but a few.

In general, the idea that bargaining is the rule in Italy is mistaken. There is no universal policy, but for the most part prices are fixed in the better shops. Where you see the sign *prezzi fissi* you can be sure that there is no bargaining to be done. There may be occasions when you will get a discount on a large purchase, however, and it is always worthwhile to ask, but don't expect the final price to be one-half of what the shopkeeper asks.

A warning is sounded against buying antiques in this country renowned for its skilled imitators. There are fascinating shops in all of the major cities, but unless you really know your antiques, don't buy without the advice of an expert or you may be throwing away money on a copy. Also, when buying fine jewelry, be sure to go to a store with a sound reputation.

There are sections called *Crafty Shopping* in some of the chapters which will tell you where some of the best places to buy handicrafts are.

There are a few general things about shopping abroad that knowledgeable shoppers will always take into account:

–Wherever possible carry your purchases home with you, especially if they are valuable or fragile.

–Find out all about customs regulations. You could be stung for a small fortune and turn a bargain into a very expensive commodity indeed.

–If you are shipping goods home, be very sure you have understood the terms, how the shipment will be made, when it should arrive . . . and get it all in writing.

FACTS AT YOUR FINGERTIPS

SECURITY

In recent years the lively art of purse-snatching has been perfected by a number of young men on motor scooters and motorcycles. One drives and the other grabs—especially in Rome, and especially in streets and piazzas frequented by tourists. Some precautions: carry your purse on the hand or shoulder farthest from the curb and keep a firm grip on it. Don't rest your purse or camera on a table or chair at a sidewalk café or restaurant; keep it on your lap, with the strap around your wrist.

Watch your luggage in stations or airports, where it may be snatched from right under your nose. Don't leave luggage in cars; if this is unavoidable, on sightseeing or meal stops, lock everything in the boot out of sight; don't leave cameras or valuables even there. Whenever possible park in daytime on guarded parking places; it is well worth the small fee; at night in a garage. Reports of smashed windows and windscreens are increasing, on top of a high rate of car-thefts.

Don't carry all your cash, travelers' checks and passport with you; leave what you don't need in the hotel safe, along with any other valuables. *Don't* leave valuables in your hotel room.

Be very wary of pickpockets in main railway stations and on trains, especially in the hectic moments of departure and arrival. If you think you might doze off on the train, secure your valuables first.

Sadly, another fiddle has been added to the list of Italian specials. This concerns the matter of change. Whenever you buy something–a rail ticket, a meal, a theater seat, a souvenir–always make a point of checking your change carefully.

Warning. This is the time to warn you about those duty-free, tax-free shops. While they *can* offer bargains, especially in liquor, cigarettes and perfume—because of the huge taxes these attract in the normal shops—the "DUTY FREE" signs can often be unpleasant hoaxes. Some airport shops charge up to 50%, sometimes even 100%, above the prices charged for exactly the same goods in town. Cameras, radios, calculators are among the goods which fall into the "Think Twice" category.

HOLIDAYS AND CLOSING TIMES. Italy takes to holidays with enthusiasm, but several were eliminated recently in an austerity drive, leaving: New Year's Day, January 6 (Twelfth Night), Easter Sunday, Easter Monday, April 25 (Liberation Day), May Day, August 15 (Assumption, known as *Ferragosto*), Dec. 8, Dec. 25 and 26. There are also local saints' days and festivals which the traveler must allow for if he wants to do any business with shops, post offices or banks. There are also long pauses in the middle of the day.

Normal business hours are about as follows, with individual variations: stores are open from 9 to 1 and from 4 to 8. Banking hours are usually from 8.30 to

1.30, mornings only, and closed on Saturdays. Exchange (*cambio* ... ever, have store hours. The Central Post Office is open until 9 P. ... operations. Branch offices open from 8 to 2. Barbers open from 8 ... and are closed Sunday afternoons and Mondays. Women's hairdresser ... 8 A.M. to 8 P.M., but most close all day Sunday and Monday.

Streetcars (trams) and buses stop running at about half an hour after midnight and recommence about 5 A.M. There are, however, skeleton services all night on the chief routes in large cities. The *EPT* or *AAST* information office, or the hall porter, for that matter, can give you the precise details for each city.

SPORTS. Both spectator and participant sports facilities exist throughout Italy. The Italians are keen motor-racing, horse-racing, bicycle-racing and football fans, and they have considerable interest in bowling. Winter sports and mountaineering opportunities abound as, naturally, do all water sports around Italy's vast coastline. Golf and tennis, fishing and hunting, are also popular.

For the equestrian-minded tourist, the *Associazione Nazionale per il Turismo Equestre,* Largo Messico 13, Rome, can furnish information on riding parties and tours of the Italian countryside.

Those interested in a golfing holiday might like to contact *Eurogolf,* 409 Hendon Way, London, NW4, who have programs taking in some of the best courses in Europe, including two in Italy.

BEACHES. Italy's beaches have a special flavor, mainly because of the laws relating to exploitation of the bathing areas. In essence, these say that anyone owning land directly adjoining the foreshore has the right to fence off the portion opposite their land and exploit it as they wish. Communes who own beach areas, as many do, also have the right to lease portions for commercial exploitation, or even to sell outright. The result is that nearly all the beaches likely to be used by bathers in any number are divided into bathing establishments usually called *Lidos.* These normally provide changing cabins or tents, restaurants, snack bars, showers and often other facilities, such as water-skiing, hire of pedalos, and the like. The admission charge may vary from as little as 750 lire to 5,000 lire. This includes the use of a changing cabin, umbrella and deckchair, with the prices varying according to the quality of the beach and the people who patronize it.

In a few recognized resorts, small areas of sand may be left open for use by the public without charge, but these are usually extremely crowded. Provided the charge for admission is not too high, you usually get quite adequate value for what you pay. It is rather a nuisance, however, when you are staying in a resort hotel to find that you can use in effect only the hotel's private strip of beach.

After the huge amount of tourist building that has gone on in almost every part of Italy, fewer and fewer unexploited beaches are left. If you find one, don't

.vax too enthusiastic about this stretch of coastline before investigating further. The sand is probably covered with sharp blades of grass and other scrub growth; it may well be lacking in shade and therefore unbearably hot; and if you want a drink you will have to cart everything down to the beach yourself in cold containers.

In the far south of the country, the government seems to have adopted a very ingenious scheme for developing these beaches. All they have done is to construct well-surfaced access roads enabling motorists to reach the sand. The roads, in many cases, have been followed by the poorest citizens from the country's mountainous interior, who have built themselves family shacks of wood (or even bamboo and sacks) along the edge of the beach. Here they are at least within reach of medical services, and enjoy a more temperate climate than the extremes of heat and cold found even 20 miles from the sea. The more enterprising of them naturally contrive to acquire a few melons, or a few bottles of Coca-Cola, which they sell to visitors. Before long a new bar is born, then a restaurant, and within a few years an entire new resort.

Once a beach is fully equipped, you naturally can make a choice between the different bathing establishments; half the art of traveling in Italy consists of knowing how to choose your spot for a day's bathing and lounging in the sun. This is something you learn only by experience. The places that charge most don't necessarily suit foreign visitors best.

Otherwise you are normally limited to the hotel's own private beach and perhaps one or two bathing establishments within easy walk. These however usually provide all the facilities you can want for an enjoyable day. The main snag is noise. The Italians love to have radios and canned music—sometimes both at the same time—operating at full power.

POLLUTION REPORT

Italy has the worst pollution problem in the Mediterranean, and you would be wise to avoid certain areas (some only at certain times) if you are looking for clean beaches, clean water or clean air. Here is a thumb-nail reading of the places most likely to be unpleasant.

The beaches near *Genoa* (though one expert says that 70% of *all* Italian beaches are a health hazard); the pine forests near *Viareggio, Versilia* and *Fregene,* dead because of urban development nearby; *Ostia,* near Rome, where the Tiber deposits its filth; the *Gulf of Gaeta* (between Rome and Naples), especially near the town of *Gaeta* (pollution from many open sewers and waste from a nuclear power plant), and for several miles south of *Gaeta,* at *Scauri, Minturo* and *Formia; Pescara, Ancona* and *Ferrara* in northeastern Italy (beaches and rivers); *Ravenna* (too much industrial pollution); *Venice,* sad to say, which suffers not only from a sinking feeling but foul fumes from the industries on the nearby mainland; the rivers south of *Milan* (full of detergent). Also bad during the kind of weather that produces smog: *Rome, Turin* and *Milan,* as bad as Tokyo or Los Angeles. And you can *forget* going near the water of the *Bay of Naples!* (Most of the sewers in Naples are so ancient that the authorities have no idea where a great many of them actually are.)

Good news! The beaches of *Western Sicily, Calabria, Apulia* (except round *Bari*), *Sardinia* (except round *Cagliari, Arbatax* and *Porto Torres*) and the *Adriatic Riviera* from *Milano Marittima* down past *Rimini* to *Cattolica* are clean. *Adriatic Riviera* beaches have been plagued lately by excess of seaweed; authorities promise to eliminate problem over next few tourist seasons.

READING MATTER. Most English newspapers and magazines are obtainable in all the big towns of Italy, the newspapers usually a day or two after publication. The *International Herald Tribune* from Paris is available on same day or next. The *Rome Daily American* offers the quickest printed news. English-language magazines and pocket books are on sale at the principal newsstands in tourist centers.

MAIL. Letters within Italy cost 200 lire up to 20 grams, about half an ounce, 300 lire within the Common Market, extra to other European countries. Air mail to the States starts at 420 lire for one thin sheet and envelope. Postcards to England are about 150 lire, to the States 270 lire air mail. Special delivery *(espresso)* is 800 lire extra in Italy, somewhat more if sent abroad, depending on the country. If there is a strike in the postal system, go to the Vatican City post office (but *only* if you are sending mail outside Italy), to the left of St. Peter's as you face it.

Telegrams and cables can be sent from any post office or from *Telegrafi* offices, which are open all night.

TELEPHONES. Pay phones in Italy can easily intimidate the uninitiated. To make a call from a pay phone: first, buy a token *(gettone)* for 100 lire at the nearest cashier. Place it in the slot at the top of the phone, with the single groove toward you. Lift the receiver; you'll hear the dial tone immediately. Dial your number. When the party replies, press the small button next to the slot. This sends the token down into the box and completes the connection. Until you do this your party cannot hear you. The newer public phones are much simpler and can be used for *teleselezione* (long-distance direct dialing): just have a handful of tokens ready (nearby machines dispense tokens).

A 3-minute phone call to London costs about 3,000 lire; to the U.S.A. about 8,000 lire. During the 24 hours of Sunday or between 11 P.M. and 11 A.M., local time, on weekdays, the rate to the U.S. is about 6,000 lire. In all cities the phone company has offices (ask for *Telefoni*) where the operators will help you.

Note. You are warned not to make long-distance phone calls from your hotel room without checking very carefully what the cost will be. Hotels frequently add several hundred percent to such calls. This is an international practice, not one confined to Italy.

CONVENIENT CONVENIENCES. All hotels, restaurants and bars have public WCs, and in most cases they're much less grim than they used to be. *Alberghi Diurni* have sparkling clean conveniences, for a modest charge. You'll find public (municipal) toilets, in varying stages of neglect, in most towns. Railway station and airport conveniences are generally good. In smaller towns WCs are known by their Italian name: *gabinetti,* or as *toelette.* If there's an attendant, a tip of 100 lire is customary.

TIPPING. Charges for service are included in all hotel bills and generally appear as a separate item on restaurant checks. Restaurant bills are probably a chief cause of misunderstandings, for the prices on handwritten menus and the cryptic entries on the check are almost always undecipherable. Such items as fresh fish, Florentine steaks and filets may be noted "s.q." (according to quantity) or "L. 700 hg.", which means in the first case that you'll be charged according to the weight of the cut you've ordered and, in the second case, that the item costs 700 lire per hectogram (3½ oz.). The check generally opens with the cover charge (*pane e coperto*—usually 700–1,500 lire per person). This charge is added whether or not you asked for, or eat, the bread that's served you. A 15% service charge usually is added into the total, unless the menu declares that service is included. In large cities and resorts, it's customary to give the waiter a 10% tip even though the service charge has already been made on the check. In general, chambermaids should be given 500–600 lire per room per day, 2,000–2,500 per week; bellboys about 600 lire per bag; doorman 400 lire for calling a cab; give the concierge about 15% of his bill for services, or from 4,000 to 10,000 lire depending on how helpful he is; tip about 500 lire for room service and valet service.

Checkroom attendants expect 300–500 lire, ushers 300–500 lire, depending on the cost of your seat. Washroom attendants get 100 lire. A 50-lire tip for whatever you drink standing up at a café, about 200–300 lire for table service. At a hotel bar, tip 400–500 for cocktails. Give a barber or hairdresser from 1,000 up to 3–4,000 for a tint or perm depending on the type of establishment.

These are average figures. In deluxe hotels and restaurants you should increase these amounts up to half, in accordance with the service given.

Railway and airport porters charge 600 lire per suitcase. If the porter is very helpful or if the suitcase is unusually heavy, an additionall 4–500 lire will be appreciated.

Service station attendants are tipped about 300 lire if they do more than fill the tank of your car.

Taxi drivers expect about 10%, with 200 lire an equitable starting point.

Guides expect about 500 lire per person for a half-day tour.

ELECTRICITY. Italian voltage is generally 220, and occasionally 115–125, and in some towns (Rome) both. Thus uniformity is not complete, and it is advisable to check before plugging anything in. British apparatus, when designed for the right voltage, can ordinarily be used for power for long periods, but American only for very short periods, since Italy follows the European 50-cycle standard and not the 60-cycle American standard. Italian plugs have round, not flat, prongs, so an adapter plug is necessary.

CLEANING SERVICES. If you are staying in a hotel, laundry services are a simple matter. Your wash will be returned within 48 hours, even sooner if you're in a rush. Dry-cleaning service usually takes about 2 days. Cleaning usually takes about 4 days. 24-hour service is available in the big-city hotels.

DRINKING WATER. Safe in all important towns. Off the beaten track, drink mineral water. Incidentally, think twice about ordering milk drinks in out-of-the-way places.

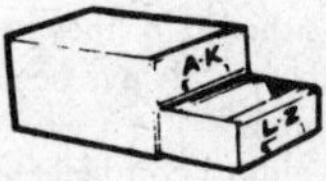

USEFUL ADDRESSES. Embassies: *American,* Via Vittorio Veneto 119, Rome; *British,* Via XX Settembre 80A, Rome; *Canadian,* Via Zara; *Irish,* Via del Pozzetto 108; *Australian,* Via Alessandria 215.

Emergency phone number for police, fire, or ambulance: 113.

For American Express offices, see *Town by Town.*

The addresses of Wagons-Lits Cook are: Via Buoncompagni 25, Rome; Piazza Strozzi 14, Florence; Piazzetta dei Leoncini 289, Venice; Via Porta degli Archi 12, Genoa; Via Depretis 126, Naples; Viale XX Settembre 45, Catania; Piazza San Carlo 132, Turin; Corso Nuvoloni 19, San Remo.

The most widespread national organization for all branches of touring is the CIT *(Compagnia Italiana Turismo)* which also has excellent interpreter service at every branch. See *Travel Agents* section above for addresses and also *Town by Town.*

TRAVELING IN ITALY

BY AIR. Because of the length of the Italian peninsula in comparison with its width, it is peculiarly suited for air travel in the north-south direction. The country is well served not only by *Alitalia* but by three other domestic airlines–*ATI, Alisarda* and *Aermed.* There are youth fares but no special excursion fares. However, one-way fares are relatively inexpensive, especially when bought locally at the favorable exchange rate. In mid-1981, sample one-way fares (all economy) from Rome were: Milan, 76,600; Venice, 68,500; Palermo, 68,500; Catania, 76,600; Cagliari, 40,500.

Getting from Airport to Town. Best, fastest and cheapest way to get from the principal airports into town is the airport buses. Fares into town terminal are: Rome, 1,750 lire; Milan, Linate 1,250; Malpena 2,500; Turin 1,250; Palermo, 1,250; Genoa, 700. At Venice, the airport bus to *Alitalia ATI* terminal at Piazzale Roma, near railway station, costs about 1,000 lire. The *Cooperativa San Marco* provides motorboat service direct from airport to San Marco for about 6,500 lire per person, including bags.

In Rome, taxi from Fiumicino airport to city, double meter amount, usually about 18,000 lire. From city to Fiumicino, meter amount plus 6,000 lire. Supplements of 200 lire for each bag, 700 lire after 10 P.M., 400 lire on holidays.

BY TRAIN. Although not endowed with the best conditions to start with—a mountainous terrain over much of the country, political divisions, economic imbalance between north and south—Italy nevertheless has a remarkably good railway system. In recent years there has been a marked improvement not only in speed but also in comfort and frequency of trains. There is now no steam haulage of passenger services left, the main lines being largely electrified, the others diesel operated. Indeed Italy has always been in the vanguard of electrification and other technical advances.

The new *direttissima* line linking Florence and Rome is almost complete with full operation planned for summer 1982. A considerable length of it has been used by express trains for some time now. In other parts of the country in the past five years there has been a big rebuilding program with slowing curves being eliminated and many miles of single line doubled.

Coupled with this, new rolling stock is being added to the system every month, all of it of the latest design. A participant in the *Trans Europ Express* network from the start, Italy now has five TEE trains entirely within its frontiers as well as sharing another five with its neighbors.

Train travel in Italy can add considerably to your holiday enjoyment even if there are times when the whole system seems to be carrying more people than it was designed for!

What to look for. The majority of Italian trains, both expresses and local, have both 1st and 2nd class carriages. However, several of the top trains (including all the TEE ones) are 1st-class only and at the other end (mainly local, suburban and stopping trains) are 2nd-class only.

Trains are classified as *rapido* (fastest services with a supplement charge dependent on the class and distance), *espresso* (fast long distance expresses), *diretto* (medium fast trains with more stops than an express but quicker than a local) and *locale* (which live up to their name, making all stops).

Most long distance overnight trains have 1st- and 2nd-class sleeping cars and 2nd-class couchettes, some with couchettes only. Of course they all have ordinary coaches as well. The sleeping cars are operated by *Wagons-Lits* and the couchettes by the railway.

2nd-class travel in Italy, particularly at weekends and on holidays of which the Italians have a large number, is often crowded. It is advisable to get there early especially if the train starts at that station. 1st class is less crowded and on limited accommodation trains where seat reservations are obligatory, standing is not permitted and this applies on all TEE trains.

Seat reservations can be made on many long distance (and all international) trains serving Italy either at main stations or through authorized travel agencies. Our advice is to do it at the station of departure.

Catering on Italian railways is done by the restaurant division of *Wagons-Lits.* Increasingly, buffet cars are being introduced although all TEEs and a selected number of other *rapidos* have full restaurant service. Mini-bar and trolley services are found on many long distance trains and all stations (other than the smaller ones) have buffets or bars, usually privately operated. However it can be a good idea to take your own provisions with you, on long journeys.

Note in some Italian cities (e.g. Milan, Turin, Genoa, Naples and Rome) there are two or more main line stations although one is usually the principal terminus or through station. *Always* check which your train will arrive at or depart from.

Fares. Italian Railways are among the cheaper in Europe, particularly if you use the reduced rate tickets. For those planning to do a lot of traveling, *Travel at Will* tickets are the best as they cover the whole system including Sicily and Sardinia. They are also valid on the ferry services between Italy and Sicily but *not* on those to Sardinia or on buses or on privately owned railways. They can be used on all *rapidos* and TEE trains without extra charge. They can be bought outside Italy (advisable) up to 60 days before date of departure and first use, or at International Frontier stations or at International airports. We recommend strongly that you obtain these tickets before going to Italy as trying to get them there involves fighting through a considerable and time-consuming bureaucratic maze.

Valid for 8, 15, 21 and 30 days, they cost respectively in 1st class $128, $162, $195, $237, and in 2nd class, $85, $103, $120, $148 at rates of exchange on going to press. Children under 14 pay half these rates.

All these tickets (except the 8-day one) can be extended on a daily basis. This must be arranged locally. A new scale of rates will be in operation by the summer of 1982, details of which were not available as we went to press. But any inceases will be modest; probably no more than $5 to $10 a day. Please note these tickets can only be obtained in Italy. Enquire at main stations.

In Italy there are also kilometric tickets for 3,000 km (1,875 miles) of travel, priced at $140 for 1st-class and $90 for 2nd-class, and valid for 30 days. In addition there are Family Tickets where four or more of the same family traveling together get 30% off both the adult and the children's fares. Proof of identity (eg passport) must be shown.

And there are numerous special excursions advertised in local stations and tourist information offices.

Italian Railways are constantly changing the numbers and conditions of *special excursion* tickets and you should inquire either from your travel agent before you leave home or at main line stations in Italy on arrival about these. In the US, write to *Italian State Railways,* 666 Fifth Ave., New York, NY 10019.

A **Eurailpass** is a convenient, all-inclusive ticket that can save you money on over 100,000 miles of railroads and railroad-operated buses, ferries, river and lake steamers, hydrofoils, with some Mediterranean crossings, in 16 countries of Western Europe (including Italy). It provides the holder with unlimited travel at the following rates—15 days $242, 21 days $300, 1 month $368, 2 months $495, 3 months $570. The Eurail Youthpass costs $320 for 2 months. Children under 12 go half-fare, under 4 go free. The prices cover first-class passage, reservation fees and TEE surcharges. Available only to those residents who live outside Europe or North Africa, the pass must be bought from an authorized agent before leaving for Europe. Apply through your travel agent, or to French National Railroads, Eurailpass Div., 610 Fifth Ave., New York, N.Y. 10020; German Federal Railroad, 11 West 42nd St., New York, N.Y. 10036 and 45 Richmond St. W., Toronto M5H 1Z2, Ontario, Canada. For complete details, write to Eurailpass, c/o WBA, 51 Ridgefield Ave., Staten Island, N.Y. 10304.

Routes within Italy. Here are six scenic routes well worth traveling over:

1. Venice or Milan to Bologna, then through the mountains to Florence and Rome. Several services daily including a number of *rapidos.* Part of journey on new super-fast *direttissima* line. Anything from 6 to 8 hours.

2. Genoa via the Ligurian coast to Pisa (connections to Florence) and then south to Rome. Again several services daily, most with buffet or dining car, some stopping at Riviera dei Levante resorts such as Rapallo. Approx. 7 hours.

3. Rome to Sicily: Best train is the *Peloritano,* a 1st class only *rapido* that goes via Naples, Salerno, Battipaglia, Reggio di Calabria and across on the train ferry to Messina where it splits, one section going to Palermo, the other to Taormina, Catania and Syracuse. Very attractive run down the Calabrian coast. Approx. 10½ hours to Palermo, less to Syracuse.

4. Rome to Rimini: One of Italy's second string main lines right across country via Orte, Terni, Foligno, Falconaro and Pesaro. Attractive mountain and rural scenery much of the way. About 6½ hours.

5. Genoa to Ventimiglia. This runs along the Italian Riviera known as the *Riviera of Flowers* serving resorts like Alassio, Diano Marina and San Remo. Ventimiglia is on the French frontier. Fast trains do the full trip in around two hours, stopping trains take an hour longer.

6. Palermo to Agrigento: Goes right across the heart of Sicily from its capital to one of its most famous classical sites. Take the morning *rapido* leaving just before 9 A.M. and you arrive in Agrigento around 11:30 A.M. Stay approx. 5 hours allowing time to do the sights and return to Palermo before 8 P.M. Similar service in opposite direction.

BY BUS. Within Italy there are a number of express bus services linking some of the main cities. These are either part of the *Europabus* network or are operated by Italian companies. Sample services:—

1. Venice-Padua-Ravenna-Bologna-Florence—daily April to October (takes about 10 hours including lunch stop).
2. Florence-Siena-Perugia-Assisi-Rome—daily April to October (takes about 10 hours including lunch stop).
3. Rome-Naples-Pompeii-Sorrento-Amalfi—daily April to October (takes about 7 hours with lunch stop).
4. Sorrento Circular Route starting at Naples and calling at Pompeii-Amalfi-Positano-Sorrento-Naples. Daily April to October (takes about 8 hours including lunch).

All the above can be used for intermediate stops on prior notice.

Further information including many useful addresses and telephone numbers on both rail and bus travel in Italy are contained in the *Travelers Handbook* published annually by the *Italian State Tourist Office* (ENIT, see *Travel Agents* for addresses) and issued free at ENIT's foreign offices.

Buses in most major towns have a flat fare of about 200 to 400 lire, but only a few are able to give change. So try to carry a few 100 lire pieces with you if you think you're going to be taking the bus. Remember also that you can be fined an on-the-spot 5,000 lire if you're caught by an Inspector without a ticket.

BY STEAMER. An extensive network of steamer services links the Italian mainland with Sicily, Sardinia and the many smaller islands off its coast. Lakes Como, Maggiore and Garda are served by passenger steamers, car ferries and hydrofoils. Times and costs variable; check locally.

BY CAR. (You will find short descriptions of local road possibilities in each area chapter under the sub-title *Road Reports.*) In most Italian towns the use of the horn is forbidden in certain if not all areas. A large notice *ZONA DE SILENZIO* indicates where. Other regulations are largely as in Britain and the US, except that the police have power to levy on-the-spot fines. Parking in *ZONA DISCO* is for limited periods. Discs can be bought at petrol stations. Outside built-up areas parking is permitted on the righthand side of the road. Fines for driving after drinking are heavy, with the additional possibility of 6 months imprisonment. There is however no fixed blood/alcohol level and no official test. One drives on the right side of the road.

The *Automobile Club of Italy (ACI),* with headquarters at Rome, Via Marsala 8, has branch offices in all major towns, and information offices at most of the frontier posts. A few small ones, to which access is over a mountain pass, are closed during the winter.

A Green Card insurance is required for driving in all European countries, plus a valid US or UK driving license supported, for Italy, by an Italian translation. These may be had free from the *AA, RAC* or *Italian State Tourist Office,* (*ENIT,* see *Travel Agents* for addresses). Motorists should also have with them their car registration papers and a red warning triangle.

Auto Fuel. Gasoline (petrol) costs about 950 lire per liter for super, a bit less for normal. Only a few gas stations are open on Sundays and most close for a couple of hours at lunchtime. There is a 130 kph speed limit on autostrade and 100 kph on other highways.

Car-Sleeper Express. Because of the long distances to be covered in Italy, motorists may wish to use one of the car-sleeper trains available within the country. These operate from Milan to Rome, San Remo, Viareggio, Bari or Brindisi (connecting with the car-ferry service for Greece); from Turin, Genoa, Bolzano or Calalzo (Cortina) to Rome; and from Rome, Naples, Milan or Turin to Villa San Giovanni (for Sicily car-ferry).

Car Hire. There are many firms from which cars can be rented. In most big cities there is a branch of *Avis, Hertz* or *Maggiore* rental agencies, which also rent chauffeur-driven and self-driven cars—reservations may be made through travel agencies or directly. Cars may be rented at airports and railway stations (Rome, Milan, Naples, Genoa, Florence, Turin, etc.). *Alitalia* has a *Jet-Drive* program with cars on tap at 15 airports—car included in the normal ticket price, with a 7-day, 2-adult minimum—and some special weekend excursions, car included.

Emergency Service. Thanks to the *Automobile Club of Italy,* breakdown service is free to foreign tourists traveling by car. It includes minor repairs of a stalled car and towing. In case of major trouble, repair charges are strictly controlled by the ACI. By dialing 116 from any telephone, any motorist whose car is disabled even on remote roads, will reach a central service station: give approximate location and, if possible, the source of the mechanical trouble, and assistance will come within a short time. Also, information is obtainable on the location of the nearest service station and where replacement parts for a particular make of car are available. In case of a road accident, this number will also reach a medical station and aid will promptly be dispatched.

Motorways. Longest of the many autostrade criss-crossing Italy is the *Autostrada del Sole* (highway no. A1, A2) from Milan to Reggio Calabria. Like all autostrade it is a toll road: the ticket issued on entering is returned on leaving, along with the toll. On some shorter motorways the toll is payable on entering.

Restaurants, snack bars and the like are found at strategic points on all motor-ways. However, they often become desperately crowded, so that using the restroom or getting a cool drink becomes a time-consuming operation.

Kilometers into Miles. This simple chart will help you to convert to both miles and kilometers. If you want to convert from miles into kilometers read from the center column to the right, if from kilometers into miles, from the center column to the left. Example: 5 miles = 8.1 kilometers, 5 kilometers = 3.1 miles.

Miles		*Kilometers*	*Miles*		*Kilometers*
0.6	1	1.6	12.4	20	32.2
1.2	2	3.2	18.6	30	48.3

Miles		*Kilometers*	*Miles*		*Kilometers*
1.9	3	4.8	24.8	40	64.4
2.5	4	6.3	31.0	50	80.5
3.1	5	8.0	37.3	60	96.6
3.7	6	9.6	43.5	70	112.3
4.3	7	11.3	49.7	80	128.7
5.0	8	12.9	55.9	90	144.8
5.6	9	14.5	62.1	100	160.9
6.2	10	16.1	124.3	200	321.9

LEAVING ITALY

CUSTOMS. If you propose to take on your holiday any *foreign-made* articles, such as cameras, binoculars, expensive timepieces and the like, it is wise to put with your travel documents the receipt from the retailer or some other evidence that the item was bought in your home country. If you bought the article on a previous holiday abroad and have already paid duty on it, carry with you the receipt for this. Otherwise, on returning home, you may be charged duty again (for British residents, VAT as well). Better still, register all such items at customs office before you leave.

Currency Declaration Form must be submitted on departure.

US Customs. At this writing, Americans who are out of the US at least 48 hours and have claimed no exemption during the previous 31 days are entitled to bring in duty-free up to $300 worth of bona fide gifts or items for their personal use. The value of each item is determined by the price actually paid (so have your receipts). Every member of a family is entitled to this same exemption, regardless of age, and the family allowance can be pooled. Purchases intended for your duty-free quota can no longer be sent home separately—they must accompany your personal baggage. For the next $600 worth of goods beyond that first $300, inspectors will assess a flat 10% duty, rather than hitting you with different percentages for different types of goods.

Not more than 100 cigars and 200 cigarettes may be imported duty-free per person, nor more than a liter of wine or liquor (none at all if your passport indicates you are from a "dry" state, or if you are under 21 years of age). Only one bottle of perfume that is trademarked in the US may be brought in, plus a reasonable quantity of other brands.

Small gifts may be mailed to friends, but not more than one package to one address and none to your own home. Notation on the package should be "Gift, value less than $25." Tobacco, liquor and perfume are not permitted.

Antiques are defined, for customs purposes, as articles manufactured over 100 years ago and are admitted duty-free. If there's any question of age, you may be asked to supply proof.

A foreign-made automobile that was ordered before your departure is subject to duty (7%) even though delivered abroad. This same rule applies to any purchase initiated in advance of your trip.

If your purchases exceed your exemption, list the items that are subject to the highest rates of duty under your exemption and pay duty on the items with the lowest rates. Any article you fail to declare cannot later be claimed under your exemption.

Do not bring home foreign meats, fruits, plants, soil, or other agricultural items when you return to the US. To do so will delay you at the port of entry. It is illegal to bring in foreign agricultural items without permission, because they can spread destructive plant or animal pests and diseases. For more information, read the pamphlet "Customs Hints", or write to *Quarantines,* US Department of Agriculture, Federal Building, Hyattsville Md, 20782, and ask for Program Aid No. 1083, Traveler's Tips on Bringing Food, Plant and Animal Products into the United States. Since 1972–73 a number of endangered species of fish, wildlife, marine mammals and plants are protected by the US government, and neither they nor any of their parts or products may be brought into the US. If in any doubt check with the US government first. There are special Customs advisors at the US embassies in London, Paris, Bonn and Rome, and at the Consulate in Frankfurt.

UK Customs. There are few concessions, and the remarks above about possible duty charges when returning home are especially valid. British subjects, except those under the age of 17 years, may import duty-free from *any* country the following: 200 cigarettes or 100 cigarillos or 50 cigars or 250 grams of tobacco; 1 liter of spirits or 2 liters of wine in excess of 38.8 proof, and 2 liters of still table wine. Also 50 grams of scent, ¼ liter of toilet water and £28 worth of other normally dutiable goods.

Returning from Italy (or any other EEC country), you may, *instead* of the above exemptions, bring in the following, provided you can prove they were not bought in a duty-free shop: 300 cigarettes or 150 cigarillos or 75 cigars or 400 grams of tobacco; 1½ liters of strong spirits (over 38.8 proof), or three liters of other spirits (under 38.8 proof) or fortified wines, plus 4 liters of still table wine; 75 grams of perfume and three-eighths liter of toilet water and £120 worth of other normally dutiable goods.

Canada. In addition to personal effects, residents of Canada may, after 7 days out of the country, and upon written declaration, claim an exemption of $150 a year plus an allowance of 40 ounces of liquor, 50 cigars, 200 cigarettes and 2 lb. of tobacco. Personal gifts should be mailed as "Unsolicited Gift—Value Under $25". For details, ask for the Canada Customs brochure "I Declare."

DUTY FREE is not what it once was. You may not be paying tax on your bottle of whiskey or perfume, but you are certainly contributing to somebody's profits. Duty free shops are big business these days and mark ups are often around 100 to 200%. So don't be seduced by the idea that because it's duty free it's a bargain. Very often prices are not much different from your local discount store and in the case of perfume or jewelry they can be even higher.

As a general rule of thumb, duty free stores on the ground offer better value than buying in the air. Also, if you buy duty free goods on a plane, remember that the range is likely to be limited and that if you are paying in a different currency to that of the airline, their rate of exchange often bears only a passing resemblance to the official one.

THE ITALIAN SCENE

ITALY—THEME AND VARIATIONS

by
LESLIE GARDINER

Leslie Gardiner is a freelance writer and broadcaster whose knowledge of Italy dates from 1942 when, as an escaped prisoner, he walked from the Alps to Sicily—a journey he has repeated, on foot and by road and rail, many times since. He has gained numerous awards for his travel articles, and won the 1976 literary competition held to celebrate Michelangelo's 500th anniversary. His books on Italy and other parts of Europe are very popular. He lives and works in Scotland.

"Your favorite foreign country?" (A radio interviewer.) Without hesitation I said "Italy" and began to wonder why. What a lot, when one comes to think about it, there is to dislike about Italy: the chaos of city traffic, the thoughtless chatter and revving up of noisy engines late at night under your bedroom window, the vanity of many men, the inanity of many women, the superstitious reverence for the arts about which most Italians know so little, the national conviction that the country has a monopoly of scenic grandeur (I have to admit they have a point there) . . . One speaks of the mass, naturally, one doesn't include one's friends.

I get so annoyed when I take a taxi out of town and find the driver hasn't the slightest idea how to read a map and is too conceited to confess it; when I see the careless indifference which people old enough to know better show towards the environment; when I notice that the foreigners who get along best are often those with the worst manners. So why should this provoking land be anyone's favorite, and why does the very word inspire a shiver of agreeable anticipation, as it evidently did to Aeneas and his friends from Troy, something like 4,000 years ago, when they tilted the salt wave to the low flat tongues of land on the Apulian shore and first raised the cry: "*Italia*"?

Andante con moto-bicicletta

Going to Italy for pleasure, we have a vested interest in the picturesque, the rustic and the primitive; and from that point of view it is not the land it used to be. Ostentatious villas line the lonely headlands where pagan temples once stood; six-lane motorways leap on concrete stilts through scenes which were known, a few years ago, only to the chamois and the eagle; the powerful, destructive torrents of the Abruzzi run with chemical waste; and a city on the Adriatic coast, where 100 years ago a British traveler could find lodging only in a hut where the sound of a woman teaching her baby a Latin prayer kept him awake half the night, has given the language a new verb, *riminizzare,* to Riminize, meaning roughly "to develop for tourism, with glass, concrete and anodized aluminum."

Young men whose fathers took mandolins under the vine pergola of their *innamorate* turn up on a motor-cycle or in a *cinquecento* Fiat, and the brrrooom-brrrooom of their exhaust is the serenade.

But, while I add up my complaints against Italy—and what are they, after all, but the sort of complaints we can make about any civilized country in the last quarter of the twentieth century?—the travelogue of memory is rolling past the mind's eye, and I halt it here and there to dwell on some vignettes. They are nothing special, they are no more than any visitors will see for themselves if they hang about in town or country; but for me they express the spirit of Italy, and maybe they help to explain why so many seasoned travelers keep a little love affair going with the idiosyncratic Italian way of life.

Aria e recitativo

At Bergamo (whose rustic actors invented the *Commedia dell'Arte* and secured immortality for a peasant named Harlequin), in a busy shopping arcade, a blind man is playing the accordion and a crowd has gathered. He is a virtuoso performer. He is swinging the Hebrew Chorus from *Nabucco* as it has never been swung before. The audience —housewives with plastic shopping bags and baby carriages, men with nothing much to occupy them for the moment—are swaying and la-la-la-ing with the tune. Two policemen in white helmets are trying to persuade the musician to move on: he is blocking the street. The audience won't let them interfere, and will not be cowed by bluster. One policeman, after a while, is seen at the back of the crowd, humbly requesting spectators to close up a little. *'Non dipende da noi,"* he keeps saying "It's not our fault, we have this job to do." His colleague has already surrendered to the rhythm of *Nabucco* and stands in the front ranks of the spectators, beating time with a white-gloved hand. Then the blind man's helper comes round, and the rattle of his collecting box achieves in a moment what the police have been powerless to achieve. The crowd melts away.

Here is a picture of some island town, I forget which one. Grass grows among the cobbles of the matchbox-sized piazza. In the shade of the plane tree, on a bench, four elderly islanders are sitting. Across the piazza, on the sunny side, the bar-tender has brought a chair to the door and is reading his newspaper. One of the four rises rheumatically and limps over for a titbit of news. He returns to his companions and they discuss it for a while in a slow, cracked, impenetrable dialect. Silence falls, punctuated by an occasional "Ma!" or *"Macchè!"*, in a resigned tone, from one or other of them. A few minutes later, the same old man rises again and totters across the square for another news item.

The next village, a stone crown on a conical hill, where Arno and Tiber converge only to part again and flow in different directions, is Caprese—Caprese Michelangelo, as it was designated earlier this century in honor of its famous son. I walk into the small general store and coffee bar. It is empty, except for a twelve-year-old girl behind the counter, and the following conversation takes place:

"What is there to see in this little village?"

"There is the birthplace of Michelangelo, *signore,* and the church where Michelangelo was baptized."

"Michelangelo? Who is he?"

"I don't understand you."

"This Michelangelo you speak of? Who is he? Some politician, or what?"

(The child takes a deep breath.) "He was none other, *signore,* than the most beautiful painter and sculptor who ever lived. And if you are ever lucky enough to see one of his works, in Florence or even in Rome, you will say that it was not done by the hand of man, but by the hand of God."

Largo, nobilmente e semplice

Italians are punctilious in rendering homage to their great men and women. Here is a passage I walked down by accident at the unfashionable end of Rome's central railway station. On this snapshot it is too dark to read the inscription on the wall tablet, but it says something to the effect that on this very spot Verdi took refuge from the enthusiasm of his admirers when he arrived in Rome to attend the première of *La Forza del Destino.*

And here, as you may guess from the brilliant light and strong colors, is Sicily. These are the gardens of Catania, beside the dead-straight thoroughfare which leads to the summit of Mount Etna, 35 miles away. The evening promenade, the perambulating marriage mart and gossip exchange of the south, is taking place. The girls are delightful in their summer dresses, the men neat and stylish in their silk shirts and flared trousers. (If we have the idea that southern Italian men are swarthy and not over-careful about their appearance, it is partly because they don't shave until early evening, for the promenade.) All over Italy, but especially in Sicily and Sardinia, men and women, young and old, take exceptional care of their looks, hair and clothes, and carry themselves and their finery with enviable dignity and panache. Back streets may be rat-infested, roadside verges a disgrace, but two compartments in the Italian's life are usually spotless: the kitchen and the wardrobe.

In the gardens, in the space of about two acres, they are holding a political rally with a pop group and several loudspeaker vans. Pistachio-nut sellers and balloon vendors are crying their wares, a rowdy open-air chess tournament is under way and a miniature train careens round the perimeter with a shrieking cargo of children. Eight o'clock chimes, and all falls magically silent. The introductory bars of *Casta diva* or some other Bellini aria steal over the populace; two minutes, and it fades, and normal activity is resumed. It happens every day, every two hours on the hour. It is the tribute Catanians pay to their fellow-citizen, the composer Vincenzo Bellini, a tribute they have paid in one form or another since his death 140 years ago.

Back to Rome. The statue of Marcus Aurelius—one of the best-known equestrian statues in the world—stood outside the Campidoglio for over 400 years. There is a myth that the horse on Emperor sits is turning slowly to gold and that when he has he will sing and announce the end of the world. The sad fact, is that gold is the last thing either horse or man are turning in polluted Roman atmosphere has done its worst and the statue, in grave danger of crumbling away, has had to be removed from its beautiful pedestal.

Molto tranquillo

The next shot comes from Tuscany and the setting is a Chianti vineyard, several clumps of cypress, a castle and a walled town of intact medieval character, spread over rolling hills: a microcosm of Italy, or what people who have never been there imagine Italy to be, from the art folders and schoolbook illustrations they have seen. Here is the typical Renaissance city, Arezzo or Cortona, Lucca or San Gimignano. In its streets life swims at an easy pace. The inhabitants move about dreamily, rather like fish in a glass tank. Tall buildings give vertical space to their narrow world, the sloping piazzas and decaying palaces are decorated with the shields of families long extinct, and with plenty of square sockets in the stonework for holding flags on days of ceremony. Of such days there are a good number. The side streets are warrens of curious trades: carpenters, goldsmiths, candle-makers, lantern-makers, makers of woodwind instruments, and they are housed in tiny antique shops, such as you would expect to find in a village.

In the faces of Tuscan citizens and farm-workers you see the expressions of those who make up the supporting cast in some of the Renaissance paintings, for the Tuscan hilltowns were hotbeds of the arts and the old masters drew on the physiognomy of fellow townsmen, and on the architecture of their surroundings, when they came to portray biblical and classical scenes. The Jerusalem of Piero della Francesca's *Legend of the Cross* is actually Sansepolcro, circa 1450 AD, the Tiber of that same painter's *Battle at the Ponte Milvio* is not the yellow Tiber of Rome but the blue-and-silver stream of the Val Tiberina, Piero's birthplace, and willows overhang it and someone drives a flock of geese along the banks and a cavalry horse, distracted by that pastorale, pauses in mid-charge and shyly dips his head to drink.

From a modest provincial town such as Arezzo, embarked in the *pullman* (bus), you can round up in the space of one day the birthplaces, and some of the masterpieces preserved in village churches and cemetery chapels, of Michelangelo, Sansovino, Piero della Francesca, Masaccio, Paolo Uccello, Luca Signorelli and Fra Angelico. And Arezzo herself is the native town of Petrarch and Vasari.

Al galoppo

This is Siena, and these are pictures of the Palio preliminaries in a city where parochial fervor goes beyond logic and every facet of urban life, every alliance or antagonism between citizens who live within a few doors of one another, is influenced by a twice-a-year horse race which lasts three minutes. Of the race itself we have no shots: it is merely a cloud of dust, kicked up by 44 hoofs on the carpet of red earth in the principal piazza. But we have a snapshot of a horse leaving the parish church, where he went to be blessed. He made a mess of the altar steps, which is why everyone wears a happy smile, for a dollop of manure in church is the best of omens. And up there, while the partisan bands roam the streets and the horses are being groomed and huge bets are changing hands and local radio interrupts its programs with bulletins on the prospects for tomorrow's race . . . up there in the Mangia tower the captains of the Siena parishes are even now carving the whole thing up among themselves. The Palio is after all a cynical charade, a typical medieval city-state intrigue, and the race is won and lost before it ever takes place.

Agitato e vivace

By these teeming streets and open-air stalls, with a scent of sprats and mussels you can almost smell from here, we know we're in Naples. On the Mezzocannone and Santa Barbara slopes things haven't changed much since Matilde Serao, a journalist on the city newspaper, wrote:

"People from the four slum zones, with no light, no air, lack of hygiene, climbing over heaps of rubbish, drinking unhealthy water and breathing nauseating fumes. These people are not idle, savage animals; they are not gloomy in their faith, nor glum in their vice, nor furious when struck by misfortune. They have an inborn gentleness, they take wreaths up to the tombs on Poggioreale, they love gay colors, they love music and sing so soulfully—their songs are heartrending and are the very essence of the nostalgia one feels when one is far away . . . "

Now I come to an anonymous scene, which might be anywhere in the south of Italy: a town's main street, just wide enough for a motorcar to pass down, provided no one wants to open a door. The street is probably called Via Roma, for in Italy all main streets lead to Rome. It is evening. Grandmas on kitchen chairs sun themselves at the threshold; behind them, indoors, the blue rectangles of television sets are flickering and a party political broadcast is coming over the radio and a number of people are shouting and screaming, though it is likely they are all on good terms with each other. Children kick footballs about, but the grandmas do not flinch because somehow the balls skim back and forth without doing any harm. Four men squat on four pieces of fallen masonry, playing cards. The house the masonry came from is temporarily banded with an iron strap, and shored up with a baulk of timber, this temporary arrangement having lasted, probably, for 20 years or more.

Two women whisper under the dilapidated tracery of a baroque balcony. Two young girls with thin black scarves on their heads pass by on their way to Vespers. From some invisible person at a top window a small boy receives a potted plant, detaches it from its 80-foot piece of string and runs off with it. A cat eases the lid off a cardboard carton full of fish-heads. A young man does a welding job on a three-wheeler truck, and showers sparks over his neighbor, who is fitting *pennacchi* (multicolored bunches of feathers) to a donkey's collar in preparation for next Sunday's parade of painted carts at the feast of the Almond in Flower . . . Scores of disconnected private activities are going on in the congested corridor of this street, all the drama of life is there. And no one gets hurt, no one gets in another's way, not even when a potential grand prix champion on a motor-scooter bursts in at full throttle and sweeps through the obstacle course in record time, near-missing everything.

I am moving on to Sardinia, like Sicily an autonomous region of Italy since the war.

"Do you call yourselves Sardinians or Italians?" I ask, remembering historical distinctions.

"We call ourselves Italians. The Italians call us Sardinians."

This hamlet, which happens to stand within a stone's throw of the costliest and most sophisticated riviera in Europe, has a path to the beach made of stones from an old cathedral and a smashed temple column. It is ringed with three lattice pylons and concave discs, one on each hilltop. The villagers, faithful to their morbid preoccupation with disaster, have christened the structures *il triangolo della morte,* the triangle of death. They believe it is part of the NATO shield, and that they are in the firing line. Actually the pylons are television repeaters, and the villagers are beneficiaries, they have clubbed together to buy a television set and the cowshed (which was formerly a church) is the viewing salon. You put a few lire in the broken font as you enter.

The hamlet, formerly so isolated, is now connected with Olbia, an unimaginable distance away, by telephone. The grey public call box stands in my hostess's living room: she wouldn't let the engineers put it outside, she admired it so much, and she and her daughter spend some time every day polishing the woodwork and the glass.

And here . . . but my viewers are fidgeting. Souvenirs of Italy mean a lot to the person who picks them up, but people want to go and pick up souvenirs of their own. I will stop at one more scene: a view of pre-Roman Italy, outcropping in the fields on the outskirts of Rome. There is a broken arch, a few fragments of an aqueduct, dry as a bone, haunted by lizards and swallowtail butterflies, and some unidentifiable humps, clothed in the rank growth of summer. Of this meadow, some 2,000 years ago, the poet Propertius was already able to write:

You, old Veii, were once the dwelling of princes,
Where on the open mart glittered the law-giver's throne;
Now your streets are filled with the fluting of wandering shepherds;
Over the graves of kings the goodman drives his plough.

I wonder whether those enigmatic Etruscans have not contributed as much to Italian life and character as all the other conquering nations in the peninsula's stormy history. They were the aboriginals, as far as we know. With their defensive League of Cities (each acting autonomously, careful to preserve its own integrity) they controlled most of the mainland. They responded to beauty and loved bright colors. They dressed smartly and moved with a dashing air. They led a cozy domestic life. They were good at plumbing: "cistern" is an Etruscan word and, if we visitors find that hotel bath-taps and ball-cocks leave something to be desired, we have to remember the fantastic waters of Tivoli and the trick fountains of the Vatican gardens and recognize the Italian genius for aquatic technology.

Above all, the Etruscans maintained a fierce civic pride which, in the end, was their undoing. In the face of foreign threat, they refused to sink petty traditional differences and combine with their neighbors. They were volatile people, they had warm hearts and a capacity for living every waking moment. Living among them you would have been alternately delighted and infuriated, you would both love them and hate them, but you could not have remained indifferent to them. The more I study the Etruscan way of life, as the frescoed tombs depict it, the more it seems to resemble everyday life in modern Italy.

Con brio e campanilismo

The Emperor Napoleon (who came to the bridge of Lodi "bearing the destiny of two centuries" and was appointed *petit caporal* by his men, who drank to his rapid promotion) disliked the shape of Italy. The land, he said, was too narrow for its length. He was considering Italy from the military and administrative angle.

Italian industrialists today make similar complaints. Their land, they have told us, resembles a giant with a good head and powerful shoulders, well fitted for thrusting his way into Europe were it not for his spindly ankles and poor feet, wobbling on the stiletto heel of Puglia and the pointed toe-cap of Calabria, tripping over the tricorne of Sicily.

The length of Italy covers eleven degrees of latitude. Her northern frontiers are on a level with Quebec, her southernmost island with North Carolina. For the visitor, her shape dictates a color and variety in life, character and scenery and in the hearts and minds of her peoples, which are not found in many lands of a similar size.

Piedmont and the Alto Adige are swept by blizzards and split by glacial torrents. Up there, your holiday home may be an Alpine chalet which is up to its windows in snow for three months in the year. Isles of the Sicilian provinces have a Moorish culture and a sub-tropical vegetation. Their dialects are Arabic and their white cubes of cottages sometimes stand in an inch or two of sand blown from the Sahara desert.

Thanks to the ladder-like arrangement of Italian motorways, you can drive from top to bottom of this country in about fifteen hours, if you must. A passage across its narrow width can take almost as long, although one or two of the villages you pass through will have a view of both the Tyrrhenian sea on the west and the Adriatic on the east, and perhaps the Ionian on the south as well. Within a couple of miles of the Calabrian coast the mountains rear up to 6,000 feet; and the *trenino* from Paola to Cosenza requires three and a half hours to accomplish a journey of 19 miles as the crow flies.

Despite the long coastline and deepwater inlets and the forbidding hinterland, the Italians have not been a maritime people since the middle ages. No Conrad or Herman Melville has emerged from their novelists. The golden treasury of Italian literature is rooted in the *terra,* a word of almost mystical significance to an Italian. It means his native soil or his community or his farm or plot of land or his province or his nation.

An irrational attachment to his *terra,* to his village belfry *(campanilismo)* or to the wider territory which is perhaps visible from it ("regionalism") has been described as both a strength and a weakness in the Italian character. As education spreads and communications improve and a media jargon supplants the innumerable dialects of the people (42 distinct dialects in the Friuli province alone), so *campanilismo* does not diminish but intensifies. It is as though, in the pressures from a larger world, the Italian sees an additional threat to the basic unit of society, which is himself.

History and topography have conditioned him. In Italy are enshrined the foundations of two important civilizations, the Etruscan and the Roman; yet, a mere 120 years ago, Italy was no more than a geographical expression, with an air of fable about it. Italy was a warring peninsula, a patchwork of many sovereign colors, a disconnected assemblage of laws and customs. In the early 19th century, the only safe way into Italy was along the shore of the south of France. You had to change your money into *scudi* at Nice and into *pistoles* at Turin. In Genoa they dealt only in *sequins.* The Lombardy currency was *paoli* and at Bologna you had to convert them to *livres.* Venice boasted two currencies, the *ducat* and the *filippo,* as did Rome with her *scudo* and *louis d'or.* Naples recognized the *onza,* but in other parts of the Bourbon domains only the *ducat* (not the Venetian *ducat*) was accepted.

Town gates closed shortly after dusk. Pioneer travelers have written with feeling of the *poste-royale* racket operated in big cities like Florence and Pisa; of the interminable delays at Siena while baggage was weighed and charged for once again; of arguments, detentions and briberies at the customs house of Rome, because the stranger hadn't written ahead for his *lascia-passare.*

Brigands, malaria, absence of roads and the ignorance of inhabitants about the country on the other side of the hill made overland journeys slow, difficult and perilous. (Salvatore Giuliano, the last brigand in Sicily, died young in 1950; Benedetto Musolino, the last brigand on the mainland, died quite recently, an old man, having spent the past 42 years in prison.) The southern seaports were often fatal to visitors because of plague. (As recently as 1884, Italy's Minister of Health announced that the whole of Naples would have to be evacuated and demolished, on account of typhoid fever.) Tourists to Italy usually hired a *felucca* in Genoa if they could, and viewed the peninsula from seaward, touching as infrequently as possible at the beautiful but deadly shore.

Italy was one long no-man's-land, dotted with walled towns and barely accessible hilltop villages where travelers, once they secured admission, stood stupefied at the perfection of medieval town-planning, the nobility of paintings, sculptures and palaces and the richness and fullness of daily life.

These were the city states, small independent powers, each operating a "foreign policy" towards the city a few miles away, a diplomacy based on semi-mythical traditions and memories of a Guelph-Ghibelline or Visconti-Sforza line-up. As many a city wall and gatehouse with portcullis survives, so does that strong, self-sufficient pride, and so do the old hereditary feuds and alliances, though you are more likely to see them manifested at football matches, crossbow-shooting contests and radio quiz shows than in brawls at the gates.

It's delightful to see the warmth and happiness of Italians in a crowd of their fellow-citizens. They prefer to live in city centers, in a dense network of apartment blocks with a porter at the entrance who takes a close personal interest in the affairs of all. At the football stadium, or when lining the streets to watch a procession, the citizens cram themselves together, chatter happily, stand patiently for hours with calm expectant faces, and exhibit none of the traumatic neuroses that overcrowding is supposed to cause.

Grandioso

Sometimes an Italian grows rich and leaves his city-center tenement and builds himself a villa in the country—as often as not, a neo-Palladian monstrosity, half-tiled with pseudo-Byzantine mosaics. He fortifies the place with high walls and iron gates and an Alsatian guard-dog; and you have the impression he is regretting the move, he is paying a high price for his independence. He should be in his community, one of the crowd; out here, he is only half a man.

But human beings are complex and paradoxical creatures, Italians more so than most. Along with his hereditary parochial loyalty and fondness for the company of the crowd, the Italian prides himself on being his own man. He prefers the solo act to the corporate endeavor. The names we call to mind on the spur of the moment, of Italians who have contributed most to mankind's enrichment, are the names of notable loners. Columbus, Dante, Marconi, Garibaldi, Puccini, Nuvolari, Machiavelli, Michelangelo, Paganini, d'Annunzio, Benedetto Croce, Pirandello . . . all have been individualists, in the mob but not of it. The artists who ushered in the Renaissance are sometimes grouped in schools, but they worked as solitary masters and their results were personally hallmarked in a way that those of, say, the Flemish masters were not.

In the international arenas of science, invention and sport (especially where mechanics was involved, for example pioneer aviation and motor-racing), Italian team efforts have generally disappointed and individual Italians have been prominent. Historians have pointed out the Italian's fondness for associating himself with success and his readiness to cheer the winner; but it has not stopped him earning reputations for brilliant solo efforts and showing that ability to rise to the big occasion which all mankind applauds.

Lamentoso

Uniformity, order and discipline don't seem to appeal to the Italians. Calls for a grand national sacrifice prompt a derisive response. "Your people," an economist tells us, "had learned to pay their taxes round about the year 1300. We Italians haven't learned it yet." (Statistics indicate that about 64 per cent of Italian taxpayers manage to avoid paying any taxes at all.) The visitor to Italy suffers, because the government has to raise a high proportion of revenue by indirect taxation. In Italy, and particularly in the south, where "mortal things touch the heart" more keenly than in other places, a good many front windows of houses and shops are plastered with mourning notices, black-edged sheets of paper bearing stereotyped tributes of the bereaved to their wives and husbands, mothers and children, nieces, nephews and cousins, grandparents and grandchildren . . . and each paper carries the 60-lire stamp, to show that duty has been paid to the state as well as the loved one. If you reside in Italy and wish to raise the matter of a blocked drain or a malfunctioning street lamp with the local council, your complaint must be made on an official form, registered, and stamp duty paid on it. Last week, when I drank my thimbleful of coffee in an Italian bar, I paid 43 separate taxes on it, starting with the impost on the sack the beans came in.

It is partly the legacy of "city-state" bureaucracy. It adds color to the Italian's existence and gives him an opportunity to dramatize his condition and be a lone adventurer, battling for survival against tremendous odds. Italians love to see themselves as the hapless victims of fate. I suspect they are never happier or more productive than in times of crises, preferably when there are hints of corrupt and malignant forces at work. Confusion in politics, a dash of anarchy, a lot of froth and glitter and an outbreak of violence, the chance of an intrigue, the *bustarella* ("little envelope") method of getting things done . . . such a situation seems to bring out the best in them.

"Come siamo ridotti! Poveri noi!" "How low we have fallen, we unhappy wretches!" is the proud, sad lament of the Italian whenever Etna or a ministerial scandal erupts, or the price of tobacco goes up.

Con spirito

All main streets, we were saying, lead to Rome. Yet national unity came to Italy not quite 120 years ago. Relatively few Italians participated in the struggle called *Risorgimento,* or understood the philosophy of that crusade. Rome was not an automatic choice for capital city, and there have since unification been other capitals of Italy than Rome.

Towards Rome, the typical Italian has a typically ambivalent attitude. He regards it as a parasitic citadel of civil servants, the source of half his troubles; and he sees it also (to use Luigi Barzini's expression) as "a great metropolis of the spirit", his spiritual home. Everyone has his own *terra,* his birthplace, and another *terra,* which is Rome; everyone, however strongly he may believe that the sun rises in his own backyard, claims a direct descendant's share in the Roman and Renaissance heritage. The penniless emigrant who stares hollow-eyed from the Munich-bound train as it pauses at some wayside stop in the of the night, the Sicilian peasant and his large family wh among their belongings (all done up with string, in cardboar at the foot of the stairs in the Maritime Terminal at Palermo, ng for tomorrow night's boat to take them to a new life in the New World, the eleven-year-old *gennarino* of Naples who works 16 hours a day in a bar (and knows he will be sacked next year, and his younger brother taken on, because the proprietor would have to pay a twelve-year-old a certain wage) . . . citizens suffering defeat in war, in football, and the humiliation of knowing they are the fifth wheel on the coach of the European Economic Community . . . all know that nothing can take from them the glory of one supreme achievement, to have come from the cradle of Western civilization and to be a citizen of Rome—not the city itself, but the spiritual metropolis, the fount of culture, religion and laws.

For economic and technological miracles, you have to go to Milan, which bears the same relationship to Rome as New York does to Washington, or Frankfurt to Bonn. Rome expresses the miracle of values. James Joyce likened Rome to a man who lives by exhibiting his grandmother's corpse—but the family ties are strong in Italy, and they have a proper reverence for the dead, and grandmother was a very wonderful old woman.

From the far north to the far south, the provincial bridegroom's dream is to take his bride to Rome for the honeymoon. In quiet country places and *montagnard* communities, a villager who has made the pilgrimage to Rome is still considered an oracle among his neighbors, and an authority on world affairs.

Allegro brillante ma con cerimonia

Crossing the road in Rome, a citizen stepped into the path of a bus. A passer-by wanted to shout a warning, but how to address him? He looked respectable, even distinguished; the passer-by took a chance and cried out: "*Commendatore!*" But the jaywalker happened to be a simple *signor,* and therefore paid no attention and was run over.

Stay a while in Italy (and, as usual, we have to add "especially in the south") and the almost ritualistic formality of address becomes noticeable. A minor pleasure, for the stranger, is to be called *dottore* or *professore,* merely because he wears glasses. Every graduate is *professore* or *dottore,* and it is customary to address professional people by their professional titles, architect, engineer, accountant and so forth, or by the rank which many hold in the last surviving order of chivalry: *cavaliere, ufficiale, commendatore.*

Hand-shaking is more widespread than in most Western countries on meeting friends after a short absence, or parting from them for a brief while, for instance. When in doubt, shake hands. Handkissing may be practiced by those who feel they can match the Italian male's ineffable grace and delicacy; but never on young women, and never in public.

Formal preliminaries introduce the foreigner to a rapid, easy, lively intimacy. He must be unusually rigid or old-fashioned if his inhibitions don't melt quickly in conversation with Italians he has just met for the first time. They are extrovert, they ask personal questions, they criticize your clothes and appearance. The foreign woman must expect to have to handle extravagant compliments without being scornful or ungracious about them: they are sincerely meant, and all this is a symptom of the Italian's interest in life and his desire to be friendly. An Italian who brings you a gift or gives you a meal will want your opinion of it, on the spot.

A few days spent in sympathetic observation of the Italians will reinforce the main point of this essay, that they are an individualistic, paradoxical and all-too-human people. The "wonderful soft brightness" that Henrik Ibsen noted when he came out of the Alpine tunnels to descend on Miramare—a brightness which set its stamp, he said, on all his subsequent work—infuses this land. Much is spotted with garish and flashy accretions. And the Italians live up to their landscape. They were Italians who built those Alpine tunnels, working in conditions too dirty and dangerous for the French and Swiss; and since then they have built the most amazing motorways in Europe. The same Italians, establishing a rural railway in the south, started off by ordering (the historians say) "enough gorgeous uniforms and swords to last the company 300 years".

They are Italians who have condemned the earthquake victims of Partanna in Sicily to live in temporary wooden huts, wrapped in blankets and apathy, for the past nine years; and Italians, right next door at Porto Empedocle, who recently roused the puppet showman in the middle of the night and forced him to go down to the theater to release the marionette Rinaldo from the dungeon in which the previous evening's episode had left him.

You may love them or hate them, but you cannot be indifferent to them. They are so whole-heartedly involved in life that every new day is like the fresh page of a thrilling story. Life in Italy—in city arcade, in backstreet tenement, in vineyard and harbor and mountain croft—is all drama. The theater of the streets is a non-stop show, in which everyone has his role and plays it with all his might. There is a part in that show for us too, the strangers, and a very important one.

Coda

Returning to my travelogue of Italian memories, I catch a glimpse of an almond tree, shedding blossom on an undulating ploughland of yellow clods. That is Etruscan soil; one day the oxen will put their feet through, and uncover marvelous frescoed tombs and ornaments. Doesn't this picture summarize Italy? The antique land which remains the country of eternal youth?

It does for me. "Youth, youth, springtime of beauty," they used to sing when I first visited Italy. It is really no surprise that we who fell for that country 40 years ago should be carrying her in our hearts. Our idea of Italy is bound up with the idea of innocence abroad, eager hopes, a taste of romance and adventure in the warm south. It was always morning when we crossed the Alps or sailed into Naples or Genoa or descended on Pisa, Venice or Rome . . . morning, and aureoles of mist on the Apennine mountain tops, and youth going places in the sunrise. One knew, every time, how the legionaries felt, returning after long exile, when they saw the torrents running towards the Mediterranean, and threw themselves down with shouts of "*Aprica! Aprica!*"—"The South, the South!"

HISTORY IN A NUTSHELL

A Young Nation with an Old Heritage

The earliest historians, the Greeks, used the word "Italy" to mean only the southern part of the peninsula. And there were no "Italians" then at all. The boot, in ancient times, was inhabited by various peoples, of differing degrees of civilization, different religious practices, different languages. In the South, they were Mediterranean; in the North, they were Alpine, or Nordic. And—then as now—there were many foreigners, who came, looked, and settled.

One such visitor, according to tradition and Virgil, was Aeneas, who may or may not have arrived in the 12th century BC. According to another, equally well-known tradition, Romulus founded Rome in 753 BC.

In any case, there were Greek settlements in Sicily and southern Italy from the 8th century before Christ. Many cities of "Magna Graecia"—Greater Greece—still exist: we know them as Naples, Paestum, Syracuse, and Agrigento. And the Phoenicians also came to settle in Sicily, at places now called Solunto and Palermo, among others.

The most important and at the same time most mysterious of pre-Roman inhabitants of Italy were the Etruscans—"the long-nosed, sensitive-footed, subtly-smiling Etruscans," as D.H. Lawrence calls them. It used to be thought that they were a central Italian tribe, confined to the area called Etruria just north of Rome, where the great tomb-cities of Tarquinia, Cerveteri and Chiusi were discovered. But recent excavations have shown that the Etruscans controlled nearly all the peninsula, from Salerno to Mantua, and that—far from being hostile to the Roman settlers—they lived in perfect amity with them for a long period.

They held Italy when Rome was a collection of mud huts. They were an artistic and a bulldog breed and in their painted wooden villas they perpetrated the worst excesses of the permissive society, such as husband and wife sitting hand-in-hand on the same couch at mealtimes, and keeping their children round them while they dined in chambers adorned with frivolous ornaments. Rome was to adopt their religious ceremonies (vestal virgins and household gods), their arts of divination (sheep's liver, thunder, the flight of birds) and their theatrical entertainments (from the flute-and-dance routine of Etruscan sacrificial captives, Roman comedy was born).

For a hundred years, until the abdication of Tarquin the Proud in 510 BC, Etruscan kings ruled Rome. After that, history speaks of another hundred years of civil war, and legends embroider it: the return of Cincinnatus from his rustic retreat to lead the people to victory; the magnanimity of the all-conquering Coriolanus, a renegade who stopped short before the city of his birth; the rape of Lucretia and the geese on the Capitol hill and how Horatio kept the bridge . . . yet the Etruscans left nothing of their civilization above ground, no clue to the language they spoke apart from a few cabalistic tablets, no clue to where they came from (some say mainland Greece, others the shores of the Black Sea) and no clue to where they disappeared to.

'You cannot dance gaily to the double flute and at the same time conquer nations," D.H. Lawrence wrote—and that was why Etruria fell. More probably, blind superstition and devotion to soothsayers was the Etruscans' undoing. The last of them vanished 2,300 years ago, but you cannot tour Italy today without being aware of him. The finest of medieval hilltowns are built on Etruscan foundations. The most admired objects in the archeological museums are Etruscan statuettes and lamps and earrings.

The Roman Republic and Empire

Then, when the Etruscan rulers were driven out, the Roman Republic was founded, about 510. Later, in 348 BC, the League broke up, and at the same time—through a series of wars—the Samnites and other southern peoples were defeated.

By destroying Pyrrhus and the Greeks at Tarentum (modern Taranto) in 272 BC, Rome completed its conquest of the mainland, but was at once involved in a series of expensive campaigns against Carthage (the Punic wars). Hannibal of Carthage, victorious at Lake Trasimene, threw away his advantage at Cannae in Puglia and Rome emerged triumphant over an "Italy" which stretched from Sicily in the south to Rimini in the northeast. Before long the whole peninsula south of the Alps was Roman "Italy".

Rome also had to contend with internal, civil and political strife. Unity was imposed by Julius Caesar, when he became dictator of the nation in 48 BC. He engaged in an ambitious program of reforms (including a new "Julian" calendar), but was unable to carry out all of them before his assassination in 44 BC. As all readers of Shakespeare know, the death of Julius was followed by a civil war. It lasted virtually twenty years, until Octavian—or Augustus, as he came to be called—restored order in 27 BC and returned much power to the Roman Senate.

After the death of Augustus, in 14 AD, the Empire was ruled for over fifty years by his heirs, some—like Tiberius—able, and some—like the notorious Caligula—disastrous. The last of the line was Nero (54–68 AD), also famous for his excesses. After his death, there was another civil war. The winner was Vespasian, who ruled from 70 to 79, followed by his sons Titus and Domitian. The boundaries of the Empire, in the ensuing reigns, were stretched to include northern Britain, lands along the Rhine and the Danube, and part of what is now Romania.

But from roughly the end of the 2nd century AD, the decline began. There were still some good emperors, but the invasions by Goths, then Franks, then Persians led to poverty, unruly armies, and general dissension. In 325, Constantine established his new capital—Constantinople—on the Bosphorus; and Rome declined even further. In 476, the barbarian Odoacer was named King of Italy. The Western Empire was at an end. Byzantium continued, but that is another story.

Constantine (whose reign went from 306 to 337) had declared Christianity the official religion of the Empire, after the Christians had been the victims of three periods of persecution: under Decius (249–51), Valerian (257–61), and Diocletian (beginning of the fourth century). After Constantine, the power of the bishop of Rome grew until the occupant of that seat became the head of the Western church. In 381, the bishop of Rome assumed the title of pope.

After the fall of the Western Empire, Italy had no real political unity again until 1870. At the end of the 5th century AD, the pattern of division was already drawn. In southern Italy, Greek was still spoken. Ravenna, bound to Byzantium, was the seat of a spearate—and important—government. In Rome, the popes exercised temporal power: they kept up the public buildings, paid the army, and ran the city and its surrounding territory.

The empire was dead, but there were pretences that it lived on. Ancient Roman titles were still used now and then. Roman law was preserved. It was, in fact, codified and imposed by Justinian, the Byzantine emperor (483–565), who—with Ravenna as his base—drove the Goths out of Italy.

But after his death there were new invaders from the north: the Lombards. Their invasion began in 568, and within a few years, they had conquered a large part of Italy (including present-day Lombardy, with its capital, Milan). They were assimilated, learned the local language, and intermarried with the inhabitants. As a reaction to their success, the popes cherished more and more their temporal power, and important city-states, especially maritime cities like Genoa, Venice, and—in the south—Amalfi, also began to develop.

In 590, Gregory the Great became Pope. A scholar and a liturgical reformer ("Gregorian" chant is named after him), he assumed the throne of Peter at a bad time: Rome had been the victim of floods, the plague, and was menaced by the Lombards. Gregory restored the city, made peace with the would-be invader, strengthening the papacy.

But the Lombards did not give up their territorial aims. In 751, they captured Ravenna and stamped out the last traces of the Byzantine rule of part of the peninsula. To combat the Lombards, the Pope (Stephen II) invited new invaders: the Franks, under Pepin, who drove the Lombards from Ravenna and gave that territory to the Pope. In 774, Pepin's son Charlemagne defeated the Lombards totally and sanctioned papal rule over what was to be known, for centuries thereafter, as the States of the Church. In 800, Pope Leo III crowned Charlemagne Holy Roman Emperor in St. Peter's.

The Holy Roman Empire

The Holy Roman Empire continued, first as a fact, then as an idea, for many centuries more. After Charlemagne's death in 814, the empire was divided up among his descendants; and this division fostered still further the growth of the independent city-states. The papacy declined until it was a kind of "hereditary Roman despotism", in the words of one historian. The great Roman families created popes from their own number, while the Saracens invaded and controlled Sicily, and, in the north, the Magyars took Lombardy.

The Saxon ruler, Otto I, with the support of the popes, invaded Italy three times, defeating the Magyars in 955, and later securing control of Rome. His son Otto II fought the Saracens, and then Otto III (son of Otto II) built himself a palace in Rome, on the Aventine hill, and sought to create a single Christian empire. But by the time of his death, in 1002, the dream had proved beyond his power to achieve.

During the 11th century, another foreign power became prominent in the south of Italy: the Normans. Skilled and unscrupulous fighters, the Normans were, first of all, mercenaries in the service of the Greeks and the Lombards. Gradually, their numbers increased and they demanded territory in payment for their war-making exploits. In 1059, Pope Nicholas II named Robert Guiscard, the Norman leader, Duke of Apulia and Calabria. Robert's son Roger won Sicily from the Saracens and in 1130 he was crowned King of Sicily in Palermo cathedral.

The Normans ruled southern Italy, with political acumen and with considerable interest in the arts (many monuments remain to prove this artistic sensitivity), almost until the end of the century.

In the confused, murky picture of the Middle Ages in Italy, bright figures—popes, emperors, artists—occasionally emerge. There was Pope Gregory VII, for example. Righteous and determined, Gregory was bent on reforming the Church and on imposing his authority on the Emperor Henry IV. In the winter of 1077, the excommunicated emperor stood for three bleak days in the courtyard of the castle of Canossa, imploring the absolution of the Pope, who was a guest there. Gregory forgave, but soon was led to excommunicate Henry again.

A more colorful emperor—Frederick I, whom the Italians called Barbarossa because of his red beard—invaded Italy from Germany in 1154, intending to bring the peninsula under his full control. But this time it was the city-states, formed into the Lombard League, that defeated him. Innocent III, who was pope from 1198 until 1216, brought the power and influence of his office, in both temporal and spiritual matters, to a peak. He gained control of Sicily, and claimed the papal right to rule most of the peninsula.

But this achievement, after Innocent's death, led to the long, bewildering struggle between popes and emperors and their respective supporters, known as Guelphs and Ghibellines. The dominant emperor of the next phase of the struggle was Frederick II (1194–1250), partly Norman and much attached to his southern Italian realm. His great castles, even today, illustrate both his political prowess and his real and intelligent love of culture and the arts.

In 1261 a Frenchman became Pope Urban IV and began to look for French support, to break for good the power of the German Hohenstaufens. Charles of Anjou was summoned to Italy, and with skillful generalship and political astuteness, he became King of Sicily and lord of southern Italy. His stern rule bred revolt, and after the "Sicilian Vespers" uprising of 1282, Sicily proper passed under the domination of the King of Aragon.

As the cities became more independent and the middle class more prominent and rich, the temporal, central power of the pope vacillated once more. The autocratic Boniface VIII tried to reaffirm it, but his papacy ended in disaster. The next pope, a Frenchman, moved to Avignon, which remained the papal residence until 1377.

During the 14th century, the eve of the Renaissance, the history of Italy is largely the story of the city-states and their battles, among themselves and against foreign influences. The most important of these little realms were Naples, the Papal States, Venice, Florence, and Milan. In Naples there was Charles of Anjou's son Robert, who was followed on the throne by his colorful, much-married daughter Joanna, then by her cousin Charles III. Eventually, in 1442, the Anjous were defeated by the Spanish, and the two Sicilies were reunited into one kingdom, ruled by Aragon.

The Papal States were, in effect, so many cities, each with its own despot. In Rome itself, chaotic and riven, the great families proved incapable of ruling; and in 1347, the unlikely Cola di Rienzo was briefly named Tribune of the People. His control of the city ended with his assassination in 1354. Pope Gregory XI returned to Rome in 1377, but ruled there only a year, and the dispute over his successor led to the Great Schism, with a pope in Rome and a rival pope in Avignon. Finally, in 1421, Martin V reestablished the Roman residency of the pope and paved the way for the city's recovery of prestige and splendor.

Venice enjoyed the most enviable government in Italy at the time, a successful, content republic, which lasted until 1797. Genoa, on the other hand, was controlled by feuding patrician families, whose incapacity led finally to the acceptance of French control in 1396.

Florence, even before the end of the Middle Ages, was the cultural center of Italy, though some of the finest Tuscan artists also worked elsewhere, and Florence's greatest poet, Dante, was condemned—for political reasons—to spend the greater part of his life in exile, until his death, in Ravenna, in 1321. A city of prosperous merchants and canny bankers, Florence began its first great building spree in the latter half of the 13th century. Monuments like the Bargello, the churches of Santa Croce and Santa Maria Novella were constructed, and before the end of the century, the cathedral and the Palazzo Vecchio were begun. In the following century Giotto built his splendid bell-tower, sculptors

Andrea Pisano and Ghiberti decorated the Baptistery, and—in 143—Brunelleschi made architectural history with his Cathedral dome.

Other great local rulers of the period, who have left their mark in history and in art, were Can Grande della Scala in Verona, the Visconti family in Milan, the Gonzagas in Mantua and the Estes in Ferrara.

The Renaissance

Unlike a dynasty or a papacy, the Renaissance cannot be given precise dates, a fixed beginning or end. Very roughly speaking, this great period of art and thought in Italy can be said to cover the 15th century. Obviously, certain "Renaissance" notions, trends can be identified earlier; and the influence of that explosion of culture and civilization lingered on, into the succeeding centuries.

In the 14th century, Florence had been often at war. The 15th century began badly: in 1400 the city was ravaged by the plague and besieged shortly afterwards by Giangaleazzo Visconti. But Visconti died, the plague receded, and the city could devote its energies to other pursuits, including the study of classical learning. Rare manuscripts were collected and translated by the Florentine humanists. The Florentines could also go back to business, and one of the most successful, in this area of activity, was Cosimo de' Medici, the banker. Cosimo, after early disappointments (including a year of exile), soon became the most politically important man in the city. Cosimo's power, at his death, was inherited by his sickly, art-loving son Piero, but Piero died only five years later.

His son was Lorenzo, later to be called "the magnificent." Like his father and grandfather, Lorenzo was a collector and a patron (and also a gifted poet in his own right). Cosimo had commissioned works from Ghiberti and Donatello; Piero had Benozzo Gozzoli paint a lovely fresco of "The Journey of the Magi" in the chapel of the Medici Palace, and he ordered works from other artists, including Paolo Uccello and Pollaiuolo.

Lorenzo, with appropriate magnificence, went even farther. He summoned foreign craftsmen, trying to revive the art of mosaic; in the garden of his palace he set up an art school whose most famous student was Michelangelo Buonarroti. Leonardo da Vinci—the archetype of the "Renaissance man"—may also have lived in Lorenzo's house.

Florence was the seat, the focus of the Renaissance; but Florentine ideas, ideals—and artists—soon moved to other Italian cities, and even abroad.

In Rome, the papacy, after the Great Schism, was resuming its longlost temporal power. It was briefly lost again, during a Roman revolt which established a republic. Pope Eugenius IV moved to Florence, and when he returned to Rome in 1443, he was accompanied by a Greek scholar, Bessarion, along with Florentine humanists, painters, and sculptors. His successor, Nicholas V, patronized Fra Angelico and the polymath Leon Battista Alberti, who supervised the dismantling of the old church of St. Peter's, in preparation for the construction of a splendid new basilica.

Perhaps the greatest Renaissance pope was Pius II (Enea Piccolomini), a man of letters, a persuasive orator, and an art-lover, whose life is described in superb frescos by Pinturicchio in the Piccolomini Library in Siena. He died as he was setting forth on a crusade.

Later 15th-century popes were more secular, but no less art-loving, and Rome continued to build, to paint, to excavate antiquities, and under Alexander VI (a Borgia), to expand its territory.

Renaissance masterpieces can be seen in villages and country houses from Tuscany northwards, as well as in towns and cities—the frescos of Giotto, Piero della Francesca, Veronese, Carpaccio and Mantegna, the bronze and stone works of Donatello, Sansovino and the della Robbias.

While the arts were flourishing, politics and wars continued. In 1455 Florence, Milan and Naples had an understanding but Lorenzo the Magnificent, grandson of Cosimo de' Medici, led Florence away. For a time this clever ruler preserved a careful balance of power between the city states but, after his death in 1492, a rapid succession of vicious and inept popes and princes reduced Italy once more to a battleground for the warring powers, France and Spain. Charles VIII of France made good his claim to Naples in 1495 but left Italy the same year, and the Spanish King, Ferdinand the Catholic, sent troops to win Naples back for the house of Aragon. The pattern of foreign invasion continued for centuries afterwards.

Italy under Foreign Control

In 1521, the Emperor Charles V, grandson of Ferdinand the Catholic, and the French King Francis I began their struggle for mastery of Italy. From his grandfather, Charles had inherited control of Sicily, Naples, and Sardinia. His aim, then, was to establish Spain as the dominant influence in Italy, leaving the native Italians to run various states. But Francis also claimed Naples and Milan. And the fight raged almost continuously until 1529, as the Italian rulers frequently shifted their allegiance from one invader to the other, in the hope of winning favors or establishing some kind of balance of power.

In 1527, leaderless Spanish and French troops occupied Rome and sacked it. The Sack of Rome is sometimes considered the end of the Renaissance. But the city, even under Spanish control, continued to build new great churches (many by Bernini and his rival Borromini). Charles V married members of his family to a Medici, who was made Duke of Tuscany, and to a Sforza, in Milan. After the death of Francesco Sforza and after more fighting, Charles made his son Philip Duke of Milan. The treaty of Câteau-Cambrésis in 1559 sealed Spanish domination, which lasted until 1713.

This period has been called one of the dreariest in Italian history. From a political point of view, it undoubtedly was. The heavy hand of the Inquisition lay on the whole peninsula, as scholars like Galileo (1564–1642) were to learn, to their dismay.

Spain's wars also affected Italy. In the War of the Spanish Succession at the beginning of the 18th century, the kingdom of Savoy, in northern Italy, rose to prominence, but the treaty of Utrecht, in 1713, substituted the Austrian Habsburgs as the chief power in Italy, in place of their extinct Spanish cousins. Some territories were given directly to the Austrian Emperor (among them Milan, Mantua, Naples and Sardinia); others were arbitrarily assigned to loyal princes. But the very arbitrariness of this arrangement, which ignored traditional ties, made the Italians even more dissatisfied with foreign domination and sowed the seeds of the process of unification under the only Italian dynasty in the century that followed.

The ambitions of the Farnese Queen of Spain soon led to new wars and changes in the Utrecht settlement. Her son received the Duchy of Parma. Savoy handed Sicily over to the Austrians and received Sardinia in exchange. In 1734, the Spanish Bourbons reconquered Naples and held it until 1860. In 1737, when the last Medici died, the Grand Duchy of Tuscany passed to Francis of Lorraine, husband of the Austrian heiress, Maria Theresa. And in 1748, after the peace of Aix-la-Chapelle, Savoy—or the Kingdom of Sardinia—was given Nice and French Savoy.

The latter half of the 18th century was peaceful, though social conditions were appalling. Brigands terrorized visitors (and inhabitants) in the south. Illiteracy was high, and so was crime. In one eleven-year period, the city of Rome—then with only 160,000 inhabitants—had more than 4,000 murders. Only Tuscany, under the enlightened Grand Duke Leopold, fared better. His reign (1765–90), till his succession as Emperor, was marked by a number of reforms; he practically dismissed his army and sold his navy—two corvettes—to Russia.

Napoleon

Then came Napoleon. The French Revolution, in 1789, affected Italy, divided in its sympathies. In 1796 Napoleon was given command of the French army of Italy and invaded the peninsula, sweeping all before him, leaving behind him a series of revolutionary republics. The Cispadane (this side of the Padana, i.e. south of the River Po) Republic was made up of Reggio, Bologna, Ferrara and Mantua. The Transpadane included Milan, Brescia, and others. Genoa became the Ligurian Republic. At Campo Formio Austria signed a peace treaty, by which it acquired Venice and its Dalmation possessions. The remainder of northern Italy was given to the French. When Napoleon went off to Egypt, unrest—and republican sentiments—spread. A republic was set up in Rome, as the Pope escaped to Tuscany.

The Bourbons in Naples, where Sir William Hamilton was British Ambassador (and his wife, Emma, was mistress of Horatio Nelson), held out; and at the end of 1798, Neapolitan forces marched on Rome, to drive away the French. The southerners managed to occupy the city for a few days, but then were ignominiously sent running back to Naples. The king, with his queen and his court, fled to Sicily. The Kingdom of Naples became the Parthenopean Republic.

The whole peninsula was, for a brief period, republican and under French control. But the situation did not last long. An Austro-Russian Army, in March of 1799, expelled the French from northern Italy. In the south, King Ferdinand, from his refuge in Palermo, asked for military help from the Russians, the Turks, and the English. With troops sent by all three nations, his representative, Cardinal Ruffo, amassed a scruffy army, including even brigands like the notorious Fra Diavolo, and besieged Naples, where the republicans were allowed to surrender conditionally. Then Nelson arrived, brushed aside the conditions, and hanged the republican Admiral Caracciolo from the yardarm of his flagship. The king was even more ruthless, and all the republican leaders—including many intellectuals—were executed. Hundreds more were imprisoned or sent into exile.

By the time the French left, there was little affection for them. All the brave talk of liberty, equality and fraternity that had accompanied their arrival had aroused enthusiasm, quickly stifled when they began to act like just another foreign tyrant. The Italians were taxed and pressed into military service; Napoleon or his agents carried off some of the country's greatest art treasures to Paris, and not all of them have yet returned.

Against the foreign oppressors (for the Austrians were just as much disliked as the French) and against their local sycophants, various clandestine organizations began to be formed, of which the most famous was the Carbonari. In their love of ritual and oaths, they resembled the Freemasons, and their influence was widespread, cutting across all class and regional distinctions.

In 1800, Napoleon won back most of northern Italy (Venice remained Austrian). A few years later, when he became emperor, Italy was turned into a kingdom, part of the Napoleonic Empire. He gradually extended its boundaries, annexing Venice, the March of Ancona, and finally Naples, where first his brother Joseph Bonaparte, then his brother-in-law Joachim Murat ruled. His son was at birth proclaimed King of Rome. But, after the fiasco of his invasion of Russia, Napoleon's star began to wane. The Austrians came back to northern Italy. The Bourbons regained Naples. The pope returned to Rome.

The Risorgimento

Napoleon's brief unification of Italy proved, at least, that the country could be a single unit. And from the Congress of Vienna in 1815, which perpetuated Italian political divisions, until Rome was taken in 1870 by the forces of King Victor Emmanuel II of Savoy, the history of Italy is a continuous struggle—with many reverses and black pages—for unification and independence.

The story is no less complex than the pages of Italian history that precede it. Many Italians, north and south, wanted the peninsula to become one nation. But there was no general agreement as to what form this nation was to take, or how its creation was to be achieved. Some believed in peaceful evolution. Some—like Mazzini—wanted to revive the splendors of the Roman Republic. Many were for a Kingdom of Italy under the house of Savoy, while the writer-priest Vincenzo Gioberti, in his *The Moral and Civil Primacy of the Italians,* argued for a federated Italy under the presidency of the pope. When Pius IX was elected pope in 1846, he was hailed as a liberal, and Gioberti's theory, for a while (until Pius proved less liberal than he had first seemed), was considered, by some Italians, a viable solution.

The year 1848 was a year of revolution throughout Europe. Rebellion in Sicily forced the king to grant a constitution. Sardinia and Tuscany quickly granted constitutions and, also in early 1848, so did the pope. When, in February, the Parisians expelled the French king and proclaimed a republic, their act was a spark that struck raging fires first in Vienna, and then, on March 17, in Milan, when the famous "five days" finally drove the Austrians from the city. A few days later, Charles Albert of Savoy sent his army to pursue the Austrians.

The first Italian war of independence thus began in March 1848, and the forces of Charles Albert were soon supported by troops from other Italian states. The pope, however, refused to declare war against Catholic Austria; and the Bourbon king, in Naples, recalled his troops and withdrew the constitution. The Austrians regained confidence and by August 7 had driven Charles Albert's army back into Piedmont. An armistice was signed. But the following spring it was denounced and fighting was resumed. This time Charles Albert was thoroughly defeated. He abdicated in favor of Victor Emmanuel and went into exile in Portugal, where he died a few months afterwards.

Venice and the Roman Republic fought on. Mazzini was the leader of the triumvirate that governed Rome, against horrendous difficulties and with true democratic spirit; Garibaldi was the commander of the city's forces. Those forces were opposed by the Neapolitans, the Austrians, and—especially—by the French, who entered the city on July 3, 1849, the day after Garibaldi had escaped across the Apennines. The following month Venice succumbed to the Austrian siege.

The Austrians had been kept out of Piedmont, which now became the one Italian state with a free press, an elected parliament, and a liberal, respected constitution. From 1852 on, when Count Camillo Cavour was prime minister, Piedmont—or the Kingdom of Sardinia, as it was properly called—also had a brilliant political leader, devoted to the Italian cause and to the monarchy.

Cavour cultivated Italian friendship with England and France, at the same time not hesitating to show his hostility to Austria. Piedmont sent troops to the Crimean war and thus won a place at the peacemaking Congress of Paris. He used it to bring the Italian question before a European forum. Though his material achievement was small, he had raised a moral issue and won further support. Two years later, in 1858, Cavour met Napoleon III secretly and came to a verbal agreement: Sardinia and France would make war against Austria; after the expected victory, an Italian kingdom would be formed for Victor Emmanuel. The price was the return of Nice and French Savoy to France.

In April 1859, after having demanded that Sardinia disarm (the demand was rejected), Austria invaded Piedmont. The French army soon came to Piedmont's support, and won victories at Magenta and Solferino. But the Austrians were not yet defeated. As the former Italian dukedoms hastened to proclaim their allegiance to Sardinia, Napoleon decided to make peace with the Austrian Emperor. The two rulers met at Villafranca. They agreed that Lombardy—with Austrian forces still in its garrisons—would become part of an Italian Federation, but the Veneto region was to go back to Austria. The dukes of Modena and Tuscany were to be reinstated.

The Italians were outraged. Cavour resigned. Tuscany and Modena refused to have their dukes back. Napoleon wanted Nice and Savoy. Recalled to power in January 1860, Cavour temporarily resolved the situation by arranging plebiscites: Nice and Savoy voted to become French, Tuscany and Modena chose Sardinia.

Already, the patriots were thinking about southern Italy. On May 5, 1860, Garibaldi and his thousand volunteers set sail from Quarto, near Genoa, for Sicily. Shortly after landing, the general declared himself dictator of the island in the name of Victor Emmanuel. After hard fighting, supported by Sicilian rebels, Garibaldi occupied Palermo. Soon reinforcements arrived, and Garibaldi led his men to the mainland. On September 7, Garibaldi entered Naples, which the king had fled the day before.

Garibaldi's intention was to continue to Rome, but a hard-won victory on the Volturno river forced him to delay. Meanwhile Victor Emmanuel and his troops, marching from the north, met the general at Teano. The question of Rome was postponed. Garibaldi retired to his little island of Caprera, and Cavour set about summoning Italy's first national parliament, which would proclaim Victor Emmanuel king. His kingdom included all of Italy except the Veneto region and Rome, with a small surrounding area.

Cavour died, suddenly, in June 1861. His loss was tragic, for no other statesman had his vision, his intelligence, or his patience. And there was much to be done: the administration of the whole peninsula had to be reorganized (or, in some cases, simply organized). Roads had to be built, standard weights and measures had to be established, the schools had to be brought into a single system.

The big problem remained Rome. The Veneto was regained from Austria after a brief, humiliatingly unsuccessful participation in the Prusso-Austrian war of 1866. But Rome, even after the French withdrew their garrison from the city, remained outside the kingdom. One party wanted to take the city by force; the conservative majority wanted to negotiate. Garibaldi attempted to seize the city, but was repulsed by papal troops and a French force, sent by Napoleon. Finally in 1870, after the Emperor's defeat at Sedan, Italian troops breached the walls of Rome, at Porta Pia, and took the city. The pope sealed himself up in the Vatican, which—for half a century—no pope ever left. "Italy is made," said Massimo d'Azeglio. "Now let us make the Italians."

Modern Italy

The final unification of Italy had been largely the work of the conservative majority in parliament, the sober, loyal, rigid Piedmontese tradition. After the government was moved to Rome, that party began to splinter; and in 1876, the left came into power. But the left, too, was not a compact organization. And the new prime minister, Agostino Depretis, showed more skill in manipulating parliament than in organizing his party or a coherent program. It was the beginning of the breakdown of the party system in Italy, with effects still discernible today.

Though tied to the apron-strings of the Dual Alliance of Germany and Austria, and by no means a great or stable country, Italy was eager for colonial adventures. In 1885 she seized Eritrea and part of Somaliland. She embarked on a disastrous ten-year war with Abyssinia (1887–96) and occupied Tripoli and some of the Greek islands (1911 and 1912). At home, under the evil genius of the prime minister, Francesco Crispi, corruption and maladministration bred desperate deeds. In 1900, Victor Emmanuel's successor, Humbert I, was assassinated.

When Giovanni Giolitti became premier in 1901, he was able to count on the open support of the clerical party (the pope, frightened by the rise of socialism, had withdrawn his veto of Catholic participation in Italian politics), and at the same time, he fostered some of the same reforms in the Socialists' program. But government grew ever more remote from the people and in 1914 Italy was a land of discontent, strikes, economic distress and mass emigration.

By the time of the First World War, the Triple Alliance had virtually lost its force. After a period of neutrality, with much vigorous nationalistic and interventionist tumult in the streets and press, Italy broke with Austria and Germany in 1915 and entered the war on the side of the Allies. Despite a searing defeat at Caporetto, the Italian Army recovered and held its own against the Austrians. After the Armistice, Italy gained new territory (though not all she wanted), including Trieste, the Trentino and Alto Adige regions, which she had been claiming for many years.

The end of the war found Italy in a parlous state: dissatisfaction with the peace terms, hostility against the army (veterans in uniform were beaten up in the streets, and officers were even killed), waves of strikes, both legal and illegal, and a series of weak governments paved the way for the advent of Fascism.

Fascism, the War and After

After asserting themselves, with unscrupulous violence, in many strongly Socialist areas, the Fascists sent Mussolini to parliament in 1921. In October of the following year, the March on Rome took place. And on October 29, 1922, the king asked Mussolini to form a cabinet.

There can be no doubt that the Fascist movement, though a minority, had considerable support, especially from the middle class and also from industrialists, who hoped to benefit from stability, at whatever cost it was achieved. At first cautiously, then blatantly, Mussolini went about eliminating the opposition. In 1926 the right to strike was abolished. The press was quickly muzzled, only the Fascist unions were allowed, and when even the brutal murder of the Socialist Giacomo Matteotti failed to bring Mussolini down, his rule was absolute. Fascism quickly penetrated every area of Italian life, from the university to sports.

In foreign affairs, Mussolini was also able to count on the support of other countries (the fact that Italian trains now were mostly on time was much admired by tourists). But his attack on Abyssinia in 1935 was almost universally decried. Flouting the sanctions of other countries, Italy pursued the war, left the League of Nations, and in 1936 formed the Axis with Hitler's Germany. When Germany seized Austria and the Sudetenland, Italy displayed her prowess by taking Albania.

When the Second World War broke out, Italy at first was "nonbelligerent" (not neutral, since she was linked by treaty to the Axis). Then, exploiting the defeat of France, Italy declared war in 1940. Both in Greece and in North Africa, the poorly equipped and unenthusiastic Italian armies were humiliated and rescued only by German assistance. After the Allied invasion of Sicily in July 1943, Fascism's days were numbered. Before the month was out, Mussolini was forced to resign, then arrested. In September, the Badoglio government announced an armistice and cooperated with the Allies as co-belligerents.

Mussolini escaped, with Nazi help, to the north and founded a puppet "Fascist republic" on the shores of Lake Como. The German armies fought tenaciously to hold the central and northern regions of the peninsula and a further eighteen months passed before, in the spring of 1945, the Allies broke through the Gothic Line south of Florence and the partisans attacked effectively in Lombardy. The escaping Mussolini was captured by partisans and executed near Lake Como on April 28. In June, a new government was formed in Rome, headed by the partisan leader Ferruccio Parri. He was shortly succeeded by Alcide De Gasperi.

In June 1946, a referendum declared against the monarchy. Italy was a republic. At the end of the following year, a new constitution was approved, creating a president (with more symbolic than political importance), a two-chamber parliament, and a cabinet and prime minister. The first general election after the approval of the constitution was held on April 18, 1948, and the Christian Democrats (De Gasperi's party) won a majority. This party has continued to control Italy's parliament ever since though Italy also has Western Europe's largest Communist party. Italy, with her genius for living with problems instead of wearing herself out seeking solutions to them, has learned to live with Communism. Up to the middle 1950s, Communism was considered an unmitigated evil. The Church was powerless to halt its progress. Efforts of the powerful ally—the United States—which Italy called upon were largely counter-productive.

The Church, as it has done so often in past history, has now subdued dogma to practical necessity and has ceased opposition to a limited cooperation. Visitors to renowned Italian centers in recent years—

Genoa (Piccola Stalingrad), Bologna, Milan, Florence and Perugia—have been horrified to learn that the administration is Communist; and reassured by the apparent continuity of party politics as usual.

Italian Communism, claiming conversion to parliamentary democracy, has its power base in northern Italy, among industrial workers, but has been gaining ground in the predominantly agricultural south, and in Sicily and Sardinia. The PCI (Italian Communist Party) is the second largest political party in Italy.

In recent years governments have been a permutation of alliances (realigned every few months) between the Christian Democrats and the Socialists, Republicans and Social Democrats. The latest variations are Christian Democratic minority governments supported by all parties except the extreme right.

The Future

What are the issues that concern Italians most as they approach the last decades of the 20th century, their first full century of nationhood? Some are old and some are new. They include the internal economy (monetary crises and rampant inflation, following the shortlived "economic miracle" of the 1960s); scandals in government; atmospheric pollution (the Seveso disaster of 1976); referenda on divorce, contraception and abortion, as the Church still plays a big part in the lives of women and children; but above all public security, especially since the dramatic assassination of the former Prime Minister and President of the Christian Democratic Party, Aldo Moro, in 1978.

The document which established the European Economic Community was signed in Rome, and Italy has been an enthusiastic member (and a major beneficiary) of that organization since the beginning. The Helsinki conference of July 1973—which discussed East-West détente—accepted Italian as one of the five official European languages. Initiatives on disarmament have long been a part of Italian foreign policy; and in the United Nations she presses for increased aid to developing countries of the Third World.

Despite dissensions among parties in power and seemingly insuperable domestic problems, an enormous topweight of bureaucracy, a tangle of antiquated laws, as well as political and organized crime unequaled for 200 years, hope remains that (to quote Barzini) "each generation is slowly advancing to the goal which some optimists thought had been triumphantly reached in 1870".

CREATIVE ITALY

A Genius for Shape and Sound

Throughout their recorded history the Italian people have been remarkable for their love of shape, color and beauty and their need to express that love with the work of their hands. No one who travels the tourist routes of the peninsula, sometimes through corridors of artisan products which seem to go on forever, can doubt that the feeling runs as deep as ever. Much craftwork on display is frothy and garish, yet frequently redeemed by the inspirational touches Italians were always famous for. Genuine craftsmen are dying out. The old trades and secret techniques which were handed down like precious heirlooms from mother to daughter and father to son will soon be found only in isolated regions of the south, and on remote islands.

Crafts

Before turning to the more internationally recognized side of the artistic life of Italy, it might be an idea to look at the crafts of the people.

Craftsmanship remains regional. Basketwork, weaving and silver-smithing are carried on in cottage and tiny workshop up and down the land, but to experts the finished item has a regional stamp, like wine, and can be identified with a particular locality.

Sicily is the land of gorgeous embroidery, lavishly decorated *carretti* (pony-carts) and harnesses and the kind of marzipan called *pasta reale*, which usually comes in fanciful and grotesque shapes, representing anything from the sea urchins to statuettes of footballers; all edible, naturally.

Homespun tweeds are a specialty of Puglia and the Romagna, and a pure weaving tradition of blankets and dress materials is the preroga-tive of several Abruzzi towns, notably Scanno. The Trentino and the Sorrentine peninsula boast a distinctive style of inlay and veneer on wood. The inlaid cabinets and trinkets of the maritime towns of Liguria are done with tortoiseshell and mother-of-pearl.

In the "*trulli*" towns of Puglia and in southern Tuscany, elaborate ironwork—gates, lamps, screens, heraldic symbols—is an ancient craft. The Lombardy towns keep alive their medieval enamel works and instrument-carving shops, producing violins, mandolins and guitars. In the Alto Adige one may still pick up the occasional wood-and-metal figurine that regional artisans were once famous for.

A rapid glance at the souvenir shops reveals Florence as the center of tooled leather (book bindings, wallets, slippers, fashion accessories), Venice of glassware (and also pottery, lace-making and filigree), Naples of glove-making. Marble sculpture is on sale almost everywhere, but especially along the Tuscan coast from Leghorn to Spezia, where the Carrara quarries provide the raw material. Terracotta statuettes and ornaments are chiefly associated with Catania in Sicily, alabaster work with the Volterra region of Tuscany, majolica with the southeast.

Buried in masses of fairground rubbish, the genuine article can still be found, and not always at a prohibitive price. It is worthwhile, particularly in the south and Sardinia, to investigate dark doorways where an aged man or woman is plying some arcane task. It may be carving picture frames, stringing gold thread for embroidery or making a raffia bag . . . whatever it may be, it probably recalls a venerable tradition of that town, that street or that house.

Painting and Sculpture

Italian art flows as naturally as its wine, its sunshine, and its *amore*, and it has been springing from the Italian spirit for nearly as long. Perhaps nowhere in the world has such a vital creative impulse flourished for almost three millennia with such variety within the noble sweep of its classic tradition. And yet, Italy lives comfortably in the midst of all these accumulated treasures. She accepts them casually and affectionately as she does her children and her flowers. True, some of her precious store has been gathered into world-famous museums, but the Italian knows best and loves most intimately the art which surrounds his every day to day activity. He goes to church among thousand-year-old mosaics, buys his groceries in a shop which has been open since the time of Columbus, picnics on the steps of a temple which was old when Christ was born, attends the opera in the same theaters where Rossini and Verdi saw their works premiered, and falls asleep in a high rise built by one of today's major architects. She wears the raiment of her heritage with a light and touching grace. She must: it is the very fabric of her life.

The first bright threads of the Italian tradition were woven into a coherent pattern by the Etruscans in Central Italy about 2,700 years ago. Their art speaks boldly of a garish and sensual life style. Etruscan towns were massively fortified mountain tops linked by roads which skimmed the highest ridges. Their temples were wooden with clay sculpture embellishments, all painted in vivid red, blue and yellow. Those few clay deities which survive are often giants whose fierce grins inspire an alarmed respect. It is, however, the careful provision for the afterlife of their dead which gives the clearest picture of Etruscan life. Their earth mound tombs were embellished with murals of lavish banquets, ecstatic dancers, cunning hunters and lusty warriors. In the center of the chamber stood the life size terracotta image of the dead man and his wife reclining on a banquet couch, partaking with a wry delight of their silent and eternal farewell party.

If Greek influence is fundamental to the fiery art of the seafaring Etruscans, the Greeks themselves were not far behind in settling and colonizing most of Southern Italy and Sicily. At Paestum near Naples and in Sicily at Agrigento, Syracuse, Selinunte and Segesta some of the best preserved Doric temples in the world stand sharp against the cobalt sky.

Rome, building upon the lessons of Etruria and Greece, both of whom she soon conquered, employed a pragmatic genius for military strategy and civic organization to impose its order on most of the known world. Cosmopolitan and eclectic, Roman art absorbed whatever its tastemakers thought modish in other cultures, but in its portraiture one detects a candor and insight which is unmistakably its own.

Daring engineers in stone and cement, Rome architects remade their Imperial capital on an awesome scale and stamped its image on every town of the provinces. Throughout Italy every major city bears some trace of Roman grandeur and technology: a battered temple column, a storied arch, the regular street plan or even the sewerage system, testifies to a civil order of universal stamp. Nowhere is this felt more powerfully than in the mother city, Rome. In spite of centuries of cannibalism for its bronze, stone and fine marbles the city's monuments still dominate. The majestic scale of the Baths of Caracalla, the eerie isolation under the one-eyed dome of the Pantheon, the menacing procession of the Colosseum arcades, and the countless temples, arches, aqueducts and ruined palaces stand silent witness above the bustling city traffic. Imposing as these monuments may be, the Roman lives for us most vividly in the multiple moods of their characterful portraits which startingly bridge the centuries in human terms.

The Christian Era Begins

Almost imperceptibly Roman confidence faded into doubt, and its anxieties bred fervid mystery cults of which Christianity proved the most enduring. When Constantine's Edict of 313 proclaimed recognition and tolerance of Christianity throughout the Empire, Christian art emerged from the dank confines of catacombs and subterranean chapels to occupy the stately basilicas in which he established Church hierarchy. Although some, like the original St. Peter's, have been razed completely and all have undergone drastic alteration, the great churches of Santa Maria Maggiore, San Giovanni in Laterano, San Paolo fuori le Mura and others preserve much of the character of the Church Triumphant.

While Rome was establishing its priority as the center of Papal authority in the West, Constantinople, today Istanbul in Turkey, became the seat of secular power and the cradle of the new Byzantine style in art and architecture. Disorder within Italy was aggravated by waves of barbarian invasions. The seat of government had been moved to Ravenna, and there, under various Gothic rulers the center of power remained for decades. After the Byzantine reconquest, Justinian, imported artists who made it one of the glories of the early phase of Byzantine art. By turns, architecturally intricate in San Vitale or the Orthodox Baptistery, or straightforward in the basilicas of Sant' Apollinare in Classe or Sant' Apollinare Nuovo, all are enhanced by the refulgent glimmer of gilded mosaic murals, among the finest concentrations of this precious art.

Constantinople continued to export the Byzantine style throughout much of the West, even to such unexpected places as Palermo where the Norman kings gave it an exotic mixture with the architectural tradition of their Moorish predecessors. Monreale, with its vast expanse of mosaic, its porphyry tombs, its bronze doors and delicate cloister is perhaps the most impressive Norman ensemble in Sicily. For mosaic of the highest quality, however, one must travel along the north coast of Sicily to Cefalù where the giant Christ in Benediction in the cathedral is profoundly moving.

As Europe's primary window to the East, the port city of Venice imported craftsmen from Constantinople to build its picturesque basilica of San Marco. They embellished it with trophies scavenged by its mercantile fleet, including the ancient bronze horses over the door, the monolithic columns in its piazza, and not least the body of St. Mark himself, thieved from Alexandria.

The Middle Ages

Even in the midst of the cultural disintegration of the feudal era and the fragmentation of Italy into city states the glorious past was never entirely forgotten, but it took a foreigner, the German Emperor Frederick von Hohenstaufen, to give nostalgia tangible form. His starkly geometric Castel del Monte and the broken fragments of his triumphal arch at Capua are fleeting reminders of the poet-Emperor's dream of a revival of antique purity in south Italy, but from this seed sprang a startingly vigorous classical style in the sculpture of Nicola Pisano.

Within the complex of Pisa cathedral, with its famous tower and handsome round baptistery, Nicola began his career with the cool but deeply felt sculpture of the baptistery pulpit and followed it with similar pulpits in Siena, Pistoia, and in Pisa cathedral, the last two the work of his son Giovanni, who replaced his father's classic concerns with a ferocious intensity of spirit which proclaims the emergence of the Gothic style in Italy.

The architecture of Pisa is but one aspect of the Romanesque in Italy. From the massy, squat brick of Sant' Ambrogio in Milan to the sunny facets of Bari cathedral, its stolid logic dominates the peninsula. Unexpected relief from this sobriety comes in Florence, where the crisp shapes and dark green and snowy marble of the baptistery and the serene harmony of San Miniato hold a promise of the coming Renaissance.

No development proclaimed the new humane mood of the Italian Church in the 12th century more clearly than St. Francis and his Order of Franciscan friars. Their gentle concern for the welfare of man and for his place in the natural order lent a warmth to the art of the Gothic era. As a memorial to the beloved saint a curious two-level church was built in his native Assisi, each a barn-like hall destined for mural paintings rather than stained glass as in French churches of the period.

Soon the major painters from various cities came to Assisi to decorate its walls: the excitable Cimabue from Florence, the urbane and courtly Simone Martini from Siena, and perhaps the young Giotto, fresh from the experience of Rome. The most famous of the scenes, the epic cycle of the life of St. Francis in the upper church, is the work of a garrulous imitator of the precocious Giotto. The master himself was traveling northward to Padua where he decorated the interior of the Scrovegni Chapel with scenes from the lives of the Virgin and Christ which, in their simplicity, clarity and faultless sense of human drama, changed the direction of Italian painting and placed it on an equal footing with its sculptural prototypes.

Siena stirred to life with the ambitious plan for the cathedral, so large that less than a quarter was ever built. Its boisterous and colorful façade teems with Giovanni Pisano's animated sculptures and its high altar was adorned with the jewel-like, multipaneled altar by Duccio, now preserved in the cathedral museum. With it, Sienese painting shook off the now decadent Byzantine style.

Rome slept out the Gothic era: the Pope was now a virtual prisoner in Avignon in Southern France and almost nothing was happening among the crumbling ruins of antiquity.

Milan flexed its military muscle but fumbled the arts in the later Middle Ages, concentrating its energies on the colossal muddle which would eventually become its cathedral five hundred years later.

After Giotto's death in 1337 Florentine artists were largely occupied with the progress of the stately cathedral for which the master had provided the design for a campanile, or bell tower. Few painters could match his achievement and most chose to concentrate on isolated aspects of his work. Furthermore, Florence was racked by financial depression and a series of virulent attacks of the Black Plague which wiped out more than half the population. Orcagna's grim and angry sculpture and painting reflects the desperate mood of the time. Only gradually, around 1400, did art recover its equilibrium with the richly naturalistic painting of Gentile da Fabriano, the iridescent pictorial fantasies of Lorenzo Monaco, and the lyrical bronze sculptures of Lorenzo Ghiberti.

The Renaissance

The Renaissance began in Florence. Renaissance means rebirth, in this case the rebirth of the classical spirit of the ancient world. But why in Florence, a city which could boast fewer Roman buildings and sculptures than many another Italian town? Perhaps it was her distinguished literary heritage which prided itself not only on the epic poetry of Dante, but the lyrics of Petrarch and the ribald prose of the father of the novel, Boccaccio. Even more significant might be the independent courage of her republican government which suggested a parallel with Roman civic virtue. Most important, however, was the long artistic tradition for a clear-sighted enquiry into the nature of man and his place in the universal order. Florentines saw the world as coherent and envisioned man as its heroic master.

As always in Florence, sculpture showed the way. Ghiberti's pliant curves took on a new logic with the study of antiquity and Nanni di Banco faithfully mimed Roman forms. It was, however, Donatello who explored a vital naturalism, first with his impudent, spring-fresh marble David and later with the calmly alert St. George for one of the outside niches of the Church of Or San Michele, a veritable showcase for the new sculptural style. By turns gently equivocal, as in the bronze David and explosively eccentric as in the Cantoria or choir gallery for the cathedral, Donatello's forceful and original sculpture won him a widespread fame and led to the Paduan bronzes for the basilica of Sant' Antonio and the equestrian monument to the general Gattamelata in the square outside. His late years saw an hysterical religious conversion best exemplified by the dessicated horror of the *Penitent Magdalen* in the Florentine Baptistery and the tremulous emotion of the bronze panels of the San Lorenzo pulpits.

Architecture entered a new era with Brunelleschi who is traditionally supposed to have invented a system of linear perspective which enabled him to prepare the ground plan, elevation and overall proportional balance of a building in advance instead of working piecemeal as had most medieval masterbuilders. Although his impressive engineering feat in raising the vast dome over Florence cathedral is his most conspicuous achievement, his elegant and reposeful churches of San Lorenzo and Santo Spirito, the refined Pazzi Chapel and the powerful original part of the Pitti Palace best represent his new ideas. In the generation which followed, Alberti developed these new ideas in design and wrote the first major theoretical treatises on architecture, as well as books on sculpture and painting.

Painting caught up and added a new dimension to the Renaissance in the work of Masaccio. Although he died in 1428 after only six years of mature activity, this rustic genius brought a pungent naturalism and a profoundly human sobriety to painting with his deeply expressive frescos of the life of St. Peter in the Brancacci Chapel of the Carmine Church. He applied Brunelleschi's classic architectural style and the device of linear perspective to project a convincing illusion of three-dimensionality in the noble Trinity mural in Santa Maria Novella.

In his wake a generation of highly individual painters brought a rich variety to his example. Fra Angelico was a delicate colorist and a reticent spokesman for religious sentiment in his work at the Monastery of San Marco, Castagno brought an explosive drama to his murals in Sant' Apollonia, Uccello had a fanatical mania for the pure geometry of perspective which dominates the dreamy Battle of San Romano in the Uffizi, Domenico Veneziano integrated pliant line and radiant color in his St. Lucy altar also in the Uffizi, and Fra Filippo Lippi's eccentric individuality lends a wistful pathos to his frescos in Prato cathedral.

Elsewhere in Italy the lessons of the Florentine Renaissance were absorbed, albeit slowly. In Northern Italy Mantegna developed the new idiom in Mantua to an antiquarian lapidary logic which was to be softened and humanized by the glowing nature poetry of his brother-in-law Giovanni Bellini who revitalized Venetian painting. Other regional centers blossomed into often vividly independent creative activity. Cosmè Tura brought craggy design and fruity color to Ferrara; Piero della Francesca left his silently enigmatic images in Arezzo, Urbino, and his native Borgo San Sepolcro; Sassetta and his Sienese followers developed the exquisite mysticism of the local tradition; Antonello da Messina in remote Sicily refined a meticulous style resembling that of the Flemings. Rome, however, remained an artistic backwater dependent for what episode activity there was on imported talent.

Leonardo, Michelangelo and Raphael

By 1475 the lessons of the new style had become second nature in Florence and artists began to explore personal byways such as the elusive linear grace of Botticelli, the every-day prose of Ghirlandaio, the fastidious decoration of Filippino Lippi, and the fierce energy of the nude in action as studied by Pollaiuolo. None, however, could match the intelligent curiosity of the young Leonardo da Vinci. When he was only about twenty years old he assisted his master, the powerful sculptor Verrocchio, in painting a picture of the Baptism of Christ; the angel head and landscape added by the youth at once eclipsed all competition in delicate loveliness.

Leonardo's restless mind ranged over experiments and inventions of every kind. As his inspiration raced ahead of his hand an impatience with the craft of painting led to the cascade of ideas which he poured forth in the *Adoration of the Magi,* only to leave the picture an incomplete sketch when he abruptly departed for Milan in 1482 to concentrate on science and technology. In this alien and unsophisticated environment he painted only occasionally but none the less produced the first masterpiece of the High Renaissance: the *Last Supper.*

Back home art remained almost untouched by Leonardo's enigmatic new style. But its revitalizing force had begun to stir a new spirit, a potential which would soon startle Florentines when a daring young sculptor named Michelangelo produced a sequence of energetic statues which culminated in the giant figure of David, the traditional symbol of heroic Florence confronting its barbaric neighbors. Leonardo's return home in this same year engendered a fierce rivalry between the now aging master and his young challenger, a confrontation which produced big plans but few tangible results. Soon the third of the great masters of the High Renaissance, Raphael of Urbino, joined them and injected his coolly ideal images into the contest.

Meanwhile the warrior Pope Julius II had determined to renew the glories of Papal Rome. His first project was to raze old St. Peter's and replace it with a colossal domed church designed by Bramante whose ingenious Milanese buildings such as Santa Maria presso Santo Satiro had set a forceful new course for architecture. Although few of his Roman projects were to be realized as planned, Bramante's perfectly balanced Tempietto at San Pietro in Montorio best exemplifies his aims.

In 1508 Julius called Michelangelo and Raphael to Rome. Leonardo soon followed, but his dilatory attention to painting and absorption with science produced few significant works. Julius set the reluctant Michelangelo the herculean task of covering the vast Sistine ceiling with a complex of scenes from the Creation. After four years of protean labor the mighty achievement was unveiled to the astonishment of Pope and public. Raphael's simultaneous fresco cycle in the Stanze of the Vatican in which he ennobled the Papacy seems by comparison a modest achievement, but its wealth of invention, superb control, and classic poise were to exert an even more powerful influence in the centuries to follow.

Within but a few years Bramante and Raphael were dead, Leonardo had retired to France and Michelangelo was frustrated with the Julius tomb, a bothersome project which was to leave scattered components in various collections but little more than the Moses on the stunted monument today in San Pietro in Vincoli. The Golden Age was passing and already stirrings of discomfort, seismic vibrations from the impending Reformation across the Alps, disturbed the ordered optimism of the Renaissance.

Mannerism

Florence, where it had begun, was to see the crisis of Renaissance style. Two young painters led the way in a revolt in which a vibrant and overheated emotionalism created the restlessly expressive style we call Mannerism. Pontormo's *Descent from the Cross* in Santa Felicità,

Florence, is a florid tangle of writhing form and incandescent color which rotates slowly in a pin-wheel of tormented anguish. Rosso's treatment of the same theme in Orvieto cathedral is a brutal hallucination of abstracted horror. Later, at Borgo San Sepolcro he painted the subject once again, this time as a ghastly nightmare haunted by demonic masks. In Siena Beccafumi explored a manner of ethereal and ghostly beauty. Introverted and highly personal, Mannerist experiment suggests anxiety and alienation in a key familiar to modern man.

Michelangelo himself created a thunderous vision of apocalyptic *Judgement* on the altar wall of the Sistine chapel and his uneasy *Medici Tombs* in Florence mirror the spiritual turmoil of the times, but his heroic challenge grew deeper with old age and concluded with the profoundly moving *Pietàs* in Florence cathedral and at the Castel Sforzesco in Milan.

In time Mannerism itself lapsed into formula and pedantry from which only the most talented could forge a personal idiom. Giulio Romano exploited illusionistic tricks of ingenious device at the Palazzo del Te in Mantua, Perino del Vaga formulated a delightfully decorative scheme for the Palazzo del Principe in Genoa, Salviati festooned the Sala del Udienza of Florence's Palazzo Vecchio with ceremonial narrative histories, and Bronzino's coldly brilliant portraits in the Uffizi exemplify the proud formality of the era. In sculpture the rhetoric of Benvenuto Cellini and the spiraling contortions of Giambologna are impressively daring.

As the Church Militant embarked on the Counter Reformation Vignola gave it an appropriate architectural setting with the Church of Il Gesù in Rome, but an even more enduring model was created by the fecund inventiveness of Sanmicheli in Verona and the lovely villas and festive churches which Palladio built in Vicenza, Venice, and the surrounding countryside.

In Venice the unfathomable mystery of Giorgione, by turns austere and remote in the Castelfranco *Madonna* and pastoral and intimate in the *Tempesta* in Venice's Accademia, parallels the ideal forms of the High Renaissance in Central Italy, but in the softly inflected cantilena of the Venetian dialect. When his brief decade of creativity was cut short by the plague in 1510, Giogione's leadership was assumed by Titian, whose extroverted sensuality gave a dynamic propulsion to Venetian painting most evident in the buoyant swirl of the *Assumption of the Virgin* in the Frari Church. Although the impact of Mannerism is perceptible in Titian's powerful ceiling paintings in the Salute Church, his healthy naturalism avoided stereotypes to arrive at a new depth of feeling in the Accademia *Pietà,* a glowing farewell by one of the supreme masters of painting.

Among the painters of the younger generation Veronese conserved the classical spirit, enriching it with a sumptuous display of physical beauty and radiant color. His decorative ensembles in Venice's Santo Sebastiano and the airy Palladian Villa Barbaro at Maser are serenely festive. Bassano gave biblical themes the touching realism of everyday life and immortalized the country landscape of his native region. Tintoretto climaxed and in effect ended the Venetian Renaissance with his volcanic pictorial explosions which engulf the ornate interiors of the Palazzo Ducale and the Scuola di Santo Rocco. By 1600 the routine acres of canvas by Palma Giovane had suffocated the tradition.

Art and architecture seemed to have sunk into lethargy in the later years of the 16th century. Only a fresh view of traditional values and a thoroughgoing reform could restore the artists' confidence. This came with the Caracci family in provincial Bologna. Annibale, its greatest member, migrated to Rome where with such epic works as the frescoed ceiling of the Palazzo Farnese he returned a fresh and tasteful buoyancy to the heritage of Raphael and Michelangelo. By contrast the roistering and hippy life style of Caravaggio produced an art which, in its unflinching truthfulness, came to influence realist painting throughout Europe.

The Baroque

Baroque sculpture owes its impetus to Bernini. His *Apollo and Daphne,* today with several other of his masterpieces in Rome's Borghese Gallery, exploits an unmatched technical facility to project a dazzlingly expansive effect of motion and emotion. As an impresario of all the arts he combined media to spectacular effect in the altar tabernacle and throne shrine in St. Peter's and the emotionally volatile *Ecstasy of Santa Teresa* in Santa Maria della Vittoria. His fountains lend a festive and cooling note to many of Rome's piazzas. Unlike Bernini, his contemporary Borromini is intimate and convoluted in style, delighting in the intricate spatial effects of San Carlo alle Quattro Fontane and Sant' Ivo. He spawned an active school, especially in far off Turin where Guarini carried on his picturesque ideas.

For a century the operatic spectacle of baroque art enriched the peninsula with such splendors as the Versailles-like palace and gardens at Caserta, the bubble domes of the Salute church in Venice, and the acrobatic ceilings of Guercino, Reni, Pietro da Cortona and a host of other inspired decorators. But like the Renaissance, the Italian baroque gradually wound down and underwent a metamorphosis in the early 18th century. In place of civic grandeur and religious fervor Italians began to prefer a quieter and more sophisticated elegance better suited to their restricted finances and diminished international influence. Charm and leisure were turned to accommodate the hordes of travelers for whom Italy was the goal of the fashionable Grand Tour. No city outdid Venice in permissiveness. In this pre-postcard era her view painters, Canaletto and Guardi, caught the nostalgic aura of the pink and blue sea-washed city in paintings to be brought home as souvenirs. Artificial and perhaps a bit tawdry in its sunset glow, Venice was still to produce one last burst of creative brilliance in Tiepolo. His magical transformations dissolved the walls of rococo interiors into cloud buoyed visions of lovely goddesses and untroubled heroes.

Modern Times

But the modern world was knocking in the person of Napoleon, and it was almost with relief that the weary princedoms left the stage and returned the darkened theater to its memories. Legend has it that Italian art ceased about 1800. Like most legends this one is only partly true. With most of Europe Italy embraced the stern principles of French Neo-Classicism, but the sculptor Canova gave it a frigidly voluptuous tone best seen in the Borghese *Venus,* surprisingly, a portrait of Napoleon's sister, Pauline Bonaparte. Canova designed a new type of tomb of which his own monument in Venice's Frari church is typical, chaste and austere in its mock pyramid and marble mourners, yet uneasily realistic and sexual in its oblique implications. His clay models, largely preserved in his studio in Possagno near Venice, are more spontaneous and inspired. A parallel with his style can be found in the severe architecture of Japelli, Valadier and Quarenghi. Painters of the time such as Appiani and Hayez are less inventive.

Although the overstuffed rhetoric of the mid-19th century endowed Italy with its share of outsized white elephants, such extravaganzas as Rome's shimmering Victor Emmanuel Monument have taken on an affectionate aura in our no-nonsense time. Victorian painters were more clear-sighted and a group called the *macchiaioli* (spatterers) produced frank and handsome landscapes, especially those of the Florentine Fattori. The gently impressionist sculpture of Medardo Rosso provides a foil to the chic dash of Boldini's society portraits.

At the beginning of our century, as cubism and other modern movements were emerging in Paris, another group of Italian painters began to experiment in depicting the old theme of movement. Called the Futurists, they explored a dynamic range of sequential action and vivid color which had a wide influence. Severini, Boccioni, Balla and their associates can best be seen at the Galleria dell'Arte Moderna in Rome. De Chirico depicted a mysterious world of empty squares and mannequin figures akin to Surrealism, and Morandi imbued his neutral still life pictures with a tender life. Under Fascism experimental painting declined, but architecture bloomed into a pompous official style which survives in the desolate vistas of Cinecittà near Rome. Stylistically vapid, Fascist architecture at least indulged engineering and in the postwar period spawned such great architects as Nervi. His exposition halls in Turin, hangar at Orbetello, sport palaces in Rome and the new Papal Audience Hall at the Vatican are a dizzying ode to the poetic potential of technology.

Although a small number of painters such as Burri, Santomaso and Afro have attracted international attention in the past twenty years, and a group of attractive sculptors of which Manzù, Greco, and Marini are the best known is widely admired, Italian contemporary artists have become more cosmopolitan, and the greater mobility of the young has resulted in an exodus of talent to other artistic centers of Europe, notably Munich, London, Paris and Amsterdam; while the gulf they have left is filled to overflowing with young foreign artists irresistibly attracted to Italy, their spiritual home. Op Art, Pop Art, Minimal Art . . . all have had their day in the Italian avant-garde, as in progressive circles the world over. Ask the Italian-in-the-street who represents the purest traditions of his country today and he will probably answer: "Henry Moore" (the British sculptor whom Florence adores).

Among new movements and new names, the color lithographs, pencil drawings and silkscreen prints of Valerio Adami currently enjoy international celebration. Adami as painter is not interested in brushwork; he erects a scaffolding of lines, and blocks in the color, in the manner of a craftsman in stained glass. He is, like several distinguished contemporaries, a political artist and his best-known works include portraits of historical statesmen and scientists—Hitler, Freud, Nietsche. Adami's portraits have something of a blown-up cartoon element, like the caricature imagery of the Pop Art from which they derive; the work is not so much cartoonery, however, as a synthesis of the biographical highlights of the subject. One of numerous artists working in similar media, Adami is based in Paris but he is a typical example of Italian ingenuity, awareness and mastery of color harmony.

Painters young and old, conventional and aggressively "modern", are found in most Italian towns and villages, inhabiting gaunt medieval tenements, ramshackle farmhouses, mountain eyries and seaside chalets. One group of four has lived and worked for some years in a boat, propelling it from harbor to harbor and setting up floating exhibitions. Schools of painters have taken over remote islands, and their canvases are the white-washed walls of fisherman's cottages. On a summer Sunday you can scarcely drive a dozen miles in Italy without coming to a painting exhibition in a community hall, devoted to local talent, much of it genuine peasant work in the primitive style of Grandma Moses.

There, as in the great galleries, you are aware of the strong color sense, the adventurousness of Italian art. The tradition is widely diffused, perhaps diluted, but it is certainly too early to write its obituary. That has been done periodically over the past twenty centuries, inevitably to the chagrin of the mistaken commentator. In the midst of the burgeoning vitality which charms and occasionally maddens the visitor the arts are not long to be neglected. Italians live the tradition too deeply.

Music

Italian music, perhaps even more than Italian art, has become part of the common cultural heritage throughout the world. It is not only the staple of hundreds of opera companies, but the unconscious possession of all who whistle a Neapolitan folk song or graduate to the Grand March from *Aida.*

The music of ancient Rome seems irretrievably lost. Lacking a written notational system, its performance tradition disintegrated at the end of the Empire leaving at best some vague literary descriptions and distant echoes in old tribal rites in the mountains of Morocco. The earliest surviving music of the Italian peninsula is that of the early Church. Chanting of the Latin mass evolved into an integral part of all services and matured as plain chant or Gregorian chant. It in turn developed into the 13th-century Ars Antigua, an increasingly complex polyphonic choral style. Ars Nova, or New Art, followed with a lively international exchange of ideas.

A friar of Arezzo in Tuscany, named Guido Monaco, invented the system of musical notation which has served the Western world for 800 years. Secular dance and madrigal forms flourished during the Renaissance and even invaded church music, a confusion corrected by the purifying Counter-Reformation polyphonist Palestrina whose severely noble choral music is the climax of this venerable tradition and a stepping stone to a richer evolution. His contemporaries in Venice, Andrea and Giovanni Gabriele, provided a gleaming brass accompaniment to the ornate late Renaissance décor.

Today it is not easy to hear professional performances of early music in Italy. With but few exceptions in Rome, church music is now at a low ebb, an often trashy and poorly performed mélange of recent sentimental tunes. If the visitor watches the posters carefully he might find one of the distinguished Florentine or Roman groups dedicated to Renaissance music performing in an atmospheric original setting.

Opera

Opera is synonymous with Italian music. It had its origin in Florence where a group of Humanists who called themselves the Camerata hoped to revive classic Greek and Roman drama by combining theater and music in Peri's *Dafne,* first heard in 1597. From this primitive beginning it was only a decade until Monteverdi created the first operatic masterpiece, *Orfeo,* an entertainment for the Gonzaga court at Mantua. The new fashion spread rapidly and found an enthusiastic public in pleasure-loving Venice where by mid-century at least eleven opera houses were in simultaneous operation. Monteverdi had moved there in 1613 and produced a long series of masses, motets, madrigals, ballets and operas. His powerfully dramatic *Incoronazione di Poppea,* one of the scant three of his operas for which we have a surviving score, was premiered in 1642, the year before his death. Monteverdi's followers, especially the talented Cavalli, rode an international wave of popularity which carried opera throughout Europe and gave every Italian city its enthusiastic fans, in particular Naples which supplanted Venice as the opera capital in the 18th century.

Composed for intimate theaters, baroque opera translates badly when performed, as it usually is in Italy, in a house seating several thousand people. Aside from an occasional reverent essay in archeological restoration which misses the fire and drama of the original, Monteverdi and his heirs are too often heard in performances tainted by the more strenuous performance tradition of later music-drama.

Simultaneously with the flowering of Italian baroque opera, orchestral and chamber music were given many definitive forms by the leading Italian composers. Frescobaldi's inventive virtuosity left an indelible mark on organ music, and Domenico Scarlatti poured forth harpsichord music of precious device. Corelli wrote for strings in a masterful style, and Vivaldi's cheerfully picturesque music evokes rococo Venice. The period also saw Italian craftsmen establish the classic shape for many instruments such as the violin. Baroque music can be heard in Italy today in polished performances by the Virtuosi di Roma, the Orchestra Alessandro Scarlatti of Naples, and other specialized ensembles as well as by a handful of good soloists, but these popular performers are more often abroad than at home.

By the mid-18th century the opera craze had placed such emphasis on lavish spectacle and the vocal pyrotechnics of the fashionable *castrati* that musical values tended to become superficial and routine. A fresh breath of humor was introduced by the comic interlude played between the acts of the ponderous classic dramas. These *opera buffa* short diversions increased in scale with Pergolesi, Cimarosa, and Paisiello to become full length comedies in their own right. The best place to hear these delightful romps as well as other small-scale baroque operas is Milan's small hall called for its great neighbor the Piccola Scala.

The Lifeblood of Italy

But opera in the present-day sense—the opera of the past 180 years—the opera that people, rightly or wrongly, call "grand" opera—is even more naturally associated with the Italians than was the baroque kind. They invented it. It is an art form peculiarly suited to their temperament. Sung in Italian, in Italy, with Italian orchestras, conductors, designers and above all producers, it has achieved its truest expression. For the most blasé theater-goer, a visit to the Italian opera is a unique experience. (And an expensive one: at La Scala in Milan you may pay forty dollars for a seat.)

Italian opera is not to every non-Italian's taste. Some think stylized acting and great singing a bad mixture esthetically; some are embarrassed by the naked emotion of it and the cliché sentimentality or incomprehensibility of the plots; and some ridicule the conventions which permit a dying heroine to rise and sing a powerful aria and perhaps an encore and lie down again to die, or a tenor to waste precious minutes (as he does in *Trovatore*) singing over and over again to his companions that mother is burning to death and there is not a moment to lose.

Riding on stirring or syrupy music, the stories are frequently violent and sexual and it has been pointed out that, if the censor dealt with opera as he does with motion pictures, only one well-known work (not an Italian one) would be passed for universal exhibition.

But, whatever foreigners may think, opera is the Italian's cultural lifeblood, a reflection of the drama of his existence, a sublimation of his personal mythology; his melodrama, burlesque, pantomime, circus and celebrity concert rolled into one. It is an art medium which grows neither old nor old-fashioned.

For the ordinary music-lover, Italian operatic history begins with the melodious trio of Rossini, Bellini and Donizetti. There is a tendency to sneer at the naïve plots and barrel-organ choruses of these pioneer composers and their librettists. It is hard to recapture the mid-19th century's passionate enthusiasm for spotless village maidens, noble prigs and unconvincing villains, the stock characters of the opera. We are more sophisticated now. Yet the sparkle of Rossini, the melodious tenderness of Bellini, the perennially rich lyricism of Donizetti, the arias crystal-clear, the recitative natural and sweet . . . these qualities, applied to the hackneyed little dramas of the times, immortalized them and can still touch the heart. The *bel canto* style—in which libretto and dramatic tension are sacrificed to virtuoso singing, and strict convention gives a certain number of set-piece arias to each singer, depending on the importance of the role—slowly passed out of fashion. The arias survive and, on the techniques those singers developed to cope with them, later composers were able to build.

Bel canto, a strictly Italian phenomenon, produced a typically Italian human being: the prima donna, haughty, tempestuous, temperamental, singer and actress combined, a despot in all her glory before whom even principal tenors (themselves a byword for pride and vanity) had to bow. Other lands acclaimed their Edmund Keans and Henry Irvings . . . Italy had her Giulia Grisi, Giuditta Pasta, Emma Nevada and Adelina Patti; and, among great 19th-century tenors, Giovanni Rubini, Luigi Lablache, Antonio Tamburini and the ever-memorable Cavaliere Mario. Operas were sometimes written for a particular diva: Bellini designed *Sonnambula* for Madame Pasta, for example, and afterwards transposed the whole thing to suit Maria Malibran, with whom he was in love.

Viva Verdi

On the heels of Giuseppe Verdi (1813–1901), a new class of operagoer arrived. Intellectuals suddenly decided that this mass spectator entertainment was no longer to be despised. Verdi introduced nobler themes and a grander style. His librettists told more credible stories. Verdi's strong plots and sincere emotions, sincerely and artistically handled, illuminated Italian opera with a brilliance which eclipsed anything that had gone before. Early Verdi is characterized by rhythmic ingenuity and splendid orchestration. The operas of his middle period—*Rigoletto, La Traviata, Il Trovatore, La Forza del Destino, Aïda*—have been for more than a hundred years the dazzling epitome of what we think of as "grand" opera, Italian style. His later work is notable for its dramatic vocal melodies and its prophetic vision of the modern principle that musical instruments, as well as voices, should have their full share in interpreting the moods and emotions of the opera.

Verdi's "tunes" (many are no more than that) are simple and catchy. The original cast of *Rigoletto* was warned not to hum *La Donna è Mobile* in public, in case the public tired of it before they heard it. But those simple tunes are not weak or banal; they have the glamor of genuine feeling in them, and Verdi is at his most impressive when embroidering them vocally and instrumentally. *La Donna è Mobile* has survived for more than a century, and we are not tired of it yet.

No composer, perhaps, has been more acclaimed in his lifetime. The word Verdi happened to be a short title for the future monarch of a united Italy, and "Verdi! Verdi!" at the opera house was both a call for the maestro and a battle cry of the Risorgimento: "*V*ittore *E*manuele, *R*e *D*'*I*talia".

Realism

As the great sun of Verdi set, a constellation of new stars ascended. (We are now at the end of the 19th century.) Leoncavallo and Mascagni were one-opera men—the short but perennially popular *Pagliacci* and *Cavalleria Rusticana* respectively. Boito is best known for *Mefistofele.* Cilea, a Calabrian, had the southerner's yearning for strong effects, but handled his tragic themes with restraint and delicacy. Of his five "gracious sisters", *Gina, Tilda, Arlesiana, Gloria* and *Adriana Lecouvreur* (all tragedies of hopeless love), only the last-named is more or less regularly revived.

These composers ushered in *verismo,* "realism", against violent diehard opposition. Giordano brought bicycles on stage in his opera *Fedora;* Leoncavallo introduced a live donkey in *Pagliacci.*

The newcomer whose picturesque and confident treatment of unlikely themes from legend, biography and stage tragedy earned him (after some initial resistance) a fame almost equal to Verdi's was Giacomo Puccini (1853–1925). It was in their Puccini roles that our fathers and grandfathers remembered the household names of yesterday—Caruso, Melba, Geraldine Farrar, Emmy Destin, Tetrazzini, Gigli—and in the same operas we have acclaimed the great singers of our own times—Callas, di Stefano, Tito Gobbi, Sutherland, Bjorling, Renata Scotto. Operas such as *La Bohème, Madame Butterfly, Tosca* and *Turandot* are the firmest of favorites in Italy and abroad, and with Puccini's freshness and sureness of romantic touch they continue to mediate in the conflicting storms of changing taste.

Opera Today

Italians are conservative about their opera, and no living composer has been elected to the pantheon which Verdi and Puccini knew in their lifetimes. There are few likely candidates. One possibility is Giancarlo Menotti, whose immensely successful *The Medium* and *The Consul,* first performed in New York just after the war, seemed to give Italian opera new vigor.

Menotti represents the contemporary Italian maestro-of-all-trades: composor, conductor, impresario. And perhaps his fame to posterity will rest as solidly on his organization of the "Two Worlds" music festival at Spoleto as on his musicianship.

The music festivals enable visitors to Italy to see authentic opera, with star singers under the batons of internationally famous conductors —the heirs of Toscanini—such as Muti, Abbado, Giulini and Alberto Erede. The most prominent opera festivals are the "Two Worlds" mentioned above (June, July at Spoleto, also includes ballet, drama, etc.) and the Maggio Musicale Fiorentino (May and June, Florence).

The official opera season is early December to mid-April. The principal opera houses are La Scala (Milan), Teatro dell' Opera (Rome), La Fenice (Venice), Teatro Comunale (Florence) and San Carlo (Naples). The audience's dress and jewelry on première nights matches the extravagant internal décor and, under huge clusters of candelabra, a full house resembles an overflowing basket of flowers—a sight to remember, even before the curtain has gone up.

Performances last all evening, with lengthy intervals. Despite the formality of the occasion, audiences are noisy and uninhibited, especially in the "second league" of opera houses, which includes the Teatro Comunale of Genoa, Teatro Regio of Parma, Teatro Massimo of Palermo, Teatro Bellini of Catania and Teatro Giuseppe Verdi of Trieste. As with old provincial music-halls, each opera house has its tradition of critical appreciation; of the Parma opera house (where Toscanini was schooled) many tales are told concerning young hopes blighted and promising careers wrecked.

Nowadays the tourists keep opera alive financially, chiefly at the summer open-air spectacles, done with typical *floridezza* at the Arena of Verona (July, August), the Baths of Caracalla in Rome (July, August), the Arena Flegrea in Naples (July), the Sferisterio at Macerata (July) and intermittently in the Castello Sforzesco of Milan.

At that season the "grand" opera houses are under dust-sheets, looking forlorn, and their exuberant baroque façades cast shadows on workmen playing cards; but you can visit them, and try out the acoustics from their vast sloping stages, and return home boasting that you've sung at La Scala or the San Carlo. Occasionally, strolling the back streets of old towns, you hear pouring out from a hundred radio sets in a hundred tiny houses the well-loved passages from *Rigoletto, Butterfly* and *Lucia di Lammermoor.* Such is the commitment of the middle-aged and elderly to their beloved Verdi, Puccini and Donizetti. It must be said that you don't hear this when there are young people in the house, when there are football matches or quiz shows on the television channels.

Literature

Compared with that of Britain and America, the Italian literary corpus is not rich. Through eighty per cent of it the same broad themes are running, two or three threads which connect Dante's victims in the *Inferno* with the latest adventure of Italo Calvino's peasant-turned-factory-worker, *Marcovaldo.* They concern folk wisdom and urban deprivation, rustic serenity and the traumatic neuroses brought on by industrialization, automation and metropolitan ambitions. The Antaeus myth, strength through contact with the good earth, is the message of Italian novelists and short-story writers, from the 19th-century classic, *Il Mulino sul Po,* to the mid-20th-century enigmas of Ugo Betti.

The *verismo* of the operatic school—"realism"—had its counterpart in literature, a reaction against the stilted romanticism of the 19th-century novelists. Giovanni Verga, a Sicilian, discovered for English-language readers by D.H. Lawrence, set out the narrow life of the peasantry in *I Malavoglia* and *Mastro Don Gesualdo.* (Sixty years later the Prince of Lampedusa's *Il Gattopardo,* a worldwide best-seller, showed striking similarities, allowing for the difference in social setting.) Antonio Fogazzaro's *Piccolo Mondo Antico* portrayed humble villagers with affection. Grazia Deledda, a Nobel prize-winner, did the same in *Marianna Sirca* for her native Sardinia.

Earlier this century, Italians were reading Francesco Chiesa's *Tempo di Marzo,* a nostalgic evocation of youth, and Renato Fucini's sketches of Tuscan life, *All' Aria Aperta.*

Impact on world opinion was first achieved by Ignazio Silone and Carlo Levi. During Mussolini's era they were cult figures of a small anti-Fascist minority, and after the war they reaped a handsome reward—Silone with *Pane e Vino* and *Fontamara,* Levi with *Cristo si è Fermato a Eboli.* Both authors portray simple southern peoples trying to come to terms with a system which offers them no hope. This all-too-popular theme of Italian writers, a sort of pilgrim's progress of the underdog, comes out strongly in Corrado Alvaro (*Quasi una Vita* and *Gente in Aspromonte*), who establishes in literature the comfortless fatalism of Calabria; and also in the living author Daniele Dolci, when he exposes Sicilian social evils in *Banditi a Partinico.*

Up to the present day, Italy's most serious novelists are, firstly, Italo Svevo, whom James Joyce encourages. *Senilità* and *La Madre* show considerable psychological insight, a rare quality in Italian writers. Luigi Pirandello, secondly, is a profound and original writer of novels *(Il fu Mattia Pascal* and *Uno, Nessuno e Centomila)* as well as of plays and short stories.

By comparison a lightweight, the Roman author Alberto Moravia is perhaps the most popular outside Italy. His best work dates back to the early 1930s, when he wrote *Gli Indifferenti.* The preoccupation with sex relationships which helps to make him so widely read is exemplified in *La Romana* and *L'Amore Coniugale.*

Futurism is the province of Massimo Bontempelli *(La Vita Intensa)* and Carlo Pavese *(Luna e Falo).* A good account of Neapolitan problems, emigrant sufferings and feudal attitudes is Giuseppe Marotta's *A Milano non fa Freddo.* Brooding violence is poetically treated in Leonardo Sciascia's *Il Giorno della Civetta,* another tale of the Sicilian Mafia.

A most engaging modern writer is Italo Calvino, who explores the points at which man's existence touches and overlaps with that of birds, animals and plants (Calvino's father was a zoologist, and he himself was brought up in a botanical garden). The most important novel to date is *Il Sentiere al Nido d'Aragno,* but his collections of *contes* devoted to one character—Marcovaldo, a naïve, good-natured countryman forced into an urban mold—are full of pathos and wry humor.

Generally speaking, Italians have done better with the short story or novella than with the full-length work. Man's struggles to better his condition, man's conflicting desires and motivations, man's acceptance of the *force majeure* of fate . . . these are the questions which interested Verga, Pirandello, Luigi Capuana and Renato Fucini in their short stories, and which continue to occupy the present-day short-story writers, Dino Buzzatti, Mario Soldati, Anna Maria Ortese and Giuseppe Marotta.

One recent work of non-fiction should be mentioned—a book written about Italy for foreigners: *The Italians,* by Luigi Barzini. This author, a former journalist, seems to have made the most successful attempt so far to explain his inexplicable fellow-countrymen to the world outside, to correct misconceptions and dispel popular fallacies in an objective and very readable way.

Poetry

The Italian poetry tradition is somewhat frail, but it has a long genealogy. Poetry bloomed in pre-Renaissance soil, when Italy was a land of leisure and formal manners for educated people. The sonnets and canzonettas of Giacomino Pugliese, Jacopo da Lentino and Ciullo d'Alcamo go back to the 12th and 13th centuries and are neat and perfect within their limitations—the limitations imposed by a language which is too rhythmical and too easy to rhyme in and perhaps too musical to sustain the expression of complex poetic imagery and ideas.

Dante Alighieri (1265–1321), however, remains one of the first half-dozen poets in anyone's world anthology, both for his *Divina Commedia* and for *La Vita Nuova,* the first and tenderest love poem of modern literature. Petrarch (1304–74) rose above a host of assembly-line sonnet-makers to survey a new sphere of mental activity, the kingdom of the post-medieval spirit, and to give Renaissance learning a new impetus. Giovanni Boccaccio (1313–75) infused the old stilted forms with a rich sensuality.

The 16th-century masters, Ariosto and Tasso, were more courtly and stylized; and Italian poetry languished like the lovesick characters who peopled it until two centuries had passed, and romantics like Alfieri, Leopardi, Carducci and Manzoni revivified the art. Of them all, only Leopardi's stature increases as time goes by; his work is vigorous and propagandist; a trifle sickly by modern standards.

Gabriele d'Annunzio has few admirers today. He was too florid and undisciplined, in life and work, for the taste of our grandfathers, but he was tremendously popular in Italy and ordinary people who once caught sight of him still treasure the memory. Interest revives in the 19th-century Roman dialect satirist Belli and in modern poets like Montale and Ungaretti, who have restored grace and delicacy to Italian poetry. But it is, and always was, an art form for which the Italian people have never had much enthusiasm.

Drama

The same might be said of Italian drama. Numerous explanations have been advanced for the comparatively thin repertory of stage plays produced by a people whose whole life is a drama: overwhelming respect paid to Greek and Roman forebears, some say, stifled native talent at a critical period; or the Italian passion for music and pageantry made opera rather than theater the favorite spectacle; or—as Moravia has suggested—Italians are so self-centered that they take no interest in characters on a stage, separated from themselves by several rows of seats. (Yet the new-style drama, with plenty of scope for audience participation, has not caught on in Italy either.)

However it may be, Italian theater-goers were for a long time content with the Harlequins and Columbines of the ritualized Commedia dell'Arte; and the old epics of the *preux chevaliers,* done with marionettes, are still watched with rapt attention.

Carlo Goldoni of Venice brought real life into the Italian theater in the 18th-century—a kind of minor Molière, smiling at human foibles; significantly, the foibles of amusing people, namely the under-privileged, as in his *La Locandiera.* Since his day there has been scarcely a playwright worth remembering until Luigi Pirandello, one of the most thoughtful and innovatory dramatists of our century. Everyone knows the title of the play which brought him fame outside Italy—*Six Characters in Search of an Author*—even if not everyone has read it. His plays deal with obscure people—characters who achieve an identity only by virtue of the reaction of events around them.

Contemporary with Pirandello and, like him, concerned with lifting the mask which convention imposes, were Luigi Antonelli *(L'Uomo che incontrò se stesso),* Dario Niccodemi (two popular comedies, *Scampolo* and *Maestrina*) and Massimo Bontempelli *(Bassano Padre Geloso),* who at the time of his death in 1960 had been lawyer, philosopher, composer and novelist as well as playwright.

Ugo Betti, who died in 1953, completes the Pléiade of the Italian dramatic Renaissance, modest as it was. In the bafflingly obscure symbolism of *Corruzione al Palazzo di Giustizia, Frana allo Scalo Nord* and *L'Aiuola,* we grasp at hints of salvation for those who recognize their human frailties; Betti wants to awaken the social conscience, but he seems to remind us that compassion is a virtue too, and that justice without mercy is not justice.

Present-day playgoers are offered limited choice of native drama—a choice between two Edoardo de Filippo plays, *Mia Famiglia* and *Napoli Milionaria* is most likely. All the theaters of Italy, regularly presenting stage plays, would not amount to the number in London's West End or on Broadway. In summer there are a great number of so-called "drama festivals", tourist-oriented. For every Italian dramatist represented, Shakespeare is represented twenty times, Sophocles and Aristophanes, Plautus and Terence about ten. The notable festivals are:

Classical drama, Syracuse (May and June), Benevento (July), Gubbio (July), Pompeii (July), Paestum (August and September), Vicenza (September); Open-air drama, Verona (July and August, principally Shakespeare), Gardone (July and August) and Portovenere (July and August).

The Cinema

Italy is the cradle of the movie camera, though the prototype, da Vinci's *camera obscura,* showed nothing more than the scene it was pointed at, reproduced upside down on the back wall of a box with a hole in it. Italy had an important role also in the pioneer days of the motion picture industry: Luigi Maggi's *Last Days of Pompeii,* produced in 1908, led through a series of spectaculars to Enrico Guazzoni's *Quo Vadis* of 1912 and eventually inspired the screen epics of Griffith and de Mille in Hollywood. Rudolph Valentino was an Italian, born in the Puglia province; but he never starred in an Italian film.

Up to the end of the Fascist era, however, the industry was in decline. Mussolini launched the Venice Film Festival—the first in the world—and one of Mussolini's sons took up movie-making as a career, without conspicuous success; but by that time all the best directors (most of whom were politically on the left) had emigrated. Cinecittà, "Movie City", built on the outskirts of Rome in 1935–6 was architecturally grand, artistically negligible. Only after it had suffered bomb damage in the war, and Italians were going in for shoestring movies in temporary corrugated-iron huts, did the industry begin to acquire a serious reputation. Cinecittá is once again a lonely place today: most movies are made in private studios.

Plays, novels and opera went through their *verismo* phases, but cinematography began with it—a disturbing phenomenon to those conditioned by Hollywood glamor. Productions like Roberto Rossellini's *Open City* (1945) and *Paisa* (1946), Vittorio de Sica's *Bicycle Thieves* (1948) and Luchino Visconti's *La Terra Trema* (1948) are still prized by the film societies. They featured that favorite character of Italian literature, the underdog, weak and helpless, picking up his life again, being exploited or corrupted in the vicious jungle of the *fin-de-guerre.*

Italian movies, a *succés d'estime* from the start, began to make money. Visconti and Pier Paolo Pasolini moved away from the humble peasant interiors and neo-realistic dialogue to the costly extravaganza with huge crowd scenes, violent color and Roman orgies. Out of the relative simplicity of de Sica's *Umberto D* (1952) came the intricate psychology of *The Garden of the Finzi-Contini* (1971); in both he was discussing the effects of rapid social and political changes on old friends and old values. Over the same period Visconti moved from the pathos of *Rocco and his Brothers* (1960) to the lavish "movie of the book" *Death in Venice* (1972).

Distant history attracted Pasolini—the biblical or mythological reconstruction, with political overtones. His Christ, in *The Gospel According to Saint Matthew* (1964), is a Marxist peasant, in contrast to the synthesis of divine, Jew and philosopher which is Zeffirelli's Christ in *Jesus of Nazareth.* Where Cecil B. de Mille would have introduced teeming streets and a complex of temples, Pasolini brought on one man and a few bare rocks and accomplished effects with "mood" music and long silences. In his later work—*Medea* (1970), *The Decameron* (1971) and *Oedipus Rex* (1974), there is much vague allegory and overt and covert sexuality.

Even fonder of barren scenery, stark metallic buildings, silence and clipped dialogue is Michelangelo Antonioni. He strips motion pictures of inessentials and makes no concessions to the restiveness of an audience. Tension builds slowly and as slowly subsides. In *L'Avventura* (1960) a hot, harsh, desolated landscape reflects the arid introspections of two who can neither live with each other or without each other. *The Eclipse* takes place on the stock exchange (1962) and *Red Desert* on an industrial site (1964)—soulless locations through which Antonioni conducts us on a roundabout journey and brings us back to the point we started from.

Producers and directors favor long associations with their successful stars. Antonioni, for example, generally used Marcello Mastroianni and Monica Vitti. The "star system" which Italy looked like developing in the 1950s, when Gina Lollobrigida and Sophia Loren became sex symbols for the Western world, is no more. Italy's greatest movie actress was Anna Magnani, a homely woman not suited to elegant roles.

Federico Fellini has pushed the Italian motion picture to the limits of fantasy (and perhaps injected the seeds of its decay) with his interpretations of the sickness of society in *La Dolce Vita* (1960), his autobiographical apologia *8½* (1963) and his dream-worlds of Roman scandals and sybaritic self-indulgence in *Satyricon* (1971) and *Casanova* (1976). Fellini's concern is with the human circus. He stresses the cynicism of the Church, the impotence of the intelligentsia, the reluctance of people to face reality. Fashionable escape routes—drink, drugs, perversions of sex—give Fellini's characters opportunities for excursions into bizarre hallucinatory situations round which a casual narrative is woven.

The big name of the mid-1970s was Bernardo Bertolucci (already famous for *The Conformist* (1970)), who achieved notoriety with his explorations of the wilder shores of physical love in *Last Tango in Paris* (1975) and a controversial epic of Italian life and character called *1900* (1976). Marco Ferreri expresses the deepest radical pessimism with his *L'ultima Donna* and *Ciao, Maschio* (1978), both based on a conviction that the male animal is finished and must disappear.

A brief survey of outstanding motion pictures must suggest that all is bleak in the Italian cinema world. Sympathy and humor, however, are not lacking, and Italian directors have learned that buffoonery can shock as successfully as brutality. The native genius for self-dramatization, the native lust for life, painful or pleasant, shines through the screen and helps to explain why such a high proportion of serious Italian movies are winners.

Satire and straight comedy, directed at suburban snobbery and antiquated conventions, is purveyed by Pietro Germi in *Divorce, Italian Style* and is given a political accent by Lina Wertmuller. Two decades ago it would have been unthinkable for a film-maker to hold Italian sexual inadequacies up for the amusement of the world.

In the more basic comedies, expensive stunts and complicated technological tricks rarely raise the action above the level of Abbott and Costello (two characters, incidentally, who are extremely popular in Italy even today). One or two excellent modern cowboy films, with an intellectual content, have been made by Sergio Leone; but on the whole the "spaghetti Western" is too crude for British and American tastes.

Cinemas are found in all communities and performances continue to a late hour at night. Seats are uncomfortable, audiences are predominantly young, male and raucous. Most provincial cinema programs are unbelievably drab and hackneyed. Violence is at a premium, heroes and heroines are generally rebellious and iconoclastic.

Cinematography: the serious movie magazine, *Bianco e Nero,* has been published since the 1930s and has a respectable circulation. The national motion picture archives are housed at the Centro Sperimentale of the cinema, at Rome. Film festivals abound. The principal international festivals are: Science Fiction Films (Trieste, July); Films of the Nations (Messina and Taormina, July and August); International Cinema Week (Sorrento, September); Survey of New Films (Pesaro, September); 16 and 8 mm Films (Salerno, September); and Social Documentaries (Florence, December). Queen of them all, however, is the Venice Film Festival (August), which recently awoke from a hibernation of several years to a fresh new lease of cinematic life.

THE FACE OF ITALY

ROME, THE ETERNAL

Treasurehouse of Western Culture

It wasn't built in a day, and all roads lead to it. These undeniable facts are the first things we learn about Rome, and if facts can grow truer with time, then these have. As the visitor sees on arrival, Rome is still being built and is turning into a vast, sprawling metropolis. Consequently, more and more roads lead to it: air routes from every continent, and new superhighways which link the Italian capital not only with the cities of Northern Europe but also with the other regions of Italy, some of which were not readily accessible in the past. Especially during the tourist season, which now lasts from early spring to late autumn, you have the feeling that Rome is still, in a way, the capital of the world.

Until just about a hundred years ago, Rome had been—in modern times—a small city, hardly more than a town. But then, as always, it was the goal of foreign visitors, and the steady stream of writers and artists who came to Rome have left their testimony to its charm and its grandeur—Goethe, Stendhal, Hawthorne, Byron. Then, in 1870, Rome became again the capital of a united Italy, and with the national government, the Roman bureaucracy appeared, and the population began its rapid modern expansion. Around the ancient core of the city stretches the Rome that this modern Italy has created.

As a result of this growth, the citizens of Rome, too, have become more heterogeneous. It is hard to find a Roman over fifty whose grandfather was born in the city; and many of today's Romans are post-war citizens of the capital, immigrants who came to Rome to work or to look for work in the second great expansion of the city in the 1940s and 1950s. Many came from the south, so the southern character of Rome has been accentuated. And, for better or worse, there is a meridional atmosphere in Rome (lamented by many northern Italians and even by some of the Romans themselves). The visitor is wise not to be in a hurry, to keep his temper, and to expect the unexpected. Part of Rome's appeal lies in its contradictions.

They are often visible: the neon sign over the baroque doorway, advertising a Western film shot in the Alban hills; the café that calls itself a snack-bar (or, because of careless spelling, a snach or a snak or even a snake bar), where the snacks are pure Italian pizzas or rustici (meat-or cheese-filled pastries) or creamy, fattening irresistible cakes. You learn to accept the fact that, in Rome, the oldest bank is the bank of the Holy Ghost and that there is a Quo Vadis filling station.

From ancient times, the Romans have been piling the present on top of the past. There is no "medieval quarter" or "baroque quarter" in Rome: ancient columns were blithely incorporated into Renaissance walls, and you can enter a gleaming, glass-and-brick modern building to be greeted by a fragment of the ancient city, uncovered by the 20th-century contractor and then left exposed to the contemporary gaze. Temples have been turned into churches, ancient baths into museums or an outdoor opera stage, some of the city's modern streets follow the ancient city plan, and the famous highways from the city are still the Via Appia, the Via Flaminia, the Via Cassia.

Rome's Origins and History

The history of Rome is a mixture of legend and reality, and both are constantly impressed on the visitor to the city. Guides in the Forum will show you the spot where, according to ancient tradition, Romulus killed Remus; and in the Capitoline Museum you can see a bronze statue, dating from Etruscan times, that shows the she-wolf nursing the two brothers as babies. Legendary or not, Romulus was not the first citizen of Rome. On the slopes of Monte Mario, the hill from which

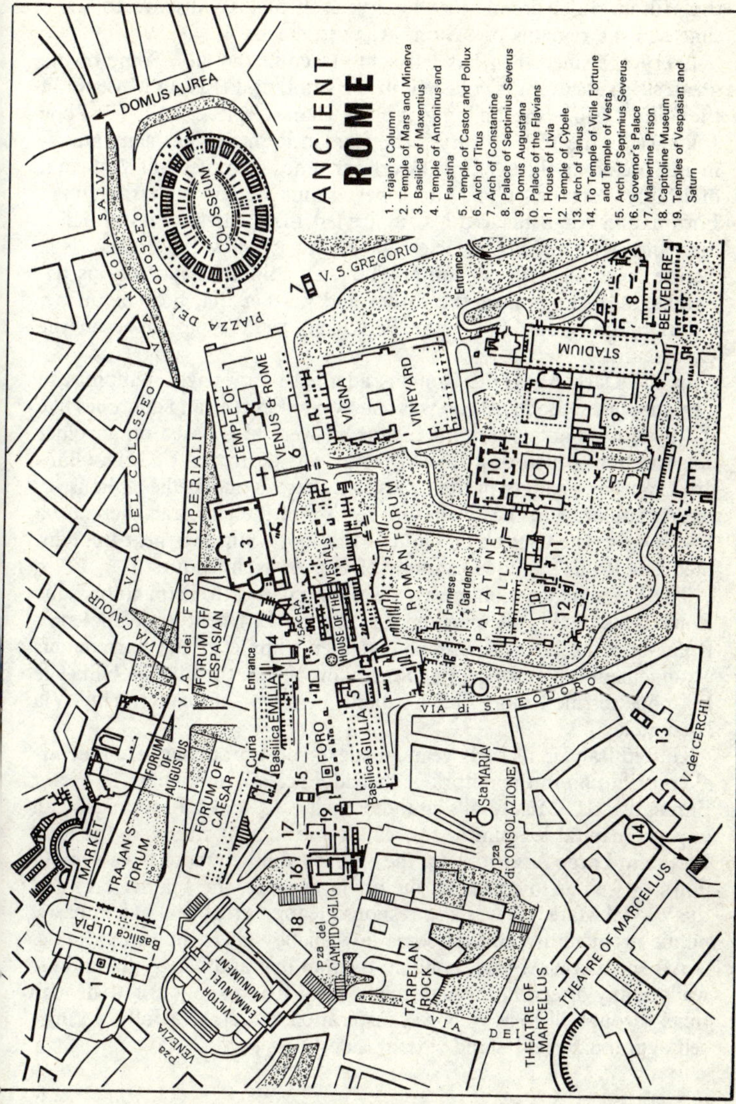
ANCIENT ROME
1. Trajan's Column
2. Temple of Mars and Minerva
3. Basilica of Maxentius
4. Temple of Antoninus and Faustina
5. Temple of Castor and Pollux
6. Arch of Titus
7. Arch of Constantine
8. Palace of Septimius Severus
9. Domus Augustana
10. Palace of the Flavians
11. House of Livia
12. Temple of Cybele
13. Arch of Janus
14. To Temple of Virile Fortune and Temple of Vesta
15. Arch of Septimius Severus
16. Governor's Palace
17. Mamertine Prison
18. Capitoline Museum
19. Temples of Vespasian and Saturn
DOMUS AUREA
VIA NICOLA SALVI
COLOSSEUM
PIAZZA DEL COLOSSEO
V. S. GREGORIO
Entrance
BELVEDERE
STADIUM
VIGNA
VINEYARD
TEMPLE OF VENUS & ROME
VIA DEL COLOSSEO
VIA dei FORI IMPERIALI
VIA CAVOUR
FORUM OF VESPASIAN
ROMAN FORUM
HOUSE OF THE VESTALS
V. SACRA
Farnese Gardens
PALATINE HILL
Entrance
Basilica EMILIA
Curia
FORO
Basilica GIULIA
VIA di S. TEODORO
FORUM OF AUGUSTUS
FORUM OF CAESAR
MARKET
TRAJAN'S FORUM
Basilica ULPIA
StaMARIA CONSOLAZIONE
V. dei CERCHI
Pza di CONSOLAZIONE
Pza del CAMPIDOGLIO
VICTOR EMMANUEL II MONUMENT
Pza VENEZIA
TARPEIAN ROCK
VIA DEI THEATRE OF MARCELLUS
THEATRE OF MARCELLUS

the Hilton Hotel dominates the city, archeologists discovered some time ago the remains of a Stone Age settlement.

Every age since then has left some trace in the city. Some of the greatest Etruscan art is collected in the stunning Etruscan Museum in the Villa Giulia (the building itself is a masterpiece, built for Pope Julius III in the 16th century). The Roman Republic left many monuments, including the two little Greek-influenced temples—of Vesta and of Manly Fortune—along the Tiber. Julius Caesar built the Julian Forum, and Augustus and his empire left the greatest series of buildings and works of art. Diocletian's Baths are now the Museo delle Terme, near the railroad station. Trajan's column, depicting his triumphs, still stands near the forum and market that bear his name. Hadrian is responsible for the Pantheon, and Vespasian began the Colosseum.

In the Dark Ages, the Romans adapted many pagan buildings to Christian uses: the Pantheon was consecrated in 609, and churches like the beautiful Santa Maria in Cosmedin were also based on an older construction. Much of medieval Rome was destroyed by Mussolini's drastic urban changes in the 1930s, but there is one medieval house—the Anguillara—in the Trastevere section of the city, and there are a few towers. The Church of Santa Maria sopra Minerva, near the Pantheon, is Rome's unique example of Gothic architecture.

The Renaissance monuments are too numerous to list, and baroque Rome is also richly documented. In the early 19th century, Napoleon's Rome-born architect Giuseppe Valadier completed the harmonious arrangement of Piazza del Popolo, linking it with the Pincian Hill. The last pope to rule Rome, Pius IX, built the ugly—but convenient—Via Nazionale.

United Italy, in its early years, made its most prominent architectural contribution in the notorious "wedding cake" monument to Victor Emmanuel II. Mussolini's grandiose plan to make Rome again an imperial capital led him to re-create some ancient sites, like the little Forum in Largo Argentina (at the expense of much regrettable demolition), as well as to construct the broad avenues, the Via del Fori and the Via del Mare. He was also responsible for a great deal of bombastic public architecture and for some now-shabby cheap housing.

All these styles blend, conflict, overlap one another. A ten-minute walk in any direction through the heart of Rome is a journey through time, through history. A pope's inspiration, a dictator's folly, a king's self-aggrandizement stand side by side.

Weather Matters

Many tourists crowd into Rome during the hot July-through-September period, yet recent years have seen the tourist season beginning earlier and earlier. Many visit Rome beginning in April. This month, May, June and early October are far and away the best months to see the city. Rome is becoming an all-year-round mecca, although November, December, January and early February are cold and it is apt to rain.

Food for Thought

Most Roman dishes make their appearance as seasonably as the weather. Exceptions are spaghetti and macaroni. But in spring, for example, the specialty is artichokes *alla giudia;* summer brings deviled chicken with peppers; winter features young roasted lamb or veal scallops seasoned with wine. Among the more common favorites: *fettucini all' uovo* (buttered egg-noodles), tripe *alla Romana, gnocchi* (potato-and-flour dumplings, with tomato sauce and cheese) and *saltimbocca* (veal-and-ham slices fried in butter, with sage leaves between). Green salads are delicious in Rome, being well-seasoned with oil, vinegar, lemon and salt. The people, however, eat their buttered dishes unsalted, and the butter itself is without it. Of Rome's highly favored cheeses, the best are *mozzarella* (white buffalo cheese), *caciotta Romana* (semi-hard, sweet sheep cheese), *pecorino* (another sheep cheese, but sharp and hard), *parmigiano vecchio* (hard and semi-sweet), *gorgonzola* (spicy, mellow). Pastas? *Spaghetti alla carbonara* or piquant *penne all'arrabbiata.*

Wines? Best of the vintage types for Rome and its environs are *Frascati, Albano, Grottaferrata* (white; not too dry); *Velletri, Montefiascone, Marino* (white; very dry); and *Marino, Cesanese, Piglio* (red). There's also another Montefiascone wine—*Est Est Est*—on which legend has it a rather notorious biship named Fugger drank himself happily to death.

Romans love to eat out, so there are plenty of good restaurants—from deluxe international ones to simple, often rustic, family-run places. With a few exceptions that include hotel dining rooms, all Roman restaurants close one day a week. Ask your hotel portiere to call and check on the place of your choice. Lunch hour begins at 1 p.m.; fashionable dinner time starts at 9 p.m., runs quite late, especially in summer.

Exploring Rome

Everyone will tell you to walk. There are good reasons. In the first place, traffic in Rome is by now so chaotic (and with no relief in sight) that your car or taxi is sure to be trapped in a jam, unless you like driving in the middle of the night. Besides, Rome is a place to be savored. Take a taxi, bus or the Metro from one vital point to another, then stroll about, keeping a sharp eye out for undisciplined drivers.

A lifetime isn't enough to see everything that is beautiful or historic or curious in Rome, so don't worry if you only have a few days, and above all, don't try to crowd too much into them. Tired eyes can't appreciate paintings or sculpture, and tired feet are an urgent distraction from even the loveliest scenes. For a first, overall notion of Rome and its riches, it might be advisable to take one of the half-day tours provided by the agencies or the low-cost sightseeing tour offered by ATAC, Rome's bus company. (Information and departure from ATAC booth in front of Termini Station).

There are also tours that will show you Rome by night, but if you can't live without nightclubs, then Rome is probably the wrong city for you anyway. In good weather, the best thing to do at night is sit down in a piazza or at an outdoor café and watch Rome go by.

It is a big city. In a nutshell, it sprawls over 62,000 acres (excluding Vatican City), plus an additional 422,000 acres in communal property supporting over 2,000,000 inhabitants who patronize some 2,000 eating places, attend 450 churches, enjoy the delights of 1,000 wineries, 1,700 bars and pastry shops, stroll through dozens of parks, gardens, national monuments . . .

Thus, obviously, you can't—and won't—see all of Rome in a one-day bus tour, a three-day stopover, or even a week or ten days. Nor will you know the city well within a year.

Well, dependent upon time available, either 1) take a few short, all-inclusive tours, 2) visit some of the city's highlights, or 3) disregard what people insist you must see and just strike out through whatever part of Rome you choose.

Self-styled travel experts, of course, advocate seeing the city as a whole first, then concentrating on its highlights if time permits. Fine. But, on the other hand, first question fired at you upon your arrival back home will be about such internationally-known spectacles as the Colosseum, St. Peter's, the balcony where Mussolini orated, etc., and if you haven't seen them, you haven't—in the minds of those at home—seen Rome. For many more tourists than you might think, this face-saving knowledge is almost as important as the visit itself. You must, in short, decide what interests you most about the city—then see it.

The Eternal City, if you like, may be divided into two parts: the old and the new. The old Rome is the true Rome today, a crowded, teeming maze of twisted alleys, musty little squares and gloomy 17th-century palaces covering 22 individual *rioni* (regions) born under the popes in their 15th-century revival of the city's ancient glory. The new Rome—apparent only since Italy united itself in 1870—is modern, lively, definitely residential, nuzzling around old Rome's perimeter, stretching outside the ancient Aurelian Wall over the city's 17 *quartieri* (quarters) in an ever-growing expanse.

A good starter might be one beginning at the city's center, in Piazza Venezia, where even the Romans still orient themselves. Stand in the middle of this square, facing the biggest thing in front of you. That's the monument to King Victor Emmanuel II, a comparatively modern work (1911) for Rome. Up the stairs, past Italy's Tomb of the Unknown Soldier and a statue of Victor Emmanuel II on horseback, a stairway winds to the top of the monument; the view of Rome on a clear day is worth your huffing and puffing to get there. And coming down into the square again, turn left into Palazzo Venezia if you want to see where Benito Mussolini once harangued his fellow countrymen jamming the square to hear longwinded speeches about Ethiopia, Spain, the tryst with Hitler, etc.

Here, then, are six exploration routes you can follow:

From the Piazza Venezia to the Colosseum

1 Behind the Victor Emmanuel Monument, on the right, steps built by no less a personage than Michelangelo himself lead upwards to the square fronting Rome's City Hall *(Campidoglio),* housed in the Senatorial Palace. This is the farthest away of the square's three buildings and is flanked by the magnificent Capitoline and Conservatori museums. After 800 years, the equestrian statue of Marcus Aurelius was removed from the Square in 1980. Pollution had restored a gilt-sheen to the bronze and thus, according to a Roman prophecy, presaging the end of the world—but more to the point, the end of the statue.

Apart from the marvellous views of the Forum that you get from the gardens at the summit, be sure to take in the two museums, the Capitoline and Conservatori. They contain a number of classical sculptures including the *Boy with a Thorn,* the *Dying Gaul* and the *Capitoline Venus.*

The Tarpeian Rock at the edge takes its name from Tarpeia, daughter of Tarpeas, governor of Rome during Romulus' time. She had fallen madly in love with a Sabine to whom she promised to open her city's gates, if the enemy army would be willing to give her "what the Sabine warriors wore on their left arms". She was alluding to their golden

ROME
ANCIENT ROME
Roman Forum
1 Temple of Saturn
2 Temple of Castor and Pollux
3 Column of Phocas
4 Temple of Antoninus and Faustina
5 Temple of Vesta
6 Basilica of Maxentius
7 Arch of Titus
Palatine
8 Temple of Cybele
9 House of Livia
10 House of Flavia
11 House of Augustus
12 Palatine Stadium
Imperial Fora
13 Trajan's Forum
14 Trajan's Column
15 Trajan's Markets
16 Augustan Forum
Other Sites
17 Mamertine Prison
18 Tarpeian Rock
19 Mausoleum of Augustus
20 The Pantheon
21 Marcellus Theater
22 Temple of Manly Fortune
23 Temple of Vesta
24 Arch of Janus
25 Column of Marcus Aurelius
26 Tiberina Island
27 Colosseum
28 Arch of Constantine
29 Baths of Caracalla
30 Baths of Diocletian
31 Nero's House of Gold
32 Temple of Minerva
Information
Palazzo Public building
Church
Museum Theater Gallery Place of Interest etc
Hospital
Police
Rail
0 yds 800
0 ms 500 1000
Città del Vaticano
Musei del Vaticano
PIAZZA S.PIETRO
V.D.CONCILIAZIONE
Castel S.Angelo
Pal.di Giustizia
VIA AURELIA
VIALE ANGELICO
VIA CRESCENZIO
VIA COLA DI RIENZO
VIALE GIULIO CESARE
VIA OTTAVIANO
Tevere (Tiber)
S.Maria d.Popolo
Pta.d.Popolo
PIAZZA DEL POPOLO
VIA FLAMINIA
PONTE MATTEOTTI
PONTE MARGHERITA
PONTE CAVOUR
PONTE UMBERTO
Museo Napoleonico
S.Maria d.Pace
S.Agostino
Chiesa Nuova
S.Maria d'Anima
S.Agnese in Agone
Piazza Navona
Pal Madama
S.Luigi d.Francesi
Museo di Roma
Pal Massimo
CORSO VITTORIO EMANUELE
Pal.d.Cancellaria
Palazzo Farnese
Museo Barracco
S Andrea d Valle
Galleria Spada
Villa Farnesina
Pal.Corsini
VIA GIULIA
VIA ARENULA
S.Maria d.Scala
S.Pietro in Montorio
S.Maria in Trastevere
VIALE TRASTEVERE
S.Cecilia
S.Francesco a Ripa
Pta. Portese
Pta S.Pancrazio
VIA PORTUENSE
Tevere
PTE GARIBALDI
PTE SISTO
PTE.SUBLICIO
Mura Aurelie
Lung.d.Vallatti
Lung Sanzio
V D LUNGARETTA
Lung.Gianicolense
Lung.d.Farnesina
Lung.dei Tebaldi
V D LUNGARA
Lung. Tor di Nona
Lung.di Castello
Lung.Prati
V.SABOTINO
VIA MAZZINI
V. SETTEMBRINI
VIA CIPRO
VIALE VATICANO
VIA CANDIA
V. A. DORIA
CIRCONV. TRIONFALE
VIA DELLA SCROFA
VIA DI RIPETTA
Pal.di Montecitorio
S Lorenzo
S.M.s.M
L.d. Cenci
V.S.M.D.PIANTO

Galleria d'Arte Moderna
Giardino Zoologico
VIALE BELLE ARTI
Galleria Borghese
Villa Borghese
Villa Medici
TRINITÀ DEI MONTI
Spanish Steps
PZA DI SPAGNA
Trinità dei Monti
CONDOTTI
P.O.
V. MERCEDE
DEL TRITONE
Fontana di Trevi
Pal. Quirinale
Museo Preistorico e Etnogr.
SS. Apostoli
V. BATTISTI
Doria
Venezia
PIAZZA VENEZIA
Emanuele II
Museo Capitolino
ROMAN FORUM
S.M. Antiqua
PALATINE
S Maria in Cosmedin
DEI CERCHI
PIAZZA DEL CIRCO MASSIMO
VIALE AVENTINO
Parco di Pta. Capena
V. DELLE TERME
VIA PINCIANA
CORSO D'ITALIA
Pta Pinciana
VIA VITTORIO VENETO
VIA BONCOMPAGNI
Pal. Margherita (U.S. Embassy)
Cappuccini
S. Maria d. Vittoria
PZA S. BERNARDO
PIAZZA BARBERINI
Pal. Barberini
QUATTRO FONTANE
VIA SISTINA
VIA NAZIONALE
S. Carlino
PZA D. QUIRINALE
V. 4 MAGGIO
PIAZZA MAGNANAPOLI
VIA MILANO
PANISPERNA
VIA D. SERPENTI
V. DEI FORI IMPERIALI
S. Francesca Romana
S. Pietro in Vincoli
V. GIOVANNI LANZA
S. Pudenziana
S. Maria Maggiore
S. Prassede
V. C. ALBERTO
VIA CAVOUR
V. DEPRETIS
Museo Nazionale Romano
S. Maria d. Angeli
PIAZZA D. REPUBBLICA
VIA XX SETTEMBRE
V. PIAVE
Pta. Pia
VIA SALARIA
VIA PO
V. TEVERE
Villa Albani
VIA NISSA
VIA REGINA MARGHERITA
VIA ARNO
CORSO TRIESTE
VIA NOMENTANA
V. degli Appennini
V. A. Torlonia
V. lla Torlonia
V. SPALLANZANI
V. DEI VILLINI
V. G. MORGAGNI
VIALE DEL POLICLINICO
Castro Pretorio
VLE CASTRO PRETORIO
VIA PALESTRO
VIA VINCENZA
VIA MARSALA
Staz. Termini
VIA GIOVANNI GIOLITTI
VIALE D. UNIVERSITÀ
V. D. SCIENZE
Università
VIALE PRETORIANO
VIALE TIBURTINO
Pta S. Lorenzo
TIBURTINA
VIALE MANZONI
Porta Maggiore
V. Cte. Verde
VIA EMANUELE FILIBERTO
VIA MERULANA
VIA STATILIA
VIA LABICANA
S. Clemente
V. S. GIOVANNI IN LATERANO
Pal. Laterano
Scala Sancta
Pta. S. Giovanni
S. Giovanni in Laterano
VIA APPIA NUOVA
V. TARANTO
VIA GALLIA
V. ETRURIA
V. d'Amba Aradam
Pta. Metronia
V. DRUSO
Via d. Navicella
S. Stefano Rotondo
S. Maria in Domenica
S. Gregorio Magno
V. CLAUDIA
SS. Giov. e Paola
VIA S. GREGORIO
Sorgio in Velabro

bracelets. But Tatius, the Sabine king, despised all traitors, even lovely ones. As he entered the city he threw his bracelet to Tarpeia, and raising her bid, he threw the heavy shield he carried on his left arm as well. His soldiers followed suit and the unfortunate Tarpeia was buried under their weight near the rock from which traitors were thrown in antiquity to their death.

For a quarter-mile back of City Hall extend Rome's greatest archeological treasures, a collection of ruins in varied states of preservation. These fall into two categories: the Imperial Fora (best overall view from a garden to the left of the Senatorial Palace) and the Roman Forum (seen best off a terrace below and to the right of the Senatorial Palace, on Via del Campidoglio).

On your way down to Via dei Fori Imperiali and the Roman Forum, don't fail to investigate the Mamertine Prison, underneath the Church of San Guiseppe del Falegnami, just to the right of the Temple of Concord. It's a gloomy, fascinating, two-celled affair, of which the upper part once served as ancient Rome's state penitentiary, with the lower dungeon being an extra-special attraction formerly reserved only for enemies of Rome who were about to be finished off in short order. Tradition has it that this was where St. Peter spent his last days, and baptized his guards from the spring which miraculously flowed forth.

Now turn into Fori Imperiali, a 100-foot-wide boulevard opened by Mussolini in 1932, which runs 2,800 feet to the Colosseum. Archeologically-minded or not, this is an overwhelming walk, with 2,000-year-old market places, forums, temples, amphitheaters, statues, and the like stretching away on both sides most of the way. Half the distance, until Via dei Fori Imperiali's intersection with Via Cavour, runs between ruins of the Imperial Fora; just after Via Cavour intersection, on your right, an entrance leads into the maze of streets lined with more ruins that constitute the Roman Forum.

A word about each of these. The original Imperial Fora were actually monumental squares erected in honor of some stupendous victory in early Roman times, each centered with a temple and surrounded by public buildings. Most impressive are Trajan's Forum, Market and Column, plus the Forums of Caesar, Augustus and Nerva. The Forum of Trajan, incidentally, became nothing more than a public pile of free building material during the Middle Ages, when home-builders sacked the place for its stone; attempts to clear the area began as late as 1924.

The Roman Forum, once nothing more than a marshy hollow, became the political and commercial center of Rome, studded with public meeting halls, shops, temples, and shrines. Gradually, however, it began to lose its importance as Rome declined; a 3rd-century fire destroyed much of the area and barbarian invasions finished it off. By the late 1700s, the Forum was again a marshy cattle pasture. Excavations began about 1870, bringing to light the principal ruins like the Temples of Castor and Pollux, Vesta, Saturn, and the Arch of Titus.

Unfortunately, air pollution has caused such deterioration of these precious marbles that the authorities have had to put under wraps (literally) such gems as Trajan's Column, The Arch of Constantine, and the Arch of Septimius Severus.

The dead end of Via dei Fori Imperiali is backstopped by what everyone seems to agree still remains the most stupendous monument of ancient Rome—the Colosseum.

The Colosseum

Consider this gigantic spectacle in three parts: as a whole, the amphitheater, and the arena. Originally known as the Flavian Amphitheater, it was begun in the year 72, opened in 80, completed in 82. Only towards the end of the 8th century, after countless gladiators were served up to the lions, did this place become known as the Colosseum. In rapid succession, it served as a 13th-century fortress, a quarry from which materials were filched to build sumptuous Renaissance churches and palaces, and finally a relic declared sacred by the popes because of the many Christian martyrs who lost their lives inside it. Statistically, the amphitheater runs 186 yards in length, 170 yards across, 159 feet high, with a circumference of 573 yards. Inside, the 250-foot-long, 160-foot-wide arena provided a huge stage for the auditorium that once seated 50,000 spectators per show. The Colosseum remains at its best when seen at dawn, sunset, or even after dark, when spotlights play along the outside walls. Walk up the staircases to the highest gallery to appreciate the size of this work. Visit the fascinating little museums on the first level and in the recently-excavated subterranean level, where all sorts of curious objects were found.

Outside the Colosseum, starting from the now-shrouded Arch of Constantine, which that emperor had built for himself about 1,600 years ago, a wide avenue—Via San Gregorio—runs arrow-like into Piazza del Massimo, where you take a turn to the left, amble through Porta Capena Park, and find on the other side of it the Baths of Caracalla. In pure grandeur, they surpass any other ruins of old Rome's public baths; like the Colosseum, they take on a particular charm early or late in the day. Squeeze your budget and stretch your timetable a bit to witness one of Rome's summer operas staged in this great stone bathing place where the ancients, in white togas, once gathered to cleanse their bodies and revel in local gossip. It's an experience you won't forget.

The Quirinale and Villa Torlonia

2 Another, somewhat different jaunt also begins at Piazza Venezia, from which you take Via Battisti into Via Quattro Novembre. At Piazza Magnanapoli, a street called Via XXIV Maggio snakes off to the left, running uphill to Piazza del Quirinale.

You can't miss this broad square, centered with a couple of statues portraying Castor and Pollux in the act of reining in their unruly horses. The square is a mixture of ancient and not-so-ancient. The statues, for example, are Roman replicas of old Greek works (4th century); the obelisk came out of the Mausoleum of Augustus; the basin was salvaged from the Roman Forum itself. Facing you, the largest building on the square is Quirinale Palace, one-time residence of Italy's king but now the "White House" of its President. You can visit the Quirinale gardens on Thursdays (2–4 P.M.); no formalities, other than passport, required.

Walk along the right side of the palace, down Via del Quirinale, past the Church of San Carlino (on your right), where the best families of Rome like to marry off their fledglings, and finally to the four-corner intersection known as Quattro Fontane (Four Fountains). There's one on each corner—four statues from ancient Roman monuments set up during the time of Pope Sixtus V, rebuilder of Rome, to spew forth the Acqua Felice water he sluiced into the city from the mountains around Tivoli outside. Keep going straight ahead for Piazza San Bernardo, and when you get there, take a minute to investigate the far corner on your right, with its Fontanone dell'Acqua Felice (Big Fountain of the Happy Water). This fountain resembles roughly a triumphal arch, and in a niche in the center of it is a statue originally intended to look like the great *Moses* by Michelangelo. A goodly number of experts are prone to regard the statue with ill-concealed contempt, labeling it a rank imitation of the real thing. Right or wrong, they must have a rather solid base for their criticism, inasmuch as history records that the unhappy sculptor who labored over this work was so ridiculed by his Roman contemporaries after he finished it that he actually committed suicide.

Via XX Settembre begins on the other side of Piazza San Bernardo to continue in a straight line past shops, bars, and cafés to Porta Pia, a huge arch built by Michelangelo in 1561. On the other side of it is the imposing monument to the Bersaglieri, Italy's plume-bonneted crack soldiers, who liven any military parade with their traditional quick-time march past the grandstand. A half-block to the left of this monument, down Corso d'Italia, you'll find a memorial column recalling the breach in the old wall through which Italian troops entered papal Rome in September, 1870, thus putting an end to the temporal power of the popes and completing the unification of Italy.

Your jaunt could very well end here. But with enough time on hand, return to the monument, take a bus heading down Via Nomentana, the boulevard that runs out from the foot of the monument, and tell the driver you want to get off at Sant' Agnese, about a mile-and-a-half distant. En route through one of Rome's better residential sections, with a half-dozen embassies and legations scattered the length of it, watch for the block-long expanse of Villa Torlonia, on your right, where Mussolini lived during his years in power, before he was deposed and arrested in 1943. At the Sant' Agnese stop, cross the street to the Church of Sant' Agnese fuori le Mura (St. Agnes Outside the Walls), built in the year 324 over a maze of catacombs where the beautiful saint was laid to rest. Go inside, down a long, cool hallway into the church nave itself, and ask to see the 3rd-century catacombs, some of the best-preserved in all of Rome. Just a few steps away in Santa Costanza, be sure to see the splendid 4th-century mosaics.

The Fountain of Trevi and Via Veneto

Trek **3** is shorter. Again from Piazza Venezia, move out along Via Cesare Battisti to Piazza Santi Apostoli, with its 1,400-year-old church of the same name. Walk to the end of the square, turn right into Vicolo del Vaccaro, then follow it through to Piazza Pilotta, from which point Via dei Lucchesi continues along to the Fountain of Trevi. (By the way, directions in Rome like this one are *not* difficult to follow; all streets are clearly marked, and well-defined landmarks help you plot your course.) This walk runs through one of the city's older sections, with small shops, market places and a number of characteristic alleys and byways interlaced along the route.

A word about the Fountain of Trevi. It's the most imposing of all Rome's more spectacular fountains. Ordered by Pope Clement XII, the work was finished by Salvi, in 1762, against a natural backdrop provided by Palazzo Poli. It features a couple of lusty marble tritons hauling a winged chariot ridden by Neptune, God of the Sea, through spurts and cascades of water that play among a maze of scenic effects when the fountain labors at full capacity. The legend attached to this fountain has it that whosoever tosses a coin into the huge basin will return to toss another one, and you can be certain the smart little Roman kids capitalize on the story during summer months when foreign tourists gather around to shell out their small change!

Leave the fountain by way of Via della Stamperia, winding into Via del Tritone, with its many shops, a busy thoroughfare. Turn right up Via del Tritone to Piazza Barberini, surrounded by hotels, stores, theaters, a hub of bustling activity from early morning to late at night. In its center is the Fountain of the Triton, designed by Bernini in 1640, a rather neat job of a triton blowing into a conch shell, with the water spurting out and upwards in a high arc. Bernini is also responsible for another fountain—this one resembling a sea shell—at the corner of the square where Via Veneto begins. Some oldsters speculate, however, that it looks more like a bee with outstretched wings; they seem to feel that the sculptor might have used the bee because it's on the coat-of-arms of the princely Barberini family, whose palace is across this square and up Via Quattro Fontane. On its top floor, by the way, is the coin collection assembled by King Victor Emmanuel III, now state property. The main floor houses an extensive art museum. One vast room was frescoed by Pietro da Cortona between 1633 and 1639.

A short way up Via Veneto, on your right, stands another of Rome's many intriguing churches—Santa Maria della Concezione (St. Mary of the Conception)—founded in 1624 and better known among Romans simply as the Church of the Capuchin Monks. Inside, tell one of the good friars you want to visit the underground chapels. He escorts you through the church, past ground-floor chapels featuring paintings like *Death of St. Francis, St. Francis Reviving a Dead Man* and *St. Francis in Ecstasy* that help create an atmosphere for the descent into five subterranean chapels where lie the whole skeletons and scattered bones of more than 4,000 (that's correct!) Capuchin monks gathered there over the centuries.

The street curves gracefully up past Palazzo Margherita, built in 1890, which now houses the US Embassy; next door is the Consulate. Ahead, continuing to the end at a tower-flanked opening in the wall called Porta Pinciana, Via Veneto covers its final stretch in a burst of cosmopolitan smugness. Past swank hotels, tea rooms, outdoor cafés and chic shops, this street was once headquarters of the *dolce vita* and *the* place to be seen in the Eternal City. Fading members of the cinema set still gather here, along with a conglomerate mixture of tourists, the poorer scions of the Roman aristocracy and new industrialists, American businessmen, several dozen of the more expensive sidewalk pick-ups of all sexes, and so on. Six o'clock in the evening finds this tourist trap portion of Via Veneto packed to the last outdoor table.

Start once more from Piazza Venezia for what is perhaps Rome's most beautiful four-hour walk, through Villa Borghese Gardens, with its fountains, green glades, statuary, scenery, museums. Set aside a part of your itinerary for this little junket, even if you have to cancel an appointment with the President of Italy. It typifies the kind of Rome you have read about.

Villa Borghese and Vicinity

4 Out of Piazza Venezia, follow Via del Corso, another of the city's busier streets, to Largo Goldoni, a small square; then turn right into

Via Condotti, nosing along past the most fashionable shops in Rome to Piazza di Spagna. With Via Condotti, two other narrow streets—Via Babuino and Via Margutta—flow into the square to form the core of what used to be Rome's bohemian quarter, a center for artists and writers of every nationality; many still gather at the century-old Caffè Greco. Via Babuino, incidentally, is lined with one antique shop after another, while Via Margutta is devoted to studio apartments and art galleries. Both streets are interesting enough to prowl through, but Via Condotti remains the top shopping district for those who would carry home something chic, distinctive—and expensive.

Standing in Piazza di Spagna, once a heart of the old Anglo-American quarter in Rome, there's a Fontana della Barcaccia (Fountain of the Boat) by Bernini, around which Romans love to cool themselves on hot summer nights. Behind it, sloping gently upwards, the famed 200-year-old flight of 137 Spanish Steps begins at a brightly-laden flower stall, between an English tea room (*Babington's*) on the left, and on the right, the house in which Britain's illustrious poet, John Keats, died in 1821. The stairs ascend gracefully to a square on the top dominated by the Church of Trinità dei Monti, built three years after Columbus discovered America, by order of King Charles VIII of France. Facing the church, move off to your left, looking for the basin-like fountain in front of the Villa Medici, the French Academy in Rome and a handsome building that regularly offers exceptional art shows free to the public.

This brings you into the Pincio, a part of the Eternal City's most beautiful gardens. They were completed in 1814 by Valadier after five years of laborious planning. No landscape gardener could possibly have chosen a better site for the project, with two of its landmarks especially outstanding. One is the *Casina Valadier,* a neo-classic combination supper club-restaurant-tearoom topped by a high balcony, frequented by darting swallows at sunset, and offering an absolutely superb view of central Rome; the other is Piazzale del Pincio, where you can walk to the edge of a low terrace and watch the sun set behind the Eternal City in a summer sky as pink as flamingo feathers. Backing off the Piazzale, several tree-shaded lanes flanked by busts of Italy's patriotic heroes twist through an area of green shrubbery, wide grassy spaces and two unique fountains—the Fountain of Moses and another with a clock keeping time as the water turns its wheels.

In front of you here, Villa Borghese sprawls forth in a series of wavy hummocks planted deep with ilex trees, umbrella pines, and magnolias. It's a favorite Sunday gathering place for Roman families, who frequent the Giardino del Lago (Lake Garden), with its tiny lake set in a well-kept botanical garden; Piazza di Siena, a pine-enclosed amphitheater where horse shows are held; and nearby, a copy of the Temple of Faustina.

Villa Borghese also boasts one of Rome's leading art galleries in the Casina Borghese. Whether or not you find either art or the Galleries that display its work particularly interesting, take time out to visit this place. The ground floor is strictly a museum, and its No. 1 attraction is Canova's nude of Pauline Borghese, sister of Napoleon, reclining on a couch. Other remarkable works include Bernini's incomparable *Rape of Proserpine, Apollo and Daphne, David Drawing the Sling,* and his *Aeneas and Anchises,* on which, at 15 years of age, he assisted his father. Upstairs in Casina Borghese, the art gallery features important works by Caravaggio. There are also paintings by Cranach, Lotto, Correggio, and a *Deposition* by Rubens, painted when the artist was in Rome, in 1605. The great treasure of the collection is Titian's *Sacred and Profane Love.*

Outside again, facing the Casina Borghese, take the street running to your left for the entrance to Rome's Zoological Gardens, rather run-down, but interesting enough.

Here is a good spot to end your jaunt, or, having rested, you can continue by the Viale Giulia to the Palazzo delle Belle Arti, housing the city's National Gallery of Modern Art, and—farther ahead—the National Museum of Villa Giulia.

Here, housed in a former papal residence set amid lovely gardens, is one of the greatest Etruscan collections in the world. This is the place to study that strange, half-understood civilization, for here are not only magnificent terracotta statues, but also jewelry, household implements, sarcophagi—a whole way of life laid out. Gold, silver and ivory, cups and dishes, dancers and satyrs, cosmetic boxes, figures smiling that eternally mysterious smile . . . it is an embarrassment of riches, among which the most precious gems are the *Apollo of Veio* and the *Sarcophagus of the Sposi.* When you have had your fill of such lovely treasures indoors, you can step out into the lovely nymphaeum, with its cool recesses, lily pools and fern-softened fountains.

Toward Vatican City

5 This walk takes you out of Piazza Venezia, along Via del Plebiscito and into Largo Argentina, where, in the middle, there are the ruins of four temples built during the early Republican era of Rome. Farther along, beyond the baroque churches of the Gesù and Sant' Andrea della Valle, beyond colonnaded Palazzo Massimo on the right and the Barocco Museum on the left, turn left into Via dei Baullari, which leads straight into Campo dei Fiori (Field of Flowers). This was once the site of public executions; now one of Rome's busiest, most popular daily markets is held here, where you'll see mountains of fruits and vegetables, some familiar, some exotic. You can poke about the stalls and carts, or listen to the bickering and shrieking of both sellers and buyers as they haggle over everything from artificial flowers to to[...] snails.

Just off Campo dei Fiori are two masterpieces of Renaissa[...]tecture—Palazzo Farnese, now the French Embassy, and Pala[...] Cancelleria, which is Vatican property. Continue along Corso V[...]o Emanuele, past the beautiful baroque façades of Chiesa Nuova and the Oratorio next door, to reach Vittorio Emanuele Bridge, which stretches across the Tiber.

Cross the bridge. This is the old Borgo region of Rome that surrounds Vatican City, once populated by high dignitaries of the storied 15th-century Papal Court who lived in fabulous luxury until their time passed with the end of the Papal State in 1870.

Look to the right along the river. That enormous round structure, with its cylindrical tower and tremendously thick walls, is the Borgo's outstanding historical monument today—Castel Sant'Angelo (St. Angel Castle). Emperor Hadrian started building it about the year 135 and Antoninus Pius finished it six years later. According to legend, the castle got its name during the plague of 590, when Pope Gregory the Great, passing by in a Catholic religious procession, saw an angel sheathing his sword appear atop the stone ramparts to predict, correctly, the plague's immediate end. Here it was, too, that Pope Clement VII took refuge in 1527 from the German mercenaries of Charles V. Outside, in a cleared enclosure around the castle, the city has laid out a public park; it provides an excellent opportunity to make a circuit of the castle, thus permitting you to judge for yourself just how immense the architectural work is and why, during the Middle Ages, it became the citadel of Rome. Inside, for a small fee, you may wander through most of Castel Sant'Angelo's many rooms, over its courtyards, and along the high-ceilinged hallways; don't fail to mount the stairs leading to the upper terrace, where, alongside the huge statue of St. Michael, you have all Rome at your feet. As a sidelight, you might be interested in spending a few minutes' worth of time exploring the Passetto Vaticano, a 15th-century arcaded passageway inside the castle grounds that links the old fortress directly with the Vatican.

In fact, moving away from Castel Sant'Angelo along Via della Conciliazione, you can see the gigantic dome of St. Peter's Basilica straight ahead. A number of 15th-century palaces line both sides of Via della Conciliazione, the most important of them being Palazzo Torlonia, built in 1496, and the 450-year-old Palazzo dei Penitenzieri.

The Pantheon and Piazza Colonna

6 For the last of these hikes around Rome, you might try one that calls for somewhat stronger arches, a good sense of direction, and the will to finish what you start.

Leave Piazza Venezia along Via del Corso and turn left into Via Lata to Piazza del Collegio Romano, with the entrance to the Doria-Pamphili Art Gallery on one side and the Collegio Romano, Rome's most famous Jesuit school for three centuries until 1870, on the other. On the far side of this square, walk along Via Piè di Marmo to reach Piazza della Minerva, which takes its name from the fact that the Church of Santa Maria sopra Minerva (St. Mary Over Minerva) you see there is actually built upon the site of an ancient temple dedicated to the goddess Minerva.

Move out of this square, centered by a sculptured elephant carrying on its back a little Egyptian obelisk dating to the 6th century BC, into Piazza del Pantheon, where stands one of Rome's most perfect, best preserved—and perhaps least appreciated—monuments of antiquity. The Pantheon was built in 27 BC by Augustus' general Agrippa, restored by Hadrian and dedicated to the seven planetary divinities. The interior of the Pantheon is infinitely more spectacular than the first glance from the square outside suggests. You pass through the original ancient bronze door into a truly majestic room studded with shrines and niches holding statues of the Virgin, the tombs of Italy's first and second kings, and the tomb of Raphael. Above, a dome 142 feet high rises mightily, diminishing in size until it becomes a mere circular opening at the top from which the Pantheon receives its only interior light.

Continue now through Via Giustiniani to the national church of France, San Luigi dei Francesi (St. Louis of the French), and follow the street just to the left of it into Corso del Rinascimento, from which point you can pass along to Piazza Navona, Rome's most typical 17th-century square. Here there are three magnificent fountains. On one side of the square, you find the Fountain of the Moors, by Bernini; on the other side is a bubbling work of art entitled Neptune Wrestling With a Marine Monster, Sea Horses and Nereids, done by Della Bitta and Zappalà. But the fountain in the center—the Fountain of the Rivers, another Bernini work and generally considered his best—is far and away the most impressive of Piazza Navona's three, with a huge basin supporting an enormous cave-pierced rock squared off by four statues of rivers representing the four corners of the world.

From Piazza Navona, make your way to Via del Corso, turn left and follow it to Piazza Colonna, with its fountain and huge column erected about 193 in honor of Emperor Marcus Aurelius. This column, made from 28 separate blocks, rises some 97 feet off the ground and is topped by a statue of St. Paul, placed there by personal order of Sixtus V. Like other ancient monuments, it's threatened by air pollution and its marvelous spirals of reliefs have had to be covered to prevent further deterioration.

Two palaces—Palazzo Wedekind and Palazzo Chigi—line Piazza Colonna. Formerly, Palazzo Chigi housed Italy's Ministry of Foreign

Affairs, which has now moved to new quarters in the Palazzo Farnesina at the foot of Monte Mario. Just beyond these fine old palaces is Palazzo Montecitorio, on its own piazza; this has been the home of the Italian Chamber of Deputies since 1871.

Back on Via del Corso again, cross over its intersection with Via del Tritone and ramble along this busy shopping street until it ends in Piazza del Popolo, Rome's largest square and traditional gathering place for mass meetings at election time. This spacious square, an oval formed by two great semi-circles, has in its center four fountains with lions and, among them, an obelisk telling all about Rameses II, one of Egypt's top men in the 13th century BC. Pass through the Porta del Popolo, an arched gateway 400 years old, and move off down Via Flaminia along the border of Rome's fashionable Parioli section to Ponte Milvio, an ancient bridge across the Tiber River which is best known for the battle fought there between Constantine and Maxentius.

Cross the Ponte Milvio, turn left along Lungotevere Maresciallo Diaz, and you can't miss on your right the grandiose Foro Italico—once much better known among Romans as the Forum of Mussolini, who built it in 1932. The place has one huge stadium after another and grounds for every sport imaginable. Like his many other efforts to make Rome a showplace of the Western world, Mussolini brandished hammer and chisel with a desire to make the new forum a Hollywood "colossal"—something in which he certainly succeeded. Take a look at the Fountain of the Spheres, or the 56-foot-high obelisk, or any one of the 60-odd statues carved in mammoth proportions which, by the way, were only fairly recently clothed in fig leaves.

Foro Italico was the headquarters of the 1960 summer Olympics; its Olympic stadium saw many records broken during the games, as did the Olympic swimming and diving pools. Its attractive tennis stadium houses international play. Nearby, a café offers an oasis of colorful umbrellas and comfortable lounge chairs under the tall pines.

The Churches of Rome

Three of Rome's 450 churches, though outside of the Vatican City, nevertheless enjoy extraterritorial status and are considered part of it. They constitute, with the Basilica of St. Peter's itself, the great quartet of Roman churches; the other three are St. John Lateran, St. Mary Major and St. Paul's Outside the Walls. (For the Vatican itself, see separate chapter following *Rome.*) Each one of these four churches must be visited by Catholic pilgrims during a Holy Year in order to gain the special indulgence remitting temporal punishment for sins.

St. John Lateran (San Giovanni in Laterano), in Piazza di Porta San Giovanni, and not St. Peter's, is the Cathedral of Rome. Adjoining it, the Lateran Palace, first of the papal residences, now houses a number of rare works within its Lateran Museum; and opposite the palace itself is a building within which you find the famed Scala Santa (Holy Stairs), traditionally the original stairway from Pontius Pilate's palace ascended by Jesus Christ on the day of His passion. The steps are worn smooth from centuries of pilgrims who climbed them on hands and knees.

St. Mary Major (Santa Maria Maggiore) stands in Piazza di Santa Maria Maggiore, where, legend says, the Blessed Virgin appeared once to Pope Liberius one night in August 352 and ordered him to build a church on the spot where he would find a heavy, unseasonal snowfall the next day. Five doors lead into the church, with the door on the extreme left being the Holy Door; inside, more priceless art works.

St. Paul's Outside the Walls (San Paolo Fuori le Mura), on Via Ostiense, is Rome's largest church after St. Peter's. Originally constructed during the time of Emperor Constantine over the tomb of St. Paul, it was destroyed by fire in 1823 and reconstructed 31 years later. Its 12th-century cloister is the richest in Rome. Along Via Ostiense, about 25 minutes on foot, you come to the Abbey of Three Fountains, where, they say, St. Paul was beheaded. The story goes that the three fountains bubbled forth at precisely the three places where St. Paul's head bounced as it fell.

Other churches include Santa Croce in Gerusalemme (Holy Cross in Jerusalem), built by St. Helena to shelter relics of the True Cross on a square of the same name—near which a Roman palace and circus almost as large as the Circus Maximus were discovered in 1959; and San Pietro in Vincoli (St. Peter in Chains), on Via San Francesco di Paola, which was reportedly founded in 442 by Empress Eudoxia to hold the chains (still there on view) that bound St. Peter in his captivity; inside is Michelangelo's masterpiece, which he described as the "tragedy of my life", the famous Moses in the unfinished tomb of Julius II. Santa Maria in Trastevere, in the city's old quarter of that name near Viale di Trastevere, was the first church in the Eternal City—and possibly for all Christianity—to be dedicated to the cult of the Holy Virgin.

One of the most fascinating churches in Rome is that of San Clemente, Via di San Giovanni Laterano. In fact, it is really three churches. Visible today from the street is an 11th-century basilica. Excavations begun in 1857 revealed a 4th-century basilica built into an even earlier palace, assumed to be that of St. Clement the Pope (90–99 AD). Beneath this is a Mithraic shrine, almost a cave, from the time of Nero.

Still another church—Santa Maria degli Angeli (St. Mary of the Angels)—rates a visit, which must include the general area in which it stands. Two long blocks from Rome's central railway station, the street opens into Piazza della Repubblica (formerly dell' Esedra), with a Fountain of the Naiads in its center that should be seen first at night, under the play of some rather remarkable lighting effects. Just beyond the fountain are the rambling remains of the Baths of Diocletian, once the largest in Rome, which were erected by Diocletian and Maximian in the year 306. St. Mary of the Angels came into being here when Pius V, deciding that some use must be made of these ruins, commissioned Michelangelo to build one part of them into a church and the remainder into a convent. The great artist adapted his new church from the largest hall of the ancient baths, giving St. Mary of the Angels a huge nave 298 feet long and 89 feet wide. To the right of the church, the National Museum, a treasurehouse of ancient sculptures, now occupies the space once used as the convent built by Michelangelo on his Papal commission.

The Jesuit Church, where the founder of the Jesuit Order, Ignatius Loyola, is buried, stands on Piazza del Gesù, off Via del Plebiscito. This rather grandiose baroque church was built at the end of the 16th century by Vignola.

Random Tours

Striking out in Rome on a pot-luck trip through the city is admittedly an adventure that may find you missing any number of the "sights" upon which the average travel agency concentrates with its organized bus and rail tours. It may also find you pleasantly ignorant of all directions, poking here and there with a trailblazer's instinct into nooks and crannies Mr. Average Visitor is certain to pass over. Naturally, any attempt to see the Eternal City along these lines has its disadvantages; but if you're willing and able to absorb a little of the bad with as much of the good, there's no better way on record of understanding one of the world's most fabulous cities and its people.

Trastevere

Take the Trastevere region, for example, one of Rome's most Roman sections, honeycombed with narrow passageways, studded with great squares like Piazza Santa Maria and Piazza Cosimato. Along with the area around Piazza Navona and Campo dei Fiori, this is a stronghold of the city's true Romans—addressed fondly as "the Romans of Rome" —a choice collection of typically uninhibited, cynical, sharp-eyed shopkeepers, horse-and-carriage drivers, masons, carpenters and artisans who ply the same trades as their fathers did generations ago. In recent years a much more heterogeneous colony—composed of foreigners, rich and poor—has moved into the quarter.

Monti

Or the Monti region. Rome's oldest and largest, stretching across three (Quirinale, Viminale, Celio) of Rome's fabled seven hills, tracing its history back into the days of the old Roman Empire, and looking down its nose upon Middle-Aged Trastevere across the Tiber River. In this sprawling area once lived such notables as Horace, Virgil, Ovid; and here, too, there once thrived the city's most evil quarter, between Colle Oppio and the Basilica of Santa Maria Maggiore, where now the changing times have left the district with little more than memories of its wicked past. Rome's largest food and fruit market functions in the Monti region at Piazza Vittorio, and the streets retain their ancient names: Via Cimara, Via del Boschetto, Via Panisperna, Via Urbana.

Created by the Popes, the older regions, like Trastevere and Monti, feature many of Rome's convents, churches, Catholic welfare institutions. Sacred images appear on almost all of their street corners; dark, crowded alleys predominate, overhung with tiny balconies crowding each other for space. It's not at all unusual to stumble upon some doorway dating back to Imperial Rome, or some unnamed fountain, some tablet dedicated when the city was still young.

The Catacombs

Other important sites that should be visited if time permits are the catacombs—the underground cemeteries of the early Christians. The term "catacomb" has a purely casual origin. The underground cemetery of San Sebastiano, which was the only one known in the Middle Ages, was located on the Via Appia near the Circus of Maxentius, where the road dips down into a hollow. This spot was known to the Romans as "catacumbas" (Greek for "near the hollow"), and they used the same name to refer to the cemetery that had existed there since the 2nd century. Later the term came to be applied to all the underground cemeteries that were discovered in Rome.

The catacombs aren't Rome's oldest cemeteries. Even before Christianity reached Rome, those who couldn't afford a fine funeral monument along one of the consular roads were either cremated or buried in necropolises outside the city gates, since an imperial law prohibited burial inside the city. During the 1st and 2nd centuries AD, Rome's Christians were buried together with their pagan brothers in these common burial grounds. As the recent excavations have revealed, St. Peter himself was buried in a necropolis on the slopes of the Vatican hill; St. Paul was laid to rest in a large burial ground along the Via Ostiense, on the left bank of the Tiber.

Since the Christians had adopted the Hebrew tradition of burying their dead, they soon required more space for this purpose and began to create cemeteries of their own, where they might also perform their religious rites. With the approval of the city fathers, they dug their cemeteries in the hilly slopes that lined the consular roads, usually in tufa formations on private land that the owner—often a Christian himself—granted for this purpose. As the need for space became more pressing, the cemeteries were extended in a series of galleries, often on two or more levels.

The general belief that the catacombs served as secret hiding places for the Christians during the persecutions that broke out with unnerving frequency during the early centuries of the Christian era is romantic, but unrealistic. Rome's early Christians may have been a little odd in their ways, but they weren't stupid. And the last place in the world they would seek refuge would be in the blind tunnels of the catacombs, whose location was common knowledge in Rome.

Between persecutions, the bodies of the martyrs who had fallen under the sword or had met death by fire, water or wild beasts were interred in the catacombs. Their remains were given a place of honor, and their presence conferred great prestige on the underground cemetery in which they lay, attracting a stream of devout pilgrims. When this came about, the catacomb was embellished with frescos and existing galleries and staircases were enlarged to accommodate the faithful. Sometimes older parts of the cemetery were dug out to make room for underground basilicas, where services in honor of the patron martyrs were held.

You'll see a great variety of tombs and decorations in the catacombs. They range from a simple rectangular niche in the wall, which was closed by bricks or marble slabs, to a sarcophagus carved out of the wall and surmounted by a niche, or a freestanding sarcophagus in terracotta, marble or lead. Off some of the galleries you'll see rooms lined with niches, where members of the same family or community were buried. Later, when space became scarce, tombs were dug in the pavement.

Each tomb was distinguished by a particular mark or sign so that the deceased's relatives could recognize it among the rows of niches. Sometimes this was an object, such as a coin or an oil lamp, sometimes an inscription. The wealthier families called in painters to decorate their tombs with frescos and ordered sculptured sarcophagi from the artisans' workshops. It's interesting to note that since the earliest catacombs date to about 150 AD, some of the frescos representing Christ or Saints Peter and Paul may well bear a fairly true resemblance to their living models. It's likely that the artists based their representations on eyewitness descriptions handed down from father to son. There is a fresco depicting St. Paul in the Catacomb of Domitilla that is generally recognized as a true likeness.

After 313, when Constantine's edict put an end to the persecutions and granted full privileges to the Christians, the construction of the catacombs flourished; they were increasingly frequented by those who wished to honor their own dead and to venerate the tombs of the early martyrs. But during the Dark Ages, when invading armies made a habit of showing up at all the gates of Rome, devastating the country-side and plundering from the living and the dead, the popes prudently decreed that the remains of the martyrs be removed from the catacombs and newly laid to rest in the relative security of Rome's churches.

With the loss of these holy relics and the appearance of the first cemeteries within the city walls, the catacombs fell into disuse, were abandoned and forgotten, with the sole exception of the catacomb of San Sebastiano on the Via Appia.

Then, in 1578, with the barbarian menace long past, some laborers digging a trench along the Via Salaria suddenly felt the ground give way beneath them and found themselves at the entrance to a series of galleries. Once they had conquered their surprise and terror, they ventured into the dark tunnels where, by the light of improvised torches, they discovered an eerie world of niches, frescos and inscriptions.

The news flashed through Rome; speculations on this strange underground city touched the limits of fantasy. But soon the learned men of the time identified these ancient remains as part of the long-forgotten catacombs, a city of the dead. The discovery spurred enthusiastic interest in further explorations, which have continued since then, slowly and painstakingly uncovering a total of almost 40 underground cemeteries encircling Rome.

Visiting the Catacombs

Of the 40 catacombs, eight are open to the public. Visitors are always accompanied by a guide, usually one of the friars charged with custody of the catacombs. The catacombs usually close at noon, reopen at 2.30 or 3. Hours vary in winter and summer.

On the Via Appia Antica.

Catacomb of San Callisto (Via Appia Antica 110; Closed Wednesday), one of the most important; many 3rd-century popes are buried here.

Catacomb of San Sebastiano (Via Appia Antica 132; Closed Thursday), originally a pagan burial ground that had previously served as a rock quarry.

On the Via Ardeatina.

Catacomb of Domitilla (Via delle Sette Chiese 282; Closed Tuesday), one of the oldest and most extensive of Rome's catacombs; named for Flavia Domitilla, who belonged to the imperial family and who donated the land for the cemetery.

On the Via Aurella.

Catacomb of San Pancrazio (under the Basilica of San Pancrazio on the Janiculum; apply to the Carmelite Fathers at the basilica), rather bare and only partly preserved.

On the Via Latina.

Catacombs "Ad decimum" (at Villa Senni; apply to the Brasilian Fathers at the monastery of Grottaferrata), on two levels, with a few frescos.

On the Via Nomentana.

Catacombs of Sant' Agnese (Via Nomentana 349, entrance in the left nave of the basilica; Open every day), on three levels.

On the Via Salaria Nuova.

Catacombs of Priscilla (Via Salaria Nuova 430; apply to the Benedictine Sisters at the Casa di Priscilla; Open every day), dates to the 2nd century and extends on two levels, with many well-preserved frescos.

On the Via Tiburtina.

Catacombs of Ciriaca or *of San Lorenzo* (Via Ciriaca, at the Basilica of San Lorenzo at Verano; apply to the sacristy at the right of the basilica), originally included a section on ground level, now occupied by the Verano cemetery.

The Ghetto

Wander into that gloomy part of old Rome bounded by Piazza Campitelli and Lungotevere Cenci, into the city's least visited but most interesting area—the ancient Jewish ghetto. Roman Jews, forming a large part of the city's poorest, most hard-working community, live along narrow, dark alleys stagnant with the poverty of centuries. The same ghetto you see today existed even in the time of Emperor Titus, who brought so many Jews out of Palestine to Rome. Within this cramped area, until 1847, all Jews of Rome were confined under a rigid, night-long curfew; at the little church opposite Quattro Capi Bridge, they were forced to attend sermons converting them to Catholicism at their own expense. Now, of course, with the old gates of the ghetto torn down and social barriers removed, Rome's Jews live where they please, and the ghetto today is a ghetto only in name.

Tip: While in the ghetto, try a delicacy all Rome has long since adopted as its own. It's the luscious *carciofi alla giudia* (artichokes Jewish style), each fried whole in olive oil until the leaves curl like golden petals. The month when artichokes are at their best is April. Swallowed with a bottle of Marino wine, they recognize no culinary equal. Two restaurants in the ghetto that specialize in carciofi alla giudia are *Giggetto* (Via di Portico d'Ottavia) and *Piperno* (Piazza Cenci).

People-Watching

Best locale for Roman types is still the area around Campo dei Fiori, Governo Vecchio, Via Giulia, in Trastevere and Monti, or along the narrow-alleyed, ill-kept Borghi parts of town behind St. Peter's Basilica and the Vatican. Physically, the men are blunt, frankly sincere, hating hypocrisy in any form; they are heavy-set, thick-chested, muscular specimens, taller than the average Italian, with jet-black hair, sharp eyes, stubborn chin, hawk-like nose. The women? Same dark hair, flashing black eyes, beautiful teeth, healthy, vigorous features, big feet and thick legs, but also lovely shoulders and the wide hips of a Hawaiian hula-dancer. Both men and women love an argument, have little delicacy, no self-control, and a passion for gambling.

One thing more: these old Romans are well-behaved towards the average tourist and infinitely more polite than when dealing with their own people. But don't get the mistaken idea that they feel servile or that their motive is merely a selfish design on the coins in your pocket. Almost all of Rome's true Roman Romans—down to the poorest and most uneducated—honestly feel that a visitor is a guest in their home and must be treated accordingly.

Flea Market

Another fascinating sidelight of Roman life is the city's flea market, at Porta Portese in Trastevere. Every Sunday morning Romans and tourists converge on this vast marketplace, which sprawls over several acres of umbrella-shaded stands selling everything from used shoes to "genuine" antiques. The quantity and infinite variety of goods on sale here is amazing; watchword for a prospective buyer is bargain, bargain, and bargain some more. The initial asking price of any item at Porta Portese is at least four times what the vendor will accept contentedly after a great deal of good-natured haggling.

EUR

Another tour leads to EUR, just outside the city on the road to Ostia, begun by Mussolini to house the Universal Exposition of Rome (hence the initials) in 1942. This world's fair never took place because of the war, and EUR was abandoned, to be reappraised in post-war years as an ideal building site for the expanding city. Strikingly modern government ministries and skyscrapers have been shooting up here, in a setting of landscaped gardens, lush parks and broad avenues.

At EUR the architect Nervi built his circular Palazzo dello Sport for the 1960 Olympics. The section is also the site of several museums, among them the Pigorini Museum, with its important prehistoric and ethnological collections. Another, the Museum of Roman Civilization, displays a very impressive plaster model, in scale, of what Rome looked like during its heyday of empire. EUR is easily reached from Rome's center by means of the city's subway—the *Metropolitana*—which runs from the central railway station all the way to the sea at Castelfusano, past Ostia.

PRACTICAL INFORMATION FOR ROME

HOTELS. Rome is a year-round city, well provided with hotels and new ones are abuilding, but it's always a good idea to make a reservation in advance. Rates are high, and in addition there are service charges, taxes, and other supplements. To get a clear picture of your total costs, ask for quotations of the inclusive rate that takes in all these extras. The top-level hotels are excellent.

Palazzo al Velabro is a CIGA apartment-hotel, administered by the Grand Hotel. Rates decrease for prolonged stays.

Some fine hotels are located near the railway station, but the area is becoming increasingly unpleasant.

Deluxe (L)

Ambasciatori, Via Vittorio Veneto 70, a member of Italhotels, is quieter, smaller than the nearby Excelsior, large, bright, beautifully furnished rooms, twin baths for doubles, plush salons.

Bernini, Piazza Barberini 23, an elegant hotel with large rooms done in bright colors or period furnishings, handsome public rooms. Excellent central location.

Eden, Via Ludovisi 49, near Via Veneto, favored by Americans, has good reputation for quiet comfort; superb view from roof bar, relatively low rates.

Excelsior, Via Vittorio Veneto 125, once a Rome tradition for style and service, it has been reported to have fallen from grace lately. A CIGA hotel, it may yet return to top standards.

Grand, Via Vittorio Emanuele Orlando 3, is a big place, like the Excelsior, catering in general to a more conservative, solid clientele. Rome's most elegant and expensive.

Hassler, Piazza Trinità de Monti 6, an Italhotel, combines all the advantages of modernity with an ancient location of remarkable picturesqueness—at the top of the spectacular Spanish Steps.

Hilton, atop Monte Mario, has splendid panoramic views from its gardens and *La Pergola* restaurant-nightclub on the roof terrace. 400 well-furnished rooms and suites, two more restaurants, pool, tennis in 7-acre park.

First Class Superior (1)

Borromini, Via Lisbona in Parioli area, ultra modern, all comforts.

Boston, Via Lombardia 47, quiet location, in Via Veneto area, top floor back rooms have balconies overlooking Borghese Gardens.

Cicerone, Via Cicerone, in Prati, shiny, modern, comfortable, bustles with groups.

De La Ville, Via Sistina 69, shares the Hassler's lovely Spanish Steps neighborhood, pleasant and comfortable, lovely garden, owned by British Grand Metropolitan group.

Delta, Via Labicana, ultra-modern building a stone's throw from the Colosseum; all comforts, including pool.

Flora, Via Vittorio Veneto 191, has rather dated décor but comfortable ample bedrooms, many with view of Villa Borghese, attentive old-world service.

Forum, Via Tor de'Conti 25, quiet, elegant, smallish rooms, all with bath, attractive dining terrace on roof overlooking the Roman Forum.

Holiday Inn, Via Aurelia, like Hilton in splendid isolation on outskirts, regular free minibus service into town. Hollywood-modern decor, big beds in ample rooms with TV, airconditioning, coffee bar, tavern, terrace, pool.

Inghilterra, Via Bocca di Leone, near the Spanish Steps, is highly recommended, attractive, recently renovated, but retaining its old-fashioned charm.

Jolly, Corso d'Italia 1, atop Via Veneto on the edge of Villa Borghese park, strikingly modern, all 200 rooms with bath, airconditioning, TV, refrigerator-bar, most expensive in category, efficient but short on atmosphere.

Londra Cargill, Piazza Sallustio, short walk from Via Veneto, elegantly modern, in renovated palazzo, 105 good-sized airconditioned rooms, attractively furnished, bright grill room restaurant, bar, handsome lounges.

Lord Byron, Via de Notaris, near Villa Borghese, quiet, airconditioned comfort in elegantly renovated villa with delightful rooftop restaurant. Outstanding, it's a *Relais et Chateaux* hotel.

Majestic, Via Vittorio Veneto 50, a well-known older hotel, traditional furnishings, airconditioned dining room.

Massimo d'Azeglio, Via Cavour 18, near railway station, one of the Bettoja group, among the best of its kind in Europe, rooms with bath, airconditioned.

Mediterraneo, Via Cavour 15, caters for groups, bit old-fashioned and dark. Airconditioned, every room with bath, finest of the Bettoja chain. Roof terrace and underground garage. Near station and air terminal.

Parco dei Medici, another Holiday Inn, same amenities, perfect for airport connections, located halfway between city limits and **Fiumicino,** free minibus service to town and airport.

Plaza, Via del Corso 126, older, comfortable, in shopping area.

Palazzo al Velabro, Via del Velabro, suitable for longer stay, apartments with kitchen, etc. Quiet, distinguished, a favorite of film stars and diplomats.

Quirinale, Via Nazionale, adjoining the Opera and close to station. Excellent garden restaurant, well-managed and attractively decorated.

Regina Carlton, Via Vittorio Veneto 72, fine location, 134 soundproofed rooms tastefully decorated in cheerful colors, spacious lounges.

Savoia, Via Ludovisi 15, off Via Veneto, all rooms with bath, freshly decorated, airconditioned.

Visconti Palace, Via Cesi, near Piazza Cavour in Prati, 246 rooms, modern.

Victoria, Via Campania 41. Quite close to the Via Veneto, this older hotel is attractive, pleasant. Room standards vary.

First Class Reasonable (1)

Anglo Americano, Via Quattro Fontane, fine location but small, dark rooms, some street noise.

Atlantico, Via Cavour 23, is very good, a Bettoja hotel.

Cardinal, Via Giulia, in picturesque Old Rome, an elegant, smallish hotel, rooms beautifully furnished and comfortable.

Carriage, Via delle Carrozze, near Piazza del Popolo, all 25 rooms with bath; modern and comfortable.

Giulio Cesare, Via degli Scipioni, in Prati, pleasant and quiet villa-hotel with good atmosphere, garden.

Palatino, Via Cavour, large modern hotel between Forum and station.

Raphael, near Piazza Navona, on Largo Febo, modern, 100 rooms with bath, tasteful furnishings, roof garden, quiet location in Old Rome but central for sightseeing.

Valadier, Via della Fontanella, a block from Piazza del Popolo, small, unpretentious and handy for everything.

Moderate (2)

In the favored Via Veneto quarter: **Internazionale,** garni, Via Sistina 29, very good; **Alexandra,** Via Veneto 18, older, reliable; **Oxford,** Via Buoncompagni 89, modern, rather flashy but comfortable, with tavern; **Tea,** Via Sardegna 149, well-run and well-furnished; **La Residenza,** garni, Via Emilia 22, converted villa in garden setting, warm atmosphere; **Gregoriana,** garni, Via Gregoriana 18, tiny, elegant, few steps from Trinità dei Monti.

In Old Rome and very central, **Bologna,** Via Santa Chiara, is solid, older hotel, as is **Tiziano,** Corso Vittorio 110. **Bolivar,** garni, Via della Cordonata, near Quirinale, recent and quiet. **Quattro Fontane,** garni, Via Quattro Fontane 149, is functional; low rates.

Between Termini station and Piazza Venezia are comfortable **Esperia,** garni, Via Nazionale 22; attractive **Britannia,** garni, Via Napoli, near Opera; **Pace Helvetia,** garni, Via Quattro Novembre 104, with elegant salons, well-furnished rooms, some inexpensive.

Near St. Peter's is **Columbus,** Via della Conciliazione, handsome old palace.

Inexpensive (3)

Dinesen, garni, Via Porta Pinciana 18; 33 immaculate rooms, Nordic atmosphere, a few steps from the Via Veneto. **Croce di Malta,** Via Borgognona 28, in the heart of smart shopping district.

Sistina, Via Sistina 136, near the Spanish Steps; **Galileo,** Via Palestro 33, quiet, but near station; **Capitol,** Via G. Amendola 77, and **Ivanhoe,** Via Ciancaleoni, near Santa Maria Maggiore, good.

Santa Prisca, Largo Gelsomini 25, in quiet but central Aventino area; **Astoria Garden,** Via Varese 8, near station but quiet, with gardens; **Aventino** and **Villa San Pio,** Via Sant'Anselmo in pleasant Aventino area, both excellent value with personalized service.

Pensions (P)

You might try these—**Veneto** (P1), Via Piemonte 63, optional airconditioning.

All (P2)—**Scalinata di Spagna,** well-run, unbeatable location atop Spanish Steps; **Sant'Anselmo,** in Aventine district; **Sicilia,** Via Sicilia 24, at Via Veneto; **Delle Legazione,** Via Barberini 11, very central, terrace restaurant; **Bellavista Milton,** Via Porte Pinciana, quiet street just off Via Veneto, pleasant.

Motels

AGIP, Via Aurelia (S.S.1.) 5 miles from city, 200 rooms, one of the best of its type on the Continent; **Belamotel,** Via Cassia, 10 miles out, 32 units, swimming pool, tennis; **Eurogarden,** Via Salaria, just off autostrada; **Americana,** 10 miles out on Via Aurelia. American-owned and managed, ultra-modern, swimming pool; **Autostella ACI,** at beginning of Via Cristoforo Colombo at EUR, halfway between Rome and the sea, has a pool.

RESTAURANTS. *Expensive (E)* **Al Vicario,** Via del Vicario 31, an elegant place, favored by the smartest of the Romans and by top-ranking politicians from the nearby Chamber of Deputies. There is a garden for summer dining.

Charly's Sauciere, Via San Giovanni in Laterano 268, offers excellent French specialties, drab decor; reserve.

Domus Aurea, at Monte Oppio, an incomparable view, especially at night, when there's dancing, too.

El Toulà, Via della Lupa 29, very smart, features Venetian specialties, exceptional risotto and seafood.

Taverna Giulia, Vicolo dell'Oro, specialties **alla genovese,** prepared and served with loving care; portions are small but their number is more than filling.

Hostaria dell'Orso, Via Monte Brianzo 93, one of Rome's most distinguished restaurants, housed in a lovely old building near the Tiber. The interior is rich without being showy, and there's a piano bar on the ground floor, dancing on the top floor. The cuisine has recently been restored to high standards.

Il Buco, Via Sant'Ignazio 8, has a straightforward atmosphere, serves tempting Tuscan specialties, including succulent steak, in two small dining rooms and a summer terrace.

Le Jardin, in Lord Byron Hotel, Via de Notaris, fairly recent, proposes a select menu in elegant atmosphere.

George's, Via Marche, behind Excelsior, considered passé by some, it's still fine, with summer garden and very dry martinis.

La Fontanella, Largo Fontanella Borghese 86 (reserve ahead, tel. 678.3849), has very smart crowd, good food.

L'Eau Vive, Via Monterone. In an elegantly rarefied atmosphere, French missionary sisters in mufti proudly serve **haute cuisine.** Service is slow but beatific, and celebrities love it.

Le Maschere, in Grand Hotel, formal, sumptuous decor, frescos of **commedia dell'arte** figures.

Le Rallye, in same hotel, posh, decorated with hunting motifs, excellent menu and service. Closed at weekends.

Carmelo, Via della Rosetta, near the Pantheon, is one of Rome's best fish restaurants, serving succulent oysters and some Sicilian specialties, too.

Passetto, Piazza Zanardelli 11, just off Piazza Navona, is a classic, hailed as having the best food in town. Cuisine and service are exceptional, though apt to decline under pressure; decor undistinguished. Closed on Sundays.

Ranieri, Via Mario de' Fiori 26, has more than a century of tradition behind it, and its **art nouveau** decor is holding up better than its cuisine. Closed Sundays.

G.B., Via delle Carceri, just off Via Giulia. Reserve for exquisite dinner in this tiny haven of refined Roman cuisine (tel. 656.9336).

Moderately Expensive (M-E)

As for the Alfredo's in Rome—there are now three, all overrated.

Alfredo's all Augusteo made the name famous in pre-war days—**fettuccine al burro** is the specialty that goes with the name.

Alfredo alla Scrofa, Via della Scrofa 104, who bought the other Alfredo out, is undoubtedly the best Alfredo's.

Alfredo in Trastevere, Piazza di Santa Maria in Trastevere, does have pretty good food however.

At **Pancrazio,** Piazza del Biscione, in the heart of old Rome, pass up the rather ordinary ground-floor rooms and go downstairs to the cool, vaulted rooms that were part of Pompey's theater 2,000 years ago.

Angelino a Tor Margana, Piazza Margana 37, is a fine trattoria on delightful square near Piazza Venezia.

On Piazza del Popolo, **Bolognese** has fine food and a summer terrace.

Apicio, Hotel Metropole, Via Principe Amedeo, near Termini station, offers consistently fine food and wide-ranging menu.

Al Moro, Vicolo delle Bollette, between Trevi Fountain and the Corso, attracts an arty crowd with hearty dishes.

Giarrosto Toscano, Via Campanina 29. Delicious hors d'oeuvres, good wines.

Nino, Via Borgognona, specializes in Tuscan dishes, but everything is good.

Mastrostefano, Piazza Navona, has the best baroque view in Rome from its outdoor tables—if you have to sit inside, it's not worth the expense.

Papa Giovanni ai Sediari, next to Piazza Navona, Roman dishes, candlelight, excellent wines.

Romagnolo, behind Pantheon, is under same management; old-time atmosphere, fine food.

Meo Patacca, in Trastevere, is still *the* place to go for fake color, rather uneven food; Ciceruacchio, opposite, is lots of fun for pizza, music

For real Roman atmosphere, go to **Piperno,** Monte dei Cenci, Ghetto, where the specialty is crisp fried artichokes **alla guidia,** plea door tables.

Sabatini, just off Piazza Santa Maria in Trastevere, is an elegantly informal place with handsome Renaissance decor and superior food.

Nearby, **Corsetti—Il Galeone,** Piazza San Cosimato, has attractive sailing ship decor, varied menu, wine-cellar pizzeria.

Moderate (M)

For some serious eating, **Giovanni,** Via Salandra 1, is one of Rome's best for typical dishes.

The same is true of **La Carbonara,** Campo de'Fiori, where they originated the spaghetti of the same name; and also **Vecchia Roma,** Piazza Campitelli.

The small **Giovanni,** Via Marche 19, two blocks behind the **Excelsior,** is good; and **Giggetto,** Via Portico d'Ottavia, in the Ghetto; true Roman food.

Antico Falcone, on Via Trionfale, 10 minutes by bus or taxi from the center, is in 14th-century way station, try their **rigatoni.**

On Piazza San Giovanni in Laterano, **Cannavota** has reasonable Roman specialties.

Near the Colosseum, the rustic **Gladiatore** and **Angelino ai Fori,** Largo Ricci, are fine.

Colline Emiliane, Via degli Avignonesi, near Piazza Barberini, haven of homemade pastas.

Barroccio, Via Pastini, near Pantheon, and **Fagiolaro,** opposite, have rustic decor, and hearty food.

Romolo, Via di Porta Settimiana 8, is a Trastevere favorite for historic atmosphere, tasty food.

On Via Ripetta, **Buca di Ripetta** is tiny and always crowded.

Outside town, pleasant on a summer afternoon or evening are the **Fattoria** on Via Flaminia, where the **antipasto** table is staggering; and **Hostaria L'Archeologia,** on Via Appia Antica, with a rustic garden. **Cecilia Metella** and **Quo Vadis,** are also on Via Appia, and both have outdoor dining in summer.

For light snacks, try a **rosticceria** or **tavola calda. Il Delfino,** Corso Vittorio Emanuele, is the best-known. **Piccadilly,** Via Barberini, reliable stand-up or sit-down food, pub, pizzeria. **Rugantino,** Trastevere, for snacks, pizza.

Such American standbys as hamburgers and hearty breakfasts are available at the **Piccadilly,** and **Wimpy** on Via Barberini, **California** on Via Bissolati.

The best **pizzerias** are—**Capricciosa,** Largo Lombardi; **La Sacrestia,** Via del Seminario; and **Ricci,** Via Genova.

At the Vatican Museums, the reasonable Vatican **cafeteria,** open only during museum hours, or on the nearby Via Germanico, **Trattoria Toscana.**

Cafés

The once-famous Via Veneto cafes—**Doney** and **Café de Paris**—have lost their luster in recent years. Now the best places for sidewalk-sitting are Piazza Navona, where **Tre Scalini** offers a grandstand view of the action and where you should try their chocolate ice-cream **tartufo,** and Piazza del Popolo, forever a favorite with artists and literati, who flock to **Rosati.** Just down Via Condotti from Piazza di Spagna, the sedate **Caffè Greco** has old-world atmosphere.

The cafés in front of the Pantheon and on Via Frattina have been decreed "in", *the* places to be seen on a pleasant evening. If it's ice cream you're after, don't miss **Giolitti,** Via Uffizi del Vicario, or **Fassi,** at Piazza Fiume.

Foreign Cooking

If you like the easygoing atmosphere of the **birrerie** (beer halls), try the **Wiener Bierhaus.** Via della Croce, or **San Marco,** Via Mazzarino 8. And for other foreign restaurants, try **La Giada,** Via IV Novembre, for the best Chinese cooking in Rome (it can be very expensive). Even more expensive is **Nihonbashi,** Via Torino, considered by some as one of the best Japanese restaurants this side of Tokyo. **Le Lapin Blond** (E), Via Visconti 39 in Prati, has won acclaim for excellent French cuisine.

Da Amato, Via Garibaldi, in Trastevere, serves Spanish dishes; **Csarda,** Via Magnanapoli, is Hungarian, complete with violins; and **Taverna Greca,** Via Sardegna, is unreservedly Greek; all are (M-E).

CINEMA. You'll find English-language films in their original versions at the **Pasquino** cinema, Vicolo della Paglia, just off Santa Maria in Trastevere.

MUSIC. *(See also Special Events).* Rome is a good city for music of all sorts, especially concerts, which are often held in its lovely old churches. In July, open-air performances begin—the Opera House stages magnificent productions in the ancient Baths of Caracalla, and the Academy of St. Cecilia organizes a series of outdoor concerts. This same Academy of St. Cecilia conducts weekly indoor concerts in winter, while others are sponsored by the Rome Philharmonic Academy and a number of Rome's better theaters.

Opera. Fans will find the Opera House at Via del Viminale—the opera season runs from November through May, with summer season at Caracalla.

Jazz. You can catch a session at **Music Inn,** Largo Fiorentini; **Centro Jazz St. Louis,** Via del Cardello; **Mississippi Jazz Club,** Borgo Angelico; and **Folkstudio,** Via Sacchi, in Trastevere.

CHURCHES. Confessions are heard in English, as well as most other languages, in **St. Peter's.** Other **Roman Catholic** churches with services in English are—**San Silvestro,** Piazza di San Silvestro; **Santa Susanna,** Piazza di San Bernardo; and **San Patrizio,** on the corner of Via Piemonte and Via Buoncompagni.

Of the **Protestant** churches, best known are—**St. Paul's Within the Walls,** Via Napoli 58, American Episcopal; **All Saint's Church,** Via del Babuino 153, Church of England; **Methodist Episcopal Church,** Via Firenze 28, American; and **Baptist Church,** Piazza San Lorenzo in Lucina.

There is an orthodox **synagogue** at Via San Francesco Desales 5.

MUSEUMS. Rome's museums are outshone by the magnificence of those within the Vatican City. Nevertheless, try some of these outstanding collections—see **Monumenti, Biblioteche, Musei** page in **Pagine Gialle,** the yellow pages volume of phone directory, for all monument and museum hours—most are open daily. National museums are usually free on Sundays, when consequently they are very crowded. Most are closed Mondays.

Academy of St. Luke, Piazza dell' Accademia di San Luca 77.

Barracco Museum, Corso Vittorio Emanuele 168. Egyptian and Greek sculpture.

Borghese Gallery and Museum (Villa Borghese), entrance from Via Pinciana.

Capitoline and Conservatori Museums, Piazza del Campidoglio.

Castel Sant' Angelo and Museums, Ponte Sant' Angelo.

Colonna Gallery, Via della Pilotta 17.

Doria Gallery, Piazza Collegio Romano.

Keats-Shelley Memorial House, Piazza di Spagna 26.

Lateran Palace Museum, Piazza San Giovanni in Laterano.

Museum of Rome (including Communal Gallery of Modern Art), Piazza San Pantaleo. Palazzo Braschi.

National Gallery (Barberini Palace), Via Quattro Fontane 13.

National Gallery of Antique Art, Via della Lungara 10.

National Gallery of Modern Art, Valle Giulia.

National Museum of Roman Antiquities, in Baths of Diocletian at Piazza della Republica.

Palazzo della Farnesina, Via della Lungara 230. Print collection.

Palazzo Venezia, Piazza Venezia, decorative arts.

Pigorini Museum of Ethnography and Pre-History, Piazza Marconi, EUR.

Rospigliosi Pallavicini Gallery, Via XXIV Maggio 45. Apply to management for admission.

Spada Gallery, Piazza Capo di Ferro 13. Paintings by Caravaggio, Titian, Rubens.

Vatican Museum, see chapter.

National Museum of Folk Art, Piazza Marconi, EUR. Exhibits of costumes and popular traditions.

Villa Giulia National Museum, Piazzale Villa Giulia 9. Outstanding Etruscan collections.

NIGHTLIFE. Cabalà, atop **Hostaria dell'Orso,** is easily Rome's most elegant spot for dancing.

Much More, Via Luciani, in Paroli, a disco that's "in" with the young crowd.

Bella Blu, Via Luciani, attracts the smart set for disco dancing.

Hippopotamus, Via Romagnosi, a swinging disco near the Piazza del Popolo.

At **La Biblioteca,** Largo del Teatro Valle, you can eat well and can dance.

Usually the last to close for the night, **Club 84,** Via Emilia 84, is always lively.

Jackie-O, Via Buoncompagni, gets a smart crowd and the doorman will turn you away if he doesn't like the look of you. Grill room (E) for supper.

Scarabocchio, Piazza dei Ponziani, in Trastevere, is an elegant little disco.

Once-swinging **Piper Club,** Via Tagliamento, has gone over to dinner and floor shows, with dancing in between.

Paradise, Via Mario dei Fiori, is a big plush place with floor show.

Just for drinks, **Harry's Bar,** atop Via Veneto, the **Blue Bar** of Hostaria dell'Orso, Via dei Soldati 25, and **Little Bar,** Via Gregoriana 54, are piano bars, or try any of the big hotel bars.

READING MATTER. The best stores in Rome for English books are the **Lion Bookshop,** 181 Via del Babuino and the **Anglo-American Bookshop,** 57 Via della Vite. You'll find lots of English paperbacks at the big newsstands on Via Veneto and at the **Economy Book Center,** 29 Piazza di Spagna. A newish bookshop, **The Open Door,** Via della Lungaretta 25, deals in both recent and second-hand books.

SHOPPING. Shopping in Rome is a thrilling experience even when your pocketbook reduces you to mere window gazing. Every store in the Via Condotti-Via Sistina area offers an abundance of taste, color and design seldom encountered elsewhere. In fashion, home decoration and jewelry, the Italians are fast becoming the world's master craftsmen, though for a price.

Note that Roman shops close on Saturday afternoon June-September, Monday mornings other months.

Via Condotti is the most fashionable street in Rome, and some enthusiasts have even called it the most elegant street in Europe. The shops you will find there offer the very finest, and they are expensive accordingly. Equally high-priced are the stores along Via Vittorio Veneto, the street made famous by its outdoor cafés. Piazza di Spagna, Via Sistina, Via del Corso, Via Frattina, Via Borgognona and Via del Tritone all offer good shopping.

For old books and prints browse through the bookstalls of Piazza Borghese.

Along with Via Babuino, Via Coronari is *the* street for antiques.

A fine selection of ceramics from the major (and some minor) ceramic-producing centers in Italy is on display at the American-owned *Bella Copia* shop, Via Coronari 8.

Pharmacies. And for the ever-necessary drugstore or chemist's shop, with English-speaking attendants and a wide range of British and American products, try the pharmacy, 417 Via del Corso; *Evans,* 63 Piazza di Spagna; *George Baker,* opposite the Grand Hotel; or the pharmacy next to Hotel Excelsior on the Via Veneto.

SPECIAL EVENTS. January 17th sees the Feast of St. Anthony, when priests at the Church of St. Eusebius bless work animals and pets, as their owners parade them past the front door. January 21st, is the day to celebrate St. Agnes at the church of the same name outside Rome's walls, where two snowy-white lambs are blessed, presented to the Pope, then sheared to provide wool for the palliums of patriarchs and archbishops.

On Palm Sunday, the Pope blesses palms sent to him by the Bresca family under a privilege granted four centuries ago. The Holy Week follows, with its processions, sacred rites in the Colosseum and Catacombs, streets filled with the influx of foreigners, always greatest at Easter.

May sees an international harpsichord festival in the city.

During the summer, the Forum is the scene of a Sound and Light spectacle given in three languages (including English).

A lively festa is held in the quarter around St. John Lateran on the eve of June 24th, when tons of stewed snails and roast suckling pig are devoured by the Romans in honor of San Giovanni.

From 16–31 July, one of Rome's oldest quarters, Trastevere, celebrates the Feast of Madonna del Carmine, with its own peculiar Festa di Noiantri—Festival of We Others—a roaring, rousing mixture of worship and carnival, managing to involve the entire city.

In September, there is an organ festival.

One of Europe's most picturesque fairs starts at Piazza Navona early in December and culminates on Epiphany Eve, when hordes of last-minute shoppers descend on the square to buy gifts for their children and welcome the Befana, a benevolent old witch, Italian equivalent of Santa Claus.

SPORTS. One of Rome's most prestigious sporting events is the international **horse show** held in May in the shade of Villa Borghese's majestic pines. There's **flat racing** at the Capanelle track starting in February for a two-month season, resuming in May for another two months and again in September through November. **Trotting races** take place at the Villa Glori track in February, June through September, and then in November.

The city has **golf courses** at Acqua Santa, off the Via Appia Nuova and at Olgiata, 12 miles out on the Via Cassia. **Tennis tournaments** are held at the tennis stadium of Foro Italico, large sports complex conceived by Mussolini and further developed for the 1960 Olympics. **Soccer games** draw crowds to the Olympic Stadium, also at Foro Italico, from September to June.

TRANSPORT. Taxis are now relatively expensive, as rates have gone up recently; there are extra charges for night service (10 P.M.-7 A.M.), for each piece of luggage, for cabs called by phone. All charges are listed on an official rate card (with English translation), displayed in the cab. Taxis don't cruise in Rome: you have to find the nearest stand (there are many, strategically located), or call your cab by phone.

Horse cabs are becoming part of Rome's past, as they can't keep pace with modern traffic. Still, they're ideal for a ride through Villa Borghese. Make terms with your driver before you start out.

Buses provide a cheap way to see the town, but avoid the rush hours. Buy an ATAC bus directory at the booth in front of Termini Station, where you can also buy tickets for an inexpensive sightseeing tour run by the city bus company.

Metro. The new *Metropolitana* runs in two directions from Termini Station, is fast and comfortable. The original line runs out to EUR district and the beach at Ostia. Another line runs to the Ostia Antica excavations.

Car Hire. *Avis* has offices at Piazza Esquilino 1, and Via Sardegna 38A; *Hertz* at Via Sallustiana 28; and *Maggiore* at Via Po 8 and Piazza della Repubblica 57. Many car rental agencies have booths at the airport; information at hotels.

USEFUL ADDRESSES. Embassies: *American,* Via Vittorio Veneto 119; *British,* Via XX Settembre 80A; *Canadian,* Via G. B. De Rossi; *Irish,* Via del Pozzetto 105; *Australian,* Via Alessandria 215.

Emergency medical phone number: 113.

American Express, Piazza di Spagna 38; *CIT,* Piazza Repubblica 64, railway station, Piazza Cola di Rienzo; *Automobile Club of Italy,* Via Marsala 8.

THE VATICAN CITY

Upon This Rock

The Lateran Treaty of February 11, 1929, signed by the Holy See and the Mussolini Government, established the Vatican City as an independent and completely sovereign state, to which diplomatic representatives are accredited from many nations.

Vatican City covers 108 acres sprawled over a hill west of the Tiber River, separated by a thick, high wall from the city of Rome that surrounds it. Inside that wall, about 1,000 people live as residents, printing their own newspaper, issuing their own stamps, striking their own money. The little state has its own flag, print shops, glass-making factory, observatory, model railway station, post office, power plant, even barracks for its armed forces. Radio Vatican, a powerful transmitting station, broadcasts in 14 different languages twice daily to six different continents. In Rome itself, outside the Vatican wall, 13 buildings enjoy extraterritorial rights; many other Papal properties within the Eternal City are exempt from taxes.

The sovereign of this little state is Pope John Paul II, till his election after a two-day conclave on October 16 1978, Cardinal Karol Wojtyla, Archbishop of Cracow. The 264th Pope of the Roman Catholic Church, the first non-Italian for 456 years and the first Pole ever, possesses full legislative, judicial, executive and military powers within his own state and is authorized to live in or move through Italian territory whenever he so desires. Pope John Paul, at 58 one of the youngest Supreme Pontiffs, heads the Roman Catholic Church and its followers throughout the world, being assisted in this capacity by the College of Cardinals, which functions somewhat like a kind of senate. The Cardinals, currently 111, are nominated and chosen by the Pope and, upon his death, elect a successor, as the world witnessed in the dramatic sequence of events that led to the election of John Paul II.

The Pope reigns over 700 million Catholics, for whom a papal audience is the highlight of a trip to Rome. The intricate rules of etiquette that were once characteristic of the Vatican have been greatly relaxed by recent Popes, especially under Pope Paul VI, and much of the Apostolic Palace has been redecorated in severely simple style. Even the Swiss Guards, whose colorful uniforms were designed by Michelangelo, appear in full costume only on special occasions.

A tour through this smallest state in the world should start with St. Peter's and might include a visit to the gardens. Save the museums and the Sistine Chapel for another day.

Formalities for Entry

To enter the territory of Vatican City, sovereign state though it is, none. When you step into the great square before St. Peter's you are on Vatican territory. You can enter the basilica and the museums without showing any papers.

At the Information Office (see map), you can book two days in advance for guided tours through the gardens; one tour includes the gardens and the Sistine Chapel, the other takes in the gardens and St. Peter's.

Exploring the Vatican City

Catholic or non-Catholic, you just don't leave without paying a visit to San Pietro in Vaticano, better known the world over as the Basilica of St. Peter, or simply St. Peter's. It is often known also as St. Peter's Cathedral, but this is incorrect. St. Peter's is not a cathedral, which means the church of a bishop. The Pope is also the Bishop of Rome,

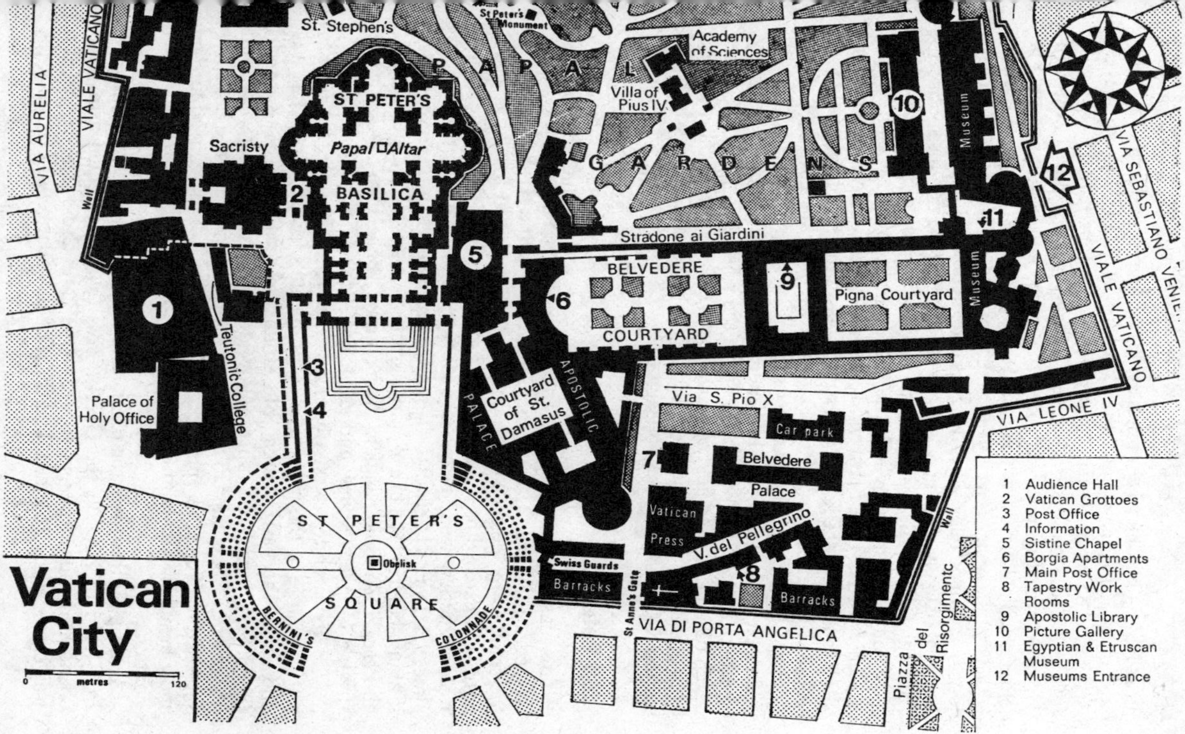
Vatican City
0 metres 120
VIA AURELIA
VIALE VATICANO
Wall
St. Stephen's
St Peter's Monument
Academy of Sciences
Villa of Pius IV
PAPAL GARDENS
Sacristy
ST PETER'S
Papal Altar
BASILICA
Stradone ai Giardini
Museum
BELVEDERE COURTYARD
Pigna Courtyard
Teutonic College
Palace of Holy Office
Courtyard of St. Damasus
APOSTOLIC PALACE
Via S. Pio X
VIA LEONE IV
VIALE VATICANO
VIA SEBASTIANO VENIER
Car park
Belvedere Palace
Vatican Press
V. del Pellegrino
Swiss Guards Barracks
St Anne's Gate
Barracks
VIA DI PORTA ANGELICA
Piazza del Risorgimento
ST PETER'S SQUARE
Obelisk
BERNINI'S COLONNADE
1 Audience Hall
2 Vatican Grottoes
3 Post Office
4 Information
5 Sistine Chapel
6 Borgia Apartments
7 Main Post Office
8 Tapestry Work Rooms
9 Apostolic Library
10 Picture Gallery
11 Egyptian & Etruscan Museum
12 Museums Entrance

but as Bishop his official church is St. John Lateran; and so it is St. John Lateran which is technically the Cathedral of Rome, though it is so overshadowed by St. Peter's that no one ever calls it that.

To get there from Piazza Venezia, follow Via del Plebiscito through Corso Vittorio Emanuele, crossing the bridge and continuing up Via della Conciliazione. Now you can see St. Peter's at the end of the Via della Conciliazione. Every year at Easter and on the New Year the Pope is shown on television giving his benediction, the *urbi et orbi,* from the papal balcony. And now you are standing on the famous spot itself. You may feel a little disappointed at first, but wait a moment—wait until you see someone climb the steps and go into the church and suddenly the contrast between his size and the enormous proportions of the square and the façade will strike you. Both are optical illusions—beautiful imperfections created by the extraordinary harmony of the volumes. Now enter the Piazza itself.

This enormous square, which Bernini built in 11 years, is generally considered one of the most beautiful in the world. An immense space, which has at one time held as many as 400,000 people, it's surrounded by a quadruple colonnade topped with a balustrade upon which are mounted some 140 statues of saints.

St. Peter's

This masterpiece of Italian Renaissance art had its beginnings about the year 319, when the Emperor Constantine built a basilica here over the tomb of St. Peter. The original basilica remained for 1,100 years, until it threatened to collapse towards the middle of the 15th century. Reconstruction work began in 1452—but it was not until 1626, or almost 200 years later, that the masterpiece stood complete as you see it today. No less than five of Italy's greatest artists—Bramante, Raphael, Peruzzi, Antonio Sangallo the Younger, Michelangelo—died while striving to erect the new and greater St. Peter's.

The first architect was Alberti and then came Bramante, who was put in charge of the plans. It was Bramante's Greek Cross that was chosen as the basic design. But Bramante died in 1514. Raphael, Guiliano, Sangallo and others followed him in the growing work until 1547, when Michelangelo took charge of the work at the age of 72. He returned to Bramante's plan, but did not live to see its realization. The most beautiful cupola in the world was completed by Della Porta and Fontana.

During all this time, the plans were significantly altered. Under the iron hand of Paul V, the Greek Cross (with four equal arms) was abandoned and the plans returned to the Latin Cross. The eastern arm was extended by 165 feet. The effect of this change was to block the view of the wonderful cupola. And now we come to the optica sions. Maderno and Bernini went to work on the square and the umns. They faked their construction: Maderno flattened the façade free the cupola, and Bernini made the square appear to be a circle, though its real form is elliptical.

In the center of the square (1,115 by 787 feet) notice the 85-foot-high obelisk brought back by Caligula from Egypt in 38 A.D. Then look at the colonnade from the vantage points marked by marble disks between it and the two fountains that are the focuses of the ellipse. There appears to be a single file of columns instead of the actual triple file of 284 columns and 88 pillars. By compressing the field of vision, Bernini enabled Maderno to keep his façade wider than it is high. It took 174 years of work before the great plan was completed. Twenty Popes reigned before the cupola and square were done.

Now enter St. Peter's itself. Five openings lead into the Portico; another five doors open into the basilica's interior, of which the last one on your right is the Porta Santa (Holy Door), officially opened only at the beginning of each Holy Year; the last one being in 1975. Once inside the basilica, pause a moment to judge its approximate size. It is difficult at first to realize just how huge it is. But walk over to the tiny cherubs clinging to a column at the left, place your arm across the sole of a cherub's foot and you will discover that it is as long as the distance from your fingers to your elbow. It is because all the proportions of this giant building are in such perfect harmony that its vast scale escapes you at first. Each of the bronze inscriptions in the marble floor indicates the approximate ground-floor dimensions of the principal Christian churches in the world; the relative length of each is measured from St. Peter's great portals, and the longest falls far short of the apse of the basilica. That should give you a vague idea of the vastness of the place, along with figures that show St. Peter's covers about 18,100 square yards, runs 212 yards in length, carries a dome which rises 435 feet and stands 138 feet across its base.

Four tremendous arches support the nave on either side, with niches in the piers holding the statues of men who founded most of Catholicism's numerous religious orders. At the far end is the High Altar, where only the Pope may celebrate mass; the Papal Altar nearby, turned towards the church's entrance, stands above the crypt where the relics of St. Peter are kept. Stroll slowly up and down the right and left aisles and transepts, noting well many of the world's finest works of art in mosaic, in sculpture, and designed with stucco. Names like Bernini, Michelangelo, Canova and Della Porta, are commonplace here.

Notice the elegant bronze throne at the back of the choir. It is Bernini's work (1656) and it covers a wooden and ivory chair that Saint Peter himself is said to have used. However, this throne cannot be older

KEY TO PLAN OF ST. PETER'S

1 Vestibule-The Ship, restored *Giotto* mosaics
2 Central Door-reliefs *Filarete c 1440*
3 Holy Door
4 Emperor Constantine-*Bernini*
5 Charlemagne-*Comacchini 1725*
6 Chapel of the Pietà; Pietà-*Michelangelo 1500*
7 Christina of Sweden monument-*Fontana*
8 Chapel of St. Sebastian-mosaic after *Domenichino;* under altar. Innocent XI tomb; on left Pius XII monument; on right, Pius XI monument
9 Chapel of the Holy Sacrament-gate des by *Borromini;* Ciborium-*Bernini;* The Trinity-*da Cortona*
10 Gregorian Chapel-*Michelangelo*
11 Altar of St. Girolamo-mosaic after *Domenichino*
12 Clemens XIII monument-*Canova c 1790*
13 Clement X monument; opp. in floor, tombs of Sixtus IV and Julius II
14 Urban VIII monument-*Bernini*
15 Gloria-*Bernini,* with St. Peter's Chair
16 Paul III monument-*della Porta*
17 Alexander VIII monument
18 Chapel of the Column: right, altar and tomb St. Leo the Great; over, Meeting of Attila and Leo-*Algardi c 1648;* opp., ancient Image of the Virgin; under altar, tombs of Leos II, III and IV; in center Leo XII
19 Alexander VII monument-*Bernini*
20 St. Joseph's Altar; right, Altar of St. Thomas the Disbeliever; left, Altar of St. Peter's Crucifixion
21 Pius V monument-*Tenerani;* below, entrance to Sacristy
22 Altar of the Lie
23 Altar of the Transfiguration-mosaic after *Raphael*
24 Clementine Chapel-*della Porta;* under altar, St. Gregory the Great tomb; left, Pius VII monument-*Thorwaldsen*
25 Leo XII monument-*Algardi c 1648;* opp., Innocent XI monument-*Monnot*
26 Chapel of the Choir
27 Pius X monument; opp., Innocent VIII monument-*Pollaiolo 1498*
28 Chapel of the Presentation; under altar, Pius X tomb; right, John XXIII monument-*Greco;* left, Benedict XV monument-*Canonica 1928*
29 Clementina Sobieski monument, opp., Pillar of the Last Stuarts-*Canova c 1820*
30 Chapel of the Baptist, Font
31 St. Peter-prov. uncertain
32 St. Longinus-*Bernini*
33 St. Helen-*Bolgi*
34 The Veronica-*Mochi*
35 St. Andrew-*Duquesnov*
36 Bronze Baldachino-*Bernini*
37 Confession-*Maderno;* Pius VI statue-*Canova*
38 1977 Bronze Door

ST. PETER'S

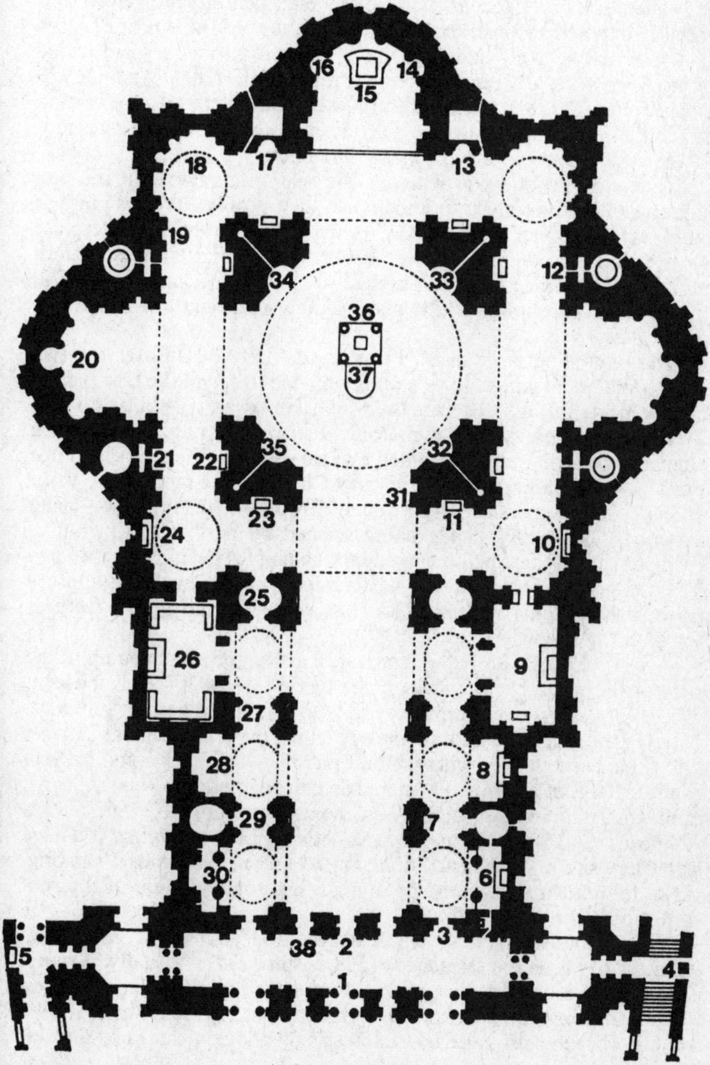
16
14
15
17
13
18
19
34
33
12
36
37
20
35
32
21
22
23
31
11
24
10
25
26
9
27
28
8
29
7
30
6
38
2
3
5
1
4

than medieval times. We come to these contradictions often. Passion far outweighs authenticity when it is a question of sacred objects. Can the remains of a "vigorous man" discovered beneath St. Peter's and recently exposed in the *tropaion* really be those of the Apostle? Does the head—most likely added in the 5th century, to a very old statue of St. Peter—actually reproduce the features of the Saint? Again it will be passion rather than reasonable argument. But see how the adoration of a million lips has completely worn down the bronze on the right foot of the statue, fixed to a pillar near the choir.

But could you question whether Michelangelo's *Pietà* (in the first side chapel on the right), sculpted when he was only 22, owes more to man's art than to an artist's faith? As we contemplate this masterpiece we are able to understand a little better that art and faith sometimes partake of the same impulse. (Tragically damaged by a maniac in 1972, the statue has been masterfully restored and screened off with shatterproof glass.)

What you should see in St. Peter's and what you will see are two entirely different things, for it's quite possible to spend the best part of a week inside without covering the whole. However, try not to miss the Treasury, wherein, among numerous other priceless objects, there's a chalice of pure platinum presented by Spain's King Charles III to Pope Pius VI and an ancient cloak they say Charlemagne might have worn at his coronation. Also, the Vatican Grottos—old and new—being actually a large cryptlike expanse formed by part of the primitive basilica that was here before anyone thought of St. Peter's as it is today. The new grotto contains a real masterpiece of early Christian sculpture in the sarcophagus of Junius Bassius, while the old grotto features tombs of numerous Popes.

Save the dome of St. Peter's for last. An elevator takes you up to the roof of the great basilica, where the dome towers 308 feet above it. There you leave the elevator and walk up a series of narrow stairways between the inner and outer domes, reaching the first gallery at 160 feet and the second at 235, with the best possible view at this point of the dome's 404-foot interior. From a little balcony here the view of Rome is magnificent, and still higher—in the copper ball itself, which holds no more than 16 persons at one time—it's even better. Unless you have good legs and a stout heart, don't try to make this climb; it's taxing. Also, the return trip takes you along a high open section of the roof with no balcony or hand rail.

Coming out of St. Peter's, the building on your left—the Vatican Palace—has been the residence of Popes since 1377. Actually, it represents a collection of individual buildings covering more than 13 acres, with an estimated (no one has ever bothered to count them!) 1,400 rooms, chapels and galleries. Interestingly enough, the Pope and his

Young visitors to Rome cool off by the Trevi Fountain, of "Three Coins" fame

The interior of Pisa Cathedral, with Pisano's pulpit and Galileo's lamp

The rich carving and banded stonework of Siena Cathedral

The end of a day's work in the Valmalenco, Lombardy

papal court occupy an infinitesimal part of the Vatican Palace; the rest is occupied by huge libraries, museums, and rooms filled with art and relics.

The Vatican Museums

One word of warning here. The Vatican museums contain the largest collection of antiquities in the world today. You could live in them for a year without becoming really familiar with what each one holds. Don't try to do St. Peter's and the Vatican museums in the same trip. It's a long, long walk around the walls of Vatican City to the museum entrance on Viale Vaticano (see map). In tourist season the Vatican runs a bus service between St. Peter's and the museum entrance.

If you're heading directly for the museums, there are city buses that stop at—or near—the entrance.

The museums, including the Sistine Chapel, are open from 9–2 except from July through September, when they stay open until 5 P.M. They close on religious holidays and on Sundays, except the last Sunday in the month, when they're free but terribly crowded. You'll find them crowded most of the time anyway, but visitors are routed through in one-way traffic. There are a snack bar and reasonably priced cafeteria for lunch, a post office and a bank.

Among the incredible artistic riches contained in the small area of Vatican City, probably the most important single spectacle is the Sistine Chapel. But you'll begin your visit at the *Pio-Clementino Museum,* a remarkable collection of antique sculptures, among them some of the best-known statues in the world, the *Laocoon,* the *Belvedere Torso,* and the *Apollo Belvedere.* Next come the *Chiaramonti Museum,* also given over to Greek and Roman sculpture, and the *Etruscan* and *Egyptian Museums,* which contain important remains of those two ancient civilizations.

You'll pass through several smaller galleries to reach the various groups of apartments that are second only to the Sistine Chapel in greatness: first are the *Raphael Rooms,* four rooms with frescos mainly by Raphael; Raphael's *Loggia,* which follows, was designed by Bramante and Raphael; *Pope Nicholas V's Chapel* is decorated with frescos by Fra Angelico; the *Borgia Apartment* (downstairs from the Raphael Rooms) consists of several rooms painted by Pinturicchio.

The *Collection of Modern Religious Art* that follows was opened in 1973 and soundly criticized by some. But it's only a way-station on the route to the magnificent *Sistine Chapel.* The ceilings and upper parts of the walls were frescoed by Michelangelo, and his enormous *Last Judgement* covers the entire wall behind the altar. He painted his own face on the wrinkled human skin in the hand of St. Bartholomew. The painting has been somewhat obscured by smoke from altar candles over the centuries. Other painters whose work decorates the wall of the Sistine Chapel are Botticelli, Ghirlandaio, Perugino and Pinturicchio. Take along a good pair of binoculars for a better look at the ceiling.

After this highlight you'll pass through some of the exhibition halls of the *Vatican Library,* one of the finest in the world, with 7,000 incunabula, precious illuminated manuscripts and an unimaginable wealth of bibliographic treasures. At this point you can stop for refreshments at the cafeteria before you go on to the *Picture Gallery,* one of the world's greatest collections of painting. It contains work by, among others, Giotto, Filippo Lippi, Fra Angelico, Leonardo da Vinci, Bellini, Titian, Caravaggio and, in particular, Raphael, represented here by many of his finest canvases, especially the *Foligno Madonna* and the recently restored *Transfiguration.* The *Gregoriano Profano Museum* displays more Greek and Roman sculptures, and the *Pio Cristiano Museum* has Early Christian and medieval art. You reach the exit via the *Ethnological Museum* and *Historical Museum,* with its carriages and armor.

Papal Audiences

Apply in advance at the Information Office for tickets to a public audience; these are generally held every Wednesday morning in architect Nervi's soaring audience hall. The entrance is to the left of the colonnade (see map). On Sunday at noon the Pope appears at his third-floor study window to address the crowd gathering in St. Peter's Square. Many kneel as he imparts the papal blessing and there's much applause and cheering as he waves goodbye. At this writing, after the shocking attempt on the Pope's life in May 1981, it's not known what, if any, restrictions may go into effect regarding his public appearances.

During the summer the Pope may retire to the cooler summer palace at Castel Gandolfo, where he continues to receive pilgrims on Wednesdays and Sundays at informal open-air audiences.

For public audiences, when any number of persons up to 10,000 might be on hand, dress conservatively, modestly, without worrying about details. However, for the *baciamano* (ring-kissing) audience, at which the Pope greets from 20 to 40 persons at a time, it's mandatory for men to wear dark suits and women to dress in black or white, with long sleeves, high neck and black veil for the head. Invitations to these audiences are extended only on special recommendation from local ecclesiastical authorities.

Religious Articles

Any number of stores around the Vatican and the major churches sell religious articles. On Via della Conciliazione are *Savelli* at no. 61, *Stocker* at 47, and *Moreschi* at 65. On Borgo Pio, to the right of St. Peter's as you face it, are *Simoncini* at no. 74 and *Comandini* at 64. You'll also find shops in the Pantheon area. Many of the shops that sell religious articles procure papal blessings on request. The *Lelli Garey* shop, Piazza Farnese 104, is particularly well stocked and helpful.

At the Vatican Post Office, next to the Information Office, you can buy Vatican-issued stamps and coins.

THE ENVIRONS OF ROME

Lazio and the Beaches

Rome's immediate environs, skirting the city from seaside to hilltop, are easily reached within an hour by road, rail or even streetcar runs. Beyond these lie other towns and villages worth visiting, still in the Lazio (Latium) region, but far enough from Rome so that it is necessary to reckon your side trips in terms of an hour-and-a-half or more. When touring Rome for a reasonable length of time, try breaking up your itinerary by mixing trips to the environs with sightseeing in the city itself; it helps prevent a certain monotonous continuity. For the outlying sidelights in Lazio, of course, specially planned junkets will be mandatory, with some possibility that you can visit two or three places on one excursion. All major tourist agencies in Rome feature bus tours through both environs and the Lazio area.

Weather Matters

If you can avoid it, don't visit in the hottest months. July and August are taxing in this region, September is almost as bad, and June sometimes is. April and May are the best months. October follows. This holds for the whole region, for though there are beaches which allow some relief from the heat, they serve chiefly as one-day or weekend escapes from the heat of Rome, so far as the tourist is concerned. Romans may settle down for long stays at the nearby beaches, but most foreigners, if they have a waterside vacation in mind, are more apt to try the Ligurian or southern coasts. Likewise, while there are skiing centers in Lazio, they are used chiefly for quick trips from Rome, usually for the weekend, and there is no skiing season which would attract visitors from any distance; they would prefer the Alps.

Road Reports

No city is better endowed with roads for the motorist than Rome; that is for one who wants to avoid it! An almost complete by-pass circle has four autostrade and two Express Highways radiating from it, besides some eight lesser roads. A new 40-mile Expressway, parallel to Via Aurelia, links the capital with its port at Civitavecchia and provides a fast road to such beach resorts as Santa Severa and Santa Marinella. A side road leads to the archeological site at Cerveteri and beyond Civitavecchia is that of Tarquinia.

Exploring Lazio

One of the simplest itineraries is a half-day ramble along the Appian Way, ancient Rome's *Queen of the Roads,* which was built more than 2,000 years ago by Appius Claudius and once ran all the way south to Brindisi. It's literally walled with ancient monuments and old Roman tombs dotted over a countryside where pines and green cypresses predominate. Here are the Catacombs of St. Calixtus and St. Sebastian, subterranean chambers where the early Christians buried their dead, venerated their martyrs and performed their rites. Along the road, a half mile out from Rome, the little Church of Domine Quo Vadis? marks the place where, according to tradition, Jesus met St. Peter fleeing from Rome and answered his query of "*Domine, quo vadis?*" ("Lord, where goest thou?") with "*Venio iterum crucifigi*" ("I go to be crucified again"), whereupon St. Peter returned to the Eternal City. And not far from this church, on Via Ardeatina, 335 Italian patriots massacred by the Germans in March 1944, lie at rest in the Fosse

Ardeatine (Ardeatine Caves). For its last four miles, past the huge, fortress-like Tomb of Cecilia Metella, the Appian Way winds through a series of ruins, sepulchral monuments and scenery that has inspired artists since man first took to the paintbrush. Patches of the original ancient pavement are evident along this last stretch if you look hard enough.

Another short trek (a mere half-hour out of Rome by car or train) brings you to Ostia, ancient and modern. The old place, once Rome's military and commercial port, is actually a whole city excavated from ruins. You can wander along its unburied streets all day if that sort of thing interests you. Modern Ostia is quite something else, being what Coney Island is to New York or what Brighton is to London. Avoid it on Sundays, when all Rome flocks to the pine groves and sandy beaches there.

Ostia Antica and the Roman Castles

One of the most interesting excavations in Italy is this "Old Town" on the outskirts of modern Ostia. Because it has been uncovered fairly recently, the elements have not yet caused much erosion and it is therefore possible to see a great deal in the remains of what ancient Roman life must have been like. Among the highlights of Ostia Antica are: the Piazzale delle Corporazioni, around which were the offices of the empire-binding commercial firms dealing in furs, grain and ships; the Forum and its Capitol, a 2nd-century building; the Caserma dei Vigili, a barracks for firemen (note the mosaic showing the sacrifice of a bull), the House of Paintings and the Museum itself. There are plenty of baths, residences and even warehouses to fascinate the visitor who has the time to take it all in.

A bit farther from Rome—but you can still see all of them on a fast trip in one day—are the Castelli Romani (Roman Castles), actually the name given to several towns and villages grouped along the slopes of the volcanic Alban Hills. Don't miss these: Albano, Frascati, Marino, Genzano, Castel Gandolfo, Rocca di Papa, Nemi, Grottaferrata, Ariccia. However, if you haven't time for all of them, take particular pains to see Albano, bordering an exquisite little lake lined with characteristic inns and eating places. And Frascati, for its typically Italian villas (Aldobrandini, Torlonia, Lancellotti, Falconieri, Mondragone; not all are open to the public), each of them architectural masterpieces and the last word in how to plan a garden. Rocca di Papa (Castle of the Pope) is the highest of the Roman castles, its stone buildings set like an angled beehive in sheer cliffs, with a good road now open for cars all the way to the top of Monte Cavo and the best possible view of Rome and its surrounding plain.

Try to see Genzano, at its best just after Easter, on the Sunday after *Corpus Domini,* when villagers stage the *Infiorata,* passing in religious procession along an entire street carpeted with hundreds of thousands of flowers arranged in intricate designs. Include, too, Castel Gandolfo, if only to sip coffee before the Swiss Guards at the entrance to the summer residence of the Popes. A new cableway runs from Castel Gandolfo down to the lakeshore, affording a good view of Lake Albano and Monte Cavo. Frascati, Marino and Grottaferrata, incidentally, are shrines for those who love good wine.

Tivoli, Fiuggi and Subiaco

Add to your trip around the Roman Castle towns one other—Tivoli. It deserves a good paragraph in itself. Once a holiday resort for wealthy patricians during the heyday of the Roman Empire, this village reached its peak about the time of Emperor Hadrian, in the 1st century. Waterfalls, ancient temples, grottos, splendid villas, a garden that's strictly out of a fairy tale—the place has everything. Wander through Hadrian's Villa, for example, which was once the largest and richest of the entire Roman world. In those ruins, the travel-wise Emperor had reproduced some of the most famous *objets d'art* in the Empire at that time. Excavations begun centuries ago and continuing today still yield the works he coveted, with 261 masterpieces of art recovered to date.

Another "must" in the area is to feast your tired eyes upon the Villa d'Este, built in 1550 for Cardinal Ippolito d'Este, with particular emphasis on the surrounding gardens. They are indescribably beautiful, descending in a series of terraces, showered by hundreds of fountains, luxuriant with shrubbery, trees and creeping vines that border dozens of footpaths and lanes. Its fountains, by the way, represent the most intricate gravity waterpipe system in the world. During the summer months, Hadrian's Villa, the Villa d'Este park and the Tivoli waterfalls are floodlit on certain evenings of the week.

About 50 miles outside Rome by train or car, you find two other towns worth a visit—Fiuggi and Subiaco—each in a different direction. The rail or highway to Fiuggi passes through Palestrina, a village so old its origin is lost in antiquity, where another terrific plastering by wartime bombardments failed to obliterate one of the finest examples of Roman mosaic in the country. The bombings, in fact, uncovered the built-over ruins of one of the vastest temples of antiquity—dedicated to Fortuna—a great part of which has now been excavated. In and near Palestrina's Palazzo Barberini can be seen some of the temple complex's original structures, along with the priceless art works found there. Fiuggi itself is Italy's top spa for kidney troubles, and some of the cures effected there have been little short of miraculous. Additionally, the hotels, mineral water establishments, golf courses, plus swimming pools, etc., help make it Lazio's leading mountain (2,037 feet) resort through the summer months. In the other direction, the road runs from Rome to Subiaco, where St. Benedict founded the Benedictine Order in the 6th century. He established his monks in 12 separate small monasteries, of which only one remains. The town is quiet, calm, giving the impression that no more appropriate place could have been chosen as a birthplace of Western monasticism.

South of Rome, along Lazio's beaches and through its mountains, Allied forces fought some of their bitterest battles of World War II. Take in just two such memorials to a recent past before you leave the area: Cassino and Anzio-Nettuno.

Cassino and Anzio

It's two hours by car or train from Rome to Cassino, and either way is scenic enough to warrant the trip. A side trip will reward you, if, instead of taking the modern motorway, you divert to Alatri, where there are architectural remains from as far back as the 4th century BC. The huge walls of the acropolis provide a good position for looking at the views over the Frosinone Valley.

On the direct route from Rome, by rail or roadway, you'll curve through heavily wooded hills and climb into the mountains, up, up—and suddenly: Cassino. A new Cassino, built slightly south of the original town which during the war died a death no less violent than ancient Pompeii. In three months—February to May 1944—the old town crumbled to charred bits under Allied air and artillery bombardments that ousted German troops from their Gustav Line stronghold street by street, house by flaming house. High above, like a gaunt beacon on a hill, St. Benedict's 1,400-year-old Abbey of Monte Cassino was also destroyed by tragic mistake, for it housed monks and refugees and not the German observation post, as believed.

The monastery has risen again and stands in its former glory. The restoration of the art works, its mosaics and frescos, the marbles of its chapels, has been done by the Benedictine monks who are also lovingly repairing the remaining manuscripts from the fabulous library. The Italian Government has spent large sums on restoring the building but by far the greater cost has been borne by the Benedictine Order.

Today, reconstruction has been completed in the Cassino area and the new village is a collection of sturdy white houses. But memories still lie thick over the soil. Memories like signs reading "Polish Cemetery" and "British Military Cemetery, 1 mile." Or the monument erected to Polish troopers who fell there. Stand alone for a moment, quietly, among the shadowy ruins, and listen to the sudden thunder that booms like cannon-fire through the valley on mid-summer days. It's an experience no other monument in all Italy can possibly offer—the passing of something great and sad and heroic in our own time.

So it is with Anzio-Nettuno, too, but on a somewhat lesser scale. The one-time twin seaside resorts of Rome's ancients, only 36 miles from the city itself, have recovered more swiftly than Cassino. Summer vacationists now fill the uninterrupted chain of bright, gay new villas between Anzio and Nettuno, two miles away. Only the sprawling cemeteries carry a thought of Cassino: the British Military Cemetery, two miles north on the road to Aprillia, and the American Military Cemetery in Nettuno, where 7,400 officers and men lie at rest.

Nearby is the rocky island of Ponza, a delightful spot, with beaches, fields, a couple of villages and some excellent underwater fishing.

The Etruscan Heartland

The new highway Rome-Civitavecchia (40 miles) brings you in less than an hour to the north coast, where there are both beach resorts—Santa Severa and Santa Marinella—and the Etruscan cities of Cerveteri and Tarquinia.

You might stop first at Santa Severa itself because recent excavations have uncovered the ruins of an Etruscan temple. (You can see these relics in the Etruscan Museum of the Villa Giulia in Rome.)

Cerveteri and Tarquinia

Cerveteri, to the southeast of Santa Severa, has many more Etruscan remains. The city was a large and important port as well as an artistic center of the Etruscans from the 7th to the 6th centuries BC. Its site is to the east of modern Cerveteri, but the Necropolis—the City of the Dead—is more to the north. The Necropolis is very important for our understanding of the Etruscans, whose civilization vanished so quickly. These tombs give us an idea of what it might have been like: they are modeled on Etruscan houses and are decorated with stuccoes representing everyday objects. If we continue to Tarquinia, located slightly north of Civitavecchia, we will have even better glimpses into Etruscan life. Tarquinia was already an important port during the reign of the Emperor Trajan and it was here that Stendhal wrote *The Charterhouse of Parma*. Before reaching Tarquinia, if you make a detour of less than 9 miles you will come upon Bracciano, a charming little town lying on the shores of Lake Bracciano and overlooked by the great Orsini castle. Visit this 15th-century castle and enjoy the sight of its interestingly decorated rooms and the splendid views from the battlements. (Open only certain days of the week; check with the Rome EPT).

Let us continue to track the Etruscans in Tarquinia. As we said, this was an important cultural and trading center and the city gave Rome her first two kings, Tarquin the Ancient and Tarquin the Proud. Today Tarquinia is a romantic little town high on a rocky plateau, overlooking the sea and the plain. It has narrow medieval streets, a Romanesque church, Santa Maria, dating from the 12th century, and the early Renaissance Vitelleschi Palace. Inside the latter there is a National Museum that contains a large collection of Etruscan relics that provide an excellent introduction to the famous Necropolis.

The Etruscans erected their tombs and tumuli on an isolated hillside 7½ miles from their city. It is easy to see how important the cult of the dead was to their civilization as we approach the Necropolis. Even though all the tombs have not yet been opened, those that you will be able to visit will give you an idea of this ancient people. The paintings that cover the walls of the sepulchers have immortalized their dead for us—we see them, cup held to lips, dancing, stalking a deer.

Allow at least two hours for a visit to the Necropolis and check on the time that visits start from the National Museum. An official guide leads a motorcade from the museum to the tombs, which are scattered around the countryside. The well-informed guides will explain the significance of tombs, paintings and ornaments dating back into a misty Oriental history.

Once in Tarquinia, by the way, remember that only 45 miles separate Tarquinia from Viterbo by bus or car (no train); so there's no reason why you can't combine both trips in one on a three- or four-day junket.

Best time for Viterbo is 3–4 September when the local people stage their traditional *Festival of Santa Rosa,* one of Italy's most colorful. It's actually a torchlight procession through town, during which the good people carry on their shoulders a 65-foot-high imitation belfry topped by the figure of their patron saint. Naturally, as with most Italian religious festivals, the solemn ceremonies are followed by local celebrations, meaning food, dancing and general merriment.

Viterbo, once a residence of the Popes in 1257, struggled with Rome for this privilege over three centuries, until the Catholic leaders went to Avignon, France. The town slipped badly then, and remained in a state of decline through the centuries. But it's now one of Lazio's favorite side trips for those who appreciate art, being replete with fine churches, palaces and graceful fountains like the Fontana Grande (Great Fountain) in a square of the same name. Undoubtedly, however, as a mere layman, you will get more out of a trip through the town by rambling at random off Via San Pellegrino into the medieval quarter, where it takes no great effort to imagine yourself transplanted back seven centuries into the late 13th.

Thirteen miles northeast of Viterbo is the Villa Orsini at Bomarzo. The Parco dei Mostri, the Monster Park, is a 16th-century fantasy created for Vicino Orsino and crowded with weird animals, heroic figures, eccentric architecture and all the phantasmagoria that the baroque age could conjure from the subconscious. The creator and his creation are the subject of a modern opera by Ginastera.

There are a thousand visual delights in the luxurious green fields flooded with sunlight around Viterbo. The Renaissance cloister of the Madonna della Quercia is right beside the Soriano road. A little farther on, at Bagnaia, you will come to the Renaissance Villa Lante with its beautiful Italian garden. Montefiascone, 10 miles to the north of Viterbo, looks out on Lake Bolsena. Stop to visit the old Romanesque church of Saint Flavian, a masterpiece of sobriety. The body of the gluttonish German prelate, Jean Fugger, lies here.

Caprarola, 11 miles south of Viterbo, is built entirely of black volcanic stone. While you are here, don't miss seeing the 16th-century villa that was the home of Alexander Farnese. It is a curious mixture of architectural styles, blending baroque with classical elegance.

At Civita Castellana, only a short distance farther, there's a cathedral begun in the 11th century and worked on well into the Renaissance. Look and see how the Romanesque style was transformed over the centuries. Keep going until you come to the famous Rocca Fortress where Alexander and Caesar Borgia held their orgies.

Rieti, further east, is set in the hollow of a valley. This lovely town will give you a sense of being in the 13th century as you explore the fortified part, the Episcopal Palace with its Gothic vaults, and the Cathedral that looks out upon the Piazza Cesare Battisti. As you sit in the shade of trees, in the public gardens, let your gaze wander to the Renaissance *loggia* of the Governmental Palace. The atmosphere surrounding the convents of Fonte Colombo and Greccio is even calmer and more serene. St. Francis celebrated the Christmas Mass for the first time flanked by a cow and a donkey at Greccio. There are many beautiful frescos here by Giotto's school to remind you of this simple priest, this *poverello,* and the first manger.

Beaches

Beaches outside Rome run north and south from it, scattered in delightful confusion over miles of open shoreline. Close by, of course, are highly commercialized ones like the city's Lido at Ostia and a popular colony resort at Fregene—both a bit too crowded for personal comfort. Also popular are those scattered from Rome north to Civitavecchia, the nearest being Ladispoli, then Santa Severa and finally Santa Marinella (lively, but little real beach).

The most beautiful stretches of beach in Lazio, curves of white sand backed up by gently climbing cliffs, lie to the south, past the too-crowded twin resorts of Anzio-Nettuno. These up-and-coming vacation towns include Sabaudia and the once chic San Felice Circeo, legendary home of Circe, now an overdeveloped bungalow haven for the Roman middle class. Quaint Terracina has Roman and medieval monuments. There's Salto di Fondi, small, still unspoiled, and picturesque Sperlonga, where fragments of an important ancient statuary group were found in the Grotto of Tiberius. Gaeta and Formia are larger, better equipped with hotels and restaurants where the specialty is, of course, fish cooked in a dozen succulent ways.

PRACTICAL INFORMATION FOR THE ENVIRONS OF ROME

HOTELS AND RESTAURANTS

Anzio. Beach resort with fine soft sand—pretty crowded. **Hotels:** All (2) are—*Dei Cesari,* recent, best, brightly furnished, pool, beach, all resort amenities; *Esperia e Parco,* and *Lido Garda* are older, unpretenious. **Restaurants:** Seafood's the specialty at *Caprera, Garda* and *Gambero,* all at the port, and all moderately priced.

Bagnaia near Viterbo. **Restaurant:** After visiting Villa Lante, lunch at *Checcarello* (M), on the piazza.

Baia Domizia. Modern Summer resort on broad sandy beach. **Hotels:** All (2) are—*Domizia Palace,* all rooms with private bath, airconditioning, excellent service, good restaurant; *Giulivo,* big modern beach hotel, all private baths, functional decor.

Cassino. Celebrated Abbey. **Hotel:** *Silvia Park* (2), fairly recent, unpretentious, swimming pool.

Restaurants: Good lunch stops at *Da Mario* and *Pavone.*

Castel Gandolfo. Pope's summer residence. This Roman Castles town provides facilities for lunching.

Restaurants: All (M) are—*I Cacciatori* is a modest restaurant with veranda overlooking Lake Albano; *Mirador,* with terrace and garden, and *Pagnanelli,* with view, are good.

Civitavecchia. Port of Rome. **Hotels:** *Mediterraneo* (2), on seafront promenade, handy to dock for Sardinia steamers, best in town proper.

At **Baia del Sole** km 69 on Via Aurelia, is the smart *Sunbay Park* (1), beach, tennis, pools, marina.

Restaurants: *Villa dei Principi* (E) overlooks the sea, specializes in fish dishes. *Taverna della Rocca* and *Gobbo,* both (M), are famous for fish soup.

Fiuggi. Important spa. **Hotels:** *Palazzo della Fonte* (L), handsome large building in quiet park, posh though old fashioned decor, pool. Both (1) are—*Vallombrosa e Majestic,* smaller, modern, 80 rooms with bath, swimming pool and gardens. *Silva Splendid,* large, tastefully modern, outdoor pool, good value.

San Giorgio (2), 80 comfortable rooms, all with bath, pleasant and good.

Formia. Beach resort. **Hotels:** Both (1) are—*Miramare,* large remodeled villa and cottage complex on private beach, tennis; *Castello Miramare,* on hillside, tiny, 10 rooms, oasis of peace and quiet.

Fagiano (2), imposing villa type, on beach.

Restaurants: All (M) are—many fine restaurants, *Hotel Miramare; Sirio; Corallo; La Quercia,* for fish; *Ciocàra,* for chicken; and *La Conchiglia,* next to hotel *Ariston.*

Frascati. Roman Castles town.

Restaurants: All (M)—several good restaurants-with-a-view in this city of wine and villas; *Cacciani* and *Spartaco* are best, with attractive dining terraces. Try *Da Blasi* on Piazza del Mercato.

Gaeta. Naval station and beach resort, with a mile-long beach of yellow sand. **Hotels:** At **Localita Serapo,** both (2) are—*Serapo,* on beach front; and *Mirasole.*

At **San Vito,** both (2) are—*Le Rocce,* modern and comfortable, with pool and beach, and *Ninfeo,* in lovely position overlooking sandy beach.

Restaurants: Both (M), simple but good, are—*Tavernetta* and *La Salute.*

Grottaferrata. Roman Castles town. Byzantine abbey.

Restaurants: All (M) are—*Tuscolo* and *Castagneto* are favorite outing spots with Romans; *Squarciarelli* attracts the tourist crowd with fine food; *Lo Spuntino,* Via Cicerone, has rustic decor; genuine Roman cuisine.

La Quercia. Near Viterbo. **Restaurant:** *Aquilante* (E), best in area.

Ostia. The Lido di Roma, Rome's Coney Island or Southend, the easiest beach to reach from the capital, and therefore the best to avoid on hot weekends, when you can hardly see the sand for the bathers. **Restaurants:** Among the best, all to be avoided on Sundays, all (M-E), *Ferrantelli,* Via Claudio, and *Capricciosa,* on beachfront avenue.

Seafood specialties (try the *mazzancolle allo spiedo,* grilled crayfish) at *Guerrino,* on the shore road, or *Il Pescatore,* just off the shore road at the canal.

At **Ostia Antica,** *Monumento,* on the piazza, is recommended, and *Sbarco di Enea* is handy for the excavations.

Palestrina. Temple town. **Restaurants:** All (M)—*Faracchiano, La Pergola* and *Stella Coccia,* all good.

Ponza. Resort on main island of Pontine Islands in Tyrrhenian Sea. **Hotels:** *Chiaia di Luna* (1), 56 rooms with shower in bungalows overlooking island's best beach, pool. *Torre dei Borboni* and *Bellavista* are comfortable hotels with beaches, sea views.

Ponzio Pilato (P1) is delightful small pension with garden, view of port. Book ahead; all except *Bellavista* closed in winter.

Sabaudia. Site of smart Baia d'Argento resort colony. **Hotels:** *Le Dune* (1) is modern white building with balconies, terraces, pool, tennis courts, on large private beach. *L'Aragosta* (P1), smallish pension on beach. Book ahead.

San Felice Circeo. An enchanting small place with a sandy beach, elegant beach resort, summer colony. **Hotels:** *Maga Circe* (1), handsome place, splendidly located, with flowered terraces overlooking sea, pool, private beach.

Both (2) are—*Carillon,* pool, beach facilities, tennis; *Punta Rossa,* quiet, popular with jet set, whitewashed bungalows, swimming pool, beach.

Sperlonga. Picturesque old town on a clifftop overlooking sea, 3 magnificent, vast and almost empty sandy beaches between here and **Gaeta.** You need a car to reach them, however—and a good deal of courage to drive during a Roman weekend. **Hotels:** *Parkhotel Fiorelle, Playa,* both (2), pool, on beach.

Restaurant: *Grotte di Tiberio* (E), outside town on shore road; wonderful view and atmosphere and a fine off-season choice, as it tends to fall apart in summer rush.

Tarquinia. Etruscan treasures. **Hotel:** *Tarconte* (2), low-slung modern hotel, comfortable rooms with fine views, recommended for panoramic position, good service and excellent restaurant.

Restaurants: All (M)—in town, *Solengo* of *Hotel Tarconte,* excellent; *Giudizi,* to the left of the museum, good; at the beach, *Velcamare* serves fish and lamb dishes, garnished with delicious local mushrooms.

Terracina. Medieval town, beach resort, the main beach is of fine deep sand, first flat, then sloping gradually, while there is a second small beach as well. **Hotels:** *L'Approdo* (1), modern, comfortable hotel on sea with beach facilities. *Riva Gaia* (2), unassuming beach hotel with tennis courts.

Restaurants: Both (M-E)—*Da Agostino,* longtime favorite for *zuppa di pesche; Grappolo d'Uva,* for *calamari* and *polipi.*

Tivoli. Restaurants: Don't miss the *Sibilla* (E), an open-air restaurant built on the side of a mountain beside the pillars of the Temple of Vesta, giving it a setting more than 2,000 years old. *Villa Gregoriana* (E) and *Eden Sirene* (M) have the same beautiful view. *Cinque Statue* (M), Via Varo, offers the best food, even on crowded Sundays.

Viterbo. Hotels: Best hotels are on the outskirts. Both (2) are—*Mini Palace,* attractive, low building with balconies, functional bedrooms with bath, fridge, radio, airy modern lounges; *Tuculca,* on Cassia highway, recent, small, motel-style, with tennis, swimming pool.

In town center, *Tuscia* (3), is modest, spotless, adequate.

Restaurants: The best restaurants here, all (M), are—*Antico Angelo, Spacca* and *Scaletta. Zi Giulia,* on the Via Tuscanese, specializes in spit-roasted game and meat.

USEFUL ADDRESSES. Tourist Offices *Anzio:* AAST, Via M. Pallostrini 3–5. *Cassino:* AAST, Via Leopardi. *Civitavecchia:* AAST, Viale Garibaldi 42, and at port; for information on boat services, Societa da Navigazione Tirrennia, Lungomare Garibaldi 42. *Fiuggi:* AAST, Via Gorizia 4. *Formia:* AAST, Via Porto Caposele. *Frascati:* AAST, Piazza G. Marconi 1. *Gaeta:* Piazza Traniella. *Tarquinia:* AAST, Piazza Cavour 1. *Terracina:* AAST, Via Lungolinea 156. *Tivoli:* AAST, Vicolo Missione 3. *Viterbo:* AAST, Piazza Verdi 4A (Palazzo Santoro); EPT, Piazzale dei Caduti 16.

SPECIAL EVENTS. *Castel Gandolfo:* A peach festival in July. *Civitavecchia:* A procession of hooded penitents on Good Friday. *Frascati:* Carnival in February. *Gaeta:* The Feast of the Sea takes place here in August. *Tivoli:* A carnival in February, and the Feast of the Madonna di Quintiliolo on the first Sunday in May. Tivoli observes the Assumption in August, and celebrates the Sagra del Pizzutello in October. *Viterbo:* The noted Festival of Santa Rosa takes place in September. *Genzano:* The *Infiorata* procession of flowers is held on the feast of Corpus Christi in mid-June, check date with Rome EPT. *Marino:* The rousing wine festival is held usually on the first Sunday of October, check date.

SPORTS. *Fiuggi:* There's a good swimming pool here; and the Fiuggi 9-hole golf course. *Ponza:* Underwater fishing is a specialty here, there are contests in July and August. *Tarquinia:* 9-hole golf course, Marina Velca.

FLORENCE

Birthplace of a New World

If all you know of Florence (Firenze) comes from books, from art history, you might be led to imagine the city as a kind of out-size museum, a place apart from contemporary life. If so, the minute you arrive in Florence, this impression will be promptly, even brutally dispelled. If you come by train, you will step off into one of Italy's finest modern buildings, the so-called "new" station, built before the last war, for many years a textbook touchstone for young Italian architects. If you come by automobile, you will arrive along the sweeping new super-highway, the Autostrada del Sole. True enough, one of the exits leads you past the 14th-century Certosa, the handsome Carthusian Monastery, but another exit leads you straight to the Supermarket. The shops in the center of the city, the stands in the open-air markets, still sell traditional Florentine products like straw mats and little tooled leather boxes or book-covers, but in other shops you can buy the latest creaof high fashion or the universal jean machine.

Florence Today

The official Italian guidebook says of Florence: "It enjoys universal fame because of its natural beauty, the aristocratic elegance of its appearance, the richness and high quality of its monuments and art collections . . . " Yes, the beauty and elegance are all there, but, along with them, the foreign visitor must be prepared for the bustle and racket of everyday life, which goes on in Florence as it does in Buffalo or Leeds or anywhere. The bustle and racket are exacerbated by the thousands, literally, of tourists who flood in for a few hours on bus tours from other large Italian cities, take in the main sights and flood out again. There are times when it is virtually impossible to get into the most famous buildings. If you can spare several days to see Florence, it is wise to try to do your visiting of these most celebrated spots at off-peak hours.

Everyone, including the inhabitants of Florence themselves, agrees that there is a special Florentine character, though it is harder to find agreement on just what it is. Ideally, the Florentine is cultivated urbane, witty. But he can also be a *becero,* "a low blackguard, a cad", according to the Cambridge Italian Dictionary, or he can be a *grullo,* "fool or chump". He is most likely to have, as a classic author said, "sharp eyes and a bad tongue". Florentine wit has been famous from the time of Boccaccio at least; along with their Madonnas and their saints, the great painters also left a store of biting caricatures. And beside the loftiest achievements of Italian literature, the Florentines produced some searing satire and rich anthologies of jests and practical jokes.

Florentine History

Florence began as a small Etruscan village, graduating through the centuries to a fair-sized Roman metropolis; by the year 1000, it had already become a city of no small importance. Some 115 years later, the city took its stand as a Guelph community, siding with Rome's popes against the emperors attempting to usurp their power, and rapidly—with the ultimate victory of the popes—it grew into an important city-state, constantly striving for supremacy over all Tuscany. Local factions fought among themselves in Florence; but, led by a circle of shrewd bankers, the city drove ahead to exert its influence eventually in much of civilized Europe.

In the 15th century, a prospering, ever-expanding Florence passed under the sway of the powerful Medici banking family. Its greatest ruler, Lorenzo the Magnificent, combined political wisdom with an artistic leadership that soon sent Florence skyrocketing to the top position of Italy's Renaissance in art—the culmination of a period that had begun as far back as the 13th century.

The work of those three centuries can be seen all over Florence: the architecture of Brunelleschi, Giotto, Alberti, Sangallo, Ammannati; the sculpture of Pisano, Donatello, Cellini, the Della Robbias; the painting of Ghirlandaio, Beato Angelico, Lippi, Botticelli, Leonardo da Vinci, Bartolomeo; the combined genius of Michelangelo, Rossellino and Benedetto da Maiano. They gave to Florence in those illustrious years a depth and power rarely—if ever—attained anywhere else.

During the 16th century, Florence became the capital of the Grand Duchy of Tuscany, which passed, on the extinction of the Medici family in 1737, to Francis of Lorraine. His descendants ruled till 1860 when Tuscany joined a united Italy, for which the city of art and culture was the capital from 1865 to 1871.

In the summer of 1944, Florence—like all of Tuscany—found itself a roaring battlefield. Allied troops ranged along the south bank of the city's bisecting Arno River; Hitler's German legions occupied positions along the north bank. Inevitably, it happened. The Germans, resisting furiously, for 18 terror-packed days, blew up all of Florence's dearly loved, world-famed bridges, excepting only the Ponte Vecchio (Old Bridge), which they blocked on either side with the ruins of demolished buildings. Reconstruction began immediately after the German retreat.

Two decades later, a new catastrophe befell the city. In the terrible floods of the late fall of 1966, countless art treasures of inestimable worth were destroyed or damaged. It is difficult to visualize the extent of the devastation, as mud-laden water, 15 feet deep or more, roared through the streets. Again the Florentines pitched in, aided from all over the world, and all the museums and monuments have been restored.

Weather Matters

Come to Florence between March 15 and June 30, or try the September-October period. Those are the city's best seasons; the weather is usually perfect and you miss the worst of the annual tourist invasion through sweltering July and August. Additionally, the main events take place in spring and fall. In May, the Maggio Musicale attracts music lovers.

Food for Thought

Cooking in Florence has a special character of its own—simple, tasty, with few spices or sauces, but based heavily upon Tuscan olive oil, which is perhaps Italy's best. Meat, poultry and vegetables become the foundations of most dishes here, while macaroni is a favorite in soups. Some of the city's specialties—served in all its restaurants—include *minestrone* or *ribollita* (a vegetable soup) and *zuppa alla Certosina* (breaded vegetable soup). Other dishes strictly Florentine: *triglie o baccalà alla Livornese* (rock mullet or dried codfish with tomato sauce), *bistecca alla Fiorentina* (grilled steak, Florentine-style; big, thick, juicy steaks famed throughout Italy), *stracotto alla Fiorentina* (stewed beef with sauce), *tortino di carciofi* (eggs with artichokes), *trippa e zampa alla Fiorentina* (tripe and calf's leg with sauce), *manzo o agnello girato al fuoco di legna* (beef or lamb roasted on a spit) and *funghi alla Fiorentina* (mushrooms served Florence-style). Roast chicken, pigeon or veal is especially well done in Florence, too.

The wines? Tuscany is the home of *Chianti,* and every table holds a flask of it. The name has become an Italian trademark throughout the world; sample a glass or two of the red with your meals to understand why. There are also excellent whites from the Chianti region. And most restaurants have in stock another delightful—if a bit strong—sweet white wine answering the name of *Vin Santo,* which is made of old dried grapes and, they say, will bring the dead back to life! Good dry red wines from this part of the country include *Rufina, Montalbano* and *Montepulciano.* An exceptional dry pink wine, if properly chilled, can challenge anything France has to offer: ask for *Vinrosa di Torre de Passeri.*

Exploring Florence

Florence hugs the banks of the Arno River where it cuts through north-central Tuscany, tucked in a bed of surrounding hills. Elegant, somewhat aloof, as if physically conscious of a past greatness, this historic center of European civilization that once represented Italy's peak in art, thought and culture, still shares with Rome the honor of first place among all Italian cities for the wealth and importance of its artistic works. Every street, every square and winding alley is a show-window of Romanesque, Gothic, and especially Renaissance architecture in churches, palaces, towers, statuary, galleries, ornate museums.

For even the most cursory tour of Florence, five days are indispensable. Consider well the fact that this city holds at least 13 monumental palaces, 19 of Italy's most beautiful churches, no less than 22 individual

Florence
Information
Palazzo/Public building
Museum/Theater/Gallery/Place of Interest
Hospital
Police
Bus stn
Rail
0yds
500
0ms
500
FORTEZZA DA BASSO
VIALE FILIPPO STROZZI
VIALE Sp.LAVAGNINI
V. E.POGGI
V. S.CATERINA
VIA DELLA FORTEZZA
PIAZZA DELLA INDIPENDENZA
VIA 27 APRILE
VIA S. ZANOBI
Villino Strozzi
VIA FAENZA
VIA NAZIONALE
Cenacolo di Fuligno
VIA FIUME
Staz S M Novella
PZA.d STAZIONE
VIA S. ANTONINO
VIA PANICALE
VIA TADDEA
VIA GUELFA
Cenacolo di S.Apollonia
V. S. REPARATA
VIA SAN GALLO
Casino d.Livia
S.Marco e Museo
VIA CAVOUR
PZA. S.MARCO
VIA LAMARMORA
Orto Botanico
VIA GINO CAPPONI
V. G.GIUSTI
Biblioteca Marucelliana
V.BATTISTI
Galleria dell' Accademia
Santissima Annunziata
PIAZZA ANNUNZIATA
Museo Archeologico
VIA LAURA
VIA DELLA COLONNA
Ospedale degli Innocenti
VIA DEGLI ALFANI
VIA DE SERVI
VIA RICASOLI
Pal.Medici Riccardi
Capelle Medicee
S.Lorenzo
S.Giovannino
Cappellone d.Spagnuoli
S.M.Novella
Biblioteca Laurenziana
B.S.LORENZO
MARTELLI
V. DE' PUCCI
Pal.Puccini
Ospedale S.M.Nuove
S.Egidio
VIA DELLA PERGOLA
PINTI
VIA DELLA SCALA
PIAZZA S.M.NOVELLA
V. PANZANI
VIA DEL GIGLIO
V de Banchi
V.CERRETANI
Battistero
PZA DUOMO
Museo dell'Opera del Duomo
V.BUFALINI
PIAZZA S.M.NUOVA
V.S.EGIDIO
Teatro Pergola
BORGO PINTI
VIA FIESOLANA
PEPI
Loggia di S.Paolo
VIA PALAZZUOLO
Pal.Antinori
Via Rondinelli
S.M.Maggiore
Pza Giovanni
Duomo
Campanile
VIA DELL' ORIUOLO
V de Agli
V de' Pecori
Loggia d Bigallo
V. VECCHIETTI
S.Gaetano
Via dei Tosinghi
Via delle Oche
S.M.in Campo
Pal.Nonfinito
Via del Sole
S.Pancrazio
Pal.Strozzi
VIA TORNABUONI
V. STROZZI
PZA.d REPUBBLICA
V.Roma
V DEI CALZAIOLI
Casa di Dante
Via del Corso
V.D.PROCONSOLO
BORGO DEGLI ALBIZI
Pal Pazzi Quaratesi
Via Pandolfini
V PALMIERI
Teatro Verdi
V. DE
Casa Buonarotti
Pal.Rucellai
V.D.VIGNA NUOVA
P.O.
V.D.Alighieri
Badia
Pal.Bargello e Museo
VIA VERDI
VIA G.
VIA GHIBELLINA
Pal.Corsini
PARIONE
S.Trinita
VIA PORTA ROSSA
Orsanmichele
Pza S.FIRENZE
Pal.Bartolini
Mercato Nuovo
PZA d.SIGNORIA
Fonte
PONTE ALLE CARRAIA
LUNGARNO CORSINI
Pal.Spini
SS.Apostoli
Loggia dei Lanzi
Pal.Vecchio
Bgo de Greci
VIA DE RUSTICI
PIAZZA S.CROCE
LUNG. GUICCIARDINI
PONTE S.TRINITA
LUNG. ACCIAIOLI
V POR S.MARIA
S.Stefano
Pal.Uffizi e Galleria
V Vinegia
Via de Neri
VIA DE BENCI
B S Croce
V MAGLIABECHI
S.Croce
V. S.GUISEPPE
VIA S. SPIRITO
Ponte Vecchio
BORGO S.JACOPO
Museo d.Storia d.Scienze
CSO. D. TINTORI
Biblioteca Nazionale
S Spirito
ARNO
LUNG. GENERALE DIAZ
Museo Horne
V. TRIPOLI
LUNG. DELLE GRAZIE
VIA MAGGIO
PIAZZA S.SPIRITO
V.GUICCIARDINI
LUNGARNO TORRIGIANI
PTE.ALLE GRAZIE
V.A MAZZETTA
PZA. d. PITTI
Via Bardi
S.Lucia d. Magnoli
COSTA
Casa Guidi
SS Giorgio e Mamiliano
Pal.Torrigiani
LUNGARNO SERRISTORI
S.Felice
Palazzo Pitti e Galleria
S. GIORGIO
Museo Bardini
S.Niccolo
VIA ROMANA
Museo di Fisica e Storia Nat
Forte di S.Giorgio in Belvedere
Porta S.Miniato
Giardino di Boboli
VIA DI BELVEDERE
Porta di S.Giorgio
Passegiata ai Colli

major gardens and public parks. You should see its Cathe-tery, Piazza della Signoria and Palazzo Vecchio, Uffizi Art argello Museum, Pitti Palace, Gallery of the Academy, louse, Piazzale Michelangelo, Medici-Riccardi Palace, ike Orsanmichele, Santo Spirito, the Carmine, Santa Maria Novella, San Lorenzo, Santa Croce, San Marco (the museum, too), San Miniato, the Badia, Santissima Annunziata, and drive along Viale dei Colli. But how?

Obviously, you won't have time to glance over more than a maximum one-half of these—even in five days—without some planning and organization. Here, then, is an itinerary for those with only one, two or three days.

One Day (morning)—Baptistery, Campanile (Bell-Tower), Cathedral, Piazza della Signoria, Uffizi Art Gallery.

(Afternoon)—Pitti Palace and Art Gallery, the drive along Viale dei Colli, Church of San Miniato, Piazzale Michelangelo, Church of Santa Croce, Church of Orsanmichele.

Two Days (morning)—same itinerary as under One Day.

(Afternoon)—Bargello Museum, Dante's House, Church of Badia, Church of Santa Croce.

(Second morning)—Church of San Lorenzo and Medici Chapels, Medici-Riccardi Palace, Gallery of the Academy (should not be missed; contains original of Michelangelo's much-copied *David*), San Marco.

(Second afternoon)—Pitti Palace and Art Gallery, Church of the Carmine, Church of Santo Spirito, the drive along Viale dei Colli, Church of San Miniato, Piazzale Michelangelo.

Three Days (morning-afternoon program for first two days)—same itinerary as under Two Days.

(Third morning)—Palazzo Vecchio, Cathedral Museum, Piazza and Church of Santissima Annunziata.

(Third afternoon)—Church of Santa Maria Novella, trip to Fiesole (visiting the village's Roman and Etruscan ruins, its cathedral, and the Church of St. Francis).

Seven Independent Tours

Specific, detailed trips about Florence, with time no object, begin from the city's center at Piazza del Duomo. In seven comparatively short tours branching away from this monumental square, you can see most of Florence as completely as you wish. Another promenade along Viale dei Colli—and you have covered the city. As every item on your visiting list is likely to have different opening hours, make sure of them when you are planning your tours. Arriving just after a building has shut is deeply frustrating. We would, also, suggest that you equip yourself with a pair of binoculars. Many of the most fascin are high up on the walls of churches and almost impossi out in detail without some kind of help.

First Tour

First, consider Piazza del Duomo itself, around which stand the great Cathedral (Duomo), the Campanile (Bell Tower) of Giotto, and the Baptistery. The lofty Cathedral of Santa Maria del Fiore, its official name, is one of the longest in the world. Begun by the great master, Arnolfo di Cambio, in 1296, work continued on the church until 1436 —some 140 years—after which it was finally consecrated. Gothic architecture predominates, with a modern façade blocked in white, green and dull red marble. Inside, the church stands as one of the most stupendous examples of Gothic architecture in Tuscany; its works and monuments of art are priceless. Over your head, a gigantic octagon-shaped dome decorated by the immense fresco, *The Last Judgement,* by Vasari and Zuccari, can be reached through a ground-floor entrance along the left aisle. Scattered through both dome and church below are numerous sculptures, frescos and paintings by such artists as Ghirlandaio, Donatello, Benedetto da Maiano, Luca della Robbia, Mino da Fiesole, Andrea del Castagno, Paolo Uccello, Nanni di Banco, and Michelangelo, whose *Pietà,* begun about 1550 and finished posthumously by Tibero Calcagni, stands in the New Sacristy, to the left of the main altar. Important ancient remains, discovered during repair work after the 1966 flood, are being excavated beneath the cathedral's nave. The vibration-damaged dome is currently being restored.

Beside the cathedral, Giotto's 14th-century Campanile, regarded as the most beautiful bell tower in the world and one of the greatest creations of Gothic art, towers 292 feet above ground. Two rows of low-reliefs line the first floor, done by Luca della Robbia and Andrea Pisano (first row) and Arnoldi and students of the Pisano-Orcagna school (second row). These are copies: the originals are now in the Museo of the Duomo. The Campanile is crowned by three more stories of magnificent windows; to reach the top, climb 414 steps for a marvelous view of Florence.

Across the square from the cathedral, you find the Baptistery of San Giovanni, featuring its three world-famous sets of bronze doors. This octagonal marble baptistery was erected in the Romanesque style in the 11th–12th centuries upon the ruins of an ancient pagan temple. Below the splendid mosaics of the cupola stand the mighty baptismal font and Donatello's tomb of the anti-Pope John XXIII. The eye-catching many-paneled bronze doors deserve a brief description:

East Door—This is the door Michelangelo called *The Gate of Paradise,* done by Ghiberti in the 27 years between 1425 and 1452 and the scenes from the Old Testament represent his greatest work.

South Door—The work of Andrea Pisano in 1326, showing his *Scenes From the Life of St. John the Baptist* and the *Theological and Cardinal Virtues.*

North Door—This earlier result of Ghiberti's efforts (1403–1424) represents his *Life of Christ* and *Evangelists and Doctors.*

Behind the cathedral, at No. 9, is its museum, known officially as the Museo dell'Opera del Duomo, with a wealth of art works, mainly sculpture, including statues by Donatello, moved here from the Campanile.

Trip No. 1 out of Piazza del Duomo takes you along Via Calzaioli to a two-storied oratory, the church of Orsanmichele, one of Florence's most interesting constructions, built between 1337 and 1404 on the former site of a storehouse for corn. Interestingly enough, this church functioned at first only on the ground floor, with the upper story being used as a granary. Its most noteworthy architectural decorations are those running around the outside. Under them are niches holding statues by Nanni di Banco, Donatello, Ghiberti and Verrocchio that constitute some of the most representative examples of Renaissance sculpture in Florence. Inside the church, see the tabernacle, a really priceless 14th-century work of art by Andrea Orcagna.

Continuing along Via Calzaioli, you soon find yourself in Piazza della Signoria, the city's largest square, with a round slab in its center marking the spot where the monk Savonarola was hanged and then burned in 1498 as a heretic. It was on the same spot a year earlier that this 15th-century version of the Ayatollah Khomeni intimidated the citizens of Florence into burning pictures, wigs, musical instruments—any outward sign of vanity. The square itself is overshadowed by Palazzo della Signoria, better known among Florentines as Palazzo Vecchio (the Old Palace), in front of which you can't miss Ammanati's huge *Fountain of Neptune.*

The Old Palace, once the home of the de' Medici family's Cosimo I and later a united Italy's seat for its Chamber of Deputies, when Florence was the Italian capital, is probably the most important civic building in the city. Built in rustic stone in the 16 years between 1298 and 1314 by Arnolfo di Cambio, then added to in subsequent centuries by artists like Buontalenti and Vasari, it is now occupied by the municipality of Florence. Entering, the figures on the steps, from the left to right, are the *Marzocco,* heraldic lion of Florence; *Judith and Holo-*

fernes, a bronze by Donatello; *David,* a copy of Michelangelo's orig and *Hercules and Cacus,* by Bandinelli. The five-centuries-old co yard holds a copy of Verrocchio's famed bronze of *Winged Gen* (original in the Bargello); inside, two floors of rooms crowded with frescos, paintings, sculptures, tapestries vary from the overwhelming to the intimate. Don't neglect the 308-foot tower, from which there's a superb view of Florence.

Next to the Old Palace, the 14th-century Loggia della Signoria, with its three semi-circular Gothic-Florentine arches, features two rows of statues known the world over. Among them are: *The Rape of the Sabines,* by Giambologna; *Rape of Polyxena,* by Fedi; *Perseus,* Cellini's masterpiece in bronze; *Ajax With Body of Patroclus,* copies from a 4th-century (BC) Greek original; and *Hercules* and *Nessus,* by Giambologna.

The Uffizi

Beyond the Old Palace and this Loggia della Signoria is the Piazza degli Uffizi, a long, narrow square almost entirely surrounded by the Palazzo degli Uffizi, in which is housed the most important collection of paintings anywhere in Italy today and one of the richest in the entire world. This fabulous collection, beautifully arranged in the Uffizi Gallery inside, was gradually developed to represent almost all the Italian (and many foreign) schools of painting, with particular stress on Tuscan schools.

You could spend days here, and enjoy every minute, but if you are pressed for time, here is a brief list of the highlights:

The *Adoration of the Magi* and *The Annunciation* by Leonardo da Vinci; *Portrait of Leo X* and *The Madonna of the Goldfinch* by Raphael; the *Urbino Venus* by Titian; *The Rest on the Flight to Egypt* by Correggio; *Portrait of Jacopo Sansovino* and *Christ and the Woman of Samaria* by Tintoretto; *Medusa, Bacchus* and the *Sacrifice of Isaac* by Caravaggio, Botticelli's *Spring* and *The Birth of Venus* (although the former is undergoing restoration and will not be back on view until 1983). At the end of the seemingly infinite series of rooms, high above the Piazza della Signoria, is a very welcome cafeteria with a fine view.

Recently re-opened, the Vasari Corridor (actually the upper level of Ponte Vecchio, a passage that once linked Palazzo degli Uffizi with Palazzo Pitti) is hung with fascinating self-portraits of the great Renaissance artists. You get a special ticket from the Uffizi ticket counter.

A walk to the far end of the palace's colonnades brings you to an excellent view over the Arno River, with San Miniato Hill above and Ponte Vecchio on your right.

Second Tour

Another, shorter trip out of Piazza del Duomo leads along Via Roma to the somewhat modern Piazza della Repubblica, in the heart of old Florence, at the far end of which you take Via Calimala to the Mercato Nuovo (New Market), covered by an arcade. This is one of the places in Florence where you can buy craft work and other souvenirs. Along one side is Tacca's bronze copy of the *Wild Boar,* commonly called the "*Porcellino*" ("Little Pig") by Florentines. Branch off Via Calimala now, moving into Via Por' Santa Maria, where, in the single night of August 3–4, 1944, German troops mined and blew up every house on the street.

The Pitti Palace

Follow Via Por' Santa Maria up to and over the 14th-century Ponte Vecchio (Old Bridge), the most ancient bridge in the city, which is lined on both sides with shops of goldsmiths, silversmiths and many of Florence's best jewelry firms. Then, on the other side of the bridge, head down Via Guicciardini, now rebuilt, into Piazza de' Pitti, which takes its name from Palazzo Pitti, a 15th-century palace once occupied by the Grand Dukes of Tuscany and considered one of the most imposing monumental palaces of the city. Its Gallery of Modern Art and Museum of Works in Silver and Palatine Gallery occupy endless rows of magnificent rooms. The collection of 16th- and 17th-century paintings hung in rich profusion in the Palatine Art Gallery fills no less than 28 rooms—not including a number of vast halls and salons draped and decorated with priceless tapestries, portraits, sculptures, and frescos. Some of the ceilings here are pure marvels. Among the highlights here, a brief list among thousands of important works of art, we can mention these: *Donna Gravida* and *Madonna del Granduca* by Raphael; *La Bella* and *The Concert* by Titian; *The Three Ages of Man* by Bellini. If you can schedule your visit to the Pitti Palace on a sunny day you will be in luck, for many of the rooms have virtually no artificial light, and the pictures are very hard to see on an overcast day.

Beside the Pitti Palace is an entrance to the Boboli Gardens, a typical Italian-style arrangement designed in 1550 by Tribolo for Eleanor of Toledo. Be sure to see the amphitheater; the Viottolone, a wide path descending to gardens between groves of laurel, cypress, oaks and pines; Neptune's Fish Pond, with its huge bronze statue of the sea god himself; and the Piazza dell'Isolotto, centered with Giambologna's Fountain of Oceanus.

From Piazza de' Pitti, follow Via Romana past the medieval Church of San Felice and the Museum of Physics and Natural History to its end at Porta Romana, a massive tower dated 1326. Way up, on the inner side, is a Madonna by Giotto's school.

Cutting across to Piazza Santo Spirito we come upon the Casa Guidi in Via Mazzetta, the one-time Florence home of Robert and Elizabeth Browning. Slated to become an office building, it was saved at the last moment by funds collected in America and England by the Browning Society.

Third Tour

A third trip could lead from Piazza del Duomo along Via de' Cerretani, past the Church of Santa Maria Maggiore, left into Via Rondinelli and into Piazza Antinori. Here is a palace of the same name, that was built during the 15th century on a design by Giuliano da Sangallo. Continuing out of Piazza Antinori along Via Tornabuoni, one of Florence's swankiest streets, you finally reach an intersection, on the left on which stands Palazzo Strozzi, built by Benedetto da Maiano in 1489, continued 17 years later by Cronaca. One of the most beautiful buildings of the Renaissance, this palace now contains artistic and cultural institutes.

It's a short walk off the intersection down Via della Vigna Nuova to Palazzo Rucellai, another Renaissance masterpiece. The palace is perhaps the greatest work Leon Battista Alberti ever did. It was his plans that Bernardo Rossellino followed to construct Palazzo Rucellai between 1446 and 1451.

Back on Via Tornabuoni again, amble along it to the end at Piazza Santa Trinità. In the center of this square is a Column of Justice brought here from the Baths of Caracalla in Rome; on the left stands Baccio d'Agnolo's 16th-century Palazzo Bartolini-Salimbeni; to the right, you have the Church of Santa Trinità. This latter is perhaps Florence's most beautiful Gothic church, rebuilt near the end of the 13th century and enlarged during the next 100 years; inside are precious works of art, among which those you must see first are the Sassetti Chapel frescos by Ghirlandaio, damaged in the 1966 flood and masterfully restored, and Luca della Robbia's Federighi tomb.

Outside the church, just opposite it in Borgo Santi Apostoli, you find one of Italy's oldest Romanesque churches, the 11th-century Church of Santi Apostoli, which has been enlarged and restored. And if you continue down the street a bit, there are the Palazzo Rosselli del Turco, done in 1517, and a group of medieval homes that are typical of the structures of those days.

Then back to Piazza Santa Trinità, crossing it to the 13th-century Palazzo Spini-Ferroni, built like a massive fortress and the city's most representative private palace during the Middle Ages, you come upon the reconstructed Bridge of Santa Trinità, replacing Ammannati's 16th-century masterpiece, which was destroyed by German mines.

Cross over the bridge into Piazza Frescobaldi, continue down Via Maggio, lined with 16th-century palaces, then turn right along Via Michelozzi into Piazza Santo Spirito. There, on the right, is the Church of Santo Spirito, one of Brunelleschi's best creations; he began it in 1444 and worked on it until his death two years later, after which the construction was continued by Manetti and finished in 1487. As in all Florentine churches, there are lovely paintings here, including a *Madonna* by Filippino Lippi.

Walk to the end of Piazza Frescobaldi, down Via Sant' Agostino, then Via Santa Monaca to reach the Church of Santa Maria del Carmine, built in 1268 and restored after a fire almost burned it to the ground in 1771. Architecturally, this church has no particular importance. The reason visitors from all over the world come to its doors is to look upon the Brancacci Chapel inside, containing one of the most celebrated series of frescos in Italian art. Done by Masaccio, who left such a tremendous impression upon Italian painting, and Masolino di Panicale, the series is divided into one upper and one lower group showing episodes in the lives of St. Peter, St. Paul, and St. John.

Fourth Tour

Trip No. 4 runs from Piazza del Duomo along Via Cerretani and Via Panzani into Piazza della Stazione, where you take Via degli Avelli, beside a church, to its end in Piazza Santa Maria Novella. Here is the entrance to the Church of Santa Maria Novella, begun by the Dominican friars, Sisto and Ristoro, in 1278 and finished by Talenti in 1360. It's a Tuscan interpretation of Gothic art, with an interior rich in precious paintings, among which some of the more famous are frescos by Ghirlandaio in the Capella Maggiore (Major Chapel), others by Nardo di Cione in the Strozzi Chapel, and a really imposing *Trinity* by Masaccio. To the left of the church is the entrance to the cloister, well worth a visit.

Across the square from this church is the Loggia of San Paolo, along the left of which runs Via de' Fossi. Follow it into Largo Goldoni. Make a short side trip here up Lungarno Corsini to Palazzo Corsini, one of the best examples of baroque architecture in Florence, and the Corsini Art Gallery inside, with certainly one of the best private collections in the city, that includes a work by Botticelli, Lippi, Signorelli,

Ghirlandaio, Fra Bartolomeo, Caravaggio, and Guido Reni. Open Sats. only, 12–1.

Back at Largo Goldini, take Lungarno Vespucci along the river across Piazza Ognissanti, noting well at the end of this square the magnificent Church of Ognissanti, which, although originally dating from 1239, was restored in the 18th century. Inside are some outstanding frescos by Botticelli and Giovanni da San Giovanni; but the most important work of all stands in the adjoining convent—Ghirlandaio's masterpiece, *The Last Supper.*

Continue along Lungarno Vespucci, past a number of swank hotels, to its end at the entrance of the Cascine, once the ancient farm lands of Tuscany's Grand Dukes, but laid out in the second half of the 18th century as a public park stretching two miles along the banks of the Arno River. To cover the park well, you need a horse-carriage for about an hour, taking one of the main avenues (Viale degli Olmi) and returning by the other (Viale dei Lecci). The Cascine runs about 2½ miles through thick woods, ending at a monument dedicated to the Indian prince Rajaram Cuttraputti, who died in Florence in 1870 and was cremated on this spot by order of relatives who knew how much he loved the city. This park, incidentally, is a favorite rendezvous for young Florentine couples, in addition to being a natural locale for picnics, hikes, tennis matches and the ever-popular bicycling runs. The city provides free bicycles.

Fifth Tour

A fifth tour takes you north from Piazza del Duomo along Via Martelli into Via Cavour, with its Medici-Riccardi Palace, built by Michelozzo between 1440 and 1460 for the Medici family, who lived there until 1540. Now a headquarters for the Florence Prefecture, its most distinctive characteristics are the beautiful Tuscan Renaissance courtyard and a series of windows designed by Michelangelo. It houses the Medicean Portrait Museum and a tiny but memorable chapel, its walls decorated with Benozzo Gozzoli's stupendous frescos, representing the *Journey of the Magi* (1459). It's a spectacular cavalcade showing the lush Florentine countryside; Lorenzo the Magnificent (on a charger) and the artist himself. This small room is frequently missed by visitors, but is one of the most lovely works of art in the city. The Palace also contains a large hall, the Gallery, with sumptuous, airy ceiling paintings. (Closed when official meetings are in progress.)

Moving to the left of the palace along Via dei Gori to Piazza San Lorenzo (another busy marketplace, with dozens of stalls offering both gimcrack rubbish and interesting craftwork), and here inspect the Church of San Lorenzo, one of Brunelleschi's most valuable works, which he did in the years between 1425 and 1446. The interior, shaped like a Latin cross, is a monumental classic in harmony. Adjoining it are the Old Sacristy, another Brunelleschi masterpiece, and the small New Sacristy, by Michelangelo, with its beautiful tombs of Giuliano Duke of Nemours, and Lorenzo, Duke of Urbino, near the burial place of Florence's famed Lorenzo the Magnificent. Note the intent expression of the statue called *The Thinker* and the perfect anatomy of *Dawn* and *Twilight,* and of the figures representing *Night* and *Day.* Famous from innumerable reproductions, these funerary monuments create an indelible impression when seen in their original setting.

Return now to Via Cavour and walk up to Piazza San Marco—to the Church of San Marco, which contains numerous 16th-century works of art. Just to the right of the church is its museum, set up in an ancient monastery built by Michelozzo in 1437 for Dominican friars. Visit this place even if you must sacrifice time elsewhere. The most important works of Fra Angelico are painted on the walls of monks' bare cells and brighten the timeworn corridors, to form an art collection rare in Italy for its interest and unity. It's a really fabulous place, with illuminated choir books, cloisters, crucifixes, and the gloomy cells in which the monk Savonarola once lived. Make certain, too, that you see Fra Angelico's famous masterpiece, *The Annunciation.*

Just below the Piazza San Marco, on the Via Ricasoli, is the Gallery of the Academy (the Accademia). Though there are some interesting primitive paintings here, it is for Michelangelo's original *David* and his *Captives* that it is most visited. The long, narrow room leading up to the *David* is often so full that you may have to fight your way. Try to get there early. Taken with the tombs in the New Sacristy and the small works in the Bargello, these massive pieces create an understanding of just why Michelangelo has exercised such a hypnotic fascination for succeeding ages.

If you like, continue out of Piazza San Marco along Via 27 Aprile to Via San Gallo, then follow it into Piazza della Libertà. Here take a streetcar or bus along the Via del Ponte Rosso to Via Stibbert, where, at No. 26, you can visit the Stibbert Museum. The place has a tremendous collection of armor and Oriental objects presented by Frederick Stibbert to the Commune of Florence—things like a set of 15th-century Italian armor mounted on a horse, a series of 14 cavaliers of the 16th century in full-dress armor, Italian costumes of the time of Napoleon I, arms and costumes of various periods from India, Persia, China and Japan.

Sixth Tour

Off Piazza del Duomo again for Trip No. 6, take Via dei Servi into Piazza Santissima Annunziata, in the center of which is Giambologna's statue of Ferdinand I, two rather curious fountains by Tacca, and a portico by Brunelleschi.

The Church of Santissima Annunziata stands on the north side of the square. It was built in 1250, then entirely rebuilt about the middle of the 15th century by Michelozzo and his helpers. In a little chapel, near the entrance, are some of the most important works of the Renaissance.

Continue along via Colonna, past the Convent of Santa Maria Maddalena dei Pazzi. *Pazzi,* the plural of *pazzo,* means lunatic. It was also the name of a famous Florentine family, belonging to the Ghibelline party, rivals of the Medici. We know about it from the history of the Pazzi Conspiracy which terminated in Giuliano de' Medici's assassination in the cathedral. We also know that Giacomo and Francesco Pazzi were caught and hanged by Lorenzo de' Medici, who had escaped being assassinated. A war followed, called the Pazzi War. The Pope (whose banker was a Roman Pazzi), Naples and Siena attacked the Medici in Florence. You may be interested to learn the origins of these family names. The Medici, for example, get their name from the word for "doctor", and from the traditional symbol of the pharmacist—his globes—that decorated their coat of arms.

But, to return to Santa Maria Maddalena dei Pazzi, which encloses the celebrated Perugino fresco, *Crucifixion and Saints,* after leaving, turn right into Via Farini, on which you will find the Florence Synagogue.

Seventh Tour

The last of these quick jaunts through Florence is, perhaps, one of the most eye-filling. This time leave Piazza del Duomo by way of Via del Proconsolo, passing Nonfinito Palace, where the National Museum of Anthropology and Ethnology is housed, and the rather elegant 15th-century Pazzi-Quaratesi Palace, with its artistic courtyard. About here, Via del Proconsolo intersects with Via Dante Alighieri, where you find the house in which Dante was born. Farther along, the street passes the Church of Badia, a Benedictine establishment founded by Marquis Hugo of Tuscany, with an interior shaped like a Greek cross; inside, the valuable works of art include a tomb of the Marquis Hugo, considered Mino da Fiesole's masterpiece, and a *Vision of St. Bernard* by Filippino Lippi.

Still farther ahead on Via del Proconsolo is the cold, fortress-like Palazzo del Podestà, built in three parts between 1254 and 1346, with a high tower and picturesque courtyard. The palace today houses Florence's National Museum, otherwise known as the Bargello Museum, and its three floors are dedicated to the works of Florentine sculptors famous during the Renaissance. Here are masterpieces by Donatello, Settignano, Verrocchio, Michelangelo, and many other great names in the world of art. It is one of those museums which reveals new surprises at every turn, and will excite anyone who loves the unusual in painting and sculpture.

Beyond the museum, through Piazza San Firenze and into Borgo dei Greci leading away from it, you come to Piazza Santa Croce, dominated by the Church of Santa Croce, largest and most beautiful of all Italy's Franciscan churches and one of the nation's most perfect examples of Gothic architecture. Probably built from designs by Arnolfo di Cambio, it dates back to 1294. Somehow, it has become customary to bury Italy's historic greats in the Church of Santa Croce, with the result that it now resembles a sort of Pantheon for Italian glories of the past. Here are the remains of illustrious personages like Galileo, Michelangelo, Machiavelli, Foscolo, Alfieri, and others. Inside, too, you find some of the city's best art works; for example, Giotto's frescos in the Bardi and Peruzzi Chapels, along with those by Maso di Banco, Taddeo and Agnolo Gaddi. The famous Cimabue crucifix, badly damaged in the flood, is on view after the exceptional restoration it underwent at Fortezza di Basso.

A View of the City

Aside from these seven short tours—but necessarily included in any visit to Florence—is a walk (about four miles) or ride along Viale dei Colli, opened in 1877 as one of the most lovely promenades in the city. If you have no car and still hesitate about hiking it all the way, take a bus from Lungarno Serristori. Best time to go is in the morning or late afternoon.

The road winds outside and above Florence to a height of 340 feet at Piazzale Michelangelo, where, in the middle, there is a bronze reproduction of his *David.* The view here from the railing covers all of Florence, the plain beyond, Pistoia, and the highest peaks of the Apennine Mountains in the far distance.

Turning away from the railing, take the stairway on your left or the road on your right up through rows of giant cypress trees to the Church of San Salvatore al Monte, built by Cronaca about 1500, then continue higher to the top of the hill. There, at about 455 feet, you will find the Church of San Miniato al Monte, one of the most beautiful and famous of Florence's many churches and a masterpiece of Romanesque architecture. It was built in 1013, during the time of Emperor Arrigo II, and finished later in the 13th century. The interior is floored in marble and covered with frescos by Spinello Aretino and the 14th and 15th-century Florentine school; there's a tabernacle by Michelozzo and a Chapel of the Cardinal of Portugal by Manetti, with Rossellino's sepulcher of the cardinal done in 1461.

Around Florence, like Rome and its environs, the hill towns and several luxurious, centuries-old villas form a rough circle, never more than four or five miles from the city's center. A bit farther beyond this rim—but easily accessible by bus or private car—are Monte Senario and Impruneta, each distinctive.

Environs of Florence

Anyone remaining in Florence for a reasonable length of time should try to alternate visits to its scattered environs with tours throughout the city itself, thus breaking the inevitable monotony derived from absorbing too much—or too many—of similar attractions, churches, art, palaces, and museums. This is rather important in most Italian cities; in Florence particularly it may mean the difference between thorough enjoyment of your visit and an irritating boredom.

See Fiesole first. It's only 20 minutes out of Florence's Piazza San Marco by bus no. 7 over a route lined with moss-grown garden walls, olive trees, cypresses, sumptuous villas, and beds of geraniums and irises.

Fiesole itself, atop a crescent-shaped hill, began as an ancient Etruscan village, later dominated the entire region, then fell prey to barbarian invasions and settled under the power of Florence. Things to see: the cathedral, built in 1028, with art by the Della Robbias, Mino da Fiesole, Nicodemo di Michelangelo, among others; the Roman Theater, uncovered in 1809, built a couple of centuries before Christ, will remind you of Rome's many ruins; the Bandini Museum, with paintings, furniture and sculptures of the 14th-16th centuries; and, above all, the Church of St. Francis, high above town on the site of an ancient Roman temple, where you can inspect the cells of monks, walk through the medieval monastery, and stand on any one of a number of terraces to catch the most beautiful view in this part of Italy.

Next, visit the "villa towns"—three out of four which are within 5 miles of Florence. There's Settignano (bus from Piazza San Marco, in the city), and its world-famous Italian garden outside the superb 17th-century Villa Gamberaia, which can be visited by arrangement a week in advance. Inquire at Florence tourist office about visiting villas. Nearby Villa I Tatti was American art critic Bernard Berenson's home; it houses the Harvard Institute for Renaissance Studies. Visit Villa astello (bus from Station Square), with another beautiful, terraced garden beside the villa once owned by the Medici family; and nearby Villa Petraia, boasting a magnificent fountain by Giambologna. A little farther out (13 miles by SACA bus line from Piazza Santa Maria Novella, or by Lazzi coach from Piazza Adua), the Villa Poggio a Caiano, bought by Lorenzo the Magnificent and decorated by artists like Sangallo and the Della Robbias, was the scene of a 16th-century tragedy when both Grand Duke Francesco Medici and his wife, Bianca Capello, died there on the same night in 1578.

Closer to Florence (about 4 miles by bus from Piazza Santa Maria Novella) is the Certosa del Galluzzo, a Carthusian monastery founded in the 14th century. Its subterranean chapels and convent hold priceless works of art. There's also a "pharmacy" where you can buy the Florentine version of Chartreuse. The liqueur comes in attractive bottles and makes an excellent and reasonably-priced souvenir.

Some 16 miles outside Florence, perched high atop Monte Senario, another monastery should be worth a place on your itinerary. Originally a hermitage, it has a chapel dating back to the 15th century.

Impruneta is a delightful hill town about half-an-hour south from Florence by bus, famous for its della Robbia terracottas and pottery workshops.

PRACTICAL INFORMATION FOR FLORENCE

HOTELS. As an important tourist center, Florence naturally has many good hotels, but you will be well advised to make reservations well in advance any time between April and November.

Knowledgeable tourists have learned to stay away from Florence during the fashion shows in October and March/April, when hotels and restaurants get too crowded for comfort.

Deluxe (L)

Excelsior Italia, Piazza Ognissanti 3, on the Arno, short walk to historic center, in imposing old palace, it has modern comforts, assiduous service, beautifully furnished, airconditioned rooms. Excellent food in *Cestello* restaurant.

Savoy is more centrally located, hardly a stone's throw from the cathedral, only slightly less grand, handsome bedrooms and public rooms.

Villa Medici, Via del Prato 42, between station and Cascine park, more modern in spirit and decor, comfortable but impersonal, pool.

First Class (1)

Aerhotel Baglioni, near station, recently redone, has a delightful roof garden with exceptional view, Renaissance decor, lots of groups.

De La Ville, Piazza Antinori, in the heart of things, is medium-sized, posh, with marble floors and rich furnishings, spacious, quiet rooms.

Croce Di Malta, Via della Scala, facing Santa Maria Novella, 120 compact, functional rooms, half overlooking garden, pool.

Jolly Carlton, overlooks Cascine park, sleekly furnished though smallish rooms, all airconditioned, pool in rooftop terrace with view of city.

Kraft, Via Solferino, has solid look, modern comforts, 70 small, well-appointed rooms, handsome lobby, rooftop terrace restaurant and swimming pool.

Lungarno, Borgo San Jacopo 12, superior modern hotel, 70 smallish, quiet, well-equipped rooms, many facing Arno with view of center, some with balcony.

Majestic, near railway station, entirely renovated to provide modern comforts, 100 rooms, all with bath and TV, elegantly done in 16th-century Florentine decor. Best in category.

Minerva, near station at Santa Maria Novella, is rather posh, with comfortable rooms, swimming pool.

Palazzo Benci, apartment hotel of CIGA chain, 31 well-furnished, fully equipped apartments, advantageous rates for stays of 7 days or more, some traffic noise.

Park Palace, Piazza Galileo, has attractive, individually furnished rooms in former villa, pool and garden, pleasant on hot days but over 2 miles from center, well served by taxis.

Plaza Lucchesi, on banks of the Arno, short walk to the Uffizi, is a favorite for traditional decor, good service, front rooms with view.

Principe, Lungarno Vespucci, has relaxed, private-home atmosphere, 22 bright, airconditioned rooms, many overlooking river, others on tiny garden.

Regency, Piazza d'Azeglio, just outside center, is a beautifully appointed villa, of *Relais* chain, where you're coddled and catered to.

Villa Cora, between autostrada and city, 18th-century villa, period furnishings but modern comforts, pool.

Villa La Massa, at *Candeli,* sumptuously decorated 15th-century country residence, pool, minibus service to town.

Moderate (2)

Berchielli, Lungarno Acciaioli 14, recommended for charming lounges, terraces, ambience, 73 rooms, those in front get traffic noise.

Continental, hard by Ponte Vecchio, 71 well-appointed though smallish rooms, bright, cheery ambience, roof garden, but lots of traffic noise.

Jennings Riccioli, Lungarno delle Grazie, overlooking river, furnishings blend antique and functional, spacious front rooms have view but noisy.

Laurus, Via Cerretani, in renovated palazzo, very central, brightly furnished in modern style, 94 airconditioned compact rooms.

Rivoli, Via della Scala, near station, 43 smallish, spotless rooms with bath or shower, pleasant public rooms, garden courtyard.

Umbria, Piazza d'Azeglio, in quiet residential zone about 10 mins. walk from center, 31 cheerful, good-sized rooms, all with bath and airconditioning, delightful garden, good restaurant.

Villa Azalee, garni, Via Fratelli Rosselli 44, just outside historic center; intimate, tasteful atmosphere in small villa-hotel with large garden.

SUBURBAN. Villa Belvedere, Via Castelli (behind Boboli Gardens), offers a splendid view of Florence from its veranda rooms, easy parking, swimming pool. **Villa San Domenico,** Via della Piazzola, 19 lushly furnished rooms in ancient convent, terrace restaurant with view. **Villa Villoresi,** officially a first-class pension, handsome 17th-century edifice, 27 spacious, frescoed rooms, period furnishings, excellent food in attractive dining rooms, pool in large park.

Inexpensive (3)

These are not beyond the pale in Florence, and you might try **Paris,** Via dei Banchi, central location, many private showers; **Aprile,** Via della Scala 6, in historic palazzo converted into comfortable hotel; nearby **Alba,** Via della Scala 22, is also reliable. **Martelli,** Via Panzani, attractive, central.

Or you might try the **Atlantico-Aquila d'Oro,** Via Nazionale 12, not far from the railroad station; or the **Ascot,** next door, more than half the rooms with bath. **Liana,** Via Alfieri, quiet, pleasant villa.

On Lungarno Zecca Vecchia is comfortable **River;** hotels with garage are—**Gioconda,** Via Panzani 2, about halfway between the railway station and the cathedral; and the **Columbia-Parlamento,** Piazza San Firenze 29; central.

Pensions (P)

All (P1) are—**Tornabuoni-Beacci,** Via Tornabuoni 3; **Embassy House,** Via Nazionale 23; as well as the small **Pitti Palace,** Via Barbadori 2. **Bretagne** (P2), Lungarno Corsini 6 and **La Residenza,** Via Tornabuoni 8, are both (P2), central, pleasant.

Two standouts: **Hermitage,** Vicolo Marzio, occupies top 4 floors of a building near Ponte Vecchio and Uffizi, bright, cheerful, inviting, with 18 tastefully furnished rooms, roof garden; **Monna Lisa,** Borgo Pinti 27, near cathedral, 26 rooms on 2 floors of ancient **palazzo,** antique Renaissance furnishings, beamed ceilings in salons, courtyard, garden. Both (P2).

RESTAURANTS. Dinner hours in Florence are earlier than those in Rome, starting at 12.30 for the midday meal, dinner from 7.30 on. Many of Florence's best restaurants are very small, especially the various Bucas, so get there early and be prepared to share a table.

For an elegant snack, try **Procacci,** Via Tornabuoni 16. A specialty shop, it has a counter that serves tiny sandwiches of white truffles with a glass of chilled white wine for a few hundred lire.

Wine shops in the heart of old Florence dispense classic Chianti and solid snacks that make an inexpensive lunch. Look for **Fratellini,** Via dei Cimatori; **Niccolino,** Volta dei Mercanti; **Bianchi,** Via dei Neri; and many more.

For a refreshing pause anytime, **Vivoli,** in Piazza San Simone, offers at least 20 flavors of freshly made ice cream.

Expensive (E)

Alfredo sull' Arno, Via Bardi at Ponte Vecchio, serves Tuscan specialties. It's locale has made it, however, very conscious of the tourist trade.

Casermetta del Forte di Belvedere, Via S. Leonardo, is a handsome place.

Doney, Via Tornabuoni 10, small, always crowded, and particularly popular with American tourists because they can get American snacks there as well as standard Italian dishes.

Harry's Bar, Lungarno Vespucci 22R, another favorite with Americans, serves good drinks but pricey food.

Le Rampe, Viale Poggi 1, offers veal in champagne and *canard à l'orange* in attractive setting with fine view. (Reserve, tel. 681.1891).

La Loggia, Piazzale Michelangelo (Reserve, tel. 287.032), also has magnificent view; classic Florentine cuisine.

Natale, on Lungarno Acciaiolo, Tuscan specialties.

Oliviero, Via delle Terme, excellent, has dinner dancing.

Very popular but a bit out of the way is **Omero,** Via Pian dei Giullari 11, on hilltop near observatory. Be sure taxi driver knows the way before starting out, and since it's always crowded, reserve (tel. 220.053).

Lo Zodiaco, Via delle Casine 2 (Reserve, tel. 672.319), specializes in fish and regional dishes concocted by Sicilian owner.

Pasquini, Via Valdilamona 2R, recommended by residents.

Pinchiorri, Via Ghibellina, exquisite food and wine, well served in a rustic 16th century wine cellar; rated one of Italy's finest for *nouvelle cuisine.* Evenings only (Reserve, tel. 210.193).

Sabatini, Via Panzani, is tops, one of Italy's best, traditional atmosphere, exceptional food (Reserve, tel. 211.559).

Villa San Domenico, Via della Piazzola 55, in lovely setting.

Villa Villoresi, 8 km from Florence (see hotel list), run by Count Luigi and family with exquisite courtesy, good food, excellent wine and oil from estate.

Moderate (M)

Buca Lapi, Via del Trebbio 1, is a big favorite with American tourists. **Paoli,** Via dei Tavolini 12, is central, attractive Gothic decor, fine pastas. **Giovacchino,** Via Tosinghi 2, is also a good restaurant.

Degli Antellesi, Piazza Santa Croce, is tops for atmosphere, really good food. Can nudge into expensive category.

Giannino in S. Lorenzo is an excellent *rosticceria* in Via Borgo S. Lorenzo (near Cathedral). **La Sostanza,** Via del Porcellana 25, is plain, small, serves hearty steaks, salads, and famous bean dishes.

13 Gobbi, Via Porcellana 9R, serves Florentine and Hungarian dishes, some pricey.

Il Fagioli, Corso Tintori 47, is an excellent trattoria with popular Tuscan specialties. Closed weekends.

Il Sasso di Dante, Piazza delle Pallottole 6R, and **Cammillo,** Borgo S. Jacopo 57R, are popular with Americans.

A well-known trattoria famous for its steaks is **Buca Mario,** Piazza degli Ottaviani 16R, just at the end of Via della Spada.

Reader-recommended is **Mamma Gina** on Borgo San Jacopo, popular, good.

A real find is the rustic **Osteria Natalino** Via Borgo degli Albizzi near Bargello, in former sacristy, closed Sunday.

Another reader discovery, **Beppino,** Via Pellicceria 28, delightful food and *simpatico* host. **Dino,** Via Ghibellina 51, near Santa Croce, is a quiet place where you may, if you wish, dine on cheese and any one of Dino's 300 kinds of wine. **Mario da Ganino,** Piazza dei Cimatori 4R, is a wine-shop serving good food.

Cantinetta Antinori, in Palazzo Antinori, offers snacks or full meals and the wines of the house.

After a gruelling morning at the Pitti, you may have a job finding somewhere to lunch. Head for Santo Spirito and **Drago Verde,** Via del Leone 50R, for a fine meal.

In the heart of town, **Croce al Trebbia,** 19 Via delle Belle Donne, is a busy trattoria with plenty of atmosphere and healthy portions.

Inexpensive (I)

You might try **Il Bargello,** Borgo dei Greci 37R; **Antico Barile,** Via dei Cerchi 40R; **Federigo,** Piazza dell'Olio; **Benvenuto,** Via dei Negri. **Frizzi,** Borgo degli Albizzi 76, is fine budget restaurant with pleasant atmosphere; **Le Cantine,** Via dei Pucci, can be reasonable if you stick with the tourist menu;

Buca Nicolini, Via Ricasoli 3, does wonders with beans and down-to-earth local specialties; **Mossacce,** Via del Proconsolo 55, tiny, busy, no lingering allowed, but the ready-to-eat food is fine and the atmosphere authentic.

MUSEUMS. Below we list some of the most outstanding museums, galleries, and palaces in Florence. Check with tourist offices for hours, as these can vary a great deal. You would be wise to plan your museum itinerary in advance (say the day before), so as to fit as many places grouped together as possible. Try to start as early as you can, to avoid the tourist busloads.

Accademia Gallery, Via Ricasoli 60. Florentine primitives; famous works by Michelangelo, including his *David.*

Archeological Museum, Piazza SS. Annunziata 9. Important Etruscan collections, Greek and Roman sculpture.

Bardini Museum and **Corsi Gallery,** Piazza de Mozzi. Outstanding private collection, including works by Tiepolo, Pollaiuolo, Uccello, etc.

Casa Buonarotti (Michelangelo's House), Via Ghibellina 70.

Davanzati Palace (Museum of the Old Florentine House), Piazza Davanzati. Home furnished as it would have been in olden times: 14th-17th century.

Fra Angelico Museum (Museum of San Marco), Piazza San Marco. Large number of works of Beato Angelico.

Medici Chapels (Church of San Lorenzo), Piazza Madonna. Tombs by Michelangelo.

Museo di Santa Maria del Fiore (Duomo), Piazza Duomo 9. Collection of outstanding works from Duomo, Baptistery and Campanile.

National Museum (Bargello), Via del Proconsolo 4. Sculptures by Donatello, Cellini, Verrocchio, and other decorative arts.

National Museum of Science History, Piazza del Giudici 1. Optical, electrical, astronomical, etc. instruments, maps, atlases.

Palazzo Medici-Riccardi, Via Cavour 1. Objects and souvenirs pertaining to the Medicis and beautiful frescos in tiny chapel.

Palazzo Vecchio (to left of Uffizi) open again. The Loeser Collection and the Della Ragione Collection; works by Vasari and Michelangelo.

Pitti Palace, with **Galleria Palatina, Galleria d'Arte Moderna** and **Museo degli Argenti,** on Piazza Pitti. Some of the most famous galleries in Italy. Site also of Boboli Gardens; new wing houses fine Contini-Bonacossi Collection.

Santa Maria Novella, Monumental Cloisters, Piazza S. Maria Novella. A number of impressive works and frescos.

Stibbert Museum, Via Stibbert 26. Wide collection, including arms and 16th-century armor.

Uffizi Gallery (Uffizi Palace), Piazza della Signoria. One of the world's great collections, particularly rich in Italian and Flemish paintings. It includes the collection of artists' self-portraits in the Vasari Corridor over Ponte Vecchio. Excellent cafeteria overlooking the Piazza della Signoria.

NIGHTLIFE. Florence is not a nightlife town, but there are a score of places where you can dine and dance. As there are frequent changes, ask your hotel porter for the latest information.

The favorites, open all year, are **Oliviero,** Via delle Terme; recently refurbished **Aer-hotel Baglioni,** Piazza del'Unità; and the attractive **Open Gate,** at Villa Monselles, Viale Michelangelo.

Among those open only in the winter season, the most frequented is **Pozzo di Beatrice,** Piazza San Trinità 5, which is not listed as a nightclub, but sometimes has an act or two. **Harry's Bar** is a popular rendezvous for English-speaking tourists. Nice British-style pub, **George and Dragon,** Borso Apostoli. Beer and banjos at the **Red Garter,** Via Benci.

Simply sitting outside a cafe, nursing a coffee or a drink and watching the world go by, is one of the best ways of enjoying a warm Florentine night.

SHOPPING. Florence is the art city of Italy and at the same time the center of the Italian artisan trade. It is the best place to buy leather goods, linens, gold jewelry and straw. Its very atmosphere is conducive to wandering and window-shopping in tiny side streets that meander off at odd angles and the central district can be happily and thoroughly explored by foot.

The most fashionable streets in Florence are Via Tornabuoni, which runs from the Arno to Via Cerretani, and Via della Vigna Nuova which angles it midway. But the most characteristic part is the medieval Ponte Vecchio, the charming bridge over the Arno River, which is crowded with small shops. It is here that the city's jewelers and silversmiths are gathered, even as they were hundreds of years ago.

Florentine jewelry has a particular quality of satin finish which characterizes it. In English it is commonly called brushed gold and in Italian *satinato.* Much of Florence jewelry is also filigree.

Cameos are another specialty of the Florentine workshop which has the trained artisans to do the intricate carving. The orange and dark shells come from Cuba and the lovely pink ones from Madagascar, but it is the artist's labor which turns these simple sea animals into delicate works of beauty. Depending on workmanship, therefore, cameos vary widely in price. Some shops will even show you the cameo being worked, and you'll understand more about this charming shell.

Also, be sure to save time for a visit to the outdoor markets, either the one at Loggia del Mercato Nuovo or the much larger one that fills the Piazza San Lorenzo. There you will find a wild mixture of plastic rubbish, cheap jeans, leather work that will bear investigation, and lots of other craft products. If you have the urge to bargain, you can certainly try, but you are not likely to come out on top.

Florence is one of the best cities in which to buy shoes. The quality is superb, and the price range wide enough to suit every pocket.

SPECIAL EVENTS. The *Scoppio del Carro,* literally translated as "Bursting of the Cart," takes place at noon on Easter Sunday in Piazza del Duomo. May and June, *Maggio Musicale,* opera, ballet and music festival. (For details write—*Maggio Musicale Fiorentino,* Teatro Communale, Via Solferino 15, 50123 Florence, tel. 262841.)

First Sunday in May and 24 June at the Boboli Gardens, and the evening of 28 June in the Piazza Santa Croce, pageants and parades and the fantastic 16th-century football game, *Gioco del Calcio.*

Summer opera in Teatro Communale (airconditioned!) in July—the winter season starts in December. 7 September, *Virgin's Nativity,* children have paper lanterns.

28 September, *Bird Fair* at the Porta Romana.

September–October, *International Antiques Fair.*

December, *International Festival of Social Documentary Films.*

TRANSPORT. Taxi charges have gone up recently; the tourist offices at Via Manzoni 16 and Via Tornabuoni 15 will provide information on rates. In addition to the meter reading there are extra charges for suitcases and night service. Taxis taken to certain outlying districts and beyond city boundaries may charge for returning empty. **Horse carriages** are fun for leisurely jaunts, but again, charges are rather complex. Ask the driver to give you an idea of what it will cost before you start out, and if you intend to keep the carriage for an hour or more make a special arrangement with him.

Car Hire. Besides drive-your-own from *Hertz, Avis,* you can hire English-speaking drivers with car or limousine from reliable *Vittorio Sulli,* Via Tartini 15, 30103.

USEFUL ADDRESSES. AAST, Via Tornabuoni 15, and Railway Station; *American Express,* SIT, Via Panzani 20R, tel. 283.825; CIT, Via Cerretani 59; *Cook's,* Via Tornabuoni 21; EPT, Via Manzoni 16.

Consulates. *American,* Lungarno Vespucci 38; *British,* Lungarno Corsini 2.

Tours enquire at EPT for program of wine tours, or villa tours (April through June) which include tea at a pleasant inn, and (Saturdays only) a visit to *I Tatti,* villa of the late Bernard Berenson.

English-speaking churches. *Catholic,* the Cathedral, San Marco, Santa Maria Novella; *Church of England,* St. Mark, Via Maggio 9; *Protestant Episcopal,* Via Rucellai 5; *Christian Science,* Via della Spada 1; *Synagogue,* Via Farini 4.

TUSCANY

Where Nature Rivals Art

Tuscany, shaped like a rough triangle, has its base along a broad stretch of Italy's west coast some miles north of Lazio and Rome, with the apex pointing inland across more than half the width of the peninsula. Along the main roads very unattractive ribbon development has encroached on the wooded hills, snow-crested peaks, vineyards, stands of cypress and olive groves, but the lovely "green valleys of Tuscany" can still be found off the beaten track. Artistically and historically, its towns are showplaces of the centuries-old Tuscan culture that brought forth masters like Michelangelo, Dante, Leonardo da Vinci, Boccaccio, Petrarch.

Tuscany is a happy blend of mountains, valleys and beaches. High mountains like the Apennines and Apuan Alps; broad valleys like those of the Arno and Serchio Rivers, emerald green in their fertility. Long, sandy stretches of beach curve along the coast through Forte dei Marmi, Viareggio, Leghorn into the pine woods of Maremma. No lakes to speak of, but plenty of streams and bubbling, fresh-water springs.

Behind this scenic wealth lie agricultural areas that pay off in livable dividends to hard-working peasants and mountaineers. The soil of Tuscany is not as rich as neighboring Emilia, for example, but its wheat, wines, oil, chestnuts and livestock help make for a reasonable prosperity. Shipping and fishing predominate through the coastal reaches; art and crafts originate higher, in mountain hamlets. Tuscany's laborers work at steel, iron, machinery, textile and chemical plants fed from considerable natural resources such as iron on the island of Elba, pyrites, tin, copper and antimony in the Maremma area, marble from Apuania, borax out of Larderello.

But the history, the art of Tuscany, the culture that has drawn educated people to this region for centuries—these are responsible for its position as a leader in the field of Italy's tourist trade. Florence symbolizes best the Tuscan pride in grace and refinement, and its deathless masterpieces of architecture, painting, sculpture and literature make it a storehouse of artistic wealth. They help create in other Tuscan cities like Siena, Pisa, Lucca, Volterra, Pistoia and Arezzo an atmosphere of the Middle Ages somehow preserved almost intact.

That, perhaps, remains the permanent characteristic of Tuscany today—a stubborn, proud refusal to change its natural beauty and way of life, so that in many of the smaller cities, in the towns and villages and isolated monasteries tucked far back through the rolling hills and valleys, you still catch something of the feeling that someone has turned the clock back.

Much of Tuscany had its origin before the dawn of history under the Etruscans, who left their art, fortified ruins and obscure civilization scattered across the region's most fertile valleys and strategic hills. The conquering Romans came next, and the lords and barons of the tempestuous Middle Ages. This combination of three distinct cultures makes itself evident wherever you wander through the Tuscan hinterland.

Unlike its southern neighbor Lazio, where Rome dominates the entire region, Tuscany is not merely Florence, but rather a sprawling chain of cities and towns rivaling each other for the right to be classified as most distinctive of the area. Florence—and possibly Siena—may have a better claim to that title; but it is impossible to consider the whole without its parts.

Central Tuscan History

The northern Tuscan cities have a somewhat similar background. Pistoia, flourishing through the 14th century, when the Guelph communes were all-powerful, went on to fall under the incredible Medici family's grasping rule; it was severely damaged during the 1944 German retreat and has since been rebuilt. Lucca, once a Roman city that later fought for—and won—her independence from 1370 to 1799, when Napoleon I handed it over to his sister, Elisa Baciocchi, eventually became the capital of a Tuscan duchy under Maria Luisa of the Bourbons in 1815. And Livorno, subjected to Florence's rule in 1421, proudly saw her famous port begun in 1571 under the rule of the Medici Duke Cosimo I—to watch it smashed by German troops and Allied bombers four centuries later and then laboriously regain its commercial position.

Pisa preserves proud memories of the 11th century, when she was the leading maritime republic holding undisputed power over Sardinia, Corsica, even the far Balearic Islands. The city, losing her sea supremacy to Genoa's fleet after the battle at Meloria in 1284, found herself forced under the rule of a succession of feudal barons, the last of whom passed her along to Florence in 1405. The astronomer Galileo Galilei, and the physicist Antonio Pacinotti, inventor of the electromagnetic ring were born here. Pisa's Romanesque architecture, which later developed a "Pisan style" of its own, spread through much of Tuscany and as far off as the Island of Sardinia.

Central Tuscany's history is best discovered in places like Volterra, first one of 12 Etruscan city-states, then a Roman municipality and finally a free and independent community from the 12th to the 15th century, with innumerable Etruscan ruins and medieval walls still evident as proof of its past. Or San Gimignano, a hilltop village right out of the Middle Ages; it flourished from the 12th century through 1357, when—like a lot of other Tuscan municipalities—it submitted to the rule of Florence's Medici family.

Of all central Tuscany, however, Siena preserves its medieval glory on the grandest scale. Of the original Etruscan village, ten miles away, which became Sena Julia under the Romans, no trace remains. In 1260 at Montaperti Siena won a stunning victory over Florence—never forgotten by her bitter rival. In 1348 Siena was decimated by a devastating plague, and 51 years later bowed to the rule of Florence. A few years later she won back her liberty for a brief period; but in 1559 Siena was officially annexed to the Duchy of Tuscany. Its architecture, an adaptation of the Gothic style to Italian taste, is still the most distinctive characteristic of the old town.

To the south, most indicative of Tuscany's history are Grosseto and Orbetello, along with Arezzo. Orbetello, too, can be traced back to the ancient Etruscans, who left the amazingly well-preserved ruins you see about three miles north of the town; in 1557, Philip II of Spain made it the capital of a short-lived military state. And Arezzo, likewise starting as an Etruscan village, subsequently became the ally of Rome, to evolve into a free community during the Middle Ages. Arezzo too made the fatal mistake of competing with Florence, under whose sway it fell in 1384.

Weather Matters

Avoid the central part of Tuscany in mid-summer. It can get very hot in the hill towns. The best of all months is May—which is why Florence has its musical festival then. June is also a good month, and then you had better skip to the September–October period. The beach resorts are, of course, overcrowded from June through September.

Road Reports

The suggested routes for train and bus travelers do equally well for tourists in their own automobiles. The area is well served by three autostrade, part of the A1, the Autostrada del Sole, connecting Florence with Bologna and Rome, passing close to Arezzo; A11 leading west from Florence, with exits to Prato, Pistoia and Lucca, meeting the coastal A12 between Viareggio and Livorno. Superstrade (no tolls) between Florence and Siena, as well as between Siena and Arezzo, make both these small cities even more logical headquarters from which to explore the enchanting and remote towns of both regions. Another superstrada connects Arezzo with Perugia (Umbria), passing Lake Trasimeno.

If you have not much time for this part of the country and want to establish yourself at a single center to explore from there, Siena would probably be the best for motorists, since Florence is no place for cars.

Travelers using the economical Alitalia Jet-Drive package can fly to Pisa for visiting the north of Tuscany including Florence, Siena and San Gimignano. Alitalia has a tie-up with Jolly Hotels at which Jet-Drive passengers can get up to 20% discount, but unfortunately there are only two Jolly Hotels in Tuscany, in Pisa and Florence.

Food for Thought

Florentine dishes are of course to be found all over Tuscany, but some of the other cities also have specialties of their own. Leghorn and Viareggio have an answer to the *bouillabaisse* of southern France in *cacciucco,* a fish soup of the same general type. Pisa likes elvers (young eels) cooked in oil, with a suspicion of sage—ask for *cieche.* Siena will give you its own special pastries for dessert—*panforti, cavallucci* and *ricciarelli,* while you will find *castagnaccio* in many parts of Tuscany—a sweet whose basis is flour made from chestnuts. Also throughout

Tuscany you will find that delicious form of *pasta* called *pappardelle con la lepre,* noodles doused in a wild hare sauce.

In addition to the wines of the Chianti district, we might call your attention to the dry red *Brolio* and the somewhat similar *Brunello di Montalcino.* Among white wines, there are two of quite distinctive flavors, that of the Island of Elba, *Bianco dell' Elba,* slightly sweet, and the *Vernaccia di San Gimignano,* which is pleasantly dry when young, quite sweet when aged. *Montepulciano* is a robust red.

Exploring Tuscany

Tuscany, as one of Italy's larger regions, demands time and considerable planning to sample its variety. A trip along its coast fits easily into the itinerary of anyone traveling through Florence to or from Rome. But the remainder of the region—north, south, and southeast—is best visited by making side trips out of Florence.

Consider the north-south coastal trip through Tuscany first, but with due consideration for an immediate side trip by car or train for those who have spare time to travel over a highly scenic route most tourists never see. This junket is especially advised for motorists, as by rail you miss some of the area's natural beauty.

Coming south from Liguria, the last city of any size through which you pass before reaching Tuscany is La Spezia, where a 76-mile highway crosses the high Apennine Mountains en route through three separate regions—Liguria, Tuscany and Emilia—to the city of Parma inland. Take this side trip if you are able. The road climbs 3,419 feet to its peak at La Cisa Pass, winding beside a five-mile-long railroad tunnel, over the unbelievably green La Magra Valley, through towns and villages that don't appear to have changed for at least four centuries. With its heavy woods, rushing streams and towering peaks, this region has so far escaped relatively unscathed from the more unwelcome aspects of tourism.

The direct route down Tuscany's coast, of course, runs out of Liguria at La Spezia and continues into the Tuscan area at Carrara, home of some of the world's most famous marble works, with excursions possible into quarries high in the Apuan Alps. There is always the chance of seeing some great sculptor at work, freeing the vision hidden inside a block of the loveliest marble on earth. The next 20 miles goes south through Massa, Forte dei Marmi and Pietrasanta. The village of Pietrasanta has a claim on the attention of anyone interested in the history of Italian art for it was from here that Michelangelo built a road up to Monte Altissimo so that he could transport the white marble he needed. Pietrasanta (and if this marble isn't a "holy stone" then no stone is sacred) is the spiritual home for sculptors and masons from all over the world. It has some lovely architecture.

The road passes along pine-bordered beaches of fine white sand to Viareggio, the largest and most crowded bathing resort on the Tyrrhenian coast. From late January to March, Italy's annual carnival time is better-evidenced here than anywhere in the country, with flower-decked parades and almost continuous weekend masquerade balls. Puccini spent his last years at nearby Torre del Lago. The great composer is buried in the park of his lakeside villa, now a museum.

Pisa

Next stop is Pisa. Between the Borgo Stretto and the Via 29 Maggio, the maze of old streets and little squares has been closed to traffic. The famous Quadrilateral, within the imposing ramparts, is best entered by the Porta Nuova (of Santa Maria), which opens on the four principal landmarks of Pisa. The ensemble is strangely lit at night by a rather green spotlight that falls on it like unreal moonlight.

The Cathedral dates back to at least the 11th century, when the architect Buscheto supervised the laying of the cornerstone. Work on it continued through the 12th and 13th centuries. Many little columns give the Rainaldo façade an airy, light look. The folding doors opposite the bell tower are especially noteworthy. Perhaps you will be surprised, after the delicacy of the exterior, by the majestic scale of its interior. Notice particularly the astonishing pulpit attributed to Nicolo and Giovanni Pisano, and the Baptistery (12th-century) designed on a circular plan and covered with marble. Look up at the pointed cupola as well.

The third landmark in the Quadrilateral is one of the best-known in the world, the Leaning Tower. Begun in 1173, the Leaning Tower sags about 14 feet off center because of a slight slip of land during its construction. Some 294 steps spiral up to a terrace on top, where the view of all Pisa is worth the hike. The delicately columned exterior is often disfigured by top-to-bottom posters.

Nearby, the Camposanto is a small cemetery, enclosed by four galleries that contain priceless but badly faded old frescos and some disgracefully dirty sculptures. A wartime shell hit the North Gallery, setting fire to the world-famous frescos of *The Triumph of Death,* which inspired Liszt's composition *The Dance of Death.* Expertly restored in a former chapel, they alone convey the somber magnificence of the original decorations.

Another site you will want to see among the many in Pisa is Piazza dei Cavalieri, one of Tuscany's finest squares architecturally, around which cluster a huge palace of the same name and the curiously named Palazzo dell'Orologio (Palace of the Clock).

Livorno and Volterra

Moving farther south along the coast again, the national highway and main north-south railroad line reach Livorno (Leghorn), home of the Italian Naval Academy. There is, however, little to see of real interest in the city, and you had better push south another 21 miles along the crowded coastal road that runs through Ardenza, Antignano and Castiglioncello to Cecina, where railway and road turn 29 miles inland to Volterra, one of the richest and most interesting of Tuscany's art cities and one-time rival of Florence. Center of antiquities here is formed by Piazza dei Priori, Palazza Pretorio (with an art gallery), and the nearby cathedral. Volterra's famed fortress is now a prison; its Etruscan Museum holds some 600 highly artistic alabaster cremation urns; Via Roma and Via Bicciarelli provide a genuine medieval atmosphere within the walls, which even boast an Etruscan gate. Balze, a huge ravine, has swallowed up numerous Etruscan tombs through the centuries. Alabaster is still being worked in Volterra (some of its streets are covered with fine white dust coming from the workshops) and constitutes one of the typical products of Italian craftsmanship.

The Cyclopean blocks of stone found at Porta all'Arco go back to Etruscan times as well.

From Cecina, it's 22 miles still south to Campiglia-Marittima—and another notable side trip. This one runs only 8 miles on road from Campiglia-Marittima to Piombino, coastal ferrying point for the Island of Elba.

Elba

Even off season, the 12-mile crossing is assured at least once a day from Piombino to Portoferraio, biggest town on Elba. The ferry service accommodates up to 60 cars. The island is 18 miles long, about 12 wide, and best known for the historical part it played as Napoleon's place of exile for ten months in 1814–15, enshrined in the famous example of palindrome "Able was I ere I saw Elba". You will still be able to see Napoleon's house—the Villa dei Mulini—located at the top of the town, as well as furnishings and other mementos kept there. He seems to have lived a rather spartan existence. His "country house" lies 3 miles away in San Martino. It contains an Egyptian room that is decorated with optical illusions showing scenes from the Egyptian campaign. The exile himself added a strange handwritten inscription that reads: "Napoleon is happy everywhere". Most likely he wasn't dreaming of the Hundred Days at that moment! He might have been looking out on the beautiful view from the terrace.

Other points of interest on the island are: Monte Capanne, which can be ascended in a *cabinovia* (a rather scary small cage)—the views from the top, especially on a clear day, are worth every effort; the thermal baths at San Giovanni; the sanctuary of Madonna di Monserrato, a

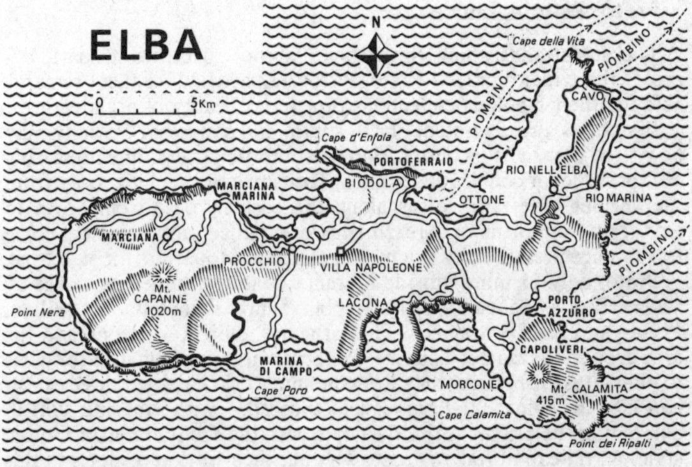

pretty, mountain setting; the churches at Santo Stefano, Poggio and Marciana Alta, all with attractive interiors and placed in scenically lovely spots. Until recently an almost unspoiled paradise, where prices were low and the visitor in some sections a curiosity, it is secluded no more. Still: thick wooded slopes, isolated beaches, and a round-the-island drive by car or bus that takes you from tremendous scenery along the edge of high, seaside cliffs to tiny towns where the sweet white wine of Elba (it's delicious, but be careful after the second glass!) comes cold and sparkling at restaurants and roadside inns. In short, it's an intimate kind of island and good for a family holiday.

Back to the mainland at Piombino, and then the main north-south railway line and highway at Campiglia-Marittima, you continue south over the Maremma, a vast expanse of reclaimed flats frequented by hunters out for the wild boar that still live there, through towns like Follonica and Grosseto to Orbetello Station, three miles from the town itself and last stop before Tuscany runs into the Lazio region and Rome. Orbetello, without monuments worth mentioning, is a possible jump-off point for a variety of scenic trips. It's built between two salt lakes on a tongue of land running out from the coast; by car or by bus, try visiting Porto Santo Stefano and Port'Ercole, two fishing villages on the peninsula's tip, "in" spots for the international set, and Ansedonia, with the impressive Etruscan remains at Cosa.

Prato, Pistoia, Lucca

The autostrada, which runs from Florence to the west coast, bypasses three major cities—Prato, Pistoia, Lucca—all of them remarkable for their fabulous collections of art and beauty of architecture.

Inland, as already noted, north, south, and southeast Tuscany may be visited best by trips out of Florence in those general directions. It's also possible, of course, to see inner Tuscany by branching away from the various cities and towns along the coastal route from north to south, or from Siena or Arezzo. However, since most travelers come to Florence first, the city is a more natural headquarters for side trips.

Prato, only 11 miles outside Florence, features numerous works by such artists as Sangallo, Della Robbia, Lippi, Donatello, Rossellino, Pisano and the Da Maianos. The cathedral, off Via Mazzoni, and the area around Piazza del Comune are representative of what the city has to offer. It is an 11th-century Romanesque work, enlarged three centuries later by Giovanni Pisano, who succeeded with amazing skill in combining the original primitive style with the then-dominant Gothic style. A roll-call of Italian artists who put their time and efforts to this immense church reads like a listing of Tuscany's most illustrious names in the history of art: frescos by Filippo Lippi, especially notable is that of Herod's feast with Salome's dance; sculptures by Donatello, Mino da Fiesole, Rossellino, Benedetto da Maiano, stained-glass windows by Lorenzo da Pelago; and the exquisite bronzes of Bruno di Ser Lapo, Pasquino da Monpulciano, Giambologna, Ferdinando Tacca.

Or wander through Prato's many other churches, where you shouldn't miss San Domenico, San Francesco, the magnificent Santa Maria delle Carceri by Sangallo, San Agostino, San Vicenzo, the paintings by Lippi in the Church of Spirito Santo, and the beautiful doorway of Santa Maria della Pietà.

Pistoia more than duplicates what you have just seen at Prato, with its centers of artistic culture scattered about the city from Piazza del Duomo to the area near the Church of Sant'Andrea. The cathedral or Duomo itself is of Pisan style, flanked by a 13th-century tower and housing some of the town's best works of art. Opposite stands a Gothic baptistery, built in alternating layers of black and white marble; elsewhere around Piazza del Duomo are the Palazzo del Podestà, adorned with coats of arms, and the rather gloomy Palazzo Comunale, now serving as a museum. Among Pistoia's churches you should try to see the two oldest—Sant'Andrea and San Giovanni, each with a priceless pulpit—San Francesco, dating back to the 13th century, and San Paolo, a 14th-century Pisan-style building.

After Pistoia, about 8 miles, the hill town of Montecatini, in season from April to November, is one of Italy's leading spas catering for stomach and liver complaints. Swank hotels and restaurants compete by the dozen.

Then beautiful Lucca, where tree-planted 16th-century ramparts are now used as delightful promenades. The Romanesque and Gothic cathedral is considered by some experts as the most spectacular monument in Tuscany today. And the Church of San Michele, with works by Lippi, Luca della Robbia and others, provides a perfect example of Pisan-Luccan architecture. Outside the old town walls are ever-expanding suburbs of beautiful private villas and gardens.

Napoleon made his sister, Elisa, Princess of Lucca and of Piombino in 1805. She held court at Lucca with her Corsican husband Baciocchi. Though she was less profligate than her better-looking sister Pauline, her interest in the arts was, nevertheless, equaled by an interest in certain writers and artists. Napoleon's abdication in 1814 forced her to leave and move to Bologna, and then, after Waterloo, to the Austrian provinces.

The art gallery—formerly the Governmental Palace—contains some remarkable paintings and sculptures. But the real beauties of Lucca are found in more out of the way places. Take a walk through the old city, for example, following this itinerary: Via Roma, Piazza del Mercato, Piazza San Pietro, and, particularly, Via Guinigi, bordered by superb little palaces, as well as the Piazza dei Servi. The second outing we recommend you make by car. You will reach the gardens of the Villa Reale very quickly, it's only 5 miles out of town. (The Office of Tourism will give you permission to visit the Villa when you are there.)

Barga, to the north, has a magnificent 11th-century cathedral, and from there you can embark on excursions into the Apuan Alps and to Lake Santo, 5,000 feet above sea-level. Camaiore also possesses an interesting church, while the spring waters of Bagni di Lucca have been taken since antiquity.

Instead of taking the superstrada south from Florence to Siena, you might detour west along the Pisa road to Empoli, turning south to include Certaldo, San Gimignano and Poggibonsi.

First stop, 21 miles out of Florence, may be at Empoli, a thriving market for its excellent works in glass. The town, also important agriculturally, has rich works of art that include the Church of Santo

Stefano and, in particular, the Collegiata, a Florentine-Romanesque building erected in 1093. Inside it, a small gallery holds paintings and sculptures by Rossellino, Fra' Bartolomeo, Botticini, the Della Robbias, and Mino da Fiesole.

Up the Elsa Valley from Empoli, some 36 miles from Florence, you reach Certaldo, the home of the writer Giovanni Boccaccio, on a flat plain backed by a hill on which the ancient Castle of Certaldo commands a view of the entire valley. This castle, incidentally, is considered one of Tuscany's best examples of a medieval stronghold. The town is dominated by the episcopal palace, also on the hill, feudal seat of the vicars, who numbered 650 down through history.

Continue southeast to Poggibonsi, famed for its wine; then take the 7-mile branch to San Gimignano, the most remarkable of all the Tuscan medieval hill towns. Time seems to have stood still there since the Middle Ages. Out of some 79 defensive towers thirteen—of various heights—are still intact and give San Gimignano a uniquely photogenic silhouette. It also has its fair share of Tuscan art treasures: beautiful frescos decorate the walls of its two churches and the *pinacoteca* houses some outstanding paintings. The pride of the Civic Museum, located in the People's Palace, is a *Virgin with Saints* by Pinturicchio, and two twin paintings by Filippino Lippi depicting *The Annunciation.* You shouldn't neglect the countryside around San Gimignano either.

Siena

Eighteen miles past Poggibonsi, set beautifully on three hills, rich in works of art, is one of Italy's best-preserved medieval towns—Siena, which amply justifies a visit of two or three days at least. The people of Siena, noted for their cordiality and their pure Italian speech—hence the Summer School of Italian Language and Culture in the 700-year-old university—are proud of the town's monumental high points: the immense unfinished cathedral, with its intarsia pavement and its stunning striped black-and-white marble, and the Palazzo Pubblico on the Piazza del Campo, flanked by the Mangia Tower, which offers a splendid view. To take in the Siena school of painting, a tour through the Art Gallery is mandatory. In fact, almost all public or church buildings in town command enough historical or architectural interest to warrant personal inspection. In particular, see Pinturicchio's animated early 16th-century frescos in the Piccolomini Library, in a wing of the cathedral whose façade is one of the most characteristic masterpieces of Italian art.

Jacopo della Quercia, Siena's most famous architect-sculptor, is responsible for the superb fonts in the Baptistry of San Giovanni. The Church of Santo Domenico is known for its frescos and paintings.

Some fine Sienese painting is in the art gallery of the Buonsignori Palace, notably works by Duccio, Simone Martini, Giovanni di Paolo and Il Sodoma.

Siena explodes in a frenzy of local rivalries on July 2 and on August 16 each year. On those two days the town celebrates its historic *Corsa del Palio* (Parade of the Banner), consisting of a full-blown, all-day festival in which representatives of Siena's 17 individual districts parade in medieval costume, compete in a horse race at Piazza del Campo, then hold open-air district banquets after the one winning the race has been awarded the year's *palio* (banner) of Siena as a prize. This has been going on for years, with one district alone already having won some 60 individual banners in keen competition that finds the entire town divided 17 different ways each year.

Sienese are also music-lovers. The Accademia Chigiana sponsors a famous international music summer-school and a brief, excellent festival, the "Sienese Week", at the beginning of September.

Worthwhile detours to the southeast are the historic townships of Montalcino, granted in 814 by the Emperor Ludovicus the Pious to the remarkable Romanesque Abbey Sant'Antonio, 5 miles south, and last mountain redoubt of the Sienese in their struggle against Florence; Pienza, built by Pope Pius II between 1459 and 1462 round the village of Corsignano, where he had been born Enea Silvio Piccolomini; Montepulciano, entirely Renaissance except for the severe Gothic Communal Palace; the mighty monastery of Monte Oliveto in a dramatic setting; to the south, the no less impressive Romanesque Abbey San Salvatore above an 8th-century crypt.

The Southeast

On the last of these suggested tours through Tuscany's interior, both railroad and the Autostrada del Sole lead to Arezzo and Cortona, with three or four notable side trips, including one to the mountaintop sanctuary of La Verna.

The most scenic road follows the Arno River to Pontassieve. Further east, amidst the heavily-forested hills, Consuma, a village of Etruscan origin, stands on the watershed of a mountain with wide panoramic views over the nearby valleys. Neat little inns along the way serve good, wholesome food—including the delicious *Casentino* ham—washed down with *Chianti* wine, served cold. One day by car will take you into any number of old villages and ancient castles straight out of storybooks.

Higher than Consuma, on the same road, the mountains spread into a succession of meadows and hills forming the Pratomagno, on the western side of which lies the magnificent forest of Vallombrosa, at

3,152 feet, with a 10th-century monastery perched even higher above it. Along the southern side of the Pratomagno is Saltino, at 3,155 feet, famous throughout all Europe for its view over the Arno River Valley, Florence, the Apuan Alps, the Adriatic Sea, mountains around Pistoia, and the Chianti Hills, covered with woods, vineyards (from which come the grapes that produce Chianti wine) and castles.

Poppi, the ancient fief of the Guidi Counts, is the point of departure for visiting the Camaldoli Hermitage, by way of Maggiona through striking countryside of great contrasts. A modern monument marks the site of the battlefield of Campaldino where the Guelphs routed the Ghibellines in 1289. The La Verna Convent—tradition attributes its origins to St. Francis of Assisi—lies east of Poppi, across a landscape of harsh beauty.

Arezzo, Cortona

Back at Pontassieve, you continue along the Arno through San Giovanni Valdarno for another 41 miles to the gentle slope of a hill upon which Arezzo rises to the Duomo and the Medici Fortress, built by Etruscan settlers hundreds of years before the ancient Roman Empire. Here, in one of Tuscany's principal towns, is the birthplace of the Italian poet Petrarch, and the home of Guido d'Arezzo, 11th-century inventor of the musical scale, to whose memory a monument has been erected in Piazza Guido Monaco. Vasari, whose talents enhanced painting, sculpture and architecture, had a beautiful house in his native town, which you can visit. You will also become acquainted with the name of another of Arezzo's famous sons, Aretino, a highly gifted and somewhat scabrous writer. But first and foremost, Arezzo is a storehouse of Tuscan art treasures.

Make certain you see the town's 14th-century Church of San Francesco, in which Piero della Francesca left a series of his frescos, entitled *Story of the Cross,* that must be listed among the most outstanding examples of Italian painting, and visit the Pieve di Santa Maria, a 12th-century Romanesque church, with its five-story belfry pierced by no fewer than 40 double windows. Three stories of narrow columns adorn a most unusual façade. Walk through the Museum of Medieval Art and its neighboring Art Gallery, if that interests you; or, not far off, an archeological museum features some really fine works in ancient Arezzo pottery. A bit farther ahead is a Roman amphitheater built in the 2nd century.

Marcillat, a 16th-century glassmaker from Bourges, spent several years in Arezzo. The Church of San Francesco and the Duomo contain beautiful stained-glass windows.

The annual festival called the Joust of the Saracen (Giostra del Saracino), which is held in Arezzo on the first Sunday in September, commemorates the town's fighting ancestors. It is a tilting competition, favorite sport of the medieval world, with four teams charging with lowered lance at a big dummy of a Saracen. It isn't without its perils as the swinging figure carries a flail tipped with lead balls that can inflict an unpleasant wound.

Sansepolcro is another example of Italy's artistic wealth. This town, on the way to the Adriatic, was the home of Piero della Francesca in the 15th century. If you wish to see his works, and those of his disciples, stop to visit the art gallery.

South of Arezzo, 63 miles from Florence, Cortona, of Etruscan origin but medieval appearance, stands on a hill towering over broad, flat stretches of the Val di Chiana plain. Cortona boasts the work of a remarkable number of Italy's artistic greats, including Sangallo, Fra Angelico, Pietro Lorenzetti, Luca Signorelli, and others. The small Diocesan museum across from the Duomo contains a strikingly rich collection of canvases, including works by Fra Angelico and Signorelli.

Outside the town gates, in the Church of Santa Margherita, patron saint of Cortona, a beautifully decorated 13th-century tomb holds her remains; and above the church, at 2,132 feet, stands the village's ancient fortress, with an excellent view over the entire countryside. The Palazzo Casali houses a representative collection of Etruscan bronzes, including a fifth-century BC lamp, as well as Roman objects excavated in the region.

The road along Lake Trasimeno leads to Chiusi, ancient Etruscan capital and paradise for archeologists. The museum, near the cathedral, houses a priceless collection of Etruscan objects; the Etruscan tombs all round the town outskirts are not easy to find, so it is best to ask at the museum for a guide.

PRACTICAL INFORMATION FOR TUSCANY

HOTELS AND RESTAURANTS

Abetone. Important winter sports center and summer resort. **Hotels:** High season, 20 Dec.–7 Jan., Easter, 25 July–22 Aug.

All (2) are—*Regina,* comfortable, old-fashioned hotel in center of town; *Palazzaccio,* also central, not much atmosphere but modern comforts; *Abetone Piramid,* seasonal, modest but adequate, nice location.

Bellavista (3), pleasant small hotel.

Restaurants. In town, *Pierone,* (M), Via Giardini, small, reserve; *Alla Casina* (I–M), well-stocked snack bar; *Caponi* or *Fernando* for pizza. Just outside town, *Bizzino* (I), is best for country-style home cooking.

Arezzo. Art city. **Hotels:** All (2) are—*Minerva,* outside town center, airconditioned, well-furnished, 82 rooms, roof-garden for summer dining; *Continental,* central, good-sized doubles; *Europa,* opposite station, rather stark but airconditioned rooms; *Graverini,* older hotel, central.

Etruria (3), opposite station, basic but airconditioned.

Restaurants. All (M) are—*Buca di San Francesco,* famous cellar restaurant in Piazza San Francesco, where you go for atmosphere, not the food; *Minerva, Continental, Graverini* are exceptionally good hotel restaurants; others are *Spiedo d'Oro,* Via Crispi; *Tonino,* Via Eritrea; *Arlecchino,* Piazza della Stazione.

Castiglioncello. Beach resort. **Hotels:** Both (2) are—*Miramare,* pleasantly located in pine grove, unpretentious decor, 63 rooms, some with sea view; *Mon Hotel,* overlooking sea, 32 airconditioned rooms, most with shower, private swimming area.

Good pensions are—*Villa St. Vincent* (P1) and *La Calanca* (P2), which has own swimming area.

Restaurants. Both (M)—On the Quercetana road, *Poggetto* and seasonal *Rugantino,* on Via Aurelia, excellent fish on seaside terrace.

Castiglione della Pescaia. Citadel town and lively beach resort. **Hotels:** *L'Approdo* (2) overlooking port, is central and comfortable. Otherwise go outside town to *Riva del Sole* (1), large resort hotel in pinewoods, facing beach.

At **Castiglione,** *David Poggiodoro* (2), comfortable, rather simple, with pool and tennis in park.

At **Roccamare,** on road to **Punta Ala,** posh *Roccamare* holiday village on good beach, with elegant class (1) hotel and class (2) bungalows in pinewoods. *Park Hotel Zibellino* (2), exclusive, 22-room beach hotel.

Restaurants. In town, both (M–E) *Romolo* and *Gambero* for fish.

Certaldo. Hill town, Boccaccio's birthplace. **Hotel/Restaurants:** A visit is likely to involve a stop for lunch. The *Osteria del Vicario,* a small hotel, has the best (and most moderately priced) restaurant, a climb by car, fine view and food.
Castello (M), is also good.

Certosa del Galluzzo. Restaurants: The number of visitors to this charterhouse has led to the establishment of two good restaurants here, the *Bianca* and the *Calamandrei,* both (M), near bridge below the monastery.

Chianciano Terme. Important spa. Hotels: Most hotels open 15 April–31 Oct. *Grand Hotel et Royal* (L), best, radio and TV in rooms, pool, tennis, garage, hotel bus at station, all rooms have bath.

Both (1) are—*Excelsior,* airconditioned, garage, hotel bus at station, close runner-up; *Michelangelo,* Via delle Piane, all rooms with bath or shower, garage, dining veranda overlooks large park; tennis, thermal pool.

Among (2) hotels, all comfortable and rather posh—*Fortuna,* in quiet park, modern decor, tennis, pool; *Boston,* traditional furnishings; *Capitol,* striking modern decor, pool on rooftop terrace; *Raffaello,* handsome, modern, with pool in attractive park.

Both (3) are—*President,* superior in category, with elegant modern appointments; *Irma,* unassuming and comfortable, almost all rooms with bath.

Consuma. Etruscan town. **Hotels:** At **Pelago,** *Laghetto nel Bosco* (2), tranquil, shares pool, tennis, riding in vast park with recent sister hotel *Parco dei Faggi* (1); both offer country villa atmosphere, only prices vary.

Cortona. Art City. **Hotels:** Both (2)—in town, *San Luca.* At **Sant'Egidio,** in hills above city, *Villa Guglielmesca,* 26 rooms, most with bath, open April–Oct.

Restaurants: *Tonino's* (M) can be good, but unsatisfactory when crowded; several good, less pretentious *trattorie;* try *La Loggetta,* off main street.

Donoratico Marina. Beach resort with wide variety of aliases (e.g., Marina di Castagneto). **Hotels:** *Club Mediterranée* center. *Ginepri* (3), basic hotel on broad sandy beach.

Elba. Largest island of Tuscan Archipelago in Tyrrhenian Sea. Most hotels open mid-April—mid-October.

At **Biodola,** *Hermitage* (1), smart, modern, right on sandy beach with pool on flowered terrace. *La Biodola* (2), 51 rooms with shower in modern building on beach, pool, tennis.

At **Capoliveri-Naregno.** *Elba International* (2). big, modern, rather impersonal, lift to beach, salt water pool. *Le Acacie* (3), 105 rooms in several buildings on beach, pool, tennis, attractive lounge and flowered dining terrace.

At **Cavoli,** *Bahia* (2), bungalows on lovely beach; it's essential to reserve way ahead for this exceptional spot.

At enchanting **Fetovaia,** off the beaten track. *Lo Scirocco* (2), tiny 12-room hotel overlooking cove.

At **Lacona,** *Lacona* (2), big, modern hotel in extensive grounds on beach, with terraces, disco, buffet-style restaurant. *Capo Sud* (P1), beautiful location near beach, 34 basic rooms in bungalows.

At **Magazzini,** *Fabricia* (2), low-slung, modern, in olive grove, 5 min. through garden to beach, 60 rooms, most with shower, balcony, salt water pool.

At **Marciana Marina.** *La Primula* (1), in town, 5 min. from beach, attractive, pleasant atmosphere. *Gabbiano Azzurro* (2), bright, friendly, 10 min. from beach. *Da Sauro* and *Rendez-Vous,* both (M-E) are cheery, good for fish.

At **Marina di Campo:** Both (2)—*Coralli,* on beach, pool, 58 rooms with shower; *Marina Due,* on hillside above town, 20 minutes from beach, all resort facilities, pool. Good choice of restaurants: *Tre Colonne* (M); *Kon Tiki* (M–E), fine, smart. *Da Gianni* (M), at Pila airport, one of island's best.

At **Ottone.** *Villa Ottone* (2), Mediterranean style with loggias, pool, tennis and water sports on bay.

At **Picchiaie,** *Picchiaie Residence* (2), quiet hillside location, handsome building with beautiful view, tennis courts and pool.

At **Porto Azzurro,** *Cala di Mola* (2), modern, well-equipped resort-style, with pool, beach. Two (M) restaurants are: *Lanterna,* on the port; *Il Pozzo,* at Barbaressa.

Portoferraio. Two (M) restaurants: *La Ferrigna,* family-run; *Jamaica,* both (M). At nearby Scaglioni, panoramic *Da Luciano* (M-E) is good.

At **Procchio:** *Del Golfo* (1), large central building contains attractive public rooms, nicely decorated bedrooms, ample grounds, large salt water pool, private white sand beach. All (2) are: *Desiree,* spacious modern hotel on private beach, airy comfortable rooms. *Monna Lisa,* quiet, modest, 10 min. from beach; *Di Procchio,* across road from beach, basic but comfortable.

Empoli. Art town, glass manufacturing center. **Hotels:** *Tazza d'Oro* (3), Via G. del Papa 16. *Sole* (3), small.

Restaurant. *Spiedo* (M), Via Livornese 178, fine reputation.

Fiesole. Art town, Florence suburb. **Hotels:** *Villa San Michele* (L), one of Italy's most distinguished hotels, in converted 15th-century monastery, partly designed by Michelangelo, expensive, recent reports cite poor service.

Aurora (2), half of its 24 rooms have bath. *Pensionato San Girolama, Bencistà,* both (P2), and *Villa Bonelli* (3), are budget value.

Restaurants. All (M) are—*Raspanti* and *Aurora,* excellent, Tuscan specialties. *Gran Terrazza,* reader-recommended for value.

And at **Maiano** (2 miles away), the excellent *Trattoria le Cave* for *tortellini* and carefully roasted meat at moderate prices.

Follonica. Jumping-off point for hunting, in the Maremma district. **Hotels:** *Golfo del Sole* (2), smallish modern hotel with beach, pool, car park.

Hotel/Restaurant. *Piccolo Mondo* (2M), noted for dining terrace on sea, (seafood *risotto,* crêpes), has 13 rather basic rooms.

Forte dei Marmi. Important, very smart beach resort. **Hotels:** High season, 15 Dec.–15 Feb., Easter, 15 June–30 Sept.

Augustus (L), in a lush park, main building and attractive bungalows contain 60 tastefully furnished rooms, smart clientele, beach club, disco, (open 10 May–10 Oct.); has annex, *Augustus Lido* (1), slightly less expensive, in former Agnelli villa, handsome ambiance, meals at *Augustus,* 50 yds. away.

All (1) are—*Hermitage,* modern, quietly located in park a short walk from beach, 40 spacious rooms with bath, pool, minibus to beach, (open 1 May–30 Sept.); *Alcione,* Viale Morin, comfortable. *Raffaelli Park* offers all resort amenities. *Byron,* attractively decorated villa with pool, garden.

All (2) are—*Astoria Garden,* quiet, pleasant; *Adams Villa Maria,* Viale Italico 10, overlooking sea, shady park; *Villa Angela,* Via Mazzini 64, very pleasant atmosphere, tennis, private beach and gardens; *Florida,* Viale Morin, comfortable; *Pleaidi,* Via Civitali, overlooks quiet gardens, (open 10 May–30 Sept.); *Alpemare,* Lungomare Italico 104, on the water, two-thirds of rooms have bath, tennis court, (1 June–31 Oct.)

Imperiale (3), Viale Mazzini 20, tennis court, garage, (open 15 May–30 Sept.)

Restaurants. Beautiful and moneyed vacationers flock to *Maitò* (E) for abundant antipasti and baked fish dishes. Another, less splashy favorite, tiny, family-run *Bruno* (M), fish only, even in your pasta. *La Barca* (E), pleasant terrace, fine food.

Giglio. Island hideaway in Tuscan Archipelago in Tyrrhenian Sea. **Hotels:** At Giglio Porto, All (2) are—*Castello Monticello,* 31 rooms, all with bath or shower; *Demo's* and *Arenella,* small.

At **Campese,** where there's a lovely beach, *Campese* (2), noisy in season.

Grosseto. Commercial center of agricultural region. **Hotels:** *Lorena* (1), airconditioned, radios in rooms. *Bastiani* (2), in town, well-equipped. *AGIP Motel* (3), Via Aurelia Sud, basic.

At **Marina di Grosseto,** all (2) are—*Nazioni* and *Mediterraneo,* on beach; *Principe,* in pine grove, tennis, private beach.

Restaurants. *Ombrone* (M), good, popular, so reserve. *La Casareccia* (M), at Poggioni. *Terzo Cerchio* (M), at Istia d'Ombrone.

Lido di Camaiore. Beach resort. **Hotels:** High season, 15 June–15 Sept; Carnival; Easter, Christmas.

Both (1) are—*Grand Hotel Riviera,* Viale Pistelli, well-furnished rooms, most with bath or shower, some with sea view; *Ariston* quietly located in large park with pool, tennis, beach facilities.

Both (2) are—*Panoramic,* modern, across road from beach, large pool in garden, summer dining terrace, pleasant, balconied rooms; *EUR* on beach boulevard, attractive garden.

Paris (3), on seafront, basic, 27 rooms with shower.

Livorno. (Leghorn) Important port but of minor interest to tourists. **Hotels:** *Palazzo* (1), Viale Italia 195, recommended, has sea view, gardens.

Granduca (2), Piazza Micheli, near ancient port, tastefully furnished. At **Stagno,** *Motel AGIP* (3).

Restaurants. All (M)—*Carducci* for *caciucco,* very good *Oscar, Parmigiana.*

Lucca. Picturesque art city. **Hotels:** Both (2) are—*Universo,* Piazza del Giglio, central, traditional furnishings, comfort, good cuisine; *Napoleon,* outside bastions, airconditioned, up-to-date.

Nuova Luna (3), Corte Campagni 12, has 35 rooms.

At **Massa Pisana,** 3 miles from Lucca, *Villa La Principessa* (1), a find; exquisitely decorated villa hotel, all comforts, park, pool.

Restaurants. If you are traveling on the road between Montecatini and Lucca (not on the *autostrada*) turn to your right about 4 miles before Lucca for the 17th-century *Villa Mansi* (E), at **Segromigno;** excellent restaurant at the beautiful manor.

All (M) are—*Buca di Sant' Antonio* on Via della Cervia 1, with the best food (risotto, *pappardelle con la lepre*) *Giglio* is agreeable; *Sergio,* Piazza Bernardini, is reasonable, recommended; *Perduca,* Via San Girolamo; *Delle Mura,* bastion Santa Maria.

At **San Macario,** just outside Lucca, *Solferino* (M), rustic, outstanding.

Marina di Massa. Beach resort. **Hotels:** All (1) are—*Tirreno,* Via Manzoni, 40 comfortable rooms, private beach; *Excelsior,* Via Vespucci, large beachfront hotel with pool, 63 airconditioned rooms.

Both (2) are—*Italia,* all rooms with shower; *Nedy* in residential quarter of **Ronchi,** 25 rooms in villa amid pines, own beach area.

Marina di Pietrasanta. Beach resort. **Hotels:** High season, 15 June–15 Sept; Christmas; Easter.

Both (1) are—*Palazzo della Spiaggia,* smart, modern resort hotel, pool in attractive garden, private beach; *Lombardi,* comfortable, 40 well-furnished rooms, pool, beach, tennis.

All (2) are—*Eden Park,* unassuming, all sports facilities; *La Riva,* pleasant, informal, doubles have balconies overlooking garden and sea; *Battelli,* Viale Versilia 171, most rooms have bath, tennis court, has annex.

Montalcino. Medieval fortress town near Siena, home of famous (expensive, even here) Brunello wine.

Restaurants. Both (M)—*Il Giglio,* modest inn, excellent fare; *Taverna dei Barbi,* country cooking.

Monte Argentario. Popular, picturesque submerged mountain peak peninsula linked to mainland by 3 tongues of land enclosing 2 saltwater lagoons.

Underwater fishing is good all along the southern stretch of Tuscan coast, from here to the island of **Giglio.**

Main towns on the peninsula are **Porto Santo Stefano** and **Porto Ercole,** both mere fishing villages years ago, but today among Europe's smartest resorts. At the base of the peninsula, 10 miles apart, **Fonteblanda** and **Ansedonia.**

Pricey, first-class hotels include the *Cala Piccola* on a handsome, secluded clifftop site at the end of a private road on the peninsula's extreme western tip, private beach, gardens; residential hotel.

Ansedonia on Aurelia highway. **Restaurants:** *Pitorsino* (E), gourmet dining (*rigatoni al gorgonzola*) in vine-shaded garden.

Fonteblanda. Hotel: *Corte dei Butteri* (1), with pool, fine beach, book in advance for this smart, secluded haven.

Orbetello, a little town in the middle of the central linking tongue, with a few modest hotels and a fine restaurant, *Egisto* (M), on Corso Italia.

Porto Ercole. Hotels: *Il Pelican,* quietly posh, informal and very expensive, with private beach and garden setting, crowded in high season, book in advance.

Both (2) are—*Don Pedro,* modern; and *Villa Letitzia,* a good buy.

Restaurants. Several good restaurants along the wharf. Both (M) are—*Al Gambero Rosso* and fine *Il Gatto e la Volpe,* on hillside.

Porto Santo Stefano. Hotels: *Filippo II* (1), attractive, pricey, on promontory, private beach, gardens, crowded in high season, book well in advance; *Vittoria* (2) is attractive; *Lucciola* (3), all rooms with shower.

Restaurants. *La Pace* (E) serves good food on a terrace overlooking sea; *Armando* and *Argentario,* both at the port, for fish specialties.

Montecatini Terme. Most important spa in Italy. **Hotels:** High season, 18 July–30 Sept. *Grand Hotel & La Pace* (1), Via Torretta, 170 rooms, all with bath, airconditioned, garage, radio and television in rooms, swimming pool, secluded situation in own pleasant grounds.

All (1) are—*Bella Vista Palace e Golf,* Viale Fedeli, smaller, also in own quiet grounds, both open April through October; *Du Park et Regina,* Viale Diaz 8, majority of rooms have bath, open 1 May–31 Oct.; *Panoramic,* Viale Bustichini, all rooms with bath; *Nizza e Suisse,* Viale Verdi 72, all rooms have bath, open 1 April–10 Nov. *Croce di Malta,* Viale IV Novembre 18, is a superior hotel, seasonal, has 2nd class annex (Aquila d'Oro); *Cristallino,* Viale IV Novembre 12, all rooms with bath, swimming pool on top of building, beautiful view, garage; in same street another pleasant new hotel, the *Tamerici e Principe.*

All (2) are—*Manzoni,* in quiet park, 55 well-furnished rooms with bath or shower, *Cappelli-Croce di Savoia,* comfortable, traditional decor. *Torretta,* comfortable, small, with garden, pool.

Reale (3), Via Palestro, central, pleasant garden, all doubles with bath.

Montepulciano. Admirably situated art city. **Hotels:** Both (3) are—*Panoramic,* all private baths, tennis; *Marzocco.*

Monte Senario. Noted monastery, near Florence. **Restaurant:** *La Giulia* (M), fine lunch stop, summer dining on terrace, winters beside huge hearth, rustic Tuscan specialties, especially *salame.*

Piombino. Jumping-off point for Elba. **Hotels:** *Centrale* (2), quarter of rooms have bath. Modest but adequate overnight halt—*Collodi* (3), in town.

Pisa. Famous art town. **Hotels:** Both (1) are—*Dei Cavalieri,* on station square, large, well-appointed, with comfortable rooms and lounges; *Duomo,* a few steps from famous tower, modern, attractive, air conditioning extra.

All (2) are—*La Pace,* at station, almost all rooms have bath; *Villa Kinzica,* Piazza Arcivescovada 4, garage, near Duomo; *Touring,* Via Puccini, good; *Terminus,* Via Colombo, has private baths; as does *Arno,* Via Crispi; *California Park Hotel,* on the Via Aurelia route from town, is the Italian version of the American motel, swimming pool.

Restaurants: All (E), *Sergio,* Lungarno Pacinotti, is attractive and very good. *Buzzino,* Via Cammeo 44, with garden, formerly top-rank, recently reported uneven. *Rosticceria Fiorentina,* Corso Italia 46, specializes in famous Tuscan steaks.

All (M) are—*Spartaco,* Piazza Vittorio, and *Emilio,* Via Roma, serve good food at lower prices; near the Leaning Tower is *Santa Maria,* also self-service; *Corzani,* Piazza Chiara Gambacorti, and *Da Nando,* Via Contessa Matilde, also good.

Pistoia. Art city. **Hotels:** *Residence Convento,* 3 mi. from town, is best, offers comfort and atmosphere (2). *Leon Bianco* (3), central.

Restaurants: Both (M)—the best place to eat here is the *Cucciolo della Montagna,* Via Pantciatichi; also good is *Nuevo Maresca,* Via Frosini, a little more expensive.

Prato. Art city. **Hotels:** All (2) are—*Palace,* newest, best, airconditioned, comfortable, pool; also good, *President,* modern; *Villa Santa Cristina,* outside town, in 17th-century villa, pool, restaurant.

Restaurants. All (M)—*Baghino,* homemade *ravioli; Stella d'Italia, ribollita* soup; *Ceppo Vecchio,* local specialties.

Punta Ala. Extensive, newly developed beach resort in bowl of low hills, villa colony, near Maremma reserve. **Hotels:** Both (1) are—*Gallia Palace,* elegant, airconditioned, open 20 May–15 Oct, all rooms with bath or shower, private beach, harbors and yacht marinas; *Cala del Porto,* low-slung modern hotel overlooking terraces, pool, sea below, attractively informal but posh, rock swimming area or hotel bus to beach, disco.

Golf (2), big, comfortable, near 18-hole course (par 72), pool, beach.

San Gimignano. Picturesque old hill town near Certaldo. **Hotels:** *La Cisterna* (2), spacious, old-fashioned rooms, fine restaurant overlooking tiled rooftops.

Opposite, on lovely square, *Leon Bianco* (3). *Bel Soggiorno* (3), is fine in category, all rooms with bath, excellent restaurant (M).

Siena. Italy's best-preserved medieval city. **Hotels:** All (1). In Siena proper —Large, palace-type, totally renovated, *Excelsior Jolly.*

Other fine hotels are on outskirts: *Park,* a CIGA hotel, handsome, 15th-century, building, antique-filled lounges and dining rooms, excellent cuisine, landscaped gardens, good-sized pool, spacious, pleasant rooms, but thin walls; *Villa Scacciapensieri,* country manor with huge fireplace, comfy sofas; some rooms in cottages in garden, pool, tennis, fine restaurant and wine cellar. *Certosa di Maggiano,* a *Relais* hotel, 14 rooms in renovated monastery, outstanding atmosphere, comfort and service; pool.

All (2) are—*Continentale,* Via Banchi di Sopra, is in heart of things, old fashioned, basic; *Minerva,* at San Lorenzo gate, adequate; *Moderno,* outside bastions, comfortable. *Athena,* good location, just inside bastions, 100 rooms, some suites.

Palazzo Ravizza (P1), few steps from cathedral, 17th-century building, fine old furnishings, garden, excellent value, reserve well ahead.

Restaurants. All (E) are—*Il Mangia,* Piazza del Campo; *Tullio-Tre Cristi,* Via Provenanzo; and the very pleasant dining rooms of hotels *Park* or *Villa Scacciapensieri.*

All (M) are—*Nello,* Via Porrione 28. Two finds: *Da Guido,* Vicolo Pettinaio, try *cannoli alla Guido;* plainer *Da Mugolone,* Via Pellegrini, delicate *crostini* (typical Tuscan canapes); Turiddu, Via Diaccetto, homey local food.

Tirrenia. Pisa's beach resort. **Hotels:** Both (1) are—*Golf,* best, pool, beach, all private baths, 9-hole golf course; *Continental,* pool, tennis.

Viareggio. Beach resort. **Hotels:** High season, 15 June–10 Sept, Carnival and Easter.

All (1) are—*Astor,* elegantly modern, well-furnished hotel overlooking beach, 66 good-sized rooms, light and airy; *Royal,* huge Renaissance-style building overlooking seaside promenade, spacious, well-furnished rooms, pool in gardens and fine beach area; *Principe di Piemonte,* palace-type, on promenade, many rooms with balcony, sea view, sumptuous public rooms, elegant sidewalk terrace, indoor pool.

All (2) are—*American,* modern, well-appointed; *Excelsior,* on shore, traditional comfort; *Garden,* attractive small hotel, short walk from beach.

Metropol (3), small, all rooms with bath or shower.

Restaurants. Both (E) are—leading restaurant, *Tito,* Molo Corrado Greco, excellent (especially for shrimp and veal scallops); as is *Buonamigo,* Via S. Andrea (for sea food antipasto and fish soup). *Il Patriarca,* Viale Carducci, or *Romano,* Via Mazzini, among best in town for fish.

All (M–E) are—*Fedi,* Via Verdi, simple but good; *Genny,* Via Zanardelli, new and popular, vast antipasto table. *Il Cancello,* Viale Carducci, reserve.

Volterra. Art city and alabaster center. **Hotel:** *Nazionale* (2), on main square.

USEFUL ADDRESSES. **Tourist Offices** *Abetone:* AAST, Piazza delle Piramidi. *Arezzo:* EPT, Piazza Risorgimento 16, Via Roma 9. *Castiglioncello:* AAST, Via Aurelia 959. *Castiglione della Pescaia:* AAST, Piazza Garibaldi. *Chianciano Terme,* AAST, Via Sabatini 7. *Cortona,* AAST, Piazza Signorelli 10 or Via Nazionale 70. *Elba:* AAST Ente Valorizzazione Elba Calata Italia 26, Portoferraio. *Fiesole:* AAST, Piazza Mina da Fiesole 45. *Follonica:* AAST, Viale Italia. *Grosseto:* EPT, Via Monterosa 206. *Livorno:* EPT, Piazza Cavour 6, Railway Station and port. *Lucca:* EPT, Piazza Guidiccioni 2, and Via V. Veneto 40. *Marina di Massa:* AAST, Viale A. Vespucci 23. *Montecatini Terme:* AAST, Viale Verdi 66. *Pisa:* EPT, Corso A. Gramsci 110. *Prato:* AAST, Via L. Muzzi 51. *Siena:* AAST, Via Bianchi di Sotto 20; EPT, Via di Città 5. *Viareggio:* AAST, Viale Carducci 10.

SPECIAL EVENTS. *Arezzo:* The 13th-century Battle of the Saracens is re-enacted on the first Sunday in September, with armored knights. *Lucca:* Festival of the Holy Cross, 13 September. *Montecatini Terme:* The annual horse show takes place in July. *Pisa:* 5 June, the historic Games of the Bridge; 16 June, the feast day of Pisa's patron saint, San Ranieri, illuminated boat processions; other events on 17 June. *Pistoia:* September sees a traditional festival, the Giostra dell'Orso, harking back to the 14th century. *Siena:* 28–30 April, the feast of St. Catherine; 2 July the first spectacle of the exciting Palio, which is run on 16 August, with the traditional procession on 14 August. *Viareggio:* The Carnival, in February, is the most important in all Italy, with a procession of grotesque gigantic papier-mâché figures and fantastic floats.

EMILIA-ROMAGNA

Princely Cities, Princely Food

Bordered on the north by the Po River and on the south by a massive section of the Appennines, the Emilia-Romagna region is really a string of little and big cities, laid out for the most part along that arrow-straight Roman road known as the Emilian Way, which runs from Milan through Piacenza, in the northwest, to Rimini, on the Adriatic, Romagna is the area from Rimini to the outskirts of Bologna, while Emilia refers to that portion between Bologna and Piacenza.

Fidenza, Parma, Reggio, Modena, Bologna, Imola, Faenza, Cesena, lie along the Emilian Way which, just short of Rimini, crosses the Rubicon. It was this river which Caesar crossed in defiance of the Fates and the Roman Senate, leading his legions on to Rome.

All the cities owe their civic origin to Rome, whose influence survived all the barbarian invasions. For this reason, the entire region is particularly rich in important monuments and works of art.

Rome built Via Emilia, the magnificent arterial way, for military and political purposes. In the centuries which followed it became the principal trade route, and was in large measure responsible for the growth of the region. A leisurely pace along this highway is recommended in order to enjoy the charming communities mellowed with age and containing much of outstanding interest and beauty.

The countryside beyond the cities and towns through which the highway runs is flat and low and often flooded, but it is a rich, fertile land. Its grape vines lacing the fruit trees, its fields of wheat and flax, its pasture for the cattle, contribute heavily to Italy's agricultural resources.

In the mountains, southwest of Bologna, ancient watchtowers still stand on seemingly inaccessible peaks where they were built by feudal lords to guard against forays into their domains. Both the Germans and the Allies used many of them as observation posts during the last war.

Weather Matters

The weather in Emilia-Romagna comes close to resembling that of Milan. From November through February it is apt to be quite damp and foggy, and July and August are usually unpleasantly hot. Spring and fall are the best seasons.

Road Reports

There could hardly be an easier region for getting from one point of interest to another. A1, the *Autostrada del Sole,* parallels the ancient Roman Via Emilia, starting north of Milan, where it crosses A4 from Turin to Venice, continuing in an almost straight line past Piacenza, Parma, Reggio Emilia, Modena, where A22 comes down from Trento and Verona, and Bologna, where it links with A13 from Venice, Padua and Ferrara, as well as A14, the *Autostrada Adriatica* to Rimini with a branch to Ravenna; A1 continues south to Florence and Rome. A coastal road leads south from Venice via Ravenna to Rimini.

If you have not much time for this part of the country, Bologna is the obvious center to explore from.

Food for Thought

The cuisine of this region, everything considered, is the finest and most famous in Italy. The most famous dish is *tagliatelle alla bolognese* or *al ragù,* thin slices of *pasta* made with eggs and served with a succulent ragout, which only the Bolognesi make properly. *Tortellini,* which resemble tiny hats, are stuffed with a mixture of pork, eggs, cheese and spices, and are served either with a ragout or in soup. *Lasagne al forno* are broad thin slices of macaroni—with cheese, tomato sauce and meat added—cooked in the oven. *Agnolotti* are squares of pasta stuffed with meat, while *ravioli* are filled with ricotta (a kind of cottage cheese) and/or such vegetables as spinach or squash.

The cooks of the region also do wonders with meat and fish dishes, *Zampone* is a pig's forefoot which has been stuffed with highly seasoned pork. This is boiled for four hours, sliced in one-inch thicknesses, and eaten with a *salsa verde* (green sauce) or mustard. *Cotoletta alla bolognese* is a veal cutlet dipped in egg, with a slice of ham and melted cheese topping it. In the Adriatic resorts you will find *brodetto,* a marvelous soup, with quantities of fish and slices of bread floating in it, usually flavored with saffron.

The wines of the region are headed by the red, sparkling *Lambrusco,* which comes both sweet and dry. The dry variety is ideal with *pasta* and meat in general. The amber-colored *Albana* goes very well with fish, and *Sangiovese* is particularly indicated for roasts. A less well-known wine is the *Vino del Bosco,* found around Ferrara. Though red and sparkling, it is good with fish.

Exploring Emilia-Romagna

Emilia-Romagna has dominated the history of Italy in some peculiar ways. Much of it was Etruscan in earliest colonization, even the names of the tribes of its earliest inhabitants being lost in the maze of prehistoric legends. The Etruscans did not last very long or implant any profound influence. When the Romans came, in the heyday of the Republic, they met little opposition on their expansion northward.

The Romans found at Bologna, for example, the Etruscan community called Felsina. They renamed it Bononia, established a powerful garrison there and moved on to the northwest, building their Via Emilia as they went. Other garrisons were established, similarly, until the long chain from Rome to Rimini, from Rimini to Milan and on to Gaul, was complete.

Discharged legionaries, after 25 years' service, were rewarded by grateful Rome with plots of marshland along the military highway. These they could, if they would, drain, cultivate and make into farms. That so many of them did is one of the major miracles of Rome's 1,000 years. The original discontent of these poor old soldiers, dumped virtually penniless onto a swamp after so much service in Rome's legions, may be the basis of Emilia's traditional unrest. Certainly the discontent has always been there. In the earliest days Hannibal found friends and allies there when he swept down through the Alps on his way to eventual defeat. But Hannibal's rear guard wasn't very popular in Emilia either and his lines of supply did not last long.

When, several hundreds of years later, the Roman Empire, beset from without by barbarian hordes and from within by corruption, disintegrated into the darkness of the Middle Ages, Emilia, in addition to contributing as usual to the fall of the forces then in power, had three distinctions. First, Ravenna became, for as long as it lasted, the capital of that refugee government which proclaimed itself the Western Empire. Second, other cities set up more rapidly than most other parts of erstwhile Rome the free city principalities which lasted for close to 1,000 years. Third, one of these free principalities became the world's oldest living republic—that of San Marino.

The Este family in Ferrara, the Pallavicini in Piacenza, the Bentivoglio in Bologna, the Polenta in Ravenna—after the Byzantine influence began to wane—and the famed Malatesta in Rimini, governed their own and nearby towns, for better or for worse, depending largely upon the incumbent ruler and the temper of the people at the moment, until late in the 16th century, when the Papal States absorbed most of them. Parma and Piacenza went over to Farnese rule instead. And the Este, losing Ferrara, managed to retain their tight hold on Modena and Reggio.

The Habsburgs took the place of the Este family, when Austria moved down into Italy and France's Bourbon monarchs won control from the Farnese. The Napoleonic conquest of Italy aroused Emilia's never dormant revolutionary feeling and turned it towards nationalism. This led to the formation of an alliance with Piedmont and the House of Savoy.

From the birth of the Kingdom of Italy until late in 1944 there is little record of any revolutionary resurgence in the province. Emilians will tell you with pride that there was always a resistance movement against Mussolini there, but if there was one it accomplished, to put it mildly, little. But, in 1944, with the Allies battering at the Apennine gateways to north Italy, Bologna and the region around it became the center of such violent partisan activity as to elicit the Nazis' most vicious reprisals.

Today Emilia continues its revolutionary history by being known as the center of Communist strength in Italy. No Emilian, not even in the "Red Capital" of Modena, can tell you why. As usual, they're just "against the government".

From Piacenza to Parma

We will assume that you are starting your journey in the northwest corner of Emilia, the natural route if you come from the north.

Your first stop, obviously, will be Piacenza. Had you been here in about 1565 you would have seen hordes of workmen laboring on the Palazzo Farnese, begun seven years previously by Vignola for the Farnese dukes, of whose dominions Piacenza was then a part. But it is still unfinished today, a colossal, massive remnant of a glory that is no more. The cathedral would have been there then, as it is today, a 12th-century Lombardian-Romanesque structure with a spectacular façade. So, too, would the Lombard Church of Sant' Antonino, and the Palazzo del Comune, in the square, dating from the 13th century. Little else remains.

Two interesting side trips from Piacenza are to Grazzano Visconti, a modern version of a medieval village, noted now for its craftwork, especially wrought-iron and hand-made furniture; and to Velleia Romana, the Roman remains of a small country town, attractively situated. Both these can be reached by bus or train.

You may stop at Fidenza to see its Romanesque cathedral, and if you like thermal baths, go up to Salsomaggiore, which is Italy's chief inland watering place, with the single exception of Montecatini.

Parma, citadel of the arts and former fief of the powerful Farnese family, is famous for having some of the most demanding opera fans in the world. They will whistle and hoot a tenor off the stage at the drop of a high C. The 12th-century Romanesque cathedral and its adjacent early Gothic baptistery form an ensemble that rivals Pisa in stylistic harmony if not in grandeur. The cathedral dome houses Correggio's fresco of the Assumption, often called one of the greatest of Renaissance masterpieces. The baptistery, built of red marble, soars five stories high above a spacious octagonal base; it ranks among Italy's finest buildings.

Not far from the Piazza del Duomo are the churches of the Madonna della Steccata and San Giovanni Evangelista, the former decorated by Parmigiano and the latter by Correggio and Parmigiano.

The Palazzo della Pilotta, built for the Farnese family, not only houses one of Italy's greatest collections of art but it does so in one of the most modern museums in Italy. It has airconditioning, excellent lighting effects and a superb collection of Italian paintings of all schools and those of other nationalities.

The famed Farnese Theater, entirely of wood, on the top floor, was so damaged in World War II that it has had to be built again piece by piece, with the original wood being utilized as much as is possible. Also in the Palazzo is the Palatine Library, with more than 40,000 volumes of precious manuscripts and incunabula, and the National Museum of Former Ages, with extremely valuable Etruscan and Roman pieces, as well as a collection of medieval and Renaissance furnishings.

Of interest also is the Glauco-Lombardi Museum. There is a collection of objects that once belonged to Napoleon's Empress Maria-Luisa, who received at the Congress of Vienna the Duchies of Parma, Piacenza and Guastalla. The garden of the Palazzo del Giardino was laid out by a French architect, Petitot.

Halfway southeast to Modena is Reggio Emilia, the Roman Forum Lepidi, with a 13th-century cathedral, several baroque churches and the Parmeggiani Gallery, containing good examples of the work of Veronese, El Greco and Van Dyck.

For lovers of music there is a pilgrimage northwest from Parma. Verdi, whose very name became the rallying cry for Italian independence, was born in Roncole, near Busseto. Busseto is itself an attractive town, with a castle. Verdi's mansion, Sant'Agata, lies on the outskirts.

Modena

A short distance on down the road is Modena, which, with Reggio, was capital of the great Duchy of Este from the end of the 13th century to the creation of the Kingdom of Italy in 1859. The city today gives ample evidence of the opulence and good taste of that 500-year rule.

Modena's outward appearance of tranquillity is enhanced by its pleasant fountains and its justly famous 14th-century bell tower—La Ghirlandina. The sacristan of Duomo, which is an exceptionally beautiful example of Romanesque style, will show you to the small museum where you can see the famous bas-reliefs that used to decorate the arched buttresses of the cathedral.

In the Palazzo dei Musei, which houses Modena's most important art collections, you will find of especial interest the Biblioteca Estense, which contains a world-famed collection of illuminated manuscripts, bookbindings, rare engravings and incunabula. Both Italian and foreign works are included. The most notable single object, perhaps, is the Borso d'Este Bible, which contains 1,200 miniatures of the Ferrara school of the 15th century. The Galleria Estense is one of Italy's largest, though not most important, art galleries. (Emilian, Venetian and Tuscan primitives; 16th-century Italian, foreign schools, etc.) The vast Ducal palace provided the setting for a brilliant Renaissance court. It is now the Italian Military Academy. A strikingly realistic terracotta *Pietà,* by Mazzoni, is to be seen in the church of San Giovanni Decollato.

Bologna

Your next stop will be Bologna. Italy's "Red capital" it is also an important economic center, a focus for learning (Marconi, the wireless inventor was born here) and has been famous for its artistic ac ments throughout the ages. It is hard to say which of all these will most attract the visitor. Scientists and students will inevitably be drawn to the university, founded in 1119, where the first lessons in human anatomy were given, and where later Galvani, by mere observations of the twitchings of dissected frogs, learned of the flow of electric current. Within the university's walls can still be seen Lelli's two famous limewood anatomical models, carved in perfection—more or less—because of the dearth and expense of actual corpses, which at that period had to be stolen.

Gourmets, and Bologna is a city of gourmets, will concentrate on the joys of the table, tasting several dishes *alla Bolognese* and drinking some of the marvellous wines of the region. Lovers of art and architecture will wander through the streets, between the Renaissance palaces, into the magnificent churches, around the famous fountains, exploring the rich monuments to Bologna's treasured past.

Of course the ideal traveler would be a rare composite of all three. He would, of course, visit the university, where he would be thrilled by the memory of the 6th-century scholars who revived the study of Roman law. Then he would lunch, very leisurely, at one of the city's fine restaurants, ordering a Bolognese luncheon, *un pranzo alla Bolognese,* and having eaten well, set forth to visit the great Church of San Petronio, one of Italy's most superb Gothic structures. Although the façade is as yet unfinished (it was only started in 1390) the center portal is adorned by Jacopo della Quercia's truly marvelous bas-reliefs of biblical episodes, the Prophets and the Virgin Mary. Within the cathedral, the chapels by Costa and Onofri and the Renaissance choir are of especial interest.

Although it was made a free city by the Emperor Henry V in 1116, Bologna nevertheless joined the Lombard league against the Hohenstaufen emperors. The leading families indulged, moreover, in endless and ruthless feuds, depending for their survival on some 200 mighty but exceedingly uncomfortable towers, of which only two remain in the Piazza di Porta Ravegnana—the Torre degli Asinelli, 350 feet high and 7 feet out of the perpendicular, and the truncated Garisenda tower, which lists a frightening 11 feet and which Dante likened to the giant Antaeus.

From the top of the Asinelli Tower you will get an excellent vista of Bologna's greatness. Nearby are the palaces of the Drapers' Company and the Loggia dei Mercanti. Then there is the Gothic Palazzo Comunale and Renaissance Palazzo del Podestà, while in the restored Palazzo di Re Enzo the son of Frederick II, King Enzo, was jailed until he died after 23 years. (For entry, enquire at the Bologna EPT tourist office.)

And there, between them, is the Piazza del Nettuno, one of Bologna's major attractions for its marvelous and magnificent Fountain of Neptune, designed by Giambologna in 1566. Seen together with the Piazza Maggiore, it forms a harmonious ensemble.

The Strada Maggiore, bounded almost entirely by medieval houses, goes down to Santa Maria dei Servi, of the 15th century, containing Cimabue's *Madonna.* Santo Stefano, a short distance away, is an array of buildings of the 11th and 12th centuries, including the Crocifisso Church, that of the Calvario and the Courtyard of Pilate in the Church of Santi Pietro e Paolo.

The most beautiful private palaces in Bologna can be found on the Via Zamboni, which leads to the Church of San Giacomo Maggiore, built in the 13th century. The Renaissance Chapel of the Bentivoglio is connected to their family palace by an underground passage. A church of the same period, San Domenico, contains a very beautiful tomb of the saint, whose life is shown on its bas-reliefs. You will certainly want to see the magnificent altarpiece in the Church of San Francesco. Bologna's Art Gallery (Pinacoteca), has a fine collection of the Bologna School and a few outstanding examples of other works such as Raphael's *The Ecstasy of St. Cecilia* and Titian's *Crucifixion* as well as works by Fragonard, and Madame Vigée-Lebrun, and members of the Bologna Academy. You may wish to visit the Museo Civico as well; it has a collection of classical and medieval pieces and a famous Etruscan *situle.*

Crossing the Rubicon

The A14 continues 66 miles southeast to the Adriatic. Imola has a few Renaisance monuments that deserve attention. Faenza is best known for its typically Italian majolica chinaware. Its International Ceramic Museum houses an imposing collection of ancient and modern ceramic pieces, including works by Picasso and Matisse. Also worth visiting is Forli, with its Romanesque Church of San Mercuriale and its powerful bell tower, the splendid tomb of Barbara Manfredi, the Ravaldino Fortress once heroically defended by Catherine Sforza, and its museums and art gallery.

At Cesena the Renaissance Malatesta Library is famed for its book treasures, priceless manuscripts and miniatures. This is a graceful Renaissance building. The Benedictine monastery and the fortress are of great architectural interest and have rich collections of paintings and old manuscripts. The harbor of Cesenatico, built as a port for Cesena, bears the mark of Leonardo da Vinci's genius.

At Savignano stop for a few moments to catch your historical breath. For here is the Rubicon, that little nearly dried-up stream you are passing almost without notice. But it is of this stream that the Roman Senate, fearing its military leaders' power, proclaimed "General or soldier, veteran or conscript, armed person whoever you may be, stop here, and let not your standards nor your arms nor your army cross the Rubicon."

Julius Caesar, weary of the oligarchic rule of the Roman plutocracy—and heavily loaded with debts and ambition—defied the senatorial edict and cried, "The die is cast," as he led his battle-scarred veterans across the Rubicon and on to take virtual imperial control of Rome.

Sigismondo Malatesta, in the 15th century, is responsible for much of Rimini's artistic fame. He preserved a number of Roman monuments and added its finest Renaissance structure when he built in honor of his then mistress, Isotta degli Atti, the Malatesta Temple. The famous Francesca da Rimini lived out her sad destiny in the 13th century and was immortalized by Dante in his *Inferno.* You will recall his line, "And that night we read no further." This contains everything about love's natural conclusion in passion, but the passage has been censored wherever it could be, from Dante's time onward. It was sometimes shown by three dots. But Dante's image of the book being put down and closed is by far the most moving conclusion to this tragic tale of Paolo and Francesca. She had married Gianciotto Malatesta by proxy and had fallen in love with Gianciotto's handsome young brother, Paolo. Her jealous husband killed them both with a single blow of his sword. The episode is also the subject for one of Ingres' finest paintings and a Tchaikovsky overture. In 1450 Alberti designed the Malatesta Temple façade, inspired by Rome's arches of triumph. Sigismondo's Castle is another historic monument of the Renaissance period.

The Bridge of Tiberius over the Marecchia River, and the Arch of Augustus represent important Roman contributions to Rimini's architecture. In addition, recent archeological discoveries have demonstrated that the Roman Amphitheater, of which little remains, was once the largest, with a seating capacity of 12,000. It is the only one visible in the Emilia-Romagna region. The Romanesque-Gothic Sant' Agostino Church contains important frescos of the Giotto school.

Oldest of Republics

Just a few miles away from Rimini—not in Emilia nor even in Italy actually by definition—is the tiny little Republic of San Marino, a hangover from the Middle Ages, which claims the honor of being the oldest republic in the world—oldest still in existence, that is. Its area is only 23 square miles.

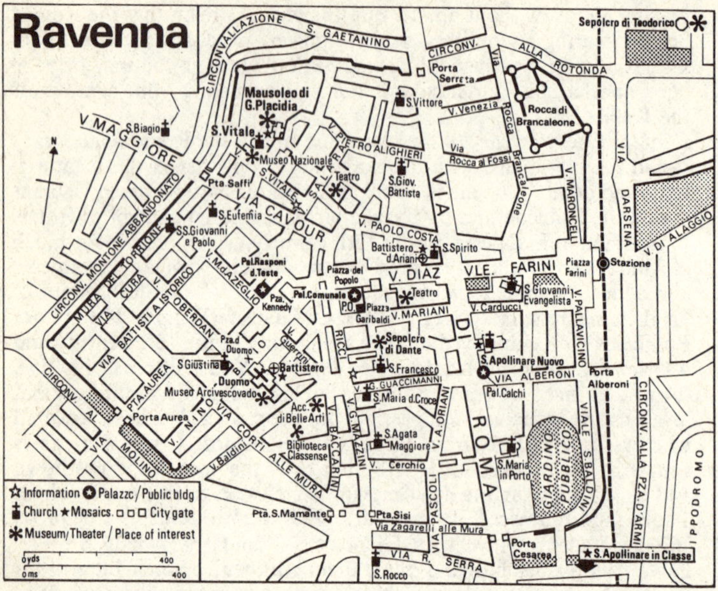

San Marino, more than 2,000 feet above Rimini's bathing beach, clings to its medieval characteristics with a somewhat pecuniary tenacity, as it is its imaginative conservation which has enabled its people to survive financially, rather than various industries ranging from ceramics to cotton yarn and paint. San Marino city boasts three castles, a Government Palace and a fine church. Despite occasional Communist governments, it has preserved its medieval pomp and circumstance; two regent captains are elected for six months to sit with members of the Grand Council. Huge crowds gather for the picturesque investiture ceremony on April 1 and October 1.

High up on Mt. Titano, the 5,000 people of the citadel-capital live by selling coins, stamps and souvenirs to the tourists who stream there, to see the fortresses and towers used by numerous motion picture companies as the location for films.

The Republic of San Marino was founded back in the 4th century by a Dalmatian stone cutter named Marino who settled as a hermit on the slopes of Titano. That it survived through all the medieval and Renaissance conflicts is due not so much to its courage as to its acumen. It never sought to expand. When Napoleon offered it more territory—

to "preserve a sample of Republic"—its citizens politely refused. They preferred their mountain, and nothing but their mountain.

At nearby San Leo is the imposing fortress, now a museum, where Cagliostro, that charming charlatan, was imprisoned and died.

Ravenna

Through Bellaria, Cervia and other seaside resorts you can go from Rimini to Ravenna, capital of the western half of the Roman Empire in the 5th century. Ater the murder of the first Germanic king, Odoacer, in 493, Ravenna became the capital of the Ostrogoth Kingdom till its reconquest by the Byzantines in 539. Ravenna was sumptuously embellished by Justinian and Theodora, while under subsequent Byzantine governors, called exarchs, the city was the final link between the Pax Romana and the Middle Ages. With the expulsion of the Byzantines by the Longobards and Franks, Europe plunged into "the thousand years of darkness".

The Churches of San Vitale and Sant' Apollinare and the Cathedral's Baptistery are world-famous examples of early Byzantine Christian art, dating back in some cases to the 5th century. San Vitale's mosaics are both unique and wonderful, their style and workmanship the finest in Byzantine art.

Ravenna's cathedral was rebuilt in 18th-century baroque, except for the 10th-century cylindrical bell tower and the 5th-century octagonal baptistery, with its two tiers of 8 arcades, which support a dome entirely covered with mosaics.

The Pulpit of St. Maximian, an Egyptian ivory work of the 6th century, is in the Archbishop's Palace behind the cathedral. In the Via Baccarini to the left of San Francesco is the tomb of Dante, who found his final safety and home here after being banished from Florence. It was in the Pineta (pine woods), toward the sea from here, that Dante meditated on the verses of his *Divine Comedy,* and it was near here that Byron was accommodated by the husband of his love, La Guiccioli.

Lovers of Byzantine art will enjoy the wonderful mosaics of the 5th-century Mausoleum of Galla Placidia and in the Chapel of St. Peter Chrysologus.

Before leaving Ravenna see the Church of Sant' Appolinare Nuovo, built by order of Theodoric, the 6th-century King of the Ostrogoths. Theodoric's tomb, a pile of square stones without mortar, covered by a monolithic dome, stands outside the Porta Serrata. Three miles away at Classe (route 19 toward Rimini) is the magnificent Basilica of Sant' Apollinare, completed in 549, with striking 6th- and 7th-century mosaics, and an impressive 9th-century bell tower.

North of Ravenna the vast marshes around the Lagoon di Comacchio have been reclaimed and the farmland has been protected by pine forests against the encroaching sand-dunes along the coastal road through the string of beach resorts to Venice. The town of Comacchio itself is interestingly picturesque, with canals, tiny bridges and fishermen whose main catch is eels.

Ferrara

From 1208 to 1598 the Este family ruled Ferrara and, although Modena was the Duchy's capital, the dukes and their court spent most of their time here.

A nobleman of the Middle Ages seemed to combine good and bad qualities that we would find incompatible in the same person today. The Este were ostentatious patrons of the arts, with unquestionably refined tastes, but they have left behind them memories of unparalleled cruelty. Nicolo III (1383–1441) killed his wife and her lover. And Ercolo I (1471–1505), his successor, tried to poison his nephew, but failed. Nicolo, the nephew, took advantage of his uncle's absence to take over the throne. However, Eleanor of Aragon, Ercolo's wife, was not to be taken by surprise and Nicolo was captured and beheaded.

Lucretia Borgia belongs in such fine company. She married Alfonso I and became, so it seems, the most enlightened and gentlest of princesses. Renée of France became the wife of Ercolo I (1534–1558). A famous poet, Ariosto (1474–1533), also lived here. His *Orlando Furioso* is still read. Another great writer, Tasso, was a local celebrity as well.

The Castello Estense, still surrounded by its 14th-century moat, is the essence of Ferrara. Four mighty towers protect its halls and salons, which once resounded to the brilliant gatherings of a sophisticated Renaissance court.

The city's 12th-century cathedral is worth a visit. So, too, is the Church of San Francesco. But many appreciate even more the Palazzo Schifanoia, once a pleasure resort for the Este princes. It was finished in 1471 and contains, in its Sala dei Mesi, some remarkable frescos by Cossa. And then there is the Palazzo di Ludovico il Moro, which Rossetti built early in the 16th century. It now contains a very fine archeological museum.

While we are speaking of museums, here are the most important: the Palazzo dei Diamanti, which houses the art gallery, a wealth of works from the Ferrara School (Garofalo, Tura, Roberti); the Museo Civico (in the Schifanoia Palace); the Cathedral Museum; to which we especially draw your attention because of its two fine paintings by the leading local painter, Cosimo Tura, *St. George Fighting the Dragon* and *The Annunciation.*

You will enjoy visiting two elegant residences, the Casa Romei (15th century, opposite the palace occupied by Renée of France), and the *palazzino* of the Marquis of Este, 16th-century patron of the arts.

The Abbey of Pomposa (30 miles from Ferrara) was originally founded in the 7th century. It has some lovely mosaics and an attractive campanile with a superb view from the top. It is one of those buildings, off the beaten track, which repay a visit by anyone who likes quiet atmosphere.

PRACTICAL INFORMATION FOR EMILIA-ROMAGNA

HOTELS AND RESTAURANTS

Bellaria. Very popular beach resort near Rimini. **Hotels:** All (2) are—**Locanda delle Dune,** top rates in category, smart, comfortable place, in quiet, isolated location right on beach; **Gambrinus,** fairly large, modern decor, with sea views, pool; **Elisabeth,** on sea, with private beach area.

Pace (3), quiet, simple but comfortable rooms, all with shower. Many inexpensive hotels and pensions.

Bellariva. Budget resort south of Rimini. **Hotels:** All (3) are—*Oceanic,* 55 rooms, all with shower, pleasant little garden for relaxing; **Acerboli,** fairly recent, functional, all rooms with shower; **Dell'Angelo,** basic but comfortable, 61 rooms.

Bologna. Hotels: Deluxe **Royal Carlton,** central, ultra-modern elegance, 240 airconditioned rooms, car park.

All (1) are—**Internazionale,** central, is attractive and efficient; **Garden,** converted monastery, central but quiet, airconditioned, with attractive cloister garden; **Elite,** big modern hotel on outskirts, sleek, functional, airconditioned rooms, suites, piano bar, excellent cuisine in **Cordon Bleu** restaurant; **Crest,** pool, also outskirts; **Milano-Excelsior,** Via Pietramellara 51, near the railway station, modern, airconditioned, reader-recommended for friendly atmosphere, thoughtful service.

All (2) are—**Alexander,** next door to **Milano-Excelsior,** excellent adjunct with first class comforts; **Nettuno,** Via Galleria, is central and comfortable; **Roma,** Via d'Azeglio 9, an inconspicuous little hotel, airconditioned, very central; **Palace,** Via Montegrappa, breakfast only; and **San Donato,** Via Zamboni, with restaurant; **Motel AGIP,** on Via Emilia, modern, standardized appointments.

All (3) are—**Lembo,** Via S. Croce 26, 38 rooms, 11 with bath; **San Felice,** Via Riva Reno 2, 33 rooms all with bath or shower; **San Giorgio,** Via Moline 17, 30 rooms with shower; **Tre Vecchi,** large, comfortable, airconditioned rooms many with bath or shower, good restaurant.

Restaurants. This is in some opinions the top gastronomic city in Italy, yet prices are not high by comparison with Paris or London.

Expensive

Al Cantunzein, Piazza Verdi, small modern; pasta (traditional or chef's own).

Diana, Via Indipendenza 24, is a culinary delight.

Don Chisciotte-Sancio Panza, excellent, Via Degli Albari 2, noted for its **lasagne** and turkey breasts.

Bacco, at Borgo Panicale, on outskirts, is well worth the trip, combines classic cuisine with creative touches.

Pappagallo, Piazza Mercanzia 3, is one of Bologna's best-known restaurants, but is overrated.

Dante, Via Belvedere (reserve, tel. 224.464), outstanding for atmosphere, service and above all fine food.

Rosteria da Luciano, Via Nazario Sauro 19, for **armonie dell' Appenino** (ravioli, cream, truffles); ask to see the wine cellar and try **Kirr** aperitif.

Royal Grill of Hotel Royal Carlton, acclaimed for impeccable interpretations of Italian regional cuisine. Reserve.

Tre Vecchi, one of Bologna's best restaurants, is at Via Indipendenza 47, a street which contains many good restaurants.

Moderate

L'Abbadia, is a gem, pheasant in cream or champagne, reserve; **Nerina,** Piazza Galileo 6; **Sampieri,** Via Sampieri 3, highly atmospheric, with its little nightclub; **Palmirani,** Via Calcavinazzi 2, a must, try green pasta with bacon; **Brunetti,** Via Caduti Cefalonia 5; **Cesarina,** Via San Stefano 19; **Ciuffe,** Via San Vilate 10; **Da Carlo,** Via Marchesana 6. **Il Tinello,** Via dei Giudei, is unpretentious and good value. **Cesoia da Pietro,** Via Massaranti 90, and **Franco Rossi,** Via delle Donzelle, can be expensive but are worth every lira.

Buca di San Pietro, Via Montegrappa, small central trattoria. **Tonino,** Corte dei Galluzzi, reader-recommended for fine food, friendly host.

Inexpensive

For a place that serves fine food at prices to meet your budget, there is **Donatello,** Via Righi; or **Augusto,** Via Testoni, near San Francesco; **Gambrinus,** Via Zamboni 11; **Mela,** Via Fusari 5; **Pepoli,** Via Pepoli 4; the excellent **Jagus,** Strada Maggiore 5; **Birreria Lamma,** Via Guidei 4, is a centrally situated beer house.

Busseto. Verdi's home and gourmet heaven. Two of Italy's finest restaurants are here: extraordinary *Cantarelli* (tel. 90.133) and renowned *Guareschi* (tel. 92.495), both (E); pleasantly rustic. A third, *Del Sole* (M) (tel. 92.243), is a close runner-up. All closed end July.

Castrocaro. Hill resort and spa near Forli. **Hotels:** Both (1)—*Delle Terme,* spa treatments at hotel, tennis court, pool; *Rosa del Deserto,* on highway, all rooms with bath. *Piccolo Hôtel* (2), comfortable, inexpensive, garage.

Restaurant. *La Frasca* (E), duck, paté, etc., with a gourmet touch. Reserve.

Cattolica. Beach resort, less smart than Rimini and Riccione. **Hotels:** Both (1) are—*Caravelle,* modern white building overlooking sea, private beach and pool, 45 rooms with bath, open May through Oct.; *Victoria Palace,* Viale Carducci, all rooms with bath, private beach.

All (2) are—*Beau Rivage,* most rooms have bath or shower, private beach; *Diplomat,* good value, beach; very comfortable are *Napoleon; Negresco; Royal,* pool, beach facilities. More basic: *Maxim,* 55 rooms; *Nettuno,* 52 rooms; *Plaza,* 63 rooms; *President,* 60 rooms; *Renzo,* 42 rooms.

Both (3) are—*Nora,* Viale Carducci 14, most rooms with bath; *Columbia,* Via Spinelli; most rooms with shower.

Restaurant. *Lampara* (M-E), at port, exquisite fish.

Cervia. Beach resort of which Milano Marittima is virtually a part, rather more elegant and cosmopolitan than Cervia proper. At **Cervia, Hotels:** All (2) are—*Beau Rivage,* Lungomare Deledda 116, best, all rooms with shower, facing sea; *Nettuno,* Lungomare G. d'Annunzio, has sea view, own beach, garden; *El Trocadero,* at no. 32, all rooms with shower; *Buenos Aires,* Lungomare G. Deledda 116, 48 rooms all with shower, new; *Excelsior,* Viale Roma 74, 34 rooms, nearly all with bath, near sea, private beach.

At **Milano Marittima,** all (1) and open 1 May–30 Sept. are—*Aurelia,* has 113 rooms, swimming pool and beach, tennis; *Gallia,* 97 rooms, most with shower, pool, tennis; recent *Mare e Pineta,* has beach, tennis, riding in own pine grove, two good annexes; *Le Palme,* smart but informal, well-furnished, in pretty garden with tennis, two steps from beach.

All (2) are—*Della Nazione,* all 50 rooms with bath or shower, good, fairly inexpensive, has excellent private beach; *Deanna,* Viale Matteotti, comfortable, pleasant rooms, tennis courts, garden, short walk from beach area; *Kent,* Viale 2 Giugno, 36 bright rooms, all with shower, garden, close to beach.

Cesenatico. Hotels: All (2) are—*Esplanade,* recent, attractively furnished and well-equipped hotel overlooking shore boulevard and beach, 56 rooms, all with shower. *Internazionale,* similar, is right on beach, pool, tennis courts; *Cristallo,* Viale Carducci 31, most rooms with bath, comfortable, overlooking sea; *Torino,* no. 56, same street but on beach, all rooms have shower; *Grande,* largest, smartest, on beach, tennis, dancing; *Des Bains,* 36 pleasant rooms, all with shower, attractive terrace, short walk from beach; *Villa Maria,* Viale Carducci 96, 34 rooms, most with shower, on the beach.

Delle Nazione (3), all private showers.

Restaurants. *Gambero Rosso* (M), on pier, a favorite for all-fish dishes; Da Vittorio (M–E), Via Pasubio, imaginative ways with fish.

Ferrara. Art City. **Hotels:** All (2)—*Astra,* Viale Cavour 55, best, most rooms with bath or shower, airconditioned: *Ferrara,* central, modern; *De la Ville,* modern, airconditioned; *Touring,* Viale Cavour 11, 36 rooms, most with bath or shower. *Europa,* Corso Giovecca, for atmosphere and antiques.

A good (3) is *Kennedy,* Via Gobetti, central, no restaurant.

Restaurants. You'll find good food here at the restaurant of Hotel *Astra,* try *pappardelle;* very good is *Da Giovanni,* Piazza Castello 32; try also *Voltini,* Via Bologna 80, and *Grotta Azzurra,* Piazza Sacrati, all (M). *Pizzeria Pulcinella,* Via Borgoleoni, is (I).

Forlì. Hotels: All (2) are—*Della Città,* Corso della Repubblica, all rooms have bath or shower; *Da Vittorino,* Via Baratti 2, good, all rooms with bath, fine restaurant; *Principe,* just outside center, modern, good.

Restaurants. The *Roma* (M) restaurant will serve you a more than adequate meal, as will *Pinin* (I), Via Mameli.

Gabicce Mare. Beach resort. **Hotels:** High season, 1 July–31 Aug. *Capo Est* (1), smart resort hotel in quiet location on hillside, with pool, tennis.

All (2) are—*Alexander,* bright modern decor, 46 rooms with bath, pool, garden; *Tre Ville,* all rooms with shower, balcony and sea view, stairs down to sandy beach, some noise from adjacent piazza; *Bahia,* modern, pool.

Igea Marina. (Bellaria) Beach resort. **Hotels:** Both (2) are—*Metropolitan,* all rooms have bath, inexpensive; *Majestic,* pool. *Touring* (3), good value.

Lido degli Estensi. Beach resort. **Hotels:** Both (2) are—*Plaza,* sea view, private beach; *Vela d'Oro,* many baths, private beach.

Lido delle Nazioni. Well-planned resort, with horse riding, nightclub and artificial lake for power-boat racing. **Hotels:** *Hotel delle Nazioni* (2), best, with pool, tennis, beach, specializes in spacious family-sized apartments which will take parents and up to four children easily, good children's recreation area.

Club Spiagga (3), tennis, beach, excellent value.

Marina di Ravenna. Beach resort. **Hotels:** *Park* (1), best, pool, tennis, access to beach through pinewoods.

Restaurant. *Maddalena* (M), seasonal.

At **Marina Romea. Hotel:** *Corallo* (2), overlooking sea and pines, pool.

Misano Adriatico. Budget beach resort. **Hotels:** *Gala* (2), small, pleasant, 27 rooms with shower.

Both (3) are—*Savoia,* comfortable, on shore boulevard; and *Alexandra,* quiet location nearby, on beach, all rooms with shower, balcony, sea view.

Modena. Hotels: Both (1) are—*Canalgrande,* central, luxurious appointments, period decor in public rooms, modern, airconditioned bedrooms with radio, TV; *Fini,* just outside center, big and bustling, bright modern decor, 93 well-appointed, airconditioned rooms.

Both (2) are—*Estense,* centrally located, modest but comfortable; *Roma,* very central, garni. *Donatello* (2), Via Giardini, is good.

San Geminiano (3), Viale Moreali, basic.

Restaurants. This city vies with Bologna for the top gastronomic position in this region. All (M) are—*Fini* ranks with the finest restaurants of Italy, try their *pasticcio di tortellini,* and if you're still hungry go on to the *cotoletta alla* *bolognese* or *zampone. Da Enzo,* Via Coltellini, noted for courtesy, quality. *Bianca* has pleasant garden; avoid on Sundays.

Parma. Hotels: Reserve early for the fairs in May and September.

All (1) are—*Palace Maria Luigia,* handsome modern furnishings, 67 rooms, all doubles, with bath or shower, optional airconditioning, attractive *Maxim's* restaurant; *Park Stendhal,* overlooks Palazzo Pilotta, 45 airconditioned rooms with bath; *Park Toscanini,* older but comfortable, car park.

All (2) are—*Bristol* and *Daniel,* both recent, good; *Torino,* very central, all rooms with shower, garage, breakfast only.

Restaurants. Here's a third city fighting hard for top honors in the food line in this region—remember Parma ham?

Highly recommended: *Maxim's* of Hotel Maria Luigia (E), reserve ahead, (tel. 21.032); local cuisine and excellent fish.

All (M) are—The *Taverna San Ambrogio,* Via San Ambrogio 3, typical atmosphere and includes a *rosticceria,* veal cutlets are the specialty; also very good is *Al Dsevod,* Via Longhi 3, for *tortellini,* pork steaks; *Filoma,* Via XX Marzo 15, for *tortellini,* stuffed veal, Lambrusco; *Greppa,* Strada Garibaldi, rustic; *Parizzi,* Strada Repubblica 71, an outstanding place.

Piacenza. Hotels: *Roma* (1), central, airconditioned, restaurant overlooks city, garage.

All (2) are—*Cappello,* good location, comfortable; *Milano,* at station, adequate, good restaurant; *Florida,* on road to **Parma.**

Restaurants. *Osteria del Teatro* (E), gourmet specialties; exceptional quality. *Peppino* (M), Piazza S. Antonio. *Bertì* (M), at outlying Quarto, rustic.

Porretta Terme. Popular spa. **Hotels:** Both (2) are—*Sassocardo,* in beautiful park, with fine view, comfortable rooms, all with bath or shower, spa treatments at hotel: *Santoli,* 48 well-furnished doubles, all with TV, bath or shower.

Ravenna. Important art city, famed for its mosaics. **Hotels:** Both (1) are—*Jolly,* near station and Sant' Apollinare, large, airconditioned, comfortable; *Bisanzio,* near San Vitale, also is good, airconditioned, breakfast only.

All (2) are—*Argentario* and *Centrale Byron,* both central for sightseeing, breakfast only; *Trieste,* short walk from center, comfortable, all doubles with bath or shower, has dining room; *Motel Romea,* 1½ miles outside town on Via Romea, 36 rooms with shower, *Ponte Nuovo* restaurant.

Restaurants. All (M) are—*Bella Venezia,* probably the best; *Scai* is good; so is *Torre;* and *Teodoro,* with *agnolotti di Ravenna* as one of its specialties. *Tre Spade,* Via Rasponi, noteworthy but can be expensive.

Reggio Emilia. (Reggio nell'Emilia) Hotels: If you have to stay overnight, these are your best bets—*Astoria* (1), Viale Nobili 4, rooms have bath or shower, overlooking park; good grillroom restaurant, airconditioned, garage.

Both (2) are—*Posta,* Piazza C. Battisti 10; *Europa,* Viale Olimpia, a bit out of the way, unassuming, recent, airconditioned, garage.

Villa al Poggio (P1), Via Boccaccio, 65 rooms with bath, pleasant, good value, hotel bus at station.

Restaurants. *La Casseruola* (M–E), Via San Carlo, is tops; host Ivano helps you choose.

All (M) are—*Zucca,* Piazza Fontanesi, wine-red walls, art nouveau decor, *tortelli di zucca; Campana* and *Cannon d'Oro* do excellent versions of regional dishes; *Ermete,* Via Emilia S. Pietro 16, in quiet courtyard, family-run, recommended. *Majorca,* Via dei Mille, traditional specialties.

Riccione. Noted beach resort, lavishly supplied with excellent accommodation. **Hotels:** All (1) are—*Atlantic,* posh modern hotel on shore boulevard, 62 well-appointed rooms, heated pool; *Lido Mediterraneo,* in heart of resort activity, 96 rooms with bath or shower, doubles have balcony, sea view, pool, beach, disco; *Savioli Spiaggia,* overlooking sea, 70 rooms with bath, heated pool; *Abner's,* modern seaside hotel with tennis, private beach; *Promenade,* richly appointed beachfront hotel, 39 rooms, attractive garden, beach facilities.

All (2) are—*Des Bains,* a few steps from beach, 77 well-furnished rooms, most with bath, pleasant dining terrace; *Bel Air,* toward end of shore boulevard away from center, light, airy public rooms, sidewalk café, all 50 rooms with bath, balcony; *Vienna Touring,* stark modern building with attractive garden in quiet residential area, well-run, tennis, beach; *Lungomare,* facing beach, 56 comfortable rooms with bath or shower.

All (3) are—*Flamengo,* attractive building in quiet area, a few steps from beach, balconied rooms, most with shower, pleasant sidewalk tables; *Alexandra Plaza,* large, modern, in garden right on beach in quiet zone bordering on Misano, 51 comfortable rooms with bath, balcony, excellent value; *Dory,* Viale Puccini, a few steps from beach, inviting, in small garden, 36 rooms most with shower, optional airconditioning.

Restaurants. Both (M) are—*Punta de l'Est,* best; *Pescatore,* Via Nievo, good.

Rimini. Cosmopolitan and often crowded beach resort. **Hotels:** There are many hotels and pensions here, which makes it difficult to single out a few. The following list is not inclusive—there are many other excellent establishments.

Grand (L), a truly deluxe establishment, beautifully appointed, most rooms have bath or shower, private beach and pool, yacht club, tennis, dance orchestra, has annex, *Residence Grand* (1), well-furnished, shares Grand's amenities.

All (1) are—*Savoia-Excelsior,* Viale A. Vespucci 44, near the sea, strikingly modern, many rooms with balconies, cheerful atmosphere; *Imperiale* and elegant *Ambasciatori,* both overlook private beaches; *Waldorf,* facing sea, open all year, comfortable rooms with bath or shower, rooftop pool, attractive terraces.

All (2) are—*Biancamano,* just behind *Grand,* a few steps from beach, comfortable, well-furnished, 68 rooms with shower, small pool in garden; *Admiral,* near beach, well-run and functional; *Villa Rosa Riviera,* near beach and shopping, 51 comfortable rooms, all with bath or shower; *Aristeo,* at end of shore boulevard toward Riccione, pleasant, 40 bedrooms with shower, pool, beach.

All (3) are—*Milton,* behind *Grand,* overlooks tennis courts, shore boulevard, pleasant terraces, all doubles with shower, balcony; *Eurogarden,* Via Lettimi, bright and modern, 27 rooms with shower; *Ciotti,* on shore boulevard toward Riccione, modern, pleasantly furnished with shady terrace, 40 rooms with shower, balcony.

Restaurants. All (M–E) are—the excellent *Vecchia Rimini,* Via Gambalunga 33, in town; *Nello al Mare,* Lungomare V. Emanuele 12, facing the sea, open in the summer; *Taverna del Marinaio,* on the harbor; *Elio,* Viale Vespucci, undistinguished looks, but top-quality food.

Riolo Terme. Spa. **Hotel:** *Cristallo* (2), modern, all rooms with shower.

Rivazzurra. Budget beach resort near Rimini. **Hotels:** All (2)—*France,* best; *Grand Meeting,* and *Artide,* both good.

Salsomaggiore Hotels. *Milano Grande Albergo* (L), Via Dante 1, big, smart, elegant, quiet location in park, with heated pool, spa treatments at hotel.

Both (1) are—*Porro,* in tranquil hillside park, 86 well-appointed rooms, indoor pool, solarium, spa treatments; *Centrale Bagni,* large, well-furnished, traditional spa hotel.

Both (2) are—*Daniel,* pleasantly modern, quiet location, all rooms with bath or shower; *Valentini,* large, with all spa facilities. *Suisse* (3) small.

Restaurants. *Al Tartufo* (E), considered one of the best in the region; *Il Guscio* (M–E), also good. Nearby, at interesting medieval town of **Castell'Arquato,** *La Rocca* (E), well worth the trip (reserve ahead; tel. 803.154).

San Marino. Southwest of Rimini, independent republic. **Hotels:** All (1) are—*Grand,* Viale Lungomonte, recent, nicely furnished, fine cuisine, airconditioned, garage, hotel bus at station; *Titano,* Via XXV Marzo, 56 rooms, most with bath; *Joli,* at station, all rooms with bath.

Hotel/Restaurants. Both (2M) are—*Tre Penne,* 18 rooms, is recommended both for accommodation and cuisine; *Diamond,* Via XXV Marzo, has a very small number of rooms, comfortable and reasonable, but is better known for its excellent restaurant.

Restaurant. *Nido del Falco, Taverna da Paolino* are both moderate.

Secchia. Near Modena **Motel:** On Autostrada del Sole, *Motel AGIP* (2), pride of the chain, big, sparkling, well-furnished, 182 rooms with shower, air-conditioning.

Sestola. Summer and winter sports resort. **Hotels:** *San Marco* (1), tennis; in quiet pinewoods, relaxing atmosphere in a converted Renaissance villa complete with Italian garden, low rates for category.

Tabiano Bagni. Spa. **Hotel:** *Farnese* (2), best; garage.

Viserba (Viserbella). Beach resort north of Rimini. **Hotels:** *Albatros* (2), rooms with shower. *Diana* (P3), on main coastal road, at seaside with own beach, pleasant, cheerful atmosphere, bar.

USEFUL ADDRESSES. Tourist Offices *Bellaria:* AAST, Via Leonardo da Vinci, at the Palazzo del Turismo. *Bologna:* EPT, Via Marconi 45; Via Leopardi 1E; Railway Station; Piazza Settembre XX; CIT, Piazza Nettuno 2; Piazza Martiri 7 (starting point for bus trips) and Stazione Centrale. American Express, Via Marconi 45 (tel. 235783, 267600). *Castrocaro:* AAST, Via Garibaldi 50. *Cattolica:* AAST, Piazza Nettuno 1. *Cervia:* AAST, Viale Roma 53. *Ferrara:* EPT, Largo Castello 28. *Forli:* EPT, Corso della Repubblica 23. *Gabicce Mare:* AAST, Viale della Vittoria 41, and Palazzo del Turismo. *Lido degli Estensi:* AAST, Viale Carducci 31. *Misano Adriatico:* AAST, Via Platini 22. *Modena:* EPT, Corso Canalgrande 3. *Parma:* EPT, Piazza Duomo 5. *Piacenza:* EPT, Via S. Siro 17, and Piazatta dei Mercanti 10. *Porretta Terme:* AAST, Viale dei Caduti 20. *Ravenna:* AAST, Via San Vitale 2; EPT, Piazza S. Francesco 7, and Autostrada A. 14 Sillaro Ovest. *Reggio Emilia:* EPT, Piazza Battisti 4. *Riccione:* AAST, Piazza Ceccarini. *Rimini:* AAST, Piazzale Indipendenza; American Express, SIT, Viale Vespucci 127 (tel. 27177 and 23779). *Riolo Terme:* AAST, Corso Matteotti 40. *Salsomaggiore:* AAST, Viale Romagnosi 7. *San Marino:* Ente Governativo del Turismo, Palazzo del Turismo. *Sestola:* AAST, Piazza Passerini 18.

SPECIAL EVENTS. *Bologna:* Opera in February, plus a children's carnival; Music Festival in June; International Book Fair in *Parma:* Food fair in September; opera winter season starts in December. *Piacenza:* opera in February; a traditional pageant in June. *Ravenna:* June "Musical Summer" in Sant' Apollinare in Classe; July to August, Organ Festival in San Vitale. *Reggio Emilia:* opera season, January through March; June, streets decorated with flower display contest; July folklore Torneo dei Maggi, repeated in August. *Salsomaggiore:* lively Children's Carnival in February; June, parade and Battle of flowers.

SPORTS. *Bologna:* 18-hole golf course. *Cattolica* and *Cervia:* both centers for sailing. *Cesenatico:* sailing and good saltwater fishing. *Riccione* and *Rimini:* both sailing and good saltwater fishing.

LIGURIA

The Two Rivieras and Genoa

The region of Liguria is contained in a narrow strip of coastline stretching 217 twisting miles from the French border to Tuscany and never more than 25 miles wide. The sea that beats upon these shores has given them their character and their history. What every schoolboy knows is that Genoa, set in the heart of this rocky coast, is the birthplace of Christopher Columbus. And America's discoverer was only one, and not the first nor the last, in a long line of seafaring men whose activity centered in the ports of the two Rivieras of Italy.

Liguria is favored by year-round mild climate; this and the ease with which it can be reached from the rest of western Europe, has helped to make it one of the most popular regions in Italy for visitors. An impressive number of foreigners—British, American, French—have permanent residences here. For centuries, its charm has inspired poets and artists, many of whom came for a brief visit and stayed on. Italians from inland cities flock to its beaches in summer or maintain their villas along its length. The flavor of the area is cosmopolitan, a mellow blend of rustic with sophisticated, provincial with smart set, primitive and old-fashioned with luxurious and up-to-date. The eye is caught, the attention is held by the contours of the coastline, curving serpentinely in an east-west arc from Ventimiglia to La Spezia; by the Ligurian Alps, plunging in sheer cliffs or sloping gradually to the sea; by the glamor and color of the resorts, the busy ports, the stately yachts against the skyline and the grandiose view across the Gulf of Genoa from a hairpin curve on the highway.

Weather Matters

Liguria is an all-year-round tourist area. A strip of coastland swinging in an arc about Genoa at its center, protected by the mountains beyond from the cool breezes of the north, it enjoys a climate allegedly milder than that of other regions in the same latitude. It is thus a region where vacationists may take refuge from the cold in winter, but the presence of the sea prevents it from being intolerably hot during the summer. The bathing beaches throughout the region are extremely crowded in July and August; in winter,too, quite a number of visitors frequent the resorts of the Riviera di Ponente, westwards from Genoa.

Road Reports

All the main points of interest in Liguria lie along the coast, threaded on the old wiggly Route 1 from the French border all the way through Genoa and La Spezia to Leghorn just south of Pisa. Countryside enthusiasts should not, however, fail to drive up the little mountain roads leading north from the coast where the views are magnificent. Boxed in by four autostrade it is something of a forgotten land, and none the worse for that. The Autostrada A12 has relieved much of the pressure on the coast road, but even now it is sometimes—mostly weekends—necessary to queue to enter such favorite spots as Portofino. Apart from reaching this region from the obvious French entry at Ventimiglia, there is a direct motorway A6 from Turin, while A8 and A9 from Varese and Como lead to Milan and thence by A7 to Genoa. It can, of course, as easily be reached from Bologna and Florence on A1 and A11.

Food for Thought

The Ligurian regional cuisine is one of the most appetizing in Italy—not too heavy, and, in keeping with the character of a coastal area, plentiful in fish. Throughout Italy you will find many fish dishes which declare their origin by the label *alla Genovese.*

One dish which can only be made by the Genoese (they say so themselves) is *pesto,* a sauce made of fresh basil and garlic, mixed by pestle and mortar with pine nuts and sharp cheese and a fine local olive oil—with variations, some very fishy (anchovies, that is). It is excellent with *lasagne* or any of the dozen forms of *pasta.*

Trenette col pesto, noodles with the sauce mentioned above. *Cima alla Genovese,* a pastry shell stuffed with meat, eggs, peas and cheese. Mushrooms grow in abundance in the Ligurian hills and a variety of dishes are made with them. Try also the *Torta Pasqualina,* of artichokes and eggs.

Liguria does not produce much wine, nor that of the best of the Italian vintages, but it has a few which might be noted. Its best wine region is that of the Cinque Terre, near La Spezia, which produces rather sweet and rather heavy white wines. All the other important wines of Liguria are also white, but in contrast with the Cinque Terre wines, extremely dry—*Polcevera, Coronata Cornigliano* and *Vermentino Ligure.*

Exploring Liguria

Liguria takes its name from the Liguri, who peopled the area 700 years before Christ. Centuries before the Liguri, prehistoric man lived in caves and left his traces in *graffiti,* rock paintings and bone implements in the Grimaldi caves of Ventimiglia, at the western end of Liguria, and on the island of Palmaria, off La Spezia.

By the 3rd century BC, when the Romans conquered Liguria, Genoa was already an important trading station. The Via Aurelia was built to link Rome and what is now France. The Middle Ages and the Renaissance saw the rise of Genoa as a great seaport, and the history of the city—jumping-off place for the Crusades, commercial center of tremendous wealth and prestige, strategic bone of international contentions—was of key importance to Europe.

Thereafter, Genoa declined in rank as a seapower. Napoleon reduced all of Liguria to an ineffective "family estate of the Bonapartes," as Tolstoy speaks of it in *War and Peace.* When the Emperor was finally defeated at Waterloo, the region became part of Piedmont and reacquired its separate identity only after the unification of Italy.

In modern times, Liguria has enjoyed unrivaled popularity among tourists as a region. The visitor to Italy is scarcely aware that Naples is in the Campania, or that Rome is in Latium; Venice, Florence and other cities are almost isolated in their greatness. But Genoa is flanked on either side by a string of resorts.

Genoa

The natives of this city have nothing to be ashamed of, really, in the old Latin saying: "*Genuensis, ergo mercator*"—Genoese, therefore merchant. Out of their maritime and commercial enterprises, they made themselves wealthy and lavished that wealth on beautifying their city. Because of its commercial reputation, Genoa is too frequently overlooked as a city of beauty rivaling that of many a recognized artistic center. But discerning writers have spoken of Genoa the Proud and of the majesty of her buildings, set in a great semi-circle around the port.

The port area, like port areas all around the world, is what tourist guides usually define as picturesque and what a sociologist will flatly call slums. Ships and installations stretch for miles on either side of the Maritime Station. From Cape Faro, on the left, to the mouth of the Polcevera, there are 12½ miles of port area: docks, freight elevators, plants, warehouses, railroad tracks and public services.

Immediately behind the docks, the lower city begins. Streets are ancient, sometimes aristocratic, like the Via Luccoli, where elegant ladies shop and promenade in the late afternoon, or they are narrow, twisting lanes called *caruggi,* lined with exotic shops.

Not far from where the liners dock is the main railway station giving on Via Balbi, which runs past the ex-Royal Palace with its much-admired Mirror Gallery and collection of art. On this street, too, is the Palazzo Durazzi, which contains paintings of the Flemish master Van Dyck. At the far end, on Piazza della Annunziata, is the 17th-century Church of the Santissima Annunziata, built by Della Porta and Scorticone.

The Genoese are proud of their Via Garibaldi (this Italian national hero was a native Ligurian), a short street, compact with princely mansions and sumptuous villas. The Palazzo Bianco (White Palace) and the Palazzo Rosso (Red Palace), facing each other on this thoroughfare, are important museums of painting and sculpture.

Piazza Fontane Marose, into which this street leads, marks the beginning of the modern center of Genoa. Branching out of it, the Via Carlo Felice leads to the Piazza De Ferrari and the Municipal Opera House.

The Church of Sant' Ambrogio at the end of the square was reconstructed in 1527 from a tiny 4th-century church. The cross-shaped interior contains priceless works by Rubens, del Piola, Merano, and other artists, and an organ by Hermann.

A block from Sant' Ambrogio is the cathedral of San Lorenzo, seat of the archbishopric of Genoa. According to legend, the cathedral was built in the 3rd century by Saint Lawrence himself. It was rebuilt, in its present Romanesque style, in 1118. The bell tower, cupola and ceiling are works of the 16th century, and the chapels full of masterpieces. What many believe to be the true Holy Grail is the cathedral's most prized treasure.

Near the cathedral, on Piazza Matteo, there is a group of ancient houses dating from the 12th century and belonging to the Doria family, one of the most important in Genoa's history. The Church of San Matteo was built in 1278; its black and white marble façade recounts the exploits of the illustrious Dorias.

The Palazzo Doria has all the flavor of Genoa's mighty days of empire, when her fleets sailed to all points of the known world and beyond, across uncharted seas on historic missions of exploration. Pomp, energy and wealth are in these doors and walls. The same is true of the Palazzo Ducale, the Palazzo Reale, the Palazzo San Giorgio, once seat of a powerful bank and money lender to European sovereigns, and the palaces of the Grimaldi and Spinola families.

Where there is a church, there is art, and Genoa has 400 churches. If you stay any length of time, visit some of these: the Madonna del Soccorso, with paintings by Van Dyck and Velazquez; Santo Stefano, where Columbus was baptized; San Donato, with a delicate octagonal campanile and a splendid triptych; Santa Maria di Castello, Saints Cosmo and Damiano, San Siro. And there is the gruesome but edifying Oratorio della Morte, dating from the 17th century, which contains, besides the art, religious objects belonging to those condemned to death and the hangman's rope.

For a change from the overpowering concentration of church art and relics, have a look at some of the special collections: the Chiossone Japanese Museum, the Naval and Archeological Museums, the Mazzini Institute, the Natural History Museum and the homes of Columbus and the fabulous violinist Paganini, whose Guarneri violin is carefully preserved by the city of Genoa and played once a year by an internationally-known violinist.

Genoa's *grattacieli* (skyscrapers) may be puny by American standards, but they are notable examples of adaptation of 20th-century architecture to a medieval and Renaissance setting. From the Capurro Grattacielo there's a fine view of city and harbor. Other vantage points are the Lanterna lighthouse (visible 27 miles out at sea); the Righi, reached by funicular from near the railway station; and the height of Nostra Signora della Guardia. Best of all is a drive along the Circonvallazione a Monte, a road that winds through the hills overlooking the city. The view changes at every turn, and on a clear day the Rivieras are visible, from La Spezia to Imperia.

Befor you leave Genoa, remember to throw a coin into the fountain of Piazza De Ferrari, to ensure your return. This is a custom borrowed from the Trevi fountain, but it's just as valid here. The money is gathered regularly and distributed to charities.

The Western (Ponente) Riviera

Approaching Liguria by car or train from France, you've barely crossed the border into the Riviera di Ponente before you come upon prehistoric and contemporary landmarks. The first structure you see on the left of the ancient Roman Aurelia highway is the Voronoff Castle, where the Russian scientist raised monkeys to use in his famous glandular experiments in rejuvenation. A little farther, on the right, a lift takes you to the Grimaldi Caves, home of prehistoric man.

Just before the border town of Ventimiglia are the Mortola Gardens, filled with the living flora of 5 continents; the entire western coastline from Ventimiglia to Genoa is known also as the Riviera of Flowers, because flower cultivation is a major industry here. The climate here is the mildest of the two Ligurian coasts. The high Maritime Alps, sloping to the sea, break the winds from the north, and the resort towns that follow—Bordighera, Ospedaletti, San Remo, Taggia, Imperia, Diano Marina—are temperate the year round.

A word about Ventimiglia: ancient *Albintimilium* was a pre-Roman settlement and contains important archeological remains in the largest museum of its kind in Liguria. In the town proper are vestiges of a Roman theater; a provincial road swings up the Nervia River valley to the lovely-sounding medieval town of Dolceaqua (Sweetwater), with a ruined castle, and Pigna, also of Roman times.

San Remo is the largest center in this half of Liguria and the most popular. Its permanent residents are dedicated to the art of tourism. Here are a hundred hotels and pensions of every category, facilities for yachts of all tonnages, miles and miles of beach, lavish public gardens, a 13th-century cathedral, swimming pools, and a funicular railway that takes you up to the Mount Bignone skiing resort (4,221 feet) in 45 minutes.

An interesting small place to visit is Coldirodi, near Ospedaletti, once the headquarters of the Knights of Rhodes, whose picture gallery contains paintings by such masters as Guido Reni, Veronese and Velazquez.

An unusual half-day excusion from San Remo leads to Bussana Vecchia, a picturesque ghost town that was partially destroyed by an earthquake in 1877. The inhabitants packed up and left en masse after the quake. Now once-lively houses are empty shells, overgrown by wild flowers and guarded by the bell tower of Bussana's church.

Bordighera, first town in Europe to grow date-palms, has a magnificent mile-long promenade with marvelous view up and down the Italian and French coasts. Here you will also find clear, quiet water, perfect for swimming. (There ia an airport here for travelers' light aircraft.)

Imperia, the provincial capital, is really two towns: Oneglia, the lower, center of Italian olive oil production, and Porto Maurizio, above it, with a broad avenue named after Theodore Roosevelt, who stayed here. From Imperia, there is a good road north to the ski runs at Monesi and nearby areas, with gradual slopes for beginners and speedier ones for practiced skiers. In August, the natives of Imperia stage a spectacular local custom: a sort of sea battle called the *Palio del Mare.*

Diano Marina, today a beach resort, is a very old town, dating back to Roman times. The fortified part has a walled castle (*castello*) that beetles over the lower city. The Knights of Malta still meet in the castle.

The province of Savona begins just beyond Imperia. It contains many of Liguria's well-known coastal resorts, like Laigueglia, Alassio, Loana, Pietra Ligure, Finale Ligure, Spotorno, and others better-known to Italian than to international tourists. This is a region which caters to English-speaking as well as French visitors. You will certain ly have no difficulty here over language, and you will probably be able to find comfortable hotels without great difficulty. But do not expect peace and quiet.

Savona is industrial. Unless you're terribly interested in one of the largest European collections of cable cars for unloading coal, it will hold no great attraction, most of the year. At Easter time, on Good Friday, there is a procession of artistically carved wooden coffers depicting episodes of the Passion. The carvings, by celebrated artists of the Genoese school, are of great value.

Pegli, on the western outskirts of Genoa, has summer homes of the old patrician Genoese families—Villa Durazzo Pallavicini, Villa Doria —that are worth seeing, set in ample parks and gardens. Here, too, there is a Naval Museum (in the Villa Doria), a Modern Art Gallery, and a fine beach.

The Eastern (Levante) Riviera

The landscape changes; the hills begin to drop sharply to the sea, the curves in the road wind tighter around sparkling little bays and inlets, and the general impression is less of sedateness, more of ruggedness.

Quarto dei Mille, in the suburbs of Genoa to the east, is of historical interest as the starting point of Garibaldi's thousand-man expedition, which liberated Sicily and led to the unification of Italy. Nervi is the oldest winter resort on the eastern Riviera. A two-mile cliff walk, chiseled out of the solid rock, is its greatest pride, and here, too, you can take hot sea baths, if that's your cup of tea. There is an underwater fishing school at Nervi (as there is farther down the coast, at Rapallo).

The towns of Bogliasco, Pieve Ligure, Sori and Recco are lively and colorful, if less exploited. Camogli is an attractive spot, noted, amongst other things, for the celebration of the *Festival of San Fortunato,* in May, when there is a wonderful fry-up of freshly caught fish in two huge frying pans, each 12 feet in diameter.

Portofino and Rapallo

At Camogli, the main road leaves the coast and goes overland to Rapallo branching down to Portofino by way of Santa Margherita and Paraggi. Of all these resorts, Portofino is without doubt the smartest place on the entire Ligurian coast. It had long been a favorite with yachtsmen and some of the more discerning members of high society, and when the Lido of Venice became too well known and began to be crowded, the leaders of society took to Portofino instead. Here they are not likely to be crowded out again, except by day trippers, who come in their hundreds, for it is a small place and it has no beach. But it has beauty—cliffs plunging down from great heights to the sea on either side of the narrow inlet where the yachts lie, the brilliant blue of the water, and clouds of flowers bedecking the buildings that climb the heights on either side. At night it is a little paradise.

Before the foreigners arrived, Portofino was a little fishing village and its cove was filled with highly-colored fishing boats, not with yachts. They are there still, side by side with the luxurious craft of the newcomers. Above, a castle broods, and in the Chapel of St. George lie bones of that saint. On his feast day, April 23, the reliquary is carried through the streets, bands bray and drums pound, and the local inhabitants have a grand time. The next day they return initiative to the millionaires.

This region is headquarters not only for the wealthy, the titled, the smart and the yachtsmen, but also for the literary set, until 1956 headed by the aloof Sir Max Beerbohm, who lived for many years at Rapallo. There are only a handful of spots in all the world of such concentrated beauty.

There are side trips you won't want to miss while you're in this region. Tradition can take you back to nearly legendary times when Richard the Lionheart passed by here and stayed at Portofino "on his way to Syria," as in the song.

But first, it's the scenery you will relish. We recommend a walk to the lighthouse at sunset. It's a pleasant walk, up the little stairway that climbs from the port toward San Giorgio. The view from this point will make you want to go farther. Walk along the lighthouse path, to the right of the church. From the lighthouse itself you will see the whole coast stretched out before you all the way to La Spezia.

San Fruttuoso is wedged right at the foot of Mount Portofino. A boat from Rapallo, Portofino or Santa Margherita will take you there, though you could follow a footpath from Portofino. But it's a good walk—from four to five hours roundtrip depending on your pace. Walking has its rewards. You'll see the fine lines of boats in the port and the Abbey built by the Benedictines of Monte Cassino. In the cloister there is the Dorias' tomb, a work that shows the transitional period between the Romanesque and Gothic styles. A little farther on you will look down and see right through the transparent waters to the bronze statue of the *Christ of the Depths,* lying sunken in the sea before the village.

Down the coast from Rapallo is Zoagli, with a thriving silk velvet industry. Chiavari is an industrial town with a messy sand-and-shingle beach that extends to Lavagna and Cavi. Ligurian sailors brought from Arabia the art of weaving macramé towels, with long, hand-knotted fringes. They still make them here, as well as craftsmanlike chairs and furniture. From Chiavari, a provincial road goes north by way of Borzonasca to the skiing resort of Santo Stefano d'Aveto at 3,295 feet.

Sestri Levante has a beach with soft, fine sand, and a wooded promontory joined to the mainland by a narrow strip of land. The promontory is the private park of a local hotel; there are other excellent hotels and boarding houses in the town itself.

From Sestri, the Via Aurelia climbs steeply through the Bracco Pass (2,000 feet), offering a broad panorama of the Gulf of Genoa before the road slides down again to La Spezia, at the southeastern tip of Liguria. Another highway, the N370, branches off just outside Sestri Levante and hugs the coast all the way to La Spezia. Well engineered, it gives you the chance of visiting all the little spots, especially those in the Cinque Terre.

The Cinque Terre

Boats take you up the coast from Portovenere to the towns of the Cinque Terre—the Five Lands—Riomaggiore, Manarola, Corniglia, Vernazza and Monterosso, most developed of the five, with its 20 hotels and pensions and good beaches. The towns are also linked by train from Genoa—about an hour's ride away. The trip by rail through the Cinque Terre is in tunnels all the way, with the train popping out briefly at each little port.

This six-mile stretch of coast below densely wooded hills is still relatively unspoilt, though possessed of picturesque fishing harbors nestling among the steep rocks, old churches, secluded coves, grapevines on terraced hillsides. You can visit all the towns by car on the N370, although you may find that one or two will need the last little spurt on foot. They are all full of character and worth seeing. Monterosso is the largest, with its twisty streets, attractive views and huge giant, like a piece of statuary left over from a de Mille epic. You can walk along the cliffs to the next town, Vernazza, though the going is a bit rough in places. In fact, if you have the legs for it, you can visit all five towns this way.

The Cinque Terre is an area we highly recommend for anyone who wants to relax in fairly simple surroundings. It is not a place to go for the high life. The isolation of centuries is only slowly being broken, and here, as in so few places in Europe, one can still enjoy the delights of local food, glorious scenery, friendly people and a gentler pace. Make sure that you go well equipped with stout shoes!

La Spezia next along the coast, is an important naval base with charms of its own that appeal to poets. Illustrious authors—Dante, Petrarch, Shelley, Byron, D'Annunzio, D.H. Lawrence—have lingered here or have written about Spezia's Gulf of Poets.

Portovenere, at the tip of the peninsula closing the Gulf of La Spezia's western side, is a picturesque fishing village. You can reach it by road along a highway winding across the tops of the cliffs overlooking the naval installations on this side of the gulf. It is already, however, a favorite excursion spot at weekends. Boat excursions can be made from here to three off-shore islands, all with ancient remains.

Lerici

On the eastern shore of Spezia Gulf is Lerici, with more than a touch of Tuscan about it. This was an old Pisan village, and its castle is a rare example of Italian medieval military architecture, with shining strips of alternating black and white stone. It was from Lerici's Villa Magni that Shelley set out on the tragic sailing trip in which he drowned. The last stretch of road from La Spezia leads southeast to the ancient episcopal town of Sarzana and the ruins of Luni, on the very edge of Tuscany. Sarzana has a number of historic churches, filled with art and relics, including that of the blood of the Savior. At Luni, the remains of an amphitheater, a basilica and baths testify that this was once a prosperous Roman settlement. In 1955, an ancient altar apparently dedicated to the worship of the moon was discovered here, but the epoch is uncertain.

The Hinterland

The hill towns and resorts are frequently disregarded by the guide books and tourist agencies. Yet a case can be made for the hinterland. For one thing, you'll meet an entirely different type of Italian locals who are less commercially minded, and vacationers who've done the more obvious beach resorts and show a friendly sense of adventure that takes them to new and unexploited places. There is contemplative peace in the wooded hills of Liguria that is lacking along the coast. And there are other activities than swimming or lolling in the sun: fishing, for instance, in gurgling mountain streams, hunting for small game and wild fowl, mountain climbing and walks along rambling paths that lead unexpectedly to a dim, cool grotto in the woods, or a rustic sanctuary or chapel, or to a breathtaking view for miles over a valley rolling leisurely to the sea. In summer, the air is cooler and you sleep better at night.

There are good roads from the seaside towns; Ventimiglia, Bordighera, San Remo, Taggia, Imperia. They wind their way amidst scenery resembling a miniature Switzerland, leading in an hour to altitudes of 3,000 to 4,000 feet above sea level, to woods of chestnut and beech trees and stately pines. Perinaldo, Baiardo and Colle di Nava are three such places in the province of Imperia; San Romolo, above San Remo, is in a pine wood at an altitude of 2,400 feet.

Sassello, due north from Savona, is 1,000 feet up in a fertile hollow, surrounded by wooded mountains. From here there are a number of walks and excursions to Madonna di Bei Baià, Mount Beigua, Mount Reixa and Bric Berton, localities which were sacred to tribal gods in a past so distant that Romans were a novelty in these parts. Other places where there are hotels are Calizzano, Bardineto, Dego, Millesimo, Stella and Urbe, all within driving distance of Savona.

The Levante Riviera is connected by several roads through mountains and forests to Piacenza, Parma and the Milan-Bologna motorway.

PRACTICAL INFORMATION FOR LIGURIA

HOTELS AND RESTAURANTS

Alassio. Beach resort. **Hotels:** All (1) are—*Diana,* Via Garibaldi 104, very good, beach, pool, some bad rail noise; *Mediterraneo Grand,* Via Roma 92, best food, 86 rooms, most with bath, on waterfront, own beach, terrace garden, open-air bar, bad highway noise; *Spiaggia,* Via Roma 104, all rooms with bath or shower, at end of beach; *Europa Concordia,* overlooking main square and beach, pleasant lounges, 56 rooms with bath, some with balcony, sea view; *Puerta del Sol,* recent, good.

All (2) are—*Beau Séjour,* overlooking beach, comfortable rooms, delightful terrace; *Idéale,* central position a short walk from beach, nicely furnished; *Regina,* beach across street, modern, 39 bright rooms, most with bath or shower, some with sea view; *Majestic,* faces beach, attractive, modern, balconied hotel, all rooms with bath or shower, private beach area; *Gallo Nero,* central, few steps from beach, well-furnished rooms, most with shower.

All (3) are—*Èden,* on beachfront, 30 rooms, some overlooking sea, pleasant dining terrace, private beach area; *Beau Rivage,* overlooking beach, comfortable, small hotel; *Torino,* reader-recommended, 21 rooms, most with bath, beach facilities.

Officially (4), but fine in all respects—*Riviera,* fairly quiet, a few steps from beach, pleasant bar-lounge, shady terrace, good bedrooms, in attractive balconied building.

Restaurants. *La Palma* (E), Via Cavour. Reserve ahead (tel. 40.314). Caters to a smart clientele with excellent food and service.

All (M)—*Stella Marina,* seafront terrace, unpretentious, fish specialties; *Excelsior,* Via Robutti, good; *La Liggia,* try *pansoti* and *fritto misto.*

Roma (I), roof garden, floor show, the town's social center.

Arenzano. Beach resort. **Hotels:** Both (1) are—*Punta San Martino,* Pineta di Arenzano, best, 16 rooms, all with bath, promontory with beautiful view of sea, outdoor dining terrace, swimming pool, tennis, very comfortable, highly recommended but expensive. *Grand,* well-appointed rooms, many with sea view, pool, tennis. Except for top hotels, uninteresting resort.

Arma di Taggia Hotels. *Vittoria* (1), new, 77 rooms with bath, beach, pool, park. *Miramare* (2), Via N. Sauro 32, has 56 rooms all with bath or shower and sea view.

Bordighera. Second most important beach resort of the Riviera di Ponente. **Hotels:** All (1) are—*Del Mare,* handsome, modern hotel in elevated position overlooking sea, 100 well-furnished rooms with bath, landscaped gardens, sea water pool, beach club, elegant panoramic restaurant, closed Nov.; *Cap Ampelio,* on hillside overlooking town and sea, smart, modern decor, 104 airconditioned rooms with bath or shower, attractive grounds, heated pool.

All (2) are—*Astoria,* small, pleasant hotel on hillside, modern, reasonable; *Centro,* on busy station square, a few steps from beach, modern functional rooms, all with bath; *Martinelli,* garden setting on edge of town, 37 rooms with bath, private beach.

All (3) are—*Parigi,* central, on shore road overlooking beach, modest but functional furnishings; *Villa Elisa,* quiet, above town, well-appointed rooms, pleasant garden; *Jean Pierre,* reader-recommended, very clean.

Restaurants. *Pinin* (E), beside San Ampeglio Chapel on San Remo road, has nice view, so-so food. *Chaudron,* Piazza Bengasi, pricey but very good.

Both (M) are—three miles out on the Dolceacqua road, *Gino,* for fish specialties; *Chez Louis,* Corso Italia, for hot or cold snacks. *Giardino,* Via Vittorio Emanuele, cheerful, simple.

Camogli. Picturesque port. **Hotels:** *Cenobio dei Dogi* (1), outstanding for quiet location overlooking gulf, elegant appointments, beautiful park and seaside terraces, pool, tennis. *Casmona* (3), 34 comfortable rooms, most with sea view. At **Ruta,** high above Camogli, *Grand Hotel Portofino Vetta,* elegant, 12-room haven of peace and quiet.

Restaurants. All (M–E) are—*Rosa,* high over the sea; *Gay,* good, on pretty piazza; *La Camogliese,* Via Garibaldi; *Tony,* reasonable.

At nearby **Recco:** *Manuelina* and *Vitturin,* both (M–E), modern, elegant, very good. Be sure to try *focaccia al formaggio.*

Cavi Hotels. All (2) are—*Park,* with attractive garden, all rooms with shower; *Mediterraneo,* sea view, nice terrace; *Astoria Grand,* large, with tennis and beach.

Celle Ligure. Beach resort. **Hotels:** All (2) are—*San Michele,* Via Monte Tabor, comfortable hotel in elevated position, 55 rooms, most with bath, pool, gardens; *Riviera,* and *Piccolo,* both pleasant, all private baths or shower.

Ancora (3), modest, but clean and quiet.

Diano Marina. Beach resort. **Hotels:** *Diana Majestic* (1), modern balconied building right on private beach, 80 smallish but bright bedrooms with bath or shower, attractive gardens, pool.

All (2) are—*Moresco,* slightly elevated position, attractive and comfortable, with pool, beach facilities; *Bellevue Méditerranée,* right on beach, pleasant rooms, many with private bath, pool and garden; *Torino,* central, modern, has pool; *Golfo e Palme,* quiet, on sandy beach, recent, all rooms with bath; *Sasso,* attractive, quiet, short walk to beach; *Tiziana,* pleasant, some rail and traffic noise.

Both (3) are—*Marinella,* good; *Gabriella,* fine, own beach.

Restaurants. Both (M–E) are—*Pesce d'Oro,* smart; *Fra Diavolo,* rustic and friendly.

Finale Ligure. Beach resort. **Hotels:** Both (1) are—*Moroni,* most rooms with bath, on sea front, private beach, reputation for good food and service; *Punta Est,* 15 rooms in pleasant villa, overlooking sea, beach facilities.

Both (2) are—*Boncardo,* across road from beach, most rooms with bath, some highway noise at back; *Colibri,* few steps from beach, comfortable, but can be noisy.

Both (3) are—*Villa Italia,* Via Torino 111, in attractive park; *Lido,* sea view, terrace restaurant.

Restaurants. *Delle Palme* (M), on seaside promenade; *Ai Torchi* (M–E), at *Pinale Borgo,* delightful old setting, fine food.

Genoa/Genova. Hotels: *Colombia-Excelsior* (L) opposite Principe station, posh public rooms, 171 handsomely furnished, airconditioned bedrooms with bath, linen sheets, impeccable.

Both (1) are—*Savoia Majestic,* facing Principe station, elegant appointments, 115 good-sized rooms with bath, airconditioning; *Bristol Palace,* in city's heart, rather traditional elegance.

All (2) are—*Eliseo,* central, excellent, 34 comfortably furnished rooms, most with bath, attractive dining terrace; *City,* very central but quiet, 71 rooms, most with bath; *Vittorio Orlandini,* near Principe station, in slightly elevated position with a view, 41 rooms with bath or shower; *Orti Sauli,* officially (P2), is very comfortable, near Brignole station, 49 pleasant rooms with bath or shower, airconditioning; *Metropoli,* central, breakfast only.

All (3) are—*Simonini Garden,* Via Balbi 33, is comfortable, smallish; *Torinese,* Via Gramsci 291R; *Bellevue,* near Principe station, many rooms with bath or shower, optional airconditioning, view of port from terrace.

Restaurants. The good restaurants here are too numerous for all to be listed.

All (E)—if you want a wonderful view along with food equally wonderful, you must try *Vittorio al Mare,* at Boccadasse, for authentic Genoese dishes (fish soup) and wines; other restaurants in the topnotch class are *La Santa,* Vico Indorati, excellent cuisine; *Marinetta,* Corso Italia 19, Boccadasse, seafood; *Pichin,* Vico Parmigiani 6; and for more fish, *Da Mario,* Via Conservatori del Mare 33R.

All (M) are—*Caravella d'Oro,* Corso Italia 15; *Punta Vagno,* Corso Italia 3, both overlooking the sea; *Ariston,* Lungo E. Vernazza; *Gino,* at both railway stations, also has snacks; near Brignole station, *Gran Gotto* is good; on the sea, try *Santa Chiara, Osvaldo* or *Gheise,* all at Boccadasse, or *Italia,* just beyond in the suburb of Quarto; *Olivio,* Piazza Raibetta 15; *Perelli,* Vico Falamonica 41; and the *Pesce d'Oro,* Piazza Caricamento 63, which makes a specialty of fish.

If you want to eat cheaply, but still well, all (I) are—*Cavanna,* Via Fieschi 37; *Due Colonne,* Piazza Matteotti 31; *La Lanterna,* Via Fieschi 78, and *Da Lino,* Via S. Martino 11R.

Imperia. Coast resort. **Hotels:** Both (2) are—*Corallo,* fine location, 36 rooms with bath or shower, some with sea view; *Croce di Malta,* pleasant, right on tiny beach.

Restaurants. We recommend *Nannina* at **Porto Maurizio** (E). *Lanterna Blu* (M), at Borgo Marina, is more basic, fine for fish.

Laigueglia. Beach resort. **Hotels:** Both (1) are—best, recently up-graded is *Laigueglia,* in quiet position overlooking sea, 55 rooms with bath, private beach; *Splendid,* set back from road, few steps to good beach, 42 rooms with bath or shower, inviting lounges, shady terrace, small pool.

All (2) are—*Del Sole,* under same management as above, also pleasant, well-equipped; *Britannia Suisse,* all 25 rooms with bath; *Bristol,* most rooms have bath, on beachfront.

Villa Ida (3), comfortable, beach facilities.

La Spezia. Large town and naval base, set in a deep bay. **Hotels:** *Jolly* (1), Via XX Settembre 2, recent, airconditioned, comfortable, all rooms have bath or shower, garage.

Palazzo San Giorgio (2), near seaside promenade, and boats to **Lerici,** nicely furnished rooms, most with bath or shower.

Restaurants. *La Posta, Carlino, Da Dina* are all (I–M), all located near public gardens on bay. *La Litoranea* (I), modest but good; lovely terrace.

Lavagna. Beach resort. **Hotels:** *Admiral Lido* (3), all rooms with bath, on the sea.

Lerici. Seaside summer resort on one arm of La Spezia's bay, famous and crowded. **Hotels:** All (2) are—*Europa,* 31 rooms with shower, gardens, view of gulf; *Byron,* very comfortable, airconditioned, all rooms with bath, but situated on main road and can be noisy in season; *Shelley,* same amenities, and same problems as Byron.

At *Panoramic* (3), good value.

Fiascherino di Lerici, just above the town is a wonderfully scenic spot. **Hotels:** Two beautifully situated hotels, both (2) are—*Nido,* 40 rooms, most with bath or shower, attractive garden; and *Cristallo,* 34 rooms, all with bath, new, well-appointed, but indifferent food.

Restaurants. All (M) are—*Calata* and *Da Paolino,* risotto di mare; *Due Corone,* at port, superb view, fish specialties. *Conchiglia,* at port, also good.

At **San Terenzo,** *Da Victor,* for *lasagna al pesto.*

Levanto. Beach resort. **Hotels:** All (2) are—*Crystal,* small, seasonal, most rooms with shower, attractive location above and outside town. *Stella d'Italia,* central, attractively furnished, well-kept, dining under arbor in delightful garden, good food, some rooms with bath, also annex (3); *Primavera,* small, all rooms with bath.

Restaurants. *Tumelin* (M–E), Via Grillo, fish specialties in handsome 12th-century salon or on terrace. *Hosteria Franco* (M).

Loano. Beach resort. **Hotels:** *Garden Lido* (1), smart, modern, on sea, 88 well-furnished rooms with bath or shower, lovely garden, pool.

Both (2) are—*Continental,* all private baths or shower, attractive terrace, private beach, reasonable; *Moderno,* Via Mazza 3, large, comfortable.

Both (3) are—*Excelsior,* many rooms with bath or shower; and *Mary,* with beach facilities.

Monterosso Al Mare. Main resort in up-and-coming Cinque Terre. **Hotels:** *Porto Roca* (1), lovely situation on headland; several smaller hotels and pensions, all good value.

Restaurants. *Claudio Il Gigante* (M-E), and *Al Pozzo* (M), are both good for fish.

Elsewhere in Cinque Terre—**Riomaggiore,** *La Grotta* (I), value-for-money restaurant; **Franceschetti** (M-E), where you top off a fine meal with American-style cheesecake. **Manarola,** *Da Aristide* (M), modest spot, Good food. **Vernazza,** *Gambero Rosso* (I-M), good fish at harborside.

At **Fegina. Hotels:** *Palme* (2), *Cinque Terre* (2), both with beach.

Nervi. Internationally known seaside resort, suburb of Genoa. **Hotels:** Both (1) are—*Savoia,* in quiet garden, 45 comfortable rooms with bath, attractive outdoor restaurant; *Astor,* smart, well-appointed.

Both (2) are—*Giardino Riviera,* 28 rooms, nearly half with bath, attractive setting, bathing area, reader-recommended (best book ahead for beachside rooms); also good, *Esperia,* new, modern, all rooms with terrace, some with bath, solarium, in own park.

Both (3) are—*Villa Bonera,* comfortable, in a lovely 17th-century villa; *Motel Milano,* 30 rooms with bath, small garden.

Restaurant. *Simona* (M-E), reserve ahead (tel. 328.635), outstanding classic cuisine; *Manuè* (M), small and satisfying.

Oneglia. Near Imperia. **Hotel:** *Kristina* (2), small hotel on quay.

Restaurant. We recommend *Salvo Cacciatori* (M–E), very good fish and game dishes.

Ospedaletti. Seaside summer resort. **Hotels:** *Le Rocce del Capo* (1), very comfortable, expensive, all rooms have shower, radio, hotel bus at station, has own beach, indoor/outdoor pools.

Petit Royal (2), Viale Regina Margherita 62, pleasantly situated, but a little old-fashioned, half of rooms with bath.

Madison (3), 20 rooms with bath. *Alexandra* (P2), pleasant little pension overlooking sea, tennis, garden.

Paraggi. Two miles from Santa Margherita Ligure, boasts a pleasantly sandy shore. **Hotel:** *Paraggi* (2), 17 rooms, 12 with bath, private beach.

Pietra Ligure. Beach resort. **Hotels:** Both (1) are—*Royal,* large, well-appointed with sea view, all rooms with bath or shower, private beach; *Paco,* modern, all rooms airconditioned, with bath or shower, pool and tennis in pleasant garden.

Portofino. Very fashionable seaside resort, with no beach. **Hotels:** *Splendido* (L), to north, very attractive location high above village, reached by a private drive, 70 rooms, most with bath, many rooms facing sea have balconies, tastefully decorated, tennis court, smart clientele, an outstanding hotel, full pension only in summer, and usually closed mid-January to mid-March.

All (2) are—*Nazionale,* at the charming port, majority of rooms have bath or shower; *Piccolo,* Frazione Paraggi, 27 rooms, many with bath; *San Giorgio,* recent, 20 rooms with bath.

Eden (3), small, all rooms with shower; garden.

Restaurants. All very (E) are—*Pitosforo,* first class menu, excellent wines, guitarists play while you eat; *Delfino* and *Stella* are good, *Navicello; Da u Bati* is a picturesque *osteria,* so popular and tiny it's booked a month ahead for summer weekends.

Porto Venere. A newly popular resort on one arm of La Spezia's bay. **Hotels:** *Royal* (1), recent, exceptional position, striking view of gulf, modern furnishings, all resort amenities.

Both (2) are—*San Pietro,* same view, more modest but still comfortable; *Della Baia,* at La Grazie, good.

Restaurants. All (M-E)—*Taverna del Corsaro* and *Iseo* have tasty food and seaside terraces. *Da Mario,* small, on port.

At **Le Grazie,** *Da Pietro,* fish caught by Pietro himself, and cooked to perfection by his wife Mafalda.

Rapallo. Favorite sandy seaside resort. **Hotels:** All (1) are—*Bristol,* Via Aurelia Orientale 309, most of its 70 rooms have bath, all rooms have balconies, swimming pool, private beach, half-pension required July–Aug; *Grand Hôtel et Europa,* Via Magioco 1, pleasantly located but beginning to show age, large rooms, half with bath; *Eurotel,* Via Aurelia Occidentale, is very up-to-date, airconditioned, has pool, all private baths, panoramic, hillside above town.

All (2) are—*Moderno e Reale,* Viale Gramsci 6, 48 rooms, most with bath, unpretentious, one minute from sea, frequented by Italian family groups. *Cuba e Milton,* Frazioni San Michele di Pagana. *Grande Italia,* Lungomare Italia 1, overlooking the sea. *Miramare,* Passeggiata a Mare, 25 rooms, most with bath, on seafront. *Riviera,* central, overlooking park, beach. *Astoria,* 24 rooms with bath, garden.

Both (3) are—*Minerva,* Via. C Colombo, near beach, 24 rooms with bath; *Mondial,* Via Ferraretto, 18 rooms with bath, garden.

Both (P2) are—*Tivoli,* Via Zunino, 23 rooms, most with bath. *Mignon Posta,* Via Boccoleri 12.

Restaurants. At the top of the eating places of this popular resort, both (E) are—*Da Fausto,* the one gastronomic must here, rivalled by *Santa Maria,* at **Santa Maria del Campo,** 1 mile away, excellent cooking.

All (M) are—*Porticciolo,* Parco Casale, for fish specialties; and *Tigullio.* Via Matteotti 80; above Rapallo, at **San Massimo,** *U Giancu,* rustic, *simpatico.*

San Fruttuoso. Atmospheric little gulf, with the old abbey of the Doria family, near Camogli. **Hotel/Restaurant:** *Da Giovanni* (4), small, modest, with good food.

San Remo. Number One resort of the Riviera di Ponente. **Hotels:** Deluxe—*Royal,* open 19 Dec.–27 Sept., in park near Casino, most rooms with bath, set in lovely grounds overlooking sea, traditional and modern furnishings, saltwater pool, tennis courts, dancing terrace, outdoor grill for *al fresco* lunches.

All (1) are—*Grand Hotel Londra,* Corso Matuzia, imposing and elegant, 140 rooms, most with bath, swimming pool in handsomely landscaped grounds; *Grand des Anglais,* Corso Imperatrice, elevated position above shore road, beach, old-world comfort and service in handsome palace-type hotel; *Miramare Continental Palace,* Corso Matuzia 9, 67 rooms, most with bath, near beach front, garden, modern furnishings, delightful restaurant, closed Oct.–Nov.; *Residence Principe,* Via Asquaciati, on hillside just above Casino, less expensive.

All (2) are—*Europe e della Pace,* Corso Imperatrice 27, is best in this class; *Nazionale,* next to Casino, many rooms with bath or shower; *Montecarlo,* 1 mile east of town, 43 rooms many with bath and terraces, family-managed, swimming pool; *Villa King,* Corso Cavallotti, small, all rooms with bath or shower, pool, garden. Closed 10 Oct.–20 Dec.

All (3) are—*Centrale,* Via Roma 16, and *Svizzera,* modern, near beach and center; *Paradiso,* Via Roccasterone, quiet location, short walk to beach, comfortable; *Juana,* Corso Matuzia 70, small, most rooms have bath; *Beau Rivage,* Lungomare Trieste, smallish, with all comforts, garden.

Marina (P3), Corso Cavallotti, small, but has private baths, garage.

Restaurants. All (E) are—one of the best places to eat is the *Casino,* as are two hotels, the *Royal* and the *Savoia; Pesce d'Oro,* known for its *lasagne al pesto,* seafood soup, grilled crabs and shrimp, is the best of the restaurants proper; *Gambero Rosso,* Via Matteotti 71, and *Caravella,* on sea, both especially for seafood; *Osteria del Marinaio,* Via Gaudio, a find, exceptional seafood salads.

All (M) are—good and less expensive, *U Nostromû,* Piazza Sardi 2; *Castel Dorio* and *Da Nico,* at port, for *gamberoni* (shrimp) *alla Bresca.*

Santa Margherita Ligure. Select seaside resort, with gently sloping beach of rocks and shingle as well as sand. **Hotels:** Deluxe—*Imperial Palace,* Via Pagana 16, largest and most expensive, all 105 airconditioned rooms with bath, amidst exotic vegetation in extensive grounds, elegance is the keynote, private beach, swimming pool, open 20 Dec.–31 Oct.

All (1) are—*Miramare,* very attractive, on shore boulevard overlooking bay, 73 rooms, most with bath, modern furnishings, disco, swimming pool, open 20 Dec.–10 Nov.; *Park Hôtel Suisse,* Via Favale 31, situated above town, 75 rooms, most with bath or shower, well-furnished, summer terrace, swimming pool, open 1 March–10 Nov.; *Continental,* above town, elegant, smart, pretty bedrooms and gardens, private beach; *Regina Elena,* recently renovated, all 64 rooms with bath, beach, gardens.

All (2) are—*Mediterraneo,* in center of town, attractive old-world villa, pleasant garden and patio; *Metropole,* in lovely park with private beach; *La Vela,* large Renaissance-style villa in elevated position with view of sea, well-furnished rooms, most with bath, good restaurant, terraces, garden.

Both (3) are—*Conte Verde,* Via Zara 1, 35 rooms; *Fiorina,* central, 55 rooms, many with bath or shower.

Restaurants. Both (E) are—smart, *Taverna del Brigantino* is costly and good; *Saltincielo,* superb view and food, disco. *Cambusa* (M-E), delicious food.

All (M) are—one of the better restaurants on the Riviera di Levante coast is the *Trattoria dei Pescatori,* which is not too expensive; also good, *La Terrazza,* Via Gramsci; *Faro,* Via Maragliano, spartan decor, absolutely fresh fish from family's 5 trawlers; *Basilico,* Via Monte Carlo, try peach flambée.

Santo Stefano d'Aveto. Summer mountain resort. **Hotels:** *Grand Hotel,* (1), quiet and pleasant, tennis court, pool. *Groppo Rosso* (2), all rooms with bath.

Savona. Hotels: All (2) are—*Riviera-Suisse,* Via Paleocapa 24, largest; *Astoria,* Via IV Novembre 38; *Motel AGIP,* modern, comfortable.

Restaurants. Both (M) are—*Ghione,* Piazza del Popolo; and *Sole,* Via Stalingrado.

Sestri Levante. Beach resort. **Hotels:** Both (1) are—*Dei Castelli,* borders on deluxe, in splendid isolated position overlooking bay and coast, medieval-style buildings with modern comforts, 42 airconditioned rooms with bath, terrace dining, natural rock pool and lift to rocky terraces on sea; *Villa Balbi,* in town, overlooking sea, richly furnished salons, half of rooms with bath, garden.

Both (2) are—*Miramare Europa,* small, terraces overlooking pretty bay; *Mimosa,* quietly situated outside town, 22 rooms with shower, pleasant pool among pines.

Restaurants. *Carmagnini* (E), *Portobello* (M).

Spotorno. Beach resort. **Hotels:** *Royal* (1) large modern hotel facing beach across road, pleasant rooms, all with bath or shower, terraces, disco, beach facilities.

All (2) are—*Delle Palme,* Via Aurelia; and *Tirreno,* same road, private beach, gardens, *Pineta,* in quiet elevated position with sea view, attractive modern building in Mediterranean style, ample terraces, bar, lovely garden, short walk from beach.

Premuda (3), on main beach.

Varazze. Beach resort. **Hotels:** All (2) are—*Cristallo,* Via Cilea 4, most rooms with bath, tennis, private beach. *El Chico,* at Invrea, quiet, comfortable, swimming pool in garden; *Eden,* pleasant, a few steps from beach; *Royal,* overlooks town and sea, 33 rooms with bath or shower.

Both (3) are—*Ideale,* 40 rooms, most with bath or shower, some with view; *Europa,* modest but comfortable.

Restaurant. *Serafino* (E) reserve ahead (tel. 90.737), well worth the 2-mile trip to **Invrea.**

Varigotti. Near Finale Ligure. **Hotels:** *Al Saraceno* (1), is attractive, unassuming, overlooking sea, 66 rooms, half with bath, private beach; *Mehari* (2), on main road, 30 rooms with bath or shower, pleasant flowered terraces.

Ventimiglia. Seaside resort. **Hotels:** All (2) are—*Francia,* downtown, majority of rooms with bath or shower.

At **Castel d'Appio,** high above town, *La Riserva,* peace and quiet, fine views, heated pool.

Sea Gull (3), overlooking sea, most rooms with bath, beach area.

Restaurants. Avoid highly overrated, expensive *La Mortola,* near French border; try *Ritrovo degli Artisti,* for local specialties; *La Capannina,* for fish, both (M), avoid Friday, chaotic market day.

Zoagli. Beach resort. **Hotels:** *Le Terrazze* (2), most rooms with bath, comfortably furnished, sea view, modest. *Le Palme* (P2), with attractive terraces, is pleasant.

USEFUL ADDRESSES. Tourist Offices: *Alassio:* AAST, Piazza Partigiani 1; American Express, Anglo-American Agency, Ufficio Viaggi e Turismo, Via Mazzini 55 (tel. 40586 and 40125. *Arenzano:* AAST, Piazza S. Bolivar 1. *Arma di Taggia:* AAST, Via Boselli. *Bordighera:* AAST, Via Roberto 1. *Camogli:* AAST, Via XX Settembre 33. *Celle Ligure:* AAST, Largo Giolitti 7. *Diano Marina:* AAST, Giardini Ardissone. *Finale Ligure:* AAST, Via San Pietro 14.

Genoa: American Express, SIT, Via San Vincenzo 22R, 16121, tel. 581368, 581886; Thomas Cook, Via Porta degli Archi 12; CIT travel organization has offices at Via XXV Aprile 16, and Principe Railway Station; EPT, Via Roma 11, information desks at both railway stations and at Cristoforo Colombo Airport; for information on *boat services,* Societa di Navigazione Tirrenia, Via Serra 8; on *air services,* Via Piaggio 15.

Imperia: AAST, Via Matteotti 22; EPT, Viale Matteotti 54. *Laigueglia:* AAST, Via Milano 33. *La Spezia:* EPT, Via Mazzini 47. *Lavagna:* AAST, Piazza della Libertà 46. *Lerici:* AAST, Via Roma 47. *Levanto:* AAST, Piazza Colombo. *Loano:* Corso Europa 19. *Nervi:* AAST, Via Casotti 1. *Ospedaletti:* AAST, Viale Regina Margherita. *Pietra Ligure:* AAST, Piazza Martiri della Libertà 31. *Portofino:* AAST, Via Roma 35. *Rapallo:* AAST, Via A, Diaz 5.

San Remo: AAST, Largo Nuvoloni 1; Thomas Cook, Corso Nuvoloni 19; EPT, Palazzo Riviera. *Santa Margherita Ligure:* AAST, Via XXV Aprile 28. *Santo Stefano d'Aveto:* AAST, Piazza del Popolo. *Savona:* EPT, Via Paleocapa 7 and 59R. *Sestri Levante:* AAST, Viale XX Settembre 33. *Spotorno:* AAST, Via Aurelia 43. *Varazze:* AAST, Via Santa Caterina 1–2. *Ventimiglia:* AAST, Via Roma 27. *Zoagli:* AAST, Piazza San Martino 8.

SPECIAL EVENTS. *Camogli:* The Fish Fair in May, when the biggest frying pans in the world (12 feet across) are used. *Genoa:* October 12, Columbus Day, is a big event here in his birthplace. *La Spezia:* August, big rowing contest, the Palio del Golfo. *Nervi:* Openair concerts throughout the summer, with the famous International Ballet Festival in July. *San Remo:* February, carnival with flower parades; regattas in April; Casino open all year round. *Savona:* January, earliest carnival celebrations; March, special Savonese Carnival; impressive Good Friday processions.

SPORTS. *Arenzano:* Della Pineta golf course, 9 holes. *Genoa:* frequent yachting regattas. *Portofino:* social center for yachtsmen. *Rapallo:* 18-hole golf course. *San Remo:* yachting regatta; Degli Ulivi, 18-hole golf course. *Santa Margherita Ligure:* frequent yachting regattas; canoe regatta for small boat handlers in July.

PIEDMONT

Italy's Window on France

Piedmont—the region of Turin and the magnificent Valle d'Aosta in the northwest corner of Italy—is one of the delightful surprises in a land of spectacular natural beauty and regional individuality. Bordering on France and Switzerland, the region has some of the characteristics of those countries blended with its basic Italian heritage—and an ever-growing number of foreign visitors are including Piedmont in their itinerary.

Geographically it combines the lure of the highest peaks of the Alps in ranges that circle fanwise along the south, west and north boundaries and the broad flat lands of the plain. Turin, its capital city, lies at the base of the mountainous circle in a level area that marks the beginning of the fertile Valley of the Po, which expands into broad plains to Milan and beyond. Its mountains and valleys provide Piedmont with some of the most beautiful scenery in Europe. In summer the peaceful towns and villages of the Alpine valleys attract many tourists in search of cool, restful holidays, where the most strenuous exertion need not be greater than a walk in the woods. For the more ambitious there is mountain-climbing. This may include the tallest in Europe, Mont Blanc, Monte Rosa, the Cervino (Matterhorn), the Gran Paradiso, and also many lesser peaks.

As for winter sports, Piedmont's mountain valleys provide the scene for some of the finest skiing in the world. For shorter stays, Piedmont offers great attractions in its heritage of historical and architectural landmarks dating from early Roman times down through medieval and baroque periods. Some of the 14th- and 15th-century castles hidden away in rugged mountain retreats were able to escape destruction through the years and remain tangible witness to more turbulent times.

The region represents the latest word in modern development, with Turin containing some of Italy's finest mass production industries. It is also the home of Borsalino hats and of vermouth. And to top it off, Piedmont offers the gourmet a treat in combining the best of French with Italian cuisine.

A Bit of History

Piedmont originally was inhabited by Celtic tribes who, when they could not beat off the encroaching invaders from Rome, ended up by joining them. As allies of the Romans, the Celts fought off Hannibal when he came down through the Alpine passes with his elephants, but finally lost, and their capital Taurasia—the present Turin—was destroyed. The Romans rebuilt the city, giving its streets the rectangular pattern which has persisted until now and which makes travelers think of an American city. Today ruins of Roman buildings are to be found in various parts of the region and particularly in the town of Aosta.

With the downfall of the Roman empire, Piedmont suffered the fate of the rest of Italy and was successively occupied and ravaged by barbarians who came from the east and the north. By the 10th and 11th centuries the area was a battleground for feuding lords. Turin was strong enough to withstand predatory knights and during the 12th and 13th centuries governed itself as a Commune—a sort of independent republic. In the 11th century a French feudal family—the Savoys—managed to rule Turin for a brief time and then came back at the end of the 13th century. Counts and dukes of this family governed the area almost continuously—Francis I of France in 1536 annexed it to his country for about 20 years—until about 1798, when the French Republican armies came down to Italy. When Napoleon's empire fell, the Savoys returned to Piedmont.

After 1848 Piedmont was one of the main centers of the Risorgimento—the revival of the spirit of Italian unity. Victor Emmanuel II became king in 1848 and under the leadership of Cavour, Garibaldi and Mazzini the movement for Italian unity and the efforts to forge an Italian nation proceeded with great patriotic fervor. In 1861 the Chamber of Deputies in Turin proclaimed the Kingdom of Italy and moved the capital to Florence until Rome could become the nation's capital.

Piedmont Today

This move marked the end of Piedmont's importance in the political sphere, but the architecture of Turin, with the regal splendor of its buildings and the stateliness of its parks, bears witness to its period as a capital city. Turin then turned to industrial and commercial pursuits and the development of arts and sciences as befitted a progressive industrial city. Today the region is the center of Italy's automobile, metal-working, chemical and candy industries. The importance of Turin is further enhanced by the fact that its industries are highly diversified. Clothing, paper and liquor manufacture also contribute widely to its commercial activities. Piedmont's industrial importance entered the political picture again during World War II when its workers opposed the Fascist and Nazi war efforts as resistance fighters both in the hills and in the city.

Piedmont offers excellent holiday facilities both in its capital city of Turin and in the many towns and villages of its Alpine valleys. Turin itself is more appealing in spring and autumn. The mountain valley towns and hamlets are best in summer, when their altitude and the breezes from glacier-topped mountain peaks provide a cool respite from summer heat. Most of the holiday resorts in Piedmont are open in winter because the terrain and abundant snow lend themselves to ideal skiing conditions.

Weather Matters

Piedmont is a two-season country, visited in the winter for skiing and other sports, in the summer for lake or mountain vacations. The period from Christmas through the first week of January is the big one for winter sports, after which resorts are quieter for about a month, entering into another lively period from February 10 to March 10. During January and February the weather is less reliable. The peak summer season runs from approximately the middle of July to the middle of August for mountain resorts like those in the Valle d'Aosta and from early July to mid-September in lake resorts like Stresa, which is politically in Piedmont but will be treated in the chapter on Lombardy, since geographically it is part of Lombardy's Lake District. Busy Turin, the capital, is best visited between the end of April and the middle of June, and again from the end of September to the middle of October.

Road Reports

It is said that the great majority of tourists visiting Piedmont make straight for a resort such as Sestriere or Stresa and stay there throughout their vacation. In which case they are missing a lot and have almost no reason to motor in the region at all, since Sestriere can be reached direct from Briançon in France, while Stresa is found immediately below the modernized Simplon Pass from Switzerland.

However, people who do want to discover Piedmont would do well to make Turin their center, pausing, perhaps, on the way down the Valle d'Aosta from the Mt. Blanc or Grand St. Bernard tunnels. This enormously historic valley has an autostrada sweeping down from Aosta to Turin, which besides providing for fast travel when necessary, means that the old road, meandering along between the castled villages, is largely free of traffic, and from it run several lesser valley roads which reward investigation. Chief among these is the Gressoney with Monte Rosa at its head; Valle del Cervino reaching towards the Matterhorn; or Val de Cogne which leads to the Gran Paradiso mountains. At the northern end, beyond Aosta there is the Grand St. Bernard road up to the monastery, and beyond Courmayeur the much more enchanting Little St. Bernard pass which is so lightly used now that it has the charm of a small country road strung with mountain villages.

Some ingenuity with a map, preferably large scale, will produce various round trips in the area. For example: Turin to Courmayeur, over the Little St. Bernard into France, down the Val-d'Isère, return to Italy over the Col du Mt. Cenis, and back to Turin; about 230 miles turning left all the time through breathtaking scenery. But except for the motorway section it is slow going all the way. On the other hand, in a southern sweep round Turin outlined by Vercelli, Cuneo and Mantua, there are such places as Limone, Acqui, Asti, Alba and Sestriere, all for their several reasons worth seeing, and in between the ubiquitous castles in a softly colored, smiling countryside.

Food for Thought

Piedmont cooking echoes the geography of the region which produced it—the basic Italian dishes are treated with French finesse, modified by a touch of the rustic quality of mountain cooking. The favorite form of *pasta* is *agnolotti,* similar to *ravioli,* small squares of dough filled with meat, spinach or cheese. *Fonduta*—melted cheese, eggs and sometimes grated truffles—is another regional specialty. The truffles are not black, but white, a specialty of Piedmont, and the cheese that goes into the dish is *fontina,* from the Valle d'Aosta. Perhaps the oddest Piedmontese dish is *cardi in bagna cauda.* This is made of edible thistles, chopped raw, and then covered with a hot sauce made of butter, oil, anchovies, cream and shredded garlic. Italian restaurants the world over put breadsticks on the table. They originated in Turin, where they are called *grissini.*

Piedmont produces many excellent wines. The reds are full-bodied and rich; among them are *Barolo, Nebiolo, Freisa* and *Barbaresco.* Best known of the whites is the champagnized *Asti Spumante,* a sweet sparkling wine that also exists in a *brut* version that is quite close to champagne (ask for *Cinzano Brut* or *President Reserve Riccadonna*). Piedmont is also the inventor of vermouth, which was developed by A. B. Carpano in 1786 and now appears under a number of brand names—*Martini, Cora, Cinzano,* etc.

In most Piedmont towns and cities you will probably eat at your hotel. In some of the Lake Maggiore centers, and in Turin itself, however, there are some good restaurants.

Exploring Turin

Although Turin, the capital of Piedmont, is a genuinely Italian city, its proximity to France and its century-old ties to the neighboring country give it a constantly recurring French accent. In fact, the peculiar Piedmontese accent you overhear in the streets will make you think it's some kind of French dialect. The Turinese say *madami* rather than *signora,* for example, and the Italians call the city their *little* Paris. Situated on the left bank of the Po, facing a hill, the city is in the midst of the plain that marks the beginning of the Po Valley. In the distance to the south, west and north are the Alps, giving a feeling of protected encirclement. From the hill across the river, Turin seems almost completely level, with the exception of the tower building called the Mole Antonelliana.

Turin is characterized by its wide streets, crossing at right angles, its many beautiful squares, its fine buildings and its modern spirit. Coming into Turin by train, the traveler gets his first contact with the city on entering the Piazza Carlo Felice, a beautifully landscaped park with a fountain in the center. Going out of the square to the north, the visitor enters Via Roma, one of the most beautiful and modern streets of the city. It connects the Piazza Carlo Felice with the Piazza San Carlo and farther along with the Piazza Castello. First opened in 1615, this street was largely rebuilt in 1931 and 1936 with shops opening onto porticos. At the entrance to the Piazza San Carlo there are the two churches of

Santa Cristina and San Carlo, which give the same effect as the two churches beside each other in the Piazza del Popolo in Rome. This square is considered by some the second best in Italy, after St. Mark's in Venice. In the center is a statue of Emanuele Filiberto sheathing his sword. Continuing north on Via Roma one comes to the Piazza Castello, which gets its name from the imposing structure in the center. Originally the location of the city gate in Roman days, the castle is an imposing combination of brick, stone and marble work.

Juvara designed the castle's splendid baroque façade and, inside it, he built a tremendous marble staircase which leads up to the royal apartments. The large assembly hall was the scene of the first Italian Senate meetings. Although it still retains the name of Palazzo Madama, for Queen Maria Cristina who made it her home in the 17th century, the building now houses the civic museum of ancient art. North of the castle is the Royal Armory, one of Europe's most important collections of armor. Nearby is the impressive new Teatro Regio.

Adjoining the castle, on Piazza San Giovanni, is the cathedral, with a façade of white marble, which was built in the 15th century. From the interior two monumental staircases lead to the black-and-white marble Chapel of the Holy Shroud; above the altar is the piece of linen, believed to be the shroud in which Jesus Christ was wounded when taken from the cross and which retains the marks of His head and body. Three-dimensional NASA photographs have proved these to be the prints of a man who had undergone flagellation. The weaving technique dates the shroud in the time of Christ, while pollen in the textile indubitably belongs to flowers of Palestine. Controversy rages about the authenticity of this relic but, argument apart, it is a mysterious and fascinating object.

South of the castle is the Via Accademia delle Scienze, which leads to the Piazza Carignano. On the right side of the latter square the visitor will see the Carignano Theater, built in 1752, and on the left is the Palazzo Carignano, which is considered a masterpiece of baroque architecture. The Italian Parliament met here from 1860 to 1865 and today it houses several museums. The most important is the Egyptian collection, which ranks third after that of London and Cairo.

From the Piazza Carignano you go on to the Piazza Carlo Alberto and to the Via Po, where in the courtyard of the university there is a plaque dedicated to Erasmus of Rotterdam, who earned his doctor's degree there in 1506. Farther along and to the left is the Via Montebello, where the Mole Antonelliana is located. This unusual structure, built in 1863, was originally intended to be a Jewish synagogue. It became a bizarre oddity, however, when the tall, thin spire was added. From the top of its 100 steps the visitor gets a wonderful view of the city, the plain surrounding it and the semi-circle of Alps beyond.

Continuing down the Via Po toward the river you come to the vast Piazza Vittorio Veneto, which leads to the city's oldest stone bridge. Across the bridge is the Church of the Great Mother of God, built on the pattern of the Pantheon in Rome. To the right, along the Corso Moncalieri is Monte dei Cappuccini, whose church, Santa Maria del Monte, and convent date from 1583.

Along the left bank of the River Po is the Parco del Valentino, which for its vastness, its gardens and its beautiful buildings is one of the most enchanting parks in Italy. The park formed part of the *Italia 61* exposition held to commemorate the centennial of Italy as a united nation. Remaining from this exposition are several decaying structures such as Nervi's Palazzo del Lavoro, once famed for their striking modern design. The better-maintained Exposition Hall houses the international automobile show each year. An outstanding building in this area is the Castello del Valentino, erected in the 17th century after the pattern of French châteaux. The interior is particularly elaborate, with frescoed walls and rich decorations. Farther along, close to the river's edge, are the medieval village and castle. Built in connection with the Turin Exposition of 1884, this collection of buildings is one of the most fascinating places in Turin. A visit to the village is a startling experience, for it gives the effect of going back to the Middle Ages. Here are houses, churches, stores, and craftsmen's shops similar to those found throughout Piedmont. But here there are no modern buildings next door. And up the hill nearby there is the castle. This does not represent any particular castle but is a composite of the features of castles extant in various parts of Piedmont.

Home of an international auto show that's held in November, Turin is also site of the fascinating Carlo Biscaretti di Ruffia Auto Museum on Corso Unità d'Italia, housing models dating back to 1893.

The suburbs of Turin consist of two distinct areas. First, there is the *collina torinese* (the hill of Turin) on the right side of the Po River, a wooded section easily accessible by auto, bus and trolley. Beyond the hill, Turin's suburbs include an interesting variety of villages, abbeys and castles that have striking historical and artistic interest.

The Rest of the Province

Ten miles from the center of Turin is the Basilica of Superga, an imposing structure marking the breaking of the French siege of 1706. The site provides a breathtaking view of the panoramic semi-circle of the Alps which rise around the Turin plain. A memorial park with a boulevard a mile and a half long lined with 10,000 trees commemorating Turin's World War I dead, leads to the *Victory Statue,* topped by a beacon light. This gigantic feminine figure, nearly 60 feet tall, is the largest cast bronze statue in the world.

Going southeast along the hill one comes to Chieri, with its vast cathedral, erected around the year 1400. Nearby are the villages of Santena, with the tomb of Camillo Cavour, one of Italy's founders, and the village of Castelnuovo Don Bosco, birthplace of Saint John Bosco, known for his work for youth. At the southern end of the hill is Moncalieri, with a 15th-century castle. West of Turin are Rivoli, also with its castle, and the medieval town of Avigliana.

In this area there are three interesting abbeys. The Abbey of San Michele was built on the peak of Mount Pirchiriano in the 11th century but later, when the monks enlarged it, they had to build part of the building on supports over 90 feet high. Architecturally noteworthy are the abbeys of St. Anthony of Ranverso and that of Vezzolano, said to have been started by Charlemagne.

Of all the castles built by the Savoy dynasty around Turin, the most elaborate is that of Stupinigi. Built in 1729 as a hunting lodge, it is more a royal villa, with many wings, landscaped gardens and forests. Its interior is sumptuously decorated and today houses the Museum of Art and Furniture.

Lesser-known attractions of the Piedmont region include a castle at Agliè containing Etruscan and Pompeian relics, as well as fine frescos and statues. Bosco Marengo is an old town still retaining vestiges of its walls and castle, whose Santa Croce Church contains works by Vasari and other Renaissance artists. At Villar San Costanzo there are fascinating rock formations. Orta San Giulio boasts its Sacred Mountain, a 16th-century sanctuary where there are 20 chapels, several oratories and a church. At Pessione, 12 miles east of Turin, is the fascinating Martini-Rossi Wine Museum.

Aosta and Asti

For the tourist or vacationist who wishes to get away from the city, the incomparable beauty of Piedmont's Alpine valleys has much to offer both in winter and summer. In scores of mountain valleys literally hundreds of villages offer a complete range of tourist facilities. Alpine crests, many with a permanent expanse of glaciers, hilltop castles, clear mountain lakes and streams, chestnut groves, pine forests and green meadows, all provide a spectacular combination of scenic beauty.

Most striking is the area called Valle d'Aosta. In 1947 this section acquired political autonomy and became a region in its own right, but from a tourist point of view it can well be considered part of the Piedmont area. Here are Europe's highest mountains, Mont Blanc, Monte Rosa, the Gran Paradiso and the Cervino, and on them or around them are the vast extensions of glaciers covering more than 200 square miles. Valle d'Aosta includes not only the valley of the Dora Baltea, but also scores of other smaller tributary valleys. The principal city—Aosta—bears witness to its Roman origin in its regular streets and many well preserved ruins. Its picturesque aspect is heightened by numerous churches, towers and buildings of the Middle Ages. Nearby there are many well preserved 14th- and 15th-century buildings, but the castles at Fenis and Issogne are the most interesting. The climate of Valle d'Aosta is particularly pleasant and healthy and has given rise to the establishment of several spas.

Other areas of Piedmont can be divided roughly into four groups of valleys which include the valleys of tributaries and mountain streams which in turn feed into them. These are Pinerolo Valley, Susa Valley, Lanzo Valley and Canavese Valley. All provide fascinating scenery, pleasant climate and scores of holiday resorts with accommodation of all types for both winter and summer visitors.

Asti, the famous wine center known for its *Asti Spumante,* and excellent red wines (*Barbera, Freisa and Grignolino*), and Alessandria, where the world-famous Borsalino hats are made, have interesting medieval buildings next door to new bustling industries. Valenza, noted for its gold and silver work, Casale Monferrato, an important cement center, Vercelli, known for its rice market, Biella, for its wool industry, and Ivrea, for its Olivetti typewriter factory, are other towns filled with striking architectural monuments of feudal times.

Mountain Sports Centers

Piedmont and Valle d'Aosta excel in facilities for winter sports. The highest mountains in Europe provide a background for skiing on their sloping approaches. Many towns and villages are equipped with hotels, cableways and chair lifts. Here are a few of the most important resorts.

Sestriére. Characterized by its "tower" hotels where every room has an outward view. This is the most famous and best equipped ski center in Piedmont. At 6,580 feet, this center has lots of sun, 74 ski runs, four cableways, 21 ski lifts, a chair lift, skating rink, and good snow from November to May. Like all of the resorts, it offers special "ski-week" rates, all-inclusive of hotel, meals, ski lessons and lifts.

Courmayeur. Against the background of the highest mountain in Europe, Mont Blanc (15,825 feet), Courmayeur, because of its position among thick pine groves, is as much a favorite in summer as in winter. It has the world's largest funicular railway. By linking the various ski areas, it helps create a total of 80 km. of ski runs.

Claviere. This French-Italian border center was among the first of the many Italian ski resorts to be developed. Claviere has excellent ski slopes and favorable snow conditions. It is particularly noted for the excursions which can be made to nearby mountains.

Breuil-Cervinia. Situated at the foot of Mount Cervino (Matterhorn), this center boasts of year-round skiing since its pasture slopes border the limits of the Cervino glacier. At 6,745 feet it is high enough to make nearby peaks more accessible. Slightly below Breuil, in the valley of the Matterhorn, is **Valtournanche,** popular with both summer and winter vacationers.

Gressoney. This is a double-barreled resort, with two settlements, Gressoney St. Jean and Gressoney La Trinité, the second (and more fashionable) 800 feet higher than the first. Like Breuil-Cervinia in the famed Valle d'Aosta section, the Gressoneys provide access to the Monte Rosa group of peaks.

Bardonecchia. Not far from the French-Italian border, this small town is on the Modane-Turin rail line. Besides skiing, it offers hockey and skating facilities.

Limone-Piemonte. This is the biggest winter sports resort of southern Piedmont. Less famous internationally than the northern places, it is popular with Italians rather than with foreigners—and for that reason is less expensive than the better-known places. Halfway between Nice and Turin, almost on the French frontier, it has the advantage also of providing a major ski center within easy reach of both the French and Italian Rivieras, a great convenience for those who want to split winter vacations between the mountains and the sea.

Sauze D'Oulx-Sportinia. 50 miles from Turin, this vacation resort has acceptable winter sports facilities and enjoys increasing popularity, especially among British skiers.

But not all of the resorts are designed for ski enthusiasts. There are good spas at Acqui and Bognanco, and a famous one at St. Vincent. This spa, on the Turin-Aosta line, also attracts visitors who come to visit the gambling casino or to enjoy a quiet vacation.

PRACTICAL INFORMATION FOR PIEDMONT

HOTELS AND RESTAURANTS

Acqui Terme. Popular spa. **Hotels:** Both (1) are—*Antiche Terme,* traditional type in park, many rooms with bath, thermal establishment, closed 1 Oct.–15 June; *Nuove Terme,* Piazza Italia 1, thermal establishment, half of rooms with bath.

All (2) are—*Ariston,* Piazza Matteotti; and *Mignon,* Via Monteverde, both fairly small, most rooms with bath; *Pineta,* new, all rooms with bath, quiet spot with view.

Da Alfredo (3), many rooms with shower, simple, but a bargain, closed Feb.

Alessandria. Second largest city. **Hotels:** All (2) are—*Alli Due Buoi Rossi,* Via Cavour, is best, good restaurant; *Europa,* Via Palestro; *Royal,* few steps from main piazza.

Restaurants: Both (M) are—*Torino,* Via Vochieri 24; *Osvaldo,* Via Casale.

Aosta. Center of the beautiful valley. **Hotels:** High season, 1 July–30 Sept., Easter and Christmas. *Valle d'Aosta* (1), a Rank hotel, on outskirts, handsome decor, 102 rooms with bath, fine mountain views.

All (2) are—*Norden,* also outside center, modern, comfortable; *Corona e Posta,* central, traditional, comfortable older hotel; *Jockey,* centrally located, most rooms with bath or shower.

Both (3) are—*Mignon,* on San Bernardo road, adequate, 22 rooms; *Rayon du Soleil,* above town, pleasant, 32 rooms with bath, attractive garden.

Restaurants: All (M-E) are—*Cheval Blanc,* delightful atmosphere; *La Croisée,* wood-paneled *Brasserie Valdotaine; Piemonte,* small, no frills.

Asti. Home of Asti Spumante. **Hotels:** *Salera* (1), on outskirts, quiet, comfortable rooms with bath, pleasant salons.

Both (2) are—*Aleramo,* modern decor, functional, 40 rooms with bath or shower, breakfast only; *Palio,* modern building in central location, all rooms with shower, no restaurant.

Restaurants: Both (M) are—*La Grotta* and the excellent family-run *Falcon Vecchio. Piuma d'Oro* (E), handsome, stately hearth, classic local cuisine.

Ayas-Champoluc. Quiet resort in Valle d'Aosta. **Hotels:** High season, 23 Dec.–8 Jan.; 10 Feb.–10 March; 10 July–31 Aug.

Both (2) are—*Monte Rosa,* Frazione Periasc, garage, tennis court; *Anna Maria,* smallish, very good, all rooms with bath, simple hearty cuisine, small park.

All (3) are—*Breithorn, Moderne* and *Alpi Rosa.*

Bardonecchia. Important year-round ski resort, with 2 chairlifts and 6 ski lifts. **Hotels:** High season, 20 Dec.–6 Jan; Carnival; Easter; 11 July–29 Aug.

Riki (1), open 5 Dec.–20 May, 29 June–31 Aug., ultra-modern, 76 rooms with bath, radio, TV, central position, garden, swimming pool, mini-golf, nightclub.

De Geneys-Splendid (2), half of rooms with bath, tennis court, garage, open winters and summers only.

Both (3) are—*Betulla,* good; and *Asplenia,* also good.

Restaurants: *Del Trau* (M), for regional specialties. *La Baucia* (M), rustic, good.

Biella. Important wool manufacturing center. **Hotels:** *Astoria* (1), recent, all well-furnished rooms with bath.

Both (2) are—*Coggiola,* most rooms with bath, garden; *Principe,* modest.

Restaurant: *Da Ferrino* (M), with terrace, has a way with chicken.

Bognanco. Spa and mountain resort. **Hotel:** High season, 15 July–30 Aug.; *Fonti e Milano* (2), best, third of rooms with bath, garage, open 1 June–30 Sept. only.

Borromean Islands. Group of four islets in Lake Maggiore.

Isola dei Pescatori, reached by boat from **Stresa. Hotel/Restaurant:** This little island is graced with one hotel, *Verbano* (2M), a quiet, delightful place, with a remarkably good restaurant, so you may lunch in peaceful, picturesque surroundings.

Isola Bella. Restaurant: *Delfino* (M) is also very good. Both close during winter.

Breuil-Cervinia. Resort in Valle d'Aosta, with three téléphériques and several ski lifts, one of which operates in summer, for you can ski here all year round on the Matterhorn glacier. **Hotels:** High season, 20 Dec.–9 January; 12 Feb.–1 May; 20 July–31 Aug.

Both (1) are—*Cristallo,* high above town, elegantly modern, tennis, open 1 Dec.–30 April, 25 June–12 Sept.; *Eurotel Cieloalto,* modern and elegant, in large complex with pool, shop, disco. Bus service into village compensates for inconvenient location.

All (2) are—*Breuil,* in village, wood-paneled comfortable rooms; high on ski slopes is *Lo Stambecco,* all rooms with bath, open 1 Nov.–10 May, 28 June–30 Sept.; *Petit Palais,* attractive rustic, modern, near ski lifts; *Planet* and new *President,* all rooms with bath. Both (3) are—*Bucaneve* and *Valdotain.*

Restaurants: *Neiges d'Antan* (E), rustic, chic, all-in price includes wine and transport. *Copa Pan* (E), chic, cosy cellar.

All (M) are—*Pavia,* good, lively; *Serenella* or *Grivola* hotel restaurants.

Brusson. **Hotels:** High season. July–August, Easter, Christmas. *Italia* (2), overlooking valley, 59 rooms with bath, open end June to end August only. *France* (3), recent, small, pool.

Claviere. Important winter and summer resort, particularly good for children and beginners, one of its three lifts serving a splendid training slope. **Hotels:** High season, 23 Dec.–10 January; March–April; Easter, 20 July–20 August.

Both (2) are—*Bellevue* and *Roccia,* good hotels with a view. *Petit* (3) is good value.

Roma (3), garage. *Miramonti* (P2), small, good.

Cogne. Winter and summer resort, spring skiing. **Hotels:** High season, 24 Dec.–6 January; July–August.

Miramonti (1), small, attractive hotel.

Both (2) are—*Bellevue* and *Roccia,* good hotels with a view. *Petit* (3), is good value.

Restaurant: *Lou Ressignon* (M–E), cozy chalet.

Courmayeur. Most important winter sports and summer resort of the valley, below Mont Blanc, with 8 cableways and 18 ski lifts. **Hotels:** High season, 23 Dec.–8 January; first two weeks in Feb.; April, July, August.

All (1) are—*Royal,* informal but elegant, modern attractive rooms, tennis, garage, open 5 Dec.–7 Nov.; *Palace Bron* and *Moderno,* all rooms with bath, both good; former is quietly posh, made for relaxing. *Pavillon,* near cableways, modern version of a chalet, attracts lively crowd.

All (2) are—*Croux,* bright, comfortable, mountain view, open 20 Dec.–30 September; *Ange et Grand Hotel,* open 20 June–20 September; *Cresta Duc,* well-appointed, 38 pleasant rooms with bath; *Majestic,* comfortable, near cable stations. *Le Bouton d'Or,* small, beautifully furnished, garni.

Both (3) are—*Svizzero,* seasonal, and *Edelweiss.*

Restaurants: All (M–E) are—*K2,* quality and atmosphere; *Torchio,* more expensive; see Entrèves. Aperitifs at quiet *Glarey* or chic *Posta.*

Cuneo. Provincial capital, art center, **Hotels:** *Augustus Minerva* (1), central, most rooms with bath or shower, breakfast only. *Royal Superga* (2), just off main piazza, good restaurant.

Restaurants: Both (M)—*Olghina,* in *Royal Superga* hotel has a flair for local dishes; *Ristoro* is good too. *Cavallo Bianco* (M) is a pleasant place.

Both (E) and excellent—*Plat d'Etain* and *Tre Citroni.*

Entrèves. Near Courmayeur. **Hotel:** *Des Alpes* (1), fine, closed Nov.

Restaurant: *Maison de Filippo* (M), a must, attractive inn, local country cooking. Second choices: *Brenva, Pilier d'Angle,* both (M).

Gressoney. Important winter sports and summer resort, with more fashionable **Gressoney La Trinité** about 800 feet higher than **Gressoney St. Jean.**

Hotels: High season, 23 Dec.–8 January; 10 February–10 March; 10 July–31 August.

At **La Trinité,** both (2) are—*Busca Thedy,* open 1 June–15 Sept., quiet, pleasant, 87 rooms, half with bath, tennis; *Residence,* alpine modern decor, all rooms with bath or shower, fine views.

At **St. Jean,** both (3) are—*Stadel,* lots of atmosphere and comfort; *Rododendro,* 14 rooms with bath.

At **Chemonal,** *Villa Tedaldi* (P2), small, intimate, garage.

Ivrea. Known for works of art and its carnival. **Hotels:** *La Serra* (1), recent, modern, very well-appointed, 61 rooms with bath or shower, terrace, indoor pool, sauna. *Sirio* (2), 1 mile away at lake, good, noted for its fine restaurant.

Restaurants: All (M) are—*Aquila Nera,* Corso Nigra; *Bolognese,* Via Aosta; or *Arancione,* Corso Vercelli 16.

Limone Piemonte, principal winter sports and summer resort of southern Piedmont. **Hotels:** *Limone* (1), recent, all rooms with bath or shower, open all year round. *Principe* (2), in quiet, panoramic position, 41 pleasant rooms with bath. *Tripoli* (3), with attractive garden terrace, many rooms with bath.

At **Colle di Tenda,** recent *Tre Amis* (2), large, modern, all comforts, swimming pool.

Restaurant: *Mac Miche* (M).

Macugnaga. Mountain-climbing center. **Hotels:** High season, 15 July–20 August; 20 Dec.–6 January.

At **Staffa,** both (3) are—*Girasole,* near cableway, nicely furnished rooms; *Zumstein,* best, many baths, park.

At **Pecetto,** both (3) are—*Lagger,* large rooms, and *Nuovo Pecetto,* recommended, charming atmosphere.

Marengo. Near Alessandria. **Hotel/Restaurant:** *Napoléon* is small, quiet, with 8 rooms.

Novara. Industrial and commercial center. **Hotel:** *Europa* (2), most rooms with bath, garage.

Restaurants: Both (M) are—*Teatro Coccia,* on main piazza; *La Cupola,* old wineshop, now a simpatico restaurant; try the *crêpes gorgonzola. Caglieri* (E) has lovely garden terrace.

Orta. Lake resort. **Hotels:** High season, Easter; 28 June–15 September. *San Rocco* (1), best, quiet, converted 17th-century convent, lakeside garden. *La Bussola* (3), overlooking lake, 17 rooms with bath, small pool in attractive garden.

Restaurants: *La Bussola* (E). *Antico Agnello* (M).

Saint Vincent. Chic spa resort, casino. **Hotels:** Deluxe—*Billia*, elegance and comfort, 132 well-furnished rooms, tennis, indoor pool, large park, fine view.

Both (2) are—*Du Parc*, near casino, attractive lounges, tennis; *Elena*, 47 comfortable rooms with shower, good restaurant.

Both (3) are—*Posta*, on bustling corner opposite funicular to spa; *Haiti*, breakfast only, budget choice.

Restaurants: All (E) are—*Posta* hotel restaurant; *Grenier* and *Batezar*.

Sauze d'Oulx. Winter resort, with a toboggan run, ski lifts, two chair lifts and a skating rink. **Hotels:** High season—4–8 Dec.; 24 Dec.–7 January; 1–20 March; Easter; August. *Palace* (1), large and noisy, sauna, nightclub.

All (2) are—*Terrazza*, better, nightclub, sun terrace; *Miravalle*, and *Holiday Debili* are comfortable, well-run. *Capricorno* (P1), in pinewoods and quiet, 5 min. by chairlift from center; favored by English skiers, excellent restaurant.

Sestriere. Top winter sports and summer resort. **Hotels:** High season, 20 Dec.–7 January; Feb.–March; Easter.

Deluxe—*Principe di Piemonte*, elegant decor, service, tennis court, heated swimming pool, garage, open December to April, one of Italy's best known.

Cristallo (1), also is smart, attractive décor, 76 rooms with bath or shower, TV, open Dec. to April. *Duchi d'Aosta* (2), striking cylindrical hotel, 154 rooms with shower, fine view, open December to April.

Both (3) are—*Olimpic* and *Miramonti*, pleasant smaller hotels also open in summer.

Restaurant: *Lo Scoiattolo* (M–E).

Turin/Torino. Regional capital, industrial and trade center, art city. **Hotels:** Deluxe (L)—Principe di Piemonte, Via Gobetti, one of Italy's leading hotels; airconditioned, elegantly furnished rooms, suites.

Expensive (1)—*City*, elegant modern decor, airconditioned rooms, no resrant; *Jolly Ambasciatori*, Corso Vittorio Emanuele, new, airconditioned, all rooms with bath and radio, garage; *Ligure*, Piazza Carlo Felice 85, most rooms with bath or shower, recommended; *Palace Hôtel Turin*, Via Sacchi 8, known for comfort and service; *Svizzera Terminus*, Via Sacchi 4, handy to station, half of rooms have bath, garage; *Villa Sassi*, recommended, across Po in quiet park, just 12 rooms in 17th-century villa, exceptional food.

Moderate (2) *Fiorina*, Via Pietro Micca 22, more than half the rooms with bath; *Rex*, very central, well-furnished, breakfast only; *Alexandra*, modern, airconditioned hotel overlooking river, walking distance of center; *Roma e Rocca Cavour*, Piazza Carlo Felice 60, nearly half of rooms with bath, garage; *Victoria* and *Luxor*, both near main station, good; *Patria*, Via Cernaia 42, half of rooms with bath, garage.

Both (3) are—*Eden*, Via Donizetti 22, most rooms with bath; *San Silvestro*, Corso Francia 1.

Europa (P1), Piazza Castello 99, nearly half the rooms have bath.

Restaurants: Expensive (E)—Best-known restaurant in Turin is the *Cambio,* Piazza Carignano, recently acquired by the Cinzano people—gilt trim, antique mirrors, excellent *fonduta.*

The most unusual is *San Giorgio,* which is in a medieval castle in the Parco del Valentino, on the shore of the Po; the setting and the food justify the prices.

Also top rank are the *Gran Giardino,* Corso d'Azeglio 11; and *Al Gatto Nero,* Corso Unione Sovietica, where the meats are spit-roasted; *Ferrero,* Corso V. Emanuele 54, very elegant.

Villa Sassi, in Via Borgofranco 47, on the hillside 2 miles from town center is a lovely villa restaurant with large gardens, antique-filled, rarefied atmosphere, very expensive; *Cont Piolett,* Strada Santa Margherita, is another sumptuous villa restaurant; (reserve at both Villa Sassi tel. 890.556; Cont Piolett tel. 831.028).

Moderate (M)—Good first-class leaders include *Rendez-vous,* Corso V. Emanuele 38; *Taverna Dantesca,* Via San Pio V; *Ostu Bacu,* Corso Vercelli; *Da Giuseppe,* Via S. Massimo, in the heart of old Turin—let host Giuseppe order for you, but insist on *profiteroles* for dessert; *Alpi Cozie,* Via Guarini 1; *Cervo,* Corso URSS 242; *Due Lampioni,* Via C. Alberto 45; *Italia,* Colle di Superga and *Pigna d'Oro,* at Pino Torinese, are in suburbs.

Inexpensive (I)—Lower in price but still excellent are *Cenacolo,* Galleria Subalpina 11; *Gli Orsi,* Via G. Amendola; *Pescatori,* Lungo Po Machiavelli 29; *Taverna Citrone,* Via M. Pietá; *Rodi,* Via Rodi 4; *Fiaschetteria,* Via XX Settembre 1; and *Tre Galline,* Via Bellezia; all typical Turin trattorias.

USEFUL ADDRESSES. Tourist Offices: *Acqui Terme:* AAST, Corso Bagni 8. *Alessandria:* EPT, Via Savona 26. *Aosta:* AAST, Piazza E. Chanoux 3; EPT, Piazza Narbonne and Piazza E Chanoux 8. *Asti:* EPT, Piazza Alfieri 34. *Ayas-Champoluc:* AAST, Piazza Centrale, Champoluc. *Bardonecchia:* AAST, Piazza Europa 15. *Bognanco:* AAST, Piazzale Giannini 5. *Brusson:* AAST, Piazza del Municipio 1. *Claviere:* AAST, Via Nazionale 30. *Cogne:* AAST, Piazza E. Chanoux 38. *Courmayeur:* AAST, Viale Monte Bianco. *Cuneo:* EPT, Corso Nizza 17. *Gressoney:* AAST, Palazzo Comunale in St. Jean; Piazza Oberte in La Trinité. *Ivrea:* AAST, Piazza di Città 1. *Limone Piemonte:* AAST, Via Roma 38. *Macugnaga:* AAST, Piazza Municipio. *Novara:* EPT, Corso Cavour 2 and Via Ravizza 6A. *Orta:* AAST, Piazza Motta. *Saint Vincent:* AAST, Via Roma 52. *Sauze D'Oulx:* AAST, Piazza Assietta. *Sestriere:* AAST, Piazza Agnelli 11. *Turin:* EPT, Via Roma 222 and 226, and main railway station; American Express, SAVET-Spa Tourist and Travel Office, Via Bruno Buozzi 10 (tel. 579444).

SPECIAL EVENTS. *Alessandria:* International Motorcycle Rally in July, and the Regatta on the Po. *Cuneo:* Winter sports events in January, February sees a carnival with a mummers parade. *Ivrea:* February, a historical carnival. *Limone Piemonte:* Winter sports events in January; a carnival in

February with "snow clowns"; the Fiaccola d'Oro, a nocturnal ski event, in December. *Sestriere:* Important winter sports events in January; international ski races and an automobile rally in February. *Turin:* Carnival in February; International Horse Show, the only "covered" one in Italy; the International Clothing Salon in April; Flowers of the World, from April to May; Sound and Light show at the Valentino Castle, from June to September; International Automobile Show, one of the world's most important, in November.

SPORTS. *Bardonecchia:* A skating rink, an Olympic ski jump and a beginner's jump. *Breuil-Cervinia:* Skiing, of course, and mountaineering; 9-hole golf course in summer. *Claviere:* Summer mountaineering; 9-hole golf course. *Courmayeur:* Skiing; mountaineering in summer; *Planpincieux,* 9-hole golf course. *Gressoney:* Mountaineering center in summer; winter sports galore. *Limone Piemonte:* Several lifts of different types, a ski school, a jump and a good skating rink; mountaineering in summer. *Orta:* Water sports, especially speedboat racing are very popular here. *Sestriere:* The best equipped winter resort of all, Sestriere has no less than 70 planned itineraries of all degrees of difficulty—30 marked descents, 4 téléphériques and 20 ski lifts, a fine skating rink with a sun room for onlookers. There are hockey matches; curling is played and lots of tennis; an 18-hole golf course.

LOMBARDY, MILAN AND THE LAKES

The Scenic North

The Lombardy area of Italy stretches gently south from the fringes of the Alps to the river Po. It is a land of industry, of pastoral tranquility, of breathtaking beauty and of a history of 2,000 years of strife.

Bergamo, Brescia, Como, Cremona, Mantua, Milan and Pavia are its chief cities and all of them have antecedents almost as ancient as those of Rome itself. Their cathedrals, their ancient and gorgeously decorated palaces, their old battle towers, their museums and the magnificent works of art which they include, comprise a wealth of incomparable magnificence.

The lake region—Como, Garda, Maggiore and Lugano—is at the foot of the Alps, which drop, seemingly almost perpendicularly, for more than 6,000 feet to the shimmering surface of the blue lakes beneath. There are good reasons for Lombardy's popularity with honeymooners!

Although some of the lake resorts fall administratively within the Piedmont area, they are included here as making for better tourist orientation.

From the Etruscans to Mussolini

More than 3,000 years ago—the date and the details are lost in the mysteries of Etruscan inscriptions—explorers from the highly civilized Etruscan kingdom of Tuscany, wandered northward beyond the River Po. The Etruscans extended their dominance into this region for some hundreds of years but left little of their culture. They were succeeded by the Cenomanic Gauls who, in turn, were conquered by the legions of Rome in the latter days of the Republic.

The region became known as Cisalpine Gaul and under the rule of Augustus it became a Roman province. Its warlike, independent people became citizens of Rome. Virgil, Catullus and both the Plinys were born in this region during this relatively tranquil era.

The decline of the Roman Empire was followed by the invasions of the Huns and the Goths, who finally brought about the destruction of the grandeur which was Rome. Attila and Theodoric in turn gave way to the Lombards, who ceded their iron crown to Charlemagne as the emblem of his vast but unstable empire.

Even before the fragile bonds which held this empire together had begun to snap, the cities of Lombardy were erecting walls in defense against the Hungarians, still on the warpath, and also against each other. These communes did, however, form the Lombard League, which in the 12th century finally defeated Frederick Barbarossa.

Once the invaders had been definitely defeated, new and even more bloody strife began. In each city the Guelphs—bourgeois supporters of the popes—and the Ghibellines—noble adherents to the so-called Emperors—clashed with each other. The communes declined and each fell under the yoke of neighboring or local powerful rulers. The Republic of Venice dominated Brescia and Bergamo. Mantua was ruled by the Gonzaga, and the Visconti and Sforza families took over Como, Cremona, Milan and Pavia.

The Battle of Pavia, at the outset of the 16th century, brought on the 200 years of Spanish occupation, when the generals of Charles V defeated the French and gave Francis I the chance to coin the famous phrase: "All is lost save honor." The Spaniards were on the whole less cruel than the local tyrants and were hardly resisted by the Lombardians.

The War of the Spanish Succession, in the early years of the 18th century, threw out the Spaniards and brought in, instead, the Austrians, whose dominion was "neither liked nor loathed" during the nearly 100 years of its existence.

Napoleon and his generals routed the Austrians. The Treaty of Campoformio resulted in the proclamation of the Cisalpine Republic, which quickly became the Republic of Italy and, just as rapidly, the Kingdom of Italy, which lasted only until Napoleon's defeat brought back the Austrians.

But Milan, as the capital of Napoleon's republic and of the Kingdom of Italy, had had a taste of glory, and the inherently independent character of its citizens, with those of the other Lombardian cities, was not slow to resent and combat the loss of its "national" pride.

From 1820 on, the Lombards joined with the Piedmontese and the House of Savoy in a perpetual struggle against the Habsburgs and, in 1859, finally defeated Austria and brought about the creation of the Kingdom of Italy two years later.

Milan and other cities of Lombardy have not lost their independence and their hatred of domination. Nowhere in Italy was the partisan insurrection against Mussolini—to whom they first gave power—and the German regime better organized or more successful. Milan itself was liberated from the Germans by its own partisan organization before the entrance of Allied troops; escaping Allied prisoners could always find sanctuary there when fighting was still going on far to the south.

Lombardians are a forthright people. They are as much inclined to taciturnity as any Italian is ever apt to be and when they do talk they mean exactly what they say. When they quote a price there is little use haggling about it. Where your Milanese is inclined to be very, very money-minded, his compatriot on the rice farm or in the mountains, although interested in dollars and pounds, is really much more interested in you as an individual.

Weather Matters

For the lake region, the favorite period for vacationists is from the beginning of July to the middle of September; but if you want to avoid the crowds and still be sure of fairly good weather, come a month or six weeks earlier. Lombardy is not as well known as a winter sport center, but it has some good resorts in the northeastern prong it thrusts into Switzerland. There the best time is from just before Christmas to the middle of January. For the countryside in general, May and June are undoubtedly the best months, with September-October following behind.

Road Reports

Farther south, all roads may lead to Rome, but here in the north they all lead to Milan. Coming into Italy from the French Riviera, the French Savoy or Switzerland, coming across northern Italy from Venice, or coming up from the south from Rome, Florence or any other point, you practically can't avoid going through Milan, whether by plane, train, bus or car. Milan is the center for excursions in all directions, but for motorists it is one of the worst cities in Europe to drive in. There are however a number of places sufficiently close to Milan to keep anyone staying in them at the hub of things. There are motels nearby, and Milan's outer circle road makes it possible to pick up the route to anywhere without going through the city. Milan is in fact crossed by the interminable east-west Autostrada 4 from Trieste to Turin; two others, A8 and A9, come in from the lakes on the north, while to the south A7 departs for Genoa and the great Autostrada del Sole sets out for Reggio Calabria.

A fairly complete view of the southern part of the region can be had by circling from Milan to Pavia, Cremona, Mantua and back by Brescia and Bergamo—about 200 miles. This is what you could call the tough part of Lombardy, whereas the lakes are gentle and lush and rich in color. Motoring around the lake region is frustrating because the quite unsuitable roads are used not only by tourists with all the time in the world, but by the traffic which has come from or is making for the most used passes out of southern Switzerland. This does not apply so much to Lake Garda, which is rather far removed from the other, bunched lakes. Because of the traffic situation, although Milan is only a few motorway miles away from Como, Lugano, Varese and Stresa, it would be more economical of time, tolls and fuel to spend a couple of days based somewhere in the lake district—nowhere could be more peacefully attractive than Orta, or elegantly geared to the tourist than Bellagio.

Food for Thought

Among the most favored specialties in Milan (where the liberal use of butter adds a distinctive flavor to the cooking) is *osso buco alla milanese,* veal knuckle served with *risotto,* rice which has been cooked until almost all the liquid has evaporated and a creamy sauce remains. *Risotto alla milanese* has saffron added, which colors the dish a rich yellow. *Costoletta alla milanese* is a breaded veal cutlet. The favorite cheese of Milan is *Gorgonzola.* Other well-known cheeses are *Bel Paese* and *Taleggio,* both mild, and *Mascarpone,* very much like cream cheese.

Milan's pastry specialty is *panettone,* a raised fluffy cake, flecked with dried raisins and a variety of candied fruit.

Other favorite dishes of Lombardy in general are the thick vegetable soup known throughout the world, *minestrone; busecca,* which is highly seasoned veal tripe, served with beans; and *risotto alla certosina,* rice accompanied by crayfish, mushrooms and peas.

Other towns than Milan have their specialties. Pavia offers its *zuppa alla Pavese,* eggs on slices of toast, over which hot broth is poured. *Polenta e osei* is shared by Bergamo and Brescia—it is small birds roasted in butter, served with *polenta,* which has to be described as corn meal mush. Cremona has two special contributions. One is *torrone,* which is a refined version of nougat. The other is *mostarda*—candied fruits in mustard syrup. This may sound rather forbidding at first thought, but actually the effect is very much like that of chutney. In addition to the cheeses mentioned in the Milan section, we might name *Stracchino* and *Crescenza,* rich and soft; *Robiola;* and *Grana Lodigiana.*

Lombardy is not wine country to the same extent as are many other regions of Italy. There are two wine producing areas, the Valtellina, from which comes *Sassella,* a very dry red, particularly worthy of attention, as well as *Grumello, Inferno, Valgella, Lugana* and others; and the Lake Garda region, whose *Chiaretto,* a rosé, is growing in popularity. Lombardy also makes *Bitter Campari,* a popular apéritif.

Exploring Milan

Milan is the industrial, banking and commercial capital of Italy, regardless of Church and State. Its art collections compare favorably with those of Rome and Florence. Its theater rivals that of Rome. Those of its historic buildings which have survived centuries of strife and destruction are carefully preserved masterpieces. Its people are proud, determined and businesslike (a very pleasant change from some other parts of Italy). They know they've wrought miracles in the past, and they are still busy performing miracles in the present—especially in the field of modern architecture, as the newer sections of the city show.

Milan is a sprawling city, a veritable nightmare to the tourist seeking to drive either in or out of its maze of inner and outer districts. But once in, with the car safely parked in a central hotel garage—where it is advisable to leave it most of the time—the traveler finds that Milanese life, art and beauty revolve around, and can be found in, a remarkably small area.

A Miracle of Delicacy

In almost the exact center of the heart of Milan is the truly great Cathedral, third largest church in the world, and the largest Gothic building in Italy. Don't be misled by its façade, one of its least attractive and most modern sections, although impressive enough. Consider that the building was started in 1386, consecrated in 1577 and not wholly completed until 1897. Walk completely around the cathedral, noting especially its 135 marble spires, the beautiful *Madonnina,* 350 feet high, surmounting them all.

Note especially the lines of the apse and its three vast and intricate windows, built in 1389 and generally attributed to Nicolas de Bonaventura, the only one of the master builders who designed and constructed this cathedral to leave his name to posterity. Note, too, but don't try to count, the 2,245 marble statues of all periods which decorate the exterior of the edifice.

The majesty and grandeur of the Cathedral's interior, with its five great aisles and enormous pillars, are best appreciated in the half-light always found there. The stained-glass windows are from the 15th and 16th centuries, and the light piercing the windows of the duomo and reflecting down onto the choir gives a superb study in the mystical effect of shadow properly used.

You will want to see the tomb of Giacomo Medici, by Leoni, in the right transept, and the choir in the presbytery, with its great bronze *ciborium* done by Pellegrini. Under this presbytery is the body of St. Carlo Borromeo, once Archbishop of Milan.

By all means either walk or take the elevator to the terraces of the cathedral. There, through a startling and amazing array of spires and statues, you can see all of Milan, all of the Lombardy plains and the Alps beyond—provided it is a clear day.

The great square in front of the cathedral, with its vari-colored tile pavement, is the Piazza del Duomo. On two sides of it are the *portici* where Milanese love to congregate. Here begins the Galleria Vittorio Emanuele, traditional gathering place with its cafés, bars, restaurants, outdoor yet sheltered tables, bookshops and, of course, souvenir shops.

Stroll through it slowly and come out into the Piazza della Scala, home of the Teatro della Scala, where Verdi's fame was established, completely renovated since World War II destruction by Allied bombs in 1943. It was reopened at a performance led by the great Arturo Toscanini himself, in 1946.

Go along the Via Verdi, now, to the Palazzo di Brera, home of the Pinacoteca di Brera, one of Italy's greatest collections of art. The 15th–18th centuries period, notable in Italian art, is especially well

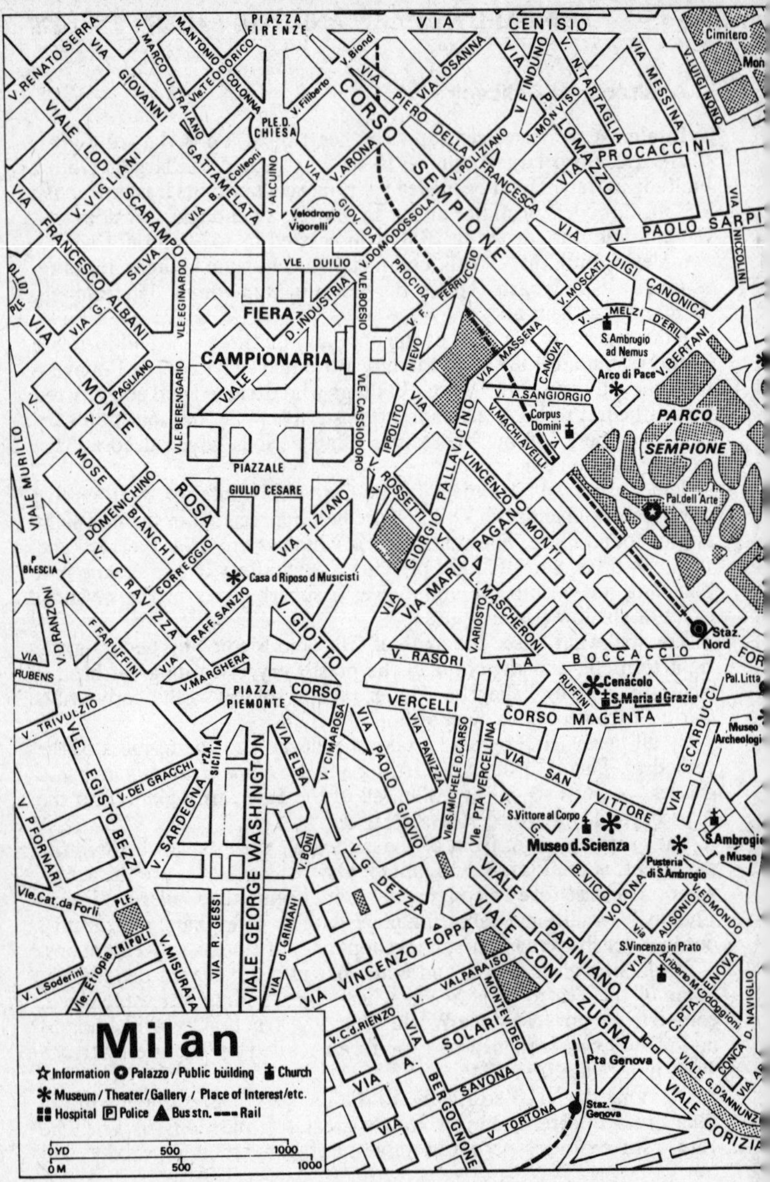
Milan
Information
Palazzo / Public building
Church
Museum / Theater / Gallery / Place of Interest/etc.
Hospital
Police
Bus stn.
Rail
0 YD
500
1000
0 M
500
1000
PIAZZA FIRENZE
VIA CENISIO
Cimitero
V. RENATO SERRA
VIA GIOVANNI
V. MARCO
U. TRAIANO
MANTONIO
Vle. TEODORICO
COLONNA
V. Biondi
V. Filiberto
VIA LOSANNA
V. F. INDUNO
V. N. TARTAGLIA
VIA MESSINA
V. LUIGI NONO
CORSO SEMPIONE
VIA PIERO DELLA FRANCESCA
P. LOMAZZO
V. MONVISO
PROCACCINI
VIALE LODI
V. VIGLIANI
PLE. D. CHIESA
GATTAMELATA
VIA B. Colleoni
V. ALCUINO
VIA
V. ARONA
V. POLIZIANO
VIA
VIA PAOLO SARPI
VIA FRANCESCO
SCARAMPO
Velodromo Vigorelli
GIOV. DA
V. DOMODOSSOLA
VIA NICCOLINI
PLE LOTTO
SILVA
ALBANI
VIA G.
VLE. EGINARDO
VLE. DUILIO
FIERA CAMPIONARIA
D. INDUSTRIA
VIALE
VLE. BOESIO
PROCIDA
FERRUCCIO
V. MOSCATI
LUIGI
CANONICA
MELZI D'ERIL
S. Ambrogio ad Nemus
Arco di Pace
V. BERTANI
VIA MONTE
PAGLIANO
VLE. BERENGARIO
VLE. CASSIODORO
V. F. NIEVO
IPPOLITO
VIA MASSENA
CANOVA
V. A. SANGIORGIO
V. MACHIAVELLI
Corpus Domini
PARCO SEMPIONE
Pal. dell'Arte
VIALE MURILLO
MOSE
DOMENICHINO
ROSA
PIAZZALE GIULIO CESARE
VIA TIZIANO
ROSSETTI
GIORGIO PALLAVICINO
VINCENZO
MONTI
BIANCHI
CORREGGIO
P. BRESCIA
V. D. RANZONI
C. RAVIZZA
Casa d Riposo d Musicisti
V. GIOTTO
VIA MARIO PAGANO
L. MASCHERONI
V. ARIOSTO
Staz. Nord
F. FARUFFINI
RAFF. SANZIO
VIA RUBENS
V. MARGHERA
V. RASORI
VIA BOCCACCIO
FORO
Pal. Litta
Cenacolo
S. Maria d Grazie
RUFFINI
PIAZZA PIEMONTE
CORSO VERCELLI
CORSO MAGENTA
V. TRIVULZIO
VLE. EGISTO BEZZI
PZA. SICILIA
VIA ELBA
V. CIMAROSA
VIA PAOLO GIOVIO
VIA PANIZZA
Vle. S. MICHELE D. CARSO
Vle. PTA VERCELLINA
VIA SAN VITTORE
G. CARDUCCI
Museo Archeologi
V. DEI GRACCHI
V. SARDEGNA
VIALE GEORGE WASHINGTON
V. BONI
V. G. DEZZA
S. Vittore al Corpo
Museo d. Scienza
S. Ambrogio e Museo
Pusteria di S. Ambrogio
V. P. FORNARI
VIA R. GESSI
VIA d. GRIMANI
VIALE CONI ZUGNA
VIALE PAPINIANO
B. VICO
V. OLONA
VIA AUSONIO
V. EDMONDO
Vle. Cat. da Forlì
PLE. TRIPOLI
V. MISURATA
VIA VINCENZO FOPPA
VALPARAISO
MONTEVIDEO
S. Vincenzo in Prato
VIA Ariberto
M. GdOggioni
C. PTA. GENOVA
D. NAVIGLIO
V. L. Soderini
Vle. Etiopia
V. C. d. RIENZO
VIA SOLARI
Pta Genova
CONCA
VIALE G. D'ANNUNZIO
VIA A. BERGOGNONE
SAVONA
V. TORTONA
Staz. Genova
VIALE GORIZIA

V. Sebenico
V. P. Borsieri
Via Confalonieri
V. VOLTURNO
V. SASSETTI
V. Bellani
MELCHIORRE GIOIA
V. GALVANI
FILZI
Staz. Centrale
V. FERR. APORTI
Soperga
P. L. da Palestina
C. Giulio
A. DORIA
PZLE. LORETO
Pergolesi
VLE.
Via
V. Dom
SETTEMBRINI
Scarlatti
MARCELLO
VIA VITRUVIO
Staz. Pta. Garibaldi
VIA G. FERRARI
V. FARINI
V. CERESIO
Grattacielo Pirelli
PZA. D. CAJA
CORSO COMO
VLE. d. LIBERAZIONE
Via Generale G. Fara
FABIO
V. PISANI
V. Carlo Tenca
SAN GREGORIO
RUGG.
LUIGI
BOSCOVICH
BENED.
BUENOS AIRES
V. PLINIO
Pta. Volta
VIA
VLE. CRISPI
Bast. di Pta. Nuova
Pta. Nuova
PZA. D. REPUBBLICA
VIALE TUNISIA
VIA LAZZARETTO
Lecco
V. Franc.
Vle. MONTELLO
VIA VOLTA
S. M. Incoronata
SOLFERINO
PTA. NUOVA
VLE VITTORIO VENETO
Bastioni di Porta Venezia
CORSO BUENOS AIRES
Viale Regina
Redi
V. LEGNANO
GARIBALDI
V. STATUTO
VIA MOSCOVA
TURATI
MANIN
ZOO
Giardino Pubblici
Planetario
Pta. Venezia
Museo di Storia Naturale
ARENA
V. Palermo
VIA SAN MARCO
V. MONTEBELLO
S. Angelo
S. Marco
CSO
Vd. Marchi
V. FILIPPO
VIA
Lambro
Giovanna
Acquario
CORSO
S. Simpliciano
V. FATEBENEFRATELLI
Galleria d'Arte Moderna
V. Sirtori
NINO BIXIO
V. PONTACCIO
Palazzo di Brera e Galleria
BORGONUOVO
V. d. Giardino
V. SENATO
CORSO VENEZIA
VIALE MAINO
VIALE PIAVE
Via C. Poerio
Via Carlo Pisacane
V. G. Modena
V. Menotti
V. Belotti
CASTELLO
V. MERCATO
S. M. d. Carmine
Brera
V. S. Spirito
Pal. del Senato
Castel Sforzesco
Museo d. Arte Antica
Via Monte di Pietà
Via dell'Orso
V. ALESS. MANZONI
Via Monte Napoleone
V. S. Andrea
Museo di Milano
CORSO
VIA MOZART
V. C. Goldoni
PZA.
BUONAPARTE
Cusani
Via Verdi
Museo Poldi-Pezzoli
Teatro Scala
Museo Teatrale
S. Fedele
S. Babila
Corso
Cso Concordia
Independenza
V. DANTE
Broletto
PZA. D. SCALA
Cso. Matteotti
CORSO MONFORTE
VLE. PREMUDA
Pal. Clerici
Pal. Marino
S. Carlo
V. MERAVIGLI
Galleria Vittorio Emanuele II
C. V. Emanuele
VLE. B. MARIA
S. M. d. Passione
Via Passione
Via G. Fiamma
Via Goff. Mameli
Maurizio
Via S. M. Fulcorina
P. O.
V. Bocchetto
V. Orefici
PIAZZA DEL DUOMO
Duomo
Cso. Europa
V. V. DI MODRONE
Casa dei Borromei
Biblioteca Ambrosiana
VIA TORINO
Fil. Corridoni
S. Pietro in Gessate
V. S. Orsola
Pal. Reale
Via Larga
Campuccio
Circo
S. Giorgio
S. Satiro
V. MAZZINI
S. Stefano
CSO. PORTA VITTORIA
Pta. Vittoria
CSO. 22 MARZO
Fontana
Via Velasca
V. FRANCESCO SFORZA
Pal. Sormani
V. Freguglia
V. MANARA
Pal. di Giustizia
VLE. REG. MARGHERITA
S. Alessandro
Università
x-Ospedale Maggiore
V. S. BARNABA
S. Maria d. Pace
V. ANFOSSI
CORSO ITALIA
SS. Paolo e Barnaba
V. D. PACE
V. SPARTACO
TICINESE
S. Lorenzo Maggiore
S. Nazzaro
V. D. COMMENDA
MONTE NERO
MAFFEI
MOROSINI
S. Eufemia
V. BERGAMO
CSO. PTA.
V. MULINO D'ARMI
S. Paolo
V. S. SOPHIA
S. Calimero
PORTA ROMANA
V. ALF. LAMARMORA
VIALE CALDARA
VIA MONTE
V. CADORE
V. E.
V. COMELICO
Via G. Mercalli
VIA ORTI
LAZIO
S. Eustorgio
Croce
S. M. d. Miracoli
S. M. d. Paradiso
BOTTA
VASARI
Via Bianca di Savoia
V. Quadronno
VIA CARLO BOSCHI
V. CIRENE
Via S. Martino
V. Carlo Crivelli
Pta. Ticinese
Pta. Romana
VLE. BEATRICE D'ESTE
Pta. Vigentina
VIA GIORGIO

represented here. Luini, Bramantino and Foppa are outstanding examples of the Lombard school. The *Dead Christ* by Mantegna is a remarkable work of the Venetian school, as is Tintoretto's *Discovery of the Body of St. Mark.* Other Venetians displayed are Veronese, Giovanni Bellini and Titian. In addition, there are fine works from other Italian schools, including Raphael and Caravaggio, and many outstanding foreign canvases, with El Greco, Rembrandt, Van Dyck and Rubens represented.

From the Castello Sforzesco to The Last Supper

Stroll back now to the Piazza del Duomo and from it along the Via Mercanti, past the ancient Palazzo della Ragione and a small medieval square and along the Via Dante to the Castello Sforzesco, dwelling of that famed family of despots, Dukes of Milan, founded by a peasant boy, who, on whim, legend says, became a soldier, a captain, a leader. *Sforza* he was nicknamed by his young comrades in arms because of his strength and his prowess at arms, and he handed down the name to his family, which grew, and remained, "the strong."

Leonardo da Vinci, Bramante and Filarete started this fierce-looking castle for Ludovico Sforza. The restoration was carried out by Beltrami. The three pyramidal stages, the heavy façade and its two towers give a true impression of strength and vigor. In the Corte Ducale you will find a magnificent collection of sculpture, including Michelangelo's last work, the *Rondanini Pietà,* interior furnishings, paintings and archeological masterpieces. The 15th-century to 18th-century paintings on the first floor are second only to those which you may have seen previously in the Pinacoteca. In this collection also are priceless examples of Japanese and Chinese art dating from 300 BC.

Later you should definitely visit the Palazzo dell'Ambrosiana, built in the early 17th century, which now houses the Ambrosiana Gallery, again with Italian paintings of the 15th–18th centuries, and a marvelous library. Notable here, in addition to Botticellis, Titians, Raphaels, etc., are 1,750 drawings by Leonardo da Vinci.

In the Via Torino, not far from the Piazza del Duomo, you will find one of the most beautiful Renaissance churches in all Italy. It is San Satiro, built by Bramante in 1480, with magnificent optical illusion used in its interior to suggest a vast spaciousness where, in truth, there is nonc. Actually it is a relatively small church for one of this type in Italy.

Quite nearby is San Lorenzo Maggiore, oldest of Milan's Christian churches. Rare 4th-century mosaics are set in the niches of its Chapel of St. Aquilinus, while the 4th-century Chapel of St. Hippolytus has two fine Roman columns.

Sant' Ambrogio, in the Piazza of the same name, is Milan's greatest medieval monument. It was founded by St. Ambrose in 386 and developed its present characteristics in the first quarter of the 12th century.

Santa Maria delle Grazie, on the Corso Magenta, is another of Milan's great church monuments which no visitor should miss. It was built in 1466, and in 1492—while Columbus was discovering America—Bramante enlarged it, adding the apse. But the chief point of this visit is not to the church itself, but to the dependency outside to its left, the Cenacolo Vinciano, once the refectory of the Dominicans. An artist decorated its wall with a scene proper to a dining room; and it is therefore here that you must come to see one of the most famous paintings ever created, Leonardo da Vinci's *Last Supper.* It is a fresco, and the wall on which it is painted has suffered from dampness and the concussions of the wartime bombardment of Milan. The incredibly delicate work of restoration was only recently completed.

Sant' Eustorgio, just outside the 14th-century gates of Porta Ticinese, contains the Portinari Chapel, just behind the apse. This chapel has been called "a perfect jewel in stone" and is the work of Michelozzo, constructed in the middle of the 15th century.

Environs of Milan

When you have more or less finished Milan, you should think a bit about the rest of Lombardy. If you are pressed for time skip everything else in the province for at least a brief tour of the lakes region.

If you have a car—or if you haven't, lots of buses are available—make a quick trip at least down to one of the world's greatest and best-known monasteries, the Certosa di Pavia, a complete masterpiece of Renaissance art of the Lombardian motif. It was finished only in the 16th century, but it was started in 1396 by the Visconti. The sculpture of the façade, with its multi-colored marble and its lacy structure, is extremely beautiful, as are the richly decorated ceilings and magnificent choir stalls of its Gothic interiors.

Only a few miles from the Charterhouse is Pavia itself, ancient Lombard capital, called Ticinum by the Romans and once a rival of Milan for domination of Lombardy, when both were free cities. It has a great history and the monumental structures of its days of glory remain, in great part, unchanged today. The cathedral was begun in 1488 by Bramante, while Leonardo da Vinci designed the majestic dome and a true early Renaissance interior. See, too, the 12th-century Church of San Michele, in which the medieval emperors received the iron crown.

San Pietro in Ciel d'Oro, another Romanesque 12th-century church, contains both the sarcophagus of the great philosopher Boethius and relics of St. Augustine. There are medieval towers, a mighty Visconti castle and the delightful university, founded in 1361.

Exploring Lombardy and the Lakes

Down the Po from Milan and Pavia, in the center of the plains of Lombardy, is Cremona, whose name has been revered and sung by musicians and all lovers of music for many generations. For it was in this medieval city that the Stradivari, Guarneri and Amati families produced the finest violins in the world. The Stradivarian Museum is rich in relics of these and of the composer Monteverdi.

The Piazza del Comune, in Cremona, is one of the most impressive of Italy's squares, with its beautiful 12th-century Duomo, huge Gothic Torrazzo—known as the tallest bell tower in Italy—octagonal Baptistery, and Loggia dei Militi.

Continuing eastward, you will come to Mantua, on the banks of the Mincio River. Near this old town the poet Virgil was born; Mantegna's tomb is in its Basilica of Sant'Andrea, while Mantua's host of medieval monuments date back chiefly to the days of the princely Gonzaga family.

Its main Piazza Sordello has two interesting 12th- and 13th-century palaces and the 18th-century façade of the cathedral which itself is early 16th. The towering mass of the Castel di San Giorgio, which was a part of the Gonzaga residence, is just behind. The battlemented walls of this castle jut out over the lakes which the Mincio forms around Mantua. Its famous 15th-century Camera degli Sposi, or Bridegroom's Chamber, is decorated with frescos of the Gonzaga family by Mantegna. Also housed here is a rare collection of Roman coins although the archeological museum has been moved to the Monastero Maggiore in Corso Magenta.

Adjoining San Giorgio, but facing on the square, is the Palazzo Ducale, once center of a brilliant court ruled by witty Isabella d'Este. Decorating its walls are Romano's rosy nudes, tapestries and paintings by Rubens, El Greco, and other great masters. Other spots to visit are Mantegna's home (housing a museum), the arcaded Piazza dell Erbe, a favorite for evening promenades, and the 15th-century Palazzo del Te outside town.

Brescia and Lake Garda

Brescia is of Roman origin, but its greatest monument is not Roman. It is the Lombard-Venetian Renaissance palace, the Loggia, in the Piazza della Loggia. Its marble decoration is outstanding. The 12th-century Rotonda church is flanked in the Piazza del Duomo by a 17th-century baroque cathedral.

Through the Via dei Musei you will find the ruins of the Capitoline Temple, dating back to Vespasian, in the year 73. It is now the site of the Roman Age Museum which contains, among other precious items, a famed 1st-century *Winged Victory.* The Museum of the Christian Age, farther along the same street, has many extremely valuable art objects—triptychs, ivory diptychs, and crosses, from the 6th and 7th centuries. In the Pinacoteca Tosio-Martinengo, in the Piazza Moretto, is a notable collection of the Brescia-Venetia school of painting of the 15th century, notably Raphael, Tintoretto, Titian and Tiepolo. Visit the medieval Castello on the hill for a splendid view of the city.

Soncino, a little-known spot, has some lovely art and architecture, notably the late 15th-century castle, built by one of the Sforzas.

Lake Garda, quite near Brescia, is worth a rather extensive visit for its beautiful scenic effects. There are three ways to see it properly, ways to suit all pocketbooks—one of course is a complete tour of the lake by private car, if you happen to have one. The second is by bus, doing the same thing, and the third is by lake steamer, which cruises leisurely along the coast, allowing ample opportunity for tranquil enjoyment of this romantic region, so highly favored by German tourists.

Desenzano del Garda is at the southernmost tip of the lake and is the best spot to start your tour. Far in the northern distance are the Alps. Stretching toward them as far as you can see, on both sides of the lake—and don't forget Garda is 32 miles long and 10 wide—are groves of olives, lemon and orange trees, at the foot of mountains often covered with snow.

There is Sirmione, where Catullus was born and to which he returned all too often to mourn the infidelities of his great love. And there is Salò, still to the west, near the spot where Gabriele D'Annunzio died and was buried. D'Annunzio's residence, the *Vittoriale*—an overpowering monument to kitsch—is now open to the public. Then Fasano, Toscolano, Bogliaco and Gargnano, in a vast green setting of olive groves.

From here on Garda narrows and is surrounded by high rugged mountains.

Now, if you have taken the steamer, you will see the cedar groves to the west, which mark your entrance into the Straits of Ponale, flanked by its cliffsides, and on to the little town of Riva, at the head of the lake—neat, tidy, beautifully located.

Bergamo Region

The part of Lombardy which lies north of the general line Bergamo-Como is not properly speaking tourist country. The amenities of civilization are definitely to be found at Clusone, at Sondrio, Bormio and at other towns and villages which nestle in the Alpine slopes and on the fringes of the streams which run down from them to the plains far beneath. And if you have the time, by all means make a trip through them. Better, if you have the time just wander up to one of them—never mind which one—take a room in some hotel or *pensione*—and you'll find all are clean and friendly—stay for as long as you can and spend your days wandering either on foot or by car through the little roads and through the hills and mountain passes. Watch the sunset behind Mt. Coca or Mt. Adamello, and sunrise behind Mt. Bernina, on the Italo-Swiss border.

The old city of Bergamo lies at the foot of the Bergamese Alps. Actually Bergamo is two cities—Lower Bergamo and Upper Bergamo. High up on the hillside, walled in by the ruins of ancient Venetian fortifications, surmounted by an ancient fortress, is Bergamo Alta. In its Piazza Vecchia, and near it are this town's principal monuments—the 12th-century Palazzo della Ragione, the massive Torre del Comune, the Duomo of Bergamo, the Church of Santa Maria Maggiore, the Colleoni Chapel and the Baptistery. The dome and the sanctuary of the Colleoni Chapel are decorated by Tiepolo's frescos of the life of St. John the Baptist.

400 feet lower, in Bergamo Bassa, in the Accademia Carrara, you will find one of Italy's greatest and most important art collections. Many of the Venetian masters are represented—Mantegna, Carpaccio, Tiepolo, Guardi, Canaletto—and there are some magnificent Bellinis and Botticellis. The citizens of Bergamo are fiercely proud that Donizetti was born there. Nor is this their only claim to musical fame, for the town is also the birthplace of the famous *bergamasque.*

Lake Como

Upon leaving Bergamo, unless you are driving and have no particular reason for retracing your steps, you'd better go back to Milan and set out from there for the Lake Country. It's easier, because both bus and rail services are much better and much more frequent.

You can, if you like, examine the various Renaissance buildings, monuments, churches, palaces, in the towns on the lakes—Locarno, Como, Stresa, Lecco. But there are thousands of better buildings to be found in other parts of Italy, while nowhere in the world will you find quite what you will find here—the sheer enchantment of living beauty.

Start with Como. Of course the town has a 14th-century cathedral, and a 13th-century palace, the Broletto, and an ancient tower. Go to the lakeside and look to the north. Look at the slopes of the hillsides bordering the lake, with their superb garden-adorned villas. Then comes Cernobbio, center of modern wealthy elegance. On a small promontory, on the east bank of the lake, is Torno, close by the still extant spring which Pliny the Younger—both Plinys were born in the Como region, which is inordinately proud of them—described so carefully in a well-known letter to a friend. The nearby Villa Pliniana has only a very remote connection with the famous Romans, as you may imagine, since it dates from the 16th century.

But take the steamer trip round Como. Pass Colonna, Sala, the famous and picturesque Island of Comacina. Go around the Avedo Promontory and along what is known as the Tremezzina Riviera, for its wonderful gardens, and on to Bellagio, where the three sections of the lake meet. Bellagio, Varenna and Menaggio are Como's prettiest resorts.

The steamer plies back and forth across the lake from Menaggio to Varenna, to Bellano and later to Dongo. That's where Italian partisans captured Mussolini in April 1945, as he was trying to escape to the north with a German convoy. Two days later they executed him and ever since then the Italian press mentions periodically the reputed "treasure of Dongo"—the vast wealth the Fascist leader was supposed to have had with him.

The names of these towns don't really matter. What you are interested in here, as you will be later at Lugano and Maggiore, is the scenery—the usually snow-capped Alps in the distance looming over the lake's shimmering waters with the little skimming boats.

Lakes Lugano and Maggiore

Lake Lugano, north of Varese, is a good bit more than half Swiss. Only that part of the shoreline between Porto Ceresio and Ponte Tresa, and the Campione region, are Italian. Lugano is Swiss. But Campione d'Italia, a kind of Italian island in Swiss territory, is an ideal little place. Further, it has an excellent casino where you have your choice of three rooms to do your gambling, depending on the limit you care to play for. Though the town belongs to Italy, Swiss money and stamps are used. There are no frontier formalities.

At Ponte Tresa the lake steamer enters the straits of Lavena. Here the Tresa River cuts the village in half and forms the exact frontier between Italy and Switzerland.

From Santa Margherita, on the south shore, take the cable railway up to Belvedere Station and go on from there a little less than a mile to Lanzo d'Intelvi, high on a pleateau and affording a view of the entire Lugano lake section, a rugged and wild region, whose ancient olive trees at the base of the mountains half shield its ultramodern hotels and aging villas.

Lake Maggiore is perhaps, next to Como, the best known of the Italian lakes, chiefly because of its west bank (Piedmontese) resorts such as Stresa, which are undoubtedly delightful but not typical of the Italian lake region. Try Stresa, however, as your headquarters for such time as you propose, or can afford, to spend on Maggiore.

Lake Maggiore is a gem. With the towering masses of Switzerland's Alps to the north, the famed Borromean Islands more or less in the center, the summer resort section of Stresa on the west, world-famed Locarno (Swiss) to the north, and Laveno to the east and south, Maggiore is a two-mile-wide ribbon of beauty connecting the plains of Lombardy with the Alps of Switzerland. Its scenery for the 40 miles of its length is so varied that it easily takes its place among the natural wonders of the world. Nowhere are the views more majestic than at Belgirate, a charming holiday spot with 11th-century castle ruins, 16th-century church containing works by Bernardino Luini, and a villa once inhabited by Napoleon's Josephine.

Take the steamer from Stresa, if you are stopping here, or from Laveno, on the Lombardian side of the lake. There are several trips available. Take them all, if you have the time, because each touches an attractive part of this lovely region. Go up to Locarno by way of Griffa, Porto Valtravaglia, and Cannero Riviera. You'll touch, too, at the village of Cannobio before you enter Switzerland's waters, then at Brisago and Ascona, and finally at Locarno.

Perhaps the loveliest of these cruises though, is that from Laveno to Stresa and Arona, or, as the case may be, from Stresa to Arona and Laveno. You will see the charming Punta Castagnola and the so-called "Gulf of Pallanza". The Borromean Islands are directly before you, with the Alps constituting the backdrop for their picturesque splendor. If you are interested in the picturesque, by the way, you should get off the boat for a while at Verbania Pallanza, whose 17th-century Palazzo Dugnani has a splendid collection of peasant costumes.

Thence you will go by Baveno and its gardens to the "Fishermen's Island"—named Isola dei Pescatori or Isola Superiore—whose untouched quaintness has made it a favorite haunt of artists and writers.

Then on to the second of the Borromeans—Isola Bella, short for "Isle of Isabella". Its gardens, its walks and its ten terraces, stretching down from the uppermost reaches of the Island's banks to the lake itself, form a sumptuous setting for the 17th-century Palazzo Borromeo, which blends into the landscape without in the least dominating it. All about you there is a profusion of exotic plants, Renaissance statuary and sparkling fountains. Isola Madre, smallest of the three islands, consists mainly of a beautiful sub-tropical garden.

And there's another, equally famous garden at Villa Taranto, 100 acres of exotic flowers, fountains, trees, and shrubs along the shore of Lake Maggiore between Pallanza and Intra. Created by a botanically-minded Scotsman, Captain Neil McEachern, these rank with Europe's most beautiful private gardens; open to the public daily (guided visits only).

PRACTICAL INFORMATION FOR MILAN

HOTELS. It is good practice to make reservations in advance, as the city is always filled with visitors. During the Trade Fair tourists are often forced to seek accommodations in fairly distant cities. Prices in Milan are expensive. Should you arrive without reservations, there is an instant telephone reservation service at the central railroad station, where a board lists over 100 hotels and pensions.

Deluxe (L)

Excelsior Gallia, Piazza Duca d'Aosta 9, has 242 rooms, most with bath, large, but often noisy, airconditioning garage. Handy for railway station.

Grand Hotel et de Milan, Via Manzoni, central, a few steps from La Scala, 90 rooms, 65 with bath. Traditional atmosphere.

Hilton, near station, atop air terminal, hostesses at concierge desk, 340 well-furnished rooms with airconditioning radio and TV. Pub-style London Bar with piano, disco.

Palace, Piazza della Repubblica 20, 222 rooms with bath, modern, convenient, quiet location. Airconditioning, garage, hotel bus at station. Delightful roof garden restaurant, smart Casanova grill room.

Principe e Savoia, Piazza della Repubblica 17, 301 rooms all with bath, airconditioned, many furnished with fine period pieces, TV. Grill room, hotel bus at station, attractive apartment annex for long stays.

First Class Superior (1)

Aerhotel Executive, Via Sturzo near air terminal, Porta Garibaldi station. Milan's most recent and one of Italy's largest hotels, it's ultra-modern, with smallish but well-furnished, airconditioned rooms, several restaurants.

Anderson, Piazza Luigi di Savoia, at station, modern, comfortable rooms with bath, TV, airconditioning.

Carlton Senato, Via Senato 5, between cathedral and main station. Bright, modern, all rooms with airconditioning, bath.

Cavalieri, Piazza Missori 1, 181 rooms, all with bath, airconditioning. Noted for its modern decor, delightful roof restaurant, and central location.

Cavour, Via Fatebenefratelli 21, same zone as above, modern decor, 98 airconditioned rooms.

De la Villc, Via Hoepli 6, 105 rooms, all with bath, airconditioning, traditional furnishings, on quiet square near cathedral.

Duomo, Via San Raffaele 1, 163 rooms, most with bath, housed in historic building opposite cathedral. Some fine duplex suites, airconditioned, grill room, garage nearby.

Jolly President, Largo Augusto 10, central, 196 rooms with bath, all amenities, airconditioning, radios in rooms, garage, rather anonymous.

Lloyd, Corso Porta Romana, modern, 52 rooms, all with bath, airconditioning, TV in rooms, garage. Pleasant decor, personalized service.

Manin, Via Manin 7, 100 rooms, modern, all rooms with bath, airconditioning, private garden.

Michelangelo, Via Scarlatti, just off station square, recent and modern, 285 comfotable rooms with bath, TV, airconditioning. Popular with Americans.

Plaza, Piazza Diaz, very central, recently renovated, tastefully decorated in contemporary style, large individually furnished rooms, some overlooking Duomo, entirely airconditioned, cozy foyer bar, no restaurant.

Select, Via Baracchini 12, 137 rooms with bath, airconditioned, very central, modern, no restaurant.

Splendido, Via Andrea Doria 4, big, modern, airconditioning, radios in rooms, private garden, no restaurant.

Touring, Via Tarchetti, 225 spacious attractive rooms, most with bath, two restaurants.

First Class Reasonable (1)

Amedei, Via Amedei, central, traditional style.

Auriga, Via Pirelli 7, 65 rooms, most with bath or shower, airconditioning, garage, near main station.

Marino alla Scala, Piazza della Scala 5, conveniently located, 79 well-furnished, airconditioned rooms, no restaurant.

Rosa, Via Pattari 5, 162 rooms, most with bath, near cathedral.

Windsor, Via Galilei, near luxury hotels, modern, all comforts.

Moderate (2)

Top-notch in category is new **Lord Internazionale,** Via Spadari 11, air conditioning, radios in rooms, central.

American, Via Finocchiaro Aprile 2, 300 rooms, all of which have shower.

Biscione, near post office, elegant small hotel, swimming pool.

The popular **Manzoni,** Via Santo Spirito 20, has 54 rooms, most with bath or shower.

Lancaster, Via Sangiorgio, pleasant small hotel at far side of Sempione park.

Mediolanum, Via Mauro Macchi, modern, comfortable, airconditioning.

Near main station **Zurigo,** Corso Italia 11A, 29 rooms, centrally located.

Monopole, Via Filzi 43, near station, has garage.

Excellent are—**Centro,** near La Scala, airconditioning, garage; **San Carlo,** facing station; **Rubens,** ideal for Fair visitors, with airconditioning, guarded car-park.

Andreola, near main station, is recommended, all rooms with bath.

Europeo, fairly central, airconditioned, pool, excellent; **Aosta** and **New York,** both very near main station.

Inexpensive (3)

Many in this category. Try the **Lux,** Via della Palla 5, small, 17 rooms; **Eden,** Via Tonale 2; **Torino,** Via Caminadella 11, or **Losanna,** Via Piero della Francesca; **Città Studi,** Van Saldini 24, pleasant, out of center, at university; **Roxy,** Via Bixio, is good.

Pensions (P)

Del Corso (P2), is in very central Galleria; **Argentario** (P2), Corso Porta Vittoria, provides meals.

RESTAURANTS. Although Milan does not have a great number of local specialties (despite the boasts of the local residents), it is one of the best cities for food in Italy. The liberal use of butter in preparing food of excellent quality adds a distinctive flavor to the Milanese cuisine. Among the most favored specialties is *osso buco alla milanese,* veal knuckle served with *risotto,* rice which has been cooked until almost all the liquid has evaporated and a creamy sauce remains. *Risotto alla milanese* has saffron added, which colors the dish a rich yellow. *Costoletta alla milanese* is a breaded veal cutlet. The favorite cheese of Milan is *Gorgonzola.* Other well known cheeses are *Bel Paese* and *Taleggio,* both mild, and *Mascarpone,* very much like cream cheese.

The regional wines are *Freccia Rossa, Grumello, Inferno, Lugana, Sassela* and *Valgella.* Milan's pastry specialty is *panettone,* a raised fluffy cake, flecked with dried raisins and a variety of candied fruit.

Expensive (E)

Alfredo—Gran San Bernardo, Via Borgese, where ex-chef of *Biffi Scala* serves *risotto al salto, filet Vornoff.* Reserve well in advance (tel. 389.000).

Biffi Scala, elegant, tea and suppers only. Reserve for after-theater.

Boeucc, Piazza Belgioioso, closed Sat. and Aug. Summer terrace, specialties *tortellini di ricotta* and *crêpes.*

Collina Pistoiese, Via Amedei, features Tuscan food, *risotto alla certosina,* its own chianti.

The **Conty Grill,** in the Hotel Continentale is outstanding and conveniently located downtown.

The classic **El Gamba de Legn,** Via Elba, authentic Milanese cooking. Reserve (tel. 463.091).

El Toulà, closed Sun. and Aug. Reserve ahead (tel. 870.302); very expensive, very chic. International and Venetian specialties.

Giannino's is one of Milan's most famous and expensive restaurants. Here you can look into the huge glass-enclosed kitchen and watch the chefs at work. The specialties are *risotto certosina* and truffled veal. Closed Sun. and Aug.

Marchesi, Via Bonvesin de la Riva, near **Giannino,** is even more expensive, very much in vogue. Average check runs 50,000 lire per person, and habitues swear it's worth it. Host Gualtiero offers "nouvelle cuisine" *all'italiana* with exquisite results. Closed Sunday, Monday noon, August. Reserve (tel. 741.246).

Scaletta, Piazzale Stazione Genova. (Reserve a week ahead, tel. 835.0290), vies with Marchesi for top quality, superb food and wines in delightful setting.

Rigolo, Via Solferino, favorite for journalists and actors, ideal for a late snack in lively company.

Savini, is in the glass-roofed Galleria, across from the cathedral, world-famous, expensive, a Milan tradition for superb food and exquisite ice-cream. Try especially *risotto milanese* and *costoletta milanese.*

Piccolo Gourmet, Corso Italia. Reserve ahead (tel. 805.3819); small, very good and quite expensive.

Taverna del Gran Sasso, closed Sun. and July. Piazza Principessa Clotilde, folksy, Abruzzese atmosphere and cooking. Reserve.

Vecchia Milano, Via Galeazzo.

At **Monza,** site of a villa built for Ferdinand of Austria, the **St. Georges Premier,** refined, expensive atmosphere in a handsome setting, international cuisine, including *crêpes alla fontina, pollo al whisky,* candlelight dining in a summer garden.

The smartest spot for drinks is the Bar of the **Principe Savoia** hotel; for tea and pastries, **Sant' Ambroeus,** Corso Matteotti 7.

Moderately Expensive (M–E)

Cavallini, on Mauro Macchi, has an attractive garden restaurant, as does **Brasera Meneghina,** Via Circo 10, one of the classic old Milan eating places.

Also excellent, **Romani,** Via Trebazio 3, especially for *truffled polenta.*

Da Piero, Via Bixio, attracts smart Milanese for *penne al salmone, scaloppine al carciofo.*

Other off-the-beaten-track places, but these in the central Brera district, are the less expensive **Soldato d'Italia** and **Franco,** both on Via Fiori Chiari, and **Ciovassino,** Via Ciovassino. In Naviglio area, earthy but pricey **Topaia,** Via Argelati.

At **La Grotte,** Via Bergamini, host Marino leads you through a sumptuous menu.

Moderate (M)

There are many moderate restaurants in Milan. To mention a few—**Rigoletto,** Via Monti 33, near castle; **Chiavacci,** outdoor dining, handy to collapse in after shopping on Via Montenapoleone; **Tantalo,** off Piazza Duomo; **Veneziano,** Via Agnello, for sea food; **San Vito da Lucco,** San Vito 5, known for its chicken *allo champagne.*

Montalcino da Edgardo, Via Valenza, near Naviglio Grande, attractive blend of fine Tuscan wines and well-prepared dishes. **Mercante,** Piazza Mercanti, central, good classic dishes.

La Pizzaccia has rustic atmosphere, down-to-earth cuisine.

At **Biffi** in the Galleria, delicious snacks and *tavola calda* for lunches. **Penny** chain offers simple, satisfying meals at counter.

Outside town: the highly recommended **Pianta** at **Corsico** (5 miles SW, leave town on Via Ludovico il Moro); **Bettolina** at **Gaggiano** (9 miles); and **San Bernardo** at **Chiaravalle,** are typical country trattorias.

MUSEUMS. Although worldfamous as an industrial center, Milan has a surprisingly large number of excellent museums. Check with concierge or at local tourist offices for hours. Among the best—

Castle of the Sforzas, Piazza Castello, with Museum of Ancient Art, painting gallery, arms collection.

Church of Santa Maria delle Grazie, Corso Magenta, Leonardo da Vinci's *Last Supper* (Cenacolo Vinciano).

Pinacoteca Ambrosiana, Piazza Pio XI, contains famous Leonardo da Vinci collection, as well as works of other masters.

Pinacoteca di Brera, Via Brera, notable 15th and 16th-century frescos of Lombard school, paintings by Mantegna, Raphael and Bronzino, among others. One of the world's great collections of painting.

Poldi-Pezzoli Museum, Via Manzoni 12, picture gallery, paintings by Botticelli, Tiepolo and others, 15th–18th-century Murano glass, 15th-century Persian carpets.

Portinari Chapel, Church of Sant'Eustorgio, Corso di Porta Ticinese, frescos depicting the life and death of St. Peter Martyr, by Foppa.

Scala Theater Museum, Piazza della Scala.

MUSIC. The most famous spectacle in Milan is the **La Scala Opera,** whose productions are among the world's most impressive. Either orchestra or chorus goes on strike occasionally, but the show goes on. The opera season runs from December to May, the concert season from October to December. The house is invariably sold out well in advance, but ask your concierge to find tickets for you; you'll have to pay for this service, but it's worth it to avoid the complicated business of getting seats.

NIGHTLIFE. Good spots—but expensive—are the roof gardens of the **Palace** and **Dei Cavalieri** hotels, with a beautiful view of the city; outdoor dancing at **Rendezvous;** the **Aretusa** discotheque, and **Hilton Hotel.**

The **Astoria Club,** Piazza Santa Maria Beltrade—with a good floor show—is one of the best in town.

The **Piccolo Bar,** Via Romagnosi, is small, elegant.

Other favorites are the noisy and lively **Porta d'Oro** in the Plaza Hotel; and **Colibri,** with strippers. There's a deafening disco **Studio 54** here, too.

SHOPPING. As the leading Italian industrial center, Milan has a great deal of wealth which is reflected in the chic of its most elegant street, Via Montenapoleone. Prices tend to be higher than in other major cities.

Silk is a good buy here, along with quality leather goods, boutique fashions are ultrasmart and expensive.

Milan rivals Rome as a marketplace for contemporary art.

For fun, go to the flea market held every Saturday on Via Calatafimi.

SPORTS. The horse racing at the **San Siro** hippodrome is first-rate. There's a beautifully kept 18-hole golf course at **Monza.** The striking new sports palace features bicycle racing and spectator sports.

TRANSPORT. Taxis are plentiful but other public transport is also good, with *buses* and a modern subway, **metropolitana,** connecting one end of the city to the other. At the Tourist Office at Piazza Duomo for a few hundred lire you can buy a ticket for unlimited travel on all trams, buses and subway lines.

USEFUL ADDRESSES. *American Express,* Via Vittor Pisani, 20124, tel. 669721; CIT, Galleria Vittorio Emanuele, the Central Station, Corso Italia 10, Corso Venezia 43; *Cook's,* Via Manzoni 10; EPT, Via Marconi 1.

Consulates: *American,* Piazza della Repubblica 32; *British,* Via San Paolo 7.

For businessmen: *World-Wide Business Centers,* Via Boccaccio 2, 20123 Milan, have secretarial, photo-copying, translating and other extremely handy services, tel: 870996.

PRACTICAL INFORMATION FOR LOMBARDY AND THE LAKES

HOTELS AND RESTAURANTS

Aprica. Summer and winter sports resort in the Bergamesque Alps. **Hotels:** *Bozzi* (2), all rooms with bath, garage. *Cristallo* (2), quiet, comfortable.

Both (3) are—*Eden* and *Ginepro.*

Baveno. Lake Maggiore resort. **Hotels:** *Splendid* (1), on lakeside, modernized, all rooms with bath and balcony overlooking lake, in park, with large pool.

Both (2) are—*Beau Rivage,* with small garden, but on main road, has annex (3); *Simplon,* in large garden on lake, near center, pool, open 1 April–30 Oct.

Rigoli (3), many private baths, lake view.

Restaurants: *Romagna* (M–E) is a pleasant place, with its dining terrace on lake.

At **Feriolo,** about 2 miles from here, *La Serenella* (M) is also good.

Belgirate. Lake Maggiore resort. **Hotels:** *Milano* (2), 54 rooms, terrace on the lake. *Villa Carlotta* (1) on main road, facing but not on lake, 68 rooms, some with bath, attractive, private beach.

Bellagio. Lake Como resort with quite a spacious beach. **Hotels:** Deluxe—Grand Hotel Villa Serbelloni, 100 rooms, most with bath, 16th-century villa on lakefront, in own park and gardens, large pool, original frescos in lounge, many suites, private beach, tennis. Courteous service, charming ambiance, open 8 April–10 Oct.

Metropole (2), pleasant, good lakeside restaurant and terraces.

All (2) are—*Du Lac,* 56 rooms, opposite landing stage, extensively modernized, excellent service, first floor restaurant with panoramic view of lake, open 1 April–31 Oct.; *Excelsior Splendido,* on lakefront, half of rooms with bath, swimming pool, also open April–Oct. *Belvedere* swimming pool, open 1 April–10 Oct.

Restaurants: Best is the excellent restaurant in *Villa Serbelloni* hotel, where you can eat on the terrace and look across rose garden to the lake.

All (M)—try *Ristorante Ferrario* or *Barchetta,* both with good cuisine, a good bet is the fish, either lake trout or *filetti de pesce persico,* freshly caught; *La Pergola* is good too, has lakeside terrace.

Bergamo. Hotels: Both (1) are—*Excelsior San Marco,* Piazza Repubblica, 150 rooms with shower, airconditioned; *Moderno,* large, older hotel.

Del Moro (2), Largo Porto Nuova, pleasant small hotel.

Both (3) are—*Agnello d'Oro,* in upper town, basic, 22 rooms with bath; *Piemontese,* near station, 55 rooms, most with shower or bath, good restaurant.

Restaurants: All (E)—In atmospheric Upper Bergamo, *Pergola* and *La Vendemmia,* both excellent, with summer terraces; *Vittorio,* near station, specializes in fish; *Angelo,* Borgo Santa Caterina, has good atmosphere and cuisine, but pricey.

Both (M) are—*Cappello d'Oro,* Viale Roma 12, short on atmosphere and elegance, but good food; *Del Sole,* specializes in game and regional dishes; Try *Agnello d'Oro* (M), Via Gombito, rustic decor, for *casoncelli* (ravioli).

Blevio. (Lombardy), near Como. **Restaurant:** A lakeside garden restaurant, *Smeraldo* (E), offers such delicacies as truffled risotto, and lake trout.

Bormio. Summer and ski resort. **Hotels:** *Palace* (1), modern and attractive.

All (2) are—*Astoria,* in center of town, all rooms with bath; *Baita dei Pini,* 46 comfortable rooms with bath or shower, garden, closed May, Oct.–Nov.; *Larice Bianco,* near ski school, cablecar, good; *San Lorenzo,* in town, all rooms with bath or shower, many with balconies, garden. *Everest* (3), pleasant small hotel with garden.

Restaurants: Both (M)—*Kuerc,* on main piazza; *Cendre.*

Brescia. **Hotels:** *Vittoria* (1), just off main piazza, well-furnished, nearby garage.

All (2) are—*Igea,* opposite station, rather basic; *Ascot,* Via Apollonio, just outside center, pleasant rooms, most with bath, cool garden; *Motor Hotel,* fine overnight, no restaurant.

Both (3) are—*Europa,* Piazzale Ospedale 7, is better than its rating would imply, 33 rooms, most with bath; *Motel AGIP,* Viale Bornata 42.

Restaurants: All (E) are—the dining room of the *Vittoria,* quite good; if you want to stuff yourself, try *Archimede,* Via Mazzini, where portions are copious; *Cuccagnina,* and *Gottardino* are both good. *La Sosta,* 16th-century atmosphere, featuring *spaghetti alla carbonara* and *Dolce Zia Giulia.*

Both (M) are *Augustus,* Via Cereto, *Ai Chiostri,* Via Einaudi.

Bargains are *Agnello,* Corso Garibaldi 20; and *Da Peppino,* Viale Venezia.

Brunate. Hill resort above Lake Como, connected by funicular with Como town. **Hotel:** *Miramonti* (3), small, above town, outstanding view, terrace restaurant, open April–October.

Cadenabbia. Resort on Lake Como, yachting center. **Hotels:** *Bellevue* (1), terrace, bathing, garage, private garden, open April–Oct.

Britannia Excelsior (2), large, comfortable old hotel in park. *Beau Rivage* (3), pleasant, bathing. Both open April–Oct.

Cannero Riviera. On Lake Maggiore. **Hotel:** *Cannero* (2), overlooking lake, old-fashioned, comfortable. Open 15 March–30 Oct.

Cannobio. Lake Maggiore resort. **Hotels:** *Villa Belvedere* (2), very comfortable, 13 rooms with shower, swimming pool, open 11 April–15 Oct. *Campagna* (3), in quiet location, many rooms with bath, lakeside beach.

Cernobbio. Lake Como resort and yachting center. **Hotels:** *Villa d'Este* (L), one of Italy's, or for that matter, the world's most luxurious hotels. Expensive. Its 171 rooms, most with bath, are arranged in the lovely Renaissance villa, built in 1568, and its annex, directly on lake. Gracious service, great tranquillity; floating pool, golf, nightclub, piano bar; an unforgettable experience.

Regina Olga (1), slightly less grand, but top-notch, well-furnished, with pool in lovely park.

Restaurants: All (E)—no surprise that the best food served here is at the *Villa d'Este,* where there are several small restaurants and trattorias, most with tables in the garden. Near the Villa d'Este, *Trattoria al Vapore* (E), at Torno, with veranda on lake, delicate fish specialties, has hearty, truly Italian atmosphere; *Terzo Crotto,* recommended, terrace dining; *Crotto Polirolo,* at the top of Mt. Bisbino.

Chiesa in Valmalenco. Summer and winter sports resorts. **Hotels:** *Grand Hotel Malenco* (1), 92 rooms, most with bath, in beautiful grounds, with panoramic view, tennis, open 25 June–2 Sept., 7 Dec.–25 April.

Rezia (2), pretty chalet-type, with indoor pool. *Tremoggia* (3), pleasant.

Clusone. Art town, summer resort, off beaten path. **Hotel:** *Erica* (3), fine for overnight.

Colico. Small Lake Como town, with a beach. **Hotels:** *Isola Bella* (3), pleasant hotel in own grounds. *Gigi* (3), only 18 rooms, modest, good. *Risi* (2) has lake view, most rooms with bath.

Comacina. Restaurant: No visit to Lake Como is complete without a visit to the beautiful little island of Comacina, and a meal eaten at the picturesque restaurant known as *Locanda del Isola* (E). Colorful tables are laid on Roman paving stones beneath the olive trees. Hire a rowboat at **Sala** to go across. Closed Nov.–Jan.

Como. Summer resort on lake and, of course, yachting center. **Hotels:** See Cernobbio for *Villa d'Este* (L).

All (1) are—*Metropole e Suisse,* Piazza Cavour 19, 70 rooms, more than half with bath, overlooking lake and harbor, modern, sidewalk café in summer; *Barchetta Excelsior,* overlooks lake, new and very comfortable, all rooms have private bath. *Villa Flori,* on Cernobbio Road, private beach and park, open April–Oct.

All (2) are—*San Gottardo,* Piazza Volta, 51 rooms, 21 with bath, central, furnishings old-fashioned, well-kept; *Engadina,* Viale Rosselli, all rooms with bath; *Como,* recent, modern and comfortable, terraces, heated pool.

Restaurants: All (E)—If you don't run over to Cernobbio for a Villa d'Este meal, you will find that you can do pretty well on the top level in Como itself, at *Lario,* Piazza Cavour; *Villa Olmo,* on the road to Cernobbio, offers very good cuisine in a peaceful lakeside setting; at least one meal at *Cassè,* on the Piazza Funicolare or at *Funicolare* itself.

Gesumin (E), in old palazzo, excellent food, cordial family ambiance. Reserve. *Celestino* (E), few steps from main piazza, pleasant and good.

All (M–E) are—*Il Fiorino; Faro,* Via Luini; *Navedano,* at nearby **Camnago;** and the *Barchetta* restaurant of the *Excelsior* hotel, Piazza Cavour.

Cremona. Hotels: All (2) are—*San Giorgio,* at the station, largest, best, 65 rooms, more than half with bath, garage; *Este,* Viale Po 131, all rooms with bath or shower; *Astoria,* Via Bordigallo, central, quiet; fully modernized behind antique façade.

Restaurants: Both (M) are—*Dordoni,* Via del Sale; and *Cigno,* both good.

Desenzano del Garda. Summer resort on Lake Garda. **Hotels:** All (2) are—*Miralago,* lakeside terrace, bathing; *Barchetta,* 36 rooms, terrace overlooking lake; *Park,* on lakeside drive, well-appointed, most rooms with bath.

All (3) are—*Vittorio,* basic, attractive lakeside location; *Vela,* lake view, gardens, bathing; *Villa Rosa,* well-equipped lakeside hotel.

Restaurants: Both (M) are—*Matarel* and *Pizzeria al Teatro,* lakeside, unpretentious.

Gardone Riviera. On Lake Garda. **Hotels:** Both (1) are—*Grand,* on lake, 213 rooms, many with bath, private jetty and bathing beach, dancing in season, pool, open 1 April–15 October; *Fasano,* 105 rooms on lake, is also good, tennis, swimming pool, open 1 April–10 October.

Both (2) are—*Villa del Sogno,* quiet, attractive, terraces with fine lake view, tennis, pool; *Monte Baldo,* lakefront, 42 rooms, many with bath, popular, private jetty, open April through October.

Good (3) is *Bellevue,* villa type, with terraces, garden, view, large spotless rooms.

Restaurants: Both (E) are—the two best eating places here, both in hotels, *Grand,* in Gardone Riviera proper; *Fasano,* in outlying quarter of the same name; a little less expensive, both excellent, *Barbarano; Bireria Wuehrer* for frankfurters and beer.

At nearby **Portese,** rustic lakeside *Piero Bello* (M), for homemade *tortellini,* freshly caught trout.

Ghiffa. On Lake Maggiore. **Hotels:** Both (2) are—*Castello di Frino,* only 13 rooms, pool, park, tennis; *Ghiffa,* on lake, private beach. Both open April through September.

Iseo. On Lake Iseo. **Hotels:** *Ambra* (2), modest, simple accommodation, with lake view.

At **Sale Marasino,** a few miles north, *Motta* (3), terraces overlooking lake. At **Pilzone,** *Europa* and *Morselli,* both (3).

Ispra. Upcoming Maggiore resort, a Euratom research center. **Hotel:** *Europa* (2), good value, private beach, garage.

Lissago. Near Varese. **Restaurant:** *Hermitage* (M), is a wonderful place to eat, not only for the food, which is superb, but for the breathtaking view.

Lodi. An attractive market town. **Restaurant:** *Isola Caprera* (M), at Borgo Adda, best, huge fireplace, lots of paintings, mirrors, try *risotto alla panna.*

Luino. Lake Maggiore resort. **Hotel:** *Internazionale* (3), is comfortable, all rooms with bath or shower.

Madesimo. Summer and winter sports resort. **Hotels:** All (2) are—*Cascata Cristallo,* comfortable, most rooms with bath, indoor pool; *Arlecchino,* pleasant, indoor pool; *Emet,* all rooms with bath or shower, small.

Ferrè (3), small, all rooms with bath or shower.

Mantua/Mantova. **Hotels:** *San Lorenzo* (1), very central, modern, attractive, all rooms with bath.

All (2) are—*Mantegna,* Via Filzi 3, modern; *Italia,* Piazza Cavalotti 8, all rooms with bath; *Apollo* and *Dante,* both no restaurant.

Restaurants: All (M) are—*Gastone,* Piazza Felice Cavalotti 14, can give you excellent cutlets Milanese; *Garibaldini,* very good for *agnolotti, cannelloni, risotto all pilota* and sausages; *Taverna del Duca,* also fine; *Due Albini,* good, try truffled turkey; *Cigno,* Piazza d'Arco, is not to be missed, one of the region's finest, frescos, antiques and genuine Mantuan specialties. *Da Baffo,* at Borgo Virgiliana, rustic dishes, homemade bread.

Menaggio. Popular Lake Como resort, with a beach. **Hotels:** All open April through October. *Victoria* (1), 98 rooms, 56 with bath, pleasant small garden, quiet situation, tennis court.

Both (2) are—*Grand e Menaggio,* 69 rooms, half with bath, small garden and private beach area. *Bellavista,* very modern, on lakeside beach.

Restaurants: All (E) are the restaurants of the *Grand e Menaggio, Principe* and *Victoria* hotels, and also good, *Pesce* (M), Piazza Garibaldi, and *Vapore* (M).

Pavia. Hotels: Both (2) are—*Rosengarten,* Piazzale Camillo Golgi 12; *Ariston,* Via Scopoli, many rooms with shower.

Restaurants: Both (E)—*Bixio* provides an excellent lunch or dinner with *Asti* wine a specialty; *Giulio,* Via Guffanti, noted for its *risotto* and *involtini. Frua* (M), near the cathedral, with regional dishes. *Pierino* (M), delightful little trattoria with terrace and garden. At **Certosa,** *Chalet* (M) is good.

Ponte di Legno. Summer and winter sports resort, with a noted ski jump. **Hotels:** Both (2) are—*Mirella,* modern, very comfortable, has indoor pool; *Excelsior,* older, traditional type, tennis.

Riva. Attractive small town at northern end of Lake Garda, with an extensive beach. **Hotels:** Both (1)—*Du Lac,* best, handsome modern hotel in sumptuous park, sauna, indoor/outdoor pools, tennis, excellent cuisine, open mid-March–October; *Lido Palace,* large, fine, pool, garden, open April–Oct.

All (2) are—*Sole,* attractive lakeside terrace; *Astoria,* pool; *Liberty,* pool, park. *Lucciola* (3), pool.

San Pellegrino Terme. Most fashionable spa in Lombardy. **Hotels:** Most hotels open 1 June–30 Sept.

Both (1) are—*Grand,* in large park, tennis court; *Terme,* Piazzale Fonti 6, almost all rooms with bath, swimming pool, private garden.

Excelsior (2), in quiet park; seasonal.

Restaurants: The two top eating places here are hotel restaurants—the *Grand* and the *Terme e Milano.* Less expensive is the *Ruspinella* (M).

Sirmione. Popular Lake Garda spa resort. **Hotels:** All (1) are—*Grande Terme,* modern, 68 rooms all with balcony, 47 with bath, in garden, on lakeshore, water sports facilities nearby, spa treatments at hotel, open April–October. The Grande Terme has a nightclub, the *Tavernetta. Sirmione,* 58 spacious rooms, salons in handsome villa, spa facilities. *Villa Cortine Palace,* older villa and modern annex, huge park, tennis, pool.

All (2) are—*Continental,* very good, all rooms with bath, private beach; *Broglia* and *Olivi,* both good value; *Giardino,* private beach. *Du Lac* (2), lakeside garden, beach. *Anna* (P2), pleasant atmosphere.

Restaurants: All (E)—hotels provide the best food here, tops being the *Terme, Sirmione* and *Catullo;* the twin *trattorie, Vecchia Lugana* and *Nuova Lugana,* are both romantic, panoramic and not quite so expensive.

Both (M-E) are the lakeside *Grifone* and *Taverna del Marinaio;* lovely views, so-so food.

Stresa. Principal summer resort on Lake Maggiore. **Hotels:** One deluxe hotel *Grand et des Îles Borromées,* on main highway to north, 146 rooms, most with bath, on lakeshore boulevard with lovely gardens and park, all front rooms with balcony, beautifully furnished, tennis courts, private beach, dancing.

Both (1) are—*Regina Palace,* Corso Umberto 1, 145 rooms, 99 with bath, on lakeshore with gardens and park, most rooms with balcony, private beach, tennis courts, dancing; slightly less expensive, *Bristol,* on main highway, most rooms with bath, former private villa facing lake, tastefully furnished, private beach. *La Palma* (1), pleasant lakeside hotel, spacious rooms, personalized service.

All (2) are—*Milano,* Piazza Marconi, lakeside situation, terrace restaurant, half of rooms have bath; *Speranza du Lac,* on main square, most rooms with bath, attractive décor, recently modernized; *Parco,* small, very good; *Della Torre,* near Mottarone cablecar; *Perla Nera* on lakeside; *Astoria,* north side on main highway, 84 rooms, most with bath, all front rooms with balcony, facing lake, comfortably furnished, swimming pool.

Both (3) are—*Italia e Svizzera* and *Primavera,* both near dock.

Best pension is *Flora* (P2), on highway, with view of Borromean Isles. Open 1 April–10 Oct.

Restaurants: Both (E)—*Il Borromeo,* of Hotel del Iles Borromées, is one of CIGA chain's best restaurants, superlative service; *Emiliano,* classic dishes cooked to perfection more than make up for desolate decor.

All (M)—the hotel restaurants, *Moderno* and *Milano* are particularly good; *Ariston* is fine; and so is *Barchetta.*

Tremezzo. Lake Como resort. **Hotels:** *Grand Hotel Tremezzo* (1), fine palace-type hotel, all front rooms with panoramic view and balcony, swimming pool lido, tennis court, dancing, open April–October.

Bazzoni (2), also good, 130 rooms with bath or shower, modern, attractive decor, restaurant with panoramic view of lake.

Azalea (3), 10 rooms, all with bath or shower, excellent cuisine.

Restaurants: Both (E)—Hotel *Tremezzo* is the best and most expensive, pleasantly cool on the terrace in even the hottest weather, for icy mountain water is kept trickling across the glass roof, the view is superb; *Azalea* offers excellent *osso buco.*

Varese. Important city, lake, mountain and skiing center. **Hotels:** *Grand Palace* (1), Via Manara 11, on Colle Campigli, quiet hilltop ½ mile north, beautiful view from shaded terrace, 110 rooms with bath, some rooms with balcony, older-style furnishings, tennis court, golf nearby, swimming pool.

City (1) and *Plaza* (2) are recent and good.

Internazionale (3), Via Morosini.

Restaurants: Both (E)—*Lago Maggiore,* elegant, classic or local cuisine and wines. At nearby Ganna, *Tre Risotti,* known for such delicacies as frogs, snails, and shrimp with hearty rice dishes.

At **Mustunate,** *Ilario* is good.

Verbania-Pallanza. Lake Maggiore summer resort, quiet, noted for its mild climate, with the best beach around. **Hotels:** *Majestic* (1), in lakeside park, tennis, swimming pool.

Belvedere (2) commands a fine view of the lake from the promontory, open April–Sept. *Astor* (2), on lakeside, fully renovated and quiet with garden restaurant. Shares *Majestic*'s sports facilities.

San Gottardo (3), same view, comfortable.

Restaurants: *Milano* (M), unpretentious place with pretty terrace and delicious food, especially cheese *ravioli.*

At **Intra,** *Miralago* (2) overlooks lake; functional modern decor.

Viggiu. Summer and autumn resort in the mountains. **Hotels:** *Viggiu* (3). *Intercontinentale* (3). *Giardino* (2).

USEFUL ADDRESSES. Tourist Offices: *Aprica:* AAST, Corso Roma, 165. *Baveno:* AAST, Piazza Dante 15. *Bellagio:* AAST, Lungolago A. Manzoni 1. *Bergamo:* AAST, Via Tasso 2; EPT, Viale Vittorio Emanuele 4. *Bormio:* AAST, Via allo Stelvio 10. *Brescia:* EPT, Corso Zanadelli 38. *Cadenabbia:* AAST, Brentano 6, Griante. *Cernobbio:* AAST, Via Regina 33B. *Chiesa in Valmalenco:* AAST, Via Roma 79. *Como:* AAST, Piazza Cavour 33; EPT, Piazza Cavour 17. *Cremona:* EPT, Gall. del Corso 3. *Desenzano del Garda:* AAST, P. Matteotti 27. *Gardone Riviera:* AAST, Viale Roma 8. *Iseo:* AAST, Lungolago G. Marconi 2. *Lanzo d'Intelvi:* AAST, Piazza Novi 1. *Luino:* AAST, Viale D. Alighieri 6. *Madesimo:* AAST, Via Carducci 15. *Mantua:* EPT, Piazza Mantehna 6. *Menaggio:* AAST, Via Lusardi 8. *Pavia:* EPT, Corso Garibaldi 1. *Ponte di Legno:* AAST, Corso Milano 39. *Riva:* AAST, Palazzo dei Congressi. *San Pellegrino Terme:* AAST, Via B. Tasso 1. *Sirmione:* AAST, Viale Marconi 2. *Stresa:* AAST, Piazzale Europa. *Tremezzo:* AAST, Piazza F. Filzi 2. *Varese:* AAST, Via Sacco 6. *Verbania-Pallanza:* AAST, Corso Zanitello 8. *Viggiu:* AAST, Piazza Risorgimento 2.

SPECIAL EVENTS. *Bergamo:* Opera from January (the birthplace of Donizetti); the Parravinci Trophy skiing competitions in April; mystery plays in the Piazza Vecchia in July. *Brescia:* Opera season starts in January. *Comacina:* 23 June, there's a boat-borne procession in costume to the island, honoring St. John, whose relics were found here centuries ago. *Como:* Opera season starts in February. *Cremona:* Opera season begins in February. *Mantua:* Opera from February and a music festival in September. *Stresa:* 25 August–20 September, music festival, details from Settimane Musicali di Stresa, Via. R. Bonghi 4, 28049 Stresa (tel. 31 195, 30 459). *Varese:* July flower festival.

SPORTS. *Bellagio:* Fun place for yachting. *Cernobbio:* Villa d'Este 18-hole golf course. *Lanzo d'Intelvi:* Lanzo 9-hole golf course. *Madesimo:* skiing and skating. *Menaggio:* Great place for freshwater yachting; 18-hole golf course. *Ponte di Legno:* Skiing and skating. *Stresa:* Lots of tennis courts; Panorama Golf, 9-hole course. *Tremezzo:* Playground for freshwater yachting. *Varese:* 18-hole golf course.

VENICE AND THE VENETIAN ARC

Empire and Decay

By the 14th century, Venice had become the most powerful of Italy's numerous little republics. It dominated the Adriatic Sea, controlled all major trade routes to the East, then opened the 16th century by reaching inland to rule over all of what is now the Venetia region, a part of Lombardy, several towns in Puglia, the city of Ravenna. The Istrian Peninsula, between present-day Italy and Yugoslavia, fell under Venetian rule, bringing her control over Trieste. Dalmatia, too, succumbed. The fabulous city, swelled to the bursting point with power and riches, extended its power even farther—into the untold wealth of the Near East.

The Byzantine trend in the Venetian arts—especially well represented by mosaic designs still evident throughout the city today—began in the early centuries, when trade with the East drew Venice into close relations with that part of the world. Later, from the 11th to the 13th century, with a growing influence of Lombard-Romanesque architecture making itself felt, there came into being the characteristic type of palace that has since made Venice famous the world over. Gothic styles during the 14th and 15th centuries helped create a new kind of Venetian-Gothic architecture and sculpture.

Only in the last half of the 15th century, however, did the real masters of Venetian painting appear upon the introduction of Renaissance art by Solari, Mantegna, Antonello da Messina, and Sansovino, the artist-sculptor. It was then that the really great school of Venetian painters soared to an all-time high through Carpaccio and the Bellinis to figures such as Titian, Tintoretto, Veronese, Giorgione da Castelfranco.

The decline of Venice began slowly, after the 16th century. For 400 years, the powerful maritime city-republic had stood firm against the Turks as a bastion of Christianity, an insurmountable rival in the battle for control of seaborne commerce. Now the tide changed. Turkey's Ottoman Empire grew steadily in the eastern Mediterranean area; a changing pattern of world affairs opened new trade routes in the Atlantic and left those of the Mediterranean far behind. Like her steadily dwindling fortunes, the art and culture of Venice also slipped away. Only her monuments to a notable past remained.

True, there was a brief 18th-century revival of art sparked by such painters as Tiepolo, Ricci, Piazzetta, Canaletto, Guardi and Longhi; but, politically and financially, the city that once represented an empire now lay weak and wasted. She had no other recourse than to bow under the pressure of a conquering Napoleon, who, in 1797, by the Treaty of Campoformio, turned Venice over to Austria. 69 years later, in 1866, the city and region finally became a part of the united Kingdom of Italy.

Weather Matters

Plan your trip to Venice either in May or between the first week of September and the first two weeks of October. It's reasonably cool then, with less chance of rain and a greater possibility that the annual rush of tourists won't crowd you out. You can visit in mid-summer, too; but don't complain when heat waves begin rippling across the canals and a bathing suit appears to be the only necessary item in your wardrobe. The single exception to the rule about avoiding Venice during the hottest months is for bathers who want to spend most of their time on the beach at the Lido, where the season runs from May to September.

If you like seeing places in a new light, you might visit Venice in January. It is a season of mists, of possible floods, of chill winds from the sea; but it is also a time when the city becomes a living entity, devoid of tourists, pursuing its own affairs and, when bathed in cold brilliant sunshine, totally captivating.

The seaside resorts of the region are at their busiest from July 1 through August. For the hill towns of the region, you had better avoid the hot months—May, June and September are the best. The spas, like Abano, Montegrotto, Recoaro, are at their liveliest in August, and continue to be well frequented until the middle of October. The Lake Garda resorts are popular from mid-June to September. The best time of year to visit the art cities of Verona, Padua, Vicenza, and Treviso is spring or fall.

Road Reports

Reaching Venetia by road from almost anywhere is the easiest thing in the world, including coming from England exclusively by motorway via Belgium, Germany and Austria, to come to Lake Garda over the Brenner Pass. And having arrived, all the great names are close by—Verona, Vicenza, Padua, Treviso, Venice—linked by the autostrade. Incidentally, the only thing to do with a car in Venice is to put it in the garage at Piazzale Roma or on one of the parking islands and forget it. The only ways to get around Venice are on foot or by boat.

Food for Thought

Venetian cooking means fish. Generally speaking, it fails to match the almost professional culinary art as practiced in cities like Rome, Florence or Bologna. But the way Venetians prepare fish is something else again. Try *granseole veneziane* (a tasty kind of local crab), prepared Venetian style, or nearby Comacchio Valley eels, served roasted or with sauce. Also delicious here are shrimps *(scampi)*. Meat specialties are *fegato alla veneziana* (fried liver and onions, as cooked by Venetian chefs), and game birds, served with excellent salads of bitter, red radicchio from Treviso. Make certain you sample, too, the *risi e bisi* (a traditional Venetian soup served with rice and peas). Also traditional is the hearty *pasta e fagioli,* a thick and tasty soup. The local *prosciutto di San Daniele* is a variety of the famous Italian dried ham.

The cooking of the entire Veneto Region follows closely the example of its capital city. We might add *gnocchi* and *polenta* as favorites of Venetia in general, especially the hill and mountain sections, where this sort of hearty rib-filling nourishment is more appropriate to the climate than it is to that of humid sea-level Venice. Lake Garda is famous for its trout, along with several other fish specialties. The countryside produces particularly fine grapes, cherries, chestnuts and apples.

For a dry red wine *Bardolino* or *Valpolicella* (the latter has the higher alcohol content of the two); while *Merlot* and *Cabernet* are dry reds from the Friuli region. Dry whites include *Soave Bianco* and *Tocai. Prosecco,* also white, despite its name nudges over towards the sweet side. In addition these regional products are worth trying: *Garganera di Gambellara,* a very white wine of moderate alcoholic content, good for warm-weather drinking; *Recioto,* a sweetish red wine, a trifle heavy, which is grown in the neighborhood of Verona; *Valpentena,* a very dry red wine; *Vini dei Colli Trevigiani,* white, very dry; *Vini dei Colli Euganei,* white and sweet. Try *grappa,* the local aquavit.

Exploring Venice

Count on a bare minimum of three days for Venice; but take a week if possible. The City of Canals, built on a lagoon three miles off the coast, supports 100,000 self-satisfied residents rabbit-warrened into an utterly impossible maze of alleys, palaces, tiny squares, bridges, old churches, hovels, marketplaces and dark waterways so much alike that you won't recognize one from another. It's not a place to hurry through.

Though protected by a seawall against the Adriatic, the high tides continue their inexorable sapping of the city's foundations, flooding the Piazza San Marco ever more often. After examining a host of extravagant plans for a decade and a half—including a rubber barrage cutting the lagoon in half but permitting ships to enter through the three openings at the Lido, at Malamocco and Chioggia—yet another commission has been appointed to study the ecological impact of preventing the tides from sweeping the canals clean. Venice may sink as much under the weight of committee reports as under the weight of water.

Based upon the three-day minimum visit, you might try a rather ambitious itinerary that will cover Venice like a blanket but, at the same time, keep you jumping. If the pace is too quick, concentrate first on Piazza San Marco, the Grand Canal tour, the Lido, the lagoon islands like Murano, Burano and Torcello, possibly picking up the other quarters later.

First Day, the Grand Canal

Up bright and early the first morning, head for the center of the city at Piazza San Marco, where, facing the Cathedral, you turn right to a

Madonna dell'Orto
Casino degli Spiriti
Fondamenta della Sensa
Fonda. d. Madonna dell'Orto
Fondamenta Ormesini
Museo Ebreo
Fondamenta della Misericordia
Abbazia della Misericordia
S.M.d.Servi
Fondamente di Cannaregio
Canal Cannaregio
S.Giobbe
Rio Terra S.Leonardo
Pal.Labia
S.Marcuola
S.Fosca
Ponte della Libertà
Carmelitani Scalzi
Lista di Spagna
S.Geremia
S.Felice
Strada Nuova
S.Stae
Staz.S.Lucia
Canal Grande
S.Simeone Grande
S.Simeone Piccolo
S.Giacomo dell Orio
S.M.Mater Domini
S.Cassiano
S.Chiara
S.Andrea
F. S.Andrea
Piazzale Roma
S Giovanni Evangelista
S.Aponal
S.Polo
I Tolentino
S Maria dei Frari
S.Rocco
Casa d.Goldoni
Riva del Carbon
S.Tomà
S.Pantalon
Pal.Contarini d.Bovolo
Calle d. Mandola
Campo S.Margherita
S.Angelo
S.Fantin
S.Stefano
Teatro La Fenice
Cpo. Morosini
S.Teresa
S.M.d.Carmine
S.Barnaba
S.Nicolò d. Mendicoli
Angelo Raffaele
Calle Avogaria
S.Sebastiano
Ognissanti
S.Trovaso
Chiesa Gesuati
S Agnese
S Gregorio
S.Maria d.Sa
Fondamente delle Zattere
Spirito Santo
Canale d. Giud
Sacca Fisola
S Eufemia
Fondamenta S.Giacomo
La Giudecca
Chiesa del Redentore

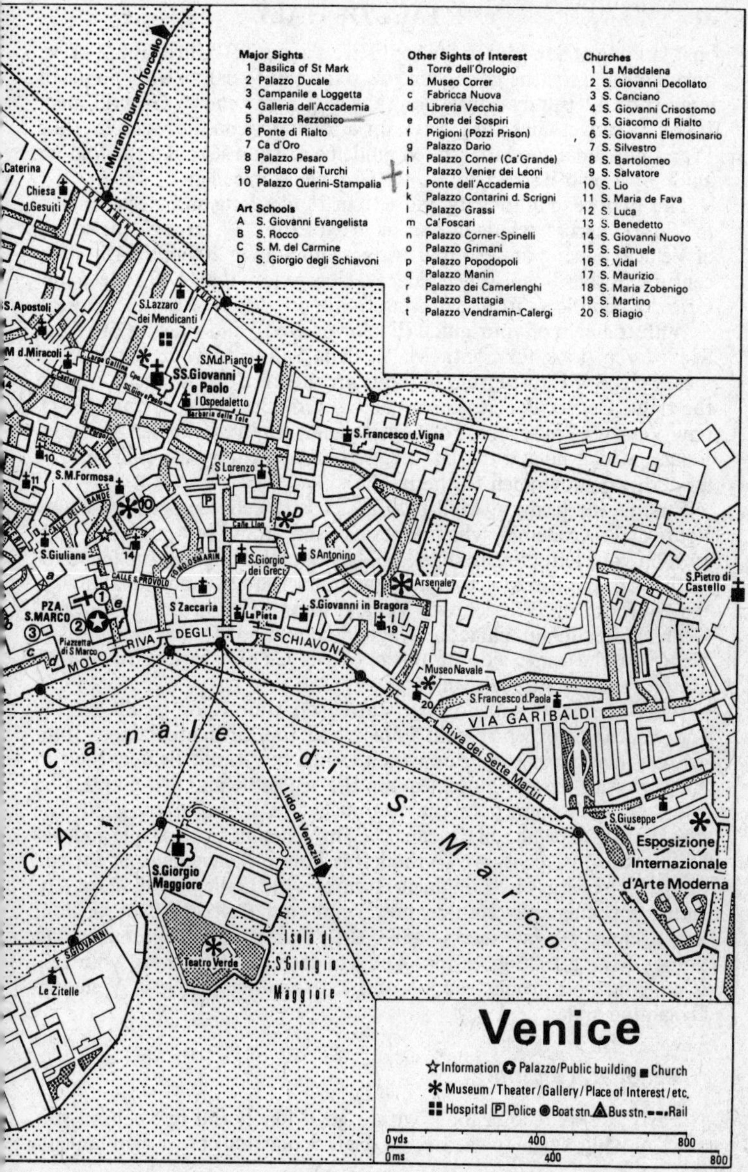

Major Sights
1 Basilica of St Mark
2 Palazzo Ducale
3 Campanile e Loggetta
4 Galleria dell'Accademia
5 Palazzo Rezzonico
6 Ponte di Rialto
7 Ca d'Oro
8 Palazzo Pesaro
9 Fondaco dei Turchi
10 Palazzo Querini-Stampalia
Art Schools
A S. Giovanni Evangelista
B S. Rocco
C S. M. del Carmine
D S. Giorgio degli Schiavoni
Other Sights of Interest
a Torre dell'Orologio
b Museo Correr
c Fabricca Nuova
d Libreria Vecchia
e Ponte dei Sospiri
f Prigioni (Pozzi Prison)
g Palazzo Dario
h Palazzo Corner (Ca'Grande)
i Palazzo Venier dei Leoni
j Ponte dell'Accademia
k Palazzo Contarini d. Scrigni
l Palazzo Grassi
m Ca'Foscari
n Palazzo Corner-Spinelli
o Palazzo Grimani
p Palazzo Popodopoli
q Palazzo Manin
r Palazzo dei Camerlenghi
s Palazzo Battagia
t Palazzo Vendramin-Calergi
Churches
1 La Maddalena
2 S. Giovanni Decollato
3 S. Canciano
4 S. Giovanni Crisostomo
5 S. Giacomo di Rialto
6 S. Giovanni Elemosinario
7 S. Silvestro
8 S. Bartolomeo
9 S. Salvatore
10 S. Lio
11 S. Maria de Fava
12 S. Luca
13 S. Benedetto
14 S. Giovanni Nuovo
15 S. Samuele
16 S. Vidal
17 S. Maurizio
18 S. Maria Zobenigo
19 S. Martino
20 S. Biagio
Murano/Burano/Torcello
Caterina
Chiesa d.Gesuiti
S.Apostoli
S.Lazzaro dei Mendicanti
M d.Miracoli
S.M.d.Pianto
SS.Giovanni e Paolo
I Ospedaletto
S.Francesco d.Vigna
S.M.Formosa
S.Lorenzo
S.Giuliana
S.Giorgio dei Greci
S.Antonino
Arsenale
S.Pietro di Castello
PZA. S.MARCO
S.Zaccaria
La Pietà
S.Giovanni in Bragora
Piazzetta di S.Marco
MOLO
RIVA DEGLI SCHIAVONI
Museo Navale
S.Francesco d.Paola
VIA GARIBALDI
Riva dei Sette Martiri
Canale di S. Marco
Lido di Venezia
S.Giuseppe
Esposizione Internazionale d'Arte Moderna
S.Giorgio Maggiore
Teatro Verde
Isola di S.Giorgio Maggiore
F. S.GIOVANNI
Le Zitelle
Venice
Information
Palazzo/Public building
Church
Museum/Theater/Gallery/Place of Interest/etc.
Hospital
Police
Boat stn.
Bus stn.
Rail
0 yds 400 800
0 ms 400 800

boat landing at San Marco Station. Hire a gondola (be firm about price, duration) and tell the gondolier you want him to call out the points of interest on a leisurely cruise along the length of Venice's Grand Canal. If you're budget-conscious, settle for a round trip on the *vaporetto* (line 1) and pick up a good illustrated guide before you set out—the foldout guide by Lucio Raccanelli, *Canal Grande,* is excellent.

This high road of the city, more than 2 miles long and measuring up to 230 feet across, winds like an inverted letter "S" through the whole of Venice, passing under three bridges and among 200-odd 14th-18th-century Gothic-Renaissance palaces. Never more than 17 feet deep, the Grand Canal flows from San Marco Station with interest all the way.

With the help of your guide (live or printed), and starting out from San Marco, look for Santa Maria della Salute to your left, domed masterpiece of 17th-century baroque architecture by Longhena, and on the right, Corner Palace, known as Ca' Grande, by Sansovino (1537), now Venice's Prefecture. To the left again, you'll see Venier dei Leoni Palace, which houses the late Peggy Guggenheim's vast collection of modern art (now open to the public).

First of the bridges you'll pass under is the contemporary wooden Ponte dell'Accademia, which takes its name from the Accademia Gallery, on your left, treasurehouse of Venetian painting. On the left, a bit farther on, the Rezzonico Palace, begun in 1660 by Longhena, houses the Museum of 17th-century Venice. Next to it, in one of the two Gothic Giustiniani palaces, Wagner composed *Tristan and Isolde.* Next, on the same side of the canal, is Ca' Foscari, 15th-century Gothic, seat of Venice's university.

After the Sant' Angelo boat station on your right, you'll see the 15th-century Corner-Spinelli Palace and the Grimani Palace, 16th-century masterpiece by Sanmicheli. After the Rialto Bridge, built in 1592 by Antonio da Ponte, leaving the vegetable and fish markets on your left, you'll come upon the magnificent Ca' d'Oro, on the right. The most beautiful palace on the canal, it's in Venetian Gothic style and was built in the 15th century. To the left is Pesaro Palace, built at the end of the 17th century by Longhena. It houses the Gallery of Modern Art. In the imposing early 16th-century Vendramin Calergi Palace, on your left, Richard Wagner died in 1883; the palace is the sumptuous winter home of the gambling casino. The Fondaco dei Turchi, on your left, is a century-old reconstruction of a 13th-century palace in Venetian-Byzantine style.

Venetian Lagoon

Early the same afternoon, with a good lunch and rest behind you, start moving again toward Riva degli Schiavoni or the Fondamenta

A decorated cart takes part in the Festival of Sant'Efisio, in Cagliari, Sardinia

The Byzantine influence is to the fore in Stilo, Calabria

The Gothic portal of Cremona Cathedral with one of its stone lions

The attractively painted 16-century Town Hall of Orta San Giulio, Piedmont

Nuova along the northcentral shore of Venice, where steamers leave for a tour of islands like San Michele, Murano, Burano and Torcello, spotted in a wavering line through the Venetian Lagoon.

Using the regular steamer service, it's best to make certain you check departure schedules at each stop *before landing* in order to know when to catch the next boat out. Consider 5 hours for the round trip.

From the Fondamenta Nuova it's a 20-minute run to the first—and smallest—of the islands at San Michele, occupied by Venice's rather unique cemetery and the Church of San Michele in Isola, built in 1478 by Coducci. Make a landing here if you want to visit either cemetery or church; otherwise, the general view of both en route is satisfactory enough. Interestingly, funeral cortèges in Venice become long lines of polished gondolas draped in black velvet and heaped with flowers.

Island No. 2 requires a little time ashore. This is Murano, actually sprawled over five small islands, where the sole major industry—glass-blowing—has been handed down from father to son for generations, making it the source of an art for which Venice has achieved a world-wide fame. Depending upon time available, see the Museo Vetrario (Museum of Works in Glass), a historical collection of glassware in the 17th-century Palazzo Giustiniani; see any of the glass-blowing establishments that extend a hearty welcome to visitors (just walk right in), along Fondamenta dei Vetrai, the main street; and the 12th-century Church of Santa Maria e Donato.

Next stop, at Burano, less than an hour on the direct run by steamer from Venice, you find a small island fishing village that for centuries has been the heart of Venice's lace industry. Here, too, most of the establishments are open to visitors who want to see just how these skilled workers accomplish the beautiful handkerchiefs, shawls, table covers, bed spreads, etc., displayed at slightly higher prices by Venetians in the shops around Piazza San Marco. Don't be fooled though; a lot of the lace on sale comes from China. You can see authentic antique pieces at the Scuola dei Merletti.

Another mile by water ends the trip at Torcello, an island on which the early Venetians first landed in their flight from barbarian hordes many centuries ago. Reportedly, it became the first colony in the Venetian Lagoon area. Torcello's cathedral was built in the 7th century, rebuilt in the 11th, when its majestic bell tower was added. It is worth a visit for its 12th- and 13th-century mosaics.

Second Day, St. Mark's and the Doges' Palace.

On your second morning, take your coffee or tea at one of the spacious outdoor cafés around Piazza San Marco. This is the heart and soul of Venice, an immense, regal square of story and legend, bordered on three sides by palatial arcades in two tiers and faced on the other by the Basilica of St. Mark, one of the world's most magnificent churches.

The mortal remains of the saint, martyred in Alexandria, were brought here by two Venetian merchants. The church was originally built as a shrine for these relics in 838, and reconstructed a century later on a Latin ground-plan. In the 11th century it was completely redone in the Byzantine manner, on a Greek-cross plan, probably inspired by the Church of the Twelve Apostles in Constantinople. The wealthy Venetians had reached the point where they could afford a church matching the splendor of those they had seen in the East.

The result was essentially what you see today: five arched and columned portals, echoed above by an arcaded story surmounting a gallery, and, finally, the five Oriental domes. The little turrets are a Gothic addition.

Inside, the incredible richness of St. Mark's is something you won't forget easily. The whole interior is faced with rare marble below and mosaics on a glittering gold background above. Hollows of the five domes alternate with barrel-like vaults to roof over the inner shape of a Greek cross that characterizes the basilica. Four great arms are divided into aisles by marble colonnades supporting galleries and a museum on the second floor. And wherever you turn, panels, colored mosaics, chapels, a golden altar, entire ceilings of masterpieces build one upon the other for supremacy in beauty and skill. To name only a few of the works, their authors, and precisely where to find them would fill a chapter in any book; English-speaking guides (names from EPT Tourist Office) offer their services at reasonable fees and know their subject well. Among others, don't fail to see the Vault of Paradise, with Titian's *Last Judgement,* and the Pala d'Oro, a 10th-century altarpiece studded with precious gems, old gold and lustrous enamel.

Stepping outside the basilica's central doorway again, turn right, where a stairway leads up past second-floor galleries (excellent view of the church's upper interior here) and a museum to the outer terrace. Here, in the center, are replicas of the four horses of gilded bronze, a Greek work dating from the 3rd century BC which once adorned the Hippodrome of Constantinople; conquering Venetians brought them home in 1207 as a symbol of their triumph and the march of Venice towards its imperial destiny. Of the five great arches you see, four are 17th-century mosaics and the one in the center is framed by Lamberti's 15th-century sculptures.

Walk downstairs now, outside the basilica, and stand before its arched central doorway with your back to it, facing Piazza San Marco. On your left is a bell tower reproduced on the same spot where its original tipped over and collapsed one day in July 1902; inside, an

St.Mark's and The Doges' Palace

Third Floor

1 Scala d'Oro
2 Atrio Quadrato
3 Sala delle Quattro Porte
4 Anticollegio
5 Sala del Collegio
6 Sala del Senato
7 Antichiesetta
8 Chiesetta
9 Sala del Consiglio dei X
10 Sala della Bussola
11 Capi del Consiglio dei X
12 Sala dei Inquisitori
13 Sala d'Armi del Consiglio dei X
14 Scala dei Censori

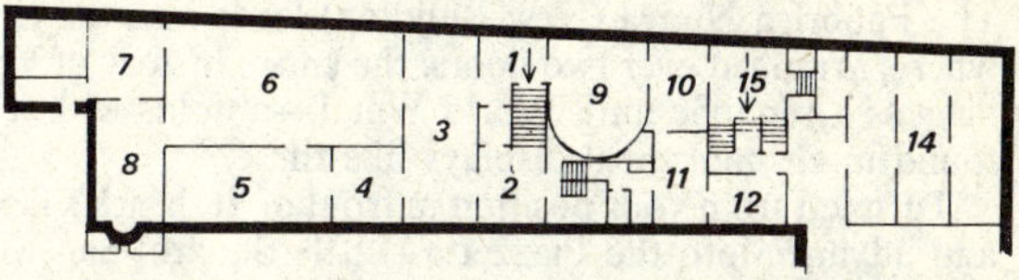

Second Floor

1 Scala d'Oro
2 Sala degli Scarlatti
3 Sala dello Scudo
4 Sala Grimani
5 Sala Erizzo
6 Sala degli Stucchi
7 Sala dei Filosofi
8 Galleria
9 Scala dei Censori
10 Audito
11 Sala della Quarantia Civil Vecchia
12 Sala del Guariento
13 Sala del Maggior Consiglio
14 Sala della Quarantia Civil Nuova
15 Sala del Scrutinio

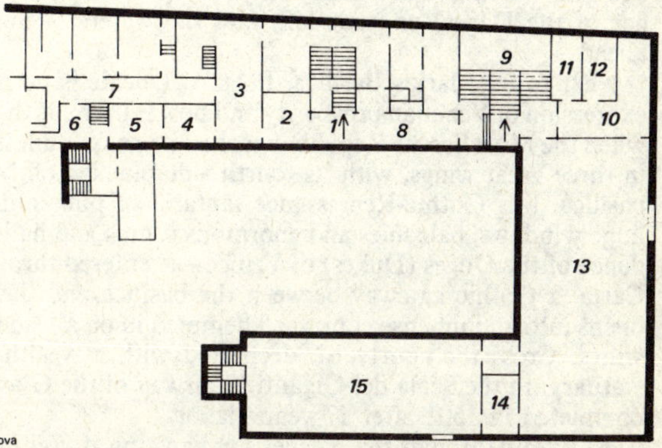

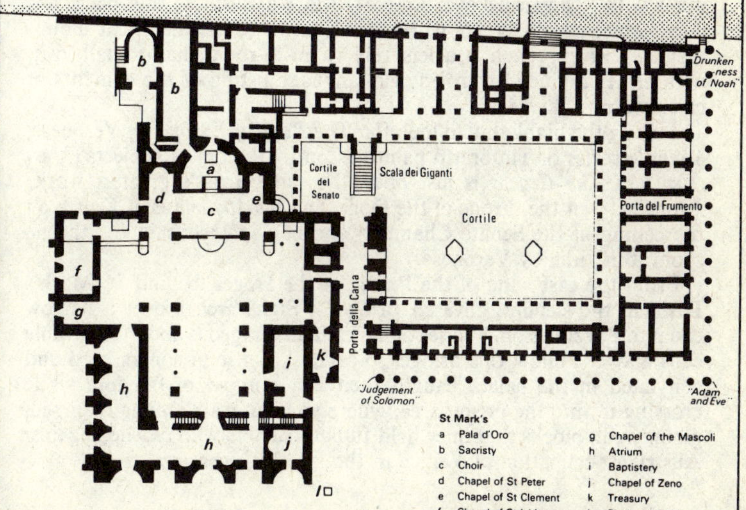

St Mark's

a Pala d'Oro
b Sacristy
c Choir
d Chapel of St Peter
e Chapel of St Clement
f Chapel of St Isidore
g Chapel of the Mascoli
h Atrium
i Baptistery
j Chapel of Zeno
k Treasury
l Pietra del Bando

elevator or stairway takes you to the top for a bird's-eye view of Venice and the lagoon area. Over there on your right, the Torre dell'Orologio (Clock Tower), built in 1496, bears a huge gilded, enameled timepiece. The Fabbrica Nuova (New Building) leads into the Correr Museum, where, arranged over two floors, the entire history of Venice—from its days as a republic until World War I—unfolds with a clarity seldom found in chronological displays like these.

Turn left from your position in front of St. Mark's facing the square, and advance into the Piazzetta (Little Square) San Marco, with the Libreria Vecchia (Old Library on your right, the Palazzo Ducale (Palace of the Doges) on your left, and the waters of St. Mark's Basin ahead.

Next to St. Mark's Basilica, Palazzo Ducale is perhaps the purest expression of Venetian prosperity and power in the 15th-century period when the Most Serene Republic reached its peak. Built like a horseshoe in three great wings, with its fourth side blocked off by a part of the basilica, this Gothic-Renaissance fantasia of pink-and-white marble, huge windows, balconies and enormous rooms and halls—former residence of the Doges (Dukes) of Venice—is entered through Porta della Carta, a Gothic gateway between the basilica and the palace, which opens into an immense courtyard hemmed in on all sides by the palace wings. Cross the courtyard, decorated with a wealth of arches and statuary, to the Scala dei Giganti (Stairway of the Giants), which was completed in 1501 after 17 years' labor.

Any tour through the palace is exhausting if you intend to absorb it all with a lingering eye. Like St. Mark's Basilica, this place has become a treasury of art works, sculptures, relics, historical monuments. Best approach is a leisurely room-to-room, hall-to-hall visit, with either a guide or an English-language listing of the contents of each room.

Among the highlights to look for: *The Rape of Europa* by Veronese; a whole series of Tintoretto paintings on mythological subjects (*Mercury and The Graces* is just one); the same artist's greatest work, *Paradise,* over the throne of the Doge, and his *Apotheosis of Venice* on the ceiling of the Senate Chamber; another *Apotheosis* in the throne room, this time by Veronese.

From the east wing of the Palace of the Doges, behind St. Mark's Basilica, the slender, covered Bridge of Sighs arches over a narrow canal to Pozzi Prison, a series of dark, dank dungeons and more livable cells above. Follow this bridge, so-called because prisoners tried and convicted in the palace caught their last glimpse of freedom while crossing it, into the prison area, where you can walk among cramped, gloomy cell blocks that once held Italian patriots who rebelled against Austrian occupation of Venice in the late 18th century.

Eastern District

Then, passing under the Clock Tower off Piazza San Marco, head into the Merceria, one of Venice's busiest streets, a favorite shopping quarter, which opens the way into the city's eastern district.

Continue along the Merceria to the Church of San Giuliano, then branch off into Calle delle Bande as far as the Church of Santa Maria Formosa, built in 1492 by Coducci. Walk around this church into the Campiello Querini-Stampalia, where a 16th-century palace of the same name has an art gallery open to the public; divided among 20 separate rooms are paintings and frescos by Donato, Palma the Younger, Bellini, Tiepolo, Longhi.

Return to the Church of Santa Maria Formosa now, following Calle di Borgolocco to Campo Santa Maria, where you turn right, cross Ponte di Cristo (Bridge of Christ) and take the Fondamenta Sanudo and Calle Castelli to the Church of Santa Maria dei Miracoli, a 15th-century Venetian Renaissance masterpiece by both the Lombardos that is even more beautiful inside. See the choir of this church in particular; it's covered with rich marble, as are the walls of the entire church.

Outside again, use Calle Gallina to reach Campo dei Santi Giovanni e Paolo, in the center of which stands a tremendous statue of Colleoni on horseback, executed mainly by Verrocchio; it portrays the great Venetian warrior in his fiercest mood; note the eyes and drawn mouth. On the same square, you find the 15th-century Gothic Church of Santi Giovanni e Paolo, which became the burial place of the Doges.

Take Barbaria delle Tole out of the square, continuing along it into Campo Santa Giustina, where you make a right turn into Calle Zon, walk over the bridge there, bear left along the canal, then right to the Church of San Francesco della Vigna, by Sansovino in 1534. From this point, directions—never easy in Venice—become rather difficult. Follow Salizzada di San Francesco and later Salizzada delle Gatte, swerving right from Campo Ugo Foscolo into Calle dei Furlani, where the 16th-century School of San Giorgio degli Schiavoni houses a collection of Carpaccio's most celebrated paintings. Up Calle Lion, across the canal called Rio di San Lorenzo, turn left as far as Ponte dei Greci (Bridge of the Greeks), then right into Fondamenta dell'Osmarin, up the street through Campo San Provolo and finally into Campo San Zaccaria, where Gambello's 15th-century Church of San Zaccaria and 13th-century Romanesque belfry constitute one of the finest churches in Venice. Take time here to look through the chapels and altars for priceless works by Bellini (especially his *Madonna*), Tintoretto and Titian.

Near the church, Sottoportico San Zaccaria leads into Riva degli Schiavoni. Take this avenue to the left, past the little Church of the Pietà, making a left turn after the next bridge into Calle del Doge, which brings you to the magnificent Church of San Giovanni in Bragora, a Gothic 15th-century structure featuring art works inside by Cima and Vivarini.

On Fondamenta dei Penini, the Arsenal, founded in 1104 as an immense dockyard from which the old Republic of Venice fleets put out to sea, still stands within the original walls that defended it. Four carved lions from ancient Greece guard the great Renaissance gateway leading inside the area, where the old *squeri* (docks) used to build Venice's war galleys remain almost intact. Near the entrance to the Arsenal is a fascinating Naval Museum, well worth a visit.

Follow the Riva dei 7 Martiri from here to the Public Gardens of Venice, exposition grounds for the city's International Exhibition of Modern Art that is held here periodically.

Smartest Beach

From the gardens, steamers leave every 10 minutes for the 15-minute trip across the Venetian Lagoon to the Lido. This is one of the most fashionable stretches of sand in Italy, one of the world's best-known seaside playgrounds, and has been so for many decades. It is a swank, chic resort which draws wealth and its hangers-on, season after season. Unless you are a guest at one of the top hotels, you are likely to find the Lido expensive, dull and disappointing.

Off the steamer, walk (buses, if you prefer) straight down Viale Santa Maria Elisabetta, the Lido's main street, which runs past dozens of tastefully decorated hotels, restaurants, villas, outdoor cafés and pensions across the island to end at the wide stretch of sand beyond.

Third Day, Western and Northern Districts

Next day, make a choice. If churches, art, sculpture, and further ramblings through the back streets and along the old canals of Venice continue to interest you, enter the western and northern district of the city, with a side trip to the island suburb of Giudecca. Or, if steamer excursions through the Venetian Lagoon to outlying points appear preferable, divide your day into two trips—morning and afternoon—to the more distant island of Chioggia and the inland village of Stra.

But if you choose the tour of churches, head out of Piazza San Marco on the third morning by way of the Merceria, crossing Rialto Bridge into Venice's western district. Five churches are spotted along the way. You should see these:

Santa Maria Gloriosa dei Frari, near the Rio Terra dei Saoneri, a Gothic structure built between 1338 and 1443 for the Franciscan Order, is one of the city's most beautiful churches. Built like a crucifix, it contains Bellini's magnificent *Madonna and Four Saints,* the Titian masterpiece entitled *Assumption,* and the sculptured tomb of Canova, one of Italy's artistic greats. Here, too, is the Church of San Rocco and, to its left, the School of San Rocco; in the latter are 56 individual paintings by Tintoretto, depicting subjects from both the Old and New Testaments, that are considered some of the greatest works of his long career. Among the highlights: a *Crucifixion* (which *he* thought was best) and an *Annunciation.* An American-based fund has financed their restoration.

Return to Piazza San Marco, then leave for a visit to the southwestern district, passing under the arcades of the Fabbrica Nuova at the far end of the square. Head for Campo Morosini, with its 14th-century Church of Santo Stefano, and see, on nearby Calle della Vida, the Palazzo Contarini del Bovolo, a 15th-century palace with the famed spiral staircase built by Candi. On the other side of the Grand Canal, at one end of the Campo Santa Margherita, is the Gothic Church of Santa Maria dei Carmine and the Scuola Grande dei Carmine, a school in which paintings by Tiepolo and Piazzetta are hung.

From here, follow the Fondamenta del Soccorso, turn left along the Fondamenta San Sebastiano, and arrive shortly at the 16th-century Church of San Sebastiano, well-known among Venetians for its paintings by Veronese, who was buried there in 1588.

The afternoon should find you leaving Piazza San Marco again through the narrow, winding Merceria, past Rialto Bridge (without crossing it this time), into Venice's northern district. Of eight churches en route, center your attention on these:

Church of the Santi Apostoli, on Calle Dolfin; Church of the Madonna dell'Orto, a 15th-century Gothic beauty, where Tintoretto is buried; it's in Calle Largo dei Mori, and was restored with British funds.

Incidentally, passage through the northern district will also bring you to Ponte delle Guglie (Bridge of the Spires), which crosses the Cannaregio, second largest canal in Venice. Turning right just before this bridge, following the Fondamenta, you cross through the old Jewish Ghetto, where there is a fascinating little museum.

If you choose the steamer excursion on this day, make an early morning trip to the Riva degli Schiavone, just off Piazza San Marco, where transportation leaves for the 2-hour, 19-mile cruise across the Venetian Lagoon to Chioggia, a small, old-worldish island at the southern tip of the estuary. It has its own canals, ancient churches, and a 17th-century cathedral built by Longhena in 1674. In all probability, however, you will prefer to ramble about the village, absorbing its atmosphere, with the satisfying knowledge that here—unlike Venice—it's a virtual impossibility to get lost.

Exploring the Venetian Arc

On the southern Venetian plain, a green carpet spotted with low, rolling hills, crops grow luxuriantly. North and south of the plain, a semicircle of gradually ascending plateaus and high meadows rises to the snow-tipped Italian Alps around Cadore and Cordevole. Rivers like the Adige begin up there, flowing down through Venetia to the sea, where ports handle shipborne commerce and fisheries dot the coastline.

But, like the Lazio region and ancient Rome, all of Venetia falls under the historical and spiritual influence of its capital at Venice. Take any city in the sprawling Venetia area—Verona, Vicenza, Padua, Treviso, Belluno, even Rovigo to the south. All repeat in one way or another the grace and refinement of Venice. No lagoons, perhaps, but the architecture, paintings, way of thinking and behaving stem from old Venice and the power she once held over this region.

Venetia, as a region, takes its name from the city of Venice, which, in turn, came into being when the Veneti people fled their mountains and plains for sheltered coastal lagoons to escape the northern barbarian invaders many centuries ago. In time, these ex-farmers and shepherds driven to the sea formed a community on canals, consolidated it, adopted seafaring ways, and created a city that ultimately became a dominant power and an arbiter of culture and the arts.

A Bit of History

The important centers of the Venetia region reflect the rise and fall of Venice, following much the same collective pattern as the region as a whole, but with small differences which account to some extent for their individual historical charm.

Verona, for example, was once an ancient Etruscan village. It grew under the Gauls, became a Roman colony in 89 BC, then rose to power and prosperity within the Roman Empire. The city continued to flourish through the guidance of leaders like Theodoric, Alboin, Pepin and Berenger I, reaching its artistic and cultural peak in the 13th and 14th centuries under the Della Scala family. In 1404, however, Verona sought security by placing itself under the control of Venice, remaining there until 1797, when Napoleon delivered the entire Venetian region to Austria.

Padua has a similar past. Originally called Patavium by the Romans, it enjoyed its heyday under the rule of the Carraresi family between 1319 and 1405, with the entrance of Tuscan Renaissance artists such as Giotto, Filippo Lippi and Donatello, whose works may still be seen in Padua today. In 1405, following Verona's example, Padua, too, sought the protection of Venice. Vicenza (Roman Vicetia) followed much the same course.

World War II touched the Venetia more lightly than many other less fortunate parts of Italy, for Allied armies driving north along the peninsula had not reached the region when Hitler's Germany surrendered. However, heavy Anglo-American bombardments did plaster cities like Treviso and Vicenza late in the war. To the northwest, high in the mountain country around Belluno, headquarters were established for Italian partisan groups which waged a ceaseless guerrilla warfare against German occupation troops.

Padua and Vicenza

The first obligatory trip out of Venice should include the chain of art cities lying westward. You leave via a 2½-mile bridge over the lagoon to reach the industrial suburb of Mestre, then continue for another 18 miles across both the Brenta and Mirano Canals into Padua, with its works of art by Giotto, Donatello and Mantegna.

Padua is worth a one-day stopover if you have the time. Concentrate on the area around Piazza del Santo. Donatello's famed statue of *Gattamelata* and more of his works are to be found inside the Basilica of Sant' Antonio, built between 1232 and 1307 over the tomb of St. Antony of Padua, whose death is still honored each June 13 by pilgrims visiting here from all parts of Italy and many foreign countries. The town's pride, however, is its university, founded in 1222, on Via 8 Febbraio. Additionally, try not to miss the 650-year-old Scrovegni Chapel (frescos by Giotto), on Corso Garibaldi, and the 13th-century Church of the Eremitani.

Another 19 miles out of Padua brings you to the town of Vicenza. Tour the Piazza dei Signori, dominated by Palladio's first major work, the *Basilica Palladiana.* Visit the 14th-century Church of San Lorenzo, with frescos by Montagna and Buonconsiglio, on Corso Fogazzaro. Walk the length of Corso Palladio, named for the artist who built so many of Vicenza's beautiful buildings; 15th-century palaces line the street. The *Teatro Olimpico,* Palladio's last work, is Vicenza's outstanding art treasure and represents an important step both in theater and scenic design.

A 20-minute walk to Monte Bèrico brings you to a baroque church dominating an 18th-century esplanade and bearing art works by Montagna and Veronese. A few minutes away by car lies the Villa Valmarana with its Tiepolo frescos. Not far off stands Palladio's *Villa Rotonda,* whose symmetrical perfection has inspired architects throughout centuries. If you plan to settle in Vicenza for a few days, you might want to run up to Asiago, at 3,300 feet, a summer-winter sports area.

Verona

Verona is perhaps second only to Venice for its classic buildings and medieval monuments. You could spend three or four days here; with time limited, try to see the Arena, Piazza delle Erbe, Tombs of the Scaligeri, the Roman Theater, the cathedral, and the Churches of Sant'Anastasia, San Fermo Maggiore and San Zeno.

The 1st-century Arena, one of the world's largest and best-preserved Roman amphitheaters, borders Piazza Brà, off which Verona's main street, Via Mazzini, leads to Piazza delle Erbe. Open-air opera performances and concerts take place there during the summer months. It comfortably seats 25,000 spectators and is so acoustically perfect that even those in the last row hear clearly. There's also the Horse and Agricultural Fair, Italy's oldest, from March 12–20, when farmers from one end of the peninsula to the other crowd into the city for the nearest thing to an old-time American fair.

The tombs of the Scaligeri honor Verona's one-time ruling Della Scala family. Located just off Piazza dei Signori, with these beautifully-sculptured 14th-century burial places you find the monument to Dante who, when Florence exiled him, was given refuge here by Bartolomeo Della Scala. In the vicinity of Piazza dei Signori, too, is the Church of Sant'Anastasia, built in Gothic style between 1290 and 1481, wherein art works by Pisanello, Montagna and Di Bartolo have been collected. Farther off, through Via Massalongo and Via Duomo, you reach the city's cathedral, a Romanesque church started in 1139, holding art by Sansovino, Sanmicheli and Titian. However, for a study of Veronese painting, it's best to visit Verona's rich Museum of Art, housed in the medieval Castelvecchio, along Corso Cavour. The Biblioteca Capitolare, near the cathedral, is one of the oldest in the world.

Romeo and Juliet? Go to the Via del Pontiere, where, not far off, they charge you a small sum to see what is alleged to be the tomb of Juliet. Or find Via Cappello 17–25, a 13th-century building in which the lovely Juliet Capulet lived. Of Romeo, alas, the landmarks are vaguer.

Approximately 20 miles north of Venice is Treviso, a small town badly damaged by World War II air raids, but well rebuilt. It is a delightful place to wander in; the streets, especially those still containing the old, overhanging houses, having much character. The surrounding ramparts give a fine view of the Alps to the north. See the area around Piazza dei Signori, with its two ancient palaces and tower; the cathedral, housing works by Titian, Bordone, Lombardo; and the

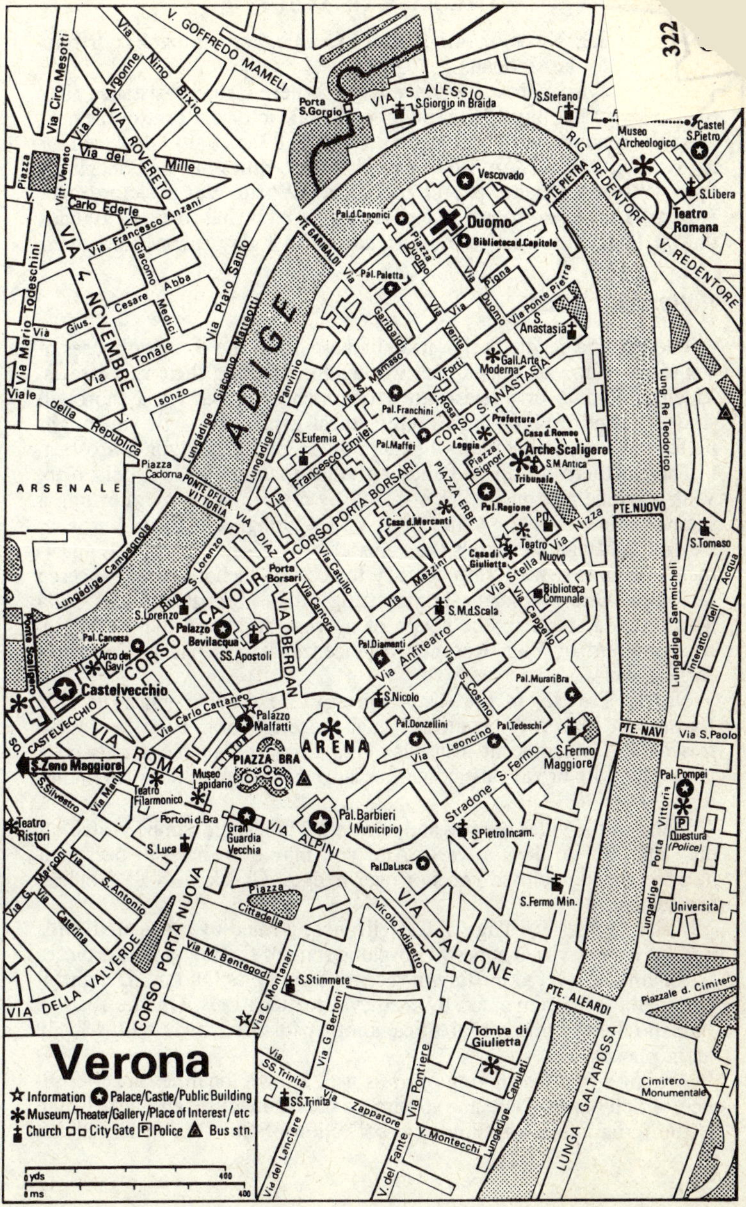
Verona
Information
Palace/Castle/Public Building
Museum/Theater/Gallery/Place of Interest/etc
Church
City Gate
Police
Bus stn.
yds
400
ms
400
ADIGE
ARSENALE
ARENA
PIAZZA BRA
Duomo
Biblioteca d.Capitolo
Vescovado
Pal.d.Canonici
Piazza Duomo
Pal.Paletta
S.Anastasia
Gall.Arte Moderna
Prefettura
Casa d.Romeo
Arche Scaligere
S.M.Antica
Tribunale
Loggia
Piazza Signori
Pal.Regione
Casa d.Mercanti
PIAZZA ERBE
Casa di Giulietta
Teatro Nuovo
Biblioteca Comunale
S.M.d.Scala
Pal.Diamanti
S.Nicolo
Pal.Donzellini
Pal.Tedeschi
Pal.Murari Bra
S.Fermo Maggiore
S.Pietro Incarn.
S.Fermo Min.
Pal.Da Lisca
Pal.Barbieri (Municipio)
Gran Guardia Vecchia
Portoni d.Bra
Museo Lapidario
Teatro Filarmonico
Palazzo Malfatti
Palazzo Bevilacqua
SS.Apostoli
S.Lorenzo
Pal.Canossa
Arco dei Gavi
Castelvecchio
S.Zeno Maggiore
Teatro Ristori
S.Luca
Porta Borsari
S.Eufemia
Pal.Maffei
Pal.Franchini
S.Stimmate
SS.Trinita
Tomba di Giulietta
Cimitero Monumentale
Piazzale d. Cimitero
Universita
Pal.Pompei
Questura (Police)
S.Tomaso
Teatro Romana
S.Libera
Castel S.Pietro
Museo Archeologico
S.Stefano
S.Giorgio in Braida
Porta S.Gorgio
PTE PIETRA
PTE GARIBALDI
PTE.NUOVO
PTE. NAVI
PTE. ALEARDI
PONTE DELLA VITTORIA
Ponte Scaligero
Piazza Cadorna
Piazza Cittadella
CORSO CAVOUR
CORSO PORTA BORSARI
CORSO S.ANASTASIA
CORSO PORTA NUOVA
VIA ROMA
VIA OBERDAN
VIA ALPINI
VIA PALLONE
VIA DELLA VALVERDE
VIA S ALESSIO
V. GOFFREDO MAMELI
VIA ROVERETO
VIA 4 NOVEMBRE
Viale della Republica
Lungadige Campagnola
Lungadige Giacomo Matteotti
LUNGA GALTAROSSA
Lung. Re Teodorico
Lungadige Sammicheli
Lungadige Porta Vittoria
V. REDENTORE
RIG. REDENTORE
Via Anfiteatro
Via Mazzini
Via Cappello
Via Stella
Via Nizza
Via Leoncino
Stradone S. Fermo
Via S.Paolo
Via Carlo Cattaneo
Via G Bertoni
Via Pontiere
Via Zappatore
V. Montecchi
Via C Montanari
Via M. Bentegodi
Vicolo Adigetto
Via Catullo
Via Cantore
Via Diaz
Via Francesco Emilei
Via Garibaldi
Via Duomo
Via Ponte Pietra
Via Verità
Via Pigna
V. Forti
Via dei Mille
Via Ciro Mesotti
Via Mario Todeschini
Via Nino Bixio
Via Piato Santo
Via Francesco Anzani
Carlo Ederle
Piazza Vitt. Veneto
Lungadige Capuleti
Via del Lanciere
V. del Fante
Via S. Antonio
Via Marconi

ıurch of San Niccolo, 14th-century Gothic, containing 40 portraits by Tommaso da Modena.

From Treviso, across the Piave River, where Italian resistance after the October retreat in 1917 brought eventual victory in June of the next year, the road winds into Conegliano, a village Venetians know well for its excellent wines. A railroad branch runs 8 miles out of Conegliano up to Vittorio Veneto, site of the Italian World War I victory over Austro-Hungarian troops; so well remembered is that battle by Italians that at least one street in most Italian cities today carries the name.

Venetian Villas

The Venetia region is rich in Palladian villas, the country houses of Venetians who vacationed here while administering their vast estates. Vicenza, Padua, or Treviso are recommended bases for a thorough study of Andrea Palladio's architectural gems, although you might prefer the smaller hamlets—Bassano di Grappa, Asolo, or Marostica.

The northern group of Palladian villas includes Villa Godi-Porto, Villa Piovene at Lonedo, approached by a steep stairway affording a splendid view over the valley, and Villa Caldogno, with its Veronese frescos. At Bagnolo there's the colossal Villa Pisani, its endless apartments decorated with 18th-century frescos by Tiepolo and Francesco Simonini. One of the most interesting villas in this region is Villa Malcontenta, built in the shape of a cross and topped by a dome. Remisniscent of Villa Rotonda in Vicenza, it was one of Palladio's earliest works.

Nearer Treviso, in the eastern group of Palladian villas, is Villa Barbaro at Maser. A beautiful Renaissance creation, it has Veronese frescos and magnificent grounds. Villa Emo at Fanzolo stands on a wide plain, its broad portico and arcades blending with its surroundings.

Many of the villas are privately owned, while some can be visited on only one or two days a week. And you may even have to peer at a number through closed gates or over hedges. Check with EPT offices for details.

Visit the nearby village of Castelfranco, girdled by crenelated walls and by water, with a superb Giorgione (one of the many masterpieces stolen and recovered in Italy in recent years) in its Duomo. Delightful Cittadella is encompassed by medieval fortifications. On the road to Bassano del Grappa is Marostica, another fortified town, with a lively main piazza.

Among other fascinating but less well-known localities are Monselice, which boasts some fine specimens of architecture, and near which is the remarkable ornithological collection of Ca' Odi; Montagnana, surrounded by a mile of wall, with 24 towers and a number of fortified gates, where you can see a fine *Transfiguration* by Veronese; Valsanzibo, near Montagnana, where the beautiful Villa Dona delle Rose basks in the sun; Adria, once an Etruscan city, which contains relics of those times; Asolo, whose beauty made it a favorite of Robert Browning; Soave, an enchanting wine center; and Costozza, the site of a series of curious grottos.

Sun, Sea and Lake

In summer, however, the beaches are almost as great an attraction as the art cities. Venice's Lido is one of Europe's most famous sand strips, but it is expensive. If you want to economize, you can take a ferry to Punta Sabbioni and enjoy the miles and miles of fine sand stretching to and beyond Lido di Jesolo. This stretch of coast is heavily developed for mass tourism, though both the state of the sea and atmosphere leaves much to be desired. Lido di Jesolo itself is a popular spot for package tours.

There is another good sand beach at Sottomarina, just beyond Chioggia, but it is not very well equipped. If you prefer fresh water to salt, Italy's largest lake, Lake Garda, is partly in Venetia—Peschiera, Bardolino, Garda, and Malcesine are favorite vacation spots on its eastern shore.

PRACTICAL INFORMATION FOR VENICE

HOTELS are no problem in Venice. A city which seems sometimes to contain no buildings other than palaces, it has converted many of them into hotels. When you go to a palace hotel in Venice, you can take the term literally. There is an instant telephone hotel reservation service at the railroad station. If you plan to stay in Venice no less than 7 days, you'll find carefree comfort in the CIGA chain's apartment-hotel, *Palazzo del Giglio,* where rates are scaled according to length of stay. *CIGA Venice Club* offers CIGA guests exchange privileges at hotel restaurants, beaches, pools; discounts on entertainments, excursions, shops.

Deluxe (L)

Danieli Royal Excelsior. The favorite among Anglo-Saxon tourists seems to be this hotel, and with good reason. It has a superb location cheek by jowl with the Doge's Palace on the Riva degli Schiavoni, looking across the lagoon to the Campanile of San Giorgio Maggiore on its private island, and with gondolas and boat landing stages just in front of it. Pleasant lounges, good food on a terrace commanding that wonderful view, and service is swift and pleasant. Airconditioned throughout. A CIGA hotel.

Bauer Grundwald shares with the Danieli the distinction of being the largest in the city. Its spacious, well-furnished rooms all have bath. Modern, elegant. Terrace restaurant on Grand Canal, roof garden for summer dancing. Swift, courteous service.

Cipriani, on tip of the Guidecca overlooking the lagoon. Five minutes from St. Mark's Square by boat provided by hotel. All rooms with bath, airconditioned, gardens and terrace restaurant. Furnished in classic Venetian style. Hotel guests use exclusive *Sea Gull Club's* pool, bar, discothèque. Open 1 April–21 Oct. Venice's smartest hotel.

Gritti Palace, of Ernest Hemingway fame, preferred by those who like a smaller, quieter hotel. It is a place of distinction, mostly suites, and all rooms have bath. Beautifully appointed, excellent management. Entirely airconditioned. Second only to Cipriani in expense. Offers gourmet cooking course, famous guest chefs. CIGA hotel.

First Class (1)

Europa e Regina, on Grand Canal, twin CIGA hotels; ample, well-furnished rooms, dining terrace. Caters to groups.

Gabrielli-Sandwirth, on Riva degli Schiavoni, overlooks lagoon, most rooms with bath, garden court; half-pension terms get you room with view.

Londra, Riva degli Schiavoni, completely renovated, attractive though smallish rooms, terrace restaurant, same impeccable management as Metropole.

Metropole, Riva degli Schiavoni, overlooking lagoon, large, airconditioned, comfortable rooms beautifully furnished in Venetian style, attentive service, excellent and recommended, some noise in front rooms from tugboats.

Monaco e Gran Canale, on Grand Canal, near St. Mark's bright, comfortable rooms, airconditioned, canal-side dining.

Park Hotel, no motor boat or gondola required to reach this hotel as it is two steps from the parking area of the only road leading from the mainland to Venice. Friendly atmosphere, American Bar, airconditioning.

Saturnia Internazionale, near Piazza San Marco, in elegant Renaissance palace, with tasteful furnishings, airconditioning, renovated, all rooms with bath, good atmosphere. Excellent restaurants (see list).

Luna, just off Piazza San Marco, an old favorite, dated decor, good service.

Moderate (2)

Hotels in this category are still good in Venice—there are none without at least some rooms with bath.

Bisanzio, Calle Bosell, quiet, rather elegant; or **Savoia e Jolanda,** on Riva degli Schiavoni.

Concordia, right at San Marco, rooms furnished in Venetian style, most with private bath; friendly service and personalized attention. Recommended.

La Fenice, central, is charming place with attractive rooms, most with bath, and pretty garden court.

Bonvecchiati has vine-covered terrace restaurant, but is erratically furnished in various styles.

Another top choice is **Cavaletto e Doge Orseolo,** comfortable, attractive, on side canal near San Marco.

If you like a small hotel, the **Patria Tre Rose,** Calle dei Fabbri, and **All' Angelo,** Calle Larga San Marco are fine, central. **Do Pozzi** and **Flora** are delightful.

Principe and **De la Ville e Austria,** both on Lista di Spagna, near station, are a bit out of the way.

MESTRE. If you haven't a hotel reservation in Venice, your best bet may be to stay at Mestre, on the mainland. The **Plaza, Tritone, Ambasciatori,** all (2), are among the best. It is only a 20-minute trolley bus ride to Venice.

Inexpensive (3)

Among the most comfortable are **Rialto,** San Marco 5147; **Malibran,** San Giovanni Crisostomo 5866, and **Paganelli,** enviable location on Riva degli Schiavoni, with terrace restaurant, view.

Smaller are 21-room **Teson,** Castello 3980, clean and quiet; the 17-room **Leonardo,** at San Leonardo 1385; and **Graspo de Ua,** San Marco 5094.

Pensions (P)

There are no first-class pensions in Venice proper and just one in the immediate vicinity: **Locanda Cipriani,** Isola di Torcello 17, 6 double rooms, airconditioned, 15 March–24 Oct., exceptional ambience, cuisine.

Also good, **Seguso** (P2), at Zattere, opposite the Giudecca Channel. **Bucintoro** (P3), Riva degli Schiavoni, 25 rooms, all with view of lagoon, no lift.

Casa Frollo (P3), on the Giudecca, is highly recommended. Large rooms in 17th-century villa.

RESTAURANTS

Expensive (E)

(Prices average about 10,000 lire higher than elsewhere.)

Antico Martini is a famous restaurant at Campo San Fantin 1981; also a nightclub with dancing from 10 P.M. A restaurant for the last 200 years, it's located in a historic palace, and is noted for *cannelloni* and fillet of sole. In summer you may dine in its courtyard. Closed for lunch.

Cipriani, new (1979) terrace restaurant in the famed Hotel Cipriani on the Giudecca; reserve. Piano bar, poolside bar and grill; free launch service from San Marco.

Caravella of Saturnia Internazionale hotel, superlative cuisine, especially *scampi* in an infinite variety of sauces, *crêpes Mona* for dessert. Old sailing ship atmosphere. Reserve.

Cortile, also in Saturnia Internazionale, attractive outdoor setting, fine food, slightly less expensive.

Harry's Bar, a nostalgic favorite with Americans and an Italian reputation for good food (especially *risotto* and shrimp dishes), same ownership as Locanda Cipriani, offers motorboat excursion to Torcello that includes lunch at the Locanda. Boat leaves at noon from Harry's.

On the island of **Torcello,** the distinguished pension, **Locanda Cipriani,** has fine specialties: *gnocchi, zuppa di pesce* and *risotto di pesce* served at tables under a grape arbor.

La Colomba is another standout at Frezzeria 1665, with seven dining rooms hung with modern paintings. Has been getting increasingly touristy and crowded.

Quadri, luxuriously furnished, in Piazza San Marco, is widely known for its exquisite food, attracts a very elegant crowd.

Taverna La Fenice, is one of Venice's truly outstanding eating places. Try their justly famous dessert of flaming peaches filled with toasted almonds.

Moderate (M)

All' Angelo, San Marco 404 (beware, *not piazza*), is highly regarded for both food and atmosphere.

Alla Quaglia, Cannaregio 4518, near Santi Apostoli, specializes in a unique pasta, *bigoli.*

Café Florian, Piazza San Marco, drips with old-world atmosphere, very popular, plush meeting place.

Graspo de Uva, San Bartolomeo 5094, offers an especially good antipasto, but otherwise overrated.

La Madonna, Calle della Madonna 594, is *the* place for seafood.

Da Ivo, small, rather elegant "trattoria" between Piazza San Marco and Campo San Luca, good food.

Others in this rank include **Al Gambero** and **All'Antica Carbonera, Vecchie Poste, Da Fiore,** near San Giacomo dell'Orio, and **Fiaschetteria Toscana,** Campo S. Giovanni Crisostomo.

The Islands: On **Murano,** *Ai Vetrai, Ai Frati, Al Corallo,* all (M), good, simple food; on **Mazzorbo,** *La Maddalena,* garden dining, fish specialties; on **Burano,** very good, is *Romano,* near Piazza Galuppi, for *risotto misto* with shellfish and *fritto misto,* tasty fish fry; *Pescatori,* for more fish.

Hotel Restaurants

These are seldom exciting, but exceptions often make the rule.

All (E)—and exceptions must be made in Venice for the terrace restaurants of the **Danieli** and of the **Gritti Palace** overlooking the Grand Canal, and the outstanding cuisine and view of the **Cipriani** on the Guidecca.

The **Gritti Palace** bar serves informal lunch or dinner at prices much lower than in the dining room.

Trattorias

Mostly moderately expensive, there are some fine ones here, among them—**Taverna dei Dogi** and **Al Malibran,** at San Giovanni Crisostomo; **Da Mondo,** Calle Racchetta 3728; Venetian cooking at **Nono Risorto,** San Cassiano 2337, and **Noemi,** Calle dei Fabbri 909; **Simionato Mario,** Calle delle Rasse; **Montin,** Fondamenta Eremiti; **Sottoprova,** Ponte delle Cadene; **Antica Latteria,** Calle Fuseri; **Pizzeria al Teatro,** at La Fenice. **Al Campanile,** just off Campo San Polo, reader-recommended for fine cooking by wife of English-speaking owner.

Wine cellar *(Enoteca):* **Al Volto,** Calla Cavalli, at Campo San Bartolomeo, more than 1,000 wines to sample, light snacks to help keep you sober.

CHURCHES. Important churches are usually open from 7 A.M. to noon and again in late afternoon. Many open only during services.

MUSEUMS. Though many insist the entire city of Venice is itself the finest museum, you will not want to miss the following outstanding collections of art. Hours are subject to change, so check at your hotel.

Accademia delle Belle Arti, in Convent and Church of Santa Maria Della Carità, on Grand Canal. The great Venetian painters.

Correr Museum, entrance under portico dell' Ascensione, on west side of Piazza San Marco. History of Venice.

Pesaro Palace, left bank of Grand Canal. Oriental and Modern art.

Querini-Stampalia Palace, near Church of Santa Maria Formosa. Art Gallery and library.

Rezzonico Palace, left bank of Grand Canal. Decorative arts, works by Guardi, Longhi, Tiepolo.

Scuola del Carmini, opposite church of same name, Tiepolo and others.

Scuola degli Schiavoni, far off in east section not far from Naval Museum. Carpaccio is the star here, in a Renaissance oratory.

Scuola di San Rocco, opposite Santa Maria Gloriosa dei Frari, 56 works by Tintoretto in beautiful 16th-century building. Great Hall is masterpiece.

Veneir dei Leoni Palace, left of the Salute. Magnificent home of the Peggy Guggenheim collection; highly recommended.

Museo Vetrario, Murano's famed glass museum, re-opened after extensive restoration; glass objects from Roman times onward.

NIGHTLIFE. *Antico Martini* restaurant is also a nightclub with dancing from 10 P.M.

From November to March, the *Casino* is open at Palazzo Vendramin Calergi, and it's well worth a visit, if only for its sumptuous decor. There's an entrance fee and a passport is required for entrance to gaming rooms. In the summer, it moves to the Lido.

SHOPPING. Venetian glassware is as famous as the city's gondolas, and from your first stroll around St. Mark's Square you will be engulfed with displays of it. Venice does make beautiful glass, but there is also a good deal of bad glass on hand, so you will do well to orient yourself before buying. Don't be discouraged by the mediocre examples you may see in window displays, or touted around with "no obligation to buy".

The trip to the glass-blowing center of **Murano** is classic, and you might want to take it and look around carefully before you invest. But *we do not* recommend buying *at* Murano *itself,* wait till you get back to Venice proper.

Ignore the self-styled "official" shills offering trips to glass and lace factories —use the *vaporetto,* line 5, to Murano.

In Murano, visit *Società Veneziana Conterie e Cristallerie* at 34 Fondamenta Navagero. *Venini* also has his own factory in Murano at 50 Fondamenta Vetrai.

In Venice, visit *Salviati & Co.,* San Gregorio 195, and Piazza San Marco 79B and 110; or *Venini* at Piazzetta Leoncini 314. You might also visit *Cenedese,* Calle San Gregorio, near San Maria della Salute, or the shop above *San Gallo* hotel, *Campo San Gallo.* To see the fashioning of Venetian glass beads go to *Mario Sanzogno* behind St. Mark's cathedral at Calle Canonica 338. *Venezia Mario,* Campo SS. Filippo e Giacomo, Calle Albanesi 42/38 has costume jewelry and Venetian beads.

Venetian lace is exquisite—and also very expensive—but whether you are in the mood to buy or merely want to look at lace and linens visit *Jesurum & Co.,* established in an old former convent just behind St. Mark's cathedral at Ponte Canonica 4310, or take another island visit—to **Burano,** famed for its needlepoint. Almost no lace is made in Venice any more, a lot of what you see is imported from abroad.

Lorenzo Rubelli & Figlio's shop, with a luscious display of precious velvets and velvet brocades, is located at Campo San Gallo 1091, right behind Piazza San Marco.

SPECIAL EVENTS. Art and cultural celebrations fit well into the May, September–October touring schedule. Realizing the disadvantages of its climate, Venice has scheduled its outstanding events for the beginning and end of the more usual tourist season, to avoid the hottest months. The International Biennial Committee now operates year-round, sponsoring shows and events in all the arts, in Venice's innumerable piazzas and palazzi.

The late summer-fall season gets under way about two-thirds of the way through August with a night fête on the Grand Canal. In September, that time of year known as the Musical Autumn opens in Venice with an historical regatta on the Canal, followed by everything from sports events (tennis, horse racing, pigeon shoots) through bridge and dancing competitions to the more serious business of symphonic concerts, theatrical performances and international music festivals. For many of these, the scene is the 158-year-old La Fenice Theater, where *Rigoletto* and *Traviata* were first performed—but December to May is the normal season.

Two traditional events outside the suggested May, September–October calendar—both commemorating the end of medieval plagues in Venice—truly capture the spirit of the city on festive occasions. More important is the Feast of the Redeemer, held on the third Sunday in July, which recalls the time in 1576 when Venetians who survived a particularly devastating plague built the Church of the Redeemer, which stands on Fondamenta San Giacomo, in the suburb of Giudecca. Venetians and visitors flock to the church for a day of worship, feasting and carnival that invariably ends with a regatta in which all the boatmen appear in local costume.

The other, less spectacular, occasion falls on November 21, the Feast of the Madonna della Salute, when solemn religious rites take place in the Church of Santa Maria della Salute, just off the Zattere quay, built in 1631 as a token of gratitude from the Venetian Republic's Senate and people for the end of a plague one year earlier.

Carnival in Venice—usually in February—is uniquely colorful.

TRANSPORT. By Train: Venice railway station looks like any other, and it's quite a shock for the first-time visitor to step out of a bustling train-filled station and instead of the customary street traffic of a city square to find himself in danger of walking straight down the station steps into the Grand Canal, at whose west end the station is located. You take a *gondola,* a *motoscafo* (motorboat) or a *vaporetto* (small steamboat) to your hotel.

By Air: take an airport bus (about 2,000 lire) to Piazzale Roma (rail station) or the Cooperativa San Marco motorboat service (about 6,500 lire per person) to San Marco, unless you plan to stay at one of the Lido hotels. (There are Air Taxis from Marco Polo Airport to the Lido.)

By Car: the motorist reaches Venice by a causeway and then must park his car either in the already crowded street or in the huge garage at Piazzale Roma or Tronchetto parking island (about 1,000 lire per day), or at the newer, cheaper terminals of Fusina or San Giuliano, from which you take a vaporetto to center.

You cannot drive in Venice. Most of the streets are water, and those that aren't are always running up and down steps over the city's hump-backed bridges. You can take your car to the Lido, however, on the car ferry that leaves from the Tronchetto landing stage.

Porters' charges are fixed according to a rather involved schedule, depending on the distance, number of bags, etc. For example, between any two points within the center of town (bounded by the railway station and Piazzale Roma), you pay 3,000 lire for one or two bags, 800 for each additional one. There's a 1,500 lire surcharge for night service.

Gondolas can be expensive; inquire at your hotel or at local tourist office for current rates, and come to terms with the gondolier before you set out. You can figure on at least 25,000 lire for a minimum of 50 minutes for 1–6 persons, 25% surcharge after 7 P.M.

Water taxis also are expensive, about 10,000 lire for groups up to 5 persons for a short ride.

Vaporetto fare is from 600–1,000 lire. After 10 P.M., a supplement of 25–30 percent is applied to all public transport, including gondolas. You can buy a tourist ticket for the vaporettos for 4,000 lire, valid for 24 hours.

For island hopping, get a copy of the timetable published by ACNIL, the water bus company, sold at most ticket booths on the landing stages. Remember that most everything on the islands closes from noon to about 2:30, so plan your day accordingly.

CIT offers two 2-hour tours of Venice, one on foot and one by gondola; a 3-hour excursion to **Murano** by motorlaunch; a full-day tour of the Venetian villas by motorcoach; and the delightful full-day *Burchiello* motorlaunch cruise up the Brenta River to **Padua** (back by bus).

USEFUL ADDRESSES. *American Express,* San Moise 1474 (tel. 700 844). *British Consulate,* Accademia 1051. *CIT,* Piazza San Marco, 48 (tel. 85 480).

Tourist Offices: AAST, Rialto 4089: EPT, Castello, Calle del Remedio 4421; San Marco, Ascensione 71C; Santa Lucia Railway Station: and Piazzale Roma 540D (summer only).

VENICE LIDO

Venice Lido is more expensive than Venice Proper. The beach is on the far side, 15 minutes by steamer from Venice—Riva degli Schiavoni, or Public Gardens. A ferry boat service for cars operates from the mainland—Piazzale Roma, motor road terminal—to the Lido.

Beach facilities range from those of the *Excelsior Palace,* open to transient sunseekers at a price, to the free beach at the other end of the Lido, a 10 minute hike from the end of the bus line.

HOTELS. Lido hotels are, with few exceptions, open only during the season, from April or May through September or October. High season, 1 July–15 Sept.

Deluxe (L)

Excelsior Palace, Lungomare Marconi 41, is the only deluxe hotel, stands on the beach itself, has 257 rooms most with bath, airconditioned, open 1 May–30 Sept. Outstanding hotel that made the Lido world-famous, with its spacious, fashionable private beach. Modern decor in rooms and suites, night-club with disco, pool, tennis, CIGA hotel.

First Class (1)

Just back from the beach is the older **Grand Hotel des Bains e Palazzo al Mare,** Lungomare Marconi 17, 303 large, well-furnished rooms, most with bath, airconditioned. Ideally situated between the sea and its own park, directly connected with its private beach by an under-passage, swimming pool. **Pagoda** restaurant on shore. Another CIGA hotel.

Moderate (2)

Petit Palais is expensive, comfortable, with private beach.

One of the most expensive moderate hotels is **Quattro Fontane,** most rooms with bath, tennis courts, open 1 April–30 Sept.

Helvetia, most rooms with bath, beach facilities, open 1 April–30 Sept.

Capelli-Wagner is large, airconditioned, has beach facilities.

Villa Mapaba, attractive, garden, lift and bar.

Villa Otello, Riviera are closed Oct.–March. Very expensive are the new **Adria Urania,** with pleasant twin villa-hotel, **Villa Nora,** both quiet, a short walk from own beach area.

Inexpensive (3)

Of the many inexpensive hotels, the best are **Atlanta** and **Buon Pesce,** which has good number of private baths.

Pensions (P)

Pensions on the Lido begin at (P2), with **La Meridiana, Albertina** and **Villa Laguna** being the most obvious choices.

RESTAURANTS. All (E)—try **Gino,** or **Belvedere,** on Piazzale Santa Maria Elisabetta. At noon, **La Taverna,** across from beach; keep check to a (relative) minimum by lunching on 17 kinds of antipasto and house wine.

At **Aberoni** try **Tavernetta Gransevola. Da Valentino** (M), Via San Gallo.

NIGHTLIFE. *Excelsior Palace* has a nightclub with disco, and the *Casino* moves from Venice to a summer home on the Lido in March.

SPORTS. There's a good 18-hole golf course at **Alberoni,** at the southernmost end of the Lido, and golfers might also like to try the *Vianello* (3), Via Ca'Rosso, 20-room hotel hard by the links.

PRACTICAL INFORMATION FOR THE VENETIAN ARC

HOTELS AND RESTAURANTS

Abano Terme. Leading spa. **Hotels:** Deluxe—*Royal Orologio,* Viale delle Terme, elegant, comfortable, airconditioned, spa treatments at hotel, swimming pool, tennis court, garage, closed Nov.–March.

All (1) are—*La Résidence,* modern, central, in large garden, all rooms soundproofed, with all amenities including stereo and terrace, closed 8 Jan.–8 Feb., roof garden, thermal pools; *Trieste Victoria,* also in center, older hotel, comfortable, well-furnished rooms, closed 10 Nov.–31 March, thermal pools, gardens; *Bristol Buja,* large, central location, well-appointed, airconditioned rooms with bath or shower, balcony, thermal pools, tennis, minigolf.

All (2) are—*Ritz,* 151 rooms, very pleasant; *Ariston Molino,* all rooms with bath or shower, swimming pool; *Terme Torino,* many rooms with bath, swimming pool, tennis court, garage, spa treatments.

All (3) are—*All' Alba,* swimming pool, spa treatments at hotel; *Salvignini,* central, swimming pool, spa treatments at hotel; *Igea Suisse,* pool, spa treatments at hotel.

Asiago. Summer and winter resort. **Hotels:** *Linta Park* (1), best, outside center, with fine view, bright, modern decor, all rooms with bath or shower, indoor pool.

Both (2)—*Croce Bianca,* traditional older hotel on main street, basic rooms, all with bath or shower, cosy bar; *Paradiso,* comfortable, medium-sized hotel in town.

Miramonti (3), at Kaberlaba ski runs, small hotel with good views.

Restaurant: *Casa Rossa* (M), at Kaberlaba, rustic.

Asolo. Hotel/Restaurant: *Villa Cipriani* (1E), excellent, elegant, only 32 well-furnished rooms in handsome building a few steps from picturesque piazza, romantic garden with beautiful view, garage, famed for outstanding cuisine in lovely setting. A CIGA hotel, reserve well in advance.

Restaurants: Both (M)—*Due Mori,* hearty, family-run trattoria; *Casonetto,* 1½ miles north. *Charly's One* (E), in town, good food, atmosphere.

Bassano del Grappa. Picturesque town, famous ceramic center. **Hotels:** *Belvedere* (2), on busy main road, short walk from all sights, comfortable, clean, ask for a quiet room.

Restaurants: All (M)—*Al Sole,* Via Vitorelli, traditional setting for Bassano's white asparagus in springtime, other specialties year round; *Amicizia,* another unhurried place where everthing is cooked to order; *Al Ponte,* overlooking famous bridge, specializes in fish.

Bosco Chiesanuova. Summer and winter sports resort. **Hotel:** Best is the modest *Fraccaroli* (3).

Chioggia. Picturesque island fishing town, simple by tourist standards. **Hotel/Restaurant:** In town itself, *Grande Italia* (2), Piazza Vigo, modest hotel, overlooking the lagoon, is *the* place for fish.

At **Sottomarina** beach: Both (2) are—*Ritz* and more modest *Capinera.* All (3) are—*Anzoletti, Capo Est* and *Florida.* All have beach facilities.

Restaurants: All (M-E)—*Speranza Nino,* on the Corso, rich *zuppa di pesce* at sidewalk tables; *El Gato,* very good. *La Piazzetta,* for authentic local specialties.

Conegliano. Art town. **Hotels:** Both (2) are—*Cristallo* and *Canon d'Oro.*

Restaurants. All (M), with good local dishes—*Tre Panoce,* garden; *Cima; Canon d'Oro,* historic building.

Garda. Lakeside summer resort. **Hotels:** *Eurotel* (1), most expensive, modern, all rooms with bath, airconditioned, swimming pool, private garden.

All (2) are—*Regina Adelaide,* good; *Flora,* attractive, comfortable, pool; *Locanda San Vigilio,* tiny, picturesque, good food.

Both (3)—*Marco Polo,* pool; and *La Perla,* pool, good value.

Restaurant: *Beati* (M), outside town, good food in old mill.

Giavera del Montello. Near Solighetto and Treviso. **Restaurants:** A real gem, *Agnoletti* (M), an inn since the 17th century, mushrooms in infinite variety and wine made by the host himself. If it's closed, go to *Bazzichet* (I), simple but good.

Lido di Jesolo. Popular beach resort. Many package tours. **Hotels:** Most hotels (2) and (3) are closed October–April.

Las Vegas (1), large modern hotel right on beach, functional bedrooms, all with balcony and sea view, terraces, pool. At Pineta, *Bellevue* (1), on beach, has pool, tennis, all rooms with shower.

All (2) are—*Beau Rivage,* Località Jesolo Pineta, tennis court; *Elpiro,* spacious, well-furnished, beach; *Majestic,* all rooms with shower, on the beach; *Byron Bellavista,* on beach, swimming pool; *Oxford,* on beach, modern, all rooms with bath, efficient and pleasant, unpretentious; *Cambridge,* all rooms with bath and balcony, on beach.

All (3)—*Ancora, Milton* and *American,* all new, all rooms with bath.

Limone sul Garda. Atmospheric lakeside town on Lake Garda, a favorite with artists. **Hotels:** Both (2), open May–Sept.—*Capo Reamol,* on lake, pool, terraces, all rooms with showers; *Roxy Park,* same amenities.

Both (3)—*Lido,* 26 rooms with shower, on lakeshore, closed 1 Oct.–10 May; *San Giorgio,* new, pool, bungalows.

Malcesine. One of the most important of the Lake Garda resorts. **Hotels:** All (2) are—*Vega,* on lakeside, with bathing area, fine view, central, sun deck, very good, radio and TV in rooms; opposite, on central square, is *Malcesine,* attractive villa-type, all rooms with bath or shower, swimming off lakeside terrace, garden, closed mid-Oct.–March; *Du Lac,* modern, overlooks lakeside promenade at southern end of town, closed mid-Oct.–March; *Excelsior Bay,* lakeside, a few minutes from town center, comfortable bedrooms with bath or shower, balcony, good-sized pool, garden.

Sirena (3), overlooking lake, has beach facilities.

Marostica. Restaurants: In incomparable setting of medieval castle above town *Taverna de Marostega* (M), offers such specialties as *roast turkey* with *pomegranate sauce.* Avoid on Sundays.

In town, *Scacchiera* (I–M), just off famous piazza.

Maser. Site of beautiful Villa Barbaro, frescoed by Veronese. Eat at nearby **Cornuda,** *Cavallino* and *Brotto,* both (M–E), seafood restaurants.

Montecchio Maggiore. You go to Montecchio Maggiore expressly to eat there, driving out from Vicenza, around 8 miles along the Verona road. **Restaurant:** *Romeo and Juliet Medieval Tavern* (E), is located in the ruins of two old fortresses, ascribed by local legend to the Montague and Capulet families, breathtaking panorama.

Montegrotto Terme. Spa. **Hotels:** Both (1) are—*Tergesteo,* large, elegantly modern hotel, well-furnished rooms, posh salons, all spa amenities, thermal pools; *Bertha International,* a little less expensive, comfortable rooms, all with bath or shower, thermal pools, tennis, garden.

Both (2) are—*Augustus,* elegantly modern, all spa facilities, park; *Terme Neroniane,* swimming pool, spa treatments, open 1 March–30 Nov.

Delle Nazioni (3), well-appointed, spa treatments, thermal pools.

Padua/Padova. Hotels: Both (1) are—*Padovanelle,* smart, modern, low-slung building in park of racetrack outside town; pool, tennis. *Plaza,* central, comfortable and efficient.

All (2) are—*Europa,* 57 rooms with bath or shower, airconditioned, good restaurant; *Milano,* modern, 45 rooms with bath or shower, TV and radio, airconditioning; *Donatello,* near the basilica, has airconditioning, very pleasant.

Restaurants: Elegant *Le Padovanelle* very (E), at race track at Ponte di Brenta, which features risotto, liver Venetian-style, and steak, is hotel restaurant (see above).

All (M)—try *Placido,* Via Santa Lucia; *Alla Fogonera,* and *Isola di Caprera,* Via Marsilio, good fish dishes. *Dotto,* best in town. *Giovanni,* Via Maroncelli, hearty portions. *Cavalca,* homey place. Three stops for a snack: opposite *Cavalca,* on Via Manin, *Panetteria Bettio* sells fresh-baked rolls with olives, walnuts or poppy seeds; *Ostricaro,* Via Marsilio 5, opens late afternoons, serves fresh mussels, cold white wine; *Café Pedrocchi,* historic old meeting place, is a must for aperitifs. *Pizzeria* (I) across from basilica is good.

Recoaro Terme. Spa and summer resort. **Hotels:** Hotels (2) and (3) have bus at station. *Dolomiti* (1), Fonti Centrali, best, half of rooms with bath, quiet, gardens.

Both (2) are—*Castiglieri,* pleasantly located on mountainside; *Parco Fortuna,* comfortable.

Augusteo, a good (3).

Soave. Home of famous wine, a picturesque medieval town. **Restaurants:** Both (M)—*Roxy* and *El Grio.*

Solighetto. About 20 miles north of Treviso. **Restaurant:** One of the best in the region is *Locanda da Lino* (M), excellent for game.

Treviso. Hotels: All (2)—*Continental,* Via Roma, best, most rooms with bath; *Carlton,* near station, fine, no restaurant; *Al Foghèr,* on the outskirts, comfortable, good restaurant.

At **Selvana Bassa,** *Carletto,* all rooms with bath, airconditioning, convenient for motorists.

Restaurants: All (M)—*Da Carletto,* a mile from town, is one of the best in the region, but is overshadowed by excellent *El Toulà* (E), where food and atmosphere are superb. Modest old inns: all (M)—*Bersagliere,* Via Barberia; *Due Mori,* Via Palestro; *Beccherie,* Piazza Ancillotto.

Val di Sogno. Near Malcesine **Hotels:** Both (2) are—very attractive, quiet, *Maximilian,* lakeside gardens; and *Olivi,* with pool.

Verona. Hotels: Deluxe—*Due Torri,* Piazza Sant' Anastasia, outstanding, site of 19th-century inn of same name, near cathedral and Adige River, all rooms have period furnishings and private baths, airconditioning, excellent service and cuisine, garage.

Best (1) is—*Colomba d'Oro,* Via Carlo Cattaneo 10, near the arena, 56 well-furnished rooms, in contemporary style, 36 with bath, airconditioned.

All (2) are—*Giulietta Romeo,* behind arena; *San Luca,* Galleria Volto San Luca, pleasant, comfortably furnished, garage; *Europa,* Via Roma 8, 44 rooms half with bath, modern, central, airconditioned, breakfast only, garage; *Ac-*

cademia, Via Scala 12, 86 rooms, half with bath, a pleasant centrally-located hotel with modern furnishings, attractive restaurant, nearby garage. *San Pietro,* recent good.

Restaurants: One of Italy's best restaurants, *Dodici Apostoli* (E), Corticella San Marco, attractive decor and atmosphere, serves excellent *pasta e fagioli,* salmon in bread crust, cutlets; a must.

Also (E), *Arche,* tiny, elegant spot near Arche Scaligere, very good food.

All (M) are—*Re Teodorico,* Piazzale Castle San Pietro, for good food and fine view; excellent pastas and roasts at *La Serra di Mamma Sinico,* Via Leoncino, in attractive garden court atmosphere, recommended; *Pedavena* has dining terrace on Arena Square.

Less expensive and good besides—*La Greppia,* Vicolo Samaritana; *Torcoloti,* Via Zambelli; *Marconi,* Vicolo Crocioni; *De' Capuleti,* Via del Pontiere.

Vicenza. Hotels: Topping the list is the *Jolly Campo Marzio* (1), 41 rooms, many with bath, opposite station, attractive restaurant and terrace, smallish rooms.

Both (2)—*Stazione,* Viale Milano, is good, well-furnished rooms most with bath, roof terrace, bar; *Continental,* Via Tressino. *Motel AGIP,* airconditioned.

Basilica (3), Piazza Erbe 9, small, modern and central, good restaurant.

At **Arcugnago,** 4 miles outside town, *Michelangelo* (2), comfortable villa, lovely rooms, sports facilities.

Restaurants: All (M)—The leading restaurant here is on the outskirts near autostrada exit at Villa Ca' Impenta, *Da Remo,* where risotto and *baccalà* are excellent. *Al Pozzo,* Via Sant'Antonio, offers mushroom soup, also has a *rosticceria* and *pizzeria; Due Mori,* Via Due Ruote, serves spit roasts; the *Birreria Pedavena,* Viale Verone, is always reliable; try also *Ristorante da Aldo.*

An inexpensive one is the *Trattoria all'Olmo,* in the locality of the same name.

Vittorio Veneto. Hotel: *Terme* (2) is comfortable, best overnight halt.

USEFUL ADDRESSES. Tourist Offices: *Abano Terme:* AAST, Via Pietro d'Abano 16. *Asiago:* AAST, Palazzo Municipale. *Bassano del Grappa;* AAST, Viale delle Fosse 9. *Bosco Chiesanuova:* AAST, Piazza Chiesa 35. *Chioggia:* AAST, Viale Veneto 32; Sottomarina Lido. *Garda:* AAST, Lungolago Regina Adelaide. *Lido di Jesolo:* AAST, Piazza Brescia 13. *Limone sul Garda:* AAST, Via Comboni. *Malcesine:* AAST, Via Capitanato. *Montegrotto Terme:* AAST, Viale della Stazione 37. *Padua:* EPT, Riviera Mugnani 8; Railway Station. AAST, Piazzatta Pedrocchi. *Recoara Terme:* AAST, Via Roma 25. *Treviso:* EPT, Via Toniolo 41. *Verona:* EPT, Via C. Montanari 14; Piazza Bra 10, in Galleria Liston. *Vicenza:* EPT, Piazza Duomo 5, and Piazza Matteotti. *Vittorio Veneto:* AAST, Piazza del Popolo.

SPECIAL EVENTS. *Marostica:* In September, a legendary chess game is played with living figures in medieval costume, every 2 years. *Treviso:* 16–24 October the city celebrates its saint. *Verona:* March brings musical events and the oldest and largest agricultural fair in Italy. The openair opera in the Roman Arena begins July. Shakespeare in the Roman Amphitheater runs July and August. For details of festivals, contact Ente Autonoma Spettacoli Lirici Arena di Verona, Piazza Bra 28, 37100 Verona (tel. 23520 and 22265). *Vicenza:* April through June is Spring in Vicenza, with drama, exhibitions, concerts, etc. In September the Teatro Olimpico houses classical drama—a must for all theater buffs.

SPORTS. *Asiago:* 9-hole golf course. *Lido di Jesole:* Fresh and salt water fishing; center for rowing and yachting; riding is popular. *Malcesine:* Coarse fishing on Lake Garda; rowing and sailing. *Treviso;* Popular spot for bowling. *Vittorio Veneto:* Consiglio, 9-hole golf course.

THE DOLOMITES

A Panoramic Playground

The international repute of the Dolomites as a tourist paradise is a fairly recent phenomenon. For years, knowing Italians and Austrians have frequented the region, going there in winter for skiing, skating and sleighing, and in summer for the cool clean air, the unspoiled mountain villages, and some of the best climbing on the Continent. The less-crowded seasons attracted those in search of scenic splendor, and crisp, dry air.

In side trips from Belluno, Trento, Bolzano, or Cortina d'Ampezzo, delightful little hideaways can be found. Accommodations range from modern luxury hotels to rooms in the spotlessly clean rustic villas. Most of the larger resort hotels, in addition, have tennis courts, swimming pools and golf courses for summer, and ski-lifts, chair-lifts, and funiculars for winter sports fans. Even in summer it is possible to ski.

As a matter of fact, one of the most important international giant slalom competitions takes place at Solda in the middle of July!

If you fish, you'll discover an abundance of trout in the torrents and cascades. Pike and golden perch are found in the mountain lakes, 300 in the Trent district alone, scattered over high meadows and in the perennial snows.

Try country walks different from anything you've experienced at home. Special paths are clearly marked out, and routes are furnished with rest huts at convenient points. These give you plenty of time to admire the toy villages, medieval castles, panoramas of wide valleys, and meadows full of bright blue gentians or pink dwarf rhododendrons. You can sample wild blueberries or pause at a friendly farmhouse to admire cheeses as big as cartwheels. The inhabitants of almost every valley still wear traditional Sunday costumes, many villages have their own bands, and popular festivals take place frequently.

Here are the highlights of this fascinating region: the southern bastion is Trent (Trento) with the lacy edge of the Brenta Dolomites behind it to the northwest. Moving north you come to Bolzano, the heart of the Alto Adige (South Tyrol to the Austrians). Farther up is the Brenner Pass to Austria. Next you arrive at Bressanone and the Gardena Valley, followed by the rail terminal town of Dobbiaco leading to Cortina d'Ampezzo. Here is the mountain group known as the Eastern Dolomites with the highest and most famous peaks. Moving east again and south you reach Belluno with its background of Cadore and some wonderful lake resorts.

Weather Matters

The Dolomites are year-round vacation territory. They provide refreshingly cool-altitude resorts during the hot weather and tingling air and sparkling snow as a background for skiing and skating in winter. In these mountains August is the most popular summer month, with the winter sports season at its height over the Christmas-New Year holidays, and then resuming towards the end of January until the middle of February.

Road Reports

To reach Cortina D'Ampezzo from Venice by car takes only 3 hours on the direct route through Treviso and Belluno. From the west take the autostrada from Milan and leave it northwards at Verona to follow the autostrada for Trento and Bolzano. This is the chief road to Austria over the Brenner Pass, and the most obvious route when coming from Britain via Germany, or if you have plenty of time, come out of Switzerland via Davos or St. Moritz over the Ofen Pass to Merano and Bolzano, then on the little road 241 over the Costalunga Pass to join route 48 for Cortina. It is a delight all the way.

Food for Thought

The cooking of the Dolomites region is, like everything else, Italian and Austrian with the accent on the latter. Some of the more popular dishes are: *Selchcarrée mit Kraut* (smoked pork with sauerkraut), *saure Suppe* (tripe soup), and *Knödl* (dumplings). *Fastenknödl* are filled with breadcrumbs, vegetables, and eggs. *Leberknödl* contain chopped liver and appeal to many visitors. A wide variety of sausages fill delicatessen windows. *Speck* is smoked raw ham, the local version of prosciutto.

There are some excellent wines in the Trentino and Alto Adige: the wines from the Val d'Isarco, *Teroldeto* from Mezzalombardo, *Riesling, Missiano, Traminer,* and *Kretzer.*

Exploring the Dolomites

Two hundred years before Christ the Romans were here, as comparative newcomers. Prehistoric remains can be seen below Trento where a lake dwellers' village, perched on stilts, was found when the water level dropped in the Lake of Ledro. Throughout the centuries different peoples and regimes have moved in and out of the area—Longobards, Franks, Habsburgs, Bonapartes, later the Bavarians and the Austrians.

This predominantly mountainous district forms the most northern part of the Italian regions known collectively as Trentino-Alto Adige. Its value as a tourist center has complicated political disputes between Italy and Austria over the area, which was originally part of Austria's Tyrol. After World Was I it was incorporated into Italy with a guarantee of autonomy in matters of education and language. Street signs are in German and Italian, and a particular political group, the Volkspartei, represents the mainly German-speaking inhabitants in Italy's parliament. But most interesting is that geographically it lies between the Mediterranean and Germanic worlds, its valleys receiving sun from the south while protected by mountains from fierce northern winds.

Besides being an important art town, Trento straddles the most important rail and bus lines from Vicenza, Venice, and Milan in Italy, and from Austria through the Brenner Pass.

For 17 years in the 16th century the eyes of the world were on Trento while Catholic dogmas were being revised by the Great Council. This was the turning point of the Counter Reformation in an attempt by

Catholics to modernize the Church and strengthen the Pope against the Protestant revolution.

The Trentino still has a quiet security about it in spite of the battles that have been fought over the territory. For instance, today you can see in Trento the moated residence of the prince-bishops who ruled here for centuries. It is charmingly named the Castello di Buonconsiglio, the Castle of Good Counsel, and is now a museum where you can profitably spend an hour. One part, although built during the Renaissance, has a collection dating from Roman times. The Gothic section has relics of various wars from the Napoleonic to World War II.

Going from the castle through the old part of the town, you reach the severely simple cathedral in the center of the city on the Piazza del Duomo. One thousand years of art and history are gathered together here. Opposite the cathedral is the medieval Palazzo Pretorio with its great tower dating from the 13th century. In the center of the square with its frescoed buildings is the glistening fountain of Neptune next to an ancient lime tree. Across from the railroad station are elaborate public gardens and the Piazza Dante crowned by a statue of the medieval poet with bronze reliefs from the *Divine Comedy.*

All around Trento are beautiful valleys and plateaus. To the southeast is the plateau of Lavarone with wide meadows, lakes, woods, and caverns full of stalactites and stalagmites. To the north are the mountains of Paganella, the most beautiful in Italy.

Valleys of Trentino

From Trento, you can reach Bolzano by heading west through the complex of valleys known as the Giudicarie instead of north by highway 12. Longer but more interesting, this route leads past Castel Toblino, an old feudal manor whose image is reflected in a picture-book lake teeming with fish. The castle has a famous love story connected with it, secret passages are excavated in the rock, and the local wine is aged in its cellars.

A turn to the right, 18 miles from Trento, takes you to Lake Molveno which feeds one of the most important hydro-electric power stations in Europe, built, incidentally, with Marshall Plan money. The picturesque village with its attractive old houses is used by mountain climbers as a base for climbing the Brenta, one of the most eerie groups of the Dolomites. The enormous Campanile Rosso darts towards the sky like a bell tower, and other peaks are just as unusual.

Back on the main road, turn north at Tione di Trento into Rendena Valley. 10 miles later you'll come to Pinzolo, 2,525 feet up. A short walk through pine woods takes you to the Church of San Vigilio. On the outside is an interesting 16th-century *Dance of Death,* a fresco 40 yards long! Near here is the Genova Valley, a wonderland of waterfalls and wild game.

Nine miles farther on a climb of 2,599 feet, the road arrives at Madonna di Campiglio, an up-to-date well-equipped resort in a high valley among forests and impressive mountain peaks. It has a lake nearby and is almost completely surrounded by the Brenta Dolomites.

After a climb of another 400 feet you go over the Campo Carlo Magno Pass where Charlemagne supposedly stopped on his way to Rome to be crowned Emperor. Then you reach the charming Val di Non with its capital Cles. Non is like something out of a fairy story, with villages that seem lost in the mountains, luxuriant orchards, and fish-filled streams.

From Cles you can visit the Lake of Tovel, 3,400 ft., surrounded by pine and fir trees, one of the world's most unusual sights. Due to micro-organisms, the lake becomes an impressive blood-red from July to September.

After returning to Cles you take highway 42 over another pass, the Mendola, open all year round. This leads into the Adige Valley by way of zig-zags through thick woods and past several castles. On the other side of the Adige is Bolzano.

Bolzano, Meeting Place of Two Nations

Bolzano is an old and modern commercial city located on the sunny, southern side of the Alps along the great passageway descending from the Brenner Pass. For over 2,000 years, this has been the main artery of traffic between the German North and the Latin South.

Bedded among orchards and vineyards and leaning against steeply rising slopes, Bolzano is protected by mountains in the north and east. Southward and westward, the green valley opens out, giving access to the Mediterranean breezes.

The city has an excellent location, a mild climate and great charm. It is well-equipped with comfortable hotels, and excellent roads make it a very convenient center for exploring the surrounding countryside.

At Bolzano's Spring festival in May–June the local dress is seen in all its splendor, Tyrolean hats, *lederhosen,* and colorful waistcoats. Festival highlights include such events as flower and dog shows, and concerts in the medieval cloister of the Franciscan monastery.

The city's architecture attests to the overlapping of German and Latin cultures. The old part of the town has high-gabled houses and narrow streets such as Via Bottai and Via Carrettai with characteristic artisan shops and wrought iron signs. At night, locals and tourists alike can enjoy the excellent native wine in centuries-old cellars.

The center of the town is Piazza Walter and the Gothic parish church with its elegant, lacy spire. At the southern end of the Via Portici, the arcaded main street, there is the Palazzo Mercantile, a beautiful, baroque building which has been the center of trade here for 200 years. Today the Chamber of Commerce is located there. At the western end of the street, one comes to the Piazza delle Erbe (fruit market) filled with activity and the delicious products of the region.

Don't miss seeing the old parish Church of Gries with its famous altar by Michael Pacher as well as the Benedictine Monastery, a fine example of baroque architecture and painting. Also to be seen is the old Dominican Convent which has a Gothic cloister and attractively-painted chapels. Near Piazza delle Erbe is the Gothic Franciscan church, with an elegant vaulted cloister and magnificient 16th-century altar, carved in wood by Hans Klocker.

Should sightseeing become too tiring, Bolzano has a "beach" with four excellent swimming pools and sports fields.

Excursions from Bolzano

Attractive as Bolzano is, it should be considered mainly as a jumping off point to other places. For example, visit Castle Roncolo (alias Runkelstein) perched on a sheer rock. The frescos inside illustrate scenes from the lives of knights of the Middle Ages.

San Genesio, 3,261 ft., is ten minutes from Bolzano by cableway via landscape dotted with orchards, larch woods, grassland, and rustic villages. There are good accommodations, a host of walks over towards the Val d'Adige and the Val Sarentina, and excellent winter sports grounds. Or you can go by mule path to Meltina in an ideal skiing area with some outstanding Romanesque and Gothic churches.

Fié and its romantic little lake (a skating rink in winter) are only an hour away. An unusual feature here is the hay baths for all kinds of arthritic pains. The tableland of Renon, 3,600 ft., is a 27-mile square natural park an hour and a half from Bolzano by cableway to the village of Soprabolzano then by electric train to Collalbo. There are some interesting 100-foot-high pyramids formed by erosion, and a panorama from the Brenta Dolomites to the Sassolungo. A longer excursion from Bolzano is southeast over the 6,500-foot Rolle Pass to San Martino di Castrozza, a fashionable resort in the heart of the Dolomites group of the same name.

In two of the valleys near Bolzano, the Val Gardena and the Val Badia, live the Ladini, descendants of soldiers sent by Emperor Tiberius to conquer this area and wipe out its Celtic inhabitants. They did so, sent for their wives and families, were forgotten, and here their descendants still remain in the long narrow *cul-de-sacs* that form the

Dolomite valleys. Here survive some of the Rhaeto-Romanic dialects known as Ladin or Romansch, derived from Latin and peculiar to parts of Switzerland and the Tyrol. But these hospitable folk usually understand German, French and Italian as well. Bus transportation is available from Bolzano northeastward to the main center of the Val Gardena at Ortisei, 5,000 ft. high. Besides a ski school, Ortisei has a notable woodcarving industry. You can visit the workshops and look at windows full of statuettes and toys. The main church is a large Byzantine building whose huge front door has a bronze knocker in the shape of a coiled snake. Gilded lamps inside are supported by carved figures of angels and saints.

The road climbs from Siusi to a vast plateau 40 miles square, also accessible by funicular from Ortisei. The highlands afford stupendous views of the Val Gardena and the Dolomite peaks. You can see about 50 miles in each direction. In spring it has the appearance of an immense flower carpet spread around the feet of rocky peaks over 7,500 ft. high. Here you find examples of the flora of the snow region, flowers not seen at lower altitudes.

Merano's "Grape Cure"

Above Bolzano, on highway 38, is a center that combines all the outdoor attractions of the Alto Adige with more worldly diversions. This is Merano, one of the few winter sports resorts that offer a combination of skiing and sun bathing in mild winter temperatures. Merano is particularly popular with the not-so-young for its amenities as well as for its health-giving qualities.

Its sheltered position gives it a superb climate, never over 80 degrees in summer, never below freezing in winter. Each winter the 9 championship tennis courts are converted into a skating rink. Skiing is within easy reach via the funicular railways that rise to the high Alpine slopes of Avelengo and San Vigilio. The first climbs from 3,600 to 7,200 feet, reaching the plateau of Avelengo in only 20 minutes.

Spring waters in Merano are recommended for digestive and circulatory diseases and have a powerful curative action on the skin. The rich sweetness of the famous Merano grapes is attributed to the radioactive soil. As a result there's a rush by health addicts to sample the district's wines: *Termeno,* extremely aromatic; *Terlano,* almost like a Rhine Wine; and a strong muscat called *Rametz.* Indeed, this "grape cure" is Merano's big attraction. In the 4th century BC Romans were mending their digestions this way, and to take the two-week cure in the fall is still considered one of the best tone-ups possible.

The old part of the city lies at the foot of Mount Benedetto. Along the narrow but sun-filled streets are houses with huge wooden doors, capped with little towers, and a 14th-century Gothic cathedral with a curious crenelated façade. The Via dei Portici is lined with arcades. Right in the center is the Castle of the Princes of Tyrol, built in the 15th century.

The Adige River—fed by 150 glaciers—is one of many streams that gurgle through the town. The Passirio River tumbles along at a terrific pace; canoe races here are as exciting as any in the world. On both sides of the river hotels and pensions, parks, gardens, and wide avenues decorated with flowers and trees jostle each other for space.

Although the city itself has a calming effect, there are all kinds of possibilities for the energetic: tennis, polo, swimming at the Lido—a huge establishment with three pools, a beach and lawns—trout fishing in the Passirio, mountain climbing, and all sorts of excursions to nearby castles, lakes, and mountain passes with some of the most spectacular views to be seen in Europe. To the west near Bormio is the tortuous Stelvio Pass. Next to the Stelvio is the Solda where you can ski in July.

Plenty of spectator sport is available, too, with national and international horse races during the summer and autumn at the Hippodrome. The Grand Prix de Merano is linked up with Italy's national lottery, making it one of the most highly staked races in Europe.

To return to Bolzano there is no need to go south over the same road again, for highway 44 takes you north through the Giovo Pass (6,900 ft.) to the little city of Vipiteno with its brightly colored houses, flower-decked verandas and balconies, and two ancient castles, the Tasso and the Pietra, with fine wainscotted rooms.

Turn south on highway 12 to Bressanone and see the Gate of the Sun, the Statue of the "*Uomo a tre teste*" (Man with Three Heads), the guard towers, the Portici Maggiori, and the medieval winding streets. A magnificent cathedral and quiet chapel have intestering cloisters, and you might take a few minutes to see the 13th-century bishop's castle. Its courtyard is filled with statues of Habsburg personalities.

Next you pass through Chiusa, which so charmed the German painter and engraver Albrecht Durer that he made it the background of his great work *Das Grosse Glück* (The Great Fortune). The village has 12th- and 13th-century houses, a great tower, the Torrione, and the famous convent of Sabiona.

Excursions into the Eastern Dolomites

From Bolzano there are three trips that can be made into the eastern Dolomites, the heart of this province. The shortest goes through Canazei to the Sella Pass and returns through the Gardena Valley. The second runs north through Bressanone, then east to Brunico and the

Pusteria region, and winds up at Dobbiaco, an important transit center. Here highway 51 branches off to the right to Cortina d'Ampezzo.

But the best route is the third, the Great Dolomites Road, with the most thrilling 68 miles of mountain travel you've ever experienced. The trip takes about three unforgettable hours. Your best bet is to rent a car with chauffeur or travel by bus. That way you can give full attention to the stupendous scenery.

Leaving Bolzano on the Brenner Road, highway 12, turn off it to the right just outside town and enter the Val d'Ega, enclosed between high walls of porphyry. A turbulent little river rushes along with you, and then you see the Castle of Carnedo perched on a cliff to the left. Rising slowly you pass through small villages until at 13 miles from Bolzano you reach Carezza, 5,360 feet high with a lake as appealing as its name, "caress." Surrounded by dark green pines dominated by the needlepointed peaks of the Catinaccio and the toothed crest of the Latemar, it looks almost too lovely to be true.

Here you begin to get the real impact of the Dolomites, jagged, broken and splintered into nighmarish forms of spires, towers, ogres, and giants. The Dolomites were the first part of the Alpine region to become ice-free. Touch the stone and you'll find a salty powder on your fingers! These coral rocks rose from the sea in ancient times. Composed of hard dolomite engrained with softer calcite, they have been formed into fantastic shapes by wind and rain through the ages. Erosion denuded the peaks, isolated the towers, and sculptured the wall faces.

After Carezza you continue up all the way for 18 miles to the Costalunga Pass (5,750 ft.) with far-flung views over the Fassa Valley. Then, down in the valley you join highway 48 and turn left for Canazei, a meeting place for climbers, 31 miles from Bolzano. Canazei is outstanding because of its dry climate. Half an hour after a thunderstorm the ground is dry again, and in summer it's not unusual to have thirteen or more hours of sunshine a day!

A long steep climb goes over the Pordoi Pass (7,536 ft.) the highest in the Dolomites. Nearby are more of the strangely shaped towers. One is 50-foot La Salsiccia (the Sausage) which guides use for training climbers. At the Val di Pan you get a superb view of the Marmolada glacier, the Sella War Memorial and the former Austrian fortress of Ruaz, now in ruins. The road runs along the steep slopes of the Col di Lana, scene of heavy World War I fighting between Austrians and Italians. The village you see from here, Livinallongo, was entirely destroyed at that time and rebuilt after 1920. The road climbs again, and Andraz castle comes into view, followed by the Sasso di Stria (the Witches' Rock). After a curving tunnel you reach the 6,946-foot Falzarego Pass.

Stop here and give yourself a chance to absorb what you've seen. The descent to come is even more awe-inspiring. Ahead are the Five Towers peaks, the almost vertical Tofana di Rozes, and in the east, the higher peaks of the Cortina mountains. Starting down, the road goes past Pocol, a resort town, into the Boito Valley. At the Crepa tunnel you'll get your first—and striking—view of Cortina and the cross-shaped Ampezzo Valley. Passing under the ropes of the cable to Belvedere Rock, a war memorial, you wind downhill past pleasant houses and broad meadows.

Cortina d'Ampezzo, Queen of the Mountains

Then 68 miles from Bolzano you arrive at Cortina (3,969 ft.), the jewel of the Dolomites in a setting worthy of Tiffany's. Here is an incredibly green basin, lush with meadows and thick forests, and surrounded by magnificent mountain ranges. All around the town are peaks; Sorapis' long subsidiary ridges are formed like tongues; Cristallo's suggest a cathedral; the curious Cinque Torri seem like five towers with crenelated ramparts; the Pelmo and the Civetta stand like guards, while the "King of Cadore", the Antelao, is distinguished by its large buttresses and its glacier. At the end of the valley are the low crags of the Montagne del Bosco Nero, the Black Forest Mountains, and pointed Becco di Mezzodi.

Besides the wood-covered Belvedere at 5,000 ft., which you passed earlier, most of the major slopes and peaks can be reached by other funiculars and lifts. One takes 10 minutes up to the 7,000-foot ridge of the Faloria. From here (wonderful skiing fields) you look out on to the castelated heights of the Pelmo. Still another line reaches up out of the valley to the Cristallo with stations built in the style of chalets. A mountain railway takes you to the top of Tofana (10,965 feet).

Cortina can now be ranked on a par with St. Moritz as one of the foremost winter sports resorts in Europe. Yet there is as much *Gemütlichkeit* about Cortina as you'll find in any Austrian resort. You can take your black coffee seated at the chestnut wood tables of the *Verzi Bar* next to mountaineers in rough khaki-colored ski suits drinking *Glühwein,* spiced hot wine. At the bar you might see a specimen of Venetian aristocracy, dark-haired and pale, while a sprinkling of Roman sportsmen argue in a corner. In the evening you can dance in the hotels or in one of the minuscule nightclubs that stay open almost until it's time to put your skis back on. The more serious sightseer should visit the church in the center of town. Its walls and floor are of light green marble and the ruby onyx font is decorated like a Grecian urn. Two unusual features are a skeleton with trinkets and gems on its fingers, and a painting of St. Peter crucified with his head towards the ground.

While Cortina has plenty to do socially, it also has some side trips worth taking. One of these takes you to Misurina, 1,800 feet higher than Cortina and 8 miles along highway 48 (the Dolomite Road) through the Tre Croci Pass. Misurina is a beautiful mountain lake with large hotels on its shores, surrounded by pine and spruce trees, and shadowed by famous peaks. Ice skating in this setting will inspire you! A road goes up to the top of Monte Piano, famous as a World War I battleground. The road ends in a vast plateau of pastureland 7,615 feet high, which in winter is transformed into magnificent snow fields.

Auronzo and the Heart of the Cadore

Return south 2 miles to highway 48 (the Alemagna), and turn east (left) 11 miles to Auronzo, situated on a small artificial lake. The town is built on a gently inclined grassgrown plain that stretches up to the spurs of the mountains; on the opposite side are magnificent spruce woods.

Auronzo has a legend typical of many in this area. Residents will point out the ancient church with its weathervane in the form of a cock, clearly showing three holes through its stomach. The people of Auronzo and Dobbiaco to the north were quarreling over their boundaries, but not wanting to fight decided to try a peaceful solution. Each town chose a young girl to set off at cockcrow with an escort of young men from the rival village and walk towards the other town. Their meeting-place, it was agreed, should be the boundary. The Auronzo girl waiting for cockcrow with her escort of young men from Dobbiaco, saw they were all asleep. Taking her knitting needle, she prodded the cock in the stomach three times so that it crowed an hour before daybreak. Thus she had an hour longer in which to walk, and to the surprise of the young woman from Dobbiaco, carried the border farther than it had ever been.

From Auronzo you enter the heart of the Cadore, the upper Piave Valley. Turn left at Cima Cogna for a pleasant trip through rolling meadowlands to Sappada, a real find in mountain resorts. Set in a hollow of grasslands among the pine woods 4,101 feet high, it has simple but good accommodations, chairlifts to the three main peaks, and a sympathetic quality about it that makes it a standout. Sappada is near the source of the Piave, the sacred river of Italy and the subject of a well-known song.

Through to Belluno

You return through San Pietro and Santo Stefano following the Piave south to Calalzo, the terminus of the narrow-gauge line from Dobbiaco and Cortina, and the junction of the railways from Padua and Venice. 2 miles south, near the artifical lake formed by the Vaiont dam (third highest in the world) is Pieve di Cadore, 19 miles from Cortina. Visit the house where Titian was born, and see one of his paintings in the cathedral. Leaving Cadore south on highway 51, you pass through the area so devastated in 1963, when some 4,000 people lost their lives after a section of Mt. Toc avalanched into the lake, spilling a tidal wave over the top of the dam, which destroyed on its way Longarone and several small villages. In less than an hour's drive you are in Belluno, situated on a plateau amidst alpine surroundings at the conflux of the Piave and Arde rivers.

Not to be missed in the town is the scenery of Rugo and Rialto at the two ends of Via Mezzaterra, the main street of the old part, characterized by Venetian-styled palaces. Belluno has a fine Civic Museum containing Roman remains and a picture gallery noted for the famous works it contains. Recommended are visits to the Piazza del Duomo with its cathedral, the Palazzo dei Rettori and the City Tower. Belluno's squares and streets are picturesque, and its buildings interesting. It was a free commune during the Middle Ages, and became a part of the Venetian dominion in the early 15th century.

A Last Round-Up

Among the fascinating but less well-known localities of the Dolomites, which we have not yet fully mentioned, are the medieval Castel Toblino, on the lake of the same name; Pinzolo, with its remarkable *danse macabre* fresco; Brunico, ancient, picturesque, a center of handicrafts and folklore festivals; and San Vigilio di Marebbe, another folklore center and also a good starting point for fishing and shooting expeditions. If you are interested in arms and armor, Sluderno has a fine collection.

PRACTICAL INFORMATION FOR THE DOLOMITES

HOTELS AND RESTAURANTS

Alleghe. Fishing center, summer and winter sports resort. **Hotel:** *Alla Posta* (2), at Caprile, handsome contemporary decor, excellent restaurant.

Auronzo. Pleasant summer and winter resort. **Hotels:** In **Auronzo di Cadore,** *Auronzo* (2), closed October.–June.

In **Misurina,** both (3) are—*Gran Misurina,* large, comfortable; *Dolomiti,* small and good.

Belluno. Hotels: *Astor* (2), Piazza del Martiri, good, all rooms with bath, radio.

Both (3)—*Dolomiti,* Via Carrera, new, all rooms with bath; *Europa,* Via V. Veneto, most rooms have shower, on outskirts.

Restaurants: All (E)—Regional dishes at *K 2,* Via Cipro; *Al Sasso,* Via Consiglio; *Zumelle Castle,* 9 miles distant, with a rustic restaurant, fine view. *Cappello* (M), budget choice.

Belluno-Nevegal. Summer and winter resort. **Hotel:** *Nevegal* (3), small and cozy, inexpensive, garage.

Bolzano. Lively mountain city. **Hotels:** *Park Hotel Laurin* (1), Via Laurino, old-time comfort and atmosphere, fine park, heated pool. *Grifone,* on central Piazza Walter, is very good; comfortable rooms, warm atmosphere, pool, gardens.

All (2) are—*Alpi,* Via Alto Adige, central and good large hotel; *Città,* central, redecorated in turn-of-century style; *Scala,* Via Brennero, pool, park.

All (3) are—*Herzog,* recommended, budget value; *Motel Kampill,* modern; and at **Ponte Roma,** an *AGIP Motel.*

Restaurants: The restaurant of the *Grifone Hotel* (E) is excellent, try *speck,* roast veal with asparagus, and a before-dinner aperitif at the bar is a must.

All (M)—*Frederic,* Via Diaz, is good; the unpretentious *Abramo* is a local favorite; *Caterpillar* is excellent; you'll share your table when they're full, in friendly little trattorias such as *Cavallino Bianco, Colomba,* and *Aquila Rossa.*

Bressanone. Hotels: Both (2)—*Elefante,* antique decor in 16th century villa, pool, park, expensive, exceptional spot; *Grasser,* lovely quiet location at fork of river.

All (3) are—*Albero Verde,* across bridge from center, clean, comfortable, pool; *Jarolim,* at station, also has pool in garden; *Corona d'Oro,* central.

Restaurants: Vying with *Andreas Hofer* (M) in **Brunico** for laurels as the finest in the region, *L'Elefante* (E) in centuries-old inn, serves Italian and Austrian specialties. For at least 6 people (you don't pay if 2 of you manage to eat it) *l'elefante* spectacular, a monumental tray of meats, rice and vegetables. For dessert, another *elefante,* this time fruit and ice cream. *Fink* (M), rustic specialties, downstairs beer hall.

Canazei. Summer and winter resort. **Hotels:** All (2) are—*Bellevue,* comfortable hotel, pleasant lounges, fine view; *Caminetto,* seasonal, attractive, all rooms with bath or shower; *Dolomiti,* well-appointed rooms, bright atmosphere.

Bernard (3), all rooms with bath or shower.

Carezza. Summer and winter resort. **Hotels:** *Karezza* (2), pleasant small hotel with nice view, indoor pool, tennis courts, open Dec.–April, June–Sept.

Cortina d'Ampezzo. Number One winter sports and summer resort of the Dolomites. **Hotels:** Deluxe—*Miramonti-Majestic,* Località Pezziè. A luxurious hotel in magnificent location; handsome and way up-market, with a touch of old-world formality; swimming pool, tennis, golf course and skating rink. Open 1 July–31 Aug., 20 Dec.–20 March.

Expensive (1)

Savoia, Via Roma 22. Also a fine hotel, somewhat less expensive than the preceding, and again a good buy for the money, half its rooms have bath or shower, swimming pool, tennis court, garage, open 20 June–10 Sept. and 20 Dec.–20 March.

Cristallo Palace, Via R. Menardi 18, large, well-kept, with lots of wood paneling, good-sized comfortable rooms, many with balconies. Swimming pool, mini-golf and tennis. A CIGA hotel. Open 20 April–15 Sept., 20 Dec.–31 March.

Bellevue, Corso Italia 165. A trifle less expensive than preceding, garden, terrace, dance bar in season.

De la Poste, on main piazza, completely rebuilt after recent fire and once again hub of local activity, its terrace is *the* place to be seen. Lovely rooms and atmosphere, attentive service. Closed 21 Oct.–20 Dec.

Moderate (2)

Corona, 10 minutes from center, quiet, attractive place, decorated with handsome modern art works, handy to ski lift.

Cortina, central, modern, attractive rooms, friendly atmosphere.

Europa, rooms small but comfortable, all with bath, shares *Cristallo's* pool, tennis.

Impero, smallish, central, attractively furnished, garni.

Concordia e Parco, Corso Italia 34, garage, annex at Corso Italia 13.

Ampezzo, central, comfortable, many rooms with bath.

Victoria, on main street, tasteful rustic decor, pleasant rooms.

Inexpensive (3)

Menardi, on outskirts, recommended; rustic decor, garden. **Montana,** very central, basic but comfortable, somewhat noisy; **Fanes,** seasonal, all rooms with bath or shower.

Restaurants: All (M–E)— **Toula** is elegant and expensive; **Foghèr** is almost as good; **Ra Stua,** simpler; so is **Capannina,** Via Sopiasez, which is known for its *risotto,* steak, and grilled mushrooms. **Camineto,** light pastas, dessert crepes. **Da Melon** (M). Unique *Rachele* (E), at Salieto, suppers for 18 by reservation only.

Fanes (M), homey. Grill rooms of *Cristallo* and *Posta* hotels (E), elegant, quite good.

Cortina-Pocol. Summer and winter resort above Cortina. **Hotels:** *Argentina, Tofana,* both (2), good.

Dobbiaco. Summer and winter resort. **Hotels:** All (2) are—*Cristallo,* panoramic location in park, indoor pool; *Park Bellevue,* comfortable rooms, many with bath; *Union,* near station, all rooms with shower, indoor pool.

Ratsberg (3), attractive alpine hotel high above town, small indoor pool.

Feltre. Art town. **Hotel:** *Casagrande* (2), modern, well-appointed hotel on main road outside town.

Foresta/Forst. 1½ miles from Merano. **Hotel:** *Castello Forst* (1), converted castle with modern comforts, handsomely furnished, indoor pool, open April–Oct.

Fragsburg. 5 miles from Merano. **Hotel:** *Castel Frieberg* (1), exchanting 14th-century castle with modern comforts, 40 rooms with bath, beautiful salons, indoor/outdoor pools, tennis, park.

La Villa. Summer and winter resort. **Hotels:** All (2) are—*Christiania,* recent, swimming pool.

At **Armentarola,** *Armentarola,* modern, pool.

At **Pedraces,** with same amenities, *Serena,* and *Sporthotel,* more luxurious.

Levico Terme. Important spa, summer and winter resort. **Hotels:** *Grand* (1), handsome building in large park, thermal pools, tennis, garage, open June–Sept.

Bellavista (2), comfortable, well-furnished rooms; and *Europa* (2).

Madonna di Campiglio. Summer and winter resort. **Hotels:** Both (1) are—*Golf,* a 9-hole golf course; 2 miles from center, smart, tranquil; *Savoia Palace,* also elegant, central, comfortable, less expensive.

All (2) are—*Caminetto,* tops, 30 bright double rooms with bath; *Oberosler,* also well-appointed, near lifts; *St. Hubertus,* pleasant, all rooms with bath, TV; *Grifone,* pleasant rooms, all with bath.

Touring (3), is good in category.

Marlengo. Summer and winter resort, just outside Merano. **Hotel:** *Oberwirt* (2) nice location, pool.

Merano. Important spa resort. **Hotels:** All (1) are: *Bristol,* Via Ottone Huber 14, highly modern, all 150 rooms on outside, with bath or shower, and spacious balconies, radios in rooms, roof terrace has swimming pool, deck chairs for sun bathing, openair dance floor for tea dances, garage, open 15 March–31 Oct.

Emma, large, central, fine reputation for comfort, service, pool in attractive garden.

Savoy, Via Rezia 1, fine Swiss-type hotel, same management as luxurious *Palace* in **Gstaad,** and *Waldhaus* in **Flims.**

Palace, very central, quiet, 150 rooms, swimming pool, spa treatments at hotel, pleasant courteous service.

Eurotel Astoria, 114 airconditioned rooms with bath, pool, member of Eurotel international chain.

Meranerhof, Via Manzoni 1, comfortable, central, swimming pool, rooms facing south have balconies, lovely garden.

Villa Mozart, a gem, 11 huge rooms with bath in *art nouveau* villa, exceptional service and restaurant.

All (2) are—*Anatol,* tranquil, all private baths, pool; *Juliane,* attractive, two pools, park; *Schloss Labers,* Via Labers, swimming pool; *Regina,* Via Cavour 101; *Irma,* Via Belvedere, and *Alla Torre* (3), Via Parrocchia, both have swimming pool in park.

Restaurants: There is a wide range of restaurants and cafés, ranging from the modern *Turri Bar* (E), to the *Municipio* (M), which is completely Italian and furnished like a country *osteria.* Other cafés have little patios and charming terraces. It is here that Austria and Italy come together in music—almost all have musicians.

All (E)—Excellent *Andrea,* Via Galilei, is small, noted for its *artichoke hearts* and *rump steak* with mushrooms, reserve; the *Palace* is a good hotel restaurant, not too expensive; don't miss the *Ca' da Bezzi,* at Via dei Portici, where the food is wonderful, has typical Tyrolean bar. *Villa Mozart* (very E), see Hotels.

Also good, both (M)—*Forsterbräu,* and *Conca d'Oro,* Corso Libertà.

All (M)—*Terlano Puts,* Via Portini, and *Algunder Weinstube,* typical. At the *Weinkost* in gaily colored Casino you can taste local wines to your heart's content while snacking on *speck* and cheese.

Moena. Budget winter and summer resort. **Hotels:** All (2) are—*Monza,* above town, bright, modern, indoor pool; *Catinaccio,* many rooms with mountain view, all with bath or shower; *De Ville,* central, well-furnished, 32 rooms with bath or shower. *Alpi,* above town, pleasant and at low end of grade.

Nova Levante. Near Carezza. **Hotel:** *Cavallino Bianco* (2), attractive resort-type, well-furnished rooms, most with bath, indoor/outdoor pools, tennis on grounds.

Ortisei. Important summer and winter resort. **Hotels:** *Aquila* (1), large garden, tennis, indoor pool, very comfortable. Open 1 Dec.–31 Oct.

All (2)—*Dolomiti Madonna; Gardena; Posta,* tennis court; *Villa Emilia,* pleasant; and *La Perla,* good, pool. *Luna* (3).

Pieve di Cadore. Dolomites summer and winter sports resorts. **Hotel:** Best hotel is *Canada* (3), at **Tai,** with pretty garden.

Restaurants: All (E) are—*Al Bosco* and *Le Maschere* top the list, then *Palatini,* specializing in *lasagne* and pheasant: *Cavallino* is good, too.

San Candido. Summer and winter resort. **Hotels:** All (2) are—*Cavallino Bianco,* comfortable, swimming pool; *Parco Sole Paradiso,* amid pines; *Posta Grand Hotel,* half of rooms with bath, garage; *Sporthotel Tyrol,* good, all private baths.

Restaurant: *Da Katti,* at Giovo, friendly, family-run.

San Martino di Castrozza. Fashionable resort. **Hotels:** Both (1)—*Dolomiti,* large, elegant, well-furnished rooms, most with bath, pool, tennis; *Excelsior Cimone,* informal, smart, 75 rooms, all with bath or shower, handy for lifts.

All (2) are—*Savoia,* well-appointed, fine view; *Colfosco,* recently modernized, gay and lively; *San Martino,* comfortable, tennis, indoor pool.

Bel Sito (3), pleasant, friendly.

Santa Cristina-Val Gardena. Important summer and winter sports resort, very atmospheric. **Hotels:** At **Monte Pana,** characteristic *Sporthotel Monte Pana* (1), swimming pool, tennis courts, garage, has a fine annex.

All (2)—*Interski* and *Posta,* have pools; *Cristallo, Carmen.* inexpensive in category.

Villa Pallua (3).

San Vito di Cadore. Summer and winter sports resport. **Hotels:** *Marcora* (1) and *Ladinia* (2) are best.

Al Pelmo (3), most rooms with bath.

Sappada. Summer and winter sports resort. **Hotels:** Best are *Ai Monti* (2), most rooms with bath, tennis court; and *Cristallo* (3).

At **Kratten—**Corona Ferrea (3).

Bellavista (P3), Borgata Cima Sappada.

Selva di Val Gardena. Summer and winter sports resort. **Hotels:** All (2) are—*Aaritz,* recent, modern, indoor pool, best; *Tyrol,* good value; *Gran Baita,* tennis; *Laurin,* good value, 30 pleasant rooms.

Siusi. Mountain resort. **Hotels:** All (2) are—*Siusi* and *Villa Hermes,* well-equipped twin hotels; *Ratzes;* and, high above town, *Eurotel Sciliar,* large resort hotel in quiet, panoramic location.

Stelvio Pass connects Valtellina with Val Venosta, just south of Swiss border. **Restaurant:** The *Albergo Passo del Stelvio* enjoys a remarkable location on the very summit of the pass. The food is good, the prices reasonable and the service excellent.

Trento. Hotels: *Trento* (1), Via Alfieri 3, all 94 rooms with bath, some with balcony, oldish furnishings, frequented by businessmen.

All (2) are—*Villa Madruzzo,* 2 miles outside town in quiet location; renovated villa, well-equipped and well-run. *Victoria,* modern, good. *Everest,* large, comfortable. *Motel AGIP,* Via Brennero.

Restaurants: All (E) are—*Castel Toblino,* 12 miles from town, recently converted to first-class hotel, fine food in elegantly restored medieval castle with magnificent location; *Castello di Pergine,* another fine castle restaurant, 10 miles from city; *Cantinotta,* Via San Marco, candlelit cellar restaurant; lunch or dinner until the wee hours, courteous waiters serve fine *risotto* with *gorgonzola* or *champagne, speck,* other specialties.

All (M)—*Chiesa,* Via San Marco, Trento's best restaurant, vaulted ceiling, courteous service, famous for entire meal using apples in many ways, but also good for *fettuccine* with walnuts, pork; *Nino,* Via Travai, a first-rate *trattoria* with varied menu including game; *Tino,* Via Santa Trinità, is simple, fine. *Port'Aquila,* Via Cervara, central, old and good.

USEFUL ADDRESSES. Tourist Offices: *Auronzo:* AAST, Viale Roma 22. *Belluno:* AAST, Piazza dei Martiri 27E; EPT, Via R. Psaro 21 and Piazza Stazione. *Bolzano:* AAST, Piazza Walter 28; EPT, Piazza Walter 8 and 22. *Bressanone:* AAST, Viale Stazione 9. *Canazei:* AAST, Via Roma 24. *Cortina d'Ampezzo:* AAST, Piazzetta S. Francesco 8. *Dobbiaco:* AAST, Via Roma. *Feltre:* AAST, Castaldi 7. *Levico Terme:* AAST, Viale D. Alighieri 6. *Merano:* AAST, Corso Libertà 45. *Nova Levante:* AAST, Via Carezza 5. *Ortisei:* AAST, P. Stetteneck. *Pieve di Cadore:* AAST, Via XX Settembre 18. *San Vito di Cadore:* AAST, Via Nazionale 9. *Sappada:* AAST, Via Bach 12. *Trento:* AAST, Via Alfieri 4; Assessorato Turismo, Corso 3 Novembre 132.

SPECIAL EVENTS. *Bolzano:* May and June the city celebrates its Spring Festival with parades, concerts and sports events. *Cortina d'Ampezzo:* January, bobsled and ice hockey events; skiing contests in January and February; August and September, alternating sporting and social events. *Merano:* Easter Monday, Farmer's Horse Race in traditional costume. *Trento:* March, spring festival with colorful regional costumes and folk dancing.

THE TRIESTE AREA

From Austria to the Adriatic

The off-the-beaten-track provinces of Italy's easternmost crescent are those of Udine, Gorizia, and Trieste—although the district as a whole is known as Friuli-Venezia Giulia. To introduce this region in a simpler way, we call it the Trieste area, thus focusing attention on its largest and most important city. The region enjoys a special autonomous status with its own elected diet, primarily because of its mixed population, with a German minority living along its northern border and a Slovenian minority along its eastern border, including the cities of Trieste and Gorizia. Also the Friulians, who represent the majority of the inhabitants, are ethnically not real Italians but have their own language, which is similar to the Rhaeto-Romanic of Switzerland and Ladin of South Tyrol. In the north, along the borders of Carinthia (the southern Austrian Federal state) and in the northeast along the frontier with Slovenia (the northwestern Yugoslav republic), the region is framed by the Carnic Alps and the West Julian Alps which descend slowly along the eastern border to the Karstic plateau between Monfalcone and Trieste. The heart of the region is formed by the rich and fertile Friulian plain reaching to the sea.

This varied area is worth exploring for its historic towns of Udine, Cividale and Aquileia, for the romantic, abruptly cut coast between Monfalcone and Trieste, for the beautifully situated city and port of Trieste, and for the splendid beaches of Grado, Caorle, Lignano and Bibione, increasingly gaining in popularity.

Weather Matters

The summer resorts located in the hill and mountain areas of the region are at their busiest from late June through August, while the seaside resorts are filled up from the middle of June through August. The winter sports season is at its height during December through February.

Road Reports

Although it is easy to get to this area by public transport, a car is greatly to be desired for touring in it. A27 to Treviso and Vittorio Veneto, A28 to Pordenone and A23 to Udine branch north from the A4 autostrada from Turin via Venice to Trieste. A23 is being extended to Tarvisio to link with the Austrian A2 as part of E7.

Food for Thought

Cooking in the Trieste area is quite varied because of the multinational background of the region, because of the different kinds of ingredients offered by mountains, plains and the sea, and because for centuries it belonged to the Austrian Empire. For seafood Trieste and Grado are among the best places in the Mediterranean; fish is prepared with olive oil in the Istrian and Dalmatian manner, grilled, fried, baked or boiled. San Daniele in Friuli is famous for its raw dried and smoked hams and Friuli also specializes in *polenta,* hares, pheasants and other small game, as well as many excellent vegetables served cooked or in salads, notably *radicchio rosso* (a special type of red salad) during the winter months. *Risotto* and *spaghetti* acquire a distinct local flavor, and the *minestra di fagioli* (bean soup) is exquisite.

Veal, pork and beef are usually prepared in the Austrian style (in Trieste you can get anything from *Wiener Schnitzel* to *Tafelspitz* and *Goulash*), while chicken, sausages and other smoked pork are mostly of Slovenian origin. Practically all the cakes and pastries are also an

Austrian and Slovenian contribution, ranging from *Apfelstrudel, Krapfen* (jelly doughnuts) and Viennese-type cakes in Trieste to *gubana* (a rolled sweet bread filled with nuts, raisins, etc.) in Cividale.

The best local wines, white and red, come from the Collio hills near Gorizia (Pinot, Tocai) and from the Cividale area (*Merlot* and the sweet *Piccolit,* which is served as a dessert wine).

Exploring the Trieste Area

Assuming that you are traveling to Friuli in a northeastern direction from Venice, passing Treviso and Conegliano, your first stop is likely to be Sacile, with a centuries-old bird fair. After the trading is over, there is a contest to see who can give the most perfectly whistled imitation of bird songs.

Next you come to Pordenone, whose arcaded main street, the Corso Vittorio Emanuele, is lined with Venetian-style patrician houses ending on a little square where stands the 13th-century town hall in Venetian-Gothic style, with a very interesting clock tower and a gallery of paintings. Next to it soars the 15th-century cathedral, with an older, Romanesque tower powerfully standing apart from it.

Udine stands on a mound supposedly erected by Attila the Hun so that he might watch the burning of Aquileia, an important Roman center 24 miles to the south. The Patriarch Elia later made it into a trading center. It has a fine art gallery, an imposing castle, and several buildings designed by Palladio. There are Tiepolo paintings in the Archbishop's Palace and in the 13th-century Romanesque cathedral, which stands on Piazza della Libertà, an arcaded square, one of the loveliest in Italy. Notice the clock tower with its lion of St. Mark, and the two figures on the top who strike the hours on the great bell. If you have time to spare, Udine reveals all sorts of pleasant little corners, especially where the Roggia River laps against the walls of the houses in scenes reminiscent of Venice.

It's 10 miles from Udine to Cividale, historically perhaps the most interesting town of the entire region. It was probably founded by Julius Caesar when he served as commander of the Roman legions at Aquileia, and for this reason the first name of the town was forum Julii. However, Cividale acquired its present name and fame when it was the capital of the Duchy of the Germanic Longobards and after 774 of Frankish Margraves; it was then called Civitas Austriae, abbreviated to Civitas and then dialectically into the present name. The most interesting historic remains of the Longobard period are found in the so-called Longobard Little Temple and in the Archeological and the Cathedral Museums. An impressive event in Cividale is the Sword Mass, celebrated every year at Epiphany. It recalls the investiture ceremony of the Patriarchs of Aquileia, who were confirmed by the Holy Roman Emperor of the German Nation, whose vassals they were. The priest wears a helmet while celebrating Mass, and presents the sword three times as a symbol of secular power.

If you're heading for Tarvisio, turn north here at Udine for the 55-mile trip up through the mountains to the 2,460-foot mark on the Austrian border where this summer and winter resort, together with several villages around it, is becoming increasingly popular. On the way to Tarvisio, you'll see what's left of Gemona and Venzone, where the 1976 earthquake destroyed interesting old churches and town fortifications. At Carnia, a side road branches off from the road to Tarvisio, taking you to the unpretentious Carnic winter and summer mountain resorts of Ravascletto, Forni Avoltri, Forni di Sotto and Forni di Sopra.

An almost continuous sand fringe sloping gently to the sea extends from Punta Sabbioni all the way to Grado, dotted with resorts accessible by branch roads from A4.

Inland, at the southern end of A28, lies Portogruaro, a small town consisting of two sinuous streets between which Lemene River flows. Features of interest: colorful porticos, a cathedral with noteworthy frescos, a leaning tower, a town hall of the 14th century in pointed arch and Renaissance style, three ancient city gates, and a museum containing a notable archeological collection. There is also the unusual experimental farm and factory project run by the Marzotto family.

Farther east, you can make a side trip to the beach resort of Lignano, one section of which is called Sabbiadoro (Golden Sands), by turning right after Latisana.

Next comes Cervignano in rich farm country. Turn right here 4 miles to the former Roman capital at Aquileia, and the beach and lagoon at Grado.

Aquileia was founded around 200 BC. Named after an eagle seen flying overhead while envoys of the Senate were planning Augustus' campaign against the Germans, it boasts an impressive basilica built in 1021, and a museum with towers, statues, tombstones, mosaics, and other relics of Roman times. A Roman forum has been discovered and partially restored. When Attila the Hun swept down on the area, the inhabitants of the town fled before him and founded Grado on an island six miles away. Its port on the lagoon commands a group of islands scattered about the estuary, and there is an attractive beach. Quays and canals run right into the center of town; the houses look out over the water. It is full of boats, fishermen, and pleasure craft, in sharp contrast to the magnificent Byzantine cathedral.

Returning from Grado to Cervignano you continue east for Monfalcone, famous for its shipyards. Shortly after, you come to Duino. This is a village populated by fishermen, small farmers and innkeepers. The remains of its old fort, standing on a cliff above the sea, originate probably from the 6th or 7th century; next to it there is the majestic "new castle", constructed in the 15th-16th century and still in the possession of the Princes of Thurn and Taxis. A little farther is the Gulf of Sistiana with fine swimming facilities and a yacht harbor. 3 miles before Trieste, in a beautiful location on a small promontory on the coast is the white castle of Miramare. A visit here is a must; from June to September a *Sound and Light* spectacle recreates the history of Archduke Maximilian of Habsburg, who for a brief period became the Emperor of Mexico and who, prior to departing for Mexico, built Miramare as his home. On view the year round are its rich collection of mementos and art objects and a large park with many trees, beautiful flower beds and romantic vistas of the sea. Before you reach Trieste itself, side roads take you down to the little bays sheltering the lovely small beach resorts of Sistiana and Grignano.

Trieste City

Modern Trieste has relics dating back to Roman times, a 2nd-century theater and an Augustan arch, but the whole city can be seen in one day. Be sure to include the 17th-century castle and the Cathedral of St. Just on their hillside esplanade, as well as the impressive Piazza Unità by the sea.

Surrounded by beautiful countryside with a rugged coastline, Trieste was until 1918 the chief port of the Austrian Empire, which built it to its present size from a small fishing town, as well as one of the leading ports of all Europe. It was awarded to Italy by the Versailles Peace Conference and has since experienced continuous decline. Its economy was revived somewhat by U.S. assistance between 1945 and 1953 when it was part of the Free Territory of Trieste, occupied by U.S. and British forces, before reverting to Italy. The best view of Trieste and the bay is from Opicina on the Karstic plateau above the city, which can be reached by cog-wheel streetcar or by a road offering beautiful vistas at every curve.

PRACTICAL INFORMATION FOR THE TRIESTE AREA

HOTELS AND RESTAURANTS

Aurisina. Near Sistiana. **Hotel:** *Europa,* (1), medium-sized resort hotel, private swimming area, open summers only.

Bibione. Popular resort similar in style to Jesolo, but smaller. **Hotels:** All (2) are—*Palace,* is recent, modern, with pool and beach; *Park,* similar resort hotel, optional airconditioning; *Bembo,* all rooms with bath or shower, has beach facilities; *Principe,* beach, tennis.

All (3) are—*Italy,* 56 rooms, on beach and near town center; *Ariston,* 33 rooms, near beach and center; *Astoria,* tennis. All open May through Sept.

Caorle. Interesting old town, with adjoining, well laid-out beach area. **Hotels:** All (2) *Airone,* overlooking sea; comfortable, well-appointed resort-type with pool, beach, tennis; *Duna Fiorita,* is attractive, isolated, on beach, pool, tennis, 24 rooms with bath or shower.

At **Santa Margherita,** 10 miles by bus or ferry, *San Giorgio,* large modern resort hotel on beach.

Restaurants: All (M)—*Da Bruno,* very good; *Al Fogher,* fisherman's trattoria; *Duilio; Eden.*

Gorizia. Border town and district. **Hotels:** Both (2)—*Palace,* modern, well-furnished; *Flora,* also recent, more unassuming.

Restaurants: Both (M) are—*Nanut,* modern, good local dishes; *Lanterna d'Oro,* within old castle, lots of atmosphere.

Gradisca d'Isonzo. Not far from Gorizia. **Restaurant:** *Taverna Leon d'Oro* (M), offers good steaks, game and chicken at very reasonable prices.

Grado. Important spa and beach resort. The beach shelves very, very gently and is perfect for children. Fine views of the mountains to the east.

Hotels: High season, 1 July—31 Aug. *Astoria* (1), Largo San Grisogono 2, large, all rooms have bath or shower, spa treatments at hotel, garage.

All (2) are—*Savoy,* Via Carducci 33, many rooms with bath, pool, gardens; *Al Bosco,* Località Rotta, private beach, park; *Tiziano Palace,* Riva Slapater; *Bellevue,* Viale dei Moreri, most of rooms with bath, lovely garden; *Fonzari,* Piazza della Vittoria 7, most of rooms with shower, some with bath.

At **La Rotta,** *Ai Pini,* all rooms with shower.

All open May through Sept.

Restaurants: *Colussi* (M), has a long and excellent seafood menu. *Adriatico,* (M), also good. *Nico* (E), atmosphere, delicious fish.

Grignano. Yachting port, near Miramare. **Hotels:** *Adriatico Palace* (1), 102 spacious rooms, all with bath or shower and radio, most with balcony overlooking sea, own swimming establishment.

Both (2)—*Riviera,* modern, own swimming establishment; near the main entrance to Miramare.

Restaurant: *Baita al Mare* (M), among the best fish restaurants in the area.

Lignano Pineta. Hotels: *Grief* (1), large, has pool, private beach.

All (2) are—*Medusa Splendid,* 56 rooms with shower; pool and beach; *Park,* same facilities; *Continental,* all rooms with shower, pool beach.

Lignano Riviera. Hotels: Both (1) are—*Eurotel,* pool, beach, garden terraces, open May–Sept. and *President,* also modern and elegant, also open May–Sept.

Lignano Sabbiadoro. Beach resort. **Hotels:** High season, 1 July–31 Aug. All open May through Sept.

All (2) are—*Atlantic,* fine location in pinewoods overlooking beach, modern well-furnished rooms with shower; *Columbus,* overlooking sea, beach facilities; *American,* bright, modern, pool, beach.

Vittoria (3), overlooks beach, comfortable.

Restaurants. All (M) are—*Al Semaforo,* and *La Sacca; El Baracuda,* in the Pineta section.

Lucinico. 2 miles out of Trieste, near Gorizia. **Restaurant:** *El Fogolar* (M), a gourmet's heaven.

Monfalcone. Restaurants: Both (M)—Try *Dal Pescatore* for fish; and *Flego* for game and Friulian dishes.

Opicina. On the Karstic plateau, above Trieste, about 7 miles away. **Hotel:** *Park Obelisko* (1), 30 well-appointed rooms with bath in smart modern resort hotel with pool and tennis in lovely park.

Restaurant: *Daneu* (M), Slovenian inn, for chicken and game, crowded on Sundays with people from the city.

Sistiana. Tiny, attractive cliff-ringed sandy beach, 10 miles north of Trieste, beyond Grignano. **Hotels:** Both (3), modest but pleasant, *Sistiana* and *Mirabel.*

Tarvisio. Summer and winter sports resort on the Austrian border. **Hotels:** High seasons, 20 Dec.–10 Jan. and 1 July–31 Aug. *Nevada* (2) and *Friuli* (3) have all rooms with shower, and are attractive, brightly furnished.

Trieste. Regional capital. **Hotels:** All (1)—Best is the modern *Duchi d'Aosta,* on handsome Piazza Unità, 52 well-furnished rooms, all with bath, airconditioning, cheerful grill room; *Jolly Cavour,* near station, 190 airconditioned rooms, most with bath, pleasant lounges.

All (2) are—*Corso,* Via San Spiridione, comfortable; *Milano,* near station, also comfortable; *Colombia,* also in station area, well-furnished, breakfast only. *Abbazia* (3), Via Geppo 20.

At **Duino,** near autostrada, *Motel AGIP* (2), good, quite recent.

Restaurants: All (E)—*Istria,* Via Milano 14, serves anything from seafood to game, *tafelspitz* and *apfelstrudel* and everything is very good; *Antica Bonavia,* Piazza Unito 2, and *Da Dante,* Via Carducci 12, two upper class restaurants offering varied food, including fish; among the best fish restaurants in the town and its suburbs, *Nastro Azzurro,* Riva Sauro 12, and *Tritone,* Viale Miramare 133.

All (M)—For beer and Austrian-type atmosphere and food, try *Birreria Forst Europa,* Via Galatti 11, *Birreria Dreher,* Via Giulia 77, which is actually a large German type beer cellar; *Suban,* Via Comici 2, very good, serves Central European fare with a Slovenian accent, especially vegetable soup and roast veal; *Bottega del Vino,* at the Castle of San Giusto, an attractive evening restaurant with music and dancing, outdoors in summer, for chicken and game you might explore any of the Slovenian inns on the Karstic plateau above Trieste, *Furlan* in **Monrupino;** *Posta* in **Basovizza** and half a dozen others—on Sundays they are crowded with Triestines.

A little bit out of the center is the *Ristorante 2002* (M), Via Settefontane 7, attractive decor and delicious pizzas; worth searching out.

In town, both (M)—*Benedetto* and *Sacra Ostaria* are very good for regional specialties.

At **Cividale,** *Zorutti* is good.

At **San Floriano,** 5 miles out, *Parco Formentini,* hearty specialties in a 15th-century castle setting.

Udine. Hotels: Both (1)—*Ambassador Palace,* Via Carducci 46, best, most rooms with bath, airconditioned; *Astoria* recent and good, airconditioned, TV in rooms.

Cristallo (2), near station, all rooms airconditioned, with bath.

Motel AGIP (2), on Vale Ledra.

Restaurants: *Vitello d'Oro* (E), famed for varied menu. Both (M), *Alla Vedova* has summer garden; *Siora Rosa* is simpler but good. *Buona Vite* (E), Via

Treppo, is elegant, expensive and specializes in seafood. *Al Lepre,* Via Poscolle (M), is family-run and does very good food.

USEFUL ADDRESSES. Tourist Offices: *Aurisina:* AAST, Riviera di Duino-Aurisina. *Bibione:* AAST, Viale Aurora 20. *Caorle:* AAST, Piazza Europa. *Gorizia:* EPT, Via Mazzini 20. *Gradisca d'Isonzo:* AAST, Via Ciotti 23. *Grado:* AAST, Vial D. Alighieri 58. *Lignano Sabbiadoro:* AAST, Via Latisana 42. *Tarvisio:* AAST, Via Roma 10. *Trieste:* AAST, Castle of San Giusto; American Express, Ufficio Centrale Viaggi, PO Box 1390, Piazza Unità; CIT, Piazza Unità; EPT, Via Rossini 6, and an information pavilion on the waterfront at Molo Audace. *Undine:* EPT, Piazza Venerio 4.

Consulates: *Trieste:* USA, Via dei Pellegrini 42; UK, Via Rossini 2.

SPECIAL EVENTS. *Trieste:* June's big event is the International Trade Fair; July, there's openair opera at the Castello San Giusto and an International Science Film Festival; summertime, a Sound and Light show is staged at the famous Miramare Castle, on the outskirts; from December, opera is staged at the Teatro Communale G. Verdi, and drama at the Politeama Rossetti Theater.

THE MARCHES

Raphael, Rossini and Rural Customs

It's quite possible that the majority of travelers to Italy will not know where to look for the Marches on the map. If you trace the Apennine backbone southwards to a point roughly opposite Florence, then look towards the Adriatic coast at the same approximate level, you will find Pesaro on that coast. From the eastern watershed of the Apennines, skirting independent San Marino, to a point just north of Pesaro, is the northern boundary of the Marches; and so, for about 110 miles going south, Apennines and Adriatic coast enclose a rectangle of land as far as the Trento River which forms the southern boundary.

It is a region of high mountains; heavy masses of them to the west—Catria, Nerone, Montefeltro—throwing across the area spurs which do not reach the sea save at one point, Conero, just below Ancona, where on that account the only good natural port is to be found. Hence the rivers are in full spate during the rainy season and when the snows melt;

while some of them are dry chasms during summer. The silt of these torrents has formed small fertile plains along their course. A region, then, of small-holders, of somewhat isolated little towns in those alluvial plains; a hard country, where the coast is of little service to man, where every inch of land has to be exploited, where vine and olive are persuaded to grow up to incredible heights; and hence, a tough population, decisive in religion and politics.

Ascoli Piceno recalls the *Picas,* the woodpecker that figured on the banners of the early tribes, chiefly Sabines, whose name, too, is rife. Metauro is the river on which the Carthaginian defeat took place and the death of Hasdrubal. Remains of Roman roads and viaducts, and Trajan's arch at Ancona (a Greek name by the way), remind one that this was a province of Augustus' Italy. The name *Marche* is of German origin; it was a frontier province, a "Mark" of the Empire of Charlemagne, who redonated it to the Church. It was already deeply imbued with Christianity, often grafted on to its pagan rites. Until 1860 the Marches were Papal dominions, and archbishops and legates were its rulers. For centuries the Church had to fight, often with fire and sword, to maintain its supremacy against imperial ambitions, against the lordlings and local squires—the Sforzas, Malatestas, Montefeltros, Della Roveres. Sometimes the Church made the best of a bad job by appointing successful lords her "vicars". The exploits of these, the fiery passage of oppressing cardinals, the fearsome scourge of Cesare Borgia—all this the country still remembers; the fact that most sizable towns were rebellious independence-seeking communes, with their own rulers, courts and civilization has given them an indefinable character which still remains; you can "feel" the personaltiy of Urbino, Tolentino, Ascoli Piceno and Osimo.

Religious and pagan usages are mingled; sheaves and baskets of grain are carried in procession with the Virgin; at Easter, a man with face and chest covered with hair, saddled, and with firecrackers exploding behind him, chases the crowd; while the "woodpecker chase" at Monterubbiano has probably survived from Sabine days. For St. Emidio, bunches of basil, blessed by the priest, are worn; in certain parts they tattoo themselves with the signs of the Passion; pilgrims carry stones up to the Mount of St. Polisia, and, heaving them into the chasm, listen for the clang of the saint's golden spinning wheel. And the wine carts, like the sails of fishing-boats, are sometimes painted with Christian and pagan symbols intertwined.

Weather Matters

The Marches are all-the-year-round country. The mild climate makes it visitable in winter—indeed, February is a favorite month along the Adriatic coast. On the other hand, it doesn't become unbearably hot in summer. The sea is at hand to provide cooling breezes for the beach resorts, and many of the hill towns are high enough up so that altitude tempers the effect of the sun.

Budget Tip: Prices throughout the region are comparatively low. The delightful resorts south of Ancona, especially Numana, Grottamare and San Benedetto del Tronto, are much greener and quieter than big crowded Adriatic resorts like Rimini, and their June or September off-season rates are real budget-savers.

Road Reports

Although it is easy enough to get to the Marches and to travel along the coast, the many extremely interesting and not too well known places which might be visited inland are fairly inaccessible without a car. The *Autostrada Adriatica* parallels the coastal road from Rimini to Pescara, bypassing Ancona, which is the pivotal point for travel in both directions; from points on either road you can visit the interior towns. From Pesaro you get to Urbino, from Ancona to Loreto; from Porto Civitanova to Macerata; from Porto d'Ascoli to Ascoli Piceno. On the west side of the region there is one main road which, so to speak, boxes it in, while in the center there is nothing but small, winding roads, slow to drive.

Food for Thought

A specialty of the coastal towns is *brodetto,* a noble edifice of fish (at least thirteen varieties, they say), on a firm foundation of toast, frescoed with carrot, celery, tomato, laurel tips and white wine. Then there's *calcioni,* an oven-baked dish which you will recognize, after you have penetrated its brown carapace, a ravioli in a slightly different guise. The Marches prefer *pasta* baked in the oven—*pasticciata* is also treated that way. Its basis is *pasta* strips, with egg in the dough, flavored with mozzarella cheese.

Typical wine of the region is the tart, greenish-white *Verdicchio* of Iesi.

Exploring the Marches

It is a good idea to set up one's headquarters on the coast. From Ancona you can reach a string of pleasant seaside resorts; Gabicce Mare, Pesaro, Fano, Senigallia, Falconara to the north, and Porto Recanati, San Giorgio and San Benedetto, to the south. These days, all of the Adriatic beaches are crowded in summer, and hotels have been built at every spot where bathing is possible. Even the mountainous background of the Monte Conero Riviera guarantees little peace—and you will certainly need a private car to reach such spots as Scoglio del Trave and Portonovo.

For the thorough and studious traveler, Ancona has the National Museum of the Marches, providing a complete historical and archeological background. Next door to it is the town's art gallery. A short walk brings you to the cathedral, bombed, but restored like other buildings in Ancona, beautifully situated, giving an excellent view of this interesting town and its colorful harbor.

The lovely white-and-rose stone door with its St. Markish lions welcomes you; the cathedral, one of the finest of Romanesque, is solid and dignified, its interior spacious. The marble Arch of Trajan, 300 yards away, is perhaps the finest Roman arch in Italy. Between cathedral and port, the old town is worth wandering in: stone ramps under Gothic arches, tiny piazzas, and giddy stairways. Southwards, all within easy walking, are: Palazzo del Senato, San Francesco delle Scale and its magnificent Gothic portal, Santa Maria della Piazza, with its beautiful cozy 13th-century façade, its little arches and majolica, like a toy church; and the exquisite twisting columns and traceried arches of the Loggia dei Mercanti. Palazzo della Pretettura is a fine, severe building that shares picturesque Piazza del Plebiscito with the Church of San Domenico.

Both Senigallia and Fano are good beach resorts for your base. The latter is also of interest for its Portico di San Francesco, Palazzo del Ragione, Cathedral and Arch of Augustus, as well as a starting point for the pleasant journey along the valley of the Metauro to Urbino (26 miles).

Urbino

This is a dream of a city, in a broad setting of rolling hills, punctuated by cypresses in a patchwork of vineyards and tilled fields. A living monument to the Renaissance, it has three great names to its credit: Frederick of Montefeltro (a broad-minded artistic prince), Raphael, and Bramante. Perched on a rock, the Ducal Palace is Urbino's sun and center. Its library with illuminated manuscripts, picture gallery with works by Uccello, Piero della Francesca, Signorelli, and Titian, object d'art, wood inlays, the finest of their kind, in Frederick's study, its courtyards and staircases, will tell you more of the bursting wealth and artistic energy of the Renaissance in Italy than all the history books can. There are interesting buildings galore in Urbino, among them Raphael's birthplace, restored in appropriate 16th-century style.

Urbino also has its share of landmarks and more of those very old and fascinating houses you have seen in other parts of the country. There's a special feeling to Urbino; you'll get to feel familiar with it as you wander about the city. We encourage you to discover its look-out points as well. From the little Church of San Giovanni you get an unusual prospect of the Ducal Palace. Go to the Monte Titano, from the Piazza Roma, and from there follow the panoramic way all along the small road which leads around to the hill facing it. You'll have a memorable view of the city and its ramparts.

Pesaro, a short distance north of Fano, is a watering-place, and an interesting old town. Its Palazzo Ducale is the chief building, and the 14th century San Francesco the most interesting church; Sant' Agostino is also worth seeing. The town boasts many art galleries—and Rossini.

The art gallery in the Municipal Museum is worth a visit, if only to see Bellini's polyptych, the *Pala di Pesaro.* You may be interested in the fine ceramic section as well.

Loreto

Loreto lives entirely on the sanctuary built around the Holy House, reputedly the home of the Virgin at the time of the Annunciation and later transported here by angels in the 13th century, when the Holy Land was overrun by Mohammedans. The church, erected in the 15th century, is a veritable museum; its later bronze doors are admirable. Special trains for sick pilgrims are run from all over Italy to Loreto. The special pilgrimage days are March 25th, August 15th, September 8th, December 8th and 10th. On the last date, *Festival of the Transference of the Holy House,* bonfires are lit all over the region.

From Loreto to Macerata is only a few miles by road, or an hour's run by a very scenic railroad from Ancona. Macerata is a pretty town; it is worth looking in at the local library and gallery and the ancient university, but there is little else except its scenery.

As you are passing by way of Recanati, stop to visit the art gallery that contains many paintings by Lorenzo Lotto. Cingoli is a little town nearly lost in the heart of the countryside—the Romans called it *Cingolum*—but its altitude, 2133 feet, offers an exciting view of the entire region all the way to the sea.

Tolentino, along the same line and road, has much more personality. It is the town where Napoleon signed the famous treaty with the Pope. Treaty-towns are almost always pleasant—Rappallo, Stresa and so on. The cathedral is interesting; but the chief monument is the Church of Santa Nicola, where the Chapel of the Saint is admirably frescoed. Still along the same route is Camerino, at 2,000 feet above sea-level—a magnificent sight to see. Ruled by the Varanis, a ducal family, for 300 years, it saw more than its share of fratricide, stranglings, and murders in church. San Venanzio (13th century) is the most interesting of its churches; the art gallery is unusually attractive.

Fabriano is one of those impressive cites, wearing the aura of past majesty like an emperor in exile. In the Middle Ages, its power and wealth were immense; and it was a center of art and learning. Moreover it was, as early as the 12th century, one of the greatest paper-making towns in the world, invented water-marks, and its paper-mills are still worth a visit. The art gallery is a revelation to those who do not know the naive and graceful work of the Marches school of painting. The Palazzo del Podestà is a noble building, the cathedral harmonious, the Church of San Benedetto is worth a visit, and the oratory of Gonfalone with its carved wooden ceiling is delightful; the 13th-century Sant' Agostino has a remarkable doorway.

The jewel of the northern Marches is Urbino; that of the southern extremity, Ascoli Piceno. If you want a seaside base from which to explore the southern part of the region, San Benedetto is to be recommended. Ascoli Piceno, on a plain at the confluence of two swift rivers, is severe from a distance, built of monumental travertine stone. But its picturesque alleys, its towers, its nobly simple buildings, its bridges are highlighted by the octagonal 12th-century baptistery, the massive dignity of the cathedral, the picture gallery in the Palazzo Comunale—these should be seen. But above all, do not miss the Piazza del Popolo, with the austere Palazzo del Popolo, whose Renaissance gate is surmounted by a statue of Pope Paul III; San Francesco, with its ascetic interior and two hexagonal towers; and next door, the graceful 16th-century Merchants' Loggia.

Ascoli Piceno is the scene of one of Italy's most colorful events, the *Tournament of the Quintana,* in early August. Townspeple in 15th-century costume take part in torchlight parades, pageants and jousts, bringing the Middle Ages to life in the perfect setting of Ascoli's piazzas.

PRACTICAL INFORMATION FOR THE MARCHES

HOTELS AND RESTAURANTS

Ancona. Chief city, major port, art town, seaside resort. **Hotels:** High season, 25 June–8 Sept.

All (1) are—*Grand Palace,* Via Vanvitelli, all private baths, airconditioned, overlooking port, attractive roof garden; *Jolly,* quiet location overlooking port, comfortable, airconditioned; *Passetto,* on beach side of promontory, 45 well-furnished rooms, sea view.

Both (2) are—*Moderno,* Via G. Bruno 1, near station, most rooms with bath; *Fortuna,* on station square, comfortable.

Motel AGIP (3), modern, on Adriatic highway.

Restaurants: *Passetto* (E), Piazza IV Novembre, try their *brodetto.* All (M) are—*Nettuno,* Via Carducci; *Giardino,* Via Filzi, classic food in lovely setting; *La Moretta,* Piazza del Plebiscito.

Ascoli Piceno. Medieval art city. **Hotels:** *Marche* (1), Viale Kennedy, recent, unassuming, all rooms with bath.

Both (2)—*Gioli,* Viale de Gasperi, most rooms with bath or shower; at **Colle San Marco,** 10 minutes from town, *Miravalle,* all rooms with shower, swimming pool, park.

Restaurants: All (M)—*Gallo d'Oro* and *Vittoria* offer local dishes; *Cantina Pennile,* just outside town, rustic; avoid on weekends; *Cantina dell'Arte,* jolly tavern; *Tornasacco.*

Fabriano. Art town. **Hotels:** *Janus* (2), modern, well-appointed, 50 rooms with bath or shower, airconditioning optional, good restaurant.

Restaurant: *Fagiano d'Oro* (M).

Fano. Important beach resort. **Hotels:** High season, 1 July–31 Aug. Elisabeth (1), recent, best, airconditioned, short walk from beach.

Both (2) are—*Continental,* on shore drive, overlooking beach, comfortable; *Beaurivage,* on beach promenade, pleasant though anonymously furnished rooms, all with bath.

Astoria (3), excellent in category, on beach.

Restaurants: All (M), *Tutta Frasaglia* for *risotto alla Rossini; Del Capitano.*

Frontone. A small hilltop village. **Restaurant:** *Taverna della Rocca* (M), atmospheric hostelry in cellars of Malatesta castle, offers good food and dancing.

Grottamare. Beach resort. **Hotels:** High season, 1 July—31 Aug. Hotels open May through September. *Europa* (2), overlooking sea, 108 rooms with shower, garden, private beach. Both (2)—*Marconi* and *Roma,* beachfront.

Iesi. Medieval walled town. **Hotels:** Both (3) are— *Mariani, Motel del Nani.*

Loreto. Pilgrimage center. **Hotels:** High seasons, 21 April–2 May; 15 July–10 Sept. and 7–12 Dec.

Both (2) are—*Marchigiano,* Piazzale Squarcia 14, largest, best, some rooms with bath; *Giardinetto,* recently remodeled, all rooms with bath.

Santuario (3), modest but adequate, 44 rooms, most with shower.

Restaurants: All (M)—Outside town, *Orlando,* dining with a view; in town, try *Centrale* or *Moro.*

Macerata. Mountain scenic resort. **Hotels:** Both (2)—*Motel AGIP,* on state highway Val di Chienti, new, 51 rooms, all with shower; and *Centrale,* best in town proper, all private baths.

Restaurant: *Da Secondo* (M), excellent *vincisgrassi* and *dolce al mascarpone.*

Numana. At southern end of Monte Conero Riviera. Two good shingly beaches, attractive village, yacht harbor.

Hotels: Both (1)—*Santa Cristiana,* smart, expensive, with pool, tennis, beach facilities; and *Numana Palace,* also good with beach.

Both (2)—*Eden Gigli* and *Scogliera,* all rooms with shower.

Restaurant: *Teresa a Mare* (M), overlooking port, modest but good for fish. Seasonal.

Pesaro. Art city, seaside resort.

Hotels: High season—1 July–31 Aug. *Vittoria* (1), attractive, smallish hotel with garden.

All (2) are—*Caravelle,* 65 rooms with bath, pool, sea view; *Mamiani,* central, modern; *Excelsior,* on beach, all private baths, pool; *Spaggia,* modern, on beach, attractive little garden, terraces, veranda overlooking beach, all private baths, balconies; *Sporting,* cheerful, modern, on main beach, all rooms with shower, balcony, Signor Marcello's personal attention.

Both (3)—*Augustus,* sea view, few steps from beach, friendly small hotel, all rooms with shower. *La Bussola,* on beach.

Restaurants: *Della Posta* (M), Via Giordano Bruno, trattoria with varied menu of meat and fish dishes. *Da Carlo,* Via Venturini, also good.

Also recommended is *Carlo a Mare* (M), Viale Trieste, for homemade soups and grilled fish. *Castiglione* (M) is good.

Porto d'Ascoli is in reality the southern part of **San Benedetto.**

Hotels: *Excelsior* (2), on beach, first-rate comforts; *International,* airconditioned, *Pierrot,* both (2), and *Mocambo* (3); all have all rooms with bath or shower.

Portonovo. Pleasant new small resort on Monte Conero Riviera near Ancona. **Hotels:** All (2)—*Fortino Napoleonico,* and *Emilia,* both quiet, unpretentious resort hotels; *Excelsior La Fonte,* 62 rooms with shower, tennis, pool.

Restaurants: Both (M–E)—*Emilia,* straightforward decor, outstanding fish specialties, *risotto con scampi,* and handsome *Fortino Napoleonico,* more sophisticated, for fish or veal, *scrigno del Fortino.*

Porto Recanati. Restaurant: *Uomo del Brodetta* (M), famous for *zuppa di pesce.*

Porto San Giorgio. Beach resort. **Hotels:** High season, 1 July–31 Aug. All (2)—*Garden,* nicely furnished, close to beach in shady garden setting, all rooms with shower; *Villa Rosa,* overlooking sea, rather modest but comfortable, garage; *Gabbiano,* good private beach; *Riviera* (3).

Restaurants: *Miramare* (E), fish only, perfectly prepared; *Nettuno* (M–E), oysters and such.

San Benedetto del Tronto. Important beach resort. **Hotels:** High season, 1 July–31 Aug. *Roxy* (1), all rooms with bath or shower, airconditioned, private garden, pool.

All (2) are—*Carniscioni,* comfortable beach hotel; *Sabbiadoro,* modern, on beach; *Arlecchino,* small, beach.

Gabbiano (3), on beach, open 1 May–30 Sept.

Restaurants: Both (M)—*Angelici, Grottino Dea,* good fish.

Senigallia. Fine beach resort. **Hotels:** High season, 25 June–8 Sept. All (1)—*City,* ultra-modern, overlooking beach, small indoor pool, rooftop restaurant; *Senbhotel,* recent, contemporary decor and comforts, private beach area. *Excelsior,* on beach promenade, bright and spacious salons, many rooms with balcony, sea view.

All (2)—*Massi,* attractive small hotel with balconies, flowered terraces, all rooms with shower, beach facilities; *Cristallo* and modern *Beaurivage,* both face sea and have beaches; *Metropol,* overlooks sea, has beach and pool.

Restaurants: *Da Bice* (I–M), Via Leopardi 105, offers good, country-style food, great *pasta e fagioli; Da Loré* (M), Via Nazionale.

Sirolo. On Monte Conero, with magnificent views of the coast. **Hotel:** *Monte Conero* (2), modest but comfortable; tennis, heated pool.

Restaurants: Both (M)—*Monte Conero Hotel* restaurant and *Taverna del Trave,* both good.

Urbino. Important Renaissance art city. **Hotels:** Both (2)—*San Giovanni,* central, in renovated medieval palazzo, basic rooms but with atmosphere. *Montefeltro,* on outskirts, adequate but anonymous.

Restaurants: Both (M)—*Fornarina,* Via Viti; and *San Giovanni,* Via Barocci.

USEFUL ADDRESSES. **Tourist Offices:** *Ancona:* AAST, Via Thaon de Revel; EPT, Via Marini 14, and Railway Station. *Fano:* AAST, Viale Battisti 10. *Grottamare:* AAST, Largo Martiri Triestini 5. *Loreto:* AAST, Via G. Solari 3. *Macerata:* EPT, Via Garibaldi 87, and Piazza della Libertà 12. *Pesaro:* AAST, Viale Trieste 164; EPT, Via Mazzolari 4. *Porto Recanati:* AAST, Corso Matteotti 111. *Porto San Giorgio:* AAST, Via Oberdan 6. *San Benedetto Del Tronto:* AAST, Via C. Colombo 3. *Senigallia:* AAST, Piazzale Morandi. *Urbino:* AAST, Piazza Duca Federico 37.

SPECIAL EVENTS. *Ascoli Piceno:* First Sunday in August, there's a famous medieval Tournament of the Quintana, a historical pageant. *Fano:* The Adriatic Carnival in February. *Loreto:* 25 March, 10 May and 15 August, feast days and pilgrimages. 8 September is the feast of the Nativity of the Virgin Mary. 8 to 10 December festival of the Transference of the Holy House, the biggest celebration of the year here. On the last day bonfires are lit throughout the Marches and solemn celebrations take place in the Sanctuary and the square. *San Benedetto del Tronto:* Carnivals in February, and a festival for the Madonna della Marina, 30 July to 1 August.

SPORTS. In *Ancona* and *Fano* there is saltwater fishing. *Grottamare* has a fine stadium for track meets; tournament tennis. *Pesaro,* saltwater fishing and tournament tennis. *Porto San Giorgio,* specializes in underwater hunting. *Senigallia,* saltwater fishing and tournament tennis.

ABRUZZI-MOLISE

Fierce Mountains and Strange Superstitions

Although the Abruzzi is better known than the Molise section of the region, both are distinctive for their natural beauty, the preservation of their old traditions, and the fact that they have been less explored than many other parts of Italy. The Abruzzi and Molise on the Adriatic side are bounded by the Marches in the north and by Apulia in the south, but in the west they are separated from the Tyrrhenian Sea by Lazio (Rome) and Campania (Naples). The region is composed almost entirely of hills and mountains belonging to the Central Apennines (the Abruzzi), and a small part to the southern Apennines (Molise), with watersheds flowing into the Adriatic Sea.

Abruzzi-Molise economy is basically agricultural and pastoral. In addition to wheat fields where the earth will allow it, potatoes and vegetables are cultivated, the latter especially in the coastal regions.

Vineyards, olive and fruit trees flourish near the coast. Sheep-raising is a traditional occupation.

Centuries ago, the tribes in this region resisted, but finally fell under Roman domination. The Lombards later added Molise to the Duchy of Benevento, and the Abruzzi to that of Spoleto. In 843, the internal central region became an autonomous country called Marsia. In the 12th century, Pope Adrian IV gave the region to Norman King William I of Sicily, but Norman domination remained only in Molise. Abruzzi lined itself up with the Swabians, and took part in the struggle between Frederick II and the Church. The rest of the history of the area revolved around individual towns, local lords and warlike bishops, and in continual insurrections against Spanish, Austrian and Bourbon regimes until 1860, when it was united with Italy.

The shepherd is the symbol of Abruzzi. Jacketed and gaitered with goatskins, carrying a weirdly-carved club, he moves with his huge flocks on the upland pastures in summer; he has stone pens for his sheep, and a hut of stone where he practices playing bagpipes and the *pifferi,* a rustic oboe. When winter approaches, he comes down to the plains, along broad primordial traditional grassy tracks; you often see his migrating flock mixed up with cursing motorists in busy lowland towns. Sometimes he makes one of a city-strolling two-man bagpipe-and-*pifferi* band; their wailing is a presage of Christmas in Rome, as "waits" are elsewhere.

Weather Matters

The best times for a visit to Abruzzi and Molise are early fall or late spring, when the snows, though they many linger on the mountains, have disappeared from the roads which wind up through the hills. But this is year-round country, for the coast enjoys a mild climate which makes it tolerable in winter, while the sea breezes temper the heat of summer.

As for the mountain resorts, many of them are high enough so that they are comfortable in summer, while in winter they offer skiing and other winter sports, though they cannot compare with the great Alpine centers.

Road Reports

To reach Abruzzi, you will be coming either from the north by the *Autostrada Adriatica,* starting at Bologna, or from Rome by the *autostrada* to L'Aquila.

L'Aquila is the best center from which to visit the region. It lies inland, among the mountains, at the center of a road network whose axis is the scenic *autostrada* between Rome and L'Aquila continuing to the coast north of Pineto, with a branch forking south well before L'Aquila to Avezzano, and eventually to Pescara. A main road leaves L'Aquila southwestwards for the Abruzzi National Park.

The Molise region is easily visited especially by traveling the 80-mile stretch which runs from Venafro through Isernia, Boiano, Campobasso, Casacalenda and Larino to Termoli.

Food for Thought

The favorite *pasta* here is known as *maccheroni alla chitarra* because the *pasta* is cut into thin strips on the strings of a guitar-shaped utensil. *Pincisgrassi* is baked pasta, alternated with layers of cheese and sauce. Suckling pig is another favorite dish. Desserts include *parrozzo,* a rich chocolate cake; *zeppole, pasta* again, but this time sweet, and a candyish confection made of dried figs, honey, almonds and nuts.

The region produces both red and white wines. Among the reds, *Cerasolo di Abruzzo* is sweet, *Montepulciano* is dry. The best dry white wine is *Trebbiano.* This district is the home of a sweetish liqueur known as *Cent' Erbe.*

Exploring the Abruzzi

Aquila is a handsome town; 2,000 feet up, it is cool in the baking Abruzzi summer, and its cold winters are brightened by lively cultural events. Two churches are of great artistic value: Santa Maria di Collemaggio, set against a magnificent background of mountains, and San Bernardino. Santa Maria's façade of harmonious pink and white marble and its rich Gothic doorways are a compensation for an over-gaudy interior, which has many reminders of Pope Celestine V, who earned Dante's contempt in the *Inferno* for laying down the triple tiara. San Bernardino's fine front shows how the Renaissance penetrated deeply into these then remote valleys; it has a lovely Della Robbia (Andrea) altarpiece, and a massive tomb of the saint. There are numerous other churches, of which the most interesting are San Silvestro, the cathedral (mainly for its St. Stephen by Domenichino) and Santa Maria del Soccorso, near the Spanish castle, which is also worth inspecting. The tourist showpiece at Aquila is the Fountain of the Ninety-Nine Spouts (each of which is a different mask) near the station.

You may want to ascend the ponderous mass of the Gran Sasso, which overawes Aquila. The best way is to take the bus to Assergi whence 15 minutes in the funicular will bring you to Campo Imperatore, at 6,000-odd feet, a place to stay awhile if you like mountain walks and comfortable climbing or good winter skiing.

Sulmona

From Aquila to Sulmona is an easy run by train or bus. The cathedral, at the somewhat depressing entrance to the town, has been often rebuilt, and has lost most of its character. It must be remembered that Abruzzi is highly subject to earthquake shocks (a score of serious ones in the last 500 years) hence the frequent use of the word "rebuilt" in descriptions of buildings. The Palace (and Church) of the Annunziata, just before you reach the main square, is a really lovely building with its graceful doors and traceried windows.

By the way, Di Carlo's shop opposite the Annunziata reminds one that Sulmona is famous for its *confetti,* those sugared almonds which people send to friends in Italy on the occasion of marriages and christenings. But in Sulmona they make *confetti* into baskets of flowers and sheaves of corn with ingenious skill.

Ovid, born in Sulmona, now spoken of there as a sorcerer rather than a poet, has a statue in the square. But, continuing along the Corso, you come to the real heart of Sulmona, the part around the old aqueduct, with San Francesco della Scarpa above and the Piazza Garibaldi with it pleasant fountain. In this Piazza a beautiful religious ceremony takes place on Easter Monday, culminating in a release of doves, fireworks and the deafening explosion of mortars and clanging bells. In this square, too, market day brings the women in from the surrounding villages, wearing their picturesque costumes. If you wish to see them at home, take a bus from Sulmona to Pettorano sul Gizio, or better, to Scanno which tumbles downhill towards a lake, a town all-of-a-piece, a work of art. Go on Sunday, when all the women wear their severe and elegant costumes.

It is thrilling to ride up on the chair-lift to the summit of Monte Rotondo (5,413 feet), from where you will have a total view over the Abruzzi.

Then follow the road which winds around the mountain mass of the Maiella overlooking Sulmona, and stop at interesting local places that take your fancy along the way. You might want to see Barrea, for example, where there is a large lake that serves as a reservoir; or Rivisondoli, where you'll find equipment for winter sports; there is the castle at Roccaraso and the medieval town of Pescocostanzo. Farther on the road winds through wooded countryside, mostly groves of pine and birch.

Before you leave the region, make a visit to Cocullo, west of Sulmona, and if you are there the first Thursday in May, you will be lucky enough to see the procession of San Domenico. Villagers decorate the saint's statue with live snakes—they are no longer poisonous—and carry it through the village streets.

On the Pescara road our first stop after Popoli will be at San Clemente de Casauria, 30 miles from Pescara, where we will find a Cistercian abbey founded in the 9th century. The abbey is late Romanesque, with some Gothic elements. It is known for its *ciborium.*

Pescara is the largest of the beach resorts strung along the coast and providing adequate, but not particularly attractive bathing. Pleasant trips can be made inland to Penne, an old village. Other trips from Pescara are to Popoli and to Lorento Aprutino.

Lanciano is neaby: a most exciting city, for in the Middle Ages it was one of the chief trading centers of Italy. Merchants came from all over Europe, from the Middle East and Africa, to buy its cloth at an annual fair which actually lasted two to three months. Its cathedral and the magnificent 13th-century Santa Maria Maggiore with its superb front, varied columns, and sculptured arches; the ancient walls and mazy alleys; and the background of Apennines and valleys: all this makes a visit to Lanciano memorable.

A visit to the Abruzzi National Park might well be made on the return journey. The railway connects Pescara with Pescina, where there are buses to various places in the park. There is also a station at Alfedena, which is a good starting-off point. Or a bus from Avezzano, an untidy town rebuilt after total destruction in the 1915 earthquake, will take you to Pescasseroli. Here the woods of beech, the wealth of flowers and vegetation (amongst which protected bear, chamois and deer roam), all set against the massive frowning mountains, might well be your last—and best—impression of a wild, haunting region.

Exploring Molise

Molise offers the traveler its own natural beauty. As one comes from the coast, famous for the beach of Termoli, to the rich and vast Larino plain, one sees the first hills covered with woods and vineyards.

Campobasso, the capital, lies in the center of a plateau from which there is an excellent view of the area. The western part is mostly mountainous, the highest points being near Capracotta (highest town in the Apennines), in the Matese mountains and in the chain of the Mainarde mountains. From here flow the larger Molise rivers—the Biferno, the Volturno and the Trigno—which are used for irrigating many parts of the section. Campobasso is a picturesque city with narrow, winding streets. At its highest point is the severe Monforte Castle, built in 1549, beneath which are the two interesting churches of San Giorgio and San Bartolomeo. The modern part of the town lies below.

Isernia, noted for lacework, is situated on a hillside between two rivers. Its cathedral, Romanesque tower and Civic Museum are well worth visiting.

Termoli's 12th-century cathedral is one of the most important monuments in Molise. Sepino has important Roman remains and an entire Roman city was discovered near here, at Altilia. Beautiful copperwork can be found in Agnone, on a good road north of Iscernia. Altogether, with its folklore, artisanship, important archeological finds and rare beauty, Molise has much to offer and all you need is a map and a camera to conquer, and be conquered by, this attractive area.

PRACTICAL INFORMATION FOR ABRUZZI-MOLISE

HOTELS AND RESTAURANTS

Aremogna. Near Roccaraso. **Hotel:** *Paradiso Aremogna* (2), all private baths, pool, outstanding value.

Campobasso. Provincial capital. **Hotels:** *Roxy* (1), Piazza Savoia, best, commands a good view, garage. *Skanderberg* (2), attractive, well-appointed, 68 rooms with bath, fine views.

Restaurants: Both (M)—*L'Abruzzese,* tasty local food; *Boccalino,* fish specialties.

Campo Imperatore. On south slope of Monte Corno/Corno Grande, summer and winter mountain resort, 6,000 feet up.

Restaurant: *Campo Imperatore* (3), the big hotel which serves this resort.

At **Fonte Cerreto,** at the foot of the Gran Sasso cableway, **Hotels:** *Portella* (2), and *Villetta* (3).

Chieti. Provincial capital. **Hotels:** High season, 20 June–31 August. *Abruzzo* (2), central, fine view of Gran Sasso range. *Sole* (2), central, older-style, delightful roof garden.

Restaurants: *Nino* (M), converted winecellar; hearty fare. *Venturini* (I–M), local specialties in tranquil old palazzo courtyard. On the main highway, *Il Carro* (I–M), is a rewarding stop.

Francavilla al Mare. Resort with a wide sandy gently-sloping beach. **Hotels:** All (2)—*Roma, Grand, Royal* and *Punta de l'Est* all have private beach. *Alcione* is modern, in attractive park setting on beach.

Giulianova. Fishing port, beach resort with a gently sloping fine sand beach. **Hotels:** *Don Juan* (1), attractive Mediterranean style, on beach, 150 airconditioned rooms with bath, most with balcony, sea view, gardens, terraces, large pool.

Both (2) are—*Smeraldo,* overlooks sea, contemporary decor, all rooms airconditioned with shower and balcony, ample pool, minibus service to center, 1 mile away; *Riviera,* similar, also on beach.

Restaurants: *Beccacci* (M–E), finest fish restaurant around, but avoid when crowded. *Torrione* (E), in old town, smart, good food and view.

Isernia. Beautifully situated town. **Hotel:** *Tequila* (2), recent and modern, in quiet spot outside center, 69 rooms with shower, pool.

Restaurants: Both (M)—*La Molisana* and *Taverna Maresca,* good local cuisine and wine.

Lanciano. Medieval city. **Hotel:** *Excelsior* (2), best, panoramic roof garden.

Restaurant: *Ranieri* (M), classic dishes and local specialties.

L'Aquila. Art city, mountain resort, chief town of the Abruzzi. 2,000 feet above sea level, far from the sea, this is also a swimming center with a fine swimming pool of national fame.

Hotels: *Grand* (1), central, traditional, well-furnished. All (2) are—*Duca degli Abruzzi,* fine, modern, 85 well-furnished rooms, rooftop restaurant; *Le Cannelle,* recent, near station, below center, comfortable, bright rooms, all with bath or shower, pool, tennis courts in garden; *Castello,* modern, facing ancient castle, attractive decor, all rooms with bath.

Restaurants: *Tetto* (E), restaurant of *Duca degli Abruzzi* hotel is elegant, and modern. All (M)—*Tre Marie,* typical, turn-of-the-century frescos and wood paneling create old-world atmosphere, try *maccheroni alla chitarra, involtini Tre Marie,* lamb dishes; *Aquila-Da Remo,* off main piazza, rustic trattoria, serves *tortelli di ricotta,* local sausages.

Montesilvano Marina. Near Pescara. **Hotels:** *Serena Majestic* (1), 216 rooms with bath or shower, modern, well-managed, it overlooks its own beach, olympic-sized pool, and tennis courts.

Both (2) are—*Sund,* tall, modern, overlooking own gardens and sea, all rooms with shower, many with balconies, pool, beach; *Montesilvano Grand,* same amenities, plus airconditioning.

Pescara. Two good mildly sloping sand beaches, and plenty of bathing establishments. **Hotels:** All (1) are—*Singleton,* overlooking sea, best, all rooms with shower; *Carlton,* on shore boulevard, pleasant, airconditioned rooms; *Esplanade,* overlooks shore boulevard, large, beach facilities, roof garden and restaurant.

All (2) are—*Maja,* modern, and *Bellariva,* both on beach; *Plaza Moderno,* on station square.

Restaurants: Both (E)—*Guerino,* on shore, is excellent for fish soup, fish fillets *al prosciutto; Cetrullo,* another winner, does wonders with tiny squid.

All (M) are—*Scaricarelle,* has lots of atmosphere, clowning waiters serve fish specialties; *Furnacelle,* Via Colle Marino, is known for great *pasta e fagioli; La Grotta,* Via Fabrizi, offers huge portions of *maccheroni* in a tiny dining room and garden; *Lu Travocche,* on shore drive, seafood.

Pescasseroli. Mountain resort. **Hotels:** *Grand del Parco* (1), big, expensive for region, magnificently situated in national park, all rooms with bath, swimming pool. *Pinguino* (2) is small, quiet, all rooms with shower.

Restaurants: *Da Leonardo* (M), *pasta alla chitarra* and exquisite lamb.

Popoli. Restaurant: *Onofrietti,* modest, does tasty things with crayfish and eels.

Rivisondoli. Summer and winter sports resort. **Hotels:** Both (2)—*Cinquemiglia,* 64 rooms with bath, dancing, terraces, swimming pool; *Impero,* many private baths, large park, excellent food.

Roccaraso. Smart summer and winter sports resort. **Hotels:** All (2) are—*Grande.* biggest, all rooms with bath; *Excelsior* and *Iris,* both good, all rooms with bath or shower, *Motel AGIP,* on highway 17.

Restaurant: *Dal Grillo* (M), *abruzzese* dishes.

Scanno. Picturesque mountain summer resort. **Hotels:** Both (2)—*Del Lago,* best, lovely location on the lake, surrounded by gardens, all rooms with bath or shower; *Mille Pini,* small, comfortable rooms, all with bath.

Restaurant: *Gli Archetti* (M), homemade pasta, roast lamb.

Silvi Marina. Small resort with a fine sand beach which drops rather steeply to the sea. **Hotels:** All (2)—*Hermitage,* strikingly modern, 100 soundproofed rooms, all with bath or shower, and balcony with sea view, on broad private beach, tennis, pool, tavern and dancing; *Abruzzo Marina,* on beach, all rooms with bath or shower, pleasant, lively atmosphere; *Orsa Maggiore,* medium-sized modern hotel, directly on beach, all rooms with shower, balcony, small pool.

Sulmona. Important mountain town. **Hotels:** Both (2)—*Artu,* best, garage. At **Campo di Giove,** nearby ski resort, *Pizzalto,* pool.

Restaurants: All (M)—*Italia* hotel restaurant is best, followed by *Clemente.* At **Passo San Leonardo.** *Taverna* serves hearty regional specialties.

Tagliacozzo. Winter sports resort. **Hotels:** *Garden* (1), all rooms with bath. *Nuovo Marina* (2), *Gatto d'Oro* (3), good.

Teramo. Provincial capital. **Hotels:** Both (2), recent, modern, all rooms with shower, pool—*Sporting* and larger *Michelangelo.*

Restaurant: *Centrale* (M), excellent local food and wine.

Termoli. Fishing and bathing resort. **Hotels:** All (2)—*Savoia,* most rooms with bath; *Corona* and *Giardino.*

Restaurants: Both (M)—*Il Drago* and *Torre Saraceno,* fine for fish.

Vasto. Rather dreary beach resort, and sailing center. If you're this far south, head for the much more rewarding Gargano beaches. **Hotels:** High season 20

June–31 August. Both (2)—*Baiocco* and *President,* both modern, anonymous beach hotels.

USEFUL ADDRESSES. Tourist Offices: *Campobasso:* EPT, Piazza della Vittoria 13. *Chieti:* EPT, Via Spaventa 29. *Francavilla al Mare:* AAST, Piazzale Sirena. *Isernia:* EPT, Via Kennedy 80. *L'Aquila:* AAST, Via XX Settembre 8; EPT, Piazza Santa Maria di Paganica 5. *Montesilvano Marina:* AAST, Viale Europa. *Pescara:* AAST, Corso Umberto 44; EPT, Via N. Fabrizi 171, and Railway Station. *Pecasseroli;* AAST, Via Principi di Napoli 32. *Roccaraso:* AAST, Viale Roma 60. *Scanno:* AAST, Piazza Santa Maria delle Valle 12. *Silvi Marina:* AAST, Via Garibaldi 38. *Sulmona:* AAST, Via Roma 21. *Tagliacozzo:* AAST, Piazza Duca degli Abruzzi. *Teramo:* EPT, Via del Castello. *Termoli:* AAST, Piazza Stazione 21. *Vasto:* AAST, Piazza del Popolo 18–20.

UMBRIA

The Mystic Province

The subtle influence of Umbria, known as the Green Heart of Italy, is difficult to recreate in words. Even among the hills, the country is undramatic, but the strange, bluish haze which diffuses the landscape and has caused so many writers to characterize Umbria as mystic and ethereal, lends the area a special charm. The colors. mostly soft tones of grays and greens, create a sense of peace. Hills covered with olive groves, or in the less cultivated parts, with pines, rise with deceptive gentleness from the flatness of the broad plain. It is only from directly below, or from one of the many towns built on them, that you realize how steep the hills really are. On the terraced lower slopes and on the plain are the famous Umbrian grape vines, carefully trained to grow over dwarf elms. Slim poplars divide the fields and shade the dusty white roads. Everything seems as motionless as if the scenery were painted.

Weather Matters

From the climatic point of view, it would be well to avoid Umbria, a centrally located district with no cooling coast, during the main tourist season of July and August, for it can get very hot then, and stick to May, June and September for your visit here. Unfortunately, some of the main events of the chief tourist attraction of Umbria, Assisi, occur in the middle of August. If you want to take them in, you have to endure the heat. However all three of the principal tourist centers—Assisi, Orvieto, Perugia—are well above 1,000 feet, and the altitude helps. And Assisi does have other events than those of August.

Road Reports

The average tourist takes in Umbria only on his way between Rome and Florence, which allows for seeing Assisi and Perugia on one route and Orvieto on another. Traveling by car, which is the ideal way for this scenically interesting country, it is possible to get all three of them in on one round trip between Rome and Florence, though it shouldn't be done in a hurry. The Fossato di Vico tunnel under the Apennines has shortened the distance between Umbria and the Adriatic coast. A super-highway links the *Autostrada del Sole* at Orte with Perugia via Terni and Todi.

Food for Thought

The most famous food specialty of Umbria is the truffle—indeed, many of the truffles you eat in France assuming they are from the Perigord, are actually imported from Umbria. The favorite *pasta* is homemade spaghetti, the favorite meat dish, suckling pig *(porchetta alla perugina).* An excellent regional dish is *carne ai capperi e acciughe:* veal with caper and herb sauce. The quality of Umbria's sausages, salami and prosciutto is famous throughout Italy. A fruit specialty is dried white figs stuffed with almonds and other nuts.

Umbria has one famous wine, *Orvieto,* which is white, but comes in both dry *(secco)* and sweet *(amabile)* varieties, the latter having the higher alcoholic content. Some lesser but honorable wines come from the Perugia region: *Sacrantino di Montefalco, Vernaccia di Cannara, Torgiano* and *Trasimeno.*

You're recommended to try the local wines throughout the region; genuine and not pasteurized, they don't travel well but are unbeatable on their home ground.

Exploring Umbria

Even in Italy, where regions rich with artistic inheritance are the rule, Umbria remains outstanding. Almost every small town contains treasures from the past. There might be a lovely Della Robbia plaque, some outstanding fresco or painting, or fine piece of sculpture. Perhaps a particularly well proportioned square, civic building, or a church is the source of local pride.

Minor arts, such as embroidery, lace-making, ceramics, and iron working, still flourish in Umbria, but in general, the current products are not to be compared with the old. Don't fail to notice the vestments in the cathedral museums. Glance up at the delicate wrought iron balconies, at the torch holders, and at the majolica plaques decorating the house-fronts.

Even the briefest crossing of Umbria will show well-preserved examples of architecture recording the passing of the Etruscans, Romans, their medieval successors and Renaissance descendants down to the present day.

Most of the surviving buildings left by those mysterious people, the Etruscans, are centered in Umbria. Several of the walled cities have portions of original Etruscan masonry incorporated into later defenses. A few gates and arches still stand. Foundations of various temples remain, some as they were laid, others with later buildings superimposed on them. The best preserved models of their skill are their family tombs.

The Romans are represented by their usual quota of temples, fora, amphitheaters and bridges, many of them adapted by citizens of later ages for their own use. Medieval castles, standing grim and alone or with walled towns clustered around them, testify to the turbulence of the history which gave them birth. Handsome palaces, marvelously decorated churches and, in contrast, narrow, twisting streets, darkened by overhanging houses, represent the Renaissance and baroque periods.

Since the majority of the Umbrian cities and towns are either placed some distance up the slope or actually crown the top of a hill, there are invariably magnificent views. You can often find restaurants at vantage points overlooking spectacular scenery. The local wines definitely add to the appreciation of the vast panorama spread below.

In addition to its natural beauty, art, history and wine, Umbria offers its share of traditional festivals. The most interesting of these is the *Feast of the Candles,* at Gubbio, while the most important religious events naturally take place in Assisi. For the music lover, operas and concerts are given in Perugia's Morlacchi Theater, and yearly, in September, there is an excellent musical festival. The Spoleto Festival (June–July) is world famous.

Perugia

Two points indicate Perugia as the logical center for short trips off the beaten path. It is the largest and richest, both materially and artistically, of the cities of Umbria, and its size and central location ensure the best regional transportation.

In the distance, Perugia displays a lovely silhouette against the sky. Built on a hill-top 1,000 feet above the plain, the city's skyline is set off to its fullest advantage. However, as one approaches, little more than its location proclaims it to be of anything but recent construction. In spite of all the beauty it contains, Perugia has sacrificed much of its charm to progress. A few of its once-numerous spires still rise, but the usual fortress is absent, and the walls are largely invisible, the city's expansion having concealed the medieval nucleus behind modern buildings.

Long before the Romans showed the first signs of civilization by assaulting the Sabines, Perugia was the site of a flourishing city, and before the first of its many recorded falls, had become one of the centers of Etruscan culture. This civilization, in conjunction with that of Greece, was to have the greatest influence in the formation of the Romans. Virtually nothing is known of these people, as their language is still largely a puzzle to the archeologists. In three fields, however, they left a distinct mark. The Etruscans were fine architects and taught much to their conquerors. They were also notable sculptors. But perhaps their most important legacy was their religious influence, and many have felt it a logical step to conclude that the intensity and mysticism of the Umbrian stems from this source.

One of the finest collections of Etruscan relics in existence is to be seen in Perugia's Museum of Etruscan and Roman Antiquities. There is an Etruscan gate (Porta Marzia) in good condition, and incidentally, about 200 feet to the right of it, one of the few stretches of the city's medieval wall still stands, unhidden by later construction.

Of the Roman period—highlighted by Octavian's sack of Perugia in 40 BC, four years after the fatal Ides of March which saw the murder of his uncle, Julius Caesar—there are few traces. Over one Etruscan gate is the inscription *Augusta Perusia,* probably dating from the rebuilding of the city at the order of its destroyer, who became Rome's first emperor, Caesar Augustus. In 1962 a 1st-century Roman reservoir was discovered under the Piazza IV Novembre.

The bulk of the old part of the city dates from the late Middle Ages and Renaissance and is concentrated around the top and upper slopes of Perugia's hill. The oldest portion is naturally nearest the top, and as the city grew, a second level developed which is known as the Lower City.

Along the highest ridge runs the city's main street, the Corso Vannucci, an odd mixture of old and new. At one extreme is the lovely square with its magnificent 13th-century fountain flanked by the cathedral and Municipal Palace. At the other end are the *Hotel Brufani-Palace,* Perugia's biggest, and a block of 19th-century buildings which can take a lion's share of the guilt for ruining the city's approach. From the same street run a series of arched tunnels and narrow alleys. These lead steeply down to the medieval town.

Two names have lent Perugia widespread familiarity. Perugina chocolate is well-known for is delicious flavor. Perugino is the nickname of the 15th-century painter Pietro Vannucci, the most distinguished figure of the Umbrian School. Along with most of the sightseeing musts of Perugia, some of the best of his work is in the Stock Exchange.

In addition to being a fine 13th-century building, the Municipal Palace contains four rooms of artistic importance, a library, and the National Gallery (Pinacoteca). On the ground floor are the rooms of the Merchants' Guild, and the Exchange with its adjoining chapel. The first is magnificently decorated with wooden panels, carved and inlaid with rare delicacy. The Exchange, also in a remarkable state of preservation, is enriched by the brush of Perugino. Its chapel is the work of his pupils. On the right side of the altar is a charming *Madonna* by Perugino's most famous pupil, Raphael. The Notary's Room, on the third floor, contains some good painting, while the Pinacoteca, on the fourth, should not be missed by anyone interested in art.

The Gothic cathedral is entered by an ornate baroque doorway. The wedding ring of the Virgin Mary, a circle of white onyx about an inch in diameter, is kept in a reliquary on a splendid silver altar in the first chapel on the left. In the Chapterhouse Museum are some finely illuminated books and a *Madonna* by Signorelli among a few paintings.

Three of Perugia's medieval streets should be mentioned as particularly interesting. The Maestà della Volte, a favorite photographic subject; the Via dei Priori, which leads to the Oratory of San Bernardino, decorated with the reliefs of Agostino di Duccio, and the Via Bagliona. The Via Bagliona is an architectural curiosity almost completely covered over by later buildings.

Perugia's Foreign University in the Gallenga Palace, the choir stalls of the Churches of San Pietro and Sant' Agostino, the curious 13th-century church of San Ercolano, and the 6th-century Sant' Angelo are all of interest if time permits.

Assisi, Home of St. Francis

On a clear day, from Perugia's upper city, Assisi can be seen to the south, compact and gray against the mass of Mt. Subasio. Assisi has such charm that other towns might seem drab by comparison. This is high praise when you consider the enormous volume of tourists and pilgrims who visit the tiny city and its important shrines.

Although Assisi lived through a history very similar to that of its neighbor and bitter enemy, Perugia (in 1492 a Perugian army led by a Baglioni sacked Assisi), it is today completely associated with the cult of St. Francis. This saint and founder of the monastic order which bears his name was born in 1182, the son of a well-to-do cloth merchant. His young manhood gave no indication of the future development of his character, for he led the life of a 12th-century rake. The great change followed a serious illness which he contracted on his return from a spell in a Perugian jail, where he was held after capture in one of the frequent clashes between the two cities.

Francis became convinced that the root of all evil lay in the desire for possessions and promptly changed his life, remodeling it on that basis. Tradition has it that not only did he himself give up all worldly things but that he tried to have his most unwilling father share his sacrifice by selling his stock of cloth and giving the proceeds to the Monastery of San Damiano.

In 1210, Francis, by then a well-known religious figure, organized the Franciscan Order of Mendicant Friars, whose basic tenets are those which he had adopted for himself, poverty and asceticism. Preaching his simple faith in an era sadly needing reform, St. Francis won many converts.

Women flocked to join the order begun by his follower St. Clare, whose first convent, incidentally, was the Monastery of San Damiano. These movements were to spread all over Europe and survive today as Fransiscans, Capuchins, Observants, Conventuals for men, and as Poor Clares for women.

Almost everything of importance to be seen in Assisi is in some way associated with the memory of the saint. The huge Basilica was started to honor him in the two years between his death in 1226 and his canonization. Originally, the land on which the church stands had served as the execution ground for condemned criminals and bore the suggestive title of Infernal Hill. St. Francis, in his humility, had asked to be buried there. His wish was granted, and by order of the Pope the name of the spot was changed to Hill of Paradise. Funds flowed in. The saint's great popularity brought many to work on his memorial without pay and the lower church was completed in the record time of 22 months. About 10 years later, the upper church and huge, double arched cloisters were added.

To prevent the saint's remains from being stolen, Francis' indefatigable follower, Brother Elias, who also seems to have been largely responsible for the building of the lower church, had the body removed to a secret vault cut in the living rock under the church. This tomb defied all attempts to locate it until 1818. Two flights below the floor of the lower church the visitor can see the coffin containing the body of the saint. The crypt is severely handsome, and its four corners hold the bodies of Francis' four closest followers.

Both the upper and lower churches, which together make up the big, two-level Basilica, are artistic treasurehouses. The lower level, dim and crypt-like on the brightest of days, is marvelously frescoed by master artists of several periods. The oldest of these paintings are classified as primitives and are attributed to a mid-13th-century artist, known only as the Master of St. Francis. Afterwards, at different times, Cimabue, Giottino (pupil of Giotto), Simone Martini, and Pietro Lorenzetti were commissioned to add to the glory of the building. Lorenzetti's fresco of the Virgin, Child Jesus, and St. Francis, to the left of the altar, is particularly sensitive and is considered to be one of the finest pieces produced by the Sienese School of that period (1330). To get the most pleasure from this visit a flashlight is invaluable.

To the left of the altar, in the sacristy, are preserved a number of relics of the saint. Among them are his patched, gray cassock, the cruel cord, made of camel hair and needles, which belted his waist, and the crude sandals which he wore when he received the Stigmata in 1224. The Stigmata, according to Roman Catholic belief, are the five wounds which Christ suffered at his crucifixion, and which can supernaturally appear on the body of an intense believer.

The top portion of the walls of the upper church are decorated with a number of frescos by unidentified artists, probably of the Roman school. More important are the 28 scenes from the life of St. Francis with which Giotto enriched the lower half of the walls of the nave. Beside the Basilica is a lovely and little-visited cloister enclosing a small cemetery.

Assisi is well worth the stiff walk up Via San Francesco to the central Piazza del Comune, flanked by 13th-century palaces and the Roman Temple of Minerva, still used as a church. In the baptismal font of the Romanesque 12th-century Cathedral of St. Rufino, St. Francis, St. Clare and the Emperor Frederick II were baptized.

The 13th-century basilica of St. Clare is most impressive in its simplicity. The saint's body, quite blackened by time, lies open to view in the crypt, while the closed cloisters of her followers adjoin the church.

In a side chapel can be seen one of the most famous and best-loved crucifixes in the world. Before this cross St. Francis prayed and first recognized his mission, and later was to have his visions of Christ and the Virgin.

In contrast, just below the town the tiny Monastery of San Damiano is full of sunshine. Originally, the cross mentioned above hung in the chapel here. The Franciscan monk acting as guide will show you the little court where St. Francis wrote, the table where St. Clare performed a miracle, and the choir with its legends. It is an exquisite spot with a glorious view.

A road climbs Mount Subasio, offering magnificent panoramas above St. Francis' favorite retreat, the Eremo delle Carceri, located in a dense forest three miles behind the town. The formidable Papal stronghold built by Cardinal Albornoz in the 14th century also is worth a visit.

Below the town is the ostentatious, frescoed Santa Maria degli Angeli, built over the cell with its adjoining chapel, the Portiuncola, where St. Francis died. Nearby is the garden where, ever since the saint rolled among the roses while wrestling with temptation, the bushes have been thornless.

Leaving Assissi we turn first south via Foligno to Spoleto and Orvieto, then west to the other two outstanding Umbrian cities.

Spoleto

Some 62 miles from Rome on the Via Flaminia, at the foot of Monteluco, Spoleto rises on the Sant' Elia hill, surrounded by a pleasant landscape which, in addition to its panoramic view, offers many opportunities for mountain and hillside excursions. Spoleto is a very old city, rich in evidence of the civilizations which succeeded one another there—from Umbrian through Roman, medieval, Renaissance to modern. Time has fused together the different periods within the town's ancient walls in an enchanting way. St. Francis, gazing at this area, said he had never seen anything as pleasing as the Spoleto valley (one of the most important autographs of the saint can be seen in the cathedral). Michelangelo stated that he found "true peace" among the oaks of Monteluco.

Among the most important and characteristic monuments in Spoleto are the fortress and the Ponte delle Torri, the Salvatore Basilica, the cathedral with Filippo Lippi frescos in the apse as well as the painter's funeral memorial, the Sant' Eufemia and San Pietro churches, the Roman theater and the Arch of Druso.

Spoleto has gained an added measure of fame with its Festival of Two Worlds, organized by Gian-Carlo Menotti. The festival presents the latest creative trends in art (music, theater, painting and sculpture) in the ancient setting of the town. Classical opera and concerts in the Piazza del Duomo are highlights of the festival. An exhibition of modern sculpture set up for the 1962 festival in Spoleto's streets and piazzas has remained as a permanent gift to the town.

If you are thinking of small tours in the area, we encourage you to go to Monteluco and to the Church of San Pietro. The Monteluco road passes right by San Pietro, whose foundations date back to the 5th century. Its 12th-century façade is adorned with remarkable Romanesque reliefs. Atop thickly wooded Monteluco you'll find a tiny monastery founded by St. Francis with an enchanting view of the valley.

Orvieto

Of all the hill cities, Orvieto has the most spectacular situation. Whether you arrive by rail or road, the city breaks into view with astonishing impact and suddenness. As you roll up the valley or wind down the steep hills, before you, in the middle of the flat plain, stand the islands of volcanic rock above whose brown cliffs the defense-minded Etruscans who founded Orvieto raised its walls. Like the *mesas* of the southwestern United States, the cliffs of this natural fortress rise sheer from the floor of the valley. Orvieto itself, largely built of the same stone that forms its foundation, blends so closely with the cliffs that it is difficult to realize the extent of the city.

Except at its approaches, Orvieto is quite flat. It preserves much of its atmosphere with its narrow, twisting streets and old houses, but it lacks the thrill of changing levels, so characteristic of the other cities. There are a number of first-rate attractions which make Orvieto worth a visit, but it has less of the power of transporting the visitor into the past than some other Umbrian towns.

Like Perugia, Orvieto has given its name to its most famous product, one of the best wines which Italy produces. Don't fail to try a glass of Orvieto at one of the wine shops in the cathedral square.

The cathedral itself, a magnificent 13th-century building of alternating stripes of black and white marble, is the pride of the city. It was designed by the Sienese architect Maitani (note the similarity with his other great work, the Cathedral of Siena) to commemorate the miracle at Bolsena. This event befell a priest who doubted the Doctrine of Transubstantiation while he was saying mass. The Host bled, proving that it really was part of Christ's body. Contrasting with the severe horizontal stripes of the sides, the façade is elaborately adorned with mosaics, bas-reliefs, carved stone work and statuary. To appreciate the full effect of its brilliant colors, the front should be seen in bright light. The most important of these decorations are the bas-relief plaques which flank the cathedral's three doors. They are probably the work of Maitani and his pupils. Note the marvelous rose window over the door.

Inside, there are some interesting frescos, the most outstanding by Lippo Memi, Fra Angelico, and Luca Signorelli. The latter painted the walls of the New Chapel, on the right of the nave. His *Last Judgement*, on the right wall, is believed to have provided Michelangelo with the inspiration for the Sistine Chapel, but is a work of strikingly macabre imagination in its own right. The cathedral's modern bronze portals were hung in 1970 amid a raging controversy as to their artistic merit and appropriateness. The viewer can judge for himself whether or not they harmonize with the magnificent façade.

To the right of the Duomo stands the handsome Palace of the Popes, for Orvieto's impregnable position provided refuge for 32 pontiff sovereigns. It is now used as a museum and houses an oddly assorted collection of relics and pottery, church vestments, painting, woodwork, and sculpture. A small but interesting Etruscan Museum is right opposite the cathedral.

The city abounds in interesting monuments. The 11th-century Palazzo Vescovile, oldest papal residence, the 12th-century Palazzo del Capitano del Popolo, the churches of San Domenico, San Francesco, Sant' Andrea, with its impressive 12-sided bell tower, and the Church of San Giovenale are all among the best of the city's monuments. Near the ruins of the fortress, another of the chain of Papal strongholds set up by the castle-building Cardinal Albornoz, is the Well of St. Patrizio. This remarkable engineering feat was commissioned by Pope Clement VII to ensure Orvieto's water supply in case of siege.

The Smaller Cities

You will find that these lesser-known cities are close enough to one another to be conveniently visited without taking too much of your scheduled time.

A trip to Città di Castello, north of Perugia, is well worthwhile. During the city's three artistically rich centuries, the Cathedral, the churches of San Domenico and San Francesco, and the Vitelli Palace were built. There are works by Raphael, Signorelli, and Andrea della Robbia in the Palace.

We have already mentioned Gubbio, also to the north, in connection with the city's annual *Feast of the Candles.* This festival takes place on May 15, beginning with a picturesque procession through the streets from the town to the Abbey of Sant Ubaldo a mile away. The local people all wear period costume, giving it a charm rather like the Sienese *palio.* The festival itself centers around a race by three teams carrying huge candle-shaped wooden pillars, through the town and up a hill to the monastery. If you miss Festival time, there are plenty of reasons for visiting Gubbio anyway. The old part of the town, the Città Vecchia, is fascinating. There's a fast flowing river, the Camignano, to wander beside and nearby, a splendid Gothic Consular Palace with a museum and art gallery. The 15th-century Ducal Palace is built of red brick and gray stone and has a very fine doorway, frescos and chimneys. From the Roman theater, going back to Augustus' time, you have a particularly fine view of the city.

To the south of Perugia, before you reach Foligno, make a stop at Spello to visit the ruins of Roman ramparts built under Augustus and to see Pinturicchio's paintings in the churches of the town.

You won't want to pass through Foligno without taking a look at the Piazza della Repubblica, or without having seen the Cathedral, the Communal Palace and the Palazza Trinci, most of which houses an art gallery. Everything is conveniently located in the center.

Right next to Foligno is Montefalco, a city with an appropriate name—it really is the Balcony of Umbria. Here you'll find frescos by Benozzo Gozzoli and work by other Umbrian painters. Beautifully situated, Montefalco is delightful not just for itself, but for the views of the surrounding countryside that it provides.

Narni is another ancient town high on a hill, from which its massive 14th-century fortress, commissioned by the ubiquitous Cardinal Albornoz, commands a thickly forested pass and the plain below. Narni's Romanesque cathedral and handsome medieval palace are a perfect backdrop for the gorgeously costumed pageant enacted each May, when horsemen representing the town's rival quarters joust for a coveted prize. Just below Narni are the ruins of the Roman bridge of Augustus.

There is much more to see in Umbria. Try to visit Todi and its Piazza de Popolo, truly an extraordinary grouping of historical buildings. The Priory Palace, the Capitanat Palace, both are excellent examples of the Gothic style. The cathedral (12th to 14th century) is Romanesque-Gothic, and it stands on the still older site of a former Roman temple.

Near Terni are the 500-foot waterfalls of Marmore which have drained the waters of the Velino into the Nera since 272 BC, but now flow only on Sundays and holidays, spectacularly illuminated at night. Citta della Pieve (the birthplace of Perugino), Gualdo Tadino, and Norcia never hide the medieval splendor of their churches and palaces. At every turn in the road you will see imposing castles crowning green hills, and readily agree that no itinerary of Italy is complete without a visit to this lovely area.

PRACTICAL INFORMATION FOR UMBRIA

HOTELS AND RESTAURANTS

Assisi. Birthplace and shrine of St. Francis. **Hotels:** All (2)—*Subasio,* best, 70 rooms, many with bath, all front rooms with balcony, garden restaurant, near Basilica; *Giotto,* 70 rooms, many with bath, overlooking valley, open-air restaurant, open 15 March–15 Nov. *Umbra,* small, central and quiet; opposite Basilica. *San Francesco; Fontebella,* recent and comfortable; *Priori,* modern, pleasant.

All (3)—*Minerva,* 29 rooms, a few with bath; *San Pietro,* small; *Excelsior,* central; *Roma,* small but nearly all rooms with bath or shower; at Santa Maria degli Angeli, *Villa Elda,* 30 rooms, all with shower.

Restaurants: All (M)—*Buca di San Francesco,* delightful atmosphere, fine local cooking; *Taverna dell'Arco,* medieval surroundings, Umbrian dishes; *Da Cecco* and *Da Carletto* are good, unpretentious trattorias; fine hotel restaurants, *Giotto* and excellent *Umbria;* for pizza, try *Del Carro,* reader recommended.

On the road to **Eremo delle Carceri,** rustic *La Stalla,* spit-roasted meat and hearth-baked bread.

Citta della Pieve. Fine buildings. **Hotel:** *Barzanti* (3), most rooms with bath, tennis, swimming pool. Excellent restaurant (M), country cooking.

Citta di Castello. Impressive churches. **Hotels:** *Villa San Donino* (2) is recent resort-type hotel with airconditioning, tennis courts, swimming pool. *Tiferno* (3), central, comfortable, all rooms with shower.

Restaurant: *Tiferno* (M) serves fine local dishes.

Corciano. Near Perugia. **Hotels:** *Colle della Trinità* (2), tennis; and *Conca del Sole* (2), pool, tennis; both all private baths.

Foligno. Art city. **Hotels:** *Umbria* (2), most rooms have bath. At **Colfiorito,** *Viaal Fiorita* (3), park, pool, tennis.

Restaurant: *Da Remo* (M), fine grilled meats.

Gubbio. Folklore center. **Hotels:** *Cappucini* (1), below town in secluded location, converted convent with attractively furnished rooms, pleasant garden court.

Both (2)—*Montegranelli,* also on outskirts, 10 rooms with bath in 18th-century villa; *Bosone,* central, recent, modern, all 33 rooms with shower; *Taverna* restaurant.

Balestrieri (3), many of its 14 rooms have bath or shower.

Restaurants: All (M)—*San Marco,* charming garden and past-century atmosphere, *risotto San Marco,* truffled specialties; *Taverna del Lupo* and *Porta Tessenaca* are near main square; *Dei Consoli,* and *Cappuccini* hotel restaurant, both very good.

Orvieto. Art city. **Hotels:** All (1)—*Maitani,* elegant, best; *Italia,* most rooms with bath, no restaurant; *La Badia,* 20 rooms, at medieval monastery that's a national monument, outside town, peaceful surroundings, tennis court, swimming pool.

Virgilio (2), recent, on Cathedral Square, small and delightful. *Posta* (3), basic in heart of town.

Restaurants: Both (E)—Best is *Morino,* Via Garibaldi, for truffled *agnolotti,* veal chops; followed by *La Badia* and *Villa Ciconia* at Orvieto Scalo.

All (M)—*Beppe,* Via Beato Angelico; *Maurizio,* Via del Duomo; *Da Cecco,* just off Piazza del Popolo.

Little wine cellar (I), across from Duomo, for hearty sandwiches, cold vino.

Perugia. Principal town, art city. **Hotels:** Both (1)—*Brufani Palace,* elegant, fine location with view, beautifully furnished salons, comfortable rooms. *Excelsior Lilli,* Piazza Garibaldi, large, very good, airconditioned, garage.

All (2)—*Grifone,* bright modern hotel on outskirts, 50 rooms with bath or shower; *Rosetta,* large, central, comfortable, cheerful place with fine restaurant; *Della Posta,* Corso Vanucci 97, many rooms with bath or shower, recently renovated; *Astor,* Piazza Vittorio Veneto, many of 44 rooms with bath or shower.

Dei Priori (3), Via Priori, modest but good, no restaurant.

Restaurants: Both (E)—*La Rosetta,* hotel restaurant, still good after changed ownership; *Ricciotto,* Piazza Dante, tasteful decor, refined menu, a touch of chic.

All (M)—*Pavone, Artisti* and *Taverna della Streghe; Sole,* with a panoramic summer terrace; *Falchetto,* try *falchetti,* delicious spinach and *ricotta* dumplings; *Lanterna,* serves local specialties, homemade *pasta.*

Spoleto. Artistic center. **Hotels:** *Dei Duchi* (2), all rooms with bath, recommended, attractive decor, view, good restaurant.

All (3)—*Lello Caro,* 42 rooms, some with bath; *Commercio,* most rooms with shower; *Nuovo Clitunno,* central, attractive, recently renovated, most rooms with shower. *Manni,* pleasant small hotel near all sights, all rooms with bath; on Via Flaminia, *Motel AGIP.*

Restaurants: Both (E)—*Pentagramma,* popular with festival crowd; *Dei Duchi,* hotel restaurant good.

All (M)—*Tartufo, Del Teatro, Pennello; Panciolle,* simple, with summer dining under the trees; and *Sciattinau,* in lower part of town.

Terni. Administrative and industrial center. **Hotels:** *Valentino* (1), recent, all rooms with bath, central, roof garden, airconditioned, radios in rooms, garage;

Garden (2), new, well-equipped hotel on outskirts; *De Paris* (2), near station, modern, comfortable.

Todi. Picturesque old town. **Hotels:** *Villa Luisa* (3), anonymous modern building on outskirts, comfortable rooms. *Zodiaco* (3), also on outskirts; simply furnished but functional.

Restaurant: *Umbria* (M–E), under arches just off main square, is an excellent terrace-restaurant, spaghetti *boscaiola, tagliatelle,* pork dishes, with a beautiful view of the blue Umbrian hills, crowded Sundays.

Trevi. Hill town. **Hotel:** *Torre* (1), below town, large modern hotel, pool, disco.

Restaurant: *Cocchetto* (M), avoid on Sunday.

USEFUL ADDRESSES. Tourist Offices: *Assisi:* AAST, Piazza del Commune 1. *Citta di Castello;* AAST, Piazza Garibaldi 2. *Foligno:* AAST, Porta Roma. *Gubbio:* AAST, Piazza Oderisi 6. *Orvieto:* Corso Cavour 36. *Perugia:* AAST, Via Mazzini 21: EPT, c/o Assessorato Regionale del Turismo, Corso Vannucci 30. *Spoleto:* AAST, Piazza della Liberta 7.

SPECIAL EVENTS. *Assisi:* Maundy Thursday sees important religious celebration; early May brings costumed troubadours into the streets for the Calendimaggio Festival; June, the Festa del Voto; August has three feast days in a row, the Festa del Perdone, the Festa di San Rufino, and the Festa di Santa Chiara, St. Clare, 10–12 Aug; 3–4 Sept. the town's festival; and sacred plays throughout the month.

Foligno: Second Sunday in September, Giostra della Quintana, revival of a 17th-century joust with 600 knights in costume, with a historical procession the night before.

Gubbio: 15 May, Festa dei Ceri or Feast of Candles, a procession in local costume when tall shrines are carried to the church on top of Mount Igino, the foremost Umbrian folklore event; 30 May, Palio Balestrieri, Crossbow Palio between Gubbio and Sansepolcro, a medieval contest with medieval costume and arms; July and August, classical drama in Roman theater.

Orvieto: Festival on 19 May. *Perugia:* Music Festival, 18 Sept.–2 Oct. details from Sagra Musicale Umbra, Casella Postale No. 341, 06100 Perugia (tel. 21374). *Spoleto:* Festival of the Two Worlds (Gian Carlo Menotti's brainchild), June and July. US/Italian festival of the arts, with no holds barred. *Todi:* Fine antique fair in April.

CAMPANIA

Naples, Pompeii and the Romantic Isles

Campania is a region of names to conjure with—Capri, Sorrento, Pompeii, Paestum—names evoking visions of cliff-shaded coves and sun-dappled waters, of mighty ruins, golden in the sunset. And Naples, a tumultuous, carefree city, the very heart of Campania, stands guard over these treasures.

Campania stretches south in flat coastal plains and low mountains from Baia Domizia, Capua and Caserta to Naples and Pompeii on the magnificent bay, past Capri and Ischia down along the rocky coast to Sorrento, Amalfi and Salerno, and farther still past the Cilento promontory to Sapri and the Calabria border. Inland lie the bleak fringes of the Apennines and the rolling countryside around Benevento.

On either side of Naples, the earth fumes and grumbles, reminding natives and visitors alike that all this beauty was born of cataclysm. Toward Sorrento, Vesuvius smolders sleepily over the ruins of Her-

..ulaneum and Pompeii, while north of Naples, beyond Posillipo, the craters of the Solfatara spew steaming gases. And nearby are the dark, deep waters of Lake Averno, legendary entrance to Hades.

With these reminders of death and destruction so close at hand, it's no wonder that the southerner in general, and the Neapolitan in particular, chooses to take no chances, plunging enthusiastically into the task of living each moment to its fullest.

Campania Today

Here in the Campania you will find a way of life—a way of life which will seem at first to be nothing more than *dolce far niente* but which is actually not that at all. It is rather the inextinguishable belief that the art of living lies in enjoying what surrounds you, not passively, but with enthusiasm—the sun, a glass of wine, a conversation, a traffic jam.

Campania was probably settled by the ancient Phoenicians, Cretans and Greeks. Traces of their presence here date back to approximately 1,000 BC, some 300 years before the legendary founding of Rome.

Herculaneum is said to have been established by the great Hercules himself and, as excavation of this once great city Greek—and later Roman—progresses, further light will be thrown on the history of the whole Campania region.

The origin of Naples, once called Parthenope and later Neapolis, presumably can be traced to what are now the ruins of Cumae nearby, which legend tells us was already in existence in 800 BC.

Greek civilization flourished for hundreds of years all along this coastline, but there was nothing in the way of centralized government until centuries later when the Roman Empire, uniting all of Italy for the first time, surged southward and absorbed the Greek colonies with little opposition.

The Romans were quick to appreciate the sybaritic possibilities of such a lovely land and it was in this region that the wealthy of the Empire built their palatial country residences. Generally the peace of the Campania was undisturbed during these centuries of Roman rule.

Naples and the Campania, with the rest of Italy, decayed with the Roman Empire and collapsed into the abyss of the Middle Ages. Naples itself regained some importance again under the rule of the Angevins in the latter part of the 13th century, and continued its progress later—in the 1440s—under Aragon rule.

The nobles who served under the Spanish viceroys in the 16th and 17th centuries, when their harsh rule made all Italy quail, enjoyed their pleasures, and the more luxurious points in the Campania began to look up. Taverns and gaming houses thrived. Business boomed, in spite of the tyranny of Spain—which, it must be added, milked the area with its taxes.

After a short-lived Austrian occupation, Naples became the capital of the Kingdom of the Two Sicilies, which the Bourbon kings established in 1738. Their rule was generally benevolent as far as Campania was concerned, and their support of the Papal authority in Rome was an important factor in the historical development of the rest of Italy. Their rule was important artistically, for not only did it contribute greatly to the architectural beauties of the region but it attracted scores of great musicians, artists and writers, who were only too willing to enjoy the easy life of court in such magnificent natural surroundings.

Finally Garibaldi launched his famous expedition, and in 1860 Naples was united with the rest of Italy.

Times were relatively tranquil through the years which followed—with tourists of one nation or another thronging to Capri, to Sorrento, to Amalfi and of course to Naples—until World War II. Allied bombings did considerable damage in Naples and the bay area. At the fall of the Fascist government, the sorely tried Neapolitans rose up against Nazi occupation troops and in four days of street fighting drove them out of the city. A monument to the *Scugnizzo*—the typical Neapolitan street urchin—celebrates the youngsters who participated in the battle.

The war ended. Artists, tourists, writers and ordinary lovers of beauty began to flow again into that Campania region which one ancient writer called "most blest by the Gods, most beloved by man". As the years have gone by, some parts have gained increased attention from the smart visitors, some have lost the cachet that they had. The balance is maintained, with a steady trend to more and more tourist development. The main tourist centers—the islands and the Sorrento and Amalfi coasts—were practically untouched by the 1980 earthquake, which shook Naples' already precarious housing situation into a desperate state.

Weather Matters

There is only one definite advantage to making your visit in summer, particularly in August, which is that the local inhabitants, who are hardened to the climate, are at their liveliest then, and many of the major religious and folklore festivals occur at this time of year. As you move southward in Italy, these celebrations become steadily more colorful and more elaborate, and it is well worth your while to try to arrange your visit to coincide with, for example, some important religious Fête. There are many ceremonies which do not have fixed dates, but may be decided upon not far ahead of time, like processions of the vial containing the dried blood of *St. Janarius* in Naples, which may or may not end in the liquefaction of the blood. Inquire at the nearest Italian tourist office in advance about the places and dates of any forthcoming festivals worth viewing. 15 July, feast of the *Madonna del Carmine,* especially revered by southern Italians, is the occasion of rousing celebrations in many towns.

It can get very hot in the region of Naples during the big vacation months, July and August, and if temperature were the only consideration, you would be well advised to try to time your visit to the Campania to miss the summer. The high season here is April, when the weather is ideal. The next best months are May, June, September and October. However, almost all the most popular places in this area lie along the seashore, if not actually in the sea (Capri, Ischia), which takes some of the curse off the heat.

Capri is *the* place to be on New Year's Eve; the island wakes from its winter sleep to welcome hordes of merrymakers for celebrations that can last for days.

Road Reports

The main north-south road in this region is the Autostrada del Sole, which connects outside Naples with the inland expressway to Salerno and with the coastal road to the Sorrento peninsula and Amalfi coast. Another superhighway turns inland toward Avellino and Bari on the Adriatic. In mid-August, traffic on the narrow Amalfi drive from Sorrento to Salerno is frequently backed up for miles. At Salerno you can join the old road which leads to Paestum and various small coastal places. Car ferries to Ischia and Capri operate from Naples, but during the August tourist rush, cars with Italian number plates are not allowed to disembark on either island.

Food for Thought

Naples is the home of *pizza,* a dish which has run around the world and should be familiar to everyone; but if you've missed it, it's an open-faced pastry shell into which almost anything may be put as filling—one favorite combination is tomatoes and anchovies, smothered under a coating of *mozzarella* (which is buffalo cheese, native to the Campania), and flavored with oregano. Naples is also a big food manufacturing city, its two specialties being various types of pasta and the tomato sauce which goes on them.

Bistecca alla pizzaiola has nothing to do with pizza; it's simply a slice of meat cooked in tomato sauce with garlic. *Don't eat uncooked shellfish in the Naples zone;* the waters of the entire bay area are notoriously polluted. Fish, cooked to choice, is generally good.

Besides *mozzarella,* the Campania produces several types of cheese, of which one, *provolone,* mild and sharp, is very well known.

Neapolitan ice cream is known the world over, of course; many standardized ice cream combinations here, *spumoni*, for being a native of Naples.

Among local specialties of other parts of the Campania the walnuts of Sorrento and the crayfish, prawns and ravioli of Capri.

Possibly the most famous wine of the Naples region is *Lacrima Christi*, "tear of Christ", from vines grown on the slopes of Vesuvius. It is a white wine, very dry. The one with the longest history is *Falerno;* the ancient Romans drank Falernian wine, though there is no way of knowing how much it resembled its modern descendant, which is also dry and white. Capri also produces good white wine, sweet or dry, and so does the island of Ischia, which produces both reds and whites.

Naples, the Heart and Soul of Campania

The best view of Naples is that from the sea, and since you'll surely take the steamer to Capri or Ischia sometime during your stay, you'll have a chance to absorb that breathtaking coastline, dominated by the lowering slopes of ever-threatening Vesuvius.

For a different perspective on the city and its surroundings, on your first morning in Naples, when the air is clear and the sun just warm enough to be comfortable, go up to the Vomero, Naples' modern residential quarter on a hillside to the west.

Down to the left is Naples, with its gently curving shoreline, docks and palm-lined, sea-side avenues. Far below is the Castel Nuovo of Charles I of Anjou, its severe and primitive shape contrasting sharply with the Hohenstaufen's Castel dell'Ovo, nearby, and with the far more modern buildings near it. Look along the bay. There is the busy port and, on the shore beyond, the industrial zone. There is the beginning of the autostrada to Pompeii and Salerno. There, a little farther along to the left if you have keen eyes, can be seen the ruins of Herculaneum. Beyond is Pompeii and Vesuvius itself, a thin wisp of smoke curling over its momentarily tranquil peak.

Back on the seashore, there is Torre Annunziata, where the highway breaks off to the right to climb to the Plain of Sorrento. You can't see the road as it winds around those hillsides in the dim distance but you can see the vague outlines of little towns, and if your eyes are very, very keen you can see Sorrento itself, perched high up on the cliff-side almost opposite you.

To your left the coast vanishes in a sharp point quite close to a mountainous little islet which seems to spring from the sea itself. That is Capri. In the dim distance is the Mediterranean—center of the earth to the pagan world. Ischia is probably a little out of sight to your right, as are Pozzuoli and Cumae.

Exploring Naples

There are a lot of places in Naples you will go back to see again, but you will probably agree—when you have seen them all—that Naples' two chief attractions are its people and its surprisingly beautiful vistas. Its four funiculars get you nicely up and down the hills.

For the first you need go nowhere in particular. Just wander through the streets, down along Via Roma, through the Umberto Gallery, or down the Via Roma to the docks and along the lovely waterfront drive, or up or down any of the little side streets which wander off in all directions. Keep your sense of humor, keep a tight grip on anything you may be carrying, watch your pocketbook, remember that if you get lost you can always get back to the waterfront by going in the general direction of Vesuvius, and then enjoy yourself. A lot of that enjoyment will come from just watching the Neapolitans, who are among the most spontaneous, volatile people on earth.

For a fine view of the city and bay go to the Certosa di San Martino. It's the Carthusian monastery up on the slopes of the Vomero, perhaps the finest example of the typically Neapolitan baroque, which now contains the Museum of San Martino. In addition to being known for its priceless works of art and for its relics of the Kingdom of Naples, it is noted for having the balcony which affords that incomparable view of the city and bay. On your way out this time take a good look at the typically Neapolitan *presepi* (cribs), which are to all Italian, but particularly Neapolitan, children what the Yule log or the Christmas tree are to ours. There's even more here we enthusiastically recommend. The Monk's Choir is a joyous baroque work you must see. Go through the audit-room to reach it. Don't miss a visit to the fortress of San Elmo. Done over by the Spaniards in the 16th century, the fortress will offer you one more magnificent view before you descend. And from the Floridiana Villa, on the rim of Vomero, you have the whole panorama before you, as well as the villa's gardens, museum and collection of porcelain, ivory and enamels.

Of course you will want to return to the Castel Nuovo, on the Piazza del Municipio, facing the harbor. Its massive bulk dominates the scene and is, for all, a focal point of interest. It was built in 1282 for Charles I of Anjou and has been restored to its original form although it was reconstructed in 1452 for Aragon's Alfonso I. Note especially the Arco di Trionfo, on the west side, between two of the three towers. It dates from 1467 and is generally considered one of the best pieces of the Italian Renaissance. It is richly ornamented with bas-reliefs and is credited to Francesco Laurana.

Naples
Information
Palazzo / Public building
Church
Museum / Theater / Gallery / Place of Interest etc
Hospital
Police
Rail
0yds 300 600 900 1200
0ms 300 600 900 1200
Palazzo e Parco di Capodimonte
Museo Nazionale
Duomo
Castel Capuano
Porta Capuana
Porta Nolana
Stazione Centrale
Stazione Circumvesuviana
Piazza Garibaldi
Piazza Mercato
Quartiere di Spacca Napoli
Staz Cumana
Castel SElmo
Certosa di SanMartino
Villa Floridiana
Villa Belvedere
Museo Naz d.Ceramica
Funicolare di Montesanto
Ferrovia Cumana
Funicolare Centrale
Funicolare di Chiaia
Vomero
Castelnuovo
Pal. Reale
Staz Marittima
Pza Trento e Trieste
Piazza Plebiscito
Piazza Municipio
Museo Pignatelli
Villa Comunale
Acquario
Monumento A.Diaz
Riviera di Chiaia
Via F Caracciolo
Galleria della Vittoria
Pizzofalcone
Chiatamone
Partenope
Castel dell'Ovo
Mergellina
Staz.di Mergellina
Piazza Piedigrotta
Tomba di Virgilio
Pza Sannazzaro
Underground
Via Toledo
Via Roma
Corso Vittorio Emanuele
Corso Umberto I
Via Nuova Marina
Via Marinella
Via A. Vespucci
Via Depretis
V.C. Colombo
Via Medina
Via Monteoliveto
V.B Croce
Via S.B. d. Librai
Via Tribunali
Via Duomo
Via Foria
Via Pessina
Via Chiaia
Via d Mille
Via Parco Margherita
Corso Francesco Crispi
Via M. Schipa
Via Tasso
Via Aniello Falcone
Via Francesco Cilea
Via Piedigrotta
Via Mergellina
Viale A. Gramsci
Via F Car cci.l.
V.S. Lucia
V. Nazario Sauro
V.C. Console
V. Acton
Places of Interest
a Accademia Belle Arti
b Galleria d. Girolamini
c Conservatorio
d Palazzo Cuomo
e Palazzo Gravina
f Universita
g Teatro Mercadante
h Galleria Umberto I
i Teatro S. Carlo
j Palazzo S. Giacomo
k Teatro Politeama
Churches
1 S.M. Donna Regina
2 S. Paolo Maggiore
3 Gerolomini
4 Gesu Nuovo (Trinita Maggiore)
5 S. Pietro Maiella
6 S. Domenico Maggiore
7 Sansevero Chapel
8 S. Gregorio Armeno
9 S. Lorenzo Maggiore
10 S. Pietro ad Aram
11 S. Giorgio Maggiore
12 S. Agostino alla Zecca
13 SS. Sossio e Severo
14 S. Giovanni Maggiore
15 S. Chiara
16 Spirito Santo
17 S.M. di Montesanto
18 S.M. d. Carmine
19 S. Eligio
20 S. Pietro Martire
21 S.M. la Nova
22 S. Anna d. Lombardi
23 S. Giacomo d. Spagnoli
24 S. Anna d. Palazzo al Rosario
25 S. Francesco da Paolo
26 S.M. di Angeli
27 S. Teresa a Chiaia
28 S. Maria in Portico
29 S. Guiseppe a Chiaia
30 S. Teresa
31 S.M. di Piedigrotta

The sprawling Palazzo Reale on the Piazza del Plebiscito dates from the 17th century. Sumptuously furnished, it houses in addition to many extremely rare tapestries and paintings, the National Library, with its treasures of incunabula. The Piazza Plebiscito itself dates from the brief reign of Napoleon's puppet king, Murat. Canova carved the statues you see in the center of the square.

No tour of Naples would be complete without a visit to the National Museum, on Piazza del Museo. Notable are the many sculptures, paintings, bronzes and both decorative and utilitarian pieces from Herculaneum and Pompeii. In addition, Grecian and Roman sculpture at their finest are found there—note especially the *Aphrodite* attributed to Praxiteles, the *Farnese Bull,* the *Drunken Satyr,* from the House of the Faun in Pompeii, the *Drunken Silenus* and the *Narcissus,* from a Praxiteles original. Recent renovations and increased attention from the authorities have made the museum much pleasanter than it used to be.

The Capodimonte Gallery specializes in the Italian school from the 14th through the 16th centuries. Titian, Botticelli, Raphael, Giovanni Bellini and Mantegna are wonderfully represented as are some of the most outstanding of the Flemish school, such as Breughel and Joos van Cleve. El Greco and Velazquez, of the Spanish school, are also included in the tremendous scope of this museum's masterpieces. The museum itself is a marvel of display techniques, perfectly lighted and well arranged, with all works clearly labeled. Its collections of porcelain and armor are worth a visit. Don't miss the view from the roof-terrace.

Naples's San Carlo Theater is of course one of the most famous opera houses in the world, as indeed well it might be in view of its location in a region renowned for *bel canto.* From its stage have come many of the most famous of the world's singers and its productions of the great Italian operas can be favorably compared with those of the Metropolitan, La Scala and Covent Garden.

Naturally the city has its share of Gothic, Renaissance and baroque churches on antique foundations. The Cathedral of San Gennaro at Olmo was erected in 1300 over the ruins of an earlier church dating back to the 5th century, which in turn was built over a Temple of Caesar. Attached to the left nave is Santa Restituta, which preserves under its baroque decorations the fourth-century basilica plan. Santa Chiara, favored by the court and the aristocracy, has been restored to its original Gothic-Provençal style.

Santi Severino e Sosio, with a 16th-century wooden choir; the Church of the Gerolimini, with its frescos and paintings of the 17th and 18th-century Neapolitan school; Santa Maria Donnaregina, with the tomb of Queen Mary of Hungary, dating from 1326; and San Domenico Maggiore, with Gothic arches from the 14th century, are probably the best of the Neapolitan churches. Others, of course, abound and each has paintings, frescos or architecture well worth a visit—but only if you have sufficient leisure.

You can't leave Naples without going into the very heart of the old city, crowded bustling Spacca. Especially since you will be able to see more fine old works as you rub elbows with the Neapolitans. Take a look at the crumbling palace on the Via San Biagio ai Librai; then wander down Via Benedetto Croce to see a 14th-century Catalonian Gothic landmark erected by the Majorcan widow of Robert the Wise of Anjou. It's worth seeing, especially the funeral monument to her husband, the king.

Exploring Campania

Once you have discovered Naples you must begin wandering afield. Take a car if you can afford it or if you happen to have one of your own. If you have no car, no matter. Trains, trams and buses abound. At the moment (mid-1981), we cannot recommend Naples as a base for visiting the region; use the coastal resorts instead.

The SITA company runs half-day bus tours of this area. CIT offers a half-day tour to Pompeii or a full-day tour that also takes in Amalfi and Sorrento. There are full-day CIT tours to Capri or Ischia.

First of all wander out to Posillipo, the long promontory separating the Bay of Pozzuoli from the Bay of Naples. Go out by the Via Acton, through the Santa Lucia quarter, past the Castel dell'Ovo, along Via Partenope and the Via Caracciolo to Mergellina. Above, at the top of a cable railway, is Posillipo, now a fashionable residential section.

From Mergellina you can take the road through the tunnel beneath Posillipo to Pozzuoli. This whole region is of volcanic origin and even in ancient days the spas of Agnano Terme and Bagnoli were well known. Solfatara still emits sulphur-charged steam jets from various apertures in the earth's crust, and sounds ominously underground. The Temple of Serapis at Pozzuoli proper also shows signs of volcanic activity. On the three columns that remain standing you can see the ancient highwater mark; the earth's crust is still rising in the Pozzuoli area. Other Roman ruins abound in the region.

An ancient doorway to Hell is just two-and-a-half miles from Pozzuoli. The Lago d'Averno, a crater 100 feet deep and 2 miles in circumference, was believed to be the direct entrance to Hades. In fact, the whole region is fraught with legend. Not far away is the Mare Morto of ancient Romans, who identified it as the Stygian Lake of the Dead, where Charon ferried souls across to the underworld. Near Lake Averno, too, is a spring which was thought to flow directly from the Styx, and it was there that Aeneas descended into Hades with the guidance of the Cumaean Sibyl. The original Styx, of course, is a river in southern Greece.

This Sibyl lived not far from Averno, just around the shores of the lake and past the oyster beds, famed among ancient gourmets. Cumae was among the first Greek colonies in the Neapolitan region, and there is no doubt whatever that the Cave of the Cumaean Sibyl existed. It still does. It is an enormous gallery, some 350 feet long, opening into a chamber where the Sibyl uttered her prophecies.

The Cumaean Acropolis is on a lava hill near the sea overlooking the lower part of the city. It's famous not only for the Sibyl but for remains of a temple to Apollo on a lower walk-way, for Jupiter's temple above it, a Greek cistern, an octagonal fountain-basin, ruins of a Christian basilica, and another glorious view of the Cape of Micena and the Gulf of Gaeta. An unanswered question is whether Cumae was the original Naples in the 8th century BC or if even older Greek colonies hadn't already preceded it. Before you leave the area, stop at Arco Felice, erected under the Emperor Domitian. The 60-foot-high archway is on the road between Cumae and Averno.

Herculaneum

Much of Herculaneum and Pompeii will be closed to visitors for some time, until the earthquake damage has been repaired. Note that all archeological sites are closed on Mondays and some Sundays; always check with EPT for details.

Hercules himself is said to have founded this city, which became a famous watering resort for the Roman elite after passing through periods of Greek and Samnite domination. It was damaged by an earthquake in 63 AD. Then, 16 years later, the gigantic eruption of Vesuvius in the year 79 buried it completely under a tide of mud and lava. Casual excavation was begun early in the 18th century, but nothing was done properly until Mussolini ordered systematic excavation in 1927.

Then it was found that the sea of mud and lava that was roughly 35 feet deep had so seeped into the crevices and niches of every building as to shut out the air and preserve their contents even better than those of Pompeii, much of which were broken or burned by the hot cinders which rained onto that city.

Naturally, most of the magnificent relics of Herculaneum and of Pompeii are now ensconced in museums throughout the world, but more than enough remains to fascinate any visitor endowed with even the smallest amount of imagination. Here, sealed and preserved for us for close on 2,000 years, are the traces of a glorious and somewhat carefree past.

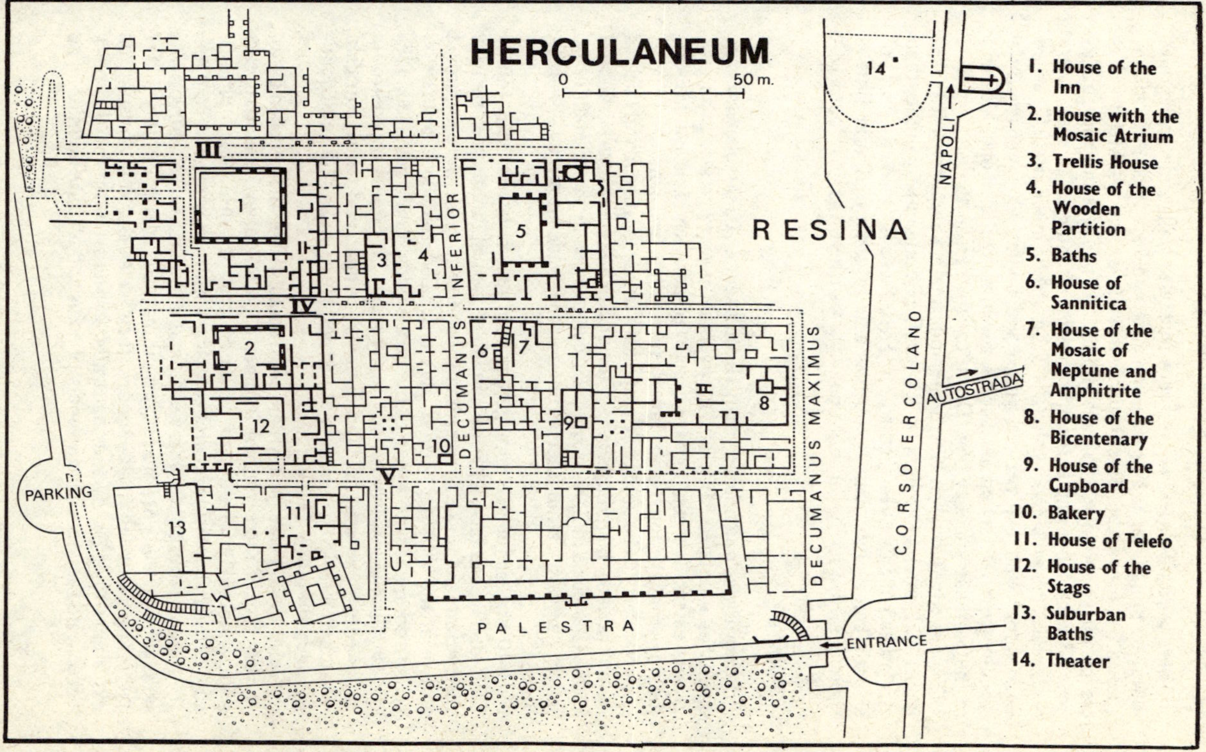

HERCULANEUM
0
50 m.
1. House of the Inn
2. House with the Mosaic Atrium
3. Trellis House
4. House of the Wooden Partition
5. Baths
6. House of Sannitica
7. House of the Mosaic of Neptune and Amphitrite
8. House of the Bicentenary
9. House of the Cupboard
10. Bakery
11. House of Telefo
12. House of the Stags
13. Suburban Baths
14. Theater
RESINA
NAPOLI
AUTOSTRADA
CORSO ERCOLANO
ENTRANCE
DECUMANUS MAXIMUS
DECUMANUS INFERIOR
PALESTRA
PARKING
III
IV
V

There were stoves and pots to cook in; styled walls and porticos and mural paintings, tapestries and brocades and hangings and clothes; gold, silver, bronze and brass ornaments and decorations. Metal-workers must have abounded. So did sculptors and painters and housebuilders, and wine-shops and baths and prostitutes and even thieves. There is the tale, perhaps apocryphal, of a discovery made in 1932, when excavators found two perfectly preserved bodies. One, apparently a wealthy patrician, lay on his face. Beside him lay the second, his hand in the patrician's money bag. Death caught him in the act.

Experts say that when Herculaneum is finally completely excavated it will shed much more light on Roman life during imperial times than any other remains unearthed so far. Here there is more of a sense of a living community than Pompeii is able to convey. If your time is short, you will likely get more out of a visit here than to Pompeii.

Pompeii

Pompeii was much larger than Herculaneum, 20,000 inhabitants as against an estimated 5,000, and excavations have progressed to a much greater extent. It seems to have been to some extent a pleasure resort, judging from the number of hotels, restaurants and bars.

Particularly to be noted in Pompeii are the decorative mural designs of four periods, including some of the finest and oldest thus far discovered. After close to 2,000 years their colors, even in the open-air *atria,* inner courtyards, retain their brilliance, the shade known as "Pompeian red".

Until the earthquake damage has been repaired, your visit will be limited. You can have a pleasant lunch at the restaurant-cafeteria near the Forum, and make a rewarding short detour to see the exceptional frescos at the Villa dei Misteri. Buy a detailed guidebook before you set out, complete with a map of the excavations. You'll get a good idea of how a provincial Roman city really lived. This one was generously endowed with an extensive forum, lavish temples and baths, patrician villas, and a thriving commercial district whose walls still carry political advertisements and notices.

Guide or no guide, you will be confronted with endless locked gates. A very few of these conceal Pompeian pornography, which appears quite innocent in these days of hard porno movies. Italy's chronic carelessness about its great archeological heritage is evident at Pompeii; the ruins are overgrown with weeds, and much is closed off. Streets and individual monuments are fairly well marked; guards on duty at the most important villas will unlock their gates for you, insisting on explaining their sights and, naturally, expecting a tip for this often unrequested service (have a supply of coins and 500-lire notes on hand

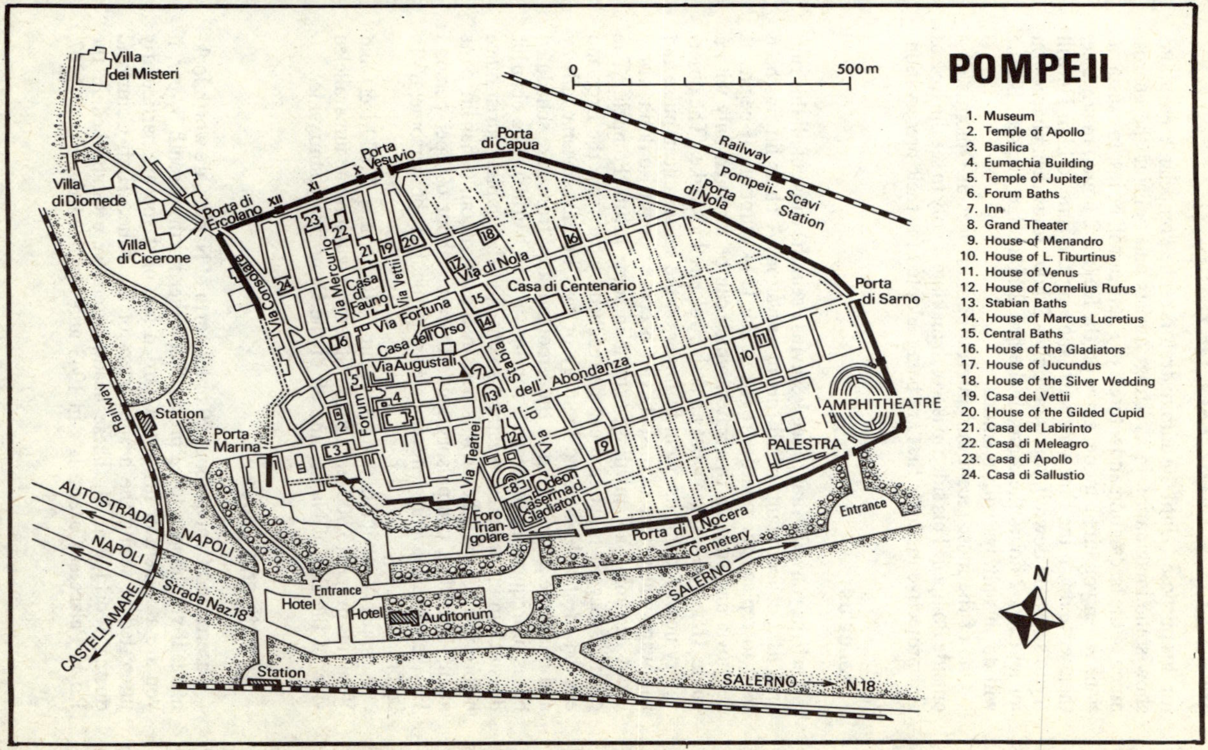
POMPEII
0
500m
1. Museum
2. Temple of Apollo
3. Basilica
4. Eumachia Building
5. Temple of Jupiter
6. Forum Baths
7. Inn
8. Grand Theater
9. House of Menandro
10. House of L. Tiburtinus
11. House of Venus
12. House of Cornelius Rufus
13. Stabian Baths
14. House of Marcus Lucretius
15. Central Baths
16. House of the Gladiators
17. House of Jucundus
18. House of the Silver Wedding
19. Casa dei Vettii
20. House of the Gilded Cupid
21. Casa del Labirinto
22. Casa di Meleagro
23. Casa di Apollo
24. Casa di Sallustio
Villa dei Misteri
Villa di Diomede
Villa di Cicerone
Porta di Ercolano
Porta Vesuvio
Porta di Capua
Porta di Nola
Porta di Sarno
Porta di Nocera
Porta Marina
Railway
Pompeii-Scavi Station
Via Consolare
Via Mercurio
Casa di Fauno
Via Vettii
Via di Nola
Casa di Centenario
Via Fortuna
Casa dell'Orso
Via Augustali
Forum
Stabia
Via dell' Abondanza
Via di Stabia
Via Teatrei
Odeon
Caserma d. Gladiatori
Foro Triangolare
AMPHITHEATRE
PALESTRA
Entrance
Cemetery
SALERNO
Station
AUTOSTRADA
NAPOLI
Strada Naz.18
CASTELLAMARE
Hotel
Auditorium
SALERNO → N.18
N

for this purpose). Until the administrators of the Pompeian excavations show some imagination in assisting tourists and policing the guards, much of the fascination and interest of Pompeii will be lost in exasperation. When you hire a guide, agree on the fee (for 2 hours) in advance, then write down the time you start, showing the time to him. He will try to slow you down if you want only a 2-hour tour, then charge you for an extra 2 hours the moment the first 2 hours has elapsed. But he will do this always with a smile.

One of the most recent and interesting finds was at Oplontis, just outside Pompeii. This sidetrip is worth making, if only to see the frescos and protective methods that are being adopted for their preservation.

Vesuvius

Perhaps you will want to see Vesuvius itself, the cause of all this ruin and, as a concomitant, of all this preservation. A chair lift has been built to replace the one destroyed in the 1944 eruption. It begins at Seggiovia and runs up the crater, which can be explored only with a guide. Here you can see what an active volcano looks like. (The observatory nearby keeps its scientific finger on the subterranean pulse and will warn when signs of misbehavior become evident, so don't worry about becoming an unwilling exhibit in some future Pompeii.) The chairlift (Seggiovia) station can be reached by car from the Ercolano exit on the Naples-Salerno highway or by Circumvesuviana railway and bus (take a local train to the Ercolano stop; from here scheduled buses, infrequent in off-season, run up to the chairlift). The chairlift doesn't run in inclement weather, so check at the Naples tourist office before you set out; the view is best in the afternoon. (Chairlift costs about 1,500 lire, compulsory guide to crater about 600 per person.) Hawkers and souvenir vendors here are particularly bothersome; try to ignore them.

Actually Vesuvius is two mountains, Mt. Somma (3,600 feet) and Vesuvius proper (3,900 feet). From either you will have an unparalleled view of the Bay of Naples and all of the Campania countryside.

Caserta and Capua

Caserta and Capua, about 20 miles north of Naples, are worth looking at if you happen to be proceeding either north or south by car, if you are a student of history, a garden fan, or if you are particularly interested in seeing the headquarters of the Allied High Command during World War II. These headquarters were established in the Royal Palace at Caserta late in 1943 and remained there until 1947.

The palace was built by Vanvitelli in 1752 for the Bourbon kings of Naples and Sicily and was intended to be more grandiose and beautiful than Versailles. It is not. Its gardens and fountains, though, are lovely, as are the somewhat tacky palace itself, the theater, the chapel and the so-called royal apartments. The town of Caserta is a dead loss.

Capua is only a few miles west of Caserta and is now just a little market village, with the ruins of its ancient wall and amphitheater which date to pre-Roman times. To the student of history this sleepy little town is fascinating. Here the Samnites made their most determined stand against the Roman legions moving southward. Here, a little later, those same Samnites, with Carthaginian and Greek aid, rebelled against Roman rule during the Carthaginian wars. Here Hannibal camped for one entire year while he waited for aid from home and while Rome mustered the strength to defeat him.

Still later, Rome established here a great school for gladiators, the school which produced the famous slave gladiator Spartacus, who led a revolt of slaves and gladiators and made Capua his fortress for two years, defying all of Rome.

Nothing remains of all of this except a museum with interesting archeological remains and a Temple of Mithras where Spartacus prayed for aid against the Roman Senate.

But let's go back south—rapidly—avoiding as much as possible the sights and scents between either Capua or Caserta and Naples. Roads from either town pass through the sordid slum fringes of Naples.

Along the Bay of Naples

From Naples you can get a fast train to Sorrento, and as the coast from Naples to Torre del Greco is depressingly industrialized, you may be wise to do so. There are some lovely views of the bay from the Naples-Sorrento superhighway, though, and you may want to take a look at Castellammare di Stabia, now a grubby, overbuilt port.

Castellammare—known then as Stabia—existed, perhaps, before Pompeii. Pliny the Elder had his villa there. Like Pompeii, it was destroyed by the eruption of Vesuvius in 79 AD, but unlike Pompeii, it was rebuilt almost immediately because of its magnificent setting as a country residence for the wealthy. Incidentally, its volcanic spring water was noted even then for its health-giving qualities.

To Sorrento

From Castellammare to Sorrento your drive curves precipitously through tiny towns, masses of flowering trees and bushes, orange and olive groves, past the site of one of Augustus' villas, the garden of

Quisisana, down onto the Sorrento plain, a vast perfumed garden on a natural terrace high above the Bay of Naples. Here, certainly, you will want to linger for a time. Emperors and kings, popes, the greatest musicians, writers and artists, have made Sorrento their preferred abode for more than 2,500 years. And one look at the view will tell you why.

Once again be sure to get a room overlooking the bay. Far down the sheer cliff on which you are perched is the crystal-clear blue water of the bay. Directly opposite and far across is Naples at its best, gleaming distantly in the brilliant sun. Off to the left, seeming only a stone's throw from the headland, is Capri, and Vesuvius lowers in the background at the base of the bay far down to the right.

At the foot of the cliff there is a little harbor, Piccolo Sant' Angelo, where the boats dock and where fishermen mend their nets. Nearby, there is a small beach from which bathers swim in water that is so high in salt content that it is next to impossible to sink.

Nearby is the vast cave called the Baths of Diana, once the scene of pagan rites. The tiny islets are the Isles of the Mermaids, famed in mythology, and all of the grottos which abound along the cliffside are called the Grottos of the Mermaids, since from time immemorial these waters have been the true habitat of those fabled beings.

The Amalfi Drive

From Sorrento, when you resume your trip, you'll continue along the Amalfi Drive, around the Campanella Point—so close to Capri—and along the Gulf of Salerno. We trust you are not driving your own car, because it is also a tortuous road, writhing its way along the coast, past caverns, little inlets, cliffs and gardens, curving sharply every 20 feet, and you will miss some stunning views.

Positano, a delightful fishing village now dedicated exclusively to tourism, slopes picturesquely down to the sea and its pebbly beach. Once hailed as the "the poor man's Capri," because it had become the haunt of writers, artists, sculptors and other impoverished appreciators of beauty, it has shared the fate of other discoveries of the artistic and is overrun by wealthier visitors, who have taken over what the artists found.

A little farther along is Praiano, a rocky little village, the Conca di Marini and, just a short distance more, Amalfi, first of the sea republics and for centuries one of the great cities of Italy. Today it is a small though noted residential resort, but in the Middle Ages its population was close to 100,000. In the 11th and 12th centuries it was a sturdy rival of Genoa and Pisa for control of the Mediterranean.

Tidal waves account in great part for Amalfi's decline, if it can be called decline. The sea there is by no means always so calm as it appears. The town straggles up the Lattari slope, but much of it once was down along the sea. In 1073 a tidal wave washed most of it away, destroying every ship in the bay. The palace of the archbishop, moderately high up the slope, vanished. Again in 1343, Petrarch tells us, the sea devoured the town, and in comparatively recent times, in 1924, it was damaged again.

The same sea which brought repeated disasters to Amalfi also carved out a beautiful grotto, known as the Grotta dello Smeraldo for the emerald light which filters through the seawater to play upon strangely shaped stalactites and stalagmites. It can be reached by elevator from the Positano-Amalfi road, but a trip to it by boat along the coast from Amalfi offers marvelous views of towering mountains and lush villas.

One fabulous remnant of Amalfi's past remains; the cathedral, towering at the top of a long stairway, its height above the sea having often been its salvation. Here in this one edifice are united Moorish, Greek, Lombard, Norman and early Gothic architectural styles in a harmonious whole. It was built in 1203, remodeled in the 18th century and contains the body of St. Andrew, brought from Constantinople early in the 13th century to rest in the crypt. On 30 November, his feast day, a miracle is said to occur occasionally, when the *Manna di Sant' Andrea,* an oily liquid, oozes from his tomb.

The Cloister of Paradise in the cathedral and the cloisters in the Hotel Luna and the Hotel Cappuccini, both former convents, are of Moorish origin, too, and date likewise from the 13th century.

The Church of Atrani, a bit farther along the road, has bronze doors as beautiful as those of the cathedral in Amalfi. Atrani is famous as the birthplace of Masaniello, the young fisherman who led a revolt against the Viceroy of Naples in 1647.

Ravello and Salerno

Ravello, beautifully situated in the folds of Monte Lattari, is one of the most picturesque spots along the Gulf of Salerno. It prospered during Amalfi's days of glory. Its bright luxuriant gardens, flowering with almost tropical vegetation, still make it one of the glories of Italy.

Visit, briefly, the Duomo di San Pantaleone, which dates from the 11th century, whose pulpit, resting on mosaic columns and sculptured wild beasts, is one of the best examples of the Cosmatesque style so common in southern Italy.

Quite nearby is the Palazzo Rufolo, built by the Rufoli family, during the 13th century. Don't be misled by the disreputable walls. Within is a scene from the earliest days of the Crusades. Norman and Arab mingle in profusion in a welter of color-filled gardens. These gardens, it is said, gave Wagner the idea of Parisifal's Home of the Flower Maidens. From Ravello's piazza, take the 20-minute walk to Villa Cimbrone, perched like an eagle's nest on the cliffs; its garden terrace offers a truly magnificent panorama of the whole bay of Salerno.

Back on the coast road, drive on past Minori and Maiori, two towns where again Arab and Norman unite. Pause to see Maiori's blue grotto, which compares favorably with that of Capri. Wind past the Capo d'Orso, where the galleons of Charles V were defeated, past Cetara, where first the Arab Saracens landed in Italy, past the twin rocks of Vietri, home of the gnomes in legend, and on to Salerno.

Salerno was the scene of the Allied landing in Italy in World War II. In medieval times it was the world capital of medicine. The monastery of the Benedictine monks, who probably founded its medical school, offered the best instruction then available. From here came the famed Four Masters—one Latin, one Hebrew, one Greek and one Arab—who gave the world of that day its greatest science.

Many times destroyed by invasion and pillage, Salerno has always been speedily rebuilt, and even today there are few traces of the ravages of those September days in 1943 when the Germans almost pushed the American forces back into the sea.

The cathedral boasts the remains of the great evangelist St. Matthew, brought back from the Holy Land by pilgrims in the 10th century. The cathedral itself dates from 1080 but was remodeled in the 18th century. Present-day Salerno is run-down and chaotic, almost Oriental.

Eboli and Paestum

Southeast from Salerno are Battipaglia and Eboli, undistinguished rural centers. Dusky water buffalo graze in the fields, and each roadside stand proclaims that its *mozzarella* is the freshest. Southward the plains stretch on along the coast to Sapri. All the towns in this region have ancient Greco-Arab origins but all today are modest little country villages. Great improvements have been made since Carlo Levi's best-selling book, *Christ Stopped at Eboli,* in which he gives an interesting account of the customs, traditions and superstitions of Lucania, where the people still believe in black magic and witchcraft as well as in the legends of ghostly bandits who once commanded the area.

Only a few miles south of Eboli is Paestum, with some of the best preserved of Greek architectural monuments, not excepting even Greece itself. Once it was a thriving Greek colony called Poseidonia, founded by settlers from Sybaris more than 600 years before Christ. Only in 173 did it become Roman and acquire its present name. Today it is a group of ruins in the lonely, tranquil plains of the Sele River.

Go to the Temple of Poseidon, a perfect example of D ture, through the Porta Aurea. Note its 35 fluted colu extraordinarily well-preserved entablature. The basilica of the oldest of Paestum's monuments, dating from ve 6th century BC. Behind it an ancient road leads to the Forum of the Roman era, near which is a single column of the Temple of Peace. A little to the north are the ruins of a Roman amphitheater and the museum, which contains important Greek frescos found in ancient tombs nearby. Off to the side is the Temple of Ceres. Try to see the temples at sunset, when the light enhances the deep gold of the stone and the air is sharp with the cries of the crows that nest high on the temples.

If you still have a day or so, push on down toward Agropoli and Santa Maria di Castellabate on the rugged Cilento promontory. Acciaroli is a delightful little fishing town, with miles of sandy beach to one side of it. Beyond the recent excavations of ancient Velia, Palinuro is a beautiful spot, "discovered" some years ago by the Club Méditerranée and more recently by Italy's well-off powerboat set. Finally, on the Calabria border, Sapri is a gentle, old-fashioned watering place on the main railway line from Naples.

Inland, should you be passing nearby Benevento, take time to see its magnificent Arch of Trajan, one of the most beautiful extant.

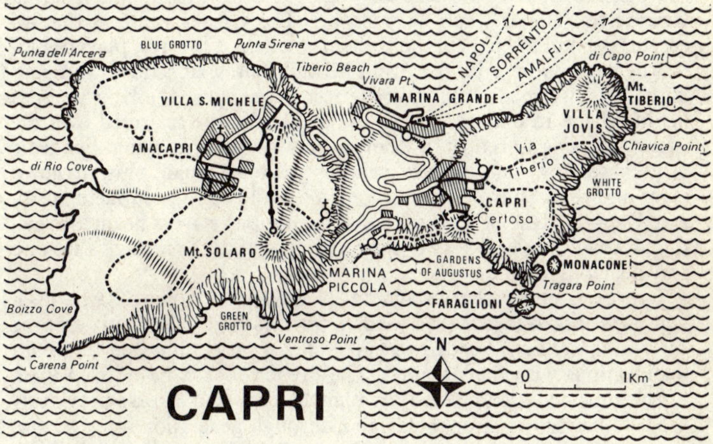

Isle of Capri

Another route that you can take from Naples is by boat to Sorrento and Capri. Take the big, comfortable steamer which meanders languid-along the coast, past the ruins of Herculaneum, past Torre Annunziata, beneath Vesuvius' menace, past Castellammare and Vico Equense, on to Sorrento. There, if you have the time, if you like the place, and above all if it is evening, we would advise breaking the trip, if only to look once again at the night scene of lighted Naples across the bay. From Sorrento you can get another boat to Capri in the morning.

So you come to Capri, the ancients' island of the goats, so-called, perhaps, because only goats, human or otherwise, dared its precipitous cliffs and slopes. But Capri has been called many things. It is truly "all things to all men," but each finds there what he seeks. The legend of Tiberius' orgies, largely discounted now, persists, as in fact do the orgies themselves among a certain element of the so-called "international set".

Capri itself never seems to change. Today, as always, it is a pint-sized paradise. It is almost 4 miles long and almost 2 miles wide and in spots more than 1,000 feet high. Unlike the other islands of the Bay of Naples, Capri is not of volcanic origin. Geologists say that it is an integral part of the limestone chain of the Apennines, left above water when some subterranean cataclysm sank its connecting links with the mainland.

The Phoenicians were its earliest settlers and to them is attributed the construction of the stairway of 159 steps which links Marina Grande to "Upper Capri"—Anacapri. The Greeks came in the 4th century BC and after them the Romans made it a favorite playground.

Augustus had a villa there and he built baths, aqueducts and conduits. Tiberius made it his favorite resort and spent the later years of his life there, in one or another of the 12 villas he scattered over the island, refusing to return to Rome even when he was dying. Fantastic grottos, soaring conical peaks, caverns great and small, plus unknown ruins and thousands of legends combine with the tales of Suetonius to give Capri a flavor of whispered and mysterious evil—a beauteous evil found nowhere else—and an intoxicating quality as heady as its rare and delicious wines.

Capri was one of the strongholds of the Barbary pirate Barbarossa, who first sacked it and then made a fortress of it. The British, in the early 19th century, wanted to make of it a small Gibraltar and built fortifications with that in mind. The French took it away from them before they could complete their plans. Moors and Greeks previously used its heights as strongholds and, through generation after generation, pirates from all corners of what was then the world made periodic depredations.

But the Roman influence was the strongest. It was not the warlike touch. Rather it was the Sybaritic influence, acquired by the Roman patricians from the earlier Greek colonists over on the mainland. Capri became, and has remained, a pleasure island.

You will go ashore from your boat at Marina Grande and then go up to your hotel at the town of Capri itself, unless you are like the Swede Axel Munthe, who, addicted by choice to Anacapri, could never forget the age-long quarrel between those two villages and never passed a night in the lower town.

Capri, the town, is highly commercial, deliberately sets out to be a tourist center, and delights in the offbeat. When it is not too crowded, it can be pleasant and relaxing. When it is packed (on national holidays, especially), it is pure purgatory, made so by too many people in too small a place.

Happily, the beauties of Capri, the island, are more than enough to compensate for the deficiencies of a relatively small percentage of its visitors, or the noisiness of the day trippers, brought by the shipload at the height of the season.

At Marina Piccola you will find the magnificent Gardens of Augustus and quite nearby the best sea-bathing on the island. The Church of Santa Costanza, of 11th-century Byzantine construction, and the Certosa of San Giacomo, 14th-century Carthusian monastery, are among the few survivals of medieval Capri. The ruins of the Castle of Castiglione, high up on the heights of San Michele, and the fabulous Castello di Barbarossa—800 steps up—are superbly sited.

You will see, of course, the impressive ruins of the Villa of Tiberius, one of the 12, and you will see the cliff from which he is falsely reported to have had his ex-favorites flung. You will see, too, the Villa Jovis, also Tiberian in origin, and, from the sanctuary above it, look out across the Bay of Naples for a truly magnificent vista.

But Capri's natural wonders are far more entrancing. The famed Blue Grotto is but one of many such caverns and some connoisseurs think it not the most beautiful. There is the Green Grotto, the Yellow Grotto and the Pink and the White. Their colors, in each case, result from the refraction of light from the walls and the waters through the varying-sized entrances. Try to visit the Blue Grotto early in the morning, when the color is unlike anything you have ever seen before, and are unlikely to see anywhere else. All these grottoes have been known and noted from the earliest days of antiquity, and were used in the days of the Greeks and the Romans, notably the Grotto dell'Arsenale, in the celebration of pagan mysteries. In 1964, two Greek statues were hauled up from the depths.

Capri is guaranteed to stir the sluggish imagination.

Isle of Ischia

The charms of Capri have long been established, and the island therefore suffers the fate of many places that become too famous—it is overrun with visitors; so those who discovered Capri in the first place, before it became crowded, have now quietly moved off to a new discovery which is rapidly going the same way. The trail blazers have simply moved across the Bay of Naples to the island of Ischia and a host of luxurious new hotels have gone up to accommodate the newcomers, with the result that Ischia, too, has problems with overcrowding in the summer months.

More than twice the size of Capri, Ischia is of volcanic origin, and the volcano, Mount Epomeo, shoots up to a height of 2,585 feet. But don't be alarmed—it hasn't erupted for 6½ centuries. In fact, there's a cableway to its summit. It starts from Porto d'Ischia, the chief settlement and a spa. Casamicciola is another favorite resort on the coast, and so is nearby Lacco Ameno. Besides scenery, the island has thermal springs.

Porto d'Ischia, where the biggest luxury hotels are found, is the usual port of debarkation. For this reason, many visitors stop here. Distances are so short that it doesn't really matter much where you put up; all parts of the island are accessible from whatever base you prefer. And Porto d'Ischia isn't one of those workaday ports of entry from which the visitor immediately takes off for more interesting parts. It's an enchanting resort whose flat-roofed oriental houses climb steeply up the hillside above the water, whose narrow streets frequently turn into flights of steps, and whose villas and gardens are topped and backed by beautiful growths of pine. If you elect to stay here, you can expect excellent bathing from the half-mile beach whose eastern end, of fine sand, is the most attractive. The slope is relatively gentle. The chief man-made features of the town are the 15th-century Castle of Ischia and a small museum.

Many visitors prefer to go on a couple of miles to Casamicciola, a popular bathing resort with a fine sandy beach next to the pier where steamers come in, and smaller beaches on either side of the town. There are mineral springs here also, some of them reaching temperatures near boiling. If you want to avoid the crowds, you might try Forio, or Sant' Angelo, on the southern coast. It has a lovely sandy beach at Lido dei Maronti.

The chief attractions of the island, besides its beaches, are the opportunities afforded for skin diving, its magnificent scenery, an unbeatable climate pleasant all year around, and perhaps not least the *Epomeo* wine produced on the slopes of the extinct volcano.

Procida

The island of Procida owes its existence to not one, but four volcanic craters. It's a wild and rugged island of great charm, a delightful spot full of sweeping views. The small population of fishermen and vineyard workers lives in beautiful little domed houses. It has a few hotels and pensions.

PRACTICAL INFORMATION FOR NAPLES

HOTELS. Reserve well in advance. *Deluxe (L)* **Excelsior,** Via Partenope 48, owned and operated by the Compagnia Italiana Grandi Alberghi; and **Vesuvio,** Via Partenope 45, a member of the Italhotels Association, both on shore drive, airconditioned, elegantly furnished, though not at same level of excellence of deluxe hotels elsewhere.

First class (1)

Majestic, Largo Vasto a Chiaia, few blocks from shore drive, very comfortable, panoramic restaurant.

Mediterraneo, just off Piazza Municipio, is central, comfortably furnished, pleasant roof garden with view of the bay.

Parker's, Corso Vittorio Emanuele, near Vomero on Posillipo hill. Old-fashioned, ornate salons, comfortable, good service.

Jolly, recent 30-story hotel. Great views, especially from rooftop restaurant; usual standardized decor, cuisine.

Moderate (2)

Cavour, on station square, is medium-sized, has many rooms with bath or shower, optional airconditioning.

Grilli, very near station and Circumvesuviana railway, large, well-equipped.

Britannique, Corso Vittorio, on slopes of Vomero, has good views, efficient and friendly service, clean rooms.

Santelmo, Via Bonito, on Vomero near funicular, and **Serius,** Viale Augusto, modern, all rooms with bath or shower.

Motel AGIP, highway 7, excellent for motorists.

Inexpensive (3)

Belvedere, on slopes of Vomero, pleasant little hotel with marvelous views.

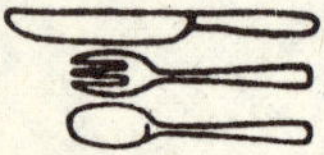

RESTAURANTS. Naples is not as good a city for eating as Bologna, Rome or Venice, unless you like pasta, pasta and more pasta. Most visitors will be attracted towards the Santa Lucia waterfront and its cluster of pleasant establishments that ring the harbor formed by the Castel dell'Ovo.

Expensive (E)

Of these, **Scialuppa di Starita** is best; try *polipi alla luciana, linguine alle vongole,* eggplant *parmigiana.*

For food with a view, you have to travel. On the Posillipo hill to the west is the elegant and excellent **Galeone,** Via Posillipo 16, and **La Sacrestia,** Via Orazio, which serves a variety of hearty Neapolitan dishes, including piquant *maccheroncini alla scarpariello.* Just beyond, at **Marechiaro, La Fazenda,** for rustic specialties.

Moderate (M)

Also on Posillipo, **Don Salvatore** is known for luscious pizzas and *linguine cosa nostra.*

Don Pasquale, practically next door, shiny modern decor, special *fettuccine* and *scaloppine.*

In a slightly different part of town, halfway up the Vomero hill, are **Le Arcate** and **D'Angelo,** both on Via Aniello Falcone and both with a view to relish. Same is true of **Sbrescia,** at Rampe di Sant'Antonio, off Via Orazio.

Just off Piazza dei Martiri, **Umberto** is a lively, neon-lit place serving Neapolitan fare.

Bergantino, just off station square, is a bustling favorite with businessmen and families, with an extensive choice of well-prepared dishes.

Ciro, Via Santa Brigida 71, is near the newspaper offices and attracts a journalistic crowd.

Al Pappagallo, Via Carlo de Cesare 14, is favorite.

Don Chisciotte, Via dell'Incoronata 29, is also good. **Rugantino,** off Via Lopez Diaz, is reader-recommended.

Dante e Beatrice, Piazza Dante, unpretentious, and according to one expert, the best *pasta e fagioli* anywhere.

Al 53, Piazza Dante, popular and worthy trattoria.

Lampara, Discesa Coroglio, high on Posillipo, serves delicious platters of mixed pastas or meats, pizzas.

Inexpensive (I)

Pizzicato, Piazza Municipio, for quick snacks, pizzas. **Osteria 'O Sfiziuso,** Via Martucci, where students go for *pasta e fagioli, baccalà.*

Luciano, Piazza San Frencesco, down-to-earth prices for seafood, especially squid.

Pizzeria Bellini, Via Santa Maria Costantinopoli, near National Museum.

MUSEUMS. There are several excellent museums in Naples, and here are some of them. More details available from Naples EPT office. Some earthquake-damaged museums will be open on a limited basis only until restorations have been completed.

Capodimonte Palace, Tondo di Capodimonte. Rich collection of paintings of Neapolitan and Roman schools, porcelains, and armor.

Castel Nuovo, Piazza Municipio, copied after Château of Angers, interesting interiors. Free entry.

Chapel of San Severo, Piazza San Domenico Maggiore, masterpieces of 18th-century sculpture.

Charterhouse of San Martino, Via Torrione di San Martino, Vomero. Convent dispensary, refectory, museum; 18th-century Neapolitan paintings; famous *presepi.*

Filangieri Museum, Via Duomo. Ancient arms, objets d'art, vases.

National Museum, Piazza del Museo. Treasures from Pompeii, Herculaneum, antique finds from all Campanian sites.

Royal Palace, Piazza del Plebiscito, royal apartments.

San Carlo Theater, Piazza Trieste e Trento.

Villa Floridiana, Via Cimarosa, Vomero, houses National Museum of Ceramics, Duca di Martina collection of porcelains and majolica.

USEFUL ADDRESSES. *American Express,* SIT, Via San Carlo 49–50, tel. 411663; *Cook's,* Via Depretis 126; CIT, Piazza Municipio 72, and Stazione Marittima, the pier; *SPAN* shipping line, Molo Beverello; for **information on boats** to Sardinia, Societa di Navigazione Tirrenia, office at the pier, Molo Angioino; *American Consulate,* Piazza della Repubblica.

Tourist Offices AAST, Palazzo Reale, and Viale Kennedy; EPT, Via Partenope 10, Railway Station, and Airport.

SPECIAL EVENTS. In July there is music at the Capodimonte Palace. For the first 10 days of September there is the Piedigrotta, a series of colorful and spectacular events; fireworks, parade of carnival floats, Neapolitan song contest. Opera begins in December at the great San Carlo Theater.

SHOPPING. Naples is famous for its coral, cameos and tortoise shell articles. The great coral factories are located at **Torre del Greco** about 10 miles south of Naples and most guided tours to **Pompeii** include a brief stop to see them.

WARNING. Do not bathe in the immediate area of Naples, and do not eat shellfish.

PRACTICAL INFORMATION FOR CAMPANIA

HOTELS AND RESTAURANTS

Acciaroli. Coast resort with vast stretches of beach. **Hotels:** Both (2)—*La Playa,* Right on beach, functional furnishings, many rooms with balcony, sea view; *Faro,* same type, on beach.

La Pineta (3), across road from beach, basic but pleasant, good for families.

Amalfi. A number of small pebbly beaches, some accessible only from the sea (friendly fishermen provide the ferries). **Hotels:** High season, May–end Sept.; crowded all along the coast at Easter and in July–August.

All (1) are—*Cappuccini-Convento,* southwest on SN 12, 62 rooms, 30 with bath, perched on cliff above town, this picturesque, old-fashioned hotel is converted convent, with cloisters, hotel bus; *Santa Caterina,* Via Nazionale, atop cliff, 50 rooms, most with bath, balcony facing sea, flower-hung terraces, lift to private swimming area and saltwater pool; pool, *Luna,* in town, 36 rooms, most with bath, also a remodeled convent, complete with cloisters, good restaurant, swimming pool and disco. *Excelsior,* isolated, high on mountain some distance from Amalfi, pool, terraces, view, minibus to town.

All (2), all short walk from town; *Miramalfi,* splendid position, 44 good-sized rooms with bath, balcony, anonymous decor, lift to pool, sea; *Bellevue,* smallish, overlooking sea, lift to swimming platform; *Cavalieri,* recent, bright modern decor, some antiques, beach; meal options at various restaurants; splendid villa annexes.

Marina-Riviera (3), on outskirts, 20 rooms, a few with bath, wonderful sea view, fresh decor.

Restaurants: Both (E) are—the dining rooms of the hotels *Santa Caterina* and *Luna.*

All (M)—Best of all is *Caravella;* also very good, *La Marinella,* on the seafront; and cheaper, *Flavio Gioia,* restaurant on stilts overlooking beach, and *Lido Azzuro,* on the port. On main street, *Da Maria* for pizza; *Da Gemma,* fine antipasto.

On road toward **Conca,** *Ciccio* (M–E), good food, lovely view.

Anacapri. Upper town on island of Capri. **Hotels:** *Europa Palace* (1) is best as well as largest, all rooms with bath or shower, pool, tennis, panoramic terraces.

San Michele (2), Via Guiseppe Orlandi 1, near Axel Munthe's villa, 36 rooms, 26 with bath, villa-type, comfortable, splendid view.

Both (3)—*Villa Patrizia* is smallish and quite pleasant; *Bella Vista,* with cleverly arranged apartments, good value.

Restaurants: All (M) are—*Vittoria,* seasonal; the café-restaurant at Monte Solarno (hour's walk or cable lift from Anacapri) offers the finest view on the island as does the terrace of *San Michele* hotel.

Avellino. Hotels: *Jolly* (1), 41 rooms, most with bath. *Patria* (2).

Restaurants: Both (M)—just off main piazza are *Soldatiello* and *Cantuccio. La Caveja* (M–E), is very good, has succulent pastas.

Benevento. Hotel: *President* (1), on central square, 76 rooms, most with bath, cheerful, modern.

Restaurants: *Taverna di Orazio* (M), favorite for local pastas and roasts. Just outside town at Piano Cappella, two trattorias for fine rustic specialties: *Pascalucci* and *Vecchia America,* both (I–M).

Capri. Main town on the small rocky island opposite the peninsula of Sorrento, the most expensive spot in Italy, crowded at Easter, avoid it during July and August.

Hotels: High season, May–end Sept. *Quisisana* (L), open Easter–Oct. 31. Now the property of the Grundig family, Capri's poshest, most expensive hostelry; central but quiet; smart international clientele; spacious, beautifully furnished rooms, fine service, pool, tennis.

All (1)—*Tiberio Palace,* 75 rooms, most with bath and many with balconies overlooking sea and town; *Regina Cristina,* 49 rooms, ultra modern, excellent service, good location, garden; *Luna,* 48 rooms with bath, excellent, garden terraces; *La Palma,* off main piazza, modern.

All (2) *Flora,* a villa and honeymooners' dream, just 14 double rooms, all with bath; *La Floridiana,* Via Campo di Teste 16, 39 rooms, most with bath, delightful spot amidst garden and pines, terrace overlooking sea; *La Pineta,* all rooms with bath, terraces, pool; *Gatto Bianco,* Via Vittorio Emanuele, 40 rooms, all with bath, central location but away from the madding crowd, open 1 April–31 Oct. *La Residenza* is simple but comfortable; *La Vega,* and *Villa delle Sirene* have all rooms with bath or shower; new *Villa Sanfelice,* central but quiet, all private baths; *Semiramis,* rooms with bath or shower; *La Pergola* has most rooms with bath or shower and terrace, quiet location, friendly service.

Villa Pina (3), swimming pool, stairs.

Among the pensions *Esperia* and *Terminus,* both (P2) are small. Pension terms at pleasant *Nuovo Reale* (2) hotel.

Restaurants: Restaurants and prices vary greatly. At the top, pricewise and for well-heeled tourists, all (E) *Pigna,* Via Roma; followed by the *Canzone del Mare,* at Marina Piccola, smart, comfortable spot where you can swim and eat till sundown, (i.e., no dinners); the chic place is *Capannina;* the bohemian one is *Glauco,* with a delightful terrace, and at both the food is excellent; still expensive, vine-clad *Faraglioni,* with good view, and at the faraglioni themselves, *Luigi,* open only for lunch (boat from Marina Piccola).

All (M)—*Grottino,* just off the piazzetta; *Da Pietro* at Marina Piccola, for shrimp, *cannelloni* and gossip with the English lady in charge, lunch only;

special mention goes to the *Pizza Maria* for its Caprese version of this famous dish; also popular, *Delle Sirene,* and *Guiseppina. Gemma,* just off the piazzetta, fine old favorite.

Good trattorias—*Michele* and *O'Saraceno,* for prawns flambé.

Casamicciola. On north coast of island of Ischia, with thermal springs, and a nice sandy beach 220 yards long. **Hotels:** Both (1)—*Cristallo Palace,* on shore drive, terraces, thermal pool, spa; *Manzi,* recent, airconditioned, on hillside, pool, gardens. *Grand Paradiso* (2), on bay, 50 rooms.

Caserta. **Hotels:** Both (1)—*Reggia Palace,* large, modern, fully airconditioned, comfortable rooms, pool, garage; *Europa,* in town, near palace, all rooms with bath or shower, good dining room.

Restaurants: Both (M) at Caserta Vecchia; *La Castellana* for such hard-to-find specialties as *minestra maritata; Da Teresa,* pastas and pizzas. In center of Caserta, *Massa* (M).

Castellammare di Stabia. Busy port, spa. **Hotel:** *Delle Terme* (2), big, swimming pool, tennis.

Castel Volturno. Brand-new sea resort about 20 miles north of Naples. **Hotel:** *Pinetamare* (2), all 200 rooms with private bath or shower and balcony, big, modern holiday center on vast sandy beach, swimming pool, tennis, nightclub.

Cava dei Tirreni. Hill resort. **Hotels:** Both (2)—*Victoria;* and *Scapolatello,* a charming spot, panoramic view from gardens, good restaurant.

Conca dei Marini. Near Amalfi. **Hotel:** *Belvedere* (1), lovely view, fine service, good food. Has swimming pool and rock bathing, highly recommended.

Forio. Port on the west coast of Ischia island. **Hotel:** *Santa Caterina* (2), lovely location, all private baths, pool.

Restaurants: *La Meridiana* (M–E) on San Francesco beach, and *Negombo* (E), on San Montano beach, are delightful.

Ischia. Town on northeast coast of Ischia Island. **Hotels:** All (1)—*Excelsior,* 67 rooms, all with bath, attractive villa with garden, private beach, swimming pool, full or half pension only; *Terme Jolly,* 220 rooms, all with bath, swimming pool, spa treatments at hotel; *Majestic,* 84 rooms, all with bath, private beach; *Parco Aurora,* all rooms with bath, on sea front, modern; *Bristol Palace,* recent, open April–Oct. all 36 well-furnished rooms have private bath or shower and balcony, pleasant public rooms, terrace, garden, a few steps from private beach; *Aragona Palace,* 40 attractive rooms.

All (2) are—*Regina Palace; Ischia; Villa Aurora,* in park, all rooms with bath; *La Perla,* pool; and *Miramare e Castello,* good, with a fine annex, *Miracastello* (3).

Villarosa (P1), special mention, gracious villa aura, pretty rooms, attentive service.

Restaurants: At **Ischia Porto,** *Nannina* and *Di Massa* are good, simple restaurants, while the first-class hotel dining rooms offer more sophisticated menus.

At **Ischia Ponte,** *Giardini Eden* (M–E) proposes rock bathing and refreshing lunches.

Lacco Ameno. On northwest coast of Ischia Island. **Hotels:** *Regina Isabella* (L), sumptuous, smart, 130 beautifully furnished rooms with bath, private beach, swimming pool, tennis, garage, spa, best on the island, a CIGA hotel.

Both (1) are—*La Reginella,* all rooms with bath or shower, tennis court, swimming pool; *San Montana,* newest, modern, elegant, on sandy cove, terraces, pool.

Restaurants: *San Montano* (E), on beach, very good or *Padrone del Mare* (M).

Maiori. Over-developed beach resort, best off-season. **Hotels:** *Reggina Palace* (1), modern balconied hotel overlooking good-sized pool in garden, beach across road. *Pietra di Luna* (2), overlooking beach across road, attractive, comfortable lounges, 85 rooms with shower, views of coast or hills.

Restaurants: Both (M)—*Reggina Palace* restaurant; or *Mammato,* try spaghetti *alle vongole.*

Marina di Camerota. Beach resort. **Hotels:** *Baia delle Sirene, America:* both (2).

Maronti Beach. On Ischia Island. **Hotels:** *Parco Smeraldo, Helios,* both (2), all amenities.

Monte Faito. Pine-covered, cool mountain resort overlooking Sorrento. **Hotel:** *Grand Hotel Monte Faito* (1), old-fashioned rooms, all with shower or tub, quiet, good food.

Ogliastro Marina. New beach resort. **Hotel:** *Punta Licosa* (2), airconditioned throughout, overlooking private beach, all rooms with bath.

Paestum. Greek temples and a vast stretch of beach. **Hotels:** All (2)—*Ariston,* pool; *Poseidon,* near temples; *Calypso,* all private baths, beach; recent *Le Palme,* resort-style with beach, pool.

Palinuro. Overbuilt resort with a vast stretch of beach. **Hotels:** *Saline* (1), modern, airconditioned resort hotel with pool, beach.

Both (2) are—*Conchiglia, La Torre.*

Pompeii. Hotels: We advise staying in either Naples or Sorrento, where the hotel choice is much better, and visiting Pompeii by the Circuvesuviana.

Restaurants: Three good, moderate restaurants are *Pompeii, Santuario,* and *Anfiteatro.*

Positano. Smart seaside resort, with a beach of sand and pebbles and stairways for streets. **Hotels:** All (1)—*San Pietro,* most striking and most expensive, on promontory outside town; lovely bedrooms with terraces, spectacular views of sea below, lift to private beach and tennis, minibus service into town. *Le Sirenuse,* smart, in town, tastefully furnished, 50 rooms, most with view; pool on terrace, some noise rises to rooms; *Miramare,* in town on cliff, small and very good, beautiful terraces; very private.

All (2) are—*Casa Albertina,* overlooking sea, short climb up from road, all rooms with bath; *Ancora,* friendly small hotel, all private baths; *Poseidon,* beautifully furnished salons, lovely garden terrace with pool, all rooms with bath, balcony. *Covo dei Saraceni,* only hotel directly on beach, balconies, pool, can be noisy. *Palazzo Murat,* handsome old villa in heart of town but in quiet garden, modern annex, breakfast only.

Villa Franca (3), good value.

Restaurants: All on beach, *Capurale* (M), good. *Buca di Bacco, Chez Black* are both (E). Best pizza at *Taverna del Leone* (M), on Praiano road. For good beach and lunch (M), take *Adolfo's* boat at pier.

Praiano. Hotel: *Tritone* (2), 54 rooms, all private baths or showers; it's a handsome hotel, built on cliffside terraces with spectacular views, in isolated position between Positano and Vettica, minibus service to Praiano, large pool, lift to beach.

Restaurant: *Gennaro* (M), pizzas, *calamari.*

Procida. Volcanic island near the entrance to the Bay of Naples. **Hotels:** All (3)—*Arcate, Oasi* and *Riviera,* all small, the only hotels on this island.

Punta Molino. On Ischia Island. **Hotels:** Both (1)—*Moresco,* hacienda-style, 43 rooms with bath, full pension only; *Grand Hotel Punta Molino,* handsome white-washed building in pines, tastefully furnished and airconditioned throughout.

Ravello. Hotels: All (2) are—*Palumbo,* tiny, excellent, old-world atmosphere, marvelous views from terraces, garage; *Caruso Belvedere,* 29 rooms, also very good, garage, produce own delicious white, red and (best) rose wine, fine terrace restaurant, gardens; and *Rufolo,* also charming, pool, gardens.

Both (3)—*Parsifal,* delightful old building, modern comforts, terraces, good value; *Villa Amore,* enchanting small hotel with garden, beautiful views.

Salerno. This bustling, almost oriental city has fallen victim to a dubious progress. The once-lovely beach is now being developed as an industrial port, and pollution has caused a ban on bathing all along the shore.

Hotels. *Jolly* (1), central, on shore drive, well-appointed, airconditioned rooms.

Both (2)—*Diana,* overlooks the sea, with a roof garden; *Montestella,* Corso Vittorio, is bright and modern.

Restaurants: *Nicola dei Principati* (M–E), Corso Garibaldi, for fish; *Caramato,* same street, and *Boccadoro* at **Santa Teresa.** Good pizzerias throughout city; try *Caminetto* (I), Via Roma.

San Giocondo. Near Sapri. **Hotel:** *Terrazze* (2), well-furnished, modern, in panoramic spot, 40 rooms with shower, beach, pool.

Sant'Agnello. Near Sorrento. **Hotels:** Good hotels, both overlooking the Bay of Naples; *Cocumella* (1), with lift to private beach, tennis courts; and *Mediterraneo* (2), which has a free bus service to Sorrento, town center. Unless you stay at one of these, you do better in terms of view and expense at Positano, Amalfi, or Ravello.

Santa Maria di Castellabate. Resort. **Hotels:** *Castelsandra* (1), at **San Marco,** excellent, all resort facilities, water sports. Other beach hotels, both (2)—*L'Approdo,* and *Santa Maria.*

Sant'Angelo. On Ischia Island. There's a good sandy beach at **Marina del Maronti** nearby. **Hotels:** *Vulcano* (1); *Apollon, San Michele,* both (2); all with pool.

Sapri. Unassuming, unpretentious, un-modernized resort. **Hotels:** *Tirreno* (3), 48 rooms, some with bath, facing the sea.

At **Villamare,** *Royal* (2), has beach, good restaurant.

Sorrento. Important beach resort, crowded at Easter. **Hotels:** High season, May–end Sept. All (1)—*Parco dei Principi,* is exceptional, includes 18th-century villa and striking modern annex, attractive rooms, beautiful views, indoor and outdoor pools, lift to private beach.

Excelsior Grand Hôtel Vittoria, a fine hotel with excellent service, cooking, and accommodations, if old-fashioned, overlooks sea, private beach.

Europa Palace, more modern, has same standout view and pleasant terrace, private beach area.

Royal, has garden and terraces on sea, lift from beach to garden; *Carlton,* attractive, enchanting orange garden, but not cliff-clinging like the first four; *Imperial Hotel Tramontano,* "living as in private villa," lift to bathing area.

Following are high above Sorrento, rather isolated, with minibus service into town: *Aminta,* marvelous views, pool; *Caesar Augustus,* 120 modern rooms, pool; *President,* attractive, all rooms with bath or shower and balcony, swimming pool and tennis courts.

All (2)—*Bellevue Syrene,* spacious rooms in 18th-century villa with garden, old-fashioned, good. *Minerva,* outside town, high above sea, attractive rooms, views, pool. *Eden,* central, friendly, bright rooms, garden.

Restaurants: All (E)—The plushiest place in town is the *Parco dei Principi,* dining room; good food at *Parrucchiano; Bottaro,* Via Correale, is gayer.

Both (M)—*Minervetta,* Via del Capo, is well known; nearby *Tonnarella,* has same view of bay, *Lasagne alla Sorrentina,* small, reserve; *Taverna del Vagabondo,* reader-recommended. *Gigino,* Via Nicotera, for pizza.

Vico Equense. Picturesque town, rather scruffy. **Hotels:** Both (1)—*Capo La Gala,* smart atmosphere, swimming pool, private beach, open June–Sept. *Le Axidie,* less expensive but delightful, modern wing on old monastery, antique-furnished, most rooms with balconies, sea view, vine-shaded terrace, pool. beach.

Restaurant: Everybody eats at *Pizza al Metro* (M), where tasty ribbons of pizza are made on an assembly line and you order by the yard.

Vietri. Beach resort with a tiny sand beach, famed for ceramics. **Hotels:** Both (1)—*Lloyd's Baia,* panoramic location above private beach; *Raito,* good, all rooms with bath or shower, beach facilities

USEFUL ADDRESSES. Tourist Offices: *Amalfi:* AAST, Corso Roma 19. *Avellino: Benevento:* EPT, Via Nicola Sala, Parco de Santis. *Capri:* AAST, Piazza Umberto 1. *Caserta:* EPT, Piazza Dante 35 and Palazzo Reale. *Castellammare de Stabia:* AAST, Nuove Terme Stabiane del Solaro. *Cava dei Tirreni:* AAST, Via M. Garzia. *Ischia:* AAST, Via Porto. *Pompeii:* AAST, Viale de 'Teatri, Pompeii Scavi. *Positano:* AAST, Via del Saracino 2. *Ravello:* AAST, Piazza Vescovado 13. *Salerno:* AAST, Piazza Amendola 8; EPT, Via Velia 15, and Piazza Ferrovia 1. *Sorrento:* AAST, Via de Maio 35. *Vico Equense:* AAST, Corso Umberto 1.

SPORTS. *Amalfi:* Sailing, rowing and underwater hunting are as popular as swimming here. *Capri:* On Capri, the beaches are Marina Grande, coarse sand and pebbles, with a steep slope; Marina Piccola, short steep pebbly patches; and minute bits of pebbly rock-strewn beach at Palazzo a Mare, Bagni di Tiberio and Marina di Ceretola. It isn't the bathing that attracts visitors to Capri, but there are bathing establishments nevertheless, with the most elaborate at Marina Piccola, and sailing, rowing, water skiing and underwater hunting are popular. The grotto-pitted rocks which plunge down to the sea are particularly well adapted to this last sport.

Ischia: The Island of Ischia offers good swimming facilities. Porto d'Ischia, where the boats come in, has several stretches of beach, one of them of fine sand with a gentle incline. *Salerno:* All water sports along nearby Amalfi coast. *Sorrento:* Some patches of beach, and besides swimming, rowing and sailing are practiced here, with a regatta during the August Fair.

THE DEEP SOUTH

Gargano, Apulia, Lucania and Calabria

Many tourists believe that with a visit to Naples, a drive round the Amalfi coast to Salerno, and possibly as far afield as Paestum, they have seen Italy's south; yet they have barely passed through the gate, however spectacular what they have seen may be. Over 400 miles of driving are needed to reach the southernmost tip of Calabria, Italy's "toe", some 20 miles beyond Reggio Calabria. On the Adriatic shore the little-known "Deep South" begins farther north at Termoli. Here old main road and new *superstrada* alike cut inland to avoid the rugged contours of the Gargano Peninsula, Italy's "spur". From Termoli, too, there's 400 miles to be done at the wheel if you follow the coast road all the way to Santa Maria di Leuca at the tip of Italy's "heel".

Italy's far south is composed of the ancient provinces of Apulia (called Puglia in modern Italy), Lucania (known also as the Basilicata), and Calabria. Apulia forms Italy's "heel", Lucania constitutes the "instep" and "arch" and the territory between, and Calabria provides the "toe". The Gargano Peninsula, the "spur", is a part of Apulia; despite recent package-tour development it is still relatively unspoilt. It should be seen before it becomes too popular. It is a wild region, yet idyllic, where olive trees stretch for mile after mile, where towns are rare and where a huge, cool forest adds a surprisingly northern touch.

But most of Apulia consists of gently rolling hills covered with olive groves and dotted with imposing castles, interesting towns, the *trulli*—simple circular dwellings, unchanged since Stone Age days (until very recently)—and some fine harbors.

Weather Matters

The inland areas of these provinces suffer from extreme heat in summer coupled with bitter cold in winter. In the southern half of Apulia, however, these extremes are tempered in both seasons by breezes from the sea—not very strong, but enough to remove a little of the season's sting. In Calabria in summer the mountain towns and resorts provide welcome coolness: after a holiday on the sea, it might be pleasant to finish at a town like Castrovillari, where you can manage without air conditioning even in mid-August.

In winter many of Calabria's mountain spots become skiing resorts. Their terrain is excellent. Though they have as yet little equipment such as skitows and lifts, they are increasingly visited by knowledgeable Italian skiers, and it is only a matter of time before they reach full international standard.

In short, you can explore Italy's deep south at any period of the year. In the heat of summer, it strikes you as extremely odd that the hoardings advertising local hotels should all stress the provision of central heating: it's about the last thing you can envisage in the summer heat. But it is definitely required in winter, even along the more temperate coasts. Only in inland Lucania does traveling in winter become a problem, and that is chiefly due to the shortage of good hotels and the difficult, tortuous, snow-covered roads.

As everywhere, the best time to visit this region is spring, when everything is green and the beautiful wild flowers native to this region are in full bloom. The last snows melt soon after mid-April. The fall, too, is mild.

Road Reports

Italy's Deep South is fundamentally car country—after you have arrived by plane, ship or train to some such base as Bari, Brindisi or Taranto. The two main lines of approach by car are the Autostrada del Sole from Rome, passing Naples and Salerno, only occasionally in view of the sea on the way to Reggio Calabria; in the east, the Autostrada Adriatica follows the coast from Rimini, Ancona and Pescara to turn inland, south of Termoli, to bypass the Gargano Peninsula on entering Apulia. The road returns to the coast (or close to it) near Barletta to terminate at Bari. From Barletta, Autostrada 17 branches west, to divide at Avellino in a spur to Naples and another to Salerno. The Autostrada del Sole sweeps through Calabria's magnificent mountain scenery, while the Adriatica passes close to Apulia's main towns, ports and beach resorts.

But, the loveliest, if slowest, drive returning from Reggio Calabria is over the Aspromonte highland, descending to the Ionian coast from Locri to Monasterace, then striking inland again to the Serra San Bruno, and after Catanzaro, through the magnificent forests of La Sila to Consenza and the autostrada. The absence of traffic makes this one of the few Italian roads where driving is still a pleasure. You should be warned that inland hotels and pensions are few and far between, and the ones along the coast are booked out in summer.

Food for Thought

Apulia offers good seafood, fish soup and oysters in season. Other specialties are roast lamb and *calzone,* a ravioli-like pasta. Calabria has trout from the mountain streams of the Sila plateau and delicious roast kid. Lucania grows artichokes.

As for wines, Apulia offers the greatest variety. The reds are *Aleatico di Puglia,* sweet, and *Castel del Monte,* dry; white are *Locorotondo,* dry, and *Malvasia di Brindisi,* sweet. In Calabria, the dry reds and whites of Cirò are exceptional and heady; *Greco di Gerace,* dry, and *Moscato di Cosenza,* sweet, are both white. Lucania produces *Aglianico dei Vulture,* red, dry, and two white wines, both sweet: *Malvasia* and *Moscato.*

The Fund for the South

Considerable improvements have been made in what has long been Italy's poorest region. The first great step was the introduction of DDT at the end of the Second World War. The entire coast of this area was so malaria-infested that only a few hardy souls could live here. Today the land is mostly fertile and well-tilled, with sugar-beet a vital, and very profitable, main crop in certain parts.

The second move was the establishment by the Italian Government of the Southern Fund, the *Cassa per il Mezzogiorno.* The Cassa's basic function was to provide capital for essential public works, such as roads, irrigation dams, and the like, and to make loans to enterprises calculated to provide employment and improve living standards. The Cassa has not always worked efficiently. Administered from Rome, its operations have been ponderous and slow. It has frequently run out of money—not primarily the administrator's fault, but upsetting to anyone depending on a promised loan. Yet the fund has already achieved a great deal towards changing the face of Italy's deep south. New roads have both opened the area to commerce and have allowed tourists to travel throughout the region in ever-increasing numbers. This increase in tourism has stimulated the need for labor-intensive operations, such as hotels, restaurants, garages and service stations, bringing both work and money at the same time.

Tourism is thus the third factor affecting Italy's extreme south. The coast resorts on the fine sandy beaches are in full development. Some places, only relatively few as yet, already possess excellent modern hotels designed to cater for different types of holiday makers. What's more, prices and hotel rates in the southern regions are low, good reason to include them in your itinerary.

Exploring the Deep South

The Gargano Peninsula is one of the surprises of southern Italy; it has breath-taking scenery, well-equipped resorts and a friendly refreshing atmosphere. Along its northern coast over 40 miles of sandy beach and dunes enclose two large lagoons, with flat fertile plains extending inland from them to the base of the limestone mountains. In summer the plains are golden with grain crops and olives cover the lower mountain slopes. By car, your jumping-off point for this region is Poggio Imperiale, south of Termoli. From San Severo, Gargano's only railway line reaches the north coast at picturesque Rodi Garganico after a *very* laborious mountain journey. Ten miles further on, it peters out at Peschici.

Rodi Garganico and Peschici are lovely white towns shut in between mountains and sea. Vieste, however, which lies on a small peninsula, is the main commercial center of this region. A coastal road runs to Porto di Mattinata, in the plain on the Gargano limestone massif's southern side, passing one cliff headland after another, uphill and downhill through the miles of olive groves that give the region much of its special character. It is not long since mules were almost the only means of transport in these parts, but today, when work in the fields is done, the local population returns home on tractors. Fishing is an important industry. Trawlers sail out of Manfredonia, smaller fishing boats out of Peschici, the most picturesque and charming town on the Gargano.

Vieste, with a magnificent, long sandy beach south of the town, is crowded with tourists during the hot summer months. The coast road from Vieste gives you tantalizing glimpses of crystal-clear water in enchanting rocky inlets. Finally, a left turn off the main road leads you to Testa del Gargano, where the Pugnochiuso promontory hosts two hotels in an internationally known holiday complex with a fine white sand beach. All along the Gargano coast the contrast of turquoise waters and white limestone cliffs topped with deep green scrub pines is breathtaking.

Smack in the middle of the Gargano peninsula stands the majestic Foresta Umbra, literally, the shady forest. The odd thing about this wood, 2,600 feet above sea level, is its density and coolness, and the fact it grows exactly the same trees as you find in the English counties of Surrey and Buckinghamshire, close to London. Emerging from its coolness into the sudden, oven-like temperature of a blazing August day is an extraordinary experience.

The only highway through the Foresta Umbra is winding and tiring. It leads from the northern coast west of Peschici to Monte Sant' Angelo, Gargano's capital, a fantastic white town, built right on top of the limestone's southernmost ridge. It is an important place of pilgrimage, for in 491 St. Michael appeared to some country shepherds in a cave here and left his red cloak behind. In the 8th century, an abbey was built on the spot, and thousands of crudaders paid homage to the angel here before embarking from the once-busy port of Manfredonia, 10 miles to the south, on the edge of the plain called the *Tavoliere* (chessboard) of Apulia.

Inland Apulia

Inland, Foggia is the plain's commercial center. It boasts a Romanesque cathedral (1179), but little else of note. San Severo, to the north, is a wine-producing center. Westwards, Lucera's chief feature is the great castle and towers built by Frederick II to protect the town. His successors transformed a Saracen mosque into a Gothic cathedral (about 1300). The ancient Roman arena can still be seen.

The autostrada and the old main road down Italy's east coast, turn inland after Termoli to dodge the Gargano Peninsula. After passing San Severo, Foggia and Cerignola they return to the coast at Barletta. Near San Severo, with its various baroque buildings, are the ruins of Castel Fiorentino, where Frederick died in 1250.

The autostrada exit at Canosa di Puglia leads northeast to the coast at Barletta, while a country lane meanders in the opposite direction to the great abode of Frederick, his favorite and most impressive castle, the Castel del Monte, rising in solitary splendor above the plain and commanding one of the finest views in southern Italy. The expertly restored octagonal construction with eight towers, has been ranked in splendor and significance with the Colosseum. Nearby, under the medieval church of Ruvo di Puglia, a 4th-century BC cemetery was unearthed in 1979, providing valuable clues to life in ancient times.

The southern part of Bari's province offers other Norman monuments in Gravina and Gioia del Colle. Within easy driving distance of Bari is Castellana Grotte, with its recently discovered underground caverns noted for their interesting stalagmites and stalactites. Altamura possesses remnants of prehistoric walls and a cathedral begun by Frederick II. Alberobello possesses a major tourist attraction in its trulli.

The trulli are considered peculiar to Apulia, but old buildings of the same style can be seen in Malta, and it is clear that something similar was used in many Mediterranean areas in bygone centuries. Basically, the trullo is a simple circular, stone-built one-roomed dwelling, roughly constructed without mortar or squaring-off of the stones. Their roofs vary. Those at Alberobello are today conical, but many old trulli in other parts of Apulia have outside stone staircases leading up to flat roofs incorporating grainstores—removed from at least the majority of rats and mice. Both types of ancient trulli have simple holes in the roof to let out the smoke of fires used for cooking.

Nowhere else is there such a large collection of these curious buildings as Alberobello, where they form almost a village on their own. This little collection is being carefully preserved. Out in the country, though, lots of old trulli are being abandoned in favor of modern variations. These latter are square, built of brick and stucco, and have proper windows and chimneys. Often, too, they are brightly colored. You see them not only in the countryside but also clustered in many coastal villages on both sides of the Salentine Peninsula, the official name of Italy's "heel". These new-style houses, which appear as if they were built from children's colored bricks, give the region an unusual and very attractive appearance. Some are rented to tourists.

Further south is Lecce, a beautiful baroque town bearing the stamp of successive Spanish governors. Greeks and Romans both held sway here, and it was an independent dukedom when the Normans captured it in the 11th century. The town center was largely built in the 16th and 17th centuries, the cathedral in 1670, bishop's palace in 1632, and seminary in 1709, all grouped together in the Piazza del Duomo (Cathedral Square). Another notable building, in fine baroque style, is the Governor's Palace (1695). There is also a 16th-century castle and two churches, Santa Croce and Sant' Irene, of similar date.

The Apulian Coast

Apulia's coast displays no less variety. Barletta is a naval base and port, with a Colossus, an enormous bronze statue, presumed to be of one of the late Roman emperors. The city also features numerous medieval churches and a superb cathedral, which is a composite of styles; Gothic, Norman and Renaissance, topped off by a fine Romanesque campanile. Two baroque palaces are complemented by one of Frederick's large castles.

Trani, Bisceglia and Molfetta all stand out because of their fine stone buildings, recalling the Venetian towns on the Yugoslav Dalmatian coast. Trani's cathedral, with splendid bronze doors, is one of the loveliest churches in Apulia. It was begun in 1094 and is more Pisan than Norman in inspiration. Bisceglie, too, boasts a fine cathedral.

Bari is by far the largest of the towns here. It consists of a tiny medieval old town on a peninsula and a vast 19th-century city built to a grid-pattern plan. Bari is a port, as well as an industrial center. Yet it is rarely given credit for what ought to be its main claim to worldwide fame; for here, in an 11th-century basilica with a later candy box painted ceiling, lie the bones of Santa Claus.

The Father Christmas of modern times was in reality a Bishop of Myra (in present day Turkey), called Nicholas, who lived nearly 1,700 years ago. His kindness to children brought him great renown and he was canonized after raising a murdered boy from the dead. In the 11th century, allegedly, some Bari sailors obtained possession of his bones and brought them home, where the church you can see today was raised for them. It is dedicated of course to St. Nicholas (San Nicola). His transmutation into Santa Claus occurred in New York. The feast of St. Nicholas on December 6th is still fêted in Holland and many other countries; in Dutch, the baby-talk version of "Sint Niklaas" (St. Nicholas) is "Sinter Klaas". It was Dutch settlers' children in New York who first transferred the saint to Christmas Day and started leaving clogs—forerunners of our modern stockings—for the kindly old bishop to deposit his presents in.

Brindisi, though smaller, is nevertheless more important as a port, a position it has held for well over 2,000 years. It's not recommended for anything more than a brief stop to see such churches as San Giovanni al Sepolcro and San Benedetto (both 11th-century), reminders of its medieval splendor. In those days, much wealth passed through the ports of southern Italy. From Brindisi, excellent sandy beaches stretch toward Bari, studded here and there with modern holiday villages. Nearby Ostuni is a picturesque town that spills over the hillside in an exotic jumble of whitewashed rooftops and arches.

Brindisi and Bari provide frequent and fast carferry crossings to Greece, but both are notorious for car thefts and for the breaking of the windows of parked cars. Take extra precautions when in either town.

From just south of Bari to the farthermost tip of the Salentine Peninsula, the coast consists almost all the way of low sandstone cliffs, whose rocks in several places have been worn into fantastic shapes. Nowhere are these more striking than at Santa Cesarea Terme, an oldfashioned spa with a modern sea bathing area. Here you can swim and sunbathe in the middle of pillars and columns and arches that look like the ruins of an old town, but are in reality merely the result of interaction between sea and sandstone.

In one or two other places, much higher cliffs of different geological composition breast the sea. Otranto, a little north of Santa Cesarea Terme, shelters in the lee of one such promontory. It is the easternmost port on the strait which gives it its name, but has lost much of its importance because of its remoteness.

The Salentine Peninsula's western coast possesses many strikingly lovely sections. The white town of Gallipoli, perched on an island reached by a causeway, is perhaps outstanding. But little Santa Caterina, with its vividly-colored box-like houses (mostly modern trulli), has a charm of a different sort—one repeated to a lesser degree in several other villages on this stretch of coast. The shore itself is edged mostly by low volcanic rocks rising only a few feet above the water's level and interspersed with sandy coves.

Taranto, even more ancient than Brindisi in its origins, is today mainly a fine 19th-century town. Its position is magnificent. It occupies a peninsula on one side of a lovely bay overlooking a narrow entrance into a large landlocked bay called the "Mare Piccola" (Small Sea). The "Mare Grande" is Taranto's even finer deepwater anchorage in the bay, created by stretching breakwaters from offshore islands so as to leave only three entrances. On the town's landward side, you have grand views towards the mountains, which once more begin to approach the coast. Taranto, the home of the Italian Crews School, retains little from the past except the 14th-century Church of San Domenico. The local museum, however, has a fine collection of classical art objects and is well worth a visit.

Lucania (The Basilicata)

Westward from Taranto a fertile coastal plain, fringed with magnificent sand, extends for 50 miles with a number of new resorts, such as Castellaneta Marina and Marina di Ginosa. In the northwest of this plain, on the wide Gulf of Taranto, the temple ruins of ancient Metapontum are a reminder that all the best harbor sites, and many other spots as well, were settled in by Greeks over 2,500 years ago. Pythagoras lived and worked at Metapontum.

Martina Franca commands a lovely panoramic view over the bowl-shaped Idria valley; its vineyards are again enlivened by trulli, and its grottos are noted for their exceedingly white stalagmites and stalactites.

Finally, at Rocca Imperiale, below one of Frederick II's great but ruined structures, road and coastal railway are hemmed in between steep mountainside and shore.

Inland Lucania is mountainous, impressive, still remote. The eccentric Emperor Frederick II, who ruled in the first half of the 13th century, bequeathed this province (and all southern Italy) a number of striking castles. Here, if you go a little way from the few main roads and penetrate into the hills, you can still see local folk threshing exactly as described by the great Roman poet Virgil in his *Georgics,* written 2,000 years ago. Life in the Basilicata is hard. Summers are scorchingly hot and winters bitterly cold, and the land is mostly poor and stony.

Located in the instep of the boot, Lucania is probably the leastknown of Italy's areas, partly because of its remoteness from the more populous centers of the country, and partly because of the absence of nature or man, though it flourished briefly during the reign of Frederick II. The scenery is varied and extraordinary, unlike any other part of Italy. Great, sandy wastelands line much of the Ionian coast; inland there are areas of forests, inhabited by wolves and wild boar. The high, wild mountains are divided by deep, rocky gorges and broad valleys.

Inland, over tortuous roads, you reach Matera, picturesquely perched on a steep slope. Much-neglected Matera contains a 13th-century cathedral and other churches, of which the oldest dates from 718. It is noted primarily, however, for its numerous rock dwellings, houses, and even churches, hewn from the solid rock on which the city rests. Worth seeing is the panorama from the high-perched village of Miglionico, a few miles southwest in whose medieval castle the feudal barons of the 15th century conspired against Ferdinand I of Aragon.

Other points of interest are Venosa, birthplace of the poet Horace; Melfi, containing churches from the 12th and 13th centuries; Acerenza, with its 12th-century cathedral; Lagopesole, another residence of Frederick—better preserved than Rocca Imperiale—and Monte Vulture, an extinct volcano whose cone dominates a huge area of the province.

The mountainous surroundings of Potenza, Lucania's capital, are more attractive than the town itself. Potenza was founded by the Romans, a vital staging post on the Via Appia from Rome to Brindisi, and from there to Rome's highly profitable eastern possessions.

The Basilicata's western coast deserves a special mention, for it includes much of the lovely Gulf of Policastro. The beaches here are not much to write home about, but the scenery is superb. The humble village of Maratea is famed for its hilltop Madonna, halfway between the resorts of Porto di Maratea and Marina di Maratea, Porto di Maratea, on the coast, is a pretty little village, and the area boasts a few good seaside hotels.

Calabria

Calabria is a strange and beautiful land, even more ruggedly mountainous than the Basilicata. It consists of coastal shelves and small alluvial plains, with magnificent sweeps of mountain inland—from some viewpoints in the Piccola Sila Range that fills the southern parts of the "toe", you have stupendous views that are also first-rate lessons in geomorphology. You can see where silt brought down by springtime torrents in gullies dry the rest of the year, has pushed the land out into the sea. You can see where land has risen in relation to the sea to leave a narrow coastal shelf or plain. In the Capo Rizzuto region, you can even see a succession of these plains, looking like a giant's garden steps. No one thinks of Calabria as a region of art towns, and indeed it cannot hold a candle to the famous places farther north. But it has plenty of spots that are worth a visit and a surprising number of ancient churches and other historical remains.

Calabria might be defined as a peninsula at the end of a peninsula, the long, thin toe at the western end of Italy's boot. The region is made up of two strips of sea coast that sandwich between them a chain of mountains and wooded areas. Calabria's history is much the same as that of the rest of southern Italy: numerous invasions succeeded one another until the area reached a low point both materially and culturally. Now beach resorts are attracting tourists, while reforestation has created valuable woodland zones. But it is still essentially an agricultural region, with the Calabrians winning a difficult living from the terraced, intensively cultivated hillsides.

The region is divided into three parts, named after the three largest Calabrian cities: Cosenza, inland in the northern half of the region; Catanzaro, near the Ionian coast, farther south; and Reggio Calabria, at the tip of Italy, across the strait from Messina. In themselves these three cities are not particularly interesting for their architecture. Reggio is entirely modern, having been rebuilt after the earthquake of 1908, which devastated Messina also. However, the three cities command excellent views of the surrounding country and emphasize what is the most absorbing feature of Calabria: its striking countryside dotted with villages.

In the province of Cosenza, one of the stops on the Naples-Reggio railroad line is Paola, a picturesque coastal town famous as the birthplace of Saint Francis di Paola, to whom a sanctuary in late Renaissance style is dedicated. The ancient square of the village is also interesting.

The road from Paola to Cosenza is famous for its great vistas of mountains and sea. In the broadest part of the Calabrian peninsula lies the Sila, a famous forest and mountainous zone, now used also for pastureland in the areas where the trees have been cut.

Of Calabria's main towns, Castrovillari, Cosenza and Catanzaro lie high in the mountains, and are therefore cool in summer. All offer fine surroundings—in particular, the circular tour round Monte Gariglione makes a stupendous day's excursion from Catanzaro, though it's decidedly hard work for the driver. You make first for Taverna, and whichever way you do the circular drive, you pass through Villagio Mancuso, a mountain resort built in the 1930s (and looking it). Drive along Lake Ampollino, and enjoy the views from close to Petilia. Tiriolo, near Catanzaro, on the narrowest part of the peninsula, commands a view including the Ionian Sea on one side, the Tyrrhenian on the other—and the famous volcano, Stromboli.

Farther north, Lakes Arvo and Cecita, artificial basins, also offer striking scenery and a restful coolness in contrast to Calabria's hot, often treeless, coasts. This is the heart of the Sila Mountains, a region that is destined to become increasingly popular in both winter and summer. The roads are excellent, and there are a few good hotels in such strategic spots as Lorica, San Giovanni in Fiore, and Camigliatello. In the center of the Sila region, San Giovanni in Fiore contains the ancient Badia Fiorense. Lying in the area where the winter snows last longest (November–March), this town is also a good stopping place for winter sports enthusiasts.

Northeast of Cosenza, in the direction of Lucania, is the town of Rossano, an important center in the Byzantine period and therefore the town of Calabria richest in Byzantine remains, among them the beautiful Church of San Marco and (not far from the town) the Monastery of Santa Maria del Patire. The Diocesan Museum possesses the *Codex Purpureus,* one of the oldest Greek illuminated manuscripts in existence.

Crossing in the direction of the Ionian coast, you arrive at Catanzaro, situated on a high, rocky cliff between two rivers that empty into the sea a short distance away. Also nearby is the town of Squillace, on the gulf of the same name, a charming village with excellent beaches. In the vicinity is the ruined Church of Santa Maria della Roccella, a majestic Norman building of the 11th century.

Other Norman and Byzantine buildings are to be seen at Santa Severina, Crotone, Vibo Valentia and Nicotera, all of them in the same general area. Farther from the coast, at Serra San Bruno, are the renowned Certosa of Saint Bruno and the Church of the Addolorata with its elegant baroque façade, the work of an unknown local architect. 12 miles away is the Ferdinandese, the restored summer residence of King Ferdinand II.

Traveling farther south and east towards the tip of the peninsula, you enter the province of Reggio Calabria, which though it is mountainous like the rest of Calabria, contains the great plains of the Aspromonte section. At Gerace visit the sumptuous cathedral, the most extensive church of Calabria. At Stilo stop to see the equally famous little Church of La Cattolica, a gem of Byzantine construction, the sister-church of San Marco (Rossano).

Reggio Calabria, almost at sea level, is less attractive than Calabria's other towns, for the narrow coastal shelf here is filled with industry, and the views all along the coast north of Reggio, though fine, are spoilt for much of the way by factories and smoke. The Sicilian village of Scilla, in a very picturesque spot, recalls the ancients' tales of Scylla and Charybdis, two harpies that devoured unhappy mariners wrecked on their threatening headlands on either side of the Strait of Messina between the mainland and Sicily. One can well imagine the sailors' fear of having to navigate clumsy, almost keel-less vessels in these narrow, rocky waters. For us, however, the region's many cliffs provide magnificent scenery—provided industrial buildings don't clutter the foreground.

Don't overlook Calabria's coast resorts. You've probably never heard of them, and their names may mystify even Italian travel agents. But some are very nice indeed, though you'll have to be selective—overbuilding has ruined some of the region's loveliest beaches.

Copanello, nestling under the sheer Punta di Stalletti, is an enchanting little place with a fine expanse of sand. Soverato, also on Calabria's Ionian (eastern) coast, also offers fine bathing. Tropea, on a sort of corn projecting from the Tyrrhenian (western) side of Italy's toe, is a town to make you dream dreams of bygone ages. Perched on the flat top of a sheer cliff, its cathedral dates from the 11th century. Its beachside hotels, however, are all moderately recent.

PRACTICAL INFORMATION FOR THE DEEP SOUTH

HOTELS AND RESTAURANTS

Acquafredda. (Lucania), near Maratea. **Hotels:** All (2) are—exceptional, in quiet location, twin hotels, excellent value, *Villa Cheta* and *Villa del Mare,* all tastefully furnished rooms with bath or shower, lift to beach below; *Gabbiano,* modest, but good.

Alberobello. (Apulia), **Hotels:** *Dei Trulli* (1), 19 rooms in *trullo*-style cottages set in pinewoods, dining terrace, pool, seasonal.

Astoria (2), all 47 rooms with bath or shower, many with balcony or terrace, rather undistinguished but comfortable modern furnishings.

Restaurants: *Cucina dei Trulli,* local olives, pastas. *Pugliese,* typical dishes. Both (M).

Bari. (Apulia), capital, important seaport. **Hotels:** Reservations are a must during Sept., for the trade fair.

Both (1)—*Jolly Palace,* central, recommended, all rooms with bath or shower and radio; *Jolly,* near station, recent, very modern; both fully airconditioned.

All (2)—*Grand Oriente,* central, traditional, airconditioned; *Boston* and *Moderno,* more moderate rates.

At Palese, near airport, *Baia* (2), on beach.

About 18 miles inland, *La Quercia,* handsome new vacation center, 80 rooms with private bath or shower and panoramic terrace, pool, tennis, pleasant restaurant and rustic *Tavernetta* for pizza.

Restaurants: *La Pignata* (E), Via Melo, is the best; *Vecchia Bari,* classic, and *Il Trullo* are fine (M). Central, very simple, folksy (M) are *Sorso Preferito, La Panca, La Buca, Mezzaluna* for pizza.

Barletta. (Apulia), interesting architecture. **Hotels:** Both (2) *Artu,* 34 rooms, most with bath or shower, near ancient castle; *Helios,* large holiday complex with beach, pool, tennis, best off season, noisy and native in July–Aug.

Restaurants: *Pierino al Fieramosca,* Via Trani (E). *Brigantino* (M).

Brindisi. (Apulia), port. **Hotels:** High season, 18 July–30 Sept. *Jolly* (1), best. Garden, car park, on station square.

All (2)—*Mediterraneo,* modern; *Motel Minerva,* pool; *Barsotti,* all rooms with bath or shower.

Restaurants: All (M)—*La Lanterna,* Piazza Vittoria, try pasta *alla contadina, La Botte,* for *orecchiette. Giubilo,* facing ferries for Greece; fine lunch stop but avoid in high season.

Castellana Grotte. (Apulia), interesting caves: **Hotels:** Both (2)—*Autostello ACI,* just 6 units, all with shower, modest.

At nearby **Putignano,** *Plaza,* 41 rooms with bath.

Castellaneta Marina. (Apulia), beach resort. **Hotels:** At **Riva dei Tessali,** *Club Residence* (1), well-managed, country club atmosphere, attractive airconditioned bungalows amid pines, large pool, sandy beach, 18-hole golf course.

All (2)—*Lisea,* overlooking private beach. At **Ginosa,** *Europa Park,* pool, all private baths, good value.

Castro Marina. (Apulia), near Santa Cesarea Terme. **Hotels:** Both (2)—*Piccolo Mondo,* 33 rooms with shower, pool, tennis; *Orsa Maggiore,* high above beach.

Roccia (P1), very pleasant small pension overlooking sea.

Castrovillari. (Calabria), colorful town. **Hotels:** Both (2)—*President Joli,* Corso Saraceni 22; and *Motel Asti,* Via Calabria, recent.

Restaurants: Well worth the 10-minute detour from Autostrada del Sole, both (M)—*Alia,* Via Roma, courteous welcome and lots of local specialties; *Motel Asti,* also known for quality of its cuisine.

Catanzaro. (Calabria), provincial capital, on fine mountain site. **Hotels:** Both (2), *Moderno* and *Grand,* both on central Piazza Matteotti. *Guglielmo* (2), central, airconditioned.

All (2)—*Motel AGIP,* modern, good value; at beach, few miles away, *Palace,* modern, airconditioned; *Niagara.*

Restaurants: Both (M)—*Quattro Lampioni,* Via Settembrini; on highway 19, *Fattoria,* rustic atmosphere, hearty food, avoid Sundays and holidays. *La Griglia* (I–M), Via Poerio, traditional local cuisine.

Cetraro. (Calabria), on sea. **Hotel:** *San Michele* (1), palatial, all rooms with bath, in imposing, isolated position high above sea, with lift to private pebbly beach, pool, tennis, superior service.

Cirella di Diamante. (Calabria). **Hotels:** All (2)—*Autostello ACI,* is bungalow style, restaurant, bar, private beach; *Agamar,* and *Guardacosta,* big resort complexes.

Copanello. (Calabria), new resort. **Hotels:** *Villaggio Guglielmo* (1) is big holiday complex on beach, tennis, water sports.

Club Hotel Vitale (2), modern chalet hotel on beach, swimming pool.

Motel Copanello (3), pleasant overnight.

Cosenza. (Calabria), provincial capital. **Hotels:** *Jolly* (1), best, right in center of town, on river, garage.

Imperial (2), central, comfortable.

Restaurants: All (M)—*Imperiale* hotel restaurant, Viale Trieste, best, courteous service, local *antipasti* and cheeses; *Villa Bernaudo* and *Giocondo,* both on Via Piave; *Elefante Rosso,* Via Don Minzoni, good.

Crotone. (Calabria). **Restaurants:** Both (M) are *Girrarosto,* good fish soup; *Bella Romagna.*

Foggia. (Apulia), regional capital. **Hotels:** *Cicolella* (1), near railway station; 170 modern rooms, optional airconditioning.

President (2), on road to airport, is modern, has indoor pool.

Restaurants: *Cicolella* hotel restaurant (E) and *La Managiatoia* (M) serve local and regional specialties, *troccoli* (pasta).

Fuscaldo Marina. (Calabria), near Guardia Piemontese Terme. **Hotels:** *Vascello* and *Sud,* both (2), resort hotels, hectic in high season.

Gallico Marina. (Calabria). **Restaurant:** *Morgana* (M), mussels a specialty.

Gallipoli. (Apulia), beautiful commercial town on coast. **Hotels:** *Costa Brada* (1), best, sparkling modern hotel, fully airconditioned, right on sandy beach, 75 rooms with shower and balcony with sea view. Minibus service into town.

Both (2)—*Lido San Giovanni,* on beach; *Le Sirenuse,* spanking white beach hotel, recent, well-furnished, airconditioned, all doubles with balcony, sea view, ample pool, garden, terraces.

Restaurants: *Marechiaro* (M), renowned *zuppa di pesce,* succulent shellfish. *Puglia Vera* (E), fine restaurant of Hotel Costa Brada.

Gambarie D'Aspromonte. (Calabria), summer and winter sports resort. **Hotel:** High season, 21 Jan.–18 Feb. and 16 July–31 Aug. *Gambarie* (2), garage.

Gioa del Colle. (Apulia), Norman architecture. **Hotel:** *Artu* (2), garage.

Restaurant: *Corte dei Sannaci* (M–E), rustic, very good.

Guardia Piemontese Lido. (Calabria), beach resort. **Hotel:** *Mediterraneo* (2), all rooms with shower, beach.

Isola di Capo Rizzuto. (Calabria), isolated Ionian coast resort. **Hotel:** *Villaggio Valtur* (2), cottage colony, all resort activities, tennis, pool, beach, good value.

Le Castella. (Calabria), **Hotel:** *Le Castella* (2), recent resort complex, chic and lively, overlooking ruined castle on sea.

Lecce. (Apulia), noted for baroque architecture. **Hotels:** *President* (1), ultramodern, airconditioned.

Both (2) are—*Patria Touring* and *Risorgimento,* both good.

Restaurants: All (M)—Restaurants of *President* and *Patria* hotels for excellent local dishes, as also at *Plaza,* Via Fanteria.

Leuca. (Apulia), Land's End of Italy's heel. At **Castrignano,** near Lecce. **Hotels:** *L'Approdo* (1) and *Terminal* (2), both have all rooms with bath or shower, private beaches.

Restaurant: *Lupo di Mare* (M–E) for oysters.

Manacore. (Apulia) near Peschici. **Hotels:** *Gusmay* (1), isolated, modern, long walk to private beach. *Paglianza* (2), atop small promontory, has pool, tennis, beach facilities.

Manfredonia. (Apulia), Gargano region. **Hotel:** *Gargano* (2), all rooms with shower, balcony, airconditioning, pool.

Restaurants: All (M)—Fish soups, local pastas at *Lanterna, Al Gambero,* restaurant of *Hotel Azzurro.*

Maratea. (Lucania). At **Porto di Maratea, Hotel:** *Santavenere* (L), all rooms with bath, swimming pool, private beach, recommended very highly, a gorgeous place.

Restaurant: *Za Mariuccia* (M), at port, family-run.

Matera. (Lucania), rock-cut dwellings. **Hotels:** Both (2) are—*President,* airconditioned, with pool; *Nicola,* all rooms with shower.

Restaurants: Both (M)—*Da Mario, Il Bocconcino* offer local dishes.

Mattinata. (Apulia) near Manfredonia. **Hotel:** *Baia delle Zagare* (2), secluded villa colony overlooking beautiful inlet; tennis, lift to beach. One of Gargano's best sites.

Restaurant: *Del Portoghese* (M), Via Pellico, modest but good.

Nicastro. (Calabria), medieval town. **Hotels:** *Savant* (2).

At **Lamezia Terme** spa is better, *Grand* (2), modern, airconditioned.

Ostuni. (Apulia), beach resort 12 miles NW of Brindisi. **Hotels:** Both (2)—*Villaggio Valtur* and *Rosa Marina,* well-organized cottage-style holiday centers on beach, pool, tennis, all sports and comforts, including shops, hairdresser, discos. *Valtur* attracts Italians; English-speaking tourists may prefer *Rosa Marina.*

Pizzo. (Calabria), picturesque coast town. **Hotel:** *Grillo* (2), resort hotel on beach.

Restaurants: *Medusa* (M), seaside terrace, *spaghetti alla Masaniello* and delicious ice cream.

Porto Cesareo. (Apulia), near Gallipoli, beach. **Hotels:** Both (2), new resort hotels—*Club Azzurro,* pool, tennis; *Lo Scoglio,* on sea.

Restaurants: Both (M)—*Lo Scoglio,* on islet; *Veliero* for *polpette.*

Portonuovo. (Apulia), near Vieste. **Hotel:** *Gargano,* attractive location on shore, modern, choice of sand beach or shoals for swimming.

Potenza. (Lucania), regional capital. Heavily damaged by 1980 earthquake. **Hotel:** *Park* (2), on outskirts, modern.

Restaurants: Both (M)—*Taverna Oraziana,* rustic decor, local dishes only, try *capretto* (kid) in season; *Da Peppe,* modest little place, excellent meals by award-winning chef-owner Giuseppe.

Praia a Mare. (Calabria), seaside resort. **Hotels:** Both (1)—*Mondial,* 66 rooms, with a view; *Germania,* open April–Sept. *Astor* (3), small and central.

Restaurant: Try *I Normanni* (M), good food and lovely view, also has a few rooms.

Reggio Calabria. (Calabria), largest city. **Hotel:** *Excelsior* (1), facing National Museum, comfortable.

All (2)—*Miramare,* Via Fata Morgana 1, largest, garage; *Lido,* Via 3 Settembre 6; *Continental,* modern, all rooms with shower; *Palace Masoanri,* recent, good.

Restaurants: All (M)—*Conti,* Via Giulia, is best; followed by *Sirena,* Piazza Garibaldi; *Baylik* Vico Leone, fish specialties.

Sangineto Lido. (Calabria), near Cirelle di Diamante. **Hotel:** *Cinque Stelle* (2), on broad sandy beach, 144 rooms with shower, small villas in holiday complex with tennis, pool, shops.

San Menaio. (Apulia). **Hotels:** *Sole* (2), with beach.

At **Rodi,** *Parco degli Aranci* (2), good, in orange grove overlooking sea, all rooms with shower, pool, tennis.

Santa Cesarea Terme. (Apulia), modest spa and fine bathing resort. **Hotels:** *Palazzo* (2), thermal treatments; *Oriente* (3).

Scilla. (Calabria), fishing village near Reggio. **Hotel:** *Matteo a Mare* (P1), delightful, well-furnished pension on sandy beach.

Restaurant: *Matteo* (M), for steaks.

Sila. Cool, scenic, mountain region, making the toe of Italy's boot. **Hotels:** At **San Giovanni in Flore,** *Dino's* (2).

At **Lorica,** *Grand* (2), overlooking lake; *Autostello ACI* (3), in pine woods, modest.

At **Camigliatello,** lively center, snow festival in Jan.—*Edelweiss, Tasso,* both (2).

At **Villaggio Mancusco,** *Faggio* (2), attractive chalet-type.

At **Tiriolo,** *Autostello ACI* (3), tiny.

Soverato Marina. (Calabria), coast resort, with fine sandy beach, sailing, etc. **Hotels:** Both (2)—*Gli Ulivi,* 50 rooms with shower, airconditioning, beach facilities; *Nettuno,* recent, all rooms with bath, hotel bus at station, private beach.

Restaurant: *Enzo* (I), Corso Umberto, for meals or snacks at all hours; unpretentious local food.

Taranto. (Apulia), naval base, magnificent situation. **Hotels:** Both (1)—*Jolly,* best, most rooms with bath or shower, pool, swimming area; *Delfino,* also good, all rooms airconditioned with bath or shower and balcony, smallish pool at water's edge.

All (2)—*Plaza,* central, 112 rooms, most with bath, breakfast only; *Bologna.* At **Lido Azzurro,** *Tritone,* tennis, pool, beach.

Restaurants: *Delfino* (E) hotel restaurant is best. Both (M)—improbably named *Gesu Cristo* is small, unpretentious, rowdy place for excellent fish; *L'Approdo,* good antipasto, fish dishes.

Testa del Gargano Region, on remote eastern tip of Gargano. **Hotels:** Both (2)—*Albergo del Faro* and *Ulivi,* comfortable, modern hotels with beach, nightclub, swimming pool, chalets. All in large, well-organized holiday complex, all sports, in beautiful setting.

Torre a Mare. (Apulia), near Bari. **Hotel:** *Motel AGIP* (1), good.

Restaurant: *Grotta della Regina* (E), with terrace on private beach, is one of the best around. Fish, naturally, but everything else is good, too.

Trani. (Apulia), noted cathedral. **Hotels:** Both (2)—*Holiday,* recent beach hotel, modern, pleasant; *Miramar,* in park, pool.

Restaurants: *Cristoforo Colombo,* and *La Grotta,* Via Cavour; both (M).

Tremiti Islands. Off Termoli in Adriatic, overcrowded in summer. **Hotel:** on **San Domino,** *Eden* (1).

Tropea. (Calabria), picturesque new beach resort beside ancient town. **Hotels:** All (2)—Above sandy beach near town, *Rocca Nettuno,* large holiday colony with all amenities, full board in season; *Pineta,* pleasant little hotel in orange grove 100 yds. from beach, breakfast only; in town, *Virgilio.*

At **Parghelia,** *Baia Parahelios,* attractive main building houses restaurant, lounges, bedrooms in cottages with terrace, fridge, in olive grove directly on sandy cove.

Sabbie Bianche (3), same type of bungalow village, all resort activities, shops, disco, beach bar-pizzeria.

Vibo Valentia. (Calabria), interesting archeological remains. **Hotels:** Both (2)—*Autostello ACI;* and *501 Hotel,* modern, pool.

Vieste. (Apulia), lively promontory town. **Hotel:** *Pizzomunno* (2), big, smart resort hotel, with all amenities, pool, tennis, sandy beach. Closed 5 Oct.–10 April.

Restaurant: *San Michele* (M), in town, hearty local dishes.

Villa San Giovanni. (Calabria), commercial center and port with shortest crossing to Sicily. **Hotels:** *Piccolo* (1) at station.

All (2)—*Castello,* converted castle hotel, all distinctively furnished rooms with bath, airconditioning, shares pool, tennis, night club, beach facilities with *Santa Trada,* residence type; *Autostello ACI.*

USEFUL ADDRESSES. Tourist Offices: *Bari:* AAST, Via A. Gimma 56; American Express, SIT, Corso Cavour 48 (tel. 339294 and 339057); EPT, Piazza Roma 33A, and Via Melo 253; CIT, Via A. Gimma 56. *Barletta:* AAST, Piazza Roma. *Brindisi:* EPT, Piazza Dionisi, Via Colombo 88; AAST, Via Duomo 4. *Catanzaro:* EPT, Via F. Spasari, Piazza Rossi. *Cosenza:* EPT, Via Tagliamento. *Crotone:* AAST, Via Firenze 47. *Foggia:* EPT, Via Perrone 17. *Guardia Piemontese Lido:* AAST, Viale Santa Lucia. *Lecce:* EPT, Via Monte San Michele 20, and Via Oberdan 63. *Manfredonia:* AAST, Corso Manfredi 26. *Maratea:* AAST, Piazza del Gesù. *Matera:* EPT, Via de Viti 9, and Piazza V. Veneto 19. *Potenza:* EPT, Via Plebiscito 4B, and Via Alienelli 4. *Reggio Calabria:* AAST, Via Roma 3; EPT, Via Tripepi 72. *Santa Cesarea Terme:* AAST, Via Roma 209. *Soverato Marina:* AAST, Via Lungomare. *Taranto:* EPT, Corso Umberto 113 and 121. *Trani:* AAST, Corso Cavour 83. *Vibo Valentia:* AAST, Piazza Diaz 8.

SPECIAL EVENTS. *Bari:* There's an impressive procession to mark Good Friday; and another for the feast of St. Nicholas, Santa Claus, 7–8 May, has nothing to do with Father Christmas as we know him: it honors chiefly the sailors of Bari who brought his bones to their town 900 years ago, and it is modern seafarers who take the largest part in the procession. The region's most important trade occasion is the Levantine Fair, held in September, lasting about two and a half weeks, it includes an automobile show and is a genuinely international event.

Brindisi: Early June, a mounted parade of gaily caparisoned horses and riders. *Cosenza:* 12 March, the picturesque feast of Madonna del Pilario, and the last ten days of May are dedicated to St. Francis of Paolo. *Matera:* 2 July, Festival of the Bruna, the dark-skinned Madonna. *Reggio Calabria:* A week-long festival of the Madonna della Consolazione in September.

SPORTS. *Santa Cesarea Terme:* Makes a specialty of clay-pigeon shooting. *Scilla:* A major base for deep-sea angling. *Tremiti:* Excellent place for underwater fishing.

SICILY

Melting Pot of the Ancient World

This fertile island lies in a strategic position in the Mediterranean. These three obvious facts constitute its importance, explain its history, and account for its suffering and the millennia of foreign domination. An island, but not enough of an island, for it is visible, across a 2-mile-wide strait, to covetous eyes on the mainland of Italy; near, yet far enough away for the Romans (who were uneasy sailors) to use it mainly as a tactical base and as a granary owned by big landlords. It represents a modern social problem only partly solved by the regional government instituted in 1947, and recent industrialization around Catania and Gela. Moreover, the island's mountains are no bulwark against armed landings, for Sicily is rich in sweeping bays and inviting inlets, her coastal plains displaying their luxuriance like a shop-window to marauding seafarers.

There are lovely, bright wild flowers everywhere for those with a botanical bent, volcanos and great lava fields for the amateur vulcanologist, the sea for swimmers and underwater explorers, colorful, earnest fishing villages for those who love fishing villages, and there are vast sweeps of scenery on all sides. A 6,000-acre area between Punta Palermo and Torre San Teodoro, rich in wildlife and fauna, is to be reserved as a nature park.

There are about a dozen off-lying islands for islomaniacs, rare, ancient coins for numismatists, mountains and hills to climb, varied and various wines for the gourmet to sample, ceramist towns for shoppers, Neolithic, Stone Age and Bronze Age sites scattered among the many others.

There are lively towns, mournful towns, baroque towns, storybook settlements, and there are the gaily-painted carts, pulled by horses or donkeys, their harnesses ajingle with myriad bells. These and flowering shrubs are *everywhere* in Sicily.

Weather Matters

For the seaside holiday-maker, Sicily is both a winter and summer playground. But the traveler who wishes to know the island had best visit it in early spring, when the mountains are still snow-covered, the meadows green, and wild flowers profuse. Summer scorches the land and brings the *sirocco,* a hot African wind which lays a three-day blanket of listlessness over the island. Popular Taormina's season is year-long, with a peak from December to April.

Because of its climate, Sicily is more apt to play host to tourists on New Year's Day than most places; it is a good time to be there, for Sicilian celebrations of this day are extremely colorful.

Road Reports

Sicily has a good road all round the coast, and a mass of small wiggly roads inland. A new superhighway connects Palermo and Catania, via Enna. To reach it in your own car you must, of course, drive the length of the Autostrada del Sole, around 775 miles, all tolled.

Food for Thought

Sicily has no typical meat dishes; its specialties run to vegetables, fish, and cereals. Order eggplant *(melanzane);* the Sicilians know dozens of ways of cooking and stuffing it—*caponatina di melanzane* will produce pleasant surprises. So will the *fritella* of artichokes. They are specialists, too, in cooking *pasta con sarde.* They delight also in the "marriage of Ceres with Neptune"—i.e., fish with *pasta.* The Arab *couscous* is still served in a Palermitan version. The special fish of Sicily is tuna served in many guises but there are any number of succulent fish caught in these waters, as well as superior shellfish.

The sweets of Sicily are famous; the monasteries still compete in the production of masterpieces: the *sfinge* of San Guiseppe, the *trionfo di gola.* And Sicily is the capital of ice cream and birthplace of *cassata.*

Wines are plentiful but not sufficiently distinguished to worry about vintage; they have the perfume of orange flowers and bergamot. The *Faro* is from the slopes of the Peloritani mountains; *Corvo,* pleasantly bitterish, has excellent dry white and red; the latter is black and purple in the glass; the fiery wine of *Etna* puts you in good humor with the world. *Marsala;* after drinking one glass of it, the Sicilians say, the abstemious Garibaldi dashed off and conquered the island in sixty days. The best-known, including those above, and *Taormina* and *Villagrande* come in white and red, the latter on the whole preferable.

A Tale of Two Cities

In a land where it is possible to ski on a snow-muffled volcano, walk among palms and orange-groves, and swim in the sea within sight of the almond-trees in flower—and all in the same day—why should the visitor to Sicily concern himself with Greeks and Carthaginians, Arabs and Normans, or the misrule of Bourbon and Aragon?

Awareness of a country's history is a very useful part of a traveler's equipment. In Sicily, such awareness is almost a necessity; only then will the visitor understand an island which is Italian, but quite unlike Italy; European, yet imbued with the color and subtlety of the East. The modern age seems to have been built on a Greek foundation, for here the heavy hand of Rome made little impression. Alertness can turn a visit to Sicily into a unique experience.

Sicily lies in one of the most strategic positions of any island on earth. In ancient times the Mediterranean was the pivot of the known world, and Sicily was the pivot of the Mediterranean. And since the world was, then as now, contended for by the opposing civilizations and ideologies of East and West, Sicily logically became their battleground. But at the beginning it was a magnet for immigrants—the America of the ancient world. But Sicily has no metals, and since the inhabitants need these, traders came to swap and remained to prey. The trading post was the first foothold of invasion.

At Pantalica, near Syracuse, there is a mighty cliff-face pitted with square hewn-out caves. This was a burial-place for the Siculi, the earliest Sicilian inhabitants of importance. They had to fight for the island against the Greeks who began to build cities there 7 or 8 centuries before Christ, and against the Carthaginians, a Semitic people from North Africa, only 80 miles away. The Siculi were soon scattered, absorbed, or enslaved by the Greeks, and the issue became a straight one between Greek and "barbarian".

The recorded history of Sicily is a tale of two cities: of Syracuse for two millennia, of Palermo for the last thousand years, the one remembering above all the name of Dionysius, the other that of Frederick II.

By the 5th century BC, Greek Sicily's history was that of Syracuse, of which most of the other cities were dependencies. One Syracusan tyrant (an absolute ruler), Dionysius, held the Carthaginians from the coast of North Africa to the south in check by building immense defensive works around his great city, which he made the most magnificent and powerful of his day, and himself the most potent of princes after the Persian king.

But even before this, Syracuse had prospered enough to sting Athens into sending a great fleet and army to destroy the city; instead, the army and fleet were themselves destroyed.

The Sicilian climate does not encourage long-sustained heroic efforts; as the Greeks grew languid, the Carthaginians resumed their aggresive tactics, and only Rome, looming large in the 3rd century, could stop them. Later, Rome took care of the Greeks also. So, by about 200 BC, Syracuse and the island were Roman, at least in name.

Byzantium revived Syracuse into a pale ghost of its former grandeur, but the tale of the first city was ended and that of the second, Palermo, began.

In the 9th century, the Arabs captured Sicily, and held it for two centuries. Their poets rhymed it, their geographers described it, they built mosques and established an Emir in Palermo, which became the apple of their eye and to which they gave a soft languid Oriental air that has never left it.

But the climate had done its work again, and the self-indulgent Arabs were easily dislodged by a small force of determined Norman adventurers; and, for a century, Robert, Roger, and William tried in vain to maintain stern Nordic virtues while enthroned at Palermo in Oriental state.

Then a Swabian dynasty came to Sicily and brought one of the most surprising figures of history, Frederick II "the astonishment of the world". His Palermo court swarmed with poets, scientists, and musicians, and the first school of Italian vernacular poetry flourished in an Orientalized city under a German prince.

The rule of the succeeding House of Anjou was cut short by the insurrection of the Sicilian Vespers (1282). For the six following centuries the Sicilians, misruled by the House of Aragon and by corrupt Spanish viceroys, tossed from Savoy to Austria and back to Spain, plotted and rebelled, were repressed and crushed, and finally took to the hills to become outlaws and bandits, a policy which later developed into a national habit. In 1860, Garibaldi landed, and Sicily became part of Italy.

Exploring Sicily

For variety and contrast, and for a number of other reasons, it may probably be best to make the journey along the northern coast, around the blunted apex by Trapani, eastwards along the Africa-facing shore, and so northwards along the "Ionic" coastal plain; this route, with a few diversions inland, will give a fairly comprehensive picture of the island.

Our itinerary assumes that the traveler will land at Messina. The strait that Hercules swam across, clinging to his sacred bulls, is now traversed by modern travelers in a swift ferry. The classical-minded person, looking northeast from the steamer deck, can see the frowning rocks and the boiling waters of Ulysses' Scylla and Charybdis, guarding the straits. He remembers that he is making for a land saturated with mythology: where Proserpina and Pluto, Arethusa, Daedalus, Titans and Cyclops, escape from school text-books and become part of the names of towns, hotels, and cafés. In fact, their deeds may still be painted, together with the exploits of King Roger and the Saracens, by illiterate artisans on gaily-colored Sicilian carts.

From Messina to Cefalù

At five o'clock in the morning of December 28th, 1908, Messina was a flourishing city of 120,000 inhabitants. A few minutes later it was a heap of rubble, shaken to pieces by an earthquake which then gathered up the waters of the Straits and flung them, together with the bulk of ships, like mighty projectiles, against the wreckage in which 80,000 people lay dead or dying.

As you approach the magnificent sickle-shaped bay, there is little evidence of that disaster—save the curious flat look of the city; for anti-earthquake precautions once placed a restriction on the height of buildings. Messina is not a city of great interest, although the traveler might well learn here to appreciate the magnificent skill of the Italians as restorers. The cathedral, for example, has been entirely rebuilt as it was originally constructed by Roger in the 11th century. The pleasant fountain in front of it has been re-erected, and the splendidly decorated marble doorway of the church pieced together again. The fine clean interior is adorned with mosaics and works of art saved from the disaster. The other Norman church, the Annunziata, stood up to the earth's trembling.

There are two interesting processions to be seen in Messina. For the *Vara,* on August 15th, monster cars loaded with figures of saints and angels move around the city; on the evening preceding this, the legendary Giants of Messina are pulled through the streets. These giant figures, in various versions, are found in many town processions on the island. They probably embody some vague folk memories of prehistoric inhabitants of gigantic stature. The Messina festival of the Madonna of the Letter takes place on June 3rd.

Two-thirds of Sicily lies above 900 feet; and the 150 or so miles of coastal road to Palermo skirt the most mountainous area. On your left as you journey are, successively, the Peloritani, the Nebrodi, and the Madonie ranges, averaging some 3,000 feet. The bare iron-grey peaks bear witness to the victimization of the forests for the galleons of millennia of seagoing peoples. The short torrential rivers, dry chasms in summer, plunge through Alpine-like uplands with poplar and ash, chestnut and almond, down to orange and lemon groves.

West of Messina, on the north coast, at a turning off to the right from the main highway, is Milazzo, a seaport town. It was founded by the Greeks, in 716 B.C., and has a rather impressive castle. But Milazzo's main interest to most travelers is that from here many people take a boat or *aliscafo* to the Aeolian (also called Lipari) Islands. On clear days you can glimpse these islands, lying to the north, all along the coast from near Milazzo to Cefalù.

Tindari and Cefalù

Tindari's sanctuary contains a Byzantine Black Madonna, reputedly miracle-working; pilgrims come from all over Sicily, especially on September 8th, to toil up the steep hill. The view, anyway, is heavenly. Tindari has, too; some Greco-Roman ruins of the old town; but unless you are an archeologist, it is better to reserve your enthusiasm for much higher-class ruins to come.

Farther along the coast there's Santo Stefano di Camastra, well known as a ceramics center. You may want to look about at a few of the shops and studios, and perhaps view one of the artisans at work. A short distance farther along the road is Castel di Tusa, where a right turning will bring you into this little, unspoiled seaside town.

Cefalù, a photographer's paradise, is an enchanting little town on a spur jutting into the sea, at the foot of an immense rock, and away to the west is the sweeping bay of Imerese. One of the finest Norman cathedrals in Sicily dominates Cefalù. It was begun by King Roger in 1131, as a thank-offering for his happy landing from a storm at sea. The cathedral is as solid as the race that built it and the rock that soars above. But it has grace, too: the elegant three-arched façade, and the slim columns and tracery set off the imposing towers. And when you walk around it, you are struck by the subtlety which diversified those massive apses with fine blind arches. Entering its solemn three-naved interior, one is hardly prepared for being overpowered by the mighty 12th-century mosaic of Christ, angels, and apostles which glimmers in the apse.

There's a small private museum down the street from the Cathedral; it can be recommended to coin collectors (who will not need to be told that Sicily minted the finest coins of antiquity) and to pottery lovers. It has a canvas by Antonello da Messina, the only painter of great stature produced by Sicily.

On past Termini Imerese, and just beyond the settlement of Fondachello, if you turn right at the small crossroads where a sign indicates Santa Flavia to the left, you can circle Cape Zafferano, with its Roman ruins at Solunto, its intriguing pastel town of Sant'Elia, and magnificent rock promontories as you round the cape. From Aspri, still on the cape, if you keep straight on, crossing Highway 113, you'll come directly into Bagheria, a dusty little city with a sense of humor and dim traceries of what must once have been elegance, for this used to be a summer outpost for the wealthy of Palermo (and still is for a few). It has a scattering of 17th- and 18th-century villas, some of which can be visited. Most intriguing is the Villa Palagonìa, its gardens full of grotesques, weird, half-animal, half-human statues, which may make you feel that you have entered a slightly distorted world. Other places to see here are Villa Valguarnera, Villa Butera, Villa Cattolicà, and several others. Unfortunately, most are in a sad state of disrepair, or downright neglect.

As you leave Bagheria you come to the Conca d'Oro (the Golden Shell), one of the loveliest bays, backed by mountains and strewn with orchards and gardens.

Palermo

Palermo is one of those cities the traveler never forgets. Externally it is unmistakable, with the great rock of Pellegrino as its landmark. Internally it has a personality of its own—cynical, yet passionate, Oriental in its languor and in the shrewdness and subtlety of its jurists and politicians. Then, too, it is a great sophisticated metropolis and port where you can enjoy yourself.

Phoenician colony, Carthaginian town, the capital of an Arab Emirate, the commercial hub of Europe and Asia under the Normans, intellectual center under Frederick II—Palermo wears all these laurels

Palermo
Information
Palazzo / Public building
Church
Museum / Theater / Gallery
Place of Interest etc.
Police
Rail
0yds 300 600 900
0ms 300 600 900
Porto
Stazione Centrale
Staz. Marittima
Palazzo d. Normanni
Cattedrale
Quattro Canti
PZA. PRETORIA
PZA. BELLINI
Teatro Massimo
Museo Archeologico
Orto Botanico
Villa Giulia
Giardino Inglese
Villa Gonzaga
Giardino Garibaldi
Villa d'Aumale
Villa Bonanno
Museo Diocesano
Pal. Sclafani
Pal. d. Zisa
Pal. di Giustizia
Palazzo Chiaramonte
Pal. Abbatellis
Palazzo Aiutmicristo
S. Giovanni d. Eremiti
La Martorana
S. Cataldo
La Magione
La Gancia
S. Francesco d'Assisi
S. Maria d. Catena
S. Giorgio d. Genovesi
S. Domenico
S. Zita
S. Agostino
S. Francesco da Paola
S. Guiseppe
S. Caterina
Gesu
Universita
Chiesa d. Olivella
Gall. d'Arte Moderna
PIAZZA RUGGERO SETTIMO
PIAZZA UCCIARDONE
Pta Nuova
VIA DELLA LIBERTÀ
VIA MONTE PELLEGRINO
VIA SAMPOLO
V. DUCA DELLA VERDURA
V. E. NOTABARTOLO
VIA MAQUEDA
VIA ROMA
CORSO VITTORIO EMANUELE
CORSO TUKORY
CORSO ALBERTO AMADEO
VIA CAVOUR
VIA DANTE
VIA DEL PORTO
V. F. CRISPI
FORO ITALICO
VIA LINCOLN
CSO DEI MILLE
VIA ORETO
VIA TIRO A SEGNO NAZIONALE
VIA RUGGERO SETTIMO
VIA MARIANO STABILE
ENRICO AMARI
CORSO DOM SCINA
VIA CARINI
VIA VOLTURNO
V. QUATTROVENTI
VIA ALLORO
V. D. SPASIMO
VIA PORTA DI CASTRO

gracefully. Its peculiarity is the happy marriage of Norman and Arab, when Mohammedan master craftsmen helped build and decorate Christian churches.

The most remarkable example of this is the Martorana church, so-called because it was donated to the nearby monastery founded by a patrician of that name, the cloister of whose adjoining house still survives. The bell-tower is a sermon in stone on tolerance: Norman solidity and Arab fancy, strength and grace combined, have created a masterpiece. The church of San Cataldo is next door. If you want to get the flavor of Palermo, wander among this group of buildings and ponder on what is there—an Arab-Norman tower, San Cataldo's stern Norman interior (with columns filched from Greek temples), red Oriental domes squatting above, Martorana's Norman interior decorated in 17th-century baroque, Greek inscriptions and a mosaic of Christ presenting the crown to Roger II, first Norman king of Sicily, who wears Oriental robes. A palm in the midst completes the picture, a commentary on all that Palermo stands for.

Two buildings dominate Palermo, the 19th-century Teatro Massimo, home of good opera, and the 12th-century cathedral, whose fortress-like dignity and strength are impressive, and even the Gothic towers add an airiness not entirely irrelevant. But examined closely, it is apt to make architects blaspheme; for a "restorer" (and Palermitans hasten to tell you that he was a Florentine) added an 18th-century dome and various other monstrosities. The interior contains the royal tombs—among them that of Frederick II. The cathedral was founded by the Archbishop of Palermo, an English priest named Walter of the Mill, comically Sicilianized as Gualtiero Offamilio.

The traveler in a hurry who prefers a few deep rather than many superficial impressions, might make his way one morning along the Via Maqueda, turning right up the Corso at the Quattro Canti (worthy of note) and, passing the cathedral, left to Piazza della Vittoria. Stopping to admire the Palazzo Sclafani on his left, he will see the Royal Palace as he rounds the Piazza. Here the Arabs built a palace for the Emirs; the Normans enlarged and beautified it (using Arab and Byzantine craftsmen), and under Frederick II, it became a European center of art and culture. Walking through its royal halls, the room of King Roger, the airy courtyards, admiring the Pisan tower, the traveler is unprepared for the sight that meets his startled eyes as he enters the Cappella Palatina. A blaze of gold, mosaics, and marble inlays glitter at him in the unreal play of light and shadow. Here Norman, Arab, and Byzantine found that they had one God in common, and glorified him. The traveler should then climb up to the observatory tower and summarize it all—the cobalt sea, the orchards, on the right the Arab castle of Favara and the buildings erected by Norman and Saracen, on the left the luxurious villas of wealthy Palermitans and, glittering where the mountains lie, Monreale, the greatest medieval cathedral of Italy.

Nearby, San Giovanni degli Eremiti is a happy adaptation of a mosque to Christianity. In the delicate-arched shadowy cloister the visitor shares what the monks saw as they sat on the marble benches to study the scriptures 8 centuries ago: roses, palms, and above, a squat, mosque-like, small-windowed building with four pink cupolas caught "in a noose of light".

There are many other things to see in the city which gave birth to that fantastic adventurer Cagliostro: the gruesome catacombs of the Capuchin convent with its thousands of fully-clothed mummified bodies, the Norman La Magione, San Francesco, the vast Pantheon-like San Domenico, Santa Zita, and the archeological museum. The Zisa, splendid Arab-Norman palace of William I, lies on the outskirts of the city, as do Santo Spirito, (where began the revolt of the Sicilian Vespers), and the beautiful Santa Maria di Gesù.

The Environs of Palermo

There are two places which must be visited: the first is Monte Pellegrino, where the Carthaginians defied the Romans for three years. The massive rock is the site of the Sanctuary of Santa Rosalia. Daughter of a duke, she became a hermit and died in the cave she chose to live in. Her bones were later found and, carried in procession through the city, caused a plague to cease. The cave has been most impressively turned into a chapel; down the bare walls trickles water that is gathered and regarded as wonder-working. Between Monte Pellegrino and Monte Gallo is Mondello, Palermo's beach resort.

The second place to be seen is Monreale, five miles out of Palermo. This glorious spot on the mountain side, once within the royal pleasure-grounds, explains why the Norman kings could not hope to maintain their strong northern virtues. William II, so the story goes, found a treasure, revealed to him in a dream by the Virgin, and with it built another treasure and another dream. The stone, color of Marsala wine, the striking apses, the well-proportioned towers of the cathedral are impressive enough, but the interior is breathtaking. The lofty, airy central nave, the slim pillars with their rich capitals are only a beginning, because a soaring imagination has attempted, succesfully, to depict in mosaic what Michelangelo's Sistine frescos did in the suppler medium of paint: the Creation, the rise and fall of man, and the triumph of the Church. 130 Pictures covering 6,000 square yards trace the events leading up to the Birth of Christ (along the central nave), His Life and Ministry (in the presbytery and side naves) and the Acts of the Apostles. The Moorish-looking cloisters and monastery are equally worth visiting.

A last word about Palermo: try to see a show at one of the puppet theaters. It is an astonishing experience.

The road to Monreale continues to Trapani. Just after passing Alcamo is Segesta. Don't be frightened by the word "ruins". Here is a Greek Doric temple almost intact; some have called it superior, for dignity and situation, to anything in Greece. The hills are bare, the view superb. 25 centuries ago slaves hauled up these immense stones from the sulphur springs below to build the 35-foot columns. Here the tyrant Agathokles murdered all the citizens who complained of his exactions. Of the city, nothing remains but the admirable Greek theater on the heights above.

From Trapani to Marsala

Trapani, living on the rapidly dimishing export of tuna or tunny-fish and salt, commands the blunted apex of the triangular island together with Marsala. The area has an aspect all its own, with its isolated bare peaks and abundant vineyards, the queer cube-like houses of fisher folk, and the little windmills which grind the sea-salt. Yet Trapani itself, neat and modern in its isthmus, seems but an appendix of Mount Erice, also called San Giuliano, the ancient Eryx (where Hercules challenged the king). The people, however, arouse interest; there are Arab, Phoenician, Norman types, and you will see peasants as Greek as any statue by Praxiteles. Pilgrims come to Trapani on March 25th to venerate the jewel-laden statue of the Madonna in the Church of the Annunziata. Most tourists, however, go to Trapani in order to buy the pretty ornaments made by skilled craftsmen of Trapani from coral, and, more especially, to ascend Mount Erice, either by car or bus.

The ancient town of Erice seems to grow out of the fierce rock 2,500 feet above Trapani. From its Cyclopean Phoenician walls the Egadi Islands can be seen, the coast of Africa is visible on a fine day, and the sunsets are fantastic almost every day. Erice has to be visited to be believed; its isolation has developed a life, a costume, and an architecture all its own. In the evening, dusk seems slowly to creep up the mountain from the coast.

Marsala is famous for its wine-making, of course, and for its memories of Garibaldi, who landed here. The English dominate the former and more profitable activity, while the Italians console themselves with their hero. The English also managed to smuggle in St. Thomas à Becket as patron saint. The Italians retorted by placing the Doric columns intended to be sent to England in the pleasant cathedral—still, however, dedicated to St. Thomas—which leaves the honors about even. The old winemaking establishments of Florio and Ingham-Whitaker can be seen, with permission. They are unusually interesting; even the Romans never made barrels of such noble proportions.

The Africa-facing coast is a sadder one. The sea coast is picturesque enough with its olives, vines, and almonds; but beyond the grain fields of the lower hills, the rounded hillocks and the little valleys, lie the bleak plateaus with weaker vegetation around grey cottages.

The road passes through pleasant Mazara and Castelvetrano, earthquake-hit, and forks right to Selinunte, an overwhelming sight. If you are interested in ancient things, just before Selinunte, at the town of Campobello, ask directions to the Cave di Cusa. This is where the stones and pillars for Selinunte were hewn from local rock, and you can see just how the Greeks, back in the 5th century BC, went about their work. The history books say it was founded 6 centuries before Christ, and that a Carthaginian army under Hannibal destroyed it. This is historian's language. The attackers may have slaughtered 16,000 of its inhabitants, but no weapons of antiquity could have scattered these 50-foot long, 10-foot thick columns, only seismic shocks could have done that.

The heart of Selinunte was the Acropolis on the shore. At its seaward limit is the Tower of Pollux, an ancient lighthouse. The Acropolis was walled, traversed by two main thoroughfares, crossed by side-streets. Of its chief temple (to Demeter), the central *Naos* or holy of holies can be seen, with the adjoining chamber where the treasure was kept. The sacramental part of the building is astonishingly small; the Greek temple was one vast public promenade, the priests remaining apart in their still, small room.

Of the three temples near the station, the Temple of Apollo is one of the most colossal Greek structures in existence. The base blocks weigh 100 tons, yet were placed one on another, joined by a central key. The mathematically-minded visitor will note the careful town-planning that went into the making of this titanic city, where digging for archeological finds is still going on.

Sciacca, farther along the road, has been known for its thermal waters for 3,000 years. If you are driving through it, go to the Piazza Scandaliato, whence the view is magnificent, or along the road locally called Panoramica.

Farther east, about 7 miles beyond Ribera, if you have a genuine interest in ancient ruins, or "digs", take the right turning to Eraclea Minoa; that is, if you don't mind about 4 miles of road which is little more than a series of potholes held together rather loosely by 2- and 3-foot stretches of pavement. Some work has been done on excavations and preservation (and there is a good, small museum), but perhaps best is to imagine what a glorious site this must have been in its "days of glory" perched here, high above the sea.

Agrigento and its Temples

Those interested in antiquity will now find fulfillment of their greatest expectations. After the lone temple of Segesta, the tremendous strewn columns of Selinunte, come the revelation of Agrigento. Egypt has its Valley of the Kings, Agrigento its Valley of the Temples. Temples, buildings, monuments, and odd works of art number a hundred or more. They are in fair state of preservation, and their setting is magnificent, particularly in late winter and early spring, when the valley is smothered with flowers and the whole vast area is alight with almond blossom. Moreover, the modern city of Agrigento, built where the Acropolis of the ancient one stood, is close at hand.

The short drive up from Porto Empedocle is a revelation of riotous scent and blossom at any season save summer. The modern port recalls the encyclopedic genius Empedocles, the most illustrious son of Agrigentum (or Greek "Akragas"), who, they say, directed the excavation of the gap separating the modern town's site from the "Athenian rock" which travelers now climb for the view across the Valley of the Temples to the sea. The city of Phalaris, the tyrant who pleasantly shut up his enemies inside a monstrous red-hot bronze bull, was erected by Carthaginian prisoners. Pindar thought it the greatest metropolis in the world, and another Greek said that its inhabitants built their temples as if they never expected to die, but lived as if they expected to die tomorrow.

The ancient city had at least ten times as great a population as the modern one. On the northeast side of the Valley of Temples, the chief buildings are the temple and sanctuary of Demeter (or Ceres), and the ancient walls. To the south are the temples of Juno, Concord, and Hercules; to the west, the temple of Jove, the 8th wonder of the world; the sacrificial altars, and the temple of Castor and Pollux.

The Temple of Concord, symbol of Agrigento, is the best preserved in the world after that of Theseus in Athens; the four columns of the Temple of Castor and Pollux (the Dioscuri) are the most photographed —they will be familiar to most people, for they are often used as symbolic of Sicily. When the almond trees around this temple are in bloom, it makes an exquisite picture. In February, the temples and almond blossom form a magnificent backdrop for an important International Folklore Festival. The temple of Juno is interesting, for the *Naos* is fairly intact.

Agrigento's modern religious festival of San Calogero, on the first Sunday of July, keeps something of the Greek festivals: a decorated mule carries sheaves of corn together with loaves shaped like the limbs or organs healed by intervention of the saint. Apart from the Convent of Santo Spirito and the interesting Church of San Nicola, modern Agrigento has no great artistic attractions. Its climate, however, is superb.

The Heart of Sicily

Time was when travelers continued on along the coast from Agrigento, but these days many dip inland, and upland, through lovely farm country, to Enna, by way of Caltanissetta. The latter is a bustling, lively town with a castle of Frederick III of Aragon perched, seemingly precariously, on a lonely crag. Beyond lies Enna, a fortress city which, at over 3,000 feet, was justifiably considered impregnable. Because of its dominance over much of this region in olden days, it has often been called the "navel of Sicily". It's a small city with a friendly atmosphere, dozens of climbing, winding streets, and incredible panoramas, including Etna. It also has a castle, built by Frederick II, which once had 20 towers. Now, with only 6 remaining, it is still impressive. Here, too, are an early 14th-century cathedral, a Swabian lookout tower, and a delightful climate.

From Enna, the road south leads through a series of pine and eucalyptus woods and lovely farmland scenery to Piazza Armerina. Some 4 miles out from town are the remains of the Emperor Maxentius' 3rd-century villa. The well-preserved mosaics are the cause of Piazza Armerina's great and growing fame.

From Piazza Armerina continue south to Caltagirone, a small city which has been turning out majolica and terracotta since the 17th century. Surprising bits and pieces appear about the town, and in the public gardens, and there is a museum showing pieces from every century. There are some interesting churches here. From Caltagirone you can dip southwest to Gela, a town of greatest interest to the archeological-minded, if you can put up with the oil refinery, or go southeast to Siracusa (Syracuse), stopping on the way at Noto, a baroque gem.

Syracuse

The east coast is placid and prosperous. The towns, drawing their livelihood from the wide fertile plain of Catania, are modern and comparatively energetic, though still conscious of their Greek past. The great earthquake of 1693 is responsible for the aspect of most of its cities, for they were rebuilt when baroque was the prevailing fashion, and the local temperament often gave this style those extra flourishes that so easily turn baroque into bad taste.

Historical imagination is needed to see Syracuse as anything more than a rather ordinary pleasantish city. It is hard to realize that here was the largest, wealthiest city of ancient Europe, bulwark of Greek civilization, where Archimedes lived and Plato taught. The modern city is almost confined to an island, the Ortigia; the ancient city occupied this and spread for miles over the surrounding country. Moreover, most of the ancient city has vanished. The great Temple of Minerva was turned into the present cathedral, and the piquant contrast between later baroque and the stern simplicity of Doric columns makes it an interesting curiosity. Walking along the fine promenade—the Marina—you may find it difficult to believe that in this modest port one of the great sea battles of antiquity was fought. Here the Athenian navy perished—largely because its commander was afraid to leave owing to an eclipse of the moon, when he might have got away. The rather brackish papyrus-fringed Arethusa well at the end of the port is the one sung by poets as that of the nymph Arethusa who was pursued by Alpheus and transformed into a fountain. Its loss may well have influenced the defeat of the thirsting Athenian army, and thus the history of the world. On this walk, the pretty Marine Gate and the fine Maniace Castle, built by Frederick II, are well worth noting. (Check with Syracuse EPT office to see if a military permit to visit castle is required.)

It is interesting to walk about the mainland north of Syracuse where the ancient city lay. The Latomie, caves whence the city's stone was quarried, are planted as gardens; one of them, with an entrance shaped like a huge ear, is known as Dionysius' Ear, for the tyrant, it is said, when interrogated prisoners would not talk, threw them in the cave and here listened to their conversation, for the caves have remarkable echoes and acoustic properties. The mighty fortress of Euryalus, built by Dionysius as a protection against the Carthaginians, was an astonishing defense system covering 15,000 square yards. One 3-mile stretch of wall was built in 20 days by 60,000 men.

The finest thing in Syracuse, however—and with the best view—is the graceful Greek Theater.

Catania and Mount Etna

The chief wonder about Catania is the fact that it is there at all. Its successive populations were deported by one Greek tyrant, sold into slavery by another, driven out by Carthaginians. Every time the city really got going again, *Force majeure* took a hand. Plague decimated the inhabitants, a mile-wide stream of lava from erupting Etna swallowed most of it in 1663 and, 30 years later, the disastrous earthquake forced the Catanese to begin all over again.

This explains Catania's 18th-century spaciousness; a well laid out city with good beaches under the superb backdrop of its old enemy Etna, to which it also owes most of its immense popularity with tourists, the fertility of its hinterland, its site (for it is built upon nine successive strata of lava), and many of its buildings, constructed from the lava as well. The city of Lava and Oranges, the Italians call it.

Catania's greatest son is Bellini the musician, but it bears the imprint of the architect Vaccarinin, who rebuilt the cathedral and the town hall round the elephant fountain, symbol of Sicily. The numerous baroque churches, the Ursino Castle, the Benedictine Convent, and the Roman and Greek remains are worth seeing, as also the fine squares and parks (Piazza Roma, Villa Bellini, Piazza Stesicoro, Piazza dell'Università).

Of the many excursions, the finest is the trip around Etna by car or bus. The scenery is extraordinarily varied and lovely. The route passes through the flowery vale of Paternò, a typical hill-town topped by a castle; the orange groves around Biancavilla; Adrano, once an important Greek city, now celebrated for its Easter Passion Play. The best scenery is perhaps on the climb up to Randazzo at 2,000 feet. At Bronte is the castle presented to Lord Nelson by the King of Naples, together with the title of Duke of Bronte. Here, too, on the slopes of Etna, are Linguaglossa, Trecastagni, Francavilla di Sicilia, and other towns, as well as the cooled lava fields which conjure somber thoughts.

As for Etna itself, the 10,000-foot giant began spewing lava again in a spectacular 1971 eruption. Rivers of molten rock flowed down to destroy the two highest stations of the funicular, but excursions may still be made, (subject to local authorization) up the slopes of the rambunctious volcano. There is fine winter and early spring skiing in the Bove Valley.

Taormina

This delightful spot is a fitting close to a tour of the island, though its natural beauty has been spoiled by overdevelopment. But the nucleus of the charming town itself has retained its distinction, the arches, columns, cupolas, dark red cliffs, Cape Sant' Andrea, the incredible rock of Sant' Alessio, Etna, which from Taormina even looks benevolent, though sometimes at night it shoots flames skyward.

The beaches below the village, a couple of miles by steep winding road, are disappointing despite the lovely setting. There are frequent bus services to romantic Isola Bella and Spisone, while Mazzaro in the middle is quickly reached by cable car. But the pebbles are hard on the feet and the water far from crystal-clear, so that several beach hotels have swimming pools.

The Corso, the main street of Taormina, is an astonishing and lively street, both social center and architectural delight. In it are many of the best places to eat and drink. Here you can shop by day and dance by night. Or just walk through the delightful, twisting alleys that climb uphill and down off the Corso, and provoke thoughts of the Saracens.

The Greek Theater is, next to that of Syracuse, the largest of the classical theaters in Sicily. Much of it remains intact. Most visitors are tempted to prove its extraordinary acoustic properties by wafting stage whispers to their friends a hundred yards away on its perimeter. The Film Festival in July is followed by the Music Festival in August, both with their respective devotees, but most impressive of all is the view.

The Palazzo Corvaia is an interesting 15th-century building with the black and white lava and pumice work characteristic of Taormina. It makes a pretty picture with its contemporary, the delightful Church of

Santa Caterina, behind which are remains of an intimate Roman theater—Taormina toned down even that grandiosely-planning people.

Almost everything to be seen in Taormina lies about the Corso, which is itself full of many-colored mansions of the 15th and 16th centuries, crammed with interesting details, many of them Moorish. Half way along the Corso is the Largo 9 Aprile, a noble square, with its 16th-century churches of Sant' Agostino and San Giuseppe, and the arched clock tower. Still following the Corso, and casting an appreciative glance at the fine door of the Ciampoli mansion, you come to the 16th-century cathedral, sturdy, squat-towered, simple, and forthright. The queer little fountain carries the emblem of Taormina (a crowned centauress holding a globe). This *Piazza* is well worth lingering in; it is backed by the hill on which the castle lies, the steps rising to the Church of the Carmine, and, to the right of the fountain, the alleys lead up to the graceful vestige of the old abbey. The 15th-century contemporary of the latter, the Palazzo Spuches, lies near, its fine windows and decorated frieze around the roof still exciting the admiration of the 20th century.

Taormina is a town for walkers and view-collectors, who satisfy both enthusiasms by making for the medieval castle, San Pancrazio, the Belvedere or the incredible little settlement of Castel Mola, perched high above Taormina, on its own rocky escarpment, which appears poised ready to soar off into space. If you are one of the latter, but not the former, buses will take you to these places. They will also transport you farther afield to the caves of Sant' Andrea, to Monte Venere, or Francavilla. And buses are really preferable to private cars, not only because of the steepness of the winding roads and alleys, but mostly because of the totally insufficient parking space on the narrow ledge.

Taormina's buildings, like Taormina, could not be imagined anywhere else, for it is extremely photogenic, in an almost theatrical way. But Taormina, like any other much lauded beauty, has become self-conscious; so have its inhabitants, and above all, its fine hotels.

Sicily's Islands

At the northeast of Sicily, reached by boat from Milazzo and Messina, and less frequently, but on regular schedule from Catania and Palermo, as well as once-weekly from mainland Naples, are the Aeolian Islands (Lipari). Their charms are beginning to be appreciated if only because they lend themselves so well to one of the newest water sports, underwater exploring and fishing. Of volcanic origin, these islands are honeycombed with grottos in which fish lurk, and the clear warm waters are ideal for the swimmer intent on stalking his prey in and about them.

One of the group has a name almost synonymous for the word "volcano"—Stromboli. The active volcano on this island is the most spectacular feature of the region. The view from the sea at night is awe-inspiring, with the never-ceasing stream of incandescent lava flowing down the flank of the mountain into the sea—the *sciara del fuoco*, the flow of fire, the inhabitants call it. In spite of the lava and the frequent explosions which toss stones and flaming projectiles into the air, there is no danger from Stromboli. It has been behaving like this since ancient times. Because the lava flows freely instead of building up pressure internally, Stromboli remains a spectacle rather than a threat.

A small companion islet nearby, Strombolicchio, is astonishing for the way its cliffs rise sheer out of the sea. They look unscalable, but a staircase has been cut out of the rock, and you can climb to the top and enjoy the remarkable view over the other islands of the archipelago.

Of these the largest is Lipari, from whose red lava rocks rise a 16th-century castle and a 17th-century cathedral on a plateau, called the Acropolis by the Liparians. Here is an incredible collection of ruins, covering almost a dozen ages of man, beginning with the prehistoric, going on through Greek steles, Corinthian ceramics, Roman relics. There are Byzantine churches, Spanish churches, and, fortunately, three museums, displaying much that has been discovered at this "melting pot" spot. Everywhere the views from Lipari are impressive, and there are delightful fishing villages, such as Canneto, in addition to the somewhat *gamin* charms of the "capital city" of Lipari.

Vulcano, from its name, might have vied with Stromboli, but its three volcanos are all extinct. It does have hot mineral springs, however. Salina is noted for the Malmsey wine it produces (Malvasia in Italian). Panarea has no volcanos, but does very well without them—besides hot springs, it has many crevices from which smoke escapes, and at times the temperature of the earth reaches 220° F. in certain spots. This does not prevent it from being a fertile producer of grapes, olives, and capers. But don't go to Panarea if you like sandy beaches and hot showers, for you'll find neither.

Filicudi, one of the smaller islands, is noted for its Sea Bull Grotto, with its exceptionally limpid water. Alicudi is even smaller. The island of Ustica lies north of Palermo and is reached by *aliscafo*. It has impressive grottos, pretty farms, lovely flowers, and fine seafood. It has established itself firmly on the tourist map for its ideal bathing and underwater fishing.

The Egadi Islands lie just west of Trapani and Erice, and are plainly visible from mainland Sicily. Here are medieval castles, villages evocative of North Africa, mysterious grottos, and a thriving tuna-fishing industry. Some say the island of Marettimo, in this group, is the Ithaka of the *Odyssey*. Pantelleria has a cone reaching up 2,742 feet, and is clothed in small forest areas and sweeps of farms. Swimming and skindiving are exceptional here.

All of Sicily's islands, especially the Aeolians, are attracting growing numbers of summer vacationers, so their much-touted tranquillity becomes strictly relative in July and August. You'll probably find them much more satisfying off-season.

PRACTICAL INFORMATION FOR SICILY

HOTELS AND RESTAURANTS

Acireale. Hotels: All (2) are—*Maugeri,* comfortable, in town. On sea: *Aloha d'Oro,* modern, pool; handsome *Perla Ionica,* 3 mi. from town.

Aci Trezza 6½ miles north of Catania. **Hotels:** *Faraglioni* (1), all rooms with shower, overlooking rocky beach. *Eden Riviera* (2) modern, overlooking sea.

Restaurants: *Nuovo Polifemo* or *Sarago,* both (M–E) for fish.

Aeolian Islands. On these small islands, just north of Sicily, there is simple but comfortable accommodation.

Lipari. Hotels: Both (2)—*Carasco,* pool, beach, island's first real resort hotel; *Giardino,* seaside, with pool, beach. *Gattopardo* (2), 19th-century villa and secluded bungalows in lovely park.

Restaurants: *Pulera, Filippino,* both (M), island specialties.

Panarea. Hotels: Here you do without hot water and often without electricity. All (3)—*Piazza,* recent, with pool, rock bathing. *Lisca Bianca,* panoramic, tranquil, meals at *Cincotta* tourist village.

Stromboli. Hotels: *Sciara Residence* (2), full-fledged resort complex, erratic electricity supply. *Sirenetta* (3), on one of the island's good beaches, quiet, basic comforts.

Vulcano. Hotels: All (2) are—*Arcipelago,* ultramodern, well-equipped resort hotel on sea, pool, rock bathing; *Eolian,* large, hacienda-style, inland location; *Sables Noirs,* pioneer hostelry on island, small, simple.

Restaurants: *Blue Moon* (M–E), food at its freshest on panoramic terrace, impromtu entertainment. *Peppino* (M), fisherman's trattoria.

Agrigento. Famous temples, so-so hotels. **Hotels:** All (1)—*Villa Athena,* newest, best, lovely airconditioned villa with pool, at the temples; *Jolly dei Templi,* near temples, quiet, airconditioned, with pool.

Both (2)—*Della Valle,* Via dei Templi, new, very good, all rooms with bath; *Akrabello,* outside town, near temples, large, quiet, airconditioned, pool.

Restaurant: *Vigneto* (M), in valley, with view of temples.

Caldura. Near Cefalu. **Hotels:** Both (2)—on the beach, the airconditioned *Kalura,* open 1 Mar.—31 Oct., an excellent buy, private beach, all rooms with bath; *Calette,* gardens, pool, bar, near beach.

Caltanissetta. Provincial capital, with Greek and Roman remains. **Hotels:** Both (2)—*Diprima,* best. *Concordia Villa Mazzone,* on outskirts, rooms comfortable, modern furnishings.

Restaurant: *Cortese* (M), try *falsomagro.*

Cannizzaro. Hotel: *Baia Verde* (1), elegant resort hotel, rock bathing, pool.

Restaurant: *La Posada* (M), seaside, really excellent seafood and sherbet.

Castellammare del Golfo. Beach resort. **Hotels:** *Punta Nord Est* (3), modern, on beach.

At **San Vito lo Capo** headland, *Cala'Mpiso* (2), resort village.

Restaurant: At Scopello, on the sea, *Torre Bennistra* (M).

Castelvetrano. Near Selinunte ruins. **Hotel:** *Zeus* (2), modern, airconditioned.

Catania. Resort with a fine sandy beach. **Hotels:** All (1) are—*Grand Hotel Excelsior,* Piazza G. Verga, central, airconditioned, all rooms with bath or shower; *Jolly,* Piazza Trento, all private baths; *Central Palace,* near sights, modern, airconditioned, well-equipped.

Both (2)—*Costa,* Via Etnea 551, pleasant, on main shopping street; *Bristol,* near cathedral.

Restaurants: All (E) and top-notch are—*Giardini,* Via Etnea 135; *Excelsior* hotel, Piazza Verga. *La Siciliana* (M–E), Viale Marco Polo.

All (M)—cheaper but good, *Finocchiaro,* Via Cestai; *Gennarino,* Piazza Manganelli; *Pagano,* behind Excelsior Hotel; tiny *Da Pietro,* Via Veneto; *Venezia,* Via Montesano. For ice cream, snacks, *Savia,* Via Etnea.

Cefalu. Delightful old town, with fine stretch of sandy beach. **Hotel:** *Baia del Capitano* (2), handsome local style, in olive grove, pool, short walk from beach.

Restaurants: Both (M)—fish specialties at *Gabbiano,* overlooking beach; and *Normanni,* just off Piazza San Francesco. *Nino* (M), Lungomare, seaside, is pleasant and very good.

Egadi Islands. Favignana, Levanzo and **Marettimo,** off the west coast of Sicily, still quite undiscovered and unspoilt.

Favignana. Hotels: *Approdo di Ulisse* (2), at **Calagrand** on beach. *Punta Fanfalo* (2), large holiday village, all resort facilities.

Enna. Fortress city at over 3,000 feet. **Hotels:** All (2)—*Belvedere,* Piazza Francesco Crispi 4, good location with a view; *Grande Sicilia,* 54 rooms with bath, pleasant; *La Giara,* 6 miles away at quiet Pergusa Lake, recent, swimming pool.

Erice. Used to be called Monte San Giuliano. **Hotels:** Both closed Nov.–March—*Jolly* (1), modern, comfortable, functionally furnished, airconditioned rooms with shower, terraces, attractive garden.

Pineta (3), 21 bungalows in lovely pine grove, restaurant and bar.

Restaurant: *Taverna di Re Aceste* (M), try *cuscus.*

At **Pizzolungo,** below Erice, on beach—*Nuovo Tirreno* (2), and *L'Approdo* (3), all private baths.

Marsala. Wine center. **Hotels:** Both adequate—*Motel AGIP* (2), 32 rooms with shower; *Cap 3000* (2), recent resort hotel.

Restaurants: *Villa Favorita* (M), classic, classy. More modest, both (M) are—*Kalos* and *Zio Ciccio,* for fish.

Mazara del Vallo. Fishing port near Marsala. **Hotel:** Recent *Hopps Hotel* (2), good, attractively modern resort hotel.

Messina. Important city, provincial capital. **Hotels:** Both (1)—*Jolly,* Corso Garibaldi 126, at very noisy port, all 99 rooms with bath, airconditioned, private launch to Reggio Calabria; *Riviera Grande,* near National Museum, modern, roof garden, all airconditioned.

Both (2)—*Europa,* at entrance to Messina-Catania autostrada, good; *Venezia,* central, comfortable, airconditioned.

Restaurants: All (M)—*Borgia,* Via Fabrizi, good; *Da Pippo,* Via U. Bassi, excellent *pasta* with *eggplant, swordfish; Lisi,* Via Maddalena; *Alberto,* Via Ghibellina, famous for antipasto, swordfish *involtini.* At Mortelle beach, excellent *Sporting,* order *pasta 'ncasciata.*

Milazzo. Port city where many embark for Aeolian Islands. **Hotel:** *Silvanetta* (2), attractive modern hotel with pool, beach, large grounds.

Restaurant: *Al Gambero* (M), very good.

Monreale. Restaurants: Both (M)—*Savoia;* on highway, rustic *La Botte.*

Naxos. Near Taormina. **Hotels:** *Holiday Inn* (2), 280 spacious, airconditioned, well-furnished rooms with balcony, most with sea view, indoor/outdoor pools, beach; *Arathena Rocks* (2), medium-sized, in quiet location overlooking sea, with pool, tennis, beach. Both are seasonal.

Ognina. Near Catania. **Hotel:** *Motel AGIP* (3), on Hwy. 114, all rooms with shower, modern, comfortable, inexpensive.

Restaurant: *Costa Azzurra* (M), overlooking port.

Palermo. Hotels: Deluxe—*Villa Igiea,* Salita Belmonte, superb comfort in gardens facing sea, swimming pool, tennis, all rooms in traditional furnishings, with bath, airconditioned, somewhat rundown but still tops.

Both (1)—*Grande Albergo e delle Palme,* central, traditional and solid in style; *Jolly,* very big, modern establishment, pool.

All (2)—*Mediterraneo,* Via Cerda, good; *Metropol,* out-of-the-way; *Sole,* airconditioned, and *Centrale,* both on Corso Vittorio, convenient for sightseeing; *Ponte,* Via Crispi, airconditioned, good; *Touring,* Via M. Stabile 136; *Motel AGIP,* Via della Regione.

Restaurants: All (E)—*Le Caprice,* Via Cavour, tops, local specialties and wines; *Charleston* is chic, open Oct. to mid-June on Piazza Ungheria, in summer it moves to Mondello; it's one of Sicily's best; *Chamade,* Via Torrearsa, recent and excellent, outstanding pastas; *Gourmand's,* Via Libertà, lives up to its name.

All (M)—*Olimpia,* Via Ruggero Settimo, specializes in Sicilian dishes; at Parco Favorita racetrack, *Scuderia,* can be pricey: *Pappagallo,* Via Granateli; *Conco d'Oro,* Corso V. Emanuele, Cortile S. Caterina; *Scudiero,* Via Turati, very good; *Al Romagnolo,* Via Messina; *Il Ficodindia,* Via Amari; *Castelnuovo,* Piazza Castelnuovo; *Giannettino,* Piazza Ruggero Settimo 11; *Gorizia,* Via Travia 39; *Napoli,* Corso Vittorio Emanuele; and *Renato,* Via Messina Marine 28; *N'Grasciata,* Via Tiro a Segno, locally famous for fish, totally unpretentious.

Palermo-Mondello. Beautiful beach area just west of city. **Hotels:** *Mondello Palace* (1), good spacious and airy salons, attractive terraces and pool, private beach area.

Hotel Splendid La Torre (2), on promontory, all rooms with bath or shower and balcony, pool, beach.

Esplanade (P2), in quiet position above bay, short walk to beach, most rooms with bath or shower and balcony, good value.

Restaurants: *Charleston Terrazze* (E), summer home of Palermo's best restaurant; both (M), *Belvedere, Miramare.*

Pantelleria Island. Off the coast of Sicily—still mercifully uncommercialized. Hotels: All (2) are— *Punta Fram,* white arches framing black lava rocks and the sea; *Di Fresco,* large resort type, with terraces, balconies, private beach. Opposite, *Cossyra,* similar. *Tre Pietre,* perched on shoals, stairs to hotel and more to bathing area.

Both (3)—*Miryam,* on beach; *Turistico,* on shoals, pool.

Restaurants: *Di Fresco* and *Cossyra* hotel restaurants (M) are excellent.

Paterno. Near summer and winter resort of **Serra La Nave,** at more than 5,000 ft. **Hotel:** *Grande Albergo Etna* (3), 30 rooms, all with shower, tennis in beautiful grounds.

Piazza Armerina. Interesting archeological center. **Hotels:** *Jolly* (1), bright, airconditioned; *Selene* (2), good alternative, all rooms with bath or shower.

Restaurants: All (M)—*Plaza,* Via Garibaldi; or *Toto,* Via Mazzini.

Ragusa. Provincial capital, minor art town. **Hotels:** All (2)—*Ionio,* with excellent restaurant (M), and *Mediterraneo,* most rooms with bath or shower. On Beach, about 15 miles away, *Kamarina,* large vacation-village, imitates local architecture, no frills, but huge pool, own "piazza", shops, etc., fine sand beach.

Randazzo. Small hill city on slopes of Etna, quite medieval. **Hotel:** *Motel AGIP* (3) on route 120, 15 rooms with shower.

Santa Lucia. Near Cefalù. **Hotels:** *Sabbie d'Oro* (2), big bungalow-type colony on beach, good value.

All (3)—*Astro, Riva del Sole,* and *Santa Lucia,* most rooms with bath or shower; *Club Méditerrannée* center.

Sciacca. Hotels: New, *Grand Hotel delle Terme* (1), 70 rooms with bath or shower, telephone, overlooking sea. Both (2)—*Garden;* and *Motel AGIP,* on highway.

Selinunte. Restaurant: *Lido Azzurro* (M), at nearby **Marinella,** fresh-caught fish on seaside terrace.

Syracuse/Siracusa. Important city with famous Greek theater. **Hotels:** Best (now that *Villa Politi* is so run-down it can no longer be recommended) is *Jolly* (1), Corso Gelone 45, modern, all rooms with bath or shower.

All (2)—*Panorama,* Via Necropoli Grotticelle, near archeological site; *Bellavista,* Viale Acradina, in park with view; *Motel AGIP,* facing excavations; *Park,* Via Filisto 22.

At nearby **Brucoli,** *Valtur Village,* low modern holiday complex on rocky point, large pool, disco, ceramic lessons.

Restaurants: All (M)—Best is *Minerva* on cathedral square, for *maccheroni* and *zuppa di pesce; L'Orologio,* Piazza Archimede; *Bandiera,* Via Eritrea. At very good *Rutta e Ciauli,* try spaghetti with tuna and stuffed pork chop.

Taormina. Hotels: Deluxe—*San Domenico,* member of the hotel group Grandi Alberghi Siciliani. Luxurious comfort is superimposed on the background of the well-preserved 15th-century Dominican monastery, complete with Renaissance cloister, which has been converted into a modern hotel. Rooms in new section are larger. Swimming pool in lush gardens. Outstanding, rather aloof.

All (1) are—*Excelsior,* most beautifully placed, dominating the bay; *Mirqmáre,* attractive, handy to funicular for beach, heated swimming pool in garden; *Timeo,* quiet position near Greek Theater, splendid views, gardens, refined atmosphere, excellent restaurant. Highly recommended. *Diodoro Jolly,* recent, all rooms with bath or shower and airconditioning, large pool, tennis on extensive grounds; recommended, *Méditerranée,* modern, rooms with spectacular view, pool, relatively low rates; *Bristol Park,* quietly modern, terraces; *Vello d'Oro,* garishly modern but comfortable, central.

All (2)—*Villa Belvedere,* pool; *Continental;* and attractive *Sole Castello,* above town, closed Nov.–Jan.

All (P1) are—*Villa San Pancrazio,* tennis; *Villa Paradiso,* rooftop restaurant with spectacular view, tennis, excellent.

La Campanella (P2), central, 12 tasteful rooms, with bath or shower, reached by flights of steps; breakfast only.

Restaurants: All (E)—The best restaurant is *Pescatore,* at Mazzarò, with seaside terrace. In town, elegant restaurant of lovely *Hotel Timeo,* eggplant *involtini,* citrus soufflés.

All (M)—*Ciclope, Gondolier, Myosotis,* all on Corso Umberto; *Le Rocce,* with pizzeria, garden and dancing; at Mazzarò beach, the fine, family-run *Delfino* or *Da Giovanni.*

For afternoon tea or drink any time, *Mocambo Tavernetta.*

Taormina-Mazzaro. Beach resort. **Hotels:** Deluxe—*Sea Palace,* new, airconditioned, attractive rooms, all with private bath or shower, front rooms with balcony, seawater pool, private beach.

Villa Sant'Andrea (1), very fine, villa-type, exceptionally well-furnished throughout, garden terraces directly on beach, friendly atmosphere.

Capo Taormina (1), on promontory, posh, all resort facilities.

All (2)—*Isola Bella,* facing sea, beach, but on noisy main road; directly on good sandy beach at **Spisone,** short walk from cablecar, *Lido Méditerranée,* modern, comfortable; *Stockholm,* airconditioned, beach restaurant.

Trapani. Provincial capital, fishing town. Best to take rooms at Erice's hotels.

Restaurants: PG (M–E), good; *Bettolaccia* (M), offers 80 different pasta dishes.

Ustica. Island off the coast of Sicily. **Hotels:** All (2)—*Diana,* modern resort hotel with terraces, pool, bathing area, 35 rooms; *Grotta Azzurra,* same type, but larger; *Punta Spalmatore,* large, 100-cottage tourist village.

USEFUL ADDRESSES. Tourist Offices: *Aci Trezza:* AAST, Corso Umberto 177. *Aeolian Islands/Lipari:* AAST, Piazza Marina Corta. *Agrigento:* AAST, Piazza V. Emanuele; EPT, Piazza Cavour 19. *Caltanissetta:* EPT, Corso V. Emanuele 109. *Catania:* American Express, SIT, Corso Sicilia 31–35, 95131 Catania (tel. 226642 and 270761); EPT, Largo Paisello 5, and Railway Station; Ventana Tours, Corso Sicilia 31–35. *Cefalù:* AAST, Corso Ruggero 114. *Enna:* AAST and EPT, Piazza Garibaldi 1. *Erice:* AAST, Viale Conte Pepoli. *Messina:* AAST, Viale San Martino 227; EPT, Via Calabria, Isolato 301, and Railway Station.

Palermo: AAST, Villa Igiea; American Express, SIT, Viale Libertà 10B (tel. 249599 and 218312); EPT, Piazza Castelnuovo 35 and Punta Raisi Airport; Wagons Lits-Cooks, Via Magliocco 31; for information on boat services, Societa di Navigazione Tirrenia, Via Roma 385. *Piazza Armerina:* AAST, Piazza Garibaldi. *Ragusa:* EPT, Via Nataletti. *Sciacca:* AAST, Corso V. Emanuele 84. *Syracuse:* AAST, Via Maestranza 33; EPT, Corso Gelone 92C. *Taormina:* AAST, Piazza Santa Caterina. *Trapani:* EPT, Corso Italia 10.

SPECIAL EVENTS. *Aci Trezza:* Showing of Christmas cribs still going on at New Year; carnivals February; week-long Feast of San Calogero starts on the first Sunday in July. *Agrigento:* Classic world reborn in February, when the Valley of Temples acts as background to the Rite of the Flowering Almonds, and folklore festival.

Caltanissetta: Carnivals in February; Maundy Thursday procession with spectacularly rich sculptured groups carried through the streets; September, the statue of St. Michael is paraded, during a fair dating from the 17th century. *Catania:* February, the Feast of St. Agatha, when the little kiosks of wood, surrounded by high candles, are paraded; puppet shows all year round. *Messina:* 13–15 August, celebrations of the Assumption, with a parade of giants; and the Trade Fair of Sicily, part of a month-long program of folklore festivals, sports and cultural events, makes up Agosto Messinese, or August in Messina. *Monreale:* A week of sacred music in April; holy feasts for the patron saint in May.

Palermo: Twelfth Night, 6 January, most famous observance in accordance with Greek rites. 13 July begins the three-day Feast of Santa Rosalia, when the streets are decked with thousands of lamps under which the cardinal-archbishop leads the procession, while spectacular fireworks herald the pilgrimage up Monte Pellegrino. Opera and concert performances in the open-air theater in August, and puppet shows all year round.

SPORTS. Three beaches worth noting on Sicily are—*Castellammare del Golfo,* a fine sandy one, less crowded than the more popular resorts. Near Messina (6 miles) is the *Lido di Mortelle,* on the Tyrrhenian Sea, a good beach. Only 6 miles from Palermo is the popular resort of Mondello, also with a good beach.

SARDINIA

Island of Strange Cults

Sardinia is, after Sicily, the largest island in the Mediterranean, yet considering its size it remains comparatively undiscovered. The Aga Khan's development of a part of the island as a plush seaside resort complex is speeding the pace, as are those of several Italian and international development companies; but to date Sardinia is a comparatively peaceful region, its people concerned with quiet occupations—farming, raising livestock, fishing—and continuing with their unique local customs. The Sardinians, a short, dark, and good-looking people, consider themselves distinct from the Italians, and the "mainland", as they refer to it, seems much farther than it really is, both because of the island's independent spirit and its semi-autonomy.

Sardinia is famous for its pocket-size donkeys, its handsome, intricate native costumes, its *pastas,* and incredible festival breads, its brooding mountain areas, its legions of fine, sandy beaches, its highly-distinctive, artistic woven baskets and rugs.

Sardinia and its nearly 1½ million people do not really belong to Europe, nor for that matter, to Italy. A common heritage links the Sards and the Italians; the official language of both is Italian, and the national dish, spaghetti, makes a kind of culinary hyphen between the mainlanders and the islanders. But the vagaries of history and the very fact of being an island has so separated the two communities that today we should really speak of two peoples under the same administration.

You will feel the difference as soon as you set foot on Sardinia from Italy. The earth feels different; you won't feel "at home" as you did in Italy, but you will feel the land's enchantment. Perhaps the reason lies in Sardinia's isolation from the waves of migrations and invasions that have taken place during the last three centuries. Sardinia has always been coveted, but she has never been colonized. Carthage and Rome tried planting colonies here. So did the Barbarians, Normans, Genovese, Pisans, Turks, Greeks and Spaniards. But Sardinia remained completely Sardinian through centuries of occupation.

If we try to be more precise about our feelings of difference, we might say that Sardinia lacks Italy's Latin exuberance. Of course you won't be so aware of this until you leave the coast. So many tourist centers have sprung up along the shore that it is no longer representative of the rest of the island. In the interior you will discover the real Sardinia. Behind quasi-Arab-looking villages, and behind the old village customs, lies a land that can only be described as Euro-African.

You won't be the first to see the desperate poverty of the Estremadura. The sun weighs down on the land so hard that it seems to slow life to a halt. The standard of living is unbelievably low. And 50 to 60% of the land-surface is quite useless because it is made of impermeable rock that the rains run right off. Even the earth dies of thirst here and there are few natural springs. Dust in the air, heat in the dust—even the huts (concealing their inhabitants' poverty) are closed up. Once in a while you may see a woman, straight-backed, proud, nothing more than a black silhouette against the sky. Walking with a haughty bearing that is accentuated by the vessel or basket she balances on her head, you might expect her to be veiled. You may find that everything around you makes you think of Moslem countries even when you know Sardinia is a Christian land.

Sardinia's Turbulent History

Even though it lay outside the main currents of European commerce, the large island of Sardinia—with its 9,298 square miles—had a turbulent past. Sardinia and southern Italy share this historical fact in common: they were almost never their own masters, not even in very distant times. We do know that the ancient warriors of Sardinia were called Nuraghese and that they were famous for attacking their enemies with stone balls. From recent artifacts unearthed at Barumini, it is believed that the Nuraghese date back to around the 11th century before Christ. There is no historical evidence to support this, however.

At any rate, it was the Phoenicians who first occupied Sardinia and gave us our first written history of the island. Then came the Carthaginians in 500 BC and the Romans in 238 BC. After the fall of the Roman Empire, Sardinia attracted still more invaders. The island was right in the Mediterranean, those days considered the center of the earth. The Vandals, the Byzantines, the Saracens, the Arabs, the Genovese, the Pisans all occupied Sardinia in their time. The Pisans "stuck" better on Sardinia than any of the others and they were well on their way to planting their beautiful Romanesque churches all over the island when it was taken from them by Aragon.

Sardinian history is no less violent until the beginning of the 18th century. Up to that time there had been nothing like enlightened rule on the island. Then in 1708 Cagliari surrendered to the English fleet and Sardinia was ceded to Austria. Soon after that, in 1720, according to the Treaty of London, the Dukes of Savoy raised their flag over Sardinia and from that time on kept the island connected with Italy. Gradually modernization took place. A system of roads was laid during the 19th century, but it wasn't until 1948 that political autonomy was granted. The postwar period brought the first waves of tourists to the island and at last the scourge of malaria was wiped out.

Weather Matters

Sardinia's climate is mild all year round, but the best period is May through October. Off-season travel can be difficult and unrewarding, as train and bus services are sketchy and many tourist attractions, especially those off the beaten track, are closed. In July and August the coast areas get very crowded with vacationing Italians. Unfortunately, the island lies in the path of some mighty winds, and when these start to blow, they don't let up for several days.

Sardinia is well noted for its fabulous feast days, mostly religious. Over 100 festivals are scattered throughout the year, with the greatest number from May through September.

Road Reports

Cars may be taken on board all the boat services from the mainland to the island. The Italian State Railways also operate modern car-passenger ferries from Civitavecchia to Golfo degli Aranci, near Olbia. Fares are lower than on private lines. As with other services to the island, return passages should be booked well in advance.

The roads are in good condition, but in some tracts roadside conveniences (filling stations, refreshment halts) are few and far between. Cars may be rented at any port or airport of entry, with or without chauffeur. Advance reservations may be made at car rental agencies on the mainland. Avis and Hertz at Costa Smeralda, and elsewhere.

Food for Thought

In Sardinia, tourists usually eat at the hotels, although, of course, there are restaurants. The typical pasta is *malloreddus;* try *zuppa cuata,* a dense, delicious oven-baked soup of bread, cheese and tomatoes; *su ziminu* is the island's fish soup. Semolina flour and saffron are used in a number of dishes. Pig roasted on a spit is popular. An interesting dessert is *sabada,* soft cheese rolled in pastry.

The dry wines of Calasetta are justly famous, as is the rather heavy *Vernaccia.*

Exploring Sardinia

Sardinia is almost 10,000 square miles in area, and an island that has very little sameness. The variety of scenes and sights is so great that something new, compelling, attractive, or awesome is bound to turn up around almost every curve of a road.

Like most of southern Italy, Sardinia has been under the control of other states. The two that have left their mark most are Pisa, responsible for the Romanesque churches that dot the island, and Piedmont, which in the 18th and 19th centuries took the first steps toward modernizing, road-building, and so on.

Topography and history have conspired rather neatly to divide Sardinia into three relatively distinct regions: south, midriff, and north. Each is fascinating, often for totally different reasons, though in each there are almost countless lovely, uncluttered beaches, little fishing villages and ancient towns.

The north, running roughly between Olbia and the Costa Smeralda on the east to Alghero and Porto Torres on the west, has mountains, but it is mainly this region's beaches and islands lying just offshore that are the centers of attraction.

If you come to Sardinia by the most common route, by boat from Civitavecchia, you will land at the little port of Olbia, a beautiful harbor, connected by a train which runs through the center of the island to Cagliari in the south. Not far from Olbia is the Golfo degli Aranci, an attractive fishing town with some splendid beaches nearby.

To the north from the town of Palau you can visit the Archipelago of La Maddalena, a group of islands, from which, in turn, there is a connection with the Island of Caprera, a rocky, barren place, where Garibaldi built a house in 1855 and where he lived intermittently until his death in 1882. The house and his tomb are now a national monument. The pretty town of Santa Teresa di Gallura, on the slopes of Punta Falcone, looks across the strait of Bonifacio to Corsica's yellow cliffs. The rugged, windswept Gallura region has a number of upcoming coastal resorts.

In the northwest is hilltop-high Sassari, the island's second city, well worth a visit during its famous festival times, and at any time to see its museum of regional arts. Sassari is largely modern, but a short distance away there is the beautiful Romanesque-Pisan Church of the Santissima Trinità di Saccargia, built in the 12th century. On the coast above Sassari, Castelsardo is a 12th-century fortress town perched on a promontory above the sea. In Porto Torres, the ruins of the so-called Palace of the Barbarian King are really Roman remains, relics of the port's past glory in imperial times. It's now an important commercial and industrial center.

Also in the area are some interesting *nuraghi,* strange stone constructions that were the houses of the earliest inhabitants of Sardinia. They date from the 18th to the 5th century BC, and though they once numbered more than 30,000 there are considerably fewer now, scattered singly and in groups throughout the island. Up to some 50 years ago some still served as dwelling places for the peasants, but now they house goats and sheep.

La Barbagia

We spoke of a vacationer's dream. Well, there are beautiful beaches all around Alghero, both west and east. Alghero itself is an attractive, lively resort with a distinctive Spanish flavor. There are also wild places, places that still give you an idea of the adventurous life in former strongholds of Sardinia's mountains, around La Barbagia. Barbagia, reached by way of Macomer, is the "land of the Barbarians", of which Nuoro is the main city. You get into the brush or *maquis* at last. The word *maquis* literally means savage or wild undergrowth. It also means, by association with its inhabitants, a kind of wasteland or noman's land for outcasts and outlaws. This is really Sardinia's somber and untamed region. We can't tell you how many men still hide out here, maybe a dozen, maybe a hundred still keeping up the old and declining custom of the *vendetta.* Such settling of accounts grows rarer today, but it still takes place around Nuoro. These men are really renegades from a former world, perhaps nostalgic for a past they feel is disappearing. This does not prevent them from indulging in the modern—or perhaps just up-dated—art of kidnapping.

Just so you won't forget that there's still violence around, there is the Barbagian funeral chant to remind you. You won't hear this song, called *l'attitù,* unless the dying man is the victim of violence. The song takes the form of a dialogue between the widow, mother or sister of the man and the *attitadora.* It's a rhymed lament, of agonizing beauty coming from the lips of these wild and almost illiterate people whose language has an innate poetic rhythm. The women all wear mourning dress as they sing praises to the deceased. They sing about the joy and sweetness of life in his presence, they weep, demanding why he is leaving them so suddenly. The chanting begins slowly and has a poignant monotony about it, only little by little mounting in pitch until the women name the murderer, condemning him and promising to revenge their kinsman. Sorrow and misfortune is a part of daily life in Sardinia, and if goodness is paid for cash down by God, evil is strictly a matter of human repayment. The *attitù* doesn't only serve to stir up the vendetta; the lament is a dramatic, social manifestation of loss and of shared tragedy.

And Nuoro isn't only a city of funerals. There is a fine museum with an outstanding collection of regional costumes collected from all over the island. From Nuoro you have many interesting side trips as well. Visit Monte Orto Bene (3,265 feet) overlooking the city, and Monte Genn Argentù, the island's highest point, viewed from Fonni, itself 3,280 feet high. Here you will discover a village built from dark stones decorated with brightly colored woodwork. Throughout this area you'll see that both men and women still wear local costumes with great nonchalance.

Then continue toward Sorgono, a stunning location with good wines, and toward the south via Aritzo. All along the way you will see more of the Nuraghi and more wonderful views.

Count on being surprised at every turn as you travel through Sardinia. Go to Dorgali on the east coast; you'll see more costumes here. Then take a look at the splendid view onto the little port of Cala Gonone and its endless sea grottos that you can explore by boat.

The coast around Cala Gonone is riddled with grottos, most important of which is the Grotta del Bue Marino. Near Dorgali at Serra Orrios lies the largest and best preserved Nuraghic village in the entire island. Craftsmen in this area faithfully reproduce the same geometric patterns and stylizations that appear in prehistoric Nuraghic art.

Arbatax is an old port where cork is put into archaic-looking small boats. Stop at Muravera, and then take the road toward Cagliari to see the strikingly wild landscape.

In the southern sector of Sardinia lies Cagliari, a whole host of lovely, pine-backdropped beaches and several nearby islands. The island of San Pietro and the peninsula of Sant' Antioco are especially fascinating for their unspoiled natural beauty; their coastlines are a succession of small beaches, intriguing coves and caves and forbidding cliffs.

Cagliari, capital of the island, port and center of various industries, is the most sophisticated and most cosmopolitan area of Sardinia. This region is not only cosmopolitan today, but has been so for untold centuries. Here, for instance, are Nora, with its Phoenician, Carthaginian and Roman ruins, and Barumini, a fine, extensive, well-excavated settlement of the little-known Nuraghic civilization, with the impressive fortress, Nuraghe su Naraxi, as its centerpiece.

In Cagliari itself are many handsome structures, some dating from the 2nd century AD. Here, too, the Aragonese and the Pisans have left their stamp. Not to be missed at Cagliari are the magnificent view from the fortress, the two Pisan towers, Torre dell' Elefante and the Torrione di San Pancrazio, and the museum, with its collection of Sardinian antiquities. The Cathedral is a mixture of styles, but contains some attractive things, not least in the crypt and in the well-stocked treasury.

We come back to Nuoro again in order to go west towards Macomer. A flawless view lies before you from the basalt plateau of Abbavanta to the mountains of Genn Argentù and Oliena. Macomer is proud of its 16th-century Church of San Pantaleo.

Now take the short trip to the artificial lake of Omodeo, and to the dam at Tirso with its falls that drop 130 feet. Then on to Abbasanta, crossroads of the region. Slightly out of town, about a mile, on the Oristano road, is the most important Nuraghe on Sardinia, a real fortress called Nuraghe Losa.

Following the same road until you reach the mouth of the river Tirso, you'll come upon Oristano, which has a memorable village carnival. Drive 12 miles from there to the ruins at Tharros, first a Carthaginian then a Roman city, located on Cape San Marco. And don't miss seeing a very old Byzantine church while you are in Sinis, San Giovanni. The jewel of the Oristano region is the 12th-century Romanesque Church of Santa Giusta.

Throughout the island there are glimpses of men astride sleek horses (Sardinians are superb horsemen), and the sight, in season, of men baling hay by hand. A completely modern church may be close by a castle or church of the 12th century. Within a few miles of each other the traveler may run the gamut from sophisticated shops to Phoenician ruins; from handsome, ultra-new resorts to Nuraghic settlements and farmhouses built on the plan of ancient Roman dwellings; from a tiny, time-honored fishing village to a harbor filled with sleek ocean-going yachts; from Genoese fortress towns and Pisan-Romanesque churches to bustling seaports or untamed mountain fastnesses.

PRACTICAL INFORMATION FOR SARDINIA

HOTELS AND RESTAURANTS

Alghero, Seaport, resort. **Hotels:** *Villa Los Tronas* (1), large mansion on promontory, spacious rooms with fine views, pool, rock bathing.

All (2) are—*Calabona,* large, modern, airconditioned rooms with bath, pool, rock bathing; *Coral,* 46 rooms, each room with private terrace, Sardinian cuisine, open 1 May–Oct. 31; *Margherita,* many balconied rooms, hotel bus to beach; *Solemar,* on shore, pleasant, airconditioned; *Catalunya,* centrally located, modern, comfortable, hotel bus to beach.

Restaurants: *Corsaro* (E), near port, justly famous. All (M) are—*La Lepanto,* attractive, good; *Uccio del Mare,* unpretentious, but excellent; *Pesce d'Oro; Diecimetri,* just off Via Roma, simpatico locale, irresistible antipasto.

Arzachena. Hotels: All (2)—*Bisaccia,* and *Club,* both seasonal, fine beach hotels; *Smeraldo Beach,* big, resort-type, beach; *Ringo,* tennis, pool.

Restaurants: Both (M–E)—*Papagallo; La Fattoria,* on Olbia, for island specialties.

Cagliari. Capital and largest city. **Hotels:** *Jolly* (1), central, Viale Regina Margherita 44, 130 rooms, most with bath or shower, airconditioned.

Both (2) are—*Moderno,* Via Roma 159, 80 rooms, many with bath; *Mediterraneo,* Lungomare Colombo, all 140 rooms with shower, most with balcony.

Motel AGIP (3).

Restaurants: All (M)—best is *Corsaro,* Viale Regina Margherita, for local-style *pasta* and *braised sausages; Rosetta,* at port; *Bruno,* Via Cavour; *Fattoria,* Via Conversi, in old monastery, *malloreddus* and *porchetta; Da Illicu,* Via Sardegna, and *Da Salvatore,* Viale Trieste, fish only.

At *Sinnai,* about 7 miles north, *Burranca* (M–E), on hillside, one of the island's best for typical dishes.

Cala Gonone. No real beach, 5 miles of hairpin curves below Dorgali. **Hotels:** All (3)—*Mastino,* high above sea; *Miramare,* and *Cala Luna,* on sea.

Calamosca. Hotel: *Capo Sant'Eliá* (2), 45 rooms with bath or shower, restaurant and terraces overlooking sea; private beach.

Capo Testa. Near Santa Teresa Gallura, on north of the island. **Hotels:** Both (2)—*Capo Testa* and *Mirage.*

Costa Smeralda/Emerald Coast. This area, lying between **Olbia** and **Arzachena,** with over 50 miles of beachfront, is continually developing. **Hotels:** Top hotels here are officially (1), but charge strictly luxury prices. Some of the new ones are splendid.

All (1) are—*Cala di Volpe,* 130 pleasantly furnished rooms, swimming pool, motor boats, private beaches, tennis, rather isolated.

Pitrizza, several villas with 2–3 suites, each with own terrace, surrounding a handsome clubhouse, heated rock-carved pool, private jetty, favored by British royalty and "Jet-setters".

Romazzino, 100 big rooms with bath and sea-view balcony, private beach, garden, water sports.

All above are seasonal hotels with personnel problems; sometimes service suffers.

Both (2)—the *Liscia di Vacca* and *La Contra. Piccolo Mondo* (E), good.

At **Cala di Voipe,** *Nibaru,* with pool.

Restaurants: In addition to the hotels listed, both (E)—the dining rooms of the *Liscia di Vacca,* and *La Contra.*

All (E) and also nice—*Rosemary; La Tartaruga; le Sporting.*

Clubs: *Castel,* on **Cavallo Island;** *Number One,* this side.

Fertilia. 4 miles from Alghero. **Hotels:** Both (2)—*Dei Pini,* among pines on sandy beach, open May–Sept. *Punta Negra,* pool, beach.

Golfo degli Aranci. Near Costa Smeralda. **Hotels:** All (2)—*Baia Caddinas,* comfortably furnished beach hotel with pool; *Gabbiano,* and small *Margherita,* are more modest, both on beach.

Restaurants: *L'Asino que ride* (E), excellent.

La Maddalena. Island off north coast, with lovely beaches. 15-minute boat trip from Palau. **Hotels:** *Excelsior* (2), 33 rooms, many with bath. *ESIT Il Gabbiano* (3), 25 rooms, some with bath. Neither is on beach.

At **Porto Massimo,** *Cala Lunga* (2), modern resort hotel, pool, beach.

Macomer. Hotel. *Motel AGIP* (2), nearby on N 131.

Monte Ortobene. Near Nuoro. **Hotels:** *ESIT* (2) 53 large rooms; *Fratelli Sacchi* (3), small, both with magnificent views.

Restaurant: *Sacchi* hotel restaurant (M) serves excellent local cuisine.

Nuoro. Hotels: *Jolly* (1), 72 rooms, most with bath, airconditioned. *Motel AGIP* (2), good, airconditioned.

Restaurants: All (M) are—*Da Giovanni,* Via Quattro Novembre, upstairs locale, and *Canne al Vento,* Viale della Repubblica, serve local specialties. *Moderno* hotel is also good.

Olbia. Seaport on Costa Smeralda, near resorts. **Hotels:** *President* (1), 44 rooms with bath or shower.

At **Marinella,** *L'Abi d'Oru* (1), very attractive, airconditioned, pool, good beach, tennis, open March–Oct.

At **Lido del Sole,** *Caprile* (2), on beach.

Restaurant: *Grazia Deledda* (E), on Baia Sardinia road, smart and good.

Oliena. 7 miles SE of Nuoro. **Restaurant:** Ask for the road to the *albergo* at *Su Gologone* (M), for traditional dishes.

Oristano. Historic town. **Hotels:** All (2)—*ISA,* airconditioned.

At **Torre Grande,** *Del Sole,* 54 rooms with shower, pool, beach.

At **Arborea,** *Ala Birdi,* cottages amid pines, on beach.

Restaurants: All (M) are—*Forchetta d'Oro* and *Il Faro,* standouts for local cuisine.

At **Torre Grande** beach, *Da Giovanni* for fish.

Palau. Port town. **Hotels:** Both (2)—*Altura,* modern, panoramic; *La Roccia.*

Restaurants: *Franco* (E) is best. *Perla Blu,* at **Punta Sardegna,** seafood soups. *Capannaccia* (M), on Santa Teresa road, excellent.

Platamona Lido. Near Sassari. **Hotels:** Both (2)—are *Del Golfo,* and *Pineta Beach,* both resort-style, with fine sea views, pool, own beaches, all rooms with bath or shower.

Restaurant: *Ernesto* (M–E), fine fish.

Porto Cervo. On Costa Smeralda. **Hotels:** *Cervo* (1), 62 rooms with bath, nightclub, small pool, lively atmosphere in heart of town, some rooms noisy.

All (2)—*Luci de la Montagna,* 79 smallish rooms, overlooks the bay; *Balocco* and *Le Ginestre,* both on beach nearby, recent and relatively expensive.

Restaurants: *St. Andrew's* (E), where the Aga Khan eats.

Both (M–E)—*Pizzeria,* for hearty *pastas;* and *Fattoria,* in the hills above the port, serves such true island fare as bread soup and spit-roasted lamb.

Porto Conte. 9 miles from Alghero. **Hotels:** Both (1)—*Eurotel,* 100 rooms, all with bath and shower and balcony facing sea, private beach, swimming pool, motor boats, open May–Sept; *El Faro,* 80 rooms, very fine, pool, rock and beach bathing.

Corte Rosada (2), pretty cottage complex, all resort facilities.

Porto Rotondo. Smarter even than Costa Smeralda centers. **Hotel:** *Sporting* (1), best, attractive, rambling place, all rooms with bath, balcony, sea view, big pool and terrace restaurant. Expensive for category.

Porto San Paolo. On Costa Smeralda, near Olbia. **Hotel:** *Don Diego* (2), 35 rooms with bath in attractive bungalows, terraces overlooking sea, pool, beach.

San Pietro Island. The main village, **Carloforte,** is very pretty. **Hotels:** Both (3)—*Riviera,* 28 rooms, many with bath or shower; and *Baia d'Argento,* all rooms with bath, on beach.

Santa Margherita di Pula. 16 miles from Cagliari. **Hotels:** *Is Morus* (1), 54 rooms with bath or shower, in pinewoods at shore, beach, pool, tennis, gardens, open 15 Apr.–Oct.

All (2)—*Forte Village,* holiday complex includes *Castello* hotel, cottages, nightclub, pools, beach, all sports and amenities such as shops, *pizzeria,* babysitting service, a fullsize golf course is available.

Flamingo, 122 rooms with bath and balcony in 6 villas and central building, all airconditioned, pools, tennis, private beach, nightclub, boutiques.

Abamar, also new, 85 rooms with bath or shower in large modern hotel on sandy beach at edge of pinewoods, pool, nightclub.

Sant'Antioco Island. Hotel: At **Calasetta** *Stella del Sud* (3), marvelous beach.

Santa Teresa Gallura. Resort at north of island. **Hotels:** *Shardana* (1), 51 rooms with bath in private bungalow furnished in rustic style, on sandy beach, rock pool, garden bar, sauna, dancing. *Moresco* (1), 53 rooms with bath, private beach, park, open June–Sept. Both (2), resort hotels outside town—*Corallaro, Li Nibbari.*

At **Costa Paradiso,** *Rosi Marini* (2), modern resort hotel.

San Teodoro. On Costa Smeralda, 15 miles south of Olbia. **Hotel:** *Bungalow San Teodoro* (2), large resort complex, pool.

Sassari. Provincial capital, second largest city. **Hotels:** *Jolly Grazia Deledda* (1), 140 rooms, airconditioned, swimming pool.

All (2) are—*Jolly Mancini,* central car park, no restaurant; *Motel AGIP,* with meals; and *Motel Marini,* both airconditioned, on outskirts.

Restaurants: All (M)—*Da Michi, Gallo d'Oro, Tre Stelle.*

Siniscola. East coast seaside resort. **Hotel:** *La Caletta* (2), 112-room beach hotel in quiet position, with pool, terraces.

Sorgono. Lovely mountain town, remote. **Hotel:** *Villa Fiorita* (3), 20 rooms, half with bath or shower, pool.

Stintino. Northwest seaside area. **Hotels:** *Grand Hotel Rocca Ruja* (2), firstclass comforts, strikingly modern hotel in quiet spot overlooking sea, beach, pool, tennis; *Cala Reale,* recent, similar.

Villasimius. Southeast side, about 40 miles from Cagliari. **Hotels:** *Grand Hotel Capo Boi* (1), 103 rooms with bath or shower, airconditioned, swimming pool, attractive wooded grounds, private beach, tennis, nightclub, open 30 Apr.–15 Oct.

Timi-Ama (2), 64 rooms with bath, airconditioned, tennis, private beach.

USEFUL ADDRESSES. **Tourist Offices:** *Alghero:* AAST, Piazza Porta Terra 9. *Cagliari:* American Express, SIT, Piazza Matteotti 12, PO Box 185, (tel. 651618 and 665205); EPT, Piazza Matteotti 1, and Piazza Deffenu 9; ESIT, Via Mameli 95; for information on boat services, Canguro Rosso Ferry Boats, Societa' Traghetti Sardi, Piazza Deffenu 4. *Nuoro:* EPT, Piazza Italia 9. *Olbia:* AAST, Via Catello Piro. *Sassari:* EPT, Piazza Italia 19.

SPECIAL EVENTS. *Cagliari:* 1–4 May, the Sagra di Sant' Efisio, one of the biggest and most colorful processions in the world, where thousands of pilgrims on foot, carts and horses, wearing costumes dating back to 1657, accompany the statue of the saint. *Macomer:* End of July, three-day Sagra di San Pantaleo, colorful fair. *Nuoro:* 29 August, Festival of the Redeemer, procession in Sardinian costume. *Oristano:* Carnivals on last Sunday and Tuesday before Ash Wednesday, with Sa S artiglia costumed parade and tournament. 11–14 September, the Sagra di Santa Croce brings people from all over the island for celebrations and gastronomic fair. *Sassari:* Ascension Thursday, mid-May, there's a Sardinian costume Cavalcade; 14 August, the Feast of the Candles.

SPORTS. *Alghero:* Swimming, fishing, water skiing and snorkeling. *Porto Cervo:* Ranks among the finest yacht harbors in the entire Mediterranean, with a regatta in mid-August; 18-hole golf course. *Porto Rotondo:* Also good for boating.

ENGLISH-ITALIAN VOCABULARY

NOTE: In the following vocabulary we have avoided those fine-sounding polite introductory phrases which bring an answering storm of swift Italian. The phrases are utilitarian, assuming that you have to make yourself understood in places where no English is spoken.

"Please" works wonders. Try to add it to the beginning or end of every question or request in the list below, and you'll see many Italian smiles and have a much better time during your visit.

PRONUNCIATION: Every letter and syllable is sounded (except *h*). The accent is on the last syllable but one, unless otherwise shown ( ).

VOWELS:

A is pronounced *ah,* e-*eh;* i-*ee;* o-*oh;* u-*ou* as in *you.* (These sounds are slightly flattened when unstressed or when followed by more than one consonant).

Double-vowels do not exist: *Austria*=ah-ou-stree-ah, *dieci*=dee-ay-chee.

CONSONANTS:

(a) **Single Consonants:** As in English, except: c—like *ch* before i or e (*cento* =chentoh; *cinque*=cheenquay); g—as in English germ before e or i. Otherwise like g in gone.

w—(occuring only in foreign words)—like English *v.*

z—like *ts:* zio=tsee-oh.

(b) **Combinations of Consonants:** Sc—like *sh* before e or i. Otherwise like *k* (*lasciare*=lashiah-reh; *scala*=scah-lah). Gl is pronounced lj: Camogli=Kahmohljee.

Read over the following words and phrases with constant reference to the above rules; then speak them slowly, clearly, and boldly, and any Italian will understand.

GENERAL

Please—Thank you—Not at all	Per favore—Gràzie—Prego.
What is this called in Italian?	Come si chiama questo in Italiano?
Here	Qui
There	Li
How much?	Quanto?
My change?	Il mio resto?
Day	il giorno
Morning	la mattina
Afternoon	il pomeriggio
Evening	la sera
Night	la notte
This morning	stamani
Sunday	domenica
Monday	lunedì
Tuesday	martedì
Wednesday	mercoledì
Thursday	giovedì
Friday	venerdì
Saturday	sabato

January	gennaio
February	febbraio
March	marzo
April	aprile
May	maggio
June	giugno
July	luglio
August	agosto
September	Settembre
October	ottobre
November	novembre
December	dicembre

NUMBERS

0	zero	11	undici	22	ventidue	80	ottanta
1	uno	12	dodici	30	trenta	81	ottantuno
2	due	13	tredici	31	trentuno	90	novanta
3	tre	14	quattordici	40	quaranta	91	novantuno
4	quattro	15	quindici	41	quarantuno	100	cento
5	cinque	16	sedici	50	cinquanta	101	cento uno
6	sei	17	diciassette	51	cinquantuno	200	duecento
7	sette	18	diciotto	60	sessanta	1,000	mille
8	otto	19	diciannove	61	sessantuno	2,000	due mila
9	nove	20	venti	70	settanta	1,000,000	un milione
10	dieci	21	ventuno	71	settantuno		

BY TRAIN

I have (want) a reserved seat.	Ho (desìdero) un posto riservato
Is there a dining car?	C'è un vagone ristorante?
What time is the first service?	A che ora è il primo servìzio?
for breakfast (lunch, dinner)?	per la colazione (il pranzo, la cena)?
When does the train leave?	A che ora parte il treno?
When does the train arrive in . . . ?	Quando arriva il treno a . . . ?
What's the name of this station?	Come si chiama questa stazione?
How far is it to . . . ?	Quanto siamo lontani da . . . ?
How long do we stay here?	Quanto ci fermiamo qui?
Take this to the check room.	Porti questa al deposito bagagli al mano.
Is there a bar in the station?	C'è un bar nella stazione?
Coffee and a sandwich.	Un caffè e un panino.
A glass (bottle) of beer. . . .	Un bicchiere (una bottiglia) di birra.
. . . to take away.	. . . da portare via.
Will you wrap these up?	Mi vuol incartare questi?

Have you English (American) newspapers?	Ha dei giornali inglesi (americani)?

BY CAR

Where is the office of the Automobile Club?	Dov'è l'ufficio dell' Automobile Club?
Where can I get gas (petrol)?	Dove posso trovare della benzina?
Twenty liters, please.	Venti litre, per favore.
Will you put some air in my tires?	Mi vuol gonfiare le gomme?
Is there a repair shop here?	C'è un' officina qui?
I need a tow to a garage.	Ho bisogno di essere rimorchiato fino al garage.
Where can I get spare parts for an English (American) car?	Dove posso trovare dei pezzi di ricambio per una macchina inglese (americana)?
Can I take this road to . . . ?	Va bene questa strada per . . . ?
I need water for my radiator.	Ho bisogno di acqua per il radiatore.
What is the name of this city (town), village?	Come si chiama questa città, questo paese?
Am I on the right road for . . . ?	Vado bene per . . . ?
Have you a road map of this region of Italy?	Ha una guida stradale di questa regione d'Italia?
One-way traffic.	Senso unico.

HOTELS

Where is there a good restaurant (hotel)?	Dove c'è un buon ristorante (albergo)?
Is there anybody who speaks English?	C'è qualcuno che parla inglese?
I want a double room,	Desìdero una camera matrimoniale,
a single room,	una camera a un letto,
for one night, two nights,	per una notte, due notti,
with bath (telephone).	con bagno (telefono).
How much, including all taxes?	Quanto costa, comprese tutte le tasse?
Name, address, coming from, nationality.	Nome, indirizzo, provenienza, nazionalità.
Where is . . .	Dov'è . . .
the bathroom?	il bagno?
the toilet?	la toiletta?
my luggage?	il mio bagàglio?
Come in!	Avanti!
Bring me soap, towels, iced water.	Mi porti del sapone, asciugamani, acqua ghiacciata.

I want this dress washed (ironed).	Desìdero far lavare (stirare) quest' abito.
When will they be ready?	Quando sarranno pronti?
Will you prepare a bath for . . . ? seven o'clock, ten o'clock, half past ten, midday, midnight.	Mi vuol prepare il bagno per . . . ? le sette, le dieci, le dieci e mezza, mezzogiorno, mezzanotte.
Call us at eight (nine).	Ci chiami alle otto (nove).
Bring us morning tea (coffee).	Ci porti il tè in camera (il caffè).

MEALS

Waiter, I want a table for three.	Cameriere, desìdero una tavola per tre.
Tea, coffee, tomato juice.	Tè, caffè, sugo di pomodoro.
Rolls and butter.	Panini e burro.
Bacon and eggs.	Pancetta affumicata e due uova.
A boiled egg.	Un uovo alla cocca.
Salt, pepper, oil, vinegar.	Sale, pepe, olio, aceto.
Bring me some more tea, coffee.	Mi dia ancora del tè, caffè.
The menu. Today's specialty.	Il menù. La specialità del giorno.
Hors d'oeuvre.	Gli antipasti.
What are the local dishes?	Quali sono le specialità del luogo?
Meat, lamb, beef, veal, steak, chicken, liver.	Carne, agnello, manzo, vitello, bistecca, pollo, fegato.
Potatoes (boiled, mashed, fried).	Patate (lesse, puree, fritte).
Fish, sole, trout, salmon.	Pesce, sogliola, trota, salmone.
Salad.	Insalata.
What kind of cheese have you?	Quali qualità di formaggio avete?
What is the local cheese?	Qual'e il formaggio locale?
Bring a bottle of good local wine.	Ci porti una bottiglia di buon vino locale.
The bill for the whole party.	Il conto complessivo.

IN TOWN

Where is the British (American Consulate?	Dov'è il consolato inglese (americano)?
Will you write the address here?	Mi vuol scrivere qui l'indirizzo?
How do I get there?	Come posso andarci?
Where is the bus (tram) stop?	Dov'è la fermata dell'autobus (tram)?
Where can I get off for . . . ?	Dove scendo per . . . ?
Where is the nearest bank?	Dov'è la banca più vicina?
What is the exchange rate for the dollar (pound)?	Cos'è il cambio del dollaro (della sterlina)?

I want to change twenty dollars (pounds).	Desìdero cambiare venti dollari (sterline).
Where is. . . .	Dov'è
a tobacconist?	il tabaccaio?
a pharmacy?	una farmacia?
a hairdresser?	un parrucchiere?
a barber?	un barbiere?
a post-office?	un ufficio postale?
I want: razorblades, a hair cut, a shave, a shampoo, to send a telegram to England (America).	Desìdero: lamette da barba, tagliare i capelli, fare la barba, uno shampoo, mandare un telegramma in Inghilterra (in America).
How much per word? ordinary rate, urgent.	Quanto viene per parola? normale, urgente.
When will it arrive?	Quando arriverà?
Where is the opera?	Dov'è. . . . (name of the theater).
Where can I buy tickets?	Dove posso comprare dei biglietti?
At what time is the box office open?	A che ora è aperto il botteghino?
I want three tickets for tomorrow night.	Desìdero tre biglietti per domani sera.
At what time does the performance begin (end)?	A che ora comincia (finisce) lo spettacolo?
What are the local products?	Quali sono i prodotti locali?
Where can I buy a	Dove posso comprare
map of the city, films?	una pianta della città? una pellicola?
Where is Piazza . . . ?	Dov'è Piazza . . . ?
the Town Hall?	il municipio?
the church of . . . ?	la chiesa di . . . ?
the . . . Museum?	il museo . . . ?
Where can I get films developed?	Dove posso far sviluppare una pellicola?
I want two prints of each.	Desìdero due copie di'ognuna.
I'd like these two enlarged.	Desìdero un ingrandimento di queste due.

TRIPS OUT OF TOWN

How do I get to . . . ?	Come faccio ad andare a . . . ?
Where is the station?	Dove la stazione?
Where does the bus start from?	Da dove parte l'autobus?
We want to go to the sea, to the mountains.	Desideriamo andare al mare, in montagna.
Two first (second) class singles to . . .	Due di prima (secònda), solo andata per . . .

Three third class returns to . . .	Tre di terza classe andata e ritorno per . . .
Do we have to change trains? Where?	Dobbiamo cambiare treno? Dove?
Is there a connection?	C'è una coincidenza?
What time is the next train? the last train? for . . .	A che ora c'è il prossimo treno? l'ultimo treno? per . . .
A bathing cabin for two, a beach umbrella, three deck-chairs.	Una cabina per due, un ombrellone, tre sedie a sdraio.
I want to hire a rowing-boat, sailing boat	Desidero affittare una barca, una barca a vela.
How much per hour? per day?	Quanto viene all' ora? Per tutto il giorno?

FELLING ILL?

I am ill.	Sono malato (malata).
My husband (my wife) is ill.	Mio marito (mia moglie) è malato (malata).
My child (my friend) is ill.	Mio bambino/a (mio amico/a) è malato (malata).
Please call a doctor.	Per piacere chiamate un medico.
Where is the hospital?	Dov'è l'ospedale?
The emergency room.	Pronto soccorso.
I need an ambulance	Ho bisogno di un'ambulanza.
Where is the pharmacy?	Dov'è la farmacia?
Can you fill this prescription?	Può prepararmi questa ricetta?
Aspirin.	Aspirina.
Antacid.	Antiacido.
Soda bicarbonate.	Bicarbonato di soda.

INDEX

INDEX

The letters H and R indicate Hotel and Restaurant listings (*See also* Practical Information sections at the end of each chapter for additional details.)

ITALY

1

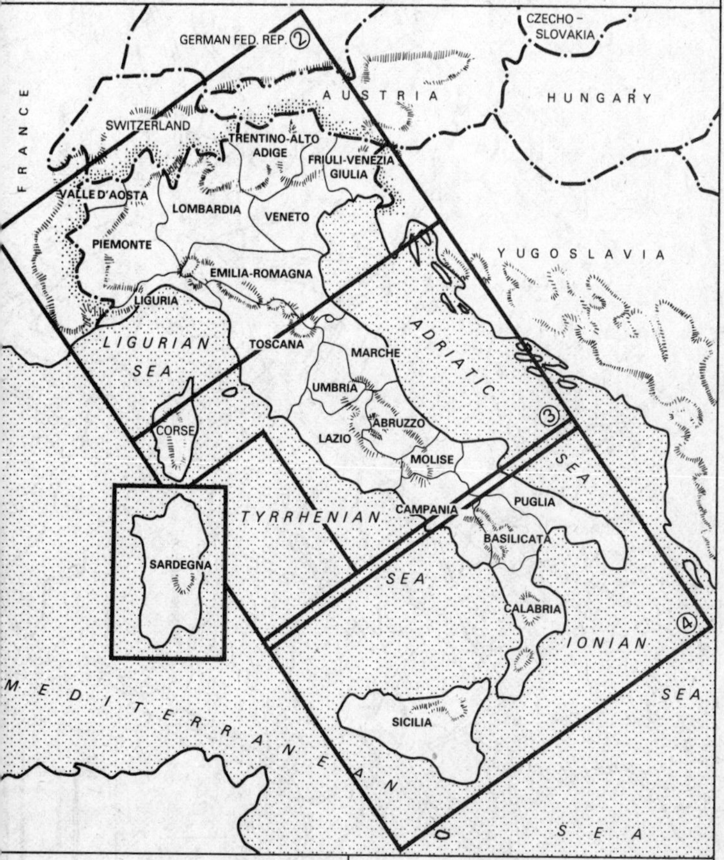

KEY

Motorways	═══
Main Roads	───
Railways	┼┼┼┼
Car Ferries	– – – –
Airports	*
Land over 1,000 m map 1 only.	

CONTENTS

MAPS

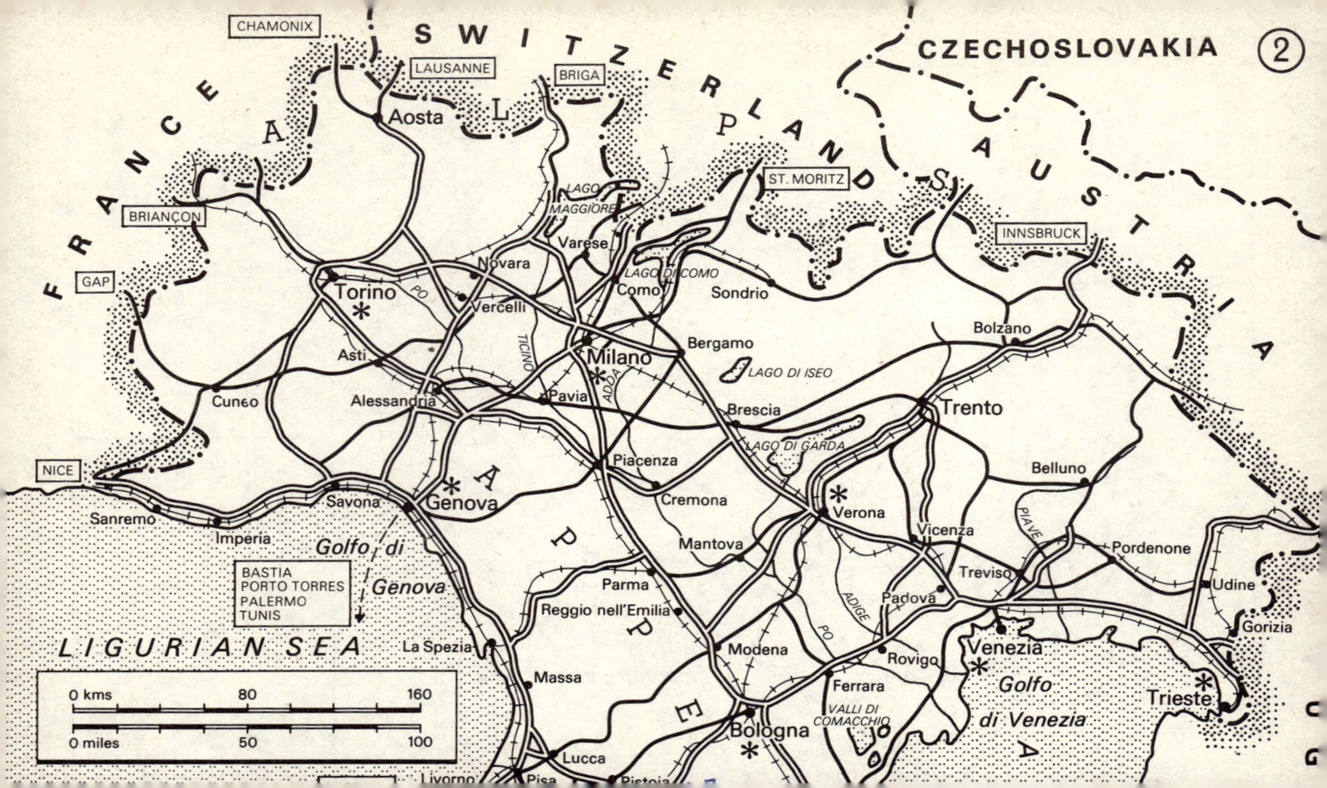

2
CZECHOSLOVAKIA
SWITZERLAND
AUSTRIA
FRANCE
ALPS
APPENNINES
CHAMONIX
LAUSANNE
BRIGA
ST. MORITZ
INNSBRUCK
BRIANÇON
GAP
NICE
Aosta
Torino
PO
Novara
Vercelli
Varese
LAGO MAGGIORE
LAGO DI COMO
Como
Sondrio
Bolzano
Milano
TICINO
ADDA
Bergamo
LAGO DI ISEO
Asti
Alessandria
Cuneo
Pavia
Brescia
Trento
LAGO DI GARDA
Piacenza
Cremona
Belluno
Verona
Genova
Savona
Sanremo
Imperia
Golfo di Genova
BASTIA
PORTO TORRES
PALERMO
TUNIS
Mantova
Vicenza
PIAVE
Pordenone
Treviso
Parma
Reggio nell'Emilia
Udine
Padova
ADIGE
Gorizia
LIGURIAN SEA
La Spezia
Modena
Rovigo
Venezia
Massa
Ferrara
Golfo di Venezia
Trieste
VALLI DI COMACCHIO
Bologna
Lucca
Pisa
Livorno
Pistoia
0 kms
80
160
0 miles
50
100

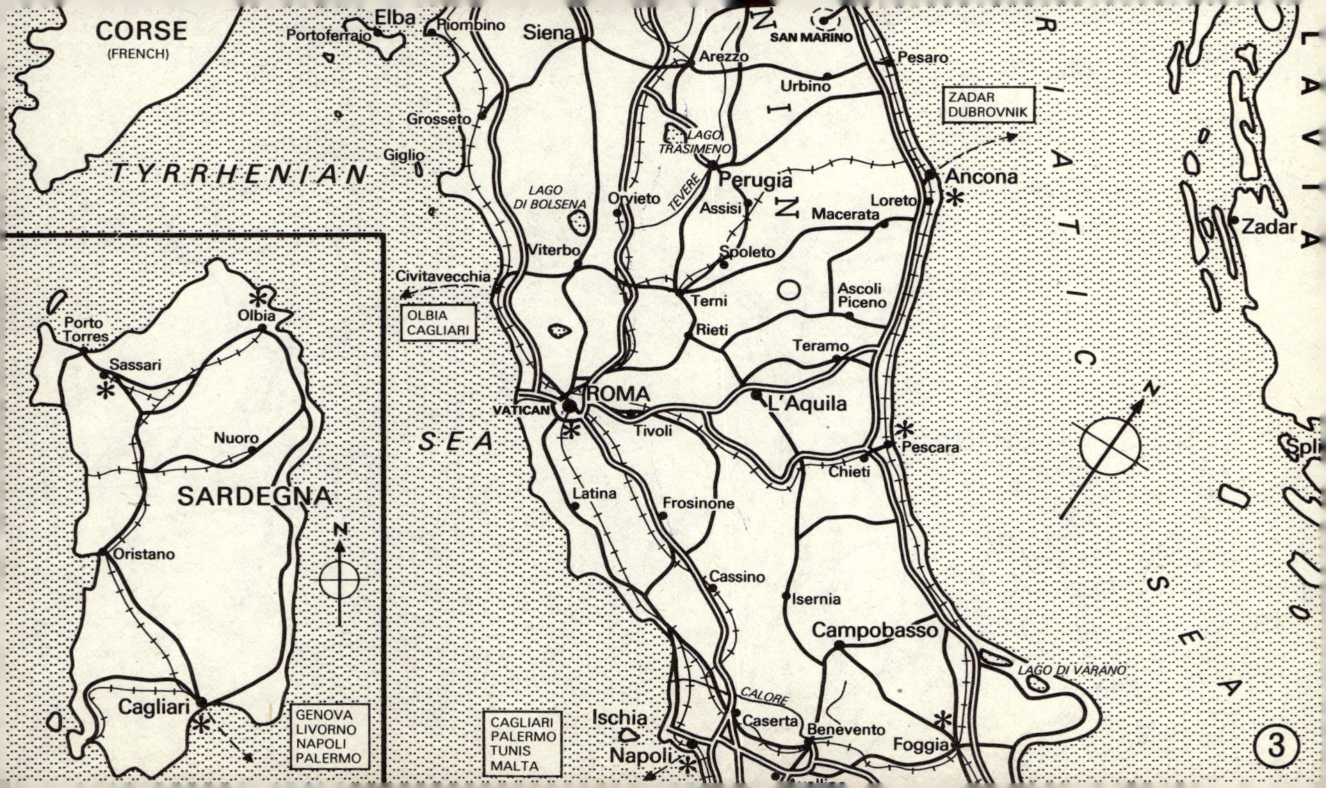
CORSE
(FRENCH)
Elba
Portoferraio
Piombino
Siena
SAN MARINO
Arezzo
Pesaro
Urbino
Grosseto
Giglio
TYRRHENIAN
SEA
LAGO TRASIMENO
Perugia
Ancona
ZADAR
DUBROVNIK
LAGO DI BOLSENA
Orvieto
TEVERE
Assisi
Loreto
Macerata
Zadar
Viterbo
Spoleto
Civitavecchia
OLBIA
CAGLIARI
Terni
Ascoli Piceno
Rieti
Teramo
ROMA
VATICAN
L'Aquila
Tivoli
Pescara
Chieti
Latina
Frosinone
Cassino
Isernia
Campobasso
LAGO DI VARANO
CALORE
Caserta
Benevento
Ischia
Napoli
Foggia
CAGLIARI
PALERMO
TUNIS
MALTA
ADRIATIC SEA
N
I
N
O
3
Porto Torres
Olbia
Sassari
Nuoro
SARDEGNA
Oristano
Cagliari
GENOVA
LIVORNO
NAPOLI
PALERMO

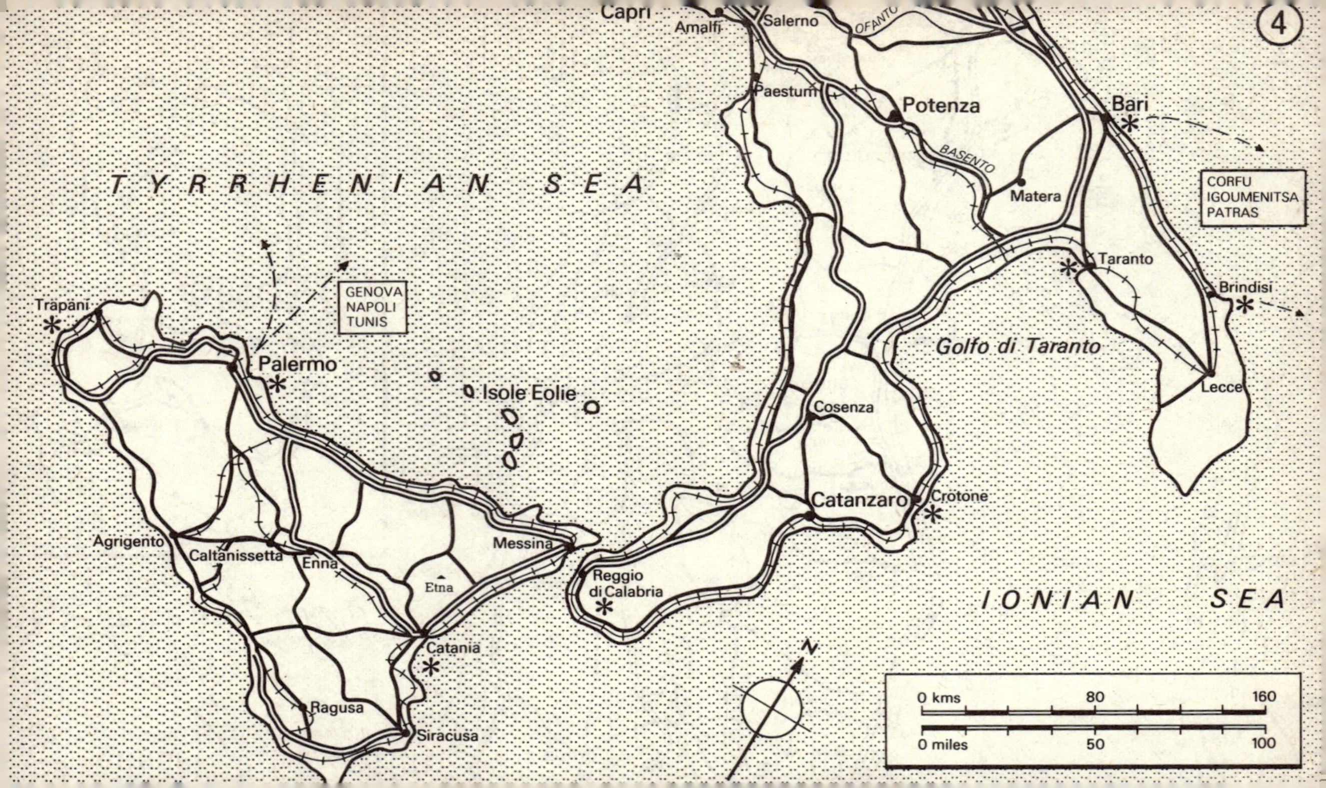
4
Capri
Amalfi
Salerno
OFANTO
Paestum
Potenza
BASENTO
Matera
Bari
CORFU
IGOUMENITSA
PATRAS
Taranto
Brindisi
Lecce
Golfo di Taranto
TYRRHENIAN SEA
GENOVA
NAPOLI
TUNIS
Trapani
Palermo
Isole Eolie
Cosenza
Catanzaro
Crotone
Agrigento
Caltanissetta
Enna
Messina
Etna
Reggio di Calabria
IONIAN SEA
Catania
Ragusa
Siracusa
N
0 kms
80
160
0 miles
50
100